Lecture Notes in Computer Science 2707

Edited by G. Goos, J. Hartmanis, and J. van Leeuwen

Springer
*Berlin
Heidelberg
New York
Barcelona
Hong Kong
London
Milan
Paris
Tokyo*

Kevin Jeffay   Ion Stoica   Klaus Wehrle (Eds.)

Quality of Service – IWQoS 2003

11th International Workshop
Berkeley, CA, USA, June 2-4, 2003
Proceedings

Springer

Series Editors

Gerhard Goos, Karlsruhe University, Germany
Juris Hartmanis, Cornell University, NY, USA
Jan van Leeuwen, Utrecht University, The Netherlands

Volume Editors

Kevin Jeffay
University of North Carolina at Chapel Hill, Department of Computer Science
Chapel Hill, NC 27599-3175, USA
E-mail: jeffay@cs.unc.edu

Ion Stoica
University of California at Berkeley
Computer Science Division, EECS Department
645 Soda Hall, Berkeley, CA 94720-1776, USA
E-mail: istoica@cs.berkeley.edu

Klaus Wehrle
International Computer Science Institute, Center for Internet Research
1947 Center Street, Suite 600, Berkeley, CA 94704, USA
E-mail: wehrle@icsi.berkeley.edu

Cataloging-in-Publication Data applied for

A catalog record for this book is available from the Library of Congress.

Bibliographic information published by Die Deutsche Bibliothek.
Die Deutsche Bibliothek lists this publication in the Deutsche Nationalbibliografie;
detailed bibliographic data is available in the Internet at <http://dnb.ddb.de>.

CR Subject Classification (1998): C.2, D.4.4, H.3.5-7, H.4, H.5.1, K.4.4, K.6.5

ISSN 0302-9743
ISBN 3-540-40281-0 Springer-Verlag Berlin Heidelberg New York

Springer-Verlag Berlin Heidelberg New York
a member of BertelsmannSpringer Science+Business Media GmbH

http://www.springer.de

© Springer-Verlag Berlin Heidelberg 2003
Printed in Germany

Typesetting: Camera-ready by author, data conversion by PTP-Berlin GmbH
Printed on acid-free paper   SPIN: 10928721   06/3142   5 4 3 2 1 0

Preface

Quality of Service continues to be an active research field, especially in the networking community. IWQoS is a successful series of workshops that aims to provide a forum for the presentation and discussion of new research and ideas on QoS. Traditionally, IWQoS workshops are cross-disciplinary and well focused, with the emphasis on innovation. As a result, a considerable amount of time is devoted to informal discussion.

In addition to the traditional QoS topics such as service guarantees and admission control, this year we aimed to expand the scope of the workshop by encouraging submissions offering research contributions related to robustness, resilience, security, and predictability in networking and distributed systems. As a result, the program included two sessions on availability, fault tolerance, and dependability. The other sessions covered routing, resource allocation, storage, Web services, incentives, and rate based QoS.

A great deal of effort as gone into putting together a high-quality program. The quality of submissions was very high, and the program committee had a difficult task to select 27 papers among many deserving papers. Special thanks to the program committee, and the outside reviewers, for their efforts and hard work in the reviewing and selection process during such a short time frame. We thank all authors who submitted papers to IWQoS, and who ultimately made this program possible.

We express our appreciation for our sponsors, NSF, the IEEE Communications Society, IFIP WG 6.1, and ACM SIGCOMM & SIGMOBILE.

Finally, we wish to thank Bob Miller for his help with organizing the workshop, and Keith Sklower for maintaining the IWQoS Web server.

April 2003   Kevin Jeffay, Ion Stoica & Klaus Wehrle

Workshop Co-chairs

Kevin Jeffay   Univ. of North Carolina
Ion Stoica   Univ. of California at Berkeley

IWQoS Steering Committee

Thomas Gross   ETH Zürich
Jorg Liebeherr   Univ. of Virginia
David Hutchison   Lancaster Univ.
Peter Steenkiste   Carnegie Mellon Univ.
Ralf Steinmetz   Darmstadt Univ. of Technology
Lars Wolf   Univ. of Braunschweig
Hui Zhang   CMU and Turin Networks

Program Committee

Nina Bhatti   Hewlett-Packard Labs
Andrew Campbell   Columbia Univ.
Anna Charny   CISCO Systems
John Chuang   Univ. of California at Berkeley
Rene Cruz   Univ. of California at San Diego
Constantinos Dovrolis   Georgia Institute of Technology
Anja Feldmann   Technical Univ. Munich
Victor Firoiu   Nortel Networks
Thomas Gross   ETH Zürich
David Hutchison   Lancaster Univ.
Shiv Kalyanaraman   Rensselaer Polytech Institute
Dina Katabi   Massachusetts Institute of Technology
Jasleen Kaur   Univ. of North Carolina
Srinivasan Keshav   Ensim Corporation
Edward Knightly   Rice Univ.
Jorg Liebeherr   Univ. of Virginia
Jane Liu   Microsoft Corporation
Nick McKeown   Stanford Univ.
Marco Mellia   Politecnico di Torino
Klara Nahrstedt   Univ. of Illinois at Urbana-Ch.
Abhay Parekh   ICSI/ICIR Berkeley
Balaji Prabhakar   Stanford Univ.
Raj Rajkumar   Carnegie Mellon Univ.
Peter Steenkiste   Carnegie Mellon Univ.
Harrick Vin   Univ. of Texas
Klaus Wehrle   ICSI/ICIR Berkeley
John Wroclawski   Massachusetts Institute of Technology
Hui Zhang   Carnegie Mellon Univ.
Zhi-Li Zhang   Univ. of Minnesota

Publicity Chair

Klaus Wehrle
Intern. Computer Science Institute

Administrative Assistant

Robert Miller
Univ. of California at Berkeley

Reviewers

Albert Banchs, NEC
Maged Beshai, Nortel Networks
Nina Bhatti, Hewlett-Packard Labs
Gordon Blair, Lancaster Univ.
Andrew Campbell, Columbia Univ.
Anna Charny, CISCO Systems
Rahul Chawathe, Rice Univ.
Shigang Chen, Univ. of Florida
Nicolas Christin, Univ. of Virginia
John Chuang, SIMS, UC Berkeley
Florin Ciucu, Univ. of Virginia
Geoff Coulson, Lancaster Univ.
Rene Cruz, Univ. of California
Filippo C. Consorzio, CNIT Italy
Constantinos Dovrolis, GeorgiaTech
Martin Dunmore, Lancaster Univ.
Anja Feldmann, TU München
Jorge Finochietto, Politecnico di Torino
Victor Firoiu, Nortel Networks
Violeta Gambiroza, Rice Univ.
Michele Garetto, Politecnico di Torino
Shravan Goorah, Lancaster Univ.
Sergey Gorinsky, Univ. of Texas, Austin
Pawan Goyal, IBM Almaden Research
Thomas Gross, ETH Zürich
David Gutierrez, Stanford Univ.
Benjamin Hardekopf, Univ. of Texas
Sugat Jain, Univ. of Texas, Austin
Kevin Jeffay, Univ. of North Carolina
Shivkumar Kalyanaraman, RPI
Vikram Kanodia, Rice Univ.
Roger Karrer, Rice Univ.
Dina Katabi, MIT
Jasleen Kaur, Univ. of North Carolina
Srinivasan Keshav, Ensim Corporation
Edward Knightly, Rice Univ.
Ravi Kokku, Univ. of Texas, Austin
Christian Kurmann, ETH Zürich
Aleksandar Kuzmanovic, Rice Univ.
Kevin Lai, UC Berkeley

Chengzhi Li, Univ. of Virginia
Jorg Liebeherr, Univ. of Virginia
Jane Liu, Microsoft Corporation
Yonghe Liu, Rice Univ.
Renato Lo Cigno, Univ. di Trento
Rui Lopes, Lancaster Univ.
King-Shan Lui, Hong-Kong Univ.
Laurent Mathy, Lancaster Univ.
Nick McKeown, Stanford Univ.
Marco Mellia, Politecnico di Torino
Jayaram Mudigonda, Univ. Texas, Austin
Klara Nahrstedt, Univ. of Illinois at U.C.
Giovanni Neglia, Univ. di Palermo
Stephen Patek, Univ. of Virginia
Dimitrios Pezaros, Lancaster Univ.
Balaji Prabhakar, Stanford Univ.
Nicholas Race, Lancaster Univ.
Ragunathan Rajkumar, Carnegie Mellon Univ.
Supranamaya Ranjan, Rice Univ.
Bahareh Sadeghi, Rice Univ.
Stefan Schmid, Lancaster Univ.
Prashant Shenoy, Univ. of Massachusetts
Steven Simpson, Lancaster Univ.
Paul Smith, Lancaster Univ.
Peter Steenkiste, Carnegie Mellon Univ.
Ion Stoica, UC Berkeley
Lakshm. Subramanian, UC Berkeley
Sandra Tartarelli, NEC
Luca Valcarenghi, Univ. di Pisa
Harrick Vin, Univ. of Texas, Austin
Jianping Wang, Univ. of Virginia
Klaus Wehrle, ICSI/ICIR, Berkeley
John Wroclawski, MIT
Mingbo Xiao, Rice Univ.
Ping Yuan, Rice Univ.
Hui Zhang, Carnegie Mellon University
Zhi-Li Zhang, Univ. of Minnesota
Shelley Zhuang, UC Berkeley

Sponsoring Institutions

IEEE Communications Society

IFIP WG 6.1

ACM SIGCOMM &
ACM SIGMOBILE

National Science Foundation (NSF)

Table of Contents

VIII Rate-Based QoS

IX Storage

I Analysis and Modeling

Network Characteristics: Modelling, Measurements, and Admission Control

Dinan Gunawardena, Peter Key, and Laurent Massoulié

Microsoft Research
7 J.J. Thomson Avenue
CB3 0FB Cambridge, United Kingdom

Abstract. Round trip delays constitute the basic network measure that can be obtained by end systems without any network support. Our aim is to design measurement-based admission control strategies for streaming applications based on such minimal feedback on network state. To this end we discuss simple statistical models of packet round trip delays accross either local or wide area networks. We observe that the delay component due to queueing scales like the reciprocal of the spare capacity, at least in a 'heavy traffic' regime where spare capacity is scarce. Our models also allow to capture the correlations between consecutive measurements. Based on these results we propose a two-stage strategy for inferring spare capacity along a network path. We show consistency of this estimate, and analyse its asymptotic variance when the number of samples becomes large. We have experimented these strategies in a local network environment. We observe a good match between theory and practice for switched Ethernets. Surprisingly, the match deteriorates only slightly when the network path comprises hubs, although the theoretical models seem to be less applicable to such technology.

1 Introduction

In IP networks, Round Trip Time (RTT) measurements constitute the basic feedback information that end hosts can use to infer the state of the network connection between them[1]. These are used in TCP Reno, explicitly to set the retransmission time out, and implicitly to trigger packet transmissions, while in TCP Vegas the variation in RTTs is monitored to stabilise the congestion window at a suitable value. Passive measurement of RTTs is considered in [8]. Many other uses of such RTT measurements have been considered, in particular for inferring the bottleneck capacity between two hosts by using active probing. Packet pair [11,12] and pathchar [6,14] are two popular methods for doing this.

The goal of the present work is to use such RTT measurements to infer the rate at which a real time connection between two hosts can be initiated, so that it does not disrupt existing connections. In contrast with previous work [10], [3], we do not rely on either loss occurring, or on the availability of ECN marks. To this end, we need to determine the spare capacity or available capacity, rather than the total capacity along

---

[1] Losses also constitute an important feedback. However their occurrence is not directly observed, but rather inferred from either triple duplicate acks, or time-outs.

K. Jeffay, I. Stoica, and K. Wehrle (Eds.): IWQoS 2003, LNCS 2707, pp. 3–20, 2003.

the path between the nodes. Related work on available capacity estimation in the wide area considers TCP as an estimator, as well as probing estimators [7]. Also relevant is the Delphi procedure, introduced in [17] to infer characteristics of cross-traffic. In contrast to most current work on network measurements, we use stochastic models of traffic and queues. A notable exception is [1]. In addition, while prior work has concentrated on the wide area context, we are also interested in small networks.

A networked home is an example of a small network (i.e. with low number of hosts, low number of segments), where a small number of devices such as servers, PCs, PDAs and other network devices may be connected using a variety of Layer 2-technologies. Switches, hubs, wireless access points and wireless bridges may be mixed together. Measuring network characteristics for such small networks is important for applications and services such as streaming multimedia across the network. For example, the available bandwidth determines whether we can safely start a new stream between two nodes in the network, and at what rate, while delay or jitter measurement may restrict the applications than can run with acceptable quality. The size of the network poses inference problems different from those for large networks.

We consider simple models for predicting the evolution of round trip times in such LANs, and observe that the queueing component of round trip times is inversely proportional to spare capacity for a wide range of background traffic. This in turn motivates probing strategies for deciding at what rate a real time streaming application can be started between the two devices. The probing strategies have to gather information without disrupting existing traffic. We consider a strategy for inferring spare capacity motivated by the maximum likelihood estimation technique. We establish consistency of this estimator, and analyse its asymptotic behaviour. We give experimental results for this strategy in switched Ethernet and Wireless LAN scenarios. These suggest that simple, robust, non-disruptive probing strategies can be found for admission control in small LANs, using current switches, hubs and home networking technologies.

Although our initial motivation lies in home environments, we believe that the statistical modeling might prove relevant in WAN situations as well. In particular, we present an analysis of correlations between observed RTTs which we use only to predict when distinct measurements can be considered independent. However such correlations do contain information which could be used to improve other estimators, such as the pathchar method for assessing bottleneck bandwidth.

The paper is organised as follows. In Section 2 we survey classical as well as novel models for the observed RTTs. In Section 3 we discuss estimation of spare capacity from such observations. Section 4 describes our experimental set-up and Section 5 the corresponding results.

2   Statistical Models for Round Trip Delays

Consider a sender/receiver pair. Assume that at time T_n, $n \geq 0$, the sender sends a packet of size p_n bytes to the receiver, which reflects it back to the sender, where it is received at time S_n. Note $\tau_n := S_n - T_n$ the corresponding round trip time. We first make simple assumptions on the physics of the transmission path. We then review a number of simple background traffic models, and results on the corresponding delay distributions. These models all exhibit short-range dependence, an assumption that is seldom met in practice (see [15]). However, these models are nevertheless useful in identifying qualitative relationships between spare capacity and observed delays.

2.1 Physical Assumptions on the Transmission Path

Single bottleneck assumption: We assume that these RTTs are fully determined by some fixed propagation time τ, plus some queueing time at a bottleneck link. We thus neglect the impact of several capacity constraints along the path, and rather assume the most stringent bottleneck alone determines the queueing times. This is appropriate in a LAN environment, where multiple bottlenecks rarely occur.

Bottleneck model: The bottleneck is supposed to be a queue with capacity C bytes/second. In addition to the packets used for measurements, the bottleneck receives background traffic. Denote by $A(s,t)$ the total amount of such background traffic received between times s and t. Let $W(t)$ denote the workload at the bottleneck at time t. We assume FIFO queueing, so that the observed transmission times read:

$$\tau_n = \tau + \frac{W(T_n^-) + p_n}{C}. \tag{1}$$

This representation relies on the assumption that the propagation time τ takes place between the bottleneck and the receiver. The impact of finite buffer capacity is discussed in 2.2 below.

2.2 Background Traffic Models

Unreactive, Poisson stream of packets: Assume that the background traffic consists in packets with independent, identically distributed (i.i.d.) sizes, that reach the bottleneck link at the instants of a Poisson process. Then the Pollaczeck-Khinchin formula (see e.g. [2]) gives the mean value of the stationary buffer content distribution. In particular, the average waiting time of a probe packet reads

$$\overline{D} = \frac{\lambda}{C} \frac{\overline{X^2}}{2(C-m)}, \tag{2}$$

where $\overline{X^2}$ is the mean of the squared packet size, λ is the packet arrival rate per second, and m is the load on the queue, given by $\lambda\overline{X}$ where $\overline{X}$ is the mean packet size. Note the inverse dependence on $C - m$.

Unreactive, white noise background traffic: Another convenient traffic model is as follows. Assume one has

$$A(s,t) = m(t-s) + \sigma \left(B(t) - B(s) \right), \tag{3}$$

where m is the mean arrival rate, σ describes the burstiness, and $B(t)$ is a standard Brownian motion (Wiener process). Such a traffic model arises naturally as a heavy traffic limit (see e.g. Reiman [16]) of a queue with short range dependent traffic. Queues with Brownian input have been extensively studied; see for instance the book [5]. For the model under consideration, the conditional distribution of the workload $W(t+h)$ at time $t+h$ given the workload at some time t is given by

$$\mathbf{P}(W(t+h) \leq x | W(t) = w) = \Phi\left(\frac{(C-m)h+x-w}{\sigma\sqrt{h}}\right)$$
$$- e^{-2(C-m)x/\sigma^2} \Phi\left(\frac{(C-m)h-x-w}{\sigma\sqrt{h}}\right), \ x \geq 0, \quad (4)$$

where $x \in \mathbb{R}$ and Φ is the cumulative distribution function of a standard normal random variable, i.e.

$$\Phi(x) = \int_{-\infty}^{x} \frac{1}{\sqrt{2\pi}} e^{-y^2/2} dy.$$

In particular, when $C > m$, it can be seen by letting h tend to infinity in the above formula that the workload $W(t)$ admits a limiting distribution given by

$$\mathbf{P}(W(t) \leq x) = \mathbf{1}_{x \geq 0} \left\{ 1 - e^{-2(C-m)x/\sigma^2} \right\}, \quad (5)$$

an exponential distribution with mean $\sigma^2/2(C-m)$. Note again the inverse dependence on the spare capacity, $C-m$. Although Equation (4) does in principle capture the correlations between the observed round trip times, it is not straightforward to derive a suitable notion of correlation time from it. This will be made easier from the analysis to follow.

Unreactive white noise, with finite buffer capacity: We now modify the previous model to incorporate a finite buffer memory. The workload process, W_t, obeys the diffusion equation

$$dW_t = -(C-m)\,dt + \sigma dB_t,$$

with reflection at 0 and b, where b represents the maximal buffer content. Here, B is a standard Brownian motion, $-(C-m)$ is the drift, and σ is as before a positive parameter describing the background traffic burstiness. The previous model is a limiting case of this one, obtained by letting b go to infinity. The results to follow are derived in the Appendix. Define the functions y_k and the numbers λ_k by letting

$$y_0(x) \equiv 1, \ y_k(x) = e^{dx/\sigma^2}\left(d\sin\left(\frac{k\pi x}{b}\right) - \frac{k\pi\sigma^2}{b}\cos\left(\frac{k\pi x}{b}\right)\right),$$
$$\lambda_0 = 0, \quad \lambda_k = \frac{1}{2\sigma^2}\left(d^2 + \frac{k^2\pi^2\sigma^4}{b^2}\right), \ k \in \mathbb{Z}_+, \quad (6)$$

where $d = C - m$. One then has:

Theorem 1. *The probability density of W_t conditionally on W_0 is specified by*

$$\pi_t(x|W_0 = z) = \mathbf{1}_{[0,b]}(x) \sum_{k \geq 0} \frac{1}{\beta_k} y_k(x) e^{-2dx/\sigma^2} y_k(z) e^{-\lambda_k t}, \quad (7)$$

where

$$\beta_0 = \frac{1 - e^{-2db/\sigma^2}}{2d/\sigma^2}, \ \beta_k = \frac{b}{2}\left[d^2 + \frac{k^2\pi^2\sigma^4}{b^2}\right], \ k > 0. \tag{8}$$

The stationary distribution is obtained by letting t go to infinity; it reads

$$\pi_{stat}(x) = \mathbf{1}_{[0,b]}(x)\frac{2d/\sigma^2}{1 - e^{-2db/\sigma^2}}e^{-2dx/\sigma^2}. \tag{9}$$

One of the insights that we derive from this result is as follows. The exponents λ_k capture the speed at which the influence of the initial value W_0 on the distribution of W_t vanishes. In particular, for times t large compared to the reciprocal of λ_1, the smallest non-zero λ_k, this influence vanishes. In this sense, that result identifies a correlation time scale for the process W_t as

$$\frac{1}{\lambda_1} = \frac{2\sigma^2}{(C - m)^2 + \frac{\pi^2\sigma^4}{b^2}}.$$

In the case where the buffer limit b is large, this critical time scale also reads

$$T_{critical} = \frac{2\sigma^2}{(C - m)^2}. \tag{10}$$

We note that this model can be used to predict the occurence of loss: indeed, a packet of size p_n would be lost according to this model when it reaches the queue and finds there a workload W such that $W + p_n$ is greater than the buffer limit b.

Poisson unreactive + reactive traffic: Now, to directly model TCP-like traffic, we assume a fixed number of packets, N say, queue at the bottleneck link together with unreactive traffic with FIFO service. After service at the bottleneck, each packet undergoes a random delay, with given mean $\bar{\delta}$, and then re-enters the bottleneck queue. Effectively these reactive packets are subject to fixed size window control. One could for instance view them as packets belonging to a number of ongoing TCP connections, assuming that the sum of the congestion windows of these TCP connections is roughly constant, and equal to N. This does not account for losses, and would be appropriate in a situation where the bottleneck buffer is large and the TCP window sizes saturate at the receive window limit.

We assume as above that unreactive packets reach the bottleneck queue at the instants of a Poisson process, with intensity λ.

For tractability, we assume that the service time of packets of both reactive and unreactive traffic at the bottleneck queue is exponentially distributed with mean denoted by $\bar{X}$. The following result is established in the Appendix.

Proposition 1. *Let $\pi(k,l)$ denote the stationary probability that there are k unreactive, and l reactive packets queued at the bottleneck. For all $k \geq 0$, all $l \in \{0, \ldots, N\}$, one has*

$$\pi(k,l) = \frac{1}{Z}\binom{k+l}{l}a^k b^l \frac{1}{(N-l)!}, \tag{11}$$

where

$$a = \frac{\lambda \overline{X}}{C}, \quad b = \frac{\overline{X}}{\delta C}, \quad Z = \frac{1}{1-a} \sum_{l=0}^{N} \left(\frac{b}{1-a}\right)^{l} \frac{1}{(N-l)!}. \tag{12}$$

In the heavy traffic limit where $1-a$ goes to 0, the stationary waiting time D satisfies the following weak convergence result:

$$\frac{C(1-a)}{\overline{X}} D \overset{W}{\to} \Gamma(N+2,1), \tag{13}$$

where $\Gamma(N+2,1)$ is the Gamma distribution with parameters $(N+2,1)$, in other words it is distributed as the sum of $N+1$ independent random variables, with exponential distribution and mean 1.

We interpret this result as follows. The impact of reactive traffic is to increase queueing delays in a *multiplicative* way, via the parameter $N+1$. More importantly, its introduction does not change the qualitative way in which spare capacity, captured by $C(1-a)$, affects delays: these are still (at least in the heavy traffic limit) proportional to the reciprocal of the spare capacity. We expect this qualitative relationship to be preserved, at least in the heavy traffic regime, for more general packet service time distributions and short range dependent exogeneous packet arrival processes.

Modelling hubs and wireless access points: Hubs behave as Ethernet segments, hence CSMA/CD models can be used to approximate their performance. Informally, the waiting time a packet sees is comprised of queueing time waiting for any packets 'in system to be cleared', plus the amount of time waiting for retransmissions. An analysis of CSMA/CD (see e.g. [2] p. 318) gives the waiting time as a deviation from from the Pollaczek-Khinchine formula

$$\overline{D} = \frac{\lambda \overline{X^2} + \beta(4.62 + 2\lambda)}{2(1 - \lambda(1 + 3.31\beta))}, \tag{14}$$

where we assume that the expected packet size $\overline{X}$ and the capacity C are normalised to 1, and β is the duration of a minislot (the time for a signal to propagate along a segment and be detected). This is small, and ignoring this term gives exactly the Pollaczek-Khinchine formula. Wireless uses CSMA/CA, and again we have approximately that the waiting time is proportional to $1/(C-m)$.

3   Spare Capacity Estimation

Our aim is to infer at what rate a real time connection can be established between two hosts, while preserving some Quality of Service constraint. If C is the capacity of the bottleneck link (or equivalent link), and the current load on the link is m, then the spare capacity is defined as $C-m$. However, this definition requires some clarification: stationarity, or 'local' stationarity is implicit in the definition, as is some assumption of timescale for which this holds. We shall take a more specific definition of available capacity, and define layer-n available capacity to be the maximum n-layer throughput that can be achieved by *unreactive* traffic, without damaging existing unreactive traffic. We now describe the model for round trip times that we adopt based on the previous section. We then analyse a specific estimator of spare capacity derived by applying the maximum likelihood method, and then discuss alternative estimates and corresponding tests.

3.1 Measurement Model

We assume that the packet send times T_n are sufficiently separated so that the sequence of workload contents $W(T_n^-)$ appearing in the expressions of the measured transmission times (1) are independent random variables. Relying on both the white noise traffic model, and the heavy traffic limit derived in Proposition 1, we assume that the observed round trip times τ_n read

$$\tau_n = \tau + \frac{1}{C-m} Z_n, \qquad (15)$$

where the random variables Z_n are i.i.d., and follow a Gamma distribution with unknown parameters, that do not depend on the background load, m. In addition to these measurements, we shall take another series of round trip time measurements, τ_n', while sending some additional unreactive traffic. This extra load, noted δm, is known to us. Noting m' the new offered load, i.e. $m' = m + \delta m$, we then have

$$\tau_n' = \tau + \frac{1}{C-m'} Z_n',$$

where the Z_n' are i.i.d., and drawn from the same Gamma distribution as the Z_n. The parameters of this Gamma distribution, which we shall denote by $N+1$ and B, as well as τ and C are a priori unknown. In the remainder of this section, we assume that there are k measurements in each sample set. We now consider the estimation of $C-m$ from these samples.

3.2 Maximum-Likelihood Estimation

Consider the Log-likelihood L of the samples $\tau_1, \ldots, \tau_k, \tau_1', \ldots, \tau_k'$. This reads

$$L = \sum_{n=1}^{k} -2\log\left(\Gamma(N+1)\right) + N \log\left((\tau_n - \tau)(\tau_n' - \tau)\right)$$
$$+ (N+1)\log\left(B^2(C-m)(C-m')\right) - B\left((C-m)(\tau_n - \tau) + (C-m')(\tau_n' - \tau)\right).$$

By differentiating, it is easy to see that the maximum likelihood estimate of the ratio $(C-m)/(C-m')$ is given by $(\overline{\tau'} - \hat{\tau})/(\overline{\tau} - \hat{\tau})$, where $\overline{\tau}$, $\overline{\tau'}$ are the sample means $k^{-1} \sum_{n=1}^{k} \tau_n$, $k^{-1} \sum_{n=1}^{k} \tau_n'$ respectively, and $\hat{\tau}$ is the maximum likelihood estimate of the shift parameter τ. Consequently, the maximum likelihood estimate of $C-m$ is given by

$$\delta m \frac{\overline{\tau'} - \hat{\tau}}{\overline{\tau'} - \overline{\tau}}.$$

As maximum likelihood estimates have desirable properties (in particular, asymptotic efficiency; see [4]) we shall rely on this specific form to infer the spare capacity. Unfortunately, no analytical expression for the maximum likelihood estimate $\hat{\tau}$ is available. We shall therefore take $\hat{\tau} = \min_{1 \leq n \leq k} (\tau_n)$ instead[2].

Introduce the relative estimation error e by letting:

$$\widehat{C-m} = \delta m \, \frac{\overline{\tau'} - \hat{\tau}}{\overline{\tau'} - \overline{\tau}} =: (C-m)(1-e). \tag{16}$$

We then have the following, which is established in the appendix:

Proposition 2. *The estimator (16) of $C - m$ is asymptotically consistent, i.e. the error e goes to zero in probability as $k \to \infty$. Assume that the random variables Z_n follow a Gamma distribution with parameters $(N+1, B)$, where $N+1$, B are two positive parameters. If N is larger than 1, as $k \to \infty$, the following weak convergence holds:*

$$k^{1/(N+1)} e \xrightarrow{W} \frac{C-m'}{C-m} X, \tag{17}$$

where X is a random variable with a Weibull distribution, specified by the complementary distribution function $\mathbf{P}(X > t) = \exp\left(-t^{N+1}/\Gamma(N+2)\right)$.

If N is smaller than 1, as $k \to \infty$, the following weak convergence holds:

$$\sqrt{k}\, e \xrightarrow{W} \frac{C-m'}{\delta m} 2(N+1)\mathcal{N}(0,1), \tag{18}$$

where $\mathcal{N}(0,1)$ denotes the standard Gaussian distribution.

This shows, on the one hand, that direct estimation of the spare capacity $C - m$ is possible without explicitly inferring the other model parameters. On the other hand, when N is larger than 1, the mean square error goes to zero as $k^{-2/(N+1)}$. This is slower than the classical scaling k^{-1} (which occurs for $N < 1$), which suggests that better estimation techniques might exist.

3.3 A General Class of Estimators

The previous section has motivated specific estimators of spare capacity. In general, we may define an estimator $S(\tau)$ of the vector $\tau = (\tau_1, ..., \tau_k)$ to be such that $(C-m)S$ is consistent for either the scale, or the location of Z. In the example above, $S(\tau) = \overline{\tau} - \tau_{\min}$ is a consistent estimator for the location of Z rescaled by $1/(C-m)$, and the standard deviation of τ is consistent for the scale. More generally we may use robust estimates of location or scale instead of just the mean or standard deviation, such as the trimmed mean or median, or other more refined M-estimates or R-estimates for the location, and similarly for the scale. We then have

$$R_{\tau,\tau} = \frac{S(\tau)}{S(\tau')} \to \frac{C-m'}{C-m}, \tag{19}$$

and hence

---

[2] Taking the minimum over both sets of samples should in principle yield a better estimate. We use the minimum over one sample instead because it simplifies the analysis to follow, and does not change its conclusions significantly.

$$\widehat{C - m} = \frac{\delta m}{1 - R_{\tau,\tau}},\qquad(20)$$

and

$$\widehat{C - m'} = \delta m \frac{R_{\tau,\tau}}{1 - R_{\tau,\tau}} = \delta m \frac{S(\tau)}{S(\tau') - S(\tau)}.\qquad(21)$$

This provides a general method for obtaining estimates of spare capacity under the model (15), which does not rely on the fact that the random variables Z_n, Z'_n follow a Gamma distribution, but applies to any arbitrary distribution instead.

These estimates lead naturally to equivalent tests. For example testing whether $C - m' > r\,\delta m$ can be based on comparing $R_{\tau,\tau}/(1 - R_{\tau,\tau})$ to r.

4   Experimental Framework and Implementation

Probing traffic can be generated by different protocol layers. For example, UDP packets could be used to generate the probing traffic. This is the protocol layer of the traffic of interest, however an implementation would then require software alteration to both the sender and receiver (a symmetric solution), and also confounds network delays with delays caused by the operating system. Using ICMP messages (which are handled at a very low level in most IP stacks) allows us to have an asymmetric solution, with measurement and probing software only required on the probing machine. The asymmetric solution is attractive for typical legacy home networks, since the probing and admission control only needs to be added to devices which act as servers or senders. To be able to reduce the effect of measurement errors and timer granularity, for small networks where the round trip time is small, we need better resolution than provided by a standard user-mode ICMP ping, and hence needed to use a kernel mode driver for accurate timestamping. Because we are looking at LANs, we avoid the problems that ICMP has in the wide area.

Our probing strategies used ICMP ping packets to generate the probing traffic and measure the network, with a kernel mode driver handling the basic probing functions. For the ping probes, echo request packet sequences were created and time-stamped by the processor cycle counter before transmission. Incoming echo replies are captured and time-stamped, giving the RTT to microsecond accuracy.

An example test configuration is shown in Figure 1, which shows a two switch (or two hub) network, with potential contention caused by traffic from the background source and the probing traffic sharing a common link. In this example, the switches (or hubs) create a single bottleneck, where the bottleneck could be between the two switches, or, if the interconnects are hubs, between the PCs and the hub. Background traffic was UDP traffic, generated at a specific nominal rate (bursts at 20ms intervals), and TCP traffic. A wireless scenario is shown in the bottom half of Figure 1, where a 802.11b Wireless Access Point is connected to wireless bridges. The switches were configured to 10Mb/s or 100Mb/s. We only report on the 10Mb/s results here. Standard switches were used from different manufacturers. The amount of buffering within each switch is typically about 128kB, giving a maximum queuing delay of about 100ms at 10Mb/s.

Experiments were run with different nominal background load (the bit-rate of the UDP background), with and without TCP traffic added, the background traffic being

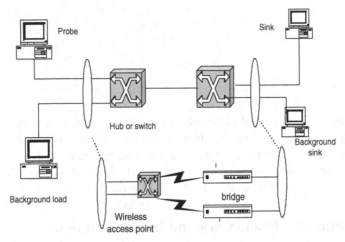

Fig. 1. Network Configuration for Experiments, showing switch/hub and wireless scenarios.

increased from 1Mb/s to 9 or 10Mb/s in 1Mb/s steps. For most of the experiments, the time between ICMPs was an exponentially distributed random variable with mean 10ms and 100ms. The two different values were used to assess the presence of correlations in the measurements.

5   Results

Consider first the switch scenario, where there are two 10Mb/s switches connecting the bottleneck link. With just UDP background load, the delay increases slightly before saturating the capacity at between 9 and 10 Mb/s. Measurements from four sets of probing, each comprising ten probes 100ms apart are summarised in the box plot in Figure 2. This plot is truncated to 200ms. In the critically loaded case (UDP load of 10Mb/s) delays as large as 500ms were observed, and 25% of the observed delays were above 350ms.

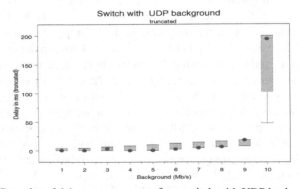

Fig. 2. Box plot of delay measurements for a switch with UDP background traffic.

With UDP background traffic alone, the transition from underload to overload is fairly sudden. In the extreme case of periodic background traffic, the delay is negligible until the switch starts to become overloaded. As the background traffic becomes more bursty, its variance increases, which increases the variability in the delay measurements (see, for example Section 2). When TCP is mixed in with UDP traffic, the delay at the 'nominal' background load (the load of the UDP traffic) increases, as does the variance, caused by the smearing effect of the TCP traffic, described analytically in Section 2. The corresponding box plot is shown in Figure 3. For a UDP load of 9 Mb/s, most measurements were below 200ms, while for a UDP load of 10Mb/s, delays as large as 1000ms were observed and 50% of the measurements were above 300ms, with some time-outs observed.

With probing at 100ms intervals, there is little correlation structure in the measurements: the autocorrelation function is plotted in Figure 4, corresponding to probing when there is a background load of 1 Mb/s (UDP) with TCP traffic also present, showing the only (just) significant correlation at lag 1. If we decrease the probing interval to 10ms, there is still little correlation structure evident. We do not present the corresponding picture, which is very similar to Figure 4.

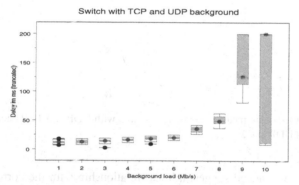

Fig. 3. Box plot of delay measurements for a switch with UDP and TCP background traffic.

A kernel density plot of the RTT delay distributions for 1, 5 and 8Mb/s background UDP mixed with TCP is given in Figure 5, suggesting that the different loadings can be inferred from the delay measurements, provided the loads are not too close. Note how both the scale and location of the densities increase with increasing load, an inverse relation with spare capacity consistent with the models of Section 2. The density shapes are not inconsistent with Gamma distributions of Proposition 1 (note that the curves shown here are based on only 40 samples, and influenced by the kernel estimator – a smoother kernel makes all three density estimates unimodal).

We now focus on the estimation of available capacity. The theoretical framework has motivated models and estimates where statistics of the round trip times are inversely related to the spare capacity. To see if this is borne out in practice for the adjusted means, we plot the logarithms of the adjusted means against the logarithm of the notional spare capacity, which should show a linear relationship with gradient -1. This is shown in

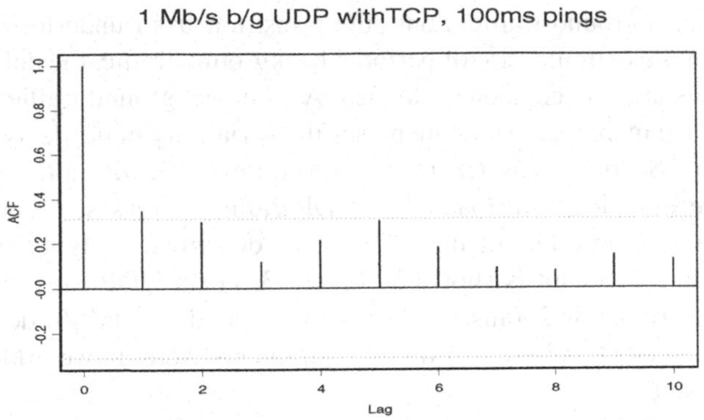

1 Mb/s b/g UDP withTCP, 100ms pings

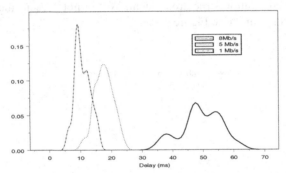

Fig. 4. Autocorrelation function of delay measurements for a switch with UDP and TCP background traffic, probes sent 100ms apart.

Fig. 5. Density plot for delay measurements for a switch with UDP and TCP background traffic, for 1, 5 and 8 Mb/s UDP load.

Figure 6, which does indeed suggest a linear relationship with the correct slope. The accuracy of the estimator (16) is shown in Figure 7, which plots the (post-probe) spare capacity estimator for different loadings (shown for the load after the probe has been admitted), where the estimate is based on 4 runs each using just 10 samples. Two different values of δm are shown: for δm equal to 1Mb/s, the estimates of spare capacity are rather noisy when there is plenty of spare capacity (which one could expect in view of Figure 3), but become more accurate the more heavily loaded the network. For δm equal to 3 Mb/s, the estimates show a good match to the spare capacity.

The set of results for a hub paint a very similar picture. Figure 8 shows a box plot of the delays. Not surprisingly, the delays increase more rapidly than for the switch, but the picture for estimation purposes is similar. The log-log plot for the spare capacity and adjusted mean is shown in Figure 9, and the capacity estimate using probing with the estimator (16) is shown in Figure 10.

For a wireless access point, the delays increase much sooner (since the effective data capacity of 802.11b is about 6 Mb/s), as shown in Figure 11. The log-log plot of adjusted mean against spare capacity in Figure 12 is again roughly linear. However, the slope is

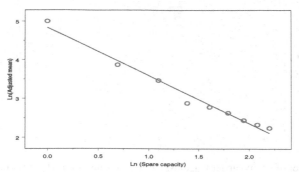

Fig. 6. Log-log plot of spare capacity against adjusted means, for 10Mb/s Switch with UDP and TCP background traffic.

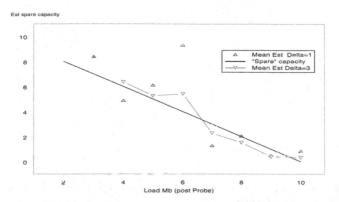

Fig. 7. Estimated (post probe) spare capacity against load (post probe), for 10Mb/s Switch with UDP and TCP background traffic.

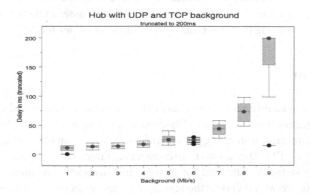

Fig. 8. Box plot of delay measurements for a hub withTCP and UDP background traffic.

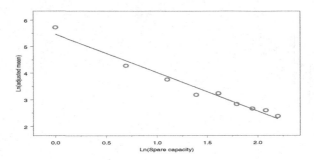

Fig. 9. Log-log plot of spare capacity against adjusted means, for a 10Mb/s hub with UDP and TCP background traffic.

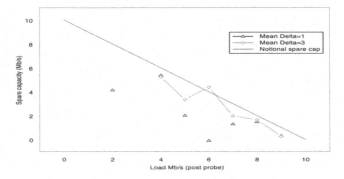

Fig. 10. Estimated (post probe) spare capacity against load (post probe), for a 10Mb/s Hub with UDP and TCP background traffic.

about -1.55, which constitutes a significant departure from the inverse dependence on which our estimator relies. Some more work is needed to assess whether this is due to noisy observations, or whether this requires a refinement of our model.

6   Conclusion

We have considered an estimate of spare capacity in a network which makes use of RTT measurements. Heavy traffic analysis of stochastic queuing models, handling a mixture of reactive and unreactive traffic, suggests an inverse relationship between spare capacity and statistics of the RTTs. This allows us to construct estimates of the spare capacity based on ratios of such statistics. The analysis is applicable to both wide area and local area networks; indeed, we would expect the results to be more accurate for larger networks. In particular, the analysis of RTT correlations presented in Theorem 1 might be used to refine existing techniques for bottleneck capacity estimation such as pathchar.

We have given some experimental results for small networks, such as those found in a networked home, and where spare capacity estimation is an essential part of any

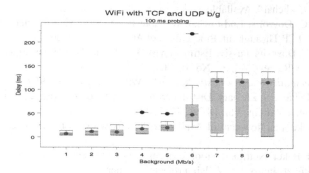

Fig. 11. Box plot of delay measurements for a wireless access point with TCP and UDP background traffic.

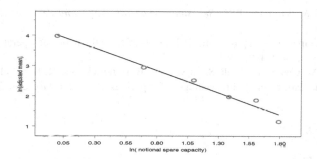

Fig. 12. Log-log plot of spare capacity against adjusted means for a wireless access point with UDP and TCP background traffic.

admission control scheme. Preliminary results are encouraging, showing a good match between theory and practice, and enabling us to design simple and robust admission control schemes. More work is required to tackle the case of wireless networks. We are currently testing a prototype admission control service for multimedia applications, based on the results of this paper, which is able to make a decision whether to admit or reject a connection within the order of 100 ms.

References

1. S. Alouf, P. Nain and D. Towsley, Inferring Network Characteristics via Moment-Based Estimators, Proceedings of IEEE Infocom, 2001.
2. D. Bertsekas and R. Gallager, *Data Networks*. Prentice Hall 1992.
3. L. Breslau, E. Knightly and S. Shenker, Endpoint Admission Control: Architectural Issues and Performance, Proceedings of ACM Sigcomm, 2000.
4. R. Davidson and J.G. MacKinnon, *Estimation and Inference in Econometrics*, Oxford University Press, 1993.
5. M. Harrison, *Brownian Motion and Stochastic Flow Systems*, John Wiley and Sons, New York, 1985.

6. V. Jacobson, "pathchar". Available at ftp://ftp.ee.lbl.gov/pathchar/.
7. M. Jain and C. Dovrolis, End-to-End Available Bandwidth: Measurement, Dynamics and Relation with TCP Throughput, Proceedings of ACM Sigcomm, 2002.
8. H. Jiang and C. Dovrolis, Passive Estimation of TCP Round-Trip Times, Sigcomm Computer Communication Review, Vol. 32, No. 1, 2002.
9. F. Kelly, *Reversibility and Stochastic Networks*, Wiley, Chichester, 1979.
10. F. Kelly, P. Key and S. Zachary, Distributed Admission Control, IEEE Journal on Selected Areas in Communications, Vol. 18, No. 12, 2000.
11. S. Keshav, Packet-pair flow control. Available at http://www.cs.cornell.edu/skeshav/doc/94/2-17.ps, 1994.
12. K. Lai and M. Baker, Nettimer: a tool for measuring bottleneck link bandwidth. Available at http://mosquitonet.stanford.edu/~laik/projects/nettimer.
13. T. Liggett, *Interacting Particle Systems*, Springer, Berlin, 1985.
14. K. Matoba, S. Ata and M. Murata, Improving Accuracy of Bandwidth Estimation for Internet Links by Statistical Methods, IEICE Transactions on Communications, Vol. E00-B, No. 6 June 2001.
15. K. Park and W. Willinger (Eds), *Self-Similar Network Traffic and Performance Evaluation*, Wiley, 2000.
16. M. Reiman, Open queueing networks in heavy traffic, Mathematics of Operations Research, Vol. 9, No. 3, pp. 441-458, 1984.
17. V. Ribeiro, M. Coates, R. Riedi, S. Sarvotham, B. Hendricks and R. Baraniuk, Multifractal Cross-Traffic Estimation, In Proceedings ITC Specialists Seminar, Monterey 2000.

7   Appendix

7.1   Proof of Theorem 1

An alternative description of the process W is via its infinitesimal generator $\mathcal{U}$ and the corresponding domain, $\mathcal{D}(\mathcal{U})$:

$$\mathcal{U}f(x) = \frac{\sigma^2}{2}f''(x) - df'(x),$$

and

$$\mathcal{D}(\mathcal{U}) = \{f \in C([0,b]) : f'' \in C([0,b]), f'(0) = f'(b) = 0\}$$

(see e.g. Liggett [13], examples 2.3 and 2.10, pages 13 and 16 respectively). Solving for the differential equation

$$\mathcal{U}f = -\lambda f, f \in \mathcal{D}(\mathcal{U}),$$

one finds that the eigenfunctions y_k and the corresponding eigenvalues $-\lambda_k$ of the generator on its domain are given by (6). We omit the details here. This thus yields the expansion

$$\mathbf{E}[f(W_t)|W_0 = z] = \sum_{k \geq 0} a_k y_k(z)e^{-\lambda_k t}, \tag{22}$$

for some coefficients a_k depending on the function f. Also, considering the scalar product $< f, g > = \int_0^b f(x)g(x)dx$ on $C([0,b])$, it is readily seen that the eigenfunctions y_k are such that $<\tilde{y}_k, \tilde{y}_l> = 0$ when $k \neq l$, where $\tilde{y}_k(x) := e^{-dx/\sigma^2} y_k(x)$. Setting $t = 0$ in (22), the left-hand side is $f(z)$; equating the scalar product of each side with $y_k(z)e^{-2dz/\sigma^2}$ yields

$$a_k = \frac{\int_0^b f(z)y_k(z)e^{-2dz/\sigma^2} dz}{\int_0^b y_k^2(z)e^{-2dz/\sigma^2} dz}.$$

. We finally obtain

$$\mathbf{E}[f(W_t)|W_0 = z] = \sum_{k \geq 0} \frac{1}{\beta_k} \left[\int_0^b y_k(x)f(x)e^{-2dx/\sigma^2} dx \right] y_k(z)e^{-\lambda_k t}, \qquad (23)$$

where the coefficients β_k are defined in (8). From Equation (23) we can read off the conditional density of W_t given $W_0 = z$, and the results of Theorem 1 follow.

7.2   Proof of Proposition 1

The formula (11) for the stationary distribution π follows from the general results in [9], Chapter 3. The normalising constant $Z(a,b)$ reads

$$Z(a,b) = \sum_{l=0}^N \frac{b^l}{(N-l)!} \sum_{k \geq 0} \binom{k+l}{l} a^k,$$

and the expression (12) thus follows from the negative binomial formula, that is

$$\sum_{k \geq 0} \binom{k+l}{l} a^k = \left(\frac{1}{1-a} \right)^{l+1}.$$

Denote by D the queueing time and by M the number of packets queued at the bottleneck. It holds that

$$D = \frac{1}{C} \sum_{m=1}^M \sigma_m,$$

where the σ_m are the sizes of the enqueued packets, and are by assumption i.i.d., exponentially distributed with mean $\overline{X}$. For any fixed real number u, one thus has

$$\mathbf{E}\left(e^{iu(1-a)\overline{X}^{-1}CD} \right) = \mathbf{E}\left(\left(\mathbf{E}e^{iu(1-a)\overline{X}^{-1}\sigma_1} \right)^M \right)$$

$$= \frac{Z(a/(1-iu(1-a)), b/(1-iu(1-a)))}{Z(a,b)}.$$

Using the formula (12) for Z in the previous expression, one readily obtains that

$$\lim_{a \to 1} \mathbf{E}\left(e^{iu(1-a)\overline{X}^{-1}CD} \right) = \left(\frac{1}{1-iu} \right)^{N+1},$$

which is the characteristic function of the $\Gamma(N+2, 1)$ distribution, thus establishing the proposition.

7.3 Proof of Proposition 2

Introduce the notations

$$\epsilon_0 = \hat{\tau} - \tau, \; \epsilon = \frac{1}{k}\sum_{n=1}^{k} Z_n - \mathbf{E}(Z), \; \epsilon' = \frac{1}{k}\sum_{n=1}^{k} Z'_n - \mathbf{E}(Z).$$

The identity $\bar{\tau} = \tau + \mathbf{E}(Z)/(C - m) + \epsilon/(C - m)$ and its analogue for $\bar{\tau}'$, used in conjunction with (16), can be used to establish that, to the first order in ϵ and ϵ', the relative error e verifies

$$e = \frac{C - m'}{\delta m\, \mathbf{E}(Z)}\left(\delta m\, \epsilon_0 - \epsilon' + \epsilon\right). \tag{24}$$

By definition, ϵ_0 reads $Z_{(1)}/(C - m)$, where $Z_{(1)}$ is the minimum of the Z_n. We now evaluate the asymptotic distribution of the minimal value $Z_{(1)}$. We need only consider the case where the second parameter B in the Gamma distribution of the Z_n is 1, as this disappears due to the division by $\mathbf{E}(Z)$ in the expression of e. The density of the Z_n is then given by $f(z) = z^N e^{-z}/\Gamma(N+1)$. It holds that

$$\mathbf{P}(Z_{(1)} > t) = (\mathbf{P}(Z_1 > t))^k.$$

Solving for $\mathbf{P}(Z_1 > t_k) = 1 - u/k$, for some fixed positive u, one finds

$$t_k \sim \left(\Gamma(N+2)\frac{u}{k}\right)^{1/(N+1)}.$$

One thus gets that

$$\mathbf{P}\left(Z_{(1)} > \left(\frac{u\Gamma(N+2)}{k}\right)^{1/(N+1)}\right) \sim e^{-u}.$$

This yields that $k^{1/(N+1)} Z_{(1)}$ follows asymptotically a Weibull distribution specified by the complementary distribution function $\exp\left(-t^{N+1}/\Gamma(N+2)\right)$. When N is larger than 1, ϵ_0 will then constitute the principal component in (24), as the other error terms are of order $1/\sqrt{k}$ by the central limit theorem. Thus, for $N > 1$, we have as $k \to \infty$ the weak convergence

$$k^{1/(N+1)} e \xrightarrow{w} \frac{C - m'}{C - m} X,$$

where X denotes a random variable with the aforementioned Weibull distribution. This establishes the first part of the proposition.

In the case where $N < 1$, the main contributions in (24) are from ϵ and ϵ'. By the central limit theorem we then obtain, as $k \to \infty$, that

$$\sqrt{k}\, e \xrightarrow{w} \frac{C - m'}{\delta m} 2(N+1)\mathcal{N}(0,1).$$

Statistical Characterization for Per-hop QoS*

Mohamed El-Gendy, Abhijit Bose, Haining Wang, and Kang G. Shin

Department of Electrical Engineering and Computer Science
The University of Michigan, Ann Arbor, MI 48109-2122
{mgendy,abose,hxw,kgshin}@eecs.umich.edu

Abstract. In Differentiated Services (DiffServ) architecture, we define the *per-hop QoS* as the throughput, delay, jitter, and loss rate experienced by traffic crossing a Per-Hop Behavior (PHB). In this paper, we use a statistical approach that is based on experiments on a real network testbed to characterize the per-hop QoS of a given PHB. Specifically, we employ a full factorial statistical design of experiments to study the effects of different PHB configurations and input traffic scenarios on per-hop QoS. We use Analysis of Variance (ANOVA) to identify the input and PHB configuration parameters that have the most significant influence on per-hop QoS. Then, multiple regression analysis is applied to construct models for the per-hop QoS with respect to these parameters. The overall approach is shown to be effective and capable of characterizing any given PHB, within the ranges of the experiments, and for construction of functional relationships for the PHB output parameters. The approach in this paper forms a "fundamental" step towards achieving predictable end-to-end QoS when applying statistical QoS control at intermediate nodes.

1 Introduction

Providing network-level Quality of Service (QoS) in large-scale IP networks is the main motivation behind the DiffServ architecture [1,2]. In this architecture, packets entering a DiffServ-enabled network are marked with different DiffServ Code Points (DSCPs), and based on these markings, they are subject to classification, traffic conditioning (such as metering, shaping, and policing), as well as to a small set of packet forwarding techniques called Per-Hop Behaviors (PHBs). The IETF DiffServ Working Group has been standardizing the building blocks of the DiffServ architecture, and a set of PHBs have been proposed in [1,3,4]. One of these PHBs, The Expedited Forwarding (EF), is a building block for low loss, low delay, and low jitter services. The Assured Forwarding (AF) PHB is proposed to offer different levels of forwarding assurance in terms of packet loss. Under AF, each packet is marked with drop precedence according to a specific marking rule or algorithm. At core routers, if the network is congested, the packets with higher precedence are preferentially dropped before packets with lower precedence.

---

* The work reported in this paper was supported in part by Samsung Electronics and the ONR under Grant N00014-99-0465.

K. Jeffay, I. Stoica, and K. Wehrle (Eds.): IWQoS 2003, LNCS 2707, pp. 21–40, 2003.
© Springer-Verlag Berlin Heidelberg 2003

Service differentiation is achieved by allocating different amounts of network resources, such as link bandwidth and buffers, to different types of traffic traversing the DiffServ-enabled routers. The output of this service differentiation at each router in terms of throughput, delay, jitter, and loss of the output traffic, is called *per-hop QoS*. Given the per-hop QoS for every node along an end-to-end path, the end-to-end[1] QoS perceived by users can be calculated. This is similar to Integrated Services [5], which uses RSVP signaling to estimate such end-to-end QoS on a hop-by-hop basis.

A PHB is the key building block of the DiffServ architecture and is realized by a variety of traffic management components, such as queues, schedulers, buffer management, policer, and filters. These components must be properly designed and implemented so that the per-hop QoS guarantees provided by the PHB can be achieved. However, it is a challenging task to assemble these building blocks together, given the complex nature of the interactions among the various components. It is becoming more important for network operators to be able to adjust the configuration parameters of network nodes within their domains to address the needs of specific services being offered, and to respond to dynamic changes of the input traffic. Characterizing a network node accurately is, therefore, an important research problem to be solved in the field of QoS. The main goal of our study is to demonstrate that careful statistical analysis coupled with an experimental framework can effectively characterize any DiffServ PHB, and extract a statistical model that can predict the per-hop QoS for this PHB.

We use a generic quantitative approach for characterizing the per-hop QoS for any PHB realization under a wide range of input traffic and configuration parameters. We first abstract the DiffServ PHBs into sets of inputs, configuration and output parameters. These parameters can be controlled and/or measured via experiments. Then, we design a set of full factorial [6] experiments to measure the effects of the inputs and configuration parameters on the output of a PHB. By performing Analysis of Variance (ANOVA) and regression analysis of the data from these experimental measurements, we can deduce functional relationships of the per-hop QoS parameters and construct a statistical model of the PHB. The results thus obtained demonstrate the effectiveness of our approach in capturing the functional dependencies of per-hop QoS on the input and configuration parameters. In addition, they point out the differences in performance guarantees provided by different PHB implementations. The potential benefits of our approach are:

1. Facilitating the control and optimization of the PHB performance. This is done by identifying the most important factors that control a certain PHB and by extracting the relationships between these factors and the output of the PHB (per-hop QoS);
2. In addition to being able to control the PHB, one can use the statistical models of the PHBs, derived in this study, in a per-hop admission control mechanism that contributes to the end-to-end admission control decision.

---

[1] Edge-to-edge Per-Domain Behaviors (PDBs) can also be quantified.

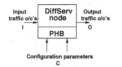

Fig. 1. Model of per-hop QoS

Fig. 2. Steps of the statistical approach

The remainder of the paper is organized as follows. Section 2 presents our strategy for characterizing a given PHB. Section 3 describes the experimental framework we use. Sample results and analysis of our study are presented in Section 4. In Section 5, we discuss some of the related work and previous studies of Diff-Serv PHBs and services. We conclude the paper with Section 6, and discuss extensions of our approach to studying larger-scale QoS problems and related protocol-level mappings.

2   Approach to Statistical Characterization

This section describes the approach we have taken to statistically characterize per-hop QoS. As shown in Fig. 1, the central idea is to abstract a given PHB as a system that consists of input (I) and output (O) traffic characteristics, and a set of configuration parameters (C). The details of the internal implementation of per-hop QoS are not considered explicitly, but their effects on the overall performance (i.e., the output traffic characteristics) are modeled. We apply statistical analysis methods to identify the most influential parameters affecting the per-hop QoS within the range and domain of our experiments and we estimate their relationships to the output. In the context of our experiments, we refer to O as the per-hop QoS attributes experienced by traffic crossing a DiffServ PHB. The basic steps of our approach are shown in Fig. 2, and can be summarized as follows.

- **Identification of the parameters in I and C that account for most of the effects on O:** In experimental design, the parameters of I and C are termed as *input factors* and the attributes of O as *response variables*. The values each factor takes are called *levels*. The most important factors are identified by calculating the percentages of the total output variation caused by the factors and their interactions. We use the Analysis of Variance (ANOVA) in this step.
- **Construction of appropriate models of the response variables based on the most important factors:** This step requires careful validation of the observed data so that the basic assumptions about the models hold for the experimental data. We use regression analysis to find such models after performing suitable transformations of the factors and response variables.

Our approach can also be used to evaluate alternative design choices. The IETF DiffServ Working Group does not specify how to design traffic control elements,

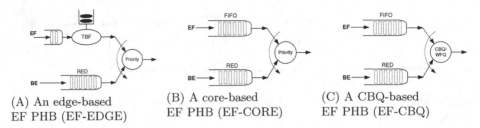

(A) An edge-based
EF PHB (EF-EDGE)

(B) A core-based
EF PHB (EF-CORE)

(C) A CBQ-based
EF PHB (EF-CBQ)

Fig. 3. Three different realizations for EF PHB sharing the a link with best-effort (BE)

such as queues, schedulers and filters for any of the proposed PHBs. One can, therefore, construct a PHB using a variety of traffic conditioning blocks as long as it conforms to the traffic handling guidelines specified in the DiffServ standard. Figures 3(A), 3(B), and 3(C) show different choices for EF PHB and best-effort (BE) sharing a single physical link. While these different implementations are expected to provide similar qualitative behavior of the aggregated output traffic, the functional relationships among the parameters are different due to the internal construction of the traffic handling blocks. We demonstrate this point further through our experiments. Next, we explain why we repeat some of the experiments by adjusting the parameters as shown in Fig. 2. For certain experiments, it is useful to start with a reduced number of levels for the full set of input factors. Once the most significant factors are identified, the number of levels corresponding to these factors are increased with the others fixed. This allows us to construct a higher-order regression model in the second stage of the analysis. This repetition of factorial analysis is shown as the "Adjust scenario parameters" step in Fig. 2. Note that our approach and framework for data collection, designing the required set of experiments, and statistical analysis, are general and mostly automated. This is a departure from most recent experimental studies of DiffServ EF and AF PHBs for multimedia traffic where a set of experiments were performed on a given testbed using a fixed configuration for traffic forwarding [7,8].

2.1 Factors and Factor Levels

As mentioned above, the parameters in I and C affect the output response (O) of a PHB. Therefore, we need to determine which parameter should be considered as factors and at what levels. The parameters of I may include both marked and unmarked input traffic.[2] We use the Dual Leaky Bucket (DLB) representation for the input traffic, as shown in Table 1. For the best-effort traffic, the ratio R_{ab} of assured traffic rate to best-effort traffic rate is more meaningful than its absolute value. Since most QoS schemes do not provide any guarantee for best-effort traffic, we are primarily interested in the performance of assured traffic. Note that some of the parameters of I depend on the PHB node itself, such as the number of input interfaces (NI). The set of configuration parameters

---

[2] Marked traffic is also called assured, and unmarked traffic is often best-effort.

Table 1. Symbolic representation of the factors in I

Factor	Symbol
Assured traffic average rate	a_r
Assured traffic peak rate	a_p
Assured traffic burst size	a_b
Assured traffic packet size	a_{pkt}
Assured traffic number of flows	a_n
Assured traffic type of traffic	a_t
Best effort traffic rate ratio	R_{ab}
Best effort traffic burst size	b_b
Best effort traffic packet size	b_{pkt}
Best effort traffic number of flows	b_n
Best effort traffic type of traffic	b_t
Number of input interfaces to the PHB node	NI

(C) usually consists of parameters such as queue length, drop probability, and scheduling parameters. Choosing the parameters of C requires either knowledge of the traffic control components of the node, or the use of vendor-supplied specifications. Alternatively, the definitions of PHBs in the IETF standard RFCs and Internet drafts can be used for this purpose. We use routers based on the open-source Linux operating system and, therefore, we have access to all the configuration parameters. The Linux traffic control module provides a flexible way to realize various PHBs with the help of a number of queueing disciplines and traffic conditioning modules. The response variables in O used in this study are throughput (BW), per-hop delay (D), per-hop jitter (J), and loss rate (L).

An important issue is the choice of the levels for the factors in designing a set of experiments, which covers the entire range of the expected performance of a PHB. It may not be possible to cover all possible ranges and various modes of operation of a specific PHB in this manner. However, the experiments should capture the expected ranges of operation for the node.[3]

A *full factorial design* utilizes every possible combination of all the factors [6] at all levels. If we have k factors, with the i-th factor having n_i levels, and each experiment is repeated r times, then the total number of experiments to perform will be $\prod_{i=1}^{k} n_i \times r$. One of the drawbacks of the full factorial analysis is, therefore, the number of experiments growing exponentially with the number of factors and their levels. Moreover, in the context of network measurements, the total duration of an experiment can be prohibitively long, and often taking several days. To reduce the number and the execution time of experiments, we use a combination of *factor clustering* and *iterative experimental design* techniques. In factor clustering, the input and configuration parameters having similar effect on the output, are grouped together. This is similar to [9] in which the authors clustered ten congestion and flow control algorithms in TCP Vegas into three groups, according to the three phases of the TCP protocol. The iterative design technique is used to investigate three distinct types of network provisioning (see Section 3).

---

[3] Given by a network administrator.

2.2 Statistical Analysis

We now briefly describe the statistical methods we used, namely, ANOVA and regression analysis. A more detailed description of these methods can be found in [6,10]. For any three factors (i.e., $k = 3$) denoted as A, B, and C with levels a, b, and c, and with r repetitions of each experiment, the response variable y can be written as a linear combination of the main effects and their interactions:

$$y_{ijkl} = \mu + \alpha_i + \beta_j + \epsilon_k + \gamma_{ABij} + \gamma_{ACik} + \gamma_{BCjk} + \gamma_{ABCijk} + e_{ijkl} \ . \tag{1}$$
$$i = 1, \ldots, a; \qquad j = 1, \ldots, b; \qquad k = 1, \ldots, c; \qquad l = 1, \ldots, r \ .$$

where
y_{ijkl} = response in the l-th repetition of experiment with factors A, B, and C at levels i, j, and k, respectively.
μ = mean response = $\bar{y}_{....}$
α_i = effect of factor A at level $i = \bar{y}_{i...} - \mu$
$\bar{y}_{i...}$ = average response at the i-th level of A over all levels of other factors and repetitions.
β_j = effect of factor B at level $j = \bar{y}_{.j..} - \mu$ γ_{ABij} = effect of the interaction between A and B at levels i and $j = \bar{y}_{ij..} - \alpha_i - \beta_j - \mu$
γ_{ABCijk} = effect of the interaction between A, B, and C at levels i, j, and k
$\quad = \bar{y}_{ijk.} - \gamma_{ABij} - \gamma_{BCjk} - \gamma_{ACik} - \alpha_i - \beta_j - \epsilon_k - \mu$
e_{ijkl} = error in the l-th repetition at levels i, j, and $k = y_{ijkl} - \bar{y}_{ijk}$
and so on. Squaring both sides of the model in (1), and summing over all values of responses (cross-product terms cancel out) we get:

$$\sum_{ijkl} y_{ijkl}^2 = abcr\mu^2 + bcr\sum_i \alpha_i^2 + acr\sum_j \beta_j^2 + abr\sum_k \epsilon_k^2 + cr\sum_{ij} \gamma_{ij}^2 + br\sum_{ik} \gamma_{ik}^2$$
$$+ ar\sum_{jk} \gamma_{jk}^2 + r\sum_{ijk} \gamma_{ijk}^2 + \sum_{ijkl} e_{ijkl}^2 \ .$$

which can be written as:

$$SSY = SS0 + SSA + SSB + SSC + SSAB + SSAC + SSBC + SSABC + SSE \ .$$

where SSE is called the sum of squared errors. The total variation of y, denoted by the sum of square total or SST, is then:

$$SST = \sum_{ijkl} (y_{ijkl} - \mu)^2 = SSY - SS0 \ .$$

The percentages of variation can be calculated as $100 \times \left(\frac{SSA}{SST}\right)$ for the effect of factor A, $100 \times \left(\frac{SSAB}{SST}\right)$ for the interaction between A and B, and so on. From these percentages of variations, we can identify the most important factors. The factors with small or negligible contributions to the total variation of the output can be removed from the model. Using ANOVA also allows us to calculate the mean square error (MSE) and compare it with the mean square of the effect of each factor to determine the significance of these effects against the experimental errors. This is called the *F-test* in ANOVA and usually leads to the same conclusion if we compare the percentage of variations of the factors with those of errors.

The above linear model used in ANOVA is based on the following assumptions [6]: (1) the effects of the input factors and the errors are additive, (2) errors are identical and independent, normally distributed random variables, and (3) errors have a constant standard deviation. Therefore, an important step after the ANOVA analysis is to validate the model by inspecting the results. This can be done using several "visual tests": (1) the scatter plot of the residuals (errors), e_{ijkl}, versus the predicted response should not demonstrate any trend and (2) the normal quantile-quantile (Q-Q) plot of residuals should be approximately linear (after removing the outliers). The ANOVA method itself does not make any assumption about the nature of the statistical relationship between the input factors and the response variables [10].

Once the most important factors have been identified, we use regression models [10] to capture possible relationships between each output response variable and the most significant input factors. Basically, we use a variant of the multiple linear regression model called the *polynomial regression* for this purpose. The justification for this is that any continuous function can be expanded into piecewise polynomials given enough number of terms. We use a number of simple transformations [6] such as inverse, logarithmic, and square root, to capture non-linearity in these relationships and convert them into linear ones. However, more complex transformations [6,10] can be used for complex models. We choose the transformation that best satisfies the visual tests, minimizes the error percentage in ANOVA, and maximizes the coefficient of determination (R^2) in the regression model. We also calculate the confidence intervals for the mean response as well as the extracted parameter estimates of the regression model. These results are presented in Section 4.

3   Experimental Framework

An automated framework is necessary to expedite our experiments due to the complexity of the tasks involved, such as the experimental scenarios setup, network elements configuration, traffic generation, and collection and analysis of very large data sets. To the best of our knowledge, our framework is the first to integrate all the essential components for large-scale network analysis.

3.1   Framework Components

Figure 4 illustrates the framework components used in our study and their locations. Each component in this framework essentially builds an abstraction for a particular service, and the components communicate with each other by exchanging messages. Such an approach allows us to incorporate new devices and replace any of the underlying software without changing the overall architecture.

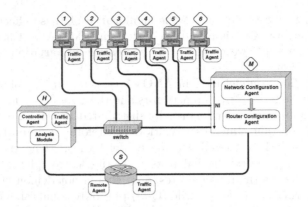

Fig. 4. Framework network

We can characterize other QoS frameworks, such as MPLS, by simply replacing the DiffServ-specific parameters in C with appropriate MPLS-specific parameters. The experimental framework components are described as follows:

Traffic Generation Agent is a modified version of Iperf [11], and it can generate both TCP and UDP traffic. UDP traffic can be optionally policed with a built-in leaky bucket so that the output traffic follows a specific average rate r and burst b. BW, D, J^4, and L are measured within the agent itself.

Controller and Remote Agents are set of distributed agents placed in the network, typically one at each host or router, that are controlled remotely through a *Controller* agent to execute and keep track of the experiment steps. The Controller agent resides on host H, as shown in Fig. 4, and reads in a scenario file, that defines the parameters (factors) and their values (levels), and run the experiments accordingly.

Network and Router Configuration Agents are placed on the router under experiments and are based on a set of APIs called DiffAgent. These APIs are used to configure the traffic control blocks in the router. Currently, our implementation is based on the traffic control (tc) APIs in the Linux kernel [12]. They receive information from the Controller agent about each test to be performed for a set of experiments and configure the router accordingly. This design allows inclusion of routers based on operating systems other than Linux, such as Cisco IOS.

Analysis Module performs ANOVA, model validation tests and polynomial regression on the experimental output data. The outcome of the module is the set of functional relationships between factors and response variables.

3.2   Network Setup and Testbed Configurations

Our network testbed consists of Linux-based software routers and end-hosts. The traffic conditioning and handling mechanisms built into the Linux kernels [12]

---

^{4} J is calculated as $J = J + (|D(i-1, i)| - J)/16$, where $D(i-1, i)$ is the delay variation between packets i and $(i-1)$.

give us two advantages: (i) a wide variety of standard traffic management components are supported, such as Token Bucket Filters (TBF), Weighted Fair Queuing (WFQ), and Priority Queuing (PQ) schedulers to name a few; and (ii) the flexibility of fine-grained specification of individual PHB components allows us to study in great detail the functional relationships between the factors and the response variables.

Figure 4 shows the network testbed used in our study. A ring topology is used so that the one-way delay can be measured without sophisticated time synchronization techniques such as GPS. Since the objective of our experiments is to characterize per-hop QoS of a single DiffServ PHB, we need only one router (M) implementing the PHB. We are primarily interested in finding out how a single EF or AF flow, which we refer to as the *designated ow*, is influenced by PHB configuration parameters, other traffic in the same aggregate, number of interfaces, etc. This *designated ow* is always generated from host H. In order to build the ring network, we add a second router S (i) to forward outgoing packets from M back to host H using *iptables* in Linux, and (ii) to act as a destination for the background traffic. The variable number of input interfaces (NI) at M is considered as one of the input factors. Hosts 1 through 6 are used to generate background traffic (both assured and best-effort) that share the links between routers M and S along with the *designated ow*.

3.3 Design of Experiments

As discussed earlier, we use clusters of input factors to reduce the parameter space and duration of the experiments. The I set can be partitioned into two subsets: the assured traffic factors (I_a), and the best-effort traffic factors (I_b). Along with these, we also choose a few parameters from the configuration set (C). If the size of C is large (depending on the particular choice of traffic components used), one may also decide to partition this set.

One can envision three different operating modes for a given PHB configuration with respect to the assured input traffic: The PHB can be *over-provisioned* (OP), *fully-provisioned* (FP), or *under-provisioned* (UP). In the OP mode, the total assured input traffic rate is less than the configured rate of the PHB. It is larger than the configured PHB rate for the UP mode. In the FP mode, they are nearly equal. These three modes can be further investigated for different scenarios of input traffic type and the degree of flow aggregation. Figure 5 illustrates the organization of the experiment scenarios for the EF PHB. In the first scenario, we investigate the interaction between sets I_a and C in the absence of any best-effort traffic. This experiment is performed for the two modes of OP and UP. The purpose of this scenario is to identify the most important factors in sets I_a and C that affect the output per-hop QoS. This is our base scenario for the assured traffic.

Next, we target a specific type of assured traffic, e.g., set I_a to certain constant values and vary the factors in I_b around these constant values. The factors in the best-effort traffic (such as rate, burst size, packet size and number of flows) range in values that include both higher and lower levels than their corresponding

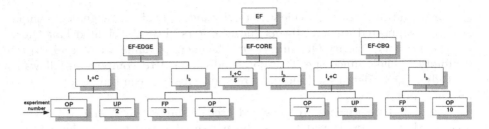

Fig. 5. Experiments scenarios for EF PHB

Table 2. "C" set for an EF PHB at edge router

Factor	Symbol
Token bucket rate	ef_r
Bucket size	ef_b
Max Transfer Unit	ef_{mtu}

Table 3. "C" set for an EF PHB based on CBQ

Factor	Symbol
EF service rate	ef_r
Burst size	ef_b
Avg packet size	ef_{avpkt}

Table 4. "C" set for the AF PHB

Factor	Symbol
Min threshold	min_{th}
Max threshold	max_{th}
Drop probability	$prob$

parameters in the assured traffic. The purpose is to investigate the effect of best-effort traffic on the assured traffic within a given range. This scenario is investigated for OP and FP modes only, since the per-hop QoS of an already-overloaded PHB is not going to change significantly due to changes in the best-effort traffic. In addition to these two scenarios, we analyze different realizations of a given PHB to investigate how the choice of different traffic conditioning elements affect the overall performance of a PHB. Different choices of schedulers, classes and filters give rise to different functional configurations and therefore, constitute different sets of parameters in C. For the EF PHB, we consider three different configurations as case studies:

- **EF-EDGE**: an edge router configuration consisting of a TBF served by a priority scheduler as shown in Fig. 3(A). Table 2 lists the parameters of C for this realization.
- **EF-CORE**: a core router configuration consisting of a single priority scheduler as shown in Fig. 3(B). The only parameter in C for this realization is the length (ef_{limit}) of the FIFO queue in the priority scheduler. The service rate for the PHB queue is the same as the link speed.
- **EF-CBQ**: a CBQ-based configuration as shown in Fig. 3(C). Table 3 lists the parameters of C for this realization.

We also repeat similar performance analysis for the AF PHB. We use a multi-color RED (or GRED) queue for each AF class served by a CBQ scheduler. Table 4 lists the C set for the AF PHB. It includes the parameters for the AF11 RED virtual queue only. We choose the AF PHB as another instance of a DiffServ PHB to demonstrate the generality of our measurement framework and analysis approach.

Table 5. Factors and their levels for EF-EDGE

	Factor (unit)	Exp1 levels	Exp2 levels	Exp4 levels
Set I_a	a_r (Mbps)	0.5,1,2,4	3,3.5,4,4.5	1 (X)
	a_p (Mbps)	6 (X)	8 (X)	2 (X)
	a_{pkt} (bytes)	100,400,600,900	800,900,1000,1200	1000 (X)
	a_b (bytes)	20000 (X)	40000 (X)	20000 (X)
	a_n (flows)	1,2,3,5	1,2,3,5	1 (X)
	NI	1,2,3,5	1,2,3,5	1,2,3,4
Set C	ef_r (Mbps)	20 (X)	2,2.2,2.5,3	3 (X)
	ef_b (bytes)	40000 (X)	20000 (X)	40000 (X)
	ef_{mtu} (bytes)	1000,1200,1400,1520	1520 (X)	1520 (X)
Set I_b	R_{ab}	(X)	(X)	2,1,0.1.0.01
	b_{pkt} (bytes)	(X)	(X)	200,1000,1200,1470
	b_b (bytes)	(X)	(X)	10000,20000,30000,40000
	b_n (flows)	(X)	(X)	1,2,3,4

Table 6. Factors and their levels for EF-CORE

	Factor (unit)	Exp7 levels	Exp10 levels
Set I_a	a_r (Mbps)	0.5,1,1.5,2	1 (X)
	a_p (Mbps)	6 (X)	2 (X)
	a_{pkt} (bytes)	100,400,600,900	1000 (X)
	a_b (bytes)	20000 (X)	20000 (X)
	a_n (flows)	1,2,3,5	1 (X)
	NI	1,2,3,5	1,2,3,4
Set C	ef_r (Mbps)	10,12,14,16	4 (X)
	ef_b (bytes)	10 (X)	10 (X)
	ef_{avpkt} (bytes)	1000,1200,1470	1000 (X)
Set I_b	R_{ab}	(X)	2,1,0.1.0.01
	b_{pkt} (bytes)	(X)	200,1000,1200,1470
	b_b (bytes)	(X)	10000,20000,30000,40000
	b_n (flows)	(X)	1,2,3,4

4   Results and Analysis

The results from our experiments are presented in the same order of the scenarios described in Section 3.3 and the chart in Fig. 5. It is important to note that the results presented in this section are examples that illustrates the applicability of our approach. We first present results for the three different implementations of the EF PHB, followed by a single configuration of the AF PHB. Unless otherwise mentioned, each experiment is repeated five times (i.e., $r = 5$) and each traffic trace is collected for 20 seconds. We use a rest period of three seconds in-between successive runs so that the network is empty of packets from a previous run. Depending on the experiment scenario, the input traffic enters router M from one or multiple input interfaces (i.e., $NI \geq 1$).

4.1   Characterizing EF PHB

For each of the EF PHB realizations, we group the results into two categories: the interaction between sets I_a and C, and the effect of background traffic (I_b) on the fixed assured traffic (I_a). The input factors (I_a and C) used in each experiment scenario are listed in Tables 5, 6, and 7 for EF-EDGE, EF-CORE, and EF-CBQ, respectively. The factors marked with (X) are not active in the

Table 7. Factors and their levels for EF-CBQ

	Factor (unit)	Exp5 levels
Set I_a	a_r (Mbps)	0.5,1,2
	a_p (Mbps)	(X)
	a_{pkt} (bytes)	100,800,1470
	a_b (bytes)	5000,10000,60000
	a_n (flows)	1,3
	NI	1,3
Set C	ef_{limit} (packets)	5,100
Set I_b	R_{ab}	(X)
	b_{pkt} (bytes)	(X)
	b_b (bytes)	(X)
	b_n (flows)	(X)

Table 8. Factors and their levels for AF PHB

	Factor (unit)	Exp levels
Set I_a	a_r (Mbps)	50,100
	a_p (Mbps)	60,100
	a_{pkt} (bytes)	600,1200
	a_b (bytes)	20000,40000
	a_n (flows)	1 (X)
	NI	3 (X)
Set C	min_{th} (Kbytes)	10,20
	max_{th} (Kbytes)	40,55
	$prob$	0.02 (X)
Set I_b	R_{ab}	0.01 (X)
	b_{pkt} (bytes)	600,1200
	b_b (bytes)	20000,40000
	b_n (flows)	2 (X)

Table 9. ANOVA results for experiment 1

Response	Trans.	a_r	a_{pkt}	a_n	(a_r,a_n)	(a_r,a_{pkt})	Error
BW	linear	48.55%	≈ 0%	34.23%	17.21%	≈ 0%	≈ 0%
D	linear	≈ 0%	83.15%	≈ 0%	≈ 0%	≈ 0%	13.53%
$1/J$	inverse	4.12%	12.52%	46.58%	≈ 0%	2.88%	25.34%

corresponding experiment. An inactive factor is a factor with one level only, and therefore, has no effect on the ANOVA results.

Over-Provisioned (OP) EF-EDGE PHB without Background Traffic: This scenario corresponds to experiment 1 in Fig. 5. The PHB is over-provisioned (OP), i.e., the throughput of the assured traffic is less than the configured rate for the PHB. The effects of significant factors and their significant interactions[5] are identified by using ANOVA and listed in Table 9. The transformation applied to each response variable, satisfying the basic assumptions of the linear ANOVA model, is indicated in the second column. The mean, standard deviation (SD), and 90% confidence interval (CI) are listed in Table 10. The loss (L) in this experiment is basically zero (no loss) since this is an over-provisioned case.

To verify the linearity of the ANOVA model, the visual tests for jitter (J), as an example, are shown in Fig. 6 and 7. After the inverse transformation, there is no trend in the residual versus predicted response scatter plot. Moreover, the errors are normal since the normal Q-Q plot is almost linear. The tests for the throughput and the delay show linearity as well. The polynomial regression models for the response variables are calculated, and the model for the BW is given in (2). The surface plot corresponding to this model is shown in Fig. 8. The coefficient of determination (R^2) is 96%.

$$BW = 299733.48 + 3246957.34a_r - 2318542.4a_n - 32371.95a_r^2 + 2223351.57a_n^2$$
$$-2815325.9a_ra_n . \tag{2}$$

Equation (3) represents the model for jitter, with the corresponding value of $R^2 = 84\%$. Note that we use the same transformation from ANOVA while per-

---

[5] We neglect any factor or interaction with a percentage of variation less than 2%.

Table 10. Mean, standard deviation (SD), and 90% confidence interval (CI) for the response variables in experiment 1

Response	Mean	SD of Mean	90% CI for Mean
BW	948.81 Kbps	0.125	(948.60,949.015)
D	0.262199 msec	0.001088	(0.260409,0.263989)
$1/J$	311.21	3.74	(305.05,317.37)

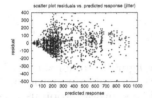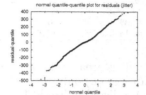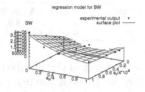

Fig. 6. Residuals vs. pre- **Fig. 7.** Normal Q-Q plot for **Fig. 8.** Response surface for dicted response for J (exp 1) J residuals (exp 1) BW (exp 1)

forming the regression analysis. We also normalize the input factors by their maximum values to provide a scaled version of the model equations.

$$1/J = 620.62 + 1343.58a_r - 1024.12a_{pkt} - 2212.85a_n - 1586.15a_r^2 - 231.39a_r a_{pkt}$$
$$-574.60a_r a_n + 913.48a_{pkt}^2 + 717.55a_{pkt}a_n + 3485.72a_n^2 + 281.31a_r^3$$
$$+583.23a_r^2 a_{pkt} + 700.89a_r^2 a_n - 133.74a_r a_{pkt}^2 - 249.64a_r a_{pkt}a_n$$
$$-51.79a_r a_n^2 - 268.81a_{pkt}^3 - 307.76a_{pkt}^2 a_n - 106.48a_{pkt}a_n^2 - 1708.39u_n^3 . \tag{3}$$

As shown in Table 9, the throughput (BW) depends mostly on the sending rate of the assured traffic (a_r) and number of EF flows (a_n). The reason for the dependency of BW on a_n is that, in this experiment, we divide the total EF rate (a_r) specified in Table 5, by the number of flows (a_n) to get an equal share for each EF flow. Because we only measure a single designated EF flow, the resulting throughput depends on the number of flows. The per-hop delay is mainly affected by the EF packet size. On the other hand, jitter is affected mostly by a_n and a_{pkt}, but little by a_r. This follows our intuition about jitter: the packets from the monitored flow have to wait in the queue because of other EF flows sharing the same queue, as well as due to the relative difference of their packet sizes. Larger values of a_n and a_{pkt} result in larger jitter. This can be seen in the regression results as well, since the corresponding coefficients are negative in the model equation given that an inverse transformation is applied to jitter. The statistical analysis also provides us with confidence intervals for each of the parameter estimates in the regression equation. The confidence intervals determine the accuracy of the models extracted, and therefore constitute an important part of model checking. However, we omit these values due to space limitation.

Under-Provisioned (UP) EF-EDGE PHB without Background Traffic: In this scenario (experiment 2), the EF PHB is under-provisioned (UP), i.e., the

Table 11. ANOVA results for experiment 2

Response	Trans.	a_r	a_n	ef_r	(a_r,a_n)	(a_r,ef_r)	(a_n,ef_r)	(a_r,a_n,ef_r)	Error
$1/L$	inverse	6.06%	20.81%	6.63%	15.1%	8.9%	16.21%	25%	$\approx 0\%$

Table 12. ANOVA results for experiment 4

Response	Trans.	b_{pkt}	b_n	R_{ab}	(b_{pkt},b_n)	(b_{pkt},R_{ab})	(b_n,R_{ab})	(b_{pkt},b_n,R_{ab})	Error
BW	linear	$\approx 0\%$	36.6%	2.65%	$\approx 0\%$	$\approx 0\%$	2.87%	4.4%	38.76%
$\log(D)$	log	3.28%	8.98%	36.3%	3.54%	10.01%	27.07%	10.69%	$\approx 0\%$
J	linear	3.36%	7.5%	39.14%	3.7%	9.72%	12.13%	22.77%	1.4%

throughput of the assured traffic is greater than the configured rate for the PHB. Here we present the results for loss (L) only. The effects of significant factors and their significant interactions are listed in Table 11. The transformation used is indicated in the second column as before. The polynomial regression model for loss is given in (4) with $R^2 = 74\%$.

$$1/L = 0.06 - 0.63a_r - 0.2a_n + 0.63ef_r + 1.48a_r^2 + 0.79a_ra_n - 2.05a_ref_r + 0.3a_n^2$$
$$-0.69a_nef_r + 0.43ef_r^2 - 1.14a_r^3 - 0.73a_r^2a_n + 2.37a_r^2ef_r - 0.42a_ra_n^2 + 1.23a_na_nef_r$$
$$-1.69a_ref_r^2 - 0.18a_n^3 + 0.46a_n^2ef_r - 0.57a_nef_r^2 + 0.57ef_r^3 . \qquad (4)$$

The model for loss clearly shows that by increasing the sending rate, the loss increases (due to the negative sign of a_r and the inverse of L). A similar effect was observed with the number of flows (a_n). Note that intuitively, the loss can be reduced by increasing the EF service rate (ef_r). The positive coefficient of ef_r in (4) clearly indicates this.

Over-Provisioned (OP) EF-EDGE PHB with Background Traffic: Next, we investigate the effect of background (e.g., best-effort) traffic on the assured traffic for the EF PHB. As shown in Table 12, the throughput (BW) of the EF traffic is affected heavily by the number of background traffic flows sharing the link with it. Since the PHB is over-provisioned, the effect of the ratio R_{ab} or the size of the background traffic itself is not dramatic. As a result of over-provisioning too, the percentage of variation due to experimental error is high. This is because of the weak interaction between the inputs and the output BW. The results also indicate that the priority scheduler does a good job in isolating the EF traffic from the background flows. There are no significant EF losses for the same reason above. Later, we will compare these results with the results of Section 5 that employs CBQ, instead of priority scheduling. Both delay and jitter values show very little experimental errors due to repetition, and strongly depend on the background traffic characteristics, such as the packet size, number of background flows, and their interactions. Note that a linear transformation fits jitter well with respect to the background traffic parameters, where a logarithmic transformation is appropriate for delay. This is different from what we found in Section 4.1 with EF-EDGE, where jitter is inversely related to the EF traffic parameters. Similar results are observed in Sections 5, 5, and 5 (to be shown).

Table 13. ANOVA results for experiment 5

Response	Trans.	a_{pkt}	a_n	(a_{pkt}, a_n)	Error
$1/J$	inverse	29.37%	18.27%	6.97%	31.78%

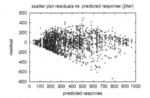 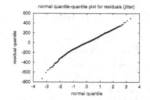 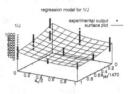

Fig. 9. Residuals vs. pre- **Fig. 10.** Normal Q-Q plot **Fig. 11.** Response surface dicted response for J (exp 5) for J residuals (exp 5)   for J (exp 5)

EF-CORE PHB without Background Traffic: The purpose of experiment 5 is to demonstrate how different implementations of a specific PHB can differ in their extracted input/output relationships. We present the results for jitter (J) as an example. The most important factors affecting J are listed in Table 13. Note that there is no effect due to a_r, unlike the scenario in Section 4.1 using EF-EDGE PHB. The visual tests are shown in Fig. 9 and 10 to test the validity of the ANOVA model. The jitter model is given in (5) with a coefficient of determination (R^2) of 64%. The response surface is shown in Fig. 11. The inverse relationship also holds here with respect to the EF traffic parameters as mentioned earlier.

$$1/J = 727.74 - 810.85a_n - 748.17a_{pkt} + 425.13a_n^2 + 322.99a_{pkt}^2 + 189.18a_{pkt}a_n . \qquad (5)$$

The negative coefficients for both a_n and a_{pkt} in the above model indicate that an increase in either of them will increase the value of jitter. A very important result can be deduced accordingly — the larger the number of flows in an EF traffic, the larger the jitter.

Over-Provisioned (OP) EF-CBQ PHB without Background Traffic: In this experiment scenario, we evaluate the EF-CBQ implementation, corresponding to experiment 7 in Fig. 5. Table 14 shows the results from the ANOVA analysis. The throughput (BW) has a square-root relationship with the input EF traffic parameters, which is different from the previous two implementations. The delay (D) model is also different. Another important difference is that the jitter is dependent on the PHB configuration parameters (C) such as ef_r for EF-CBQ, where as neither EF-EDGE nor EF-CORE shows such dependency. On the other hand, the jitter (J) still has an inverse relationship with the input EF traffic parameters.

Over-Provisioned EF-CBQ PHB with Background Traffic: The purpose of experiment 10 is to investigate the effect of the background traffic on EF traffic. The characteristics of the background traffic are listed in Table 7. As shown in Table 15, the delay and jitter models, with respect to the input background

Table 14. ANOVA results for experiment 7

Response	Trans.	a_r	a_{pkt}	a_n	ef_r	(a_{pkt},a_n)	(a_n,ef_r)	Error
$\sqrt{BW}$	square	96.73%	$\approx 0\%$	$\approx 0\%$	$\approx 0\%$	$\approx 0\%$	$\approx 0\%$	$\approx 0\%$
$1/D$	inverse	$\approx 0\%$	94.55%	$\approx 0\%$	$\approx 0\%$	$\approx 0\%$	$\approx 0\%$	2.51%
$1/J$	inverse	$\approx 0\%$	14.1%	37.5%	6.8%	2.0%	2.0%	22.55%

Table 15. ANOVA results for experiment 10

Response	Trans.	b_{pkt}	b_n	R_{ab}	(b_{pkt},b_n)	(b_{pkt},R_{ab})	(b_n,R_{ab})	(b_{pkt},b_n,R_{ab})	Error
BW	linear	10.64%	$\approx 0\%$	15.76%	7.97%	31.44%	8.53%	23.65%	0.4%
$\log(D)$	log	$\approx 0\%$	$\approx 0\%$	83.23%	2.34%	3.53%	2.04%	7%	0.1%
J	linear	11.88%	$\approx 0\%$	22.01%	5.63%	35.6%	5.68%	16.93%	0.27%
$\sqrt{L}$	sqrt	8.87%	2.38%	36.89%	5.14%	25.84%	4.8%	15.45%	0.53%

traffic parameters, are similar to those in Section 5, where the delay (D) logarithmically depends on the background traffic volume and the jitter (J) linearly depends on the three factors, b_{pkt}, b_n, and R_{ab}. The EF-CBQ implementation also cannot protect the EF traffic against packet losses. The loss (L) depends mostly on the volume of the background traffic and the interaction with other factors, as shown in Table 15. The polynomial regression model for delay is presented in (6) with a coefficient of determination (R^2) of 89%.

$$\log(D) = 1.91 - 46.65R_{ab} + 2.33b_n - 6.03b_{pkt} + 121.86R_{ab}^2 + 1.89R_{ab}b_n + 2.74R_{ab}b_{pkt} - 5.25b_n^2$$
$$+1.19b_n b_{pkt} + 8.61b_{pkt}^2 - 78.24R_{ab}^3 - 1.34R_{ab}^2 b_n + 0.51R_{ab}^2 b_{pkt} + 0.79R_{ab}b_n^2$$
$$+1.99b_n^2 b_{pkt} - 1.88b_n b_{pkt}^2 - 3.44b_{pkt}^3 - 1.89R_{ab}b_n b_{pkt} - 1.96R_{ab}b_{pkt}^2 + 1.90b_n^3 . \qquad (6)$$

Although the delay does not depend on individual factors, such as b_{pkt} and b_n as seen from the ANOVA table, it is dependent on their interactions with R_{ab} and their interactions. Therefore, we need to include b_{pkt} and b_n into the regression model.

$$\log(D) \approx 1.91 - 46.65R_{ab} + 121.86R_{ab}^2 + 1.89R_{ab}b_n + 2.74R_{ab}b_{pkt} - 78.24R_{ab}^3$$
$$-1.34R_{ab}^2 b_n + 0.51R_{ab}^2 b_{pkt} + 0.79R_{ab}b_n^2 - 1.89R_{ab}b_n b_{pkt} - 1.96R_{ab}b_{pkt}^2 . \qquad (7)$$

However, when comparing the coefficients values, we find that the coefficients for R_{ab} and their powers are orders-of-magnitude larger than the other factors, which is consistent with the ANOVA analysis. Given that the normalized values of b_n and b_{pkt} are in the range of $(0,1)$, we can exclude them from the model and approximate the model as shown in (7).

4.2   Characterizing AF PHB

We present results for the AF PHB to show the generality of our approach and to provide an insight into the behavior of the AF PHB. The relevant per-hop QoS attributes, according to the IETF standard, are throughput (BW) and loss (L). However, some applications may also impose delay and jitter requirements on AF-based services, so we present results for them as well. In this experiment, we mark the designated flow with AF11 DSCP; and the background traffic (filling

Table 16. ANOVA results for AF PHB

Res.	a_r	a_p	a_{pkt}	max_{th}	min_{th}	(a_r,a_p)	(a_r, max_{th})	(a_r, min_{th})	(a_p, max_{th})	(a_{pkt}, b_{pkt})	(a_r, a_p, max_{th})
BW	51.38%	12.51%	$\approx 0\%$	2.67%	2.38%	13.27%	3.27%	2%	2%	$\approx 0\%$	2.37%
D	38.2%	25.42%	2.85%	$\approx 0\%$	3.1%	25.06%	$\approx 0\%$	$\approx 0\%$	$\approx 0\%$	$\approx 0\%$	$\approx 0\%$
$1/J$	14.75%	17.35%	34.82%	$\approx 0\%$	$\approx 0\%$	18.94%	$\approx 0\%$	$\approx 0\%$	$\approx 0\%$	4.09%	$\approx 0\%$
L	29.32%	17.12%	$\approx 0\%$	7.14%	4.17%	16.98%	7.4%	3.89%	3.91%	$\approx 0\%$	4.03%

up the rest of the network capacity) with AF12 and AF13 DSCPs. The input factors and their levels are listed in Table 8. Table 16 lists[6] the ANOVA results for the four QoS attributes. The results indicate that the throughput (BW) depends mostly on the average and peak sending rates, and their interactions. They also exhibit some dependency on the threshold levels of the AF11 virtual queue. In another experiment (not shown here), we find this dependency increases with the increase of the drop probability for the virtual queue. The results for loss (L), delay (D), and jitter (J) show similar dependencies, although the percentages vary with each of the QoS parameters. We notice a small, but non-trivial, interaction between the packet size of the designated and that of the background traffic contributing to the jitter of the assured traffic.

4.3   Discussion

From the above results, we can capture the functional relationships of a number of PHBs and identify the differences in their dependencies on the various input factors. To summarize: for the EF PHB cases, the results for jitter (J) indicate an inverse relationship with the factors in set I_a, and a direct relationship with the factors in set I_b. The delay (D) has a direct relationship with factors in set I_a and a logarithmic one with factors in set I_b. Also, different PHB realizations exhibit different relationships among their inputs and the outputs. For example, delay has a direct relationship with factors in set I_a in EF-EDGE and EF-CORE PHBs, while it has an inverse relationship with I_a in EF-CBQ PHB. The throughput (BW) has a square root relationship with I_a for EF-CBQ only, but it has a direct relationship in the other EF PHBs.

Note that the purpose of the present study is not to cover all possible performance ranges or configurations for a particular PHB. Instead, we present a technique for analyzing the PHB performance under different situations. The levels of factors used in the experimental analysis represent only a certain range of the PHB operation. Additional parameters – such as the expected loads, the type of physical links connected to the PHB node, etc. – should be considered when applying this technique to characterize PHBs in real-world networks.

It is worth mentioning that the errors in our study can be divided into three categories as follows:

1. *Experimental errors* are due to the experimental methods and we use a reasonable number of repetitions to minimize them. These errors are captured in the ANOVA analysis.

---

[6] The error column is not shown due to space limitation.

2. *Model errors* are due to factor truncation. When we discard the insignificant factors and perform regression with the most significant ones, small errors can be potentially introduced.
3. *Statistical or tting errors* are due to difference between the fitted regression model and the actual data. The regression usually fits an approximate model to the actual data by using the least-square fit to minimize the deviation from the actual data.

Finally, we provide an example of the potential benefit of the statistical approach we proposed. This example is beneficial for network operators as it provides a proof of using the above results in controlling the per-hop QoS of a PHB. From the results of Section 5, we observe that for $b_{pkt} = 600$ Bytes, b_n = 1 and $R_{ab} = 2$, the average delay experienced by the designated EF flow is 0.4136 msec. Now, suppose we increase the number of background flows from 1 to 3, and the average packet size of the background traffic from 600 to 1470 Bytes. Can the PHB configuration be controlled in such a way that it provides the same delay value to the assured traffic as in the first case? Basically, we have to find the right value for R_{ab} which drives the PHB to deliver the same delay. By applying the delay model in (7) to the two sets of levels, we calculate the required value for R_{ab} to be 0.494. Substituting this value back into the model, we get a delay value of 0.3652 msec which is within the accuracy $(1 - R^2$ or $11\%)$ of the model. Now, when we run the experiment again with this acquired value of R_{ab}, we get the same delay as the original controlled value. Therefore, by simply controlling the factors in the derived model, we can achieve predictable per-hop QoS. Such scenario is quite realistic. Consider the assured flow that belongs to a delay-sensitive application such as video-streaming. The adjusted R_{ab} value suggests that the streaming rate at the server needs to be lower for guaranteeing the same delay bound. Although, the focus of our experiments is per-hop QoS while guaranteeing delay bounds for applications requires an end-to-end approach, such per-hop delay bounds are essential for satisfying the end-to-end guarantees.

5   Related Work

Very few previous studies used ANOVA for experimental analyses and modeling of IP QoS networks. The authors of [13] applied a full factorial design and ANOVA to compare a number of marking schemes for TCP acknowledgments in a DiffServ network. Their results suggested an optimal strategy for marking the acknowledgment packets for both assured and premium flows. The performance of AF PHB was analyzed in [14] using the ANOVA method where the authors compared the performance of different techniques for bandwidth and buffer management. Compared with these previous studies, our approach is more general in studying the per-hop QoS of any QoS-enabled node. The authors of [15,16] utilized a *ring* network topology, which is similar to the one used here for experimental studies on the EF PHB. Their findings can be summarized as follows. The EF burstiness was greatly affected by the number of EF streams and packet loss. Moreover, WFQ was found to be more immune to burstiness of traffic than PQ, when used for scheduling, but had less timely delivery guarantees. Our work complements these studies and provide a more rigorous way to identify these affects. The authors of [8] conducted an experimental analysis of the EF PHB by incorporating a part of the Internet2 QBone and using the QBone Premium Service (QPS). They used the same QoS metrics (throughput, delay, jitter and packet loss) we use. The difference, however, is that their metrics are measured as end-to-end quantities, while ours are per-hop quantities. Moreover, they did not provide any functional relationships or models for designing premium services over Internet2. A rigorous theoretical study to find probabilistic bounds for EF was presented in [17]. The authors used a combination of queueing theory and network calculus to obtain delay bounds for backlogs of heterogeneous traffic as well as traffic regulated by a leaky bucket. They also derived bounds on loss ratio under statistical multiplexing of EF input flows. Our approach is purely experimental; instead of providing bounds on delay or packet loss, we seek to identify the parameters necessary to construct simple performance models of per-hop QoS mechanisms, and eventually to control their run-time behavior. The AF PHB has been studied in [18] among other studies as well. The authors used modeling techniques to evaluate the performance of AF-based services with respect to Round Trip Time (RTT), number of microflows, size of target rate, and packet size. The performance metric was the throughput perceived by the AF traffic. Collectively, these studies identified important effects on the performance of the AF PHB. By contrast, we have attempted to build simple mathematical models to calculate the performance and response surfaces applying statistical procedures on the experimental data.

6   Conclusions and Extensions

In this paper we have presented a framework for statistically characterizing the outcome of a PHB — the per-hop QoS. We have conducted an experimental study followed by rigorous statistical analysis, including ANOVA and regression models, to find the functional relationships for the per-hop QoS. We point out operational differences among the different PHB implementations, and explain these differences based on the internal structure of the PHBs. Our framework for measurement and experimental design is automated – the configuration of the PHBs and the measurement of the corresponding output parameters are automatically performed. Our results are promising since they can further quantify the end-to-end QoS by concatenating per-hop QoS attributes along the path. However, more careful analysis has to be done for such complex multi-hop case.

The approaches presented in Sections 2 and 3 can be extended to more complex systems, e.g., edge-to-edge QoS building blocks such as a Per-Domain Behavior or PDB in DiffServ, especially if the PDB is constructed by concatenation of multiple similar PHBs. Although we focused on per-hop QoS at the network layer, the statistical characterization approach can be applied to parameters across the entire protocol stack, with suitable instrumentation of the related layers. This will allow us to study end-to-end QoS parameters for any distributed application in different network topologies and QoS frameworks. We are also exploring the use of statistical control methods based on the most important factor(s) for controlling per-hop QoS of network nodes. We aim to validate our approach using stochastic network calculus in future work and discuss more practical issues on real-networks.

References

1. Blake, S., Black, D., Carlson, M., Davis, E., Wang, Z., Weiss, W.: An architecture for differentiated services. RFC 2475, IETF (1998)
2. Nichols, K., Jacobson, V., Zhang, L.: A two-bit differentiated services architecture for the Internet. RFC 2638, IETF (1999)
3. Davie, B., et al.: An expedited forwarding PHB (per-hop behavior). RFC 3246, IETF (2002)
4. Heinanen, J., Baker, F., Weiss, W., Wroclawski, J.: Assured forwarding PHB group. RFC 2597, IETF (1999)
5. Braden, R., Clark, D., Shenker, S.: Integrated services in the internet architecture: an overview. RFC 1633, IETF (1994)
6. Jain, R.: The Art of Computer Systems Performance Analysis. John Wiley & Sons, Inc. (1991)
7. Ashmawi, W., Guerin, R., Wolf, S., Pinson, M.: On the impact of policing and rate guarantees in diff-serv networks: A video streaming application perspective. In: Proceedings of ACM SIGCOMM'01. (2001)
8. Mohammed, A., et al.: Diffserv experiments: Analysis of the premium service over the Alcatel-NCSU internet2 testbed. In: proceedings of the 2nd European Conference on Universal Multiservice Networks ECUMN'2002, CREF. (2002)
9. Hengartner, U., Bolliger, J., Gross, T.: TCP vegas revisited. In: Proceedings of IEEE INFOCOM'00. (2000)
10. Neter, J., Wasserman, W., Kutner, M.: Applied Linear Statistical Models: Regression, Analysis of Variance, and Experimental Designs. Homewood, R.D. Irwin, Inc. (1985)
11. Iperf 1.1.1: http://dast.nlanr.net/projects/iperf/ (2000)
12. Almesberger, W.: Linux network traffic control – implementation overview. In: Proceedings of the 5th Annual Linux Expo. (1999)
13. Papagiannaki, K., et al.: Preferential treatment of acknowledgment packets in a differentiated services network. In: Proceedings of the IWQoS 2001. (2001)
14. Goyal, M., Durresi, A., Jain, R., Liu, C.: Performance analysis of assured forwarding. draft-goyal-diffserv-afstdy.txt, Internet draft (work on progress) (2000)
15. Ferrari, T.: End-to-end performance analysis with traffic aggregation. Computer Network Journal, Elsevier 34 (2000) 905–914
16. Ferrari, T., Chimento, P.: A measurement-based analysis of expedited forwarding PHB mechanisms. In: Proceedings of IWQoS'00, IEEE 00EXL00. (2000)
17. Vojnovic, M., Boudec, J.L.: Stochastic analysis of some expedited forwarding networks. In: proceedings of INFOCOM'02. (2002)
18. Seddigh, N., Nandy, B., Pieda, P.: Bandwidth assurance issues for TCP flows in a differentiated services network. In: proceedings of GLOBECOM'99. (1999)

Performance Analysis of Server Sharing Collectives for Content Distribution

Daniel Villela and Dan Rubenstein*

Columbia University, Dept. of Electrical Engineering
500 W. 120th Street
New York, NY 10027
{dvillela,danr}@ee.columbia.edu

Abstract. Demand for content served by a provider can fluctuate with time, complicating the task of provisioning serving resources so that requests for its content are not rejected. One way to address this problem is to have providers form a collective in which they pool together their serving resources to assist in servicing requests for one another's content. In this paper, we determine the conditions under which a provider's participation in a collective reduces the rejection rate of requests for its content - a property that is necessary for the provider to justify participating in the collective. We show that all request rejection rates are reduced when the collective is formed from a homogeneous set of providers, but that some rates can increase within heterogeneous sets of collectives. We also show that asymptotically, growing the size of the collective will sometimes, but not always resolve this problem. We explore the use of thresholding techniques, where each collective participant sets aside a portion of its serving resources to serve only requests for its own content. We show that thresholding allows a more diverse set of providers to benefit from the collective model, making collectives a more viable option for content delivery services.

1 Introduction

Content providers profit from servicing their clients' requests for their content. If a provider's serving resources (e.g. servers and bandwidth) are insufficient, it will be forced to turn away a large number of requests during periods when the content reaches its peak in popularity. The amount of serving resources needed during a peak period, however, is often much larger than what would be needed on a regular basis. Hence, a provider that provisions resources for these peak periods will pay for equipment that sits by idly most of the time, reducing profits.

A recent solution used by many providers has been to contract third party content distribution networks (CDN) that host and service their content during peak periods. The provider, however, pays the CDN for its assistance, which again can reduce profits.

* This material was supported in part by the National Science Foundation under Grant No. ANI-0117738 and CAREER Award No. 0133829. Any opinions, findings, and conclusions or recommendations expressed in this material are those of the authors and do not necessarily reflect the views of the National Science Foundation. Daniel Villela received scholarship support from CNPq-Brazil (Ref. No. 200168/98-3).

K. Jeffay, I. Stoica, and K. Wehrle (Eds.): IWQoS 2003, LNCS 2707, pp. 41–58, 2003.
© Springer-Verlag Berlin Heidelberg 2003

Instead of relying on CDNs during peak periods, an overlooked alternative is for groups of providers to form *collectives* and host one another's content. When the demand for content that originated at provider A peaks, exceeding its own serving abilities, it can redirect requests to other members of the collective whose available serving resources can handle these requests. In return, when the demand for content that originates at some other provider peaks, provider A's serving resources can be used to help serve this other content.

It is well known that systems that pool together resources can outperform the performance of their individual components. For instance, load can more easily be balanced among the pooled resources, and overloads (dropping requests) are less likely to occur [1,2,3,4,5]. The problem we consider here, however, has an important distinction from these traditional works and from the CDN model: *each service provider "profits" only from requests for its own content.* While the collective more efficiently serves the aggregate demand (over all providers), because a provider's resources may be used to help serve other providers' content, there may not be enough resources in the collective to serve its own client demand. This leaves open the possibility that the rejection rate of requests for an individual provider's content can be higher within the collective than if that provider operated in isolation. Since the provider profits only from requests for its originating content, this increase in rejection rate can deter its participation in the collective. The Content Distribution Internetworking (CDI) charter [6] at the IETF describes similar concepts and requirements for interconnection of content networks to collectives. The CDI work in progress, however, lacks a performance analysis of the benefits of such a system.

In this paper, we identify from a performance perspective when these collectives are a viable alternative. In particular, we address the following questions:

- Under what conditions do all provider participants in a collective benefit from their membership to the collective?
- Are there any mechanisms that can be introduced into the collective architecture that will increase the range of conditions under which all participating providers benefit?

To enable us to focus on the performance aspects of this question, we start at the point where a set of providers have agreed to form a collective, have made copies of one another's content, and can redirect requests for a particular content object to any server within the collective with sufficient available capacity. When no server has available capacity, the request is dropped.

For each provider in the collective, we compare the rejection rate for its content (that it originated) when served within the collective to when it serves its content in isolation. Each provider is described in terms of its capacity (number of jobs it can serve simultaneously) and its intensity (the rate of requests for its content divided by the rate at which it serves requests). We find that collectives reduce rejection rates of **all** provider participants by several orders of magnitude when the collective is formed from a homogeneous set of providers with identical capacities and intensities. However, even slight variations in intensity among providers yield heterogeneous collectives in which the lower intensity participants achieve significantly lower rejection rates in isolation than within the collective.

We next consider whether all providers' needs can be met by growing the size of the collective, i.e., can the rejection rate be brought arbitrarily close to zero by simply increasing the membership to the collective? We identify a simple rule that is a function of the average intensity and the average capacity that determines whether the rejection rate converges to zero or to a positive constant. A convergence to zero implies that all providers would benefit from participating in very large collectives. However, when the rate converges to a positive constant, some providers may still be better off participating in isolation.

To accommodate providers whose rejection rates are lower in isolation, we consider the application of thresholding techniques within the collective. Thresholding allows each provider to set aside a portion of its serving resources to be used exclusively to service its own clients' requests. We demonstrate that often, by appropriately setting thresholds, all providers in a collective will experience lower rejection rates than when they operate in isolation, even if this property did not hold within the threshold-free version of that collective. Our work demonstrates that from a performance standpoint, collectives that utilize thresholds often offer a viable, cheaper alternative to overprovisioning or utilizing CDN services.

The rest of the paper is structured as follows. In Section 2, we briefly overview related work. In Section 3 we present our general model for server collectives and evaluate collectives for fixed–rate sessions. We evaluate for elastic file transfers in Section 4. Section 5 evaluates a suite of thresholding techniques. We conclude and elaborate on open issues in Section 6.

2   Related Work

Several works analyze systems that pool server resources to improve various performance aspects of content delivery. For instance, [3,4,5] investigate the practical challenge of maintaining consistency among distributed content replicas. The study in [7] investigates the placement of content in the network to minimize delivery latencies. Other studies [1,2] investigate load sharing policies. These approaches keep the processing load on a set of hosts relatively balanced while keeping redirection traffic levels low. The Oceano project [8] provides a set of servers that can be spawned and managed to meet additional server resources for customers. After servers are allocated to customers they are used exclusively by contracted customers without concurrent system sharing. An analytical study of these types of systems appears in [9].

The goal in these previous works differs from ours in that there is no notion of individual, competing objectives as there is within a server collective. In other words, in these other works, the only objective is to improve the greater good of the entire system.

The problem of alleviating rapid and unpredictable spikes in request demands ("flash crowds") has generated much attention recently. Jung et al. propose a re-assignment of servers within a CDN infrastructure to handle such events [10]. Recent proposals in this area [11,12,13] approach this problem using peer–to–peer solutions, in which clients communicate directly with one another to retrieve the desired content. Here, clients have nothing to gain by serving content. The effectiveness of these approaches simply relies on the goodwill of those who receive content to also transmit the content to others when requested to do so.

The Content Distribution Internetworking (CDI) charter at the IETF has been working towards an initiative whose direction is closer to our work. The CDI model currently concentrates on the definition of requirements and concepts that allow interconnection of CDNs for common content delivery across different content networks [6]. The performance of these systems, however, has not been analyzed.

3   Collectives General Model

In this section, we develop the model that allows us to explore the fundamental performance tradeoff that collectives offer to content providers. Namely, we investigate if participating in a collective reduces the rejection rate of requests for a provider's content. Our goal is to develop a model that is simple, elegant, and amenable to a performance analysis. To accomplish this task, we assume that a set of providers has already agreed to form a collective and has distributed each content object to each server within the collective. The network core is well-provisioned such that the server's processing capabilities or its access link to the network are what limit the number of jobs that can be served simultaneously. Hence, a client's position in the network does not affect the server's ability to serve that client.

An example of how a collective, once established, can reduce the rate at which requests for a provider's content are rejected is depicted in Figure 1. Servers s_1, s_2, and s_3 are deployed by three distinct content providers in both Figures 1(a) and 1(b). The number of sessions a server can host simultaneously is indicated by the number of boxes. Shaded boxes indicate a session being supported and clear boxes indicate available resources. In Figure 1(a) three different providers operate in isolation (i.e., they do not participate in a collective and do not host one another's content). The server labeled s_3 cannot service all requests and is forced to drop a request. A logical view of the collective involving these three servers is shown in Figure 1(b). Here, server s_3 redirects the request it cannot service itself to server s_2, which has the capacity to process the request. As a result, by participating in the collective, fewer requests for s_3's content are rejected.

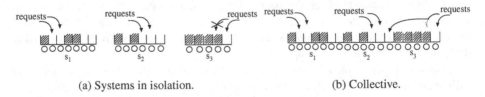

(a) Systems in isolation.   (b) Collective.

Fig. 1. Collective example compared to systems in isolation.

Our model of a server collective consists of content providers, servers, clients, commodities, and sessions. *Commodities* are the content/information goods offered by content providers. For instance, multimedia lectures are the commodities of an online course offering. The *content provider* (or simply *provider*) is the entity that offers commodities to customers via the Internet. A *client* requests commodities, and a *server* interfaces with the network to deliver commodities to clients. When a server accepts a client request for a commodity, a *session* (or content transfer) is initiated to deliver the content from the server to the client.

We consider a set of content providers $\mathcal{Y} = \{y_1, y_2, ...y_n\}$ where a given provider's commodities are files whose lengths are described by i.i.d. random variables. The set of servers that belong to provider y_i are modeled as a single serving system, s_i. We refer to any commodity that originated at provider y_i as v_i. We develop separate models for two classes of content. The first class consists of *fixed rate* transfers, such as streaming audio or video, where each transfer consumes a fixed amount of server bandwidth per unit time, such that the length of a session is independent of the number of files served concurrently by the server. The second class consists of *elastic transfers*, such as data files, where the amount of bandwidth consumed per unit time is inversely proportional to the number of files served concurrently. In both classes, the number of files that a server will simultaneously transmit is bounded to ensure that transfer rates proceed above a minimum rate. For fixed rate transfers, we make a simplifying assumption that each commodity (across providers) requires the same rate of transfer, such that each server s_i is capable of hosting a fixed number, k_i, of sessions simultaneously, where this number is independent of the set of commodities currently being hosted. The request rate for each provider's commodities, $v_i \in \mathcal{V}$ is modeled as a Poisson process with rate λ_i and each request receives service immediately if there is an idle processor at the receiving server. The service times for instances of transfers of commodity v_i are i.i.d. random variables B_i with mean $E[B_i]$. The service times of the instances of transfers over the set of all commodities are independent. Under these conditions, each serving system can be modeled as an $M/G/k/k$ queueing system. If the server in a collective cannot host an arriving request for its commodity, the server forwards the request to an available server (when one exists) in the collective. Otherwise, the request is dropped. Note that if a server operates in isolation, then when it has no additional room to service a request, the request must be dropped. Note that the collective can also be modeled as an $M/G/k/k$ queueing system with arrival rate $\sum_{i=1}^{n} \lambda_i$, mean service time $(\sum_{i=1}^{n} \lambda_i E[B_i])/(\sum_{i=1}^{n} \lambda_i)$, and that can service up to $\sum_{i=1}^{n} k_i$ sessions simultaneously.

We assume that a provider chooses to participate in a collective as long as the rejection rate of requests for its content is lower than when the provider operates in isolation. However, we also consider a provider willing to participate when the rejection rate is higher within the collective if this rate falls below a *tolerance limit*, l_i. The tolerance limit is a rejection rate that is considered to be negligible by the provider. For instance, if $l_i = 10^{-5}$ for provider y_i, y_i contributes its resources to collectives as long as the collective keeps the rejection rate for commodity v_i below 10^{-5}. When a provider is "willing" to join a collective, we say that the provider is *favorable*.

3.1   Computing the Rejection Rate of a Collective

While collectives are useful to handle sudden spikes of demand, we are interested only in spikes that last for non-negligible portions of time. Thus, the rejection rate can be determined by observing the steady state statistics of the serving system.

We define $p_{n,i}$ to be the rejection rate of provider y_i's content in a collective composed of n servers (e.g., a set of providers $\{y_1, y_2, ...y_n\}$ employing servers $s_1, \cdots, s_n$).[1] A single provider operating in isolation from other providers has rejection rate given by $p_{1,i}$, or simply p_1. For provider y_i in isolation, $i = 1, ...n$, the Erlang loss formula (also known as Erlang B formula) applies directly [14]:

$$p_1 = \frac{\rho_1^{k_1}/k_1!}{\sum_{j=0}^{k_1}(\rho_1)^j/j!} \tag{1}$$

where $\rho_1 = \lambda_1 E[B_1]$.

We extend this formula to the rejection rate of a two–server collective $p_{2,i}$, $i = 1, 2$. First, we define the random variables N_i, $i = 1, 2$, that describe the number of sessions for each of the commodities v_i, $i = 1, 2$. Since such a loss system is a symmetric queue [15], the stationary distribution for each state $P(N_1 = x, N_2 = z)$, where x (z) is the number of commodities of type v_1 (v_2) actively being processed, can be expressed in product–form: $P(N_1 = x, N_2 = z) = \pi_x \pi_z c_2$, where $\pi_x = \rho_1^x/x!$, $\pi_z = \rho_2^z/z!$, and c_2 is a normalizing constant such that $\sum_{x \geq 0, z \geq 0, z+x \leq k_1+k_2} \pi_x \pi_z c_2 = 1$. Hence we find the rejection rate of a two–server collective to be

$$p_2 = P(N_1 + N_2 = k_1 + k_2) = \sum_{x=0}^{n} P(N_1 = k_1 + k_2 - x, N_2 = x)$$

$$= \sum_{x=0}^{n} \frac{1}{x!}\rho_1^x \frac{1}{(k_1 + k_2 - x)!}\rho_2^{k_1+k_2-x} c_2 = (\rho_1 + \rho_2)^{k_1+k_2} \frac{1}{(k_1 + k_2)!}c_2, \tag{2}$$

where $\rho_i = \lambda_i E[B_i]$, $i = 1, 2$. We refer to ρ_i as the *intensity* for provider i. Noting that (2) is in the form of (1) with ρ_1 replaced by $\rho_1 + \rho_2$ and k_1 replaced by $k_1 + k_2$ we can repeat this process recursively to compute the rejection rate for a collective composed by n providers.

$$p_n = \frac{1}{(\sum_{j=1}^{n} k_j)!} \left(\sum_{j=1}^{n} \rho_j \right)^{\sum_{j=1}^{n} k_j} c_n. \tag{3}$$

where c_n is once more the normalizing constant for this distribution such that

$$\sum_{x_1 \geq 0, x_2 \geq 0, ..., \sum_{j=1}^{n} x_j \leq \sum_{j=1}^{n} k_j} P(N_1 = x_1, ..., N_n = x_n) = 1.$$

When $\rho_i/k_i = \rho_j/k_j$ for all i, j, $1 \leq i < j \leq n$, the collective is said to be homogeneous.

3.2   Evaluation of Scenarios under Fixed-Rate Transfers

We begin by evaluating collectives as a function of number of participating providers and the provider intensities. Figure 2(a) plots rejection rates of n–provider systems p_n,

---

[1] Whenever $\forall y_i, y_j \in \mathcal{Y}, i \neq j, p_{n,i} = p_{n,j}$, $p_{n,i}$ can be written as p_n.

$n = 2, 5, 10$, where each server can simultaneously service 100 commodities ($k_i = 100$, $i = 1, 2$).[2] The results are a direct application of Equation (3).

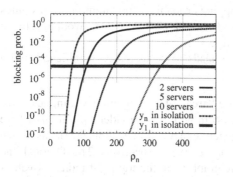
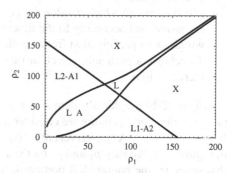

(a) Rejection rate in collectives scenario compared to servers in isolation.

(b) Areas of comparison between two–server collectives and servers in isolation.

Fig. 2. Evaluation of collectives under the model of fixed-rate transfers.

First, we fix the configurations of $n-1$ providers while we vary the traffic intensity of the other, referred to as y_n. The value of $\rho_i = 65$ is chosen such that requests for v_i exhibit a rejection rate of approximately 10^{-5} when y_i operates in isolation, $1 \leq i < n$. On the x–axis, we vary ρ_n, the provider intensity for provider y_n. The y–axis plots rejection rates for various system configurations. The curve labeled "y_n in isolation" depicts the rejection rate of requests for commodities v_n when provider y_n stays in isolation. The constant line at $p_1 \approx 10^{-5}$, labeled "y_1 in isolation", plots rejection rate of requests for commodity v_1 for provider y_1 when y_1 operates in isolation (results for providers $y_2, \cdots, y_{n-1}$ are identical). The remaining curves labeled "n servers", $n = 2, 5, 10$, depict the rejection rate for all providers that participate in an n–provider collective. From the figure, we observe that:

- For the range of values of ρ_n shown, the rejection in the collective for commodity v_n is smaller than its rejection rate in isolation. Therefore, regardless of its own provider intensity, a provider is willing to participate in a collective when the other providers have sufficiently low provider intensities.
- Ranges for ρ_n exist, $0 \leq \rho_n \leq 110$, $0 \leq \rho_n \leq 175$,and $0 \leq \rho_n \leq 330$ for $n = 2, 5, 10$, respectively, where the rejection rate in the collective for commodity $v_i, i < n$, is smaller than the rejection rate when s_i operates in isolation. Hence, the collective benefits provider $y_i, i < n$ even when all other providers in the collective have larger provider intensities.
- Beyond the range described above, requests for commodity $v_i, i < n$ are dropped with greater probability in collectives. However, as long as $\rho_n < 120$, $\rho_n < 200$,

---

[2] In practice limitations on the server side can also be due to license restrictions. For instance, today RealNetworks [16] offers its basic streaming server (free of charge) with maximum capacity of 1 Mbit/s. Their $1,999–dollar license server (Helix Universal Server – standard) has maximum capacity of 4 Mbit/s. The maximum number of sessions is then given by the maximum transmission throughput divided by the average transmission rate of delivery sessions.

$\rho_n < 350$, for $n = 2, 5, 10$, respectively, the rejection rate in the shared system remains small, i.e., below the tolerance limit $l_n = 10^{-4}$. Hence, content provider y_i is favorable.

- When ρ_n assumes higher values, the dropping probability for commodities becomes excessive, and according to the described criteria, y_i, $1 \leq i \leq n$, would prefer to withdraw its participation from a collective.
- To achieve a particular rejection rate, ρ needs to be increased significantly with increases in n.

Figure 2(b) graphically demonstrates the "areas of participation willingness" for two providers. In this figure we consider a system with two providers, y_1 and y_2 where $k_i = 100, i = 1, 2$. A two-server collective generates a two-dimensional picture as shown in Figure 2(b). We vary ρ_1 and ρ_2 on the $x-$ and $y-$axis, respectively. The diagonal line that separates the bottom–left portion of the graph from the top right indicates values of ρ_1 and ρ_2 where a collective drops requests at a rate of 10^{-4}. Below this line, the collective offers a lower aggregate intensity, resulting in a drop rate below the tolerance limit of 10^{-4}. The top curve that goes from the bottom–left to the top–right of the graph is the set of values of (ρ_1, ρ_2) where content provider y_1 experiences the same rejection rate regardless of whether it operates in isolation or participates within the collective, i.e., $p_{1,1} = p_2$. Above this curve, $p_{1,1} < p_2$: the rejection rate is reduced for y_1 by operating in isolation, and below, $p_{1,1} > p_2$. Similarly, the lower curve that runs from the bottom left to the top right is formed from the points where $p_{1,2} = p_2$. Below this curve, $p_{1,2} < p_2$, and above, $p_{1,2} > p_2$.

In Figure 2(b), each area between the various curves receives one or more labels to indicate the "willingness" of y_1 and y_2 to form a collective. A label of 'Li', $i = 1, 2$, indicates an area in which rejection rate for y_i's content is smaller in a collective than in isolation, i.e., $p_2 < p_{1,i}$. An 'Ai' label, $i = 1, 2$, indicates an area where $p_2 < l_i$. When both providers mark an area similarly, the pair of labels 'A1', 'A2' are replaced by 'A', and 'L1', 'L2' are replaced by 'L'. 'X' marks the areas where a content provider is not favorable in collectives. We see that there is a significant region in which both providers can benefit simultaneously by participating in a collective. We note, however, that both providers tend to benefit only in "near-homogeneous" configurations (in this case defined by the line $\rho_2 = \rho_1$), especially when intensities range from moderate to high. As the difference in intensities widens, the win–only property ceases to hold. In fact, we observe a rapid increase in the rejection rate in Figure 2(a) for a collective of 2 servers in the range $85 \leq \rho_n \leq 150$. In addition, we note that there is no area in which the rejection rates of both content providers are higher in the shared system than in isolation, i.e., at least one provider is willing to participate in the collective in any area marked by an 'X'.

3.3   Asymptotic Limits of Collectives: The ρ/k Factor

We turn to the performance of an n–server collective as the number of servers n tends to ∞. In practice a very large collective requires also very large storage units in each of the collective participants. There are, however, important insights to be gained from studying the impact on performance as a collective grows. In fact, just a small number of providers forming a collective can be enough to lead the performance of the collective close to the asymptotic limit.

We assume that there are n_c different classes of providers, where all provider systems in the same class exhibit the same provider intensity ρ_i and have the same bound, k_i, on the number of jobs that can simultaneously be serviced. We let f_i represent the fraction of providers in class i, $1 \leq i \leq n_c$. Equation 3 can be reformulated as

$$p_n = \frac{\frac{\left(\sum_{j=1}^{n_c}(nf_j\rho_j)\right)^{\sum_{j=1}^{n_c} nk_j f_j}}{\left(\sum_{j=1}^{n_c} nk_j f_j\right)!}}{\sum_{i=0}^{\sum_{j=1}^{n_c} nf_j k_j} \frac{\left(\sum_{j=1}^{c_n}(nf_j\rho_j)\right)^i}{i!}} \tag{4}$$

which is simplified via the constants $\hat{\rho} = \sum_{j=1}^{n_c} f_j\rho_j$ and $\hat{k} = \sum_{j=1}^{n_c} f_j k_j$ to $p_n = \frac{(n\hat{\rho})^{n\hat{k}}/(n\hat{k})!}{\sum_{j=0}^{n\hat{k}}(n\hat{\rho})^j/j!}$. As n tends to ∞, the asymptotic limit of the rejection rate is [17]:

$$\lim_{n \to \infty} p_n = \begin{cases} 0, & \text{if } \hat{\rho}/\hat{k} \leq 1 \\ 1 - \hat{k}/\hat{\rho}, & \text{if } \hat{\rho}/\hat{k} > 1 \end{cases} \tag{5}$$

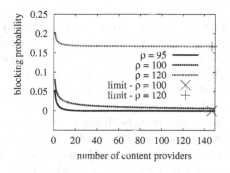

(a) Rejection rate when increasing the number of providers.

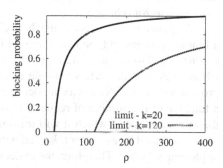

(b) Asymptotic rejection rate for $n \to \infty$.

Fig. 3. Asymptotic observations on rejection rate for fixed–rate transfer collectives.

Figure 3 illustrates the behavior of an n–server collective as n grows large. For simplicity, we show only the case where only one class of servers exists, i.e., $n_c = 1$ in which each provider's system can simultaneously handle $k = 100$ transmissions. In Figure 3(a), we vary the number of participating providers along the x–axis, plotting the rejection rate along the y–axis, where each curve depicts a collective where an average provider intensity, ρ, is exhibited. We use Equation 3 to plot the curves for $\rho = 95$, $\rho = 100$, and $\rho = 120$. The asymptotic limits are marked with two distinct points. Using Equation 5, the asymptotic limit for $\rho = 100$ is effectively 0, and for $\rho = 120$, the limit is approximately $1/6$. The asymptotic limits observed here fit the claims of Equation 5. In particular, for $\rho < k$, the rejection rate converges to 0, whereas for $\rho > k$, we observe the rejection rate converging to the limit given by Equation 5. The figure demonstrates (for a homogeneous collection of providers) that the most dramatic benefits from a collective result from clustering small numbers of providers together, and that incorporating additional providers further reduces rejection rates, but at a quickly diminishing rate.

In Figure 3(b) we apply Equation 5 to plot the asymptotic rejection rate of a collective as a function of ρ. The curve on the left is the asymptotic rejection rate for the case where $k = 20$. The curve on the right is for the case where $k = 120$. We notice for $k = 120$ a slower increase in the asymptotic rejection rate.

In conclusion, even when participants in a collective are homogeneous but individually overloaded ($\rho_i > k_i$), their rejection rate for requests for their content remains bounded by $1 - k/\rho$.

4   Collectives for Elastic Transfers

In this section we consider collectives receiving a type of traffic whose service rate is proportional to $1/w_n$, where w_n is the number of customers simultaneously in service across all n servers that comprise the collective. For such a model load is equally balanced across the collective. This can be accomplished in practice, for instance, with parallel downloading technology [18], which is commonplace today in peer-to-peer downloading tools such as Morpheus.

We again consider a model in which client arrivals to each provider are described by a Poisson process and the load imposed by each commodity is described by a general distribution. Using the same argument as before, we collapse the model to the case where each provider offers a single commodity and uses a single server. We apply a processor sharing (PS) service model to capture the behavior of the transmission rate as a function of the number of requests in service. We assume that each server s_i bounds the minimum rate at which it will transmit data to clients by bounding the number of clients accepted by a constant, k_i, and will turn away (or redirect) any additional clients requesting service.[3] Therefore, the collective under the PS model can be modeled as an $M/G/1/k_i/PS$ queue. As before, we assume that jobs are never queued when service is unavailable, but are simply turned away (dropped). In addition to rejection rate as a metric, we also measure job completion time.

We have derived the rejection rate of sessions under this model [19]. While the distribution of an unbounded queueing system that uses a processor sharing discipline is known to be geometric [14], for a finite queueing system we find the following law:

$$p_n = (\lambda E[B])^k \frac{1 - \lambda E[B]}{1 - (\lambda E[B])^{k+1}} \tag{6}$$

where $\lambda = \sum_{j=1}^n \lambda_j$ (λ_j is the request rate for commodity v_j), $k = \sum_{j=1}^n k_j$, and $E[B]$ is the mean size of the request to the collective. For an n–server collective, the amount of work can be described for each individual job B_n in the collective as a function of the work, B, introduced in isolation for $\{y_1\}$ where $B_n = k_1 B/(\sum_{j=1}^n k_j)$.

---

[3] In the context of parallel downloading, the sum of all fractional components serviced should add up to k_i.

Assuming $\lambda_i = \lambda_j = \lambda, k_i = k_j, \forall i, j$, it is easy to show that, for $\rho = \lambda E[B]$, when the number of content providers n tends to ∞, the rejection rate converges to $\lim_{n\to\infty} p_n = 1 - \frac{1}{\rho}$. For a collective formed from n providers, the expected completion time of a session d_n is obtained using Little's Law, as the fraction of requests accepted to the system $(1 - p_n)\lambda$. We also define the number of servicing sessions as a random variable N. Therefore,

$$d_n = \frac{\bar{w}_n}{(1 - p_n)\lambda}, \tag{7}$$

where the expected number of simultaneous sessions is $\bar{w}_n = \sum_{z=0}^{k} z P(N = z)$.

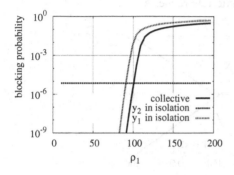 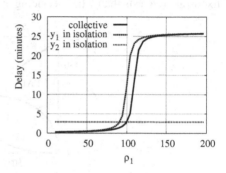

(a) Rejection rate under a processor sharing discipline.

(b) Mean completion time under a processor sharing discipline.

Fig. 4. Evaluation of a collective for elastic transfers.

4.1 Numerical Evaluation

Here we study conditions under which providers would be *favorable* participants within a collective that consist of providers whose transfer rates are elastic. We apply the same criteria described in Section 3 as to determine whether providers are favorable. For instance, Figure 4 illustrates a scenario in which we vary ρ_1 and maintain ρ_2 fixed at $\rho_2 = 91$. Figure 4(a) and 4(b) plot the rejection rate and average completion time, respectively, of the providers in collectives as well as of providers in isolation as a function of ρ_1. The curves labeled "collective", "y_1 in isolation", and "y_2 in isolation" respectively plot p_2, $p_{1,1}$, and $p_{1,2}$ (the last being constant). We observe the rejection rate of providers within the collective to be almost 4 orders of magnitude smaller than $p_{1,1}$ when ρ_1 and ρ_2 are approximately equal. However, the benefits become marginal with increasing $|\rho_1 - \rho_2|$. This again supports the intuition that a collective is useful for elastic transfers only when the intensities imposed by providers are approximately the same.

Figure 5 depicts areas of interest computed via application of Equation 6. The parameters $\rho_1 = \lambda_1 E[B_1]$ and $\rho_2 = \lambda_2 E[B_2]$ are varied respectively along the x– and y–axis. We use the same labeling convention as in Section 3.2. In comparison to Figure

2(b), we see that a collective in elastic environments favors both providers for a wider variation of their respective intensities when both intensities are small (i.e., the bubble in the bottom-left corner is bigger). However, when intensities are large, the difference in provider intensities over which both providers are favorable is reduced. Intuitively, this may be due to the fact that when the system is under high loads, the average completion time of a job increases. Bringing in additional capacity (but with a proportional load) does not reduce completion times of admitted jobs significantly when load is high. It will, however, reduce completion times when load is light. Since a collective formation is most useful when intensities are high (e.g., in Figure 5, the bulb lies almost completely within a range of rejection rates that are below the providers' tolerance limits), we conclude that collectives can tolerate more heterogeneity in systems when servicing fixed-rate requests than when servicing elastic-rate requests.

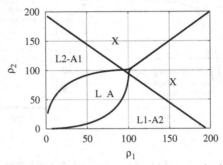

Fig. 5. Area of benefit for collectives under processor sharing discipline

5   Resource Bounding with Thresholds

Here, we evaluate *thresholding* techniques as a means to limit the amount of server resources a provider contributes to a collective. We show how thresholding can be used to bound the rejection rates.

Let h_i be a *threshold*, $0 \le h_i \le k_i$ for server s_i such that s_i refuses any requests to service other provider's commodities whenever it is actively servicing h_i commodities that are not v_i. This guarantees that the provider will maintain space to service simultaneously at least $k_i - h_i$ requests of its own commodity at any given time. We call this threshold type D1. We also evaluate a variant of this thresholding technique. A D2 type threshold denies a request at server s_i for another provider's commodity v_j, $j \ne i$, whenever the available space for commodity transmission at server s_i falls below h_i (i.e., $k_i - x_i$ where x_i is the number of sessions in service). For both types of thresholding, setting $h_i = 0$, $1 \le i \le n$, is equivalent to n providers operating in isolation and setting $h_i = k_i$ for all i is equivalent to a collective described in previous sections where providers fully share their resources.

5.1 Analytical Evaluation of D1 Thresholding

We begin by evaluating server collectives in which an ongoing session re-assignment (also called switching) is enabled: for any i, if there are fewer than k_i jobs servicing commodity v_i, then all these jobs are serviced by s_i. Therefore, if a processor within s_i becomes available, some ongoing transmission for commodity v_i is reassigned from an s_j to s_i if such a j exists, $j \neq i$. We shall see shortly (comparing simulation results) that enabling switching has little impact on rejection rate.

For the sake of analysis, we assume that service times are exponentially distributed.[4] This allows us to model the 2–provider collective as a truncated Markov chain with states described by the pair (N_1, N_2), where N_i is the number of sessions servicing commodity v_i in the system, $i = 1, 2$, $0 \leq N_1 \leq k_1 + \min(k_2 - N_2, h_2)$, and $N_2 \leq k_2 + \min(k_1 - N_1, h_1)$. A crucial difference from previous models is that here, since the decision to accept a request depends on the identity of the commodity being requested, the rejection rates for the differing commodities can differ within a collective. The Markov chain transitions are as follows:

- From $(x - 1, z)$ to (x, z) with rate λ_1, for $1 \leq x \leq k_1 + \min(k_2 - z, h_2)$.
- From (x, z) to $(x - 1, z)$ with rate $x\mu_1$, for $1 \leq x \leq k_1 + \min(k_2 - z, h_2)$.
- From $(x, z - 1)$ to (x, z) with rate λ_2, for $1 \leq z \leq k_2 + \min(k_1 - x, h_1)$.
- From (x, z) to $(x, z - 1)$ with rate $z\mu_2$, for $1 \leq z \leq k_2 + \min(k_1 - x, h_1)$.

The above conditions satisfy the requirements that allow computation of the steady-state probabilities as a product-form solution for truncated Markov chains [20]: $P(N_1 = x, N_2 = z) = \pi_{x,z} = \pi_x \pi_z c_2$, where $\pi_x = \rho_1^x / x!$, $\pi_z = \rho_2^z / z!$, and c_2 is a normalizing constant such that $\sum_{x=0}^{k_1+h_2} \sum_{z=0}^{k_2+\min(h_1, k_1 - z)} \pi_{x,z} = 1$.

We use the probabilities $\pi_{i,j}$ to compute the probabilities of all states for which $N_i = k_i + \min(k_j - w, h_j)$, given that $N_j = w$, $i = 1, 2$, $j = 1, 2$, $j \neq i$. The rejection rate of provider y_i's content in the collective, $p_{2,i}$, is:

$$
\begin{aligned}
p_{2,i} &= \sum_{x=k_i}^{k_i+h_j} \pi_{x, k_i+k_j}\ x \ + \sum_{z=0}^{k_j\ h_j\ 1} \pi_{k_i+h_j, z} \\
&= \sum_{x=k_i}^{k_i+h_j} \frac{(\lambda_i/\mu_i)^x}{x!} \frac{(\lambda_j/\mu_j)^{k_i+k_j}\ x}{(k_i + k_j - x)!} c_2 + \frac{(\lambda_i/\mu_i)^{k_i+h_j}}{(k_i + h_j)!} \sum_{z=0}^{k_j\ h_j\ 1} \frac{(\lambda_j/\mu_j)^z}{z!} c_2. \quad (8)
\end{aligned}
$$

Figure 6 depicts respective rejection rates experienced for requests of commodities v_1 and v_2 for various intensities and D1 threshold levels with switching, where providers y_1 and y_2 apply the same threshold, i.e., $h_1 = h_2$. Each of them has a server with total capacity for $k_i = 100$, $i = 1, 2$ concurrent sessions. On the x–axis, we vary ρ_1. Instead of fixing ρ_2, we set $\rho_2 = 0.2\rho_1$ such that the intensities that both providers contribute to the collective increase along the x–axis, but y_1's intensity remains much larger than that of y_2. The various curves depict rejection rates for the two commodities for differing threshold levels. The curves for the systems in isolation are represented with thicker lines.

---

[4] Note that our reduction of a provider's server system to a single server with a single commodity still holds without loss of generality.

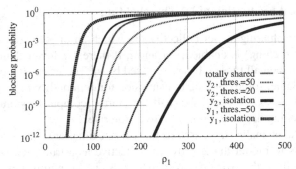

Fig. 6. Respective rejection rate experienced on requests for providers y_1's and y_2's content and different thresholds.

The curve labeled "totally shared" is the rejection rate for both commodity requests when the thresholds are set to maximum values $h_1 = h_2 = 100$. The remaining curves' labels indicate the provider whose content's rejection rate is being plotted and the value to which the threshold is set.

The most important conclusion here is that changing the threshold value can lead to significant variations in rejection rate for a collective. In fact, when the intensity of a provider is small enough that the provider can meet its desired rejection rate operating by itself, that provider can then use thresholds in a collective to allow other content providers the use of its resources without raising its own rejection rate above the undesired level.

5.2   Comparison of Thresholding Techniques

We resort to simulation to evaluate non-switching and D2–threshold configurations. We model arrivals by a Poisson process, but service times here are described by a lognormal distribution, as has been observed in practice [21,22,23,24]. The probability density function of the lognormal distribution is given by $\frac{e^{-(\log(x)-\mu)^2/(2\sigma^2)}}{x\sigma\sqrt{2\pi}}$, where $\log(x)$ is the natural logarithm and μ and σ are the standard parameters used within the lognormal distribution. We used the mean and standard deviation of 26 and 46 (minutes) observed in [21], respectively, to derive the parameters μ and σ.

Based on measurements from [21], we conduct simulations with $\lambda = 3.5$ requests per minute and $E[B] = 26$ minutes giving a value $\rho_2 = 91$ for commodity v_2. Figure 7 plots rejection rates obtained from the previous analysis (Equation 8, for the case of D1 thresholding with switching) and simulations (for the other cases) in which $h_i = 40$ for $i = 1, 2$. Figure 7(a) plots rejection rates for commodity v_1, and Figure 7(b) plots rejection rates for commodity v_2. Here ρ_1 is varied along the x–axis in both Figure 7(a) and Figure 7(b). The curves in each figure labeled "D1+switching", "D1+non–switching", "D2+switching", and "D2+non–switching" depict the various collective thresholding configurations formed by alternating between the use of non-switching and switching methods, and between the use of D1 and D2 thresholding techniques.

In Figure 7(a), we observe little difference in rejection rate for commodity v_1 as we vary the configuration. In Figure 7(b), we observe the rejection rates of provider y_2's content (commodity v_2). The horizontal line depicts the rejection rate for commodity

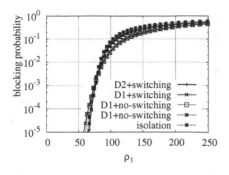

(a) Rejection rate of provider y_1's content.

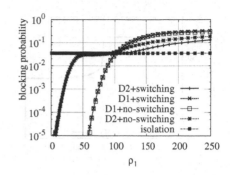

(b) Rejection rate of provider y_2's content.

Fig. 7. The use of D1–thresholding and D2–thresholding/switching.

v_2 when y_2 operates in isolation. For $\rho_1 < 40$ the two curves with sharp increases correspond to the collective with D2–thresholds. The two curves are indistinguishable except for $\rho_1 > 100$ where the switching system exhibits a rejection rate that is slightly lower than the non-switching system. The two curves with sharp increases in the range $60 < \rho_1 < 100$ correspond to the collective with D1–thresholds. When operating in the collective, the rejection rate for commodity v_2 drops by as much as three orders of magnitude in the range where $\rho_1 < 50$ using D2 and $\rho_1 < 100$ using D1–thresholds. In the range $\rho_1 > 100$ the rejection rates for commodity v_2 increase at a slower rate when using D2–thresholds than when using D1–thresholds. This is because under D2 thresholding, commodity v_2 is less likely to be serviced by server s_1. In contrast, when using D1-thresholding the exhibited rejection rates are much lower than those exhibited when using D2 thresholding when $\rho_1 < 100$. Hence, D1 thresholding should be used when the competing system's intensity is expected to be higher, and D2 thresholding should be used when the competing system's intensity is expected to be lower.

We further observe that there is little difference in the results obtained when ongoing session switching is enabled from when it is not. This suggests that analytical results for rejection rate from a switching system can be used to approximate the rejection rate within non-switching systems.

5.3 Adaptive Thresholding

Motivated by the results in previous sections, we consider an ideal scenario in which a provider, y_i, adapts its threshold as a function of the provider intensities imposed on the collective. By doing so it contributes the maximum amount of its own server resources (i.e., the highest threshold possible) without the rejection rate for its own commodity, v_i, exceeding its tolerance limit, l_i.

We apply our analysis of D1–type thresholding systems with switching to a 2–provider collective in which providers y_1 and y_2 accept a maximum of $k_1 = 100$ and $k_2 = 20$ concurrent sessions, respectively. Provider y_1 receives a fixed intensity of $\rho_1 = 20$. Provider y_1 adjusts its threshold h_1 to the maximum integer value (via Equation

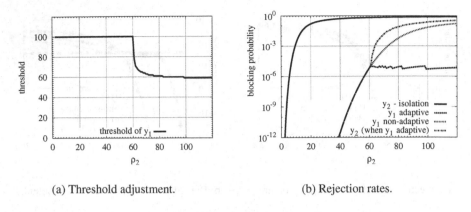

(a) Threshold adjustment.   (b) Rejection rates.

Fig. 8. Ideal adaptive thresholding.

8) such that the rejection rate for commodity v_1 remains below its tolerance limit of $l_1 = 10^{-5}$. Provider y_2 enables its server to fully share its resources, i.e., $h_2 = k_2 = 20$.

In Figure 8(a) we vary ρ_2 in the x-axis and plot the largest value of h_1 along the y-axis as a function that maintains $p_{2,1} < l_1$. We see that for $\rho_2 \leq 60$, the threshold remains at 100. As ρ_2 crosses 60, the threshold drops rapidly, then continues to reduce, but at a much slower rate. In Figure 8(b) we vary ρ_2 along the x–axis, and the rejection rate along the y–axis. Figure 8(b) shows rejection rates of various configurations as a function of ρ_2. The left-most curve plots the rejection rate of provider y_2's content when y_2 operates in isolation (obtained from Equation 1). The remaining three curves (which differ only when $\rho > 60$) plot, from top to bottom are, respectively, the rejection rate of provider y_2's content when participating in the collective with the adaptive threshold- ing, the rejection rate for all commodities when participating in the collective without thresholding (obtained from Equation 2), and the rejection rate of provider y_1's content when participating in the collective with the adaptive thresholding.

The bottom curve verifies that with thresholding, rejection rates of commodity v_1 remain below $l_1 = 10^{-5}$. By comparing the remaining two curves from the collective to the curve for the case where y_2 is in isolation, we see that, even with thresholding, participating in the collective significantly reduces provider y_2's rejection rate. We see that, while thresholding increases the rejection rate for commodity v_2 in comparison to a threshold-free collective, provider y_1 is favorable only when the thresholding is applied, and provider y_2 experiences a rejection rate that is orders of magnitude smaller than if y_2 operates in isolation.

6   Conclusion

We have analyzed the performance of resource sharing via the formation of server collec- tives as a means to reduce rejection rates in content distribution services. Providers can benefit by participating in collectives but should avoid situations in which their resources are overused servicing requests on the behalf of other collectives members, worsening the delivery quality of their own content. Our analysis and simulation via fundamental queueing models yields to the following results and insights:

- We modeled fixed and elastic rate transfers within collectives and compared the rejection rates and completion times of these transfers to the case where providers operate in isolation. We then used our models to determine the conditions under which a provider benefits from participating in collectives. In particular, we determine the conditions for which all participants simultaneously benefit from their participation in collectives.
- In some circumstances, we observe significant reduction of rejection rates by comparing collectives to systems in isolation. For instance, we show a 4-order-of-magnitude reduction in rejection rates when comparing an isolated system to a two-server collective. Furthermore, a 10-server collective has a 7-order-of-magnitude reduction in comparison to an isolated system. As the number of servers increases the relative reduction of rejection rate becomes less dramatic.
- We found asymptotic results as the number of collective providers tends to ∞. If the factor ρ/k given by the average provider intensity ρ and the maximum number of concurrent sessions in the system k is less than one, then the system's rejection rate is 0 in the limit. Otherwise, the rejection rate converges to $1 - k/\rho$.
- When demands on providers' contents are high, composing a collective (without thresholding) can reduce the rejection rate of all participants for a greater variation in intensities among participating systems supporting fixed-rate transfers than can be tolerated within systems supporting elastic-rate transfers.
- Even a small degree of heterogeneity among participants in a collective can lead to situations in which one or more providers achieve a lower rejection rate for their content by operating in isolation. An expected consequence is that such providers would refrain from participating in collectives in these unfavorable circumstances.
- We analyzed two thresholding techniques that enable heterogeneous sets of server systems (different intensities and numbers of slots) to form a collective in which requests for all participants' commodities are dropped at a rate lower than when the systems operate in isolation. We show that, in conjunction with thresholding, the ability to dynamically swap a transmission to the server that profits directly from the servicing of the content has little impact on the rejection rate. Thresholding therefore encourages providers to participate in collectives who otherwise would not do so, extending the range of heterogeneity in providers for which server collectives are applicable.

Acknowledgements. We would like to thank Ed Coffman for valuable discussions and comments on this article, Predrag Jelenkovic and Vishal Misra for valuable discussions regarding this work. We are also thankful to Ward Whitt for pointing out a reference on asymptotic behavior of loss systems.

References

1. D. Eager, E. Lazowska, and J. Zahorjan, "A comparison of receiver-initiated and sender-initiated adaptive load sharing," *Performance Evaluation*, vol. 16, May 1986.

2. D. Eager, E. Lazowska, and J. Zahorjan, "Adaptive load sharing in distributed systems," *IEEE Transactions on Software Engineering*, vol. 12, May 1986.
3. M. Dahlin, R. Wang, T. Anderson, and D. Patterson, "Cooperative caching: Using remote client memory to improve file system performance," in *Proc. of OSDI'94*, 1994.
4. G. Voelker, H. Jamrozik, M. Vernon, H. Levy, and E. Lazowska, "Managing server load in global memory systems," in *Proc. of 1997 ACM Sigmetrics*, June 1997.
5. G. Voelker, E. Anderson, T. Kimbrel, M. Feeley, J. Chase, A. Karlin, and H. Levy, "Implementing cooperative prefetching and caching in a global memory system," in *Proc. of the 1998 ACM Sigmetrics Conference*, June 1998.
6. M. Day, B. Cain, G. Tomlinson, and P. Rzemski, "A model for content internetworking (CDI)," Tech. Rep. draft-ietf-cdi-model-02, IETF, Nov. 2002. work in progress.
7. J. Kangasharju, J. W. Roberts, and K. W. Ross, "Object replication strategies in content distribution networks," in *Proceedings of Sixth International Workshop on Web Caching and Content Delivery*, June 2001.
8. IBM. Research, "Oceano project." http://www.research.ibm.com/oceanoproject/.
9. L. Golubchik and J. C. S. Lui, "Bounding of performance measures for threshold-based systems: Theory and application to dynamic resource management in video-on-demand servers," *IEEE Transactions of Computers*, pp. 353–372, Apr. 2002.
10. J. Jung, B. Krishnamurthy, and M. Rabinovich, "Flash crowds and denial of service attacks: Characterization and implications for cdns and web sites," in *Proc. of WWW Conference*, (Honolulu, HI), May 2002.
11. V. N. Padmanabhan, H. J. Wang, P. A. Chou, and K. Sripanidkulchai, "Distributing streaming media content using cooperative networking," in *Proc. of NOSSDAV'02*, (Miami Beach, FL), May 2002.
12. T. Stading, P. Maniatis, and M. Baker, "Peer-to-peer caching schemes to address flash crowds," in *1st International Workshop on Peer-to-Peer Systems (IPTPS 2002)*, Mar. 2002.
13. R. J. B. Jr., A. Somani, D. Gruhl, and R. Agrawal, "Youserv: A web hosting and content sharing tool for the masses," in *Proc. of WWW-2002*, 2002.
14. S. Ross, *Stochastic Processes*. John Wiley & Sons, Inc., 1983.
15. R. W. Wolff, *Stochastic Modeling and the Theory of Queues*, ch. 6, pp. 334–341. Prentice Hall, 1988.
16. Real Networks, Inc., "http://www.real.com." web-site.
17. K. Ross, *Multiservice loss models for Broadband Telecommunications Networks*. Springer, 1995.
18. J. Byers, M. Luby, and M. Mitzenmacher, "Accessing multiple mirror sites in parallel: Using tornado codes to speed up downlaods," in *Proc. of IEEE INFOCOM'99*, 1999.
19. D. Villela and D. Rubenstein, "A queueing analysis of server sharing collectives for content distribution," Tech. Rep. EE2002-04-121, Columbia University – Department of Electrical Engineering, Apr. 2002.
20. D. Bertsekas and R. Gallager, *Data Networks*. Prentice-Hall, 2 ed., 1992.
21. J. M. Almeida, J. Krueger, D. L. Eager, and M. K. Vernon, "Analysis of educational media server workloads," in *Proc. of NOSSDAV*, pp. 21–30, June 2001.
22. J. Padhye and J. Kurose, "An empirical study of client interactions with a continuous-media courseware server," *IEEE Internet Computing*, Apr. 1999.
23. M. Chesire, A. Wolman, G. M. Voelker, and H. M. Levy, "Measurement and analysis of a streaming-media workload," in *Proceedings of the Third USENIX Symposium on Internet Technologies and Systems*, Mar. 2001.
24. S. Jin and A. Bestavros, "Gismo: Generator of streaming media objects and workloads," *Performance Evaluation Review*, 2001.

An Approximation of the End-to-End Delay Distribution

Han S. Kim and Ness B. Shroff

School of Electrical and Computer Engineering
Purdue University
West Lafayette, IN 47907
{hkim,shroff}@ecn.purdue.edu
http://yara.ecn.purdue.edu/~newsgrp

Abstract. In this paper we propose an approximation for the end-to-end (queueing) delay distribution based on endpoint measurements. We develop a notion of the end-to-end capacity which is defined for a path of interest. We show that the end-to-end path can be represented by a single-node model with the end-to-end capacity in the sense that the single-node model is equivalent to the original path in terms of the queue-length and the departure. Our study is motivated by the case where the end-to-end delay distribution can be approximated by an appropriately scaled end-to-end queue-length distribution. We investigate the accuracy of our approximation and demonstrate its application to admission control providing end-to-end QoS.

1   Introduction

There are a plethora of papers that have analyzed the queue-length distribution and loss probability for a single node [1] [2] [3] [4] [5] [6]. However, if we simply apply the single-node analysis to each node on the end-to-end path for the end-to-end QoS guarantee, it could result in an inefficient utilization of network resources, and also cause a scalability problem. For example, suppose that the QoS requirement per each flow is to maintain the end-to-end delay violation probability with threshold D less than ϵ, and that we have a tool for estimating the delay violation probability only for single-node systems. A simple way to guarantee the end-to-end QoS is to estimate the delay violation probability with threshold $D' = D/n$ (where n is the number of nodes on the path) at each node on the path and maintain it less than ϵ. This may result in an unnecessarily small end-to-end delay violation probability and, hence an unnecessary waste of network resources. Moreover, it will also cause a scalability problem because per-flow delay violation probability would need to be managed even at the core nodes inside the network that serve a very large number of flows.

There has been an attempt to reduce the unnecessary waste of network resources by optimally setting the QoS level at each node depending on traffic models and the type of the QoS metric [7]. It has been investigated via a simulation study that the convolution of delay distributions of all the nodes on the

K. Jeffay, I. Stoica, and K. Wehrle (Eds.): IWQoS 2003, LNCS 2707, pp. 59–75, 2003.

path is quite close to the actual end-to-end delay distribution [8]. But such approaches still have the scalability problem. Moreover, in the latter approach, to estimate the end-to-end delay violation probability at one point of threshold D, the delay distribution of each node need to be calculated for the entire range of the convolution.

In this paper we propose an approximation of the end-to-end (queueing) delay distribution[1] based on endpoint measurements. The underlying idea is the following. We define the end-to-end capacity as the maximum capacity that can be allocated to the path for the given traffic and connections. Then, a single-node model with the end-to-end capacity is equivalent to the original path in the sense that they have the same end-to-end queue length, and hence, they also have the same departure and end-to-end delay. On the other hand, it is well known that when the capacity is constant, say c, the delay violation probability, $\mathbb{P}\{W > x\}$, is equal to the tail probability scaled by c, $\mathbb{P}\{Q > cx\}$, for integer x in a discrete-time FIFO queue, i.e., $\mathbb{P}\{W > x\} = \mathbb{P}\{Q > cx\}$. We find a similar relationship in the case of non-constant capacity, $\mathbb{P}\{W > x\} \approx \mathbb{P}\{Q > \bar{c}x\}$, where $\bar{c}$ is the mean of the capacity. In particular, we have shown that for any $\delta > 0$, $\mathbb{P}\{Q > (\bar{c} + \delta)x\} \leq \mathbb{P}\{W > x\} \leq \mathbb{P}\{Q > (\bar{c} - \delta)x\}$ for all sufficiently large x. Precise definitions of these quantities will be provided later. Based on these results, we first estimate the queue-length distribution in the single-queue model by endpoint measurements in order to avoid the scalability problem, and then, obtain the end-to-end delay distribution.

The main contributions of this paper are:
(i) We propose an approximation for the end-to-end delay distribution based on endpoint measurements. Our approach is the first attempt to estimate the end-to-end delay distribution itself.
(ii) We show that the end-to-end path can be represented by a single-node with the end-to-end capacity in the sense that they are identical in terms of the end-to-end queue length.
(iii) We apply the above results to admission control.

This paper is organized as follows. In Section 2 we define the end-to-end capacity and the end-to-end queue-length and motivate our study. In Section 3, we provide estimation methods for the end-to-end capacity and the end-to-end queue-length distribution, and then, based on these estimates, we approximately compute the end-to-end delay distribution. We provide simulation results showing how the approximation works and demonstrate its applicability to admission control in Section 4. In Section 5 we validate our approach by showing certain properties of the end-to-end capacity. In Section 6 we discuss our approach comparing with related works. We conclude in Section 7. All proofs are provided in the Appendix.

---

[1] Throughout the paper we consider only the queueing delay unless stated otherwise. The constant factors of the end-to-end delay such as the transmission time and the propagation delay are ignored.

2   System Model

We consider a discrete time system. Define a path as a set of links and nodes connecting the source to the destination.

2.1   Definitions

- N_p := set of nodes belonging to path p
- f_p := first node (ingress node) of path p
- l_p := last node (egress node) of path p
- A_l := set of flows on node l
- $B_p := \bigcap\limits_{l \in N_p} A_l$ = set of flows traversing path p
- c_l := capacity of node l
- D_p^l := constant delay between node l and the last node of path p, excluding the queueing delay
- $r_i^l(t)$:= rate (or the number of packets) of flow i entering node l at time t
- $d_i^l(t)$:= rate of flow i departing node l at time t
  (If flow i moves from node 1 to node 2 with delay D, $r_i^2(t) = d_i^1(t - D)$.)
- $a_l(t) := c_l - \sum_{i \in A_l} d_i^l(t)$ = unused capacity of node l at time t
- $c_p(t) := \sum_{i \in B_p} d_i^{f_p}(t) + \min\limits_{l \in N_p} a_l(t - D_l)$ = end-to-end capacity of path p

  (defined as the maximum capacity that can be allocated to the path for given flows and connections)
- $q_p(t) := \sum_{k=1}^{t} \sum_{i \in B_p} r_i^{f_p}(k - D_{f_p}) - \sum_{k=1}^{t} \sum_{i \in B_p} d_i^{l_p}(t)$ = end-to-end queue length of path p (the summation of the number of packets, belonging B_p, at each node on path p)
- $w_p(t) := \min\{s : \sum_{k=1}^{t} \sum_{i \in B_p} r_i^{f_p}(k - D_{f_p}) - \sum_{k=1}^{t+s} \sum_{i \in B_p} d_i^{l_p}(k) \le 0\}$ = end-to-end (queueing) delay[2] of path p

2.2   Motivation

We have empirically found that the end-to-end queue-length distribution scaled by $\bar{c}_p := \mathbb{E}\{c_p(t)\}$ closely matches the end-to-end delay distribution. Fig. 1 shows an example. The path consists of two nodes as in Fig. 5, $r_1(t) = 100$ on-off sources[3], $c_1(t)$ = Gaussian process with mean 45(or 53) and $\text{Cov}(t) = 10 \times 0.9^t$, and $c_2(t)$ = Gaussian process with mean 47(or 53) and $\text{Cov}(t) = 10 \times 0.8^t$ (the resulting $\bar{c}_p$ is 42(or 51)). This figure is obtained assuming the perfect knowledge of $c_p(t)$. In practice, however, $c_p(t)$ is not known without information from all nodes on the path, and should be estimated by endpoint measurements. From Fig. 1, we can see that $\mathbb{P}\{Q_p > x\} \approx \mathbb{P}\{W_p > x/\bar{c}_p\}$ where Q_p and W_p represent the steady state versions of the end-to-end queue length and the end-to-end delay,

---

[2] $w_p(t)$ defined here is the delay seen by the last packet arriving at the first node at time slot t.

[3] The same traffic parameters in [6] are used.

respectively. Hence, we can approximate the end-to-end delay distribution by means of the end-to-end queue-length distribution and the end-to-end capacity. The reason we are first dealing with the queue-length distribution (which is later scaled to approximate the end-to-end delay distribution) rather than directly handling the delay distribution is that the end-to-end queue length at time t can be represented by the summation of the queue length at each node at time t. However, the end-to-end delay seen by the last packet of time slot t at the first node is not the simple sum of the delays seen by the last packet of time slot t at each node because last packets at different nodes will be different.

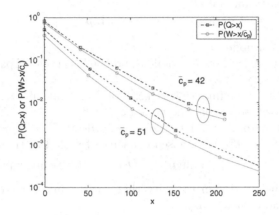

Fig. 1. Comparison of $\mathbb{P}\{Q_p > x\}$ and $\mathbb{P}\{W_p > x/\bar{c}_p\}$.

3　Estimation of the End-to-End Delay Distribution

In this section, we propose an approximation of the end-to-end delay distribution. As illustrated in Fig. 1, once we have the mean end-to-end capacity and an estimate of the end-to-end queue-length distribution, we can approximate the end-to-end delay distribution by scaling the end-to-end queue-length distribution.

3.1　MVA Approximation for Delay

We first estimate the tail of the end-to-end queue-length distribution. We treat the path p as a virtual single node with input $\sum_{i \in B_p} r_i^{f_p}(k - D_p^{f_p})$ and capacity $c_p(t)$. For simplicity, we rewrite the input as $r_1(t - D)$ to represent the aggregate input $\sum_{i \in B_p} r_i^{f_p}(k - D_p^{f_p})$. We then estimate the tail probability of the virtual single node queue-length distribution by applying an existing single-node technique. It has been found that the Maximum Variance Asymptotics (MVA) approach (first named in [4]) provides an accurate estimate of the tail probability. Although the net input $r_1(t - D) - c_p(t)$ may not be modeled as Gaussian, which is assumed in the MVA approach, it have been investigated that the MVA method also works well for non-Gaussian cases including a case where a small number of flows are multiplexed [4] [6]. Hence, we estimate the tail probability by

$$\mathbb{P}\{Q_p > x\} \approx e^{-m_x/2} \tag{1}$$

where

$$m_x := \min_{t \geq 1} \frac{(x + (\bar{c}_p - \bar{r}_1)t)^2}{\text{Var}\{X(1,t)\}}, \tag{2}$$

and $X(1,t) = \sum_{k=1}^{t}[r_1(k - D) - c_p(k)]$. An important question is how to obtain $\bar{c}_p$ and $\text{Var}\{X(1,t)\}$. They are estimated from the measurement during the *busy period*. This will be explained in the following subsection.

Then, as Fig. 1 suggests, we approximate the end-to-end delay by

$$\mathbb{P}\{W_p > x\} \approx e^{-m_{\bar{c}_p x}/2}, \tag{3}$$

and we call this *MVA approximation for delay*.

3.2   Measuring the Moments of $X(1,t)$

The MVA method requires the first two moments of $X(1,t)$. We assume that $c_p(t)$ and $r_1(t)$ are independent, and hence, we estimate their moments separately and add their variance to get $\text{Var}\{X(1,t)\}$.[4] We assume that the ingress node inserts timestamps to record the arrival time of packets [10] [11]. Then, there will be no problem in measuring the moments of $r_1(t)$.

We now explain how to measure the moments of $c_p(t)$. If a minimally backlogging probe packet which makes $\min_{l \in N_p} a_l(t - D_p^l) = 0$ were inserted to the path, the departure would be exactly $c_p(t)$. But determination of such input itself would be problematic because it also requires the knowledge of all flows at each node. Inspired by the idea in [10],[5] we define the busy period as an interval in which the end-to-end queue length $q_p(t)$ is greater than 0. The determination of the busy period can be done by comparing the accumulated input and departure, assuming that $D_p^{f_p}$ is known since it is fixed for a given path. Since the departure is equal to $c_p(t)$ during the busy period, the moments of $c_p(t)$ can be estimated by measuring the departure during the busy period.

One may wonder how well the moments measured during the busy period represent the actual moments. We have found that the moments are a little underestimated compared to their actual values but the errors tend to compensate

---

[4] Though $c_p(t)$ and $r_1(t)$ are somewhat correlated, $\text{Var}\{X(1,t)\}$ is quite close to the sum of $\text{Var}\{\sum c_p(t)\}$ and $\text{Var}\{\sum r_1(t)\}$. We have also found empirically that as $r_1(t)$ becomes smaller compared to the capacity, their statistics become independent.

[5] In [10], the service envelope is measured during a backlogging interval in which there is at least one more packet arrival between the departure time and the arrival time of each packet.

each other because the first moment is the numerator and the second moment is the denominator in (1). We have also found that the estimation during busy period becomes more accurate as $c_i(t)$ has relatively smaller variance (compared to the mean) and less correlation, which is expected as the system size increases.

4   Numerical Experiments

In this section we investigate how the MVA approximation for delay performs and how it can be applied for admission control.

4.1   Approximation of the End-to-End Delay

In this experiment, we use a five node network with 4 paths (Fig. 2). Each path is carrying voice and video traffic: 800 voice and 14 video sources for path 1, 1000 voice and 9 video sources for path 2, 700 voice and 14 video sources for path 3, 500 voice and 19 video sources for path 4. The capacities are: $C_1 = C_2 = C_4 =$

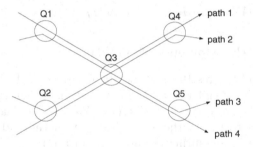

Fig. 2. Five node network

$C_5 = 210$pkt/slot, $C_3 = 420$pkt/slot, which are chosen for a 45Mbps link with 2ms time slot and 53byte packet.[6] We use the on-off model as a voice source[7] and the real MPEG trace (007 movie) as a video source. The propagation delay is set to 0. From Fig. 3 we can see that the approximation bounds the actual delay within an order of magnitude. As will be demonstrated in Section 4.2, such an approximation can be used for admission control and the achievable utilization will be conservative but quite close to the maximum utilization for given QoS.

4.2   Application to Admission Control

Many admission control algorithms are based on single-node analysis [12] [13] [14] and the admission decision is made by estimating the QoS at a node, for

---

[6] If we are interested in rare events of delay violation with large threshold, the impact of the slot size is negligible. We choose 2ms slot size here, but the result with 10ms slot size is almost same.

[7] The same traffic parameters in [6] are used.

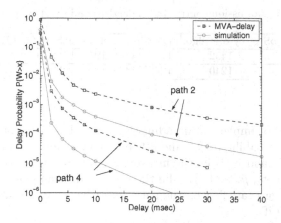

Fig. 3. Approximation of the end-to-end delay for path 2 and 4.

example, the overflow probability that the aggregate flow rate is greater than the capacity of the node. In order to provide a sort of end-to-end QoS, this type of test need to be performed at all nodes on the path including core routers that serve a large number of flows, thus causing a scalability problem. We can apply the concept of the end-to-end capacity and the end-to-end delay distribution to admission control without the scalability problem because admission control is done only by edge nodes.

One way of implementing admission control is based on the end-to-end overflow probability. Once a new flow request for a path arrives, the edge node on that path will estimate the end-to-end overflow probability, which is defined as the probability that the aggregate input to the path is greater than the end-to-end capacity. In this experiment we use Gaussian approximation for the estimation of the overflow probability. Let μ and σ^2 be the mean and variance of a new flow, $\hat{c}_p$ and $\hat{\sigma}_c^2$ be the measured mean and variance of the end-to-end capacity, $\hat{\mu}_r$ and $\hat{\sigma}_r^2$ be the measured mean and variance of the existing aggregate flow on the path, and ϵ be the target QoS. Then, a new flow is admitted if

$$Q\left(\frac{\hat{c}_p - \hat{\mu}_r - \mu}{\sqrt{\hat{\sigma}_c^2 + \hat{\sigma}_r^2 + \sigma^2}}\right) < \epsilon \tag{4}$$

where $Q()$ is the complementary cdf of a standard Gaussian random variable, $N(0,1)$. In this experiment, we fix path 2,3, and 4 with 1400 voice flows, and do the admission control for path 1 in the same five node network in Fig. 2. Table 1 compares the number of flows admitted by the proposed algorithm with the maximum obtained by simulation. From Table 1, we can see that the number of admitted flows by our algorithm is conservative but close to the maximum and the target QoS is met.

Table 1. Admission control by the end-to-end overflow probability

target QoS	# by our algo.	max #	actual QoS at Q_1, Q_3, Q_4
10^{-3}	1452	1466	$8.6 \times 10^{-4}, 1.2 \times 10^{-4}, 8.3 \times 10^{-4}$
10^{-4}	1240	1249	$2.6 \times 10^{-5}, 4.2 \times 10^{-6}, 1.9 \times 10^{-5}$

Another way of implementing admission control is based on the end-to-end delay violation probability. Let μ and $v(t)$ be the mean and the variance function[8] of a new flow, $\hat{c}_p$ and $\hat{v}_c(t)$ be the measured mean and variance function of the end-to-end capacity, $\hat{\mu}_r$ and $\hat{v}_r(t)$ be the measured mean and variance function of the existing aggregate flow on the path, and ϵ be the target QoS. Then, a new flow is admitted if

$$\sup_{t \geq 1} \frac{\hat{v}_c(t) + \hat{v}_r(t) + v(t)}{[x + (\hat{c}_p - \hat{\mu}_r - \mu)t]^2} > -2 \log \epsilon. \tag{5}$$

In this experiment, we fix path 2, 3, and 4 with 35 video flows, and do the admission control for path 1 in the same five node network in Fig. 2. We set D to 20, i.e., $40ms$. From the result in Table 2, we can see that the number of admitted flows by our algorithm is again conservative but close to the maximum and the target QoS is met.

Table 2. Admission control by the end-to-end delay violation probability

target QoS	# by our algo.	max #	actual QoS
10^{-5}	32	33	3.4×10^{-7}
10^{-6}	29	31	1.6×10^{-8}

5   Properties of the End-to-End Capacity

We now provide some theoretical properties on the end-to-end capacity that further support our methodology. More specifically, we show that the single-node model with the end-to-end capacity has the identical queue length with the original path, and that the end-to-end capacity plays a role like a lower bound to the capacities of the nodes on the path in some sense.

5.1   Equivalent Single-Queue Representation

For simplicity, start with a path of two nodes as shown in Fig. 4. $r'_1(t)$ and $r'_2(t)$ are cross traffic, and $d'_1(t)$ and $d'_2(t)$ are the corresponding departures. Assume

---

[8] The variance function $\hat{v}(t)$ is defined as the variance of the accumulated input during $[1, t]$.

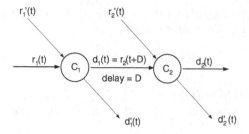

Fig. 4. Original path

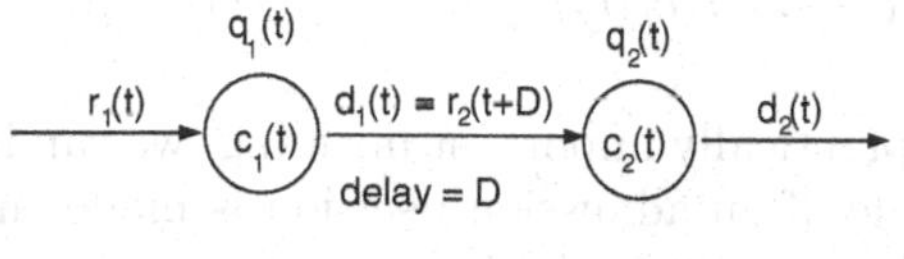

Fig. 5. Two-node model

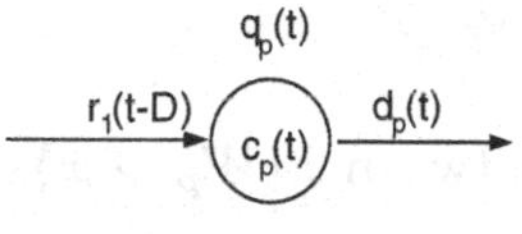

Fig. 6. Single-node model

that the departure of the first node arrives at the second node D time slots later. By replacing $c_i(t) = C_i - d'_i(t), i = 1, 2$, we can re-draw the path as if the cross traffic were a part of the capacity (Fig. 5). We will compare this(Fig. 5) with the single-node model(Fig. 6) where $c_p(t) = d_2(t) + \min\{a_1(t - D), a_2(t)\}$.

Proposition 1. *Assume that* $q_1(0) = q_2(D) = q_p(D) = 0$. *Then,* $q_1(t - D) + q_2(t) = q_p(t)$, *and* $d_2(t) = d_p(t)$, $\forall t \geq D$.

Proposition 1 tells us that once both queues become empty, which is ensured as long as the system is stable, the single-node model is identical with the original path thereafter.

We have considered so far a path with two nodes. It can be easily extended to a path of more than two nodes. Find $c_p(t)$ for the last two nodes, and replace them with a single node. Then, repeat this for the new last two nodes. We can also extend this to multi-class cases simply by treating other classes as cross traffic.

5.2 Properties of $c_p(t)$

Note that $c_p(t) = \min\{c_1(t - D) + q_2(t - 1), c_2(t)\}$. Hence, it is possible that $c_p(t) > c_1(t - D)$ for some instants. However, we have the following result.

Proposition 2. *Assume that all ows are stationary and ergodic, and that* $\mathbb{E}\{r_i(t) + r_i'(t)\} < C_i$ *for stability. Then,*

$$\mathbb{E}\{c_p(t)\} \leq \min_{i=1,2} \mathbb{E}\{c_i(t)\}.$$

Since $\mathbb{E}\{c_i(t)\} = \mathbb{E}\{C_i - d_i'(t)\} = C_i - \mathbb{E}\{r_i'(t)\} \geq \mathbb{E}\{c_p(t)\}$, we also have $\mathbb{E}\{r_1(t - D) - c_p(t)\} \geq \mathbb{E}\{r_i(t) + r_i'(t) - C_i\}$, and we expect that the following conjecture is true.

Conjecture A:

$$\mathbb{P}\{r_1(t - D) > c_p(t)\} \geq \max_{i=1,2} \mathbb{P}\{r_i(t) + r_i'(t) > C_i\}. \tag{6}$$

Conjecture A has a practically important meaning. we can infer from the conjecture that, for example, if an admission decision is made such that the overflow probability of the single-node model is less than ϵ, the overflow probability at each node on the path is also less that ϵ (it has been demonstrated in numerical experiments).

5.3   The Relationship between $\mathbb{P}\{W_p > x\}$ and $\mathbb{P}\{Q_p > \bar{c}_p x\}$

To support the approximation, $\mathbb{P}\{W_p > x\} \approx \mathbb{P}\{Q_p > \bar{c}_p x\}$, we investigate the relationship between $\mathbb{P}\{W_p > x\}$ and $\mathbb{P}\{Q_p > \bar{c}_p x\}$. Though we believe that they are asymptotically similar (which is obvious when c_p is constant), we have shown so far for a particular case only. For a heavy-tailed case where $\mathbb{P}\{Q_p > x\}$ is decaying slower than exponential, i.e., $\lim_{x \to \infty} \frac{e^{-\alpha x}}{\mathbb{P}\{Q_p > x\}} = 0$ for any $\alpha > 0$, we have the following result.

Proposition 3. *Assume that* $\{c_p(t)\}_{t \geq 1}$ *are independent of* $Q_p(0)$ *and* $\frac{1}{\sqrt{x}} \sum_{t=1}^{x} c_p(t)$ *converges in distribution to a Gaussian, and that for any* $\alpha > 0$ $\lim_{x \to \infty} \frac{e^{-\alpha x}}{\mathbb{P}\{Q_p > x\}} = 0$. *Then, for any* $\delta > 0$, *there exist an* x_0 *such that*

$$\mathbb{P}\{Q_p > (\bar{c}_p + \delta)x\} \leq \mathbb{P}\{W_p > x\} \leq \mathbb{P}\{Q_p > (\bar{c}_p - \delta)x\}, \qquad \forall x \geq x_0. \tag{7}$$

6   Discussion

6.1   Related Work

Our approach is motivated by empirical observations. Nevertheless, it is valuable because the MVA approximation for delay is the first attempt to estimate the end-to-end delay distribution itself. Existing works on delay have focused on a deterministic end-to-end delay bound [15], or a statistical per-node delay bound [16] [17]. In [15], the maximum (or worst-case) end-to-end delay is calculated for regulated traffic. In [16] and [17], an upper bound to the delay distribution at a single node is obtained when the amount of input is statistically bounded by a traffic envelope.

The admission control algorithm in [10] is based on the end-to-end delay violation probability. Based on this algorithm, a new flow with peak-rate envelope $r(t)$ is admissible with delay bound x and confidence level $\Phi(\alpha)$ if

$$t\bar{R}(t) + tr(t) - \bar{S}(t + x) + \alpha\sqrt{t^2\sigma^2(t) + \psi^2(t + x)} < 0 \qquad (8)$$

for all interval lengths $0 \leq t \leq T$, and $\lim_{t\to\infty} \bar{R}(t) + r(t) \leq \lim_{t\to\infty} \frac{\bar{S}(t)}{t}$, where the existing aggregate flow on the path has a maximum arrival envelope with mean $\bar{R}(t)$ and variance $\sigma^2(t)$ and the end-to-end path has a minimum service envelope with mean $\bar{S}(t)$ and variance $\psi^2(t)$, T is the length of the measurement window, $\Phi(\alpha) = \exp(-\exp(-\frac{\alpha-\lambda}{\delta}))$, $\delta = \sqrt{\frac{6}{\pi^2}(t^2\sigma^2 + \psi^2(t + x))}$, and $\lambda = t\bar{R}(t) + tr(t) - \bar{S}(t + x) - 0.577726$. Hence, we can infer from the result of [10] that $\mathbb{P}\{W_p > x\} \leq 1 - \min_{0\leq t\leq T}\Phi(\alpha_x)$ where α_x is the minimum value such that (8) is satisfied for given x. This is an upper bound on the end-to-end delay distribution. Since the bound is obtained by the *maximum* arrival envelope and the *minimum* service envelope, it could be quite loose in terms of predicting the actual delay probability. The performance of this algorithm also depends on the value of T. In [12], the impact of T has been investigated when only the arrival envelope is used. Considering both arrival envelope and service envelope, what we have found is that the performance for different values of T can be quite different, and that either very small or very large values of T may cause a significant error. It is expected that a very large T will result in significant underutilization because the envelopes become deterministic as T goes to ∞ so that the delay bound provided by the test (8) will be the worst-case delay.

Based on (2), it seems that $\text{Var}\{X(1,t)\}$ needs to be evaluated for the entire range of t due to the *min* operation over $\{t \geq 1\}$. Fortunately, it has been shown that the value of t (or the *dominant time scale*) at which $\frac{(x+(\bar{r}_p - \bar{r}_1)t)^2}{\text{Var}\{X(1,t)\}}$ takes its minimum can be determined by measuring $\text{Var}\{X(1,t)\}$ for values of t only up to a bound on the dominant time scale [19]. This makes the MVA approach amenable for on-line measurements.

It has been shown that core nodes serving large flows with large capacity compared to edge nodes can be ignored for the end-to-end analysis [18] [20]. Thanks to this, it is possible to improve the accuracy in measuring moments of $c_p(t)$ at the cost of additional functionality in the ingress node. When the ingress node f_p inserts a timestamp for each arriving packet to record its arrival time, it could insert one more to denote the amount of unused capacity at the previous time slot. Then, for a departing packet with timestamp t, the egress node l_p can determine $c_p(t + D_p^{f_p} - 1)$ by comparing its own unused capacity, $a_{l_p}(t + D_p^{f_p} - 1)$, with the value recorded in the packet, $a_{f_p}(t - 1)$, and it does not have to check the busy period. This comparison only needs to be done at least for one packet per path per time slot. If no packet of path p with time stamp t is found at the egress node, simply set $c_p(t + D_p^{f_p} - 1) = a_{l_p}(t + D_p^{f_p} - 1)$. Since the unused capacity $a_l(t)$ is the same for all paths on node l, the implementation complexity is not that high.

6.2   Direct Measurement of $\mathbb{P}\{W_p > x\}$

One may ask why not directly measure the delay (or queue-length) distribution when the estimation is based on *measurements* after all. The problem in directly measuring the delay distribution is that it may require too long time to measure a small value. For example, measuring a value of 10^{-6} requires more than 10^7 samples. If the link speed is 45Mbps and the packet size is 53Bytes, 10^7 packet time is about 100sec which is too long. However, measuring moments of flows, which is required in the MVA method, can be done in shorter duration with more reliability. Table 3 shows the result of an experiment comparing the length of time to measure(or estimate) the delay probability within the 90% confidence interval less than an order of magnitude. In this experiment, 200 on-off sources and an AR Gaussian input with mean 30 and covariance $\text{Cov}(t) = 10 \times 0.9^t$ are multiplexed in a queue with capacity 118. When the target value becomes 10 times smaller (changed from 10^{-5} to 10^{-6}), direct measuring requires 50 times longer duration while moments measuring for the MVA method requires only 4 times longer duration.

Table 3. Comparison of the required simulation cycles

target value	direct measuring	moments measuring
10^{-5}	2×10^6 cycles	2×10^4 cycles
10^{-6}	1×10^8 cycles	8×10^4 cycles

7   Conclusion

We have shown that the end-to-end path can be represented by a single-node with a certain end-to-end capacity. These two systems are identical in terms of the end-to-end queue length. Thus, they also have the same departure and the same end-to-end delay. Further, we have empirically found that $\mathbb{P}\{W_p > x\} \approx \mathbb{P}\{Q_p > \bar{c}_p x\}$. We have also shown for a particular case that for any $\delta > 0$, $\mathbb{P}\{Q_p > (\bar{c}_p + \delta)x\} \leq \mathbb{P}\{W_p > x\} \leq \mathbb{P}\{Q_p > (\bar{c}_p - \delta)x\}$ for all sufficiently large x.

Based on these results, we have proposed an estimation technique for the end-to-end delay distribution (*MVA approximation for delay*). In particular, we estimate the delay distribution for the single-node model that is equal to the end-to-end delay distribution for the original path. We obtain the estimation of the delay distribution for the single-node model by estimating the queue-length distribution first and then scaling it by the mean end-to-end capacity. Since the estimation is done by endpoint measurements only, the scheme is scalable. We have also validated our estimation by numerical experiments. Unlike existing works on the delay that have focused on the maximum (or worst-case) end-to-end delay [15] or a bound on the per-session delay distribution at a single node

[16] [17], our approach is the first attempts to estimate the end-to-end delay distribution itself.

References

1. Addie, R. G. and Zukerman, M.: An Approximation for Performance Evaluation of Stationary Single Server Queues. *IEEE Transactions on Communications* **42**, (1994) 3150–3160.
2. Duffield, N. G. and O'Connell, N.: Large Deviations and Overflow Probabilities for the General Single Server Queue, with Application. *Proc. Cambridge Philos. Soc.* **118**, (1995) 363–374.
3. Glynn, P. W. and Whitt, W.: Logarithmic Asymptotics for Steady-State Tail Probabilities in a Single-Server Queue. *Journal of Applied Probability* (1994) 131–155.
4. Choe, J. and Shroff, N. B.: A Central Limit Theorem Based Approach for Analyzing Queue Behavior in High-Speed Networks. *IEEE/ACM Transactions on Networking* **6**, (1998) 659–671.
5. Likhanov, N. and Mazumdar, R. R.: Cell-Loss Asymptotics in Buffers fed with a Large Number of Independent stationary sources. In *Proceedings of IEEE INFOCOM*. San Francisco, CA (1998).
6. Kim, H. S. and Shroff, N. B.: Loss Probability Calculations and Asymptotic Analysis for Finite Buffer Multiplexers. *IEEE/ACM Transactions on Networking* **9**, (2001) 755–768.
7. Nagarajan, R., Kurose, J. and Towsley, D.: Local Allocation of End-to-End Quality-of-Service in High-Speed Networks. *IFIP Transactions C-Communication Systems* **15**, (1993) 99–118.
8. Yates, D., Kurose, J. and Towsley, D.: On Per-Session End-to-End Delay and the Call Admission Problem for Real-Time Applications with QOS Requirements. *Journal of Highspeed Networks* **3**, (1994) 429–458.
9. Kim, H. S.: Queueing Analysis of Network Multiplexers: Loss Ratio and End-to-End Delay Distribution. *PhD thesis*. School of Electrical and Computer Engineering Purdue University, West Lafayette, IN (2003).
10. Cetinkaya, C., Kanodia, V. and Knightly, E.: Scalable Services via Egress Admission Control. *IEEE Transactions on Multimedia* **3**, (2001) 69–81.
11. Yuan, P., Schlembach, J., Skoe, A. and Knightly, E.: Design and Implementation of Scalable Admission Control. *Computer Networks Journal:Special Issue on Quality of Service in IP Networks* **37**, (2001) 507–518.
12. Qiu, J. and Knightly, E.: Measurement-Based Admission Control with Aggregate Traffic Envelopes. *IEEE/ACM Transactions on Networking* **9**, (2001) 199–210.
13. Grossglauser, M. and Tse, D.: A Time-Scale Decomposition Approach to Measurement-Based Admission Control. In *Proceedings of IEEE INFOCOM*. New York, NY (1999).
14. Bianchi, G., Capone, A. and Petrioli, C.: Throughput Analysis of End-to-End Masurement-based Admission Control in IP. In *Proceedings of IEEE INFOCOM*. Tel Aviv, Israel (2000).
15. Cruz, R. L.: A Calculus for Network Delay, Part II : Network Analysis. *IEEE Transactions on Information Theory* **37**, (1991) 132–142.
16. Kurose, J.: On Computing Per-Session Performance Bounds in High-Speed Multi-Hop Computer Networks. In *Proceedings of ACM SIGMETRICS*. (1992) 128–139.

17. Zhang, H. and Knightly, E. W.: Providing End-to-End Statistical Performance Guarantee with Bounding Interval Dependent Stochastic Models. In *Proceedings of ACM SIGMETRICS.* (1994) 211–220.
18. Eun, D., Kim, H. S. and Shroff, N. B.: End-to-End Traffic Analysis in Large Networked Systems. In *Proceedings of Allerton Conference.* Monticello, IL (2001).
19. Eun, D. and Shroff, N. B.: A Measurement-Analytic Approach for QoS Estimation in a Network based on the Dominant Time Scale. *IEEE/ACM Transactions on Networking* (2003) to appear.
20. Eun, D. and Shroff, N. B.: Simplification of Network Analysis in Large-Bandwidth Systems. In *Proceedings of IEEE INFOCOM.* San Francisco, CA (2003).
21. Feller, W.: An Introduction to Probability Theory and its Applications I. John Wiley & Son, New York (1968).

Appendix

Proof of Proposition 1: We will prove by mathematical induction.

When $t = D$, $q_1(0) + q_2(D) = 0 = q_p(D)$. Suppose $q_1(t - D - 1) + q_2(t - 1) = q_p(t - 1)$ for $t \geq D + 1$.

$$
\begin{aligned}
q_1(t - D) + q_2(t) &= (q_1(t - D - 1) + r_1(t - D) - c_1(t - D))^+ + (q_2(t - 1) \\
&\quad + r_2(t) - c_2(t))^+ \\
&= (q_1(t - D - 1) + r_1(t - D) - d_1(t - D)) + (q_2(t - 1) + d_1(t - D) \\
&\quad - d_2(t)) \\
&= q_1(t - D - 1) + q_2(t - 1) + r_1(t - D) - d_2(t) \\
&= q_p(t - 1) + r_1(t - D) - d_2(t) \quad (9) \\
q_p(t) &= (q_p(t - 1) + r_1(t - D) - c_p(t))^+ \\
&= (q_p(t - 1) + r_1(t - D) - d_2(t) - \min\{a_1(t - D), a_2(t)\})^+ \quad (10)
\end{aligned}
$$

We will show that (10) is equal to (9).

Case 1) $a_1(t - D) = 0$ or $a_2(t) = 0$:

$$
\begin{aligned}
q_p(t) &= (q_p(t - 1) + r_1(t - D) - d_2(t) - \min\{a_1(t - D), a_2(t)\})^+ \\
&= (q_p(t - 1) + r_1(t - D) - d_2(t))^+ \\
&= q_p(t - 1) + r_1(t - D) - d_2(t) \\
&= q_1(t - D) + q_2(t) \quad (\Leftarrow \text{from (9)})
\end{aligned}
$$

Case 2) $a_1(t - D) > 0$ and $a_2(t) > 0$: Note that $q_1(t - D) = q_2(t) = 0$ in this case.

$$
\begin{aligned}
d_1(t - D) &= q_1(t - D - 1) + r_1(t - D), \\
d_2(t) &= q_2(t - 1) + r_2(t) = q_2(t - 1) + d_1(t - D) \\
&= q_2(t - 1) + q_1(t - D - 1) + r_1(t - D) \\
&= q_p(t - 1) + r_1(t - D).
\end{aligned}
$$

Thus,

$$q_p(t) = (q_p(t-1) + r_1(t-D) - d_2(t) - \min\{a_1(t-D), a_2(t)\})^+$$
$$= (d_2(t) - d_2(t) - \min\{a_1(t-D), a_2(t)\})^+$$
$$= (-\min\{a_1(t-D), a_2(t)\})^+$$
$$= 0 = q_1(t-D) + q_2(t).$$

So we have $(10) \equiv (9)$, from which it follows that $d_2(t) = d_p(t)$.

$$d_2(t) = r_2(t) + q_2(t-1) - q_2(t)$$
$$= d_1(t-D) + q_2(t-1) - q_2(t)$$
$$= r_1(t-D) + q_1(t-D-1) - q_1(t-D) + q_2(t-1) - q_2(t)$$
$$= r_1(t-D) + [q_1(t-D-1) + q_2(t-1)] - [q_1(t-D) + q_2(t)]$$
$$= r_1(t-D) + q_p(t-1) - q_p(t)$$
$$= d_p(t).$$

∎

Proof of Proposition 2:

Note that $c_p(t) = \min\{c_1(t-D) + q_2(t-1), c_2(t)\}$. Hence, $\mathbb{E}\{c_p(t)\} \leq \mathbb{E}\{c_2(t)\}$.

For a given sample path, let I be an interval from the time when $q_2(t)$ becomes positive to the time when $q_2(t)$ becomes zero. Because of stability, there will be infinitely many intervals, and index them as $I_k, k = 1, 2, \cdots$. Let t_k be the last moment of I_k. Note that $q_2(t) > 0$ and $c_p(t) = c_2(t)$ for all $t \in I_k - \{t_k\}$, and $q_2(t_k) = 0$. Then, for all $t \notin \bigcup_k I_k, q_2(t-1) = 0$, and hence, $c_p(t) = \min\{c_1(t-D), c_2(t)\} \leq c_1(t-D)$. Now, to show that $\sum_{t \in I_k} c_p(t) \leq \sum_{t \in I_k} c_1(t-D)$ will complete the proof.

$$q_2(t_k - 1) = \sum_{t \in I_k - \{t_k\}} (r_2(t) - c_2(t)) = \sum_{t \in I_k - \{t_k\}} (d_1(t-D) - c_1(t))$$
$$\leq \sum_{t \in I_k - \{t_k\}} (c_1(t-D) - c_1(t)) = \sum_{t \in I_k - \{t_k\}} (c_1(t-D) - c_p(t)).$$

Thus,

$$\sum_{t \in I_k - \{t_k\}} c_1(t-D) \geq \sum_{t \in I_k - \{t_k\}} c_p(t) + q_2(t_k - 1).$$

$$\sum_{t \in I_k} c_p(t) = \sum_{t \in I_k - \{t_k\}} c_p(t) + c_p(t_k)$$
$$= \sum_{t \in I_k - \{t_k\}} c_p(t) + r_2(t_k) + q_2(t_k - 1) + \min\{a_1(t-D), a_2(t)\}$$
$$\leq \sum_{t \in I_k - \{t_k\}} c_1(t-D) + r_2(t_k) + \min\{a_1(t-D), a_2(t)\}$$
$$\leq \sum_{t \in I_k - \{t_k\}} c_1(t-D) + c_1(t_k - D) = \sum_{t \in I_k} c_1(t-D).$$

∎

Proof of Proposition 3:

Since we are interested in the asymptotics, assume that x is integer for simplicity. Let σ^2 be the variance of $c_p(t)$, $F_Q()$ be the distribution function of Q_p, and $F_Z()$ be the distribution function of $Z := \frac{\sum_{t=1}^{x} c_p(t) - \bar{c}x}{\sigma\sqrt{x}}$.

Note that $\{W_p > x\} = \{\sum_{t=1}^{x} c_p(t) < Q_p(0)\}$. Since $\{c_p(t)\}_{t\geq 1}$ are independent of $Q_p(0)$,

$$
\mathbb{P}\{W_p > x\} = \int_0^\infty \mathbb{P}\left\{ \sum_{t=1}^{x} c_p(t) < Q_p(0) \middle| Q_p(0) \right\} dF_Q(q)
$$

$$
= \int_0^\infty \mathbb{P}\left\{ \sum_{t=1}^{x} c_p(t) < q \right\} dF_Q(q)
$$

$$
= \int_0^\infty \mathbb{P}\left\{ \frac{\sum_{t=1}^{x} c_p(t) - \bar{c}x}{\sigma\sqrt{x}} < \frac{q - \bar{c}x}{\sigma\sqrt{x}} \right\} dF_Q(q)
$$

$$
= \int_0^\infty F_Z\left(\frac{q - \bar{c}x}{\sigma\sqrt{x}} \right) dF_Q(q).
$$

First we prove the left inequality: $\mathbb{P}\{Q_p > (\bar{c}_p + \delta)x\} \leq \mathbb{P}\{W_p > x\}$.

$$
\int_0^\infty F_Z\left(\frac{q - \bar{c}x}{\sigma\sqrt{x}} \right) dF_Q(q) \geq \int_{(\bar{c}+\delta)x}^\infty F_Z\left(\frac{q - \bar{c}x}{\sigma\sqrt{x}} \right) dF_Q(q)
$$

$$
\geq \int_{(\bar{c}+\delta)x}^\infty F_Z\left(\frac{\delta x}{\sigma\sqrt{x}} \right) dF_Q(q)
$$

$$
= F_Z\left(\frac{\delta}{\sigma}\sqrt{x} \right) \mathbb{P}\{Q > (\bar{c} + \delta)x\}.
$$

Since Z converges (in distribution) to a standard Gaussian random variable as x goes to ∞, $F_Z(\frac{\delta}{\sigma}\sqrt{x})$ can be arbitrarily close to 1 for sufficiently large x, say, larger than $1 - \epsilon$. Thus, $F_Z(\frac{\delta}{\sigma}\sqrt{x})\mathbb{P}\{Q > (\bar{c}+\delta)x\} \geq (1-\epsilon)\mathbb{P}\{Q > (\bar{c}+\delta)x\}$ for all sufficiently large x, and we have the left inequality.

We next prove the right inequality: $\mathbb{P}\{W_p > x\} \leq \mathbb{P}\{Q_p > (\bar{c}_p - \delta)x\}$.

$$
\int_0^\infty F_Z\left(\frac{q - \bar{c}x}{\sigma\sqrt{x}} \right) dF_Q(q) = \int_0^{(\bar{c}-\delta)x} F_Z\left(\frac{q - \bar{c}x}{\sigma\sqrt{x}} \right) dF_Q(q)
$$

$$
+ \int_{(\bar{c}-\delta)x}^\infty F_Z\left(\frac{q - \bar{c}x}{\sigma\sqrt{x}} \right) dF_Q(q)
$$

$$
\leq \int_0^{(\bar{c}-\delta)x} F_Z\left(\frac{-\delta x}{\sigma\sqrt{x}} \right) dF_Q(q)
$$

$$
+ \int_{(\bar{c}-\delta)x}^\infty F_Z\left(\frac{q - \bar{c}x}{\sigma\sqrt{x}} \right) dF_Q(q)
$$

$$
\leq F_Z\left(\frac{-\delta}{\sigma}\sqrt{x} \right) + \int_{(\bar{c}-\delta)x}^\infty F_Z\left(\frac{q - \bar{c}x}{\sigma\sqrt{x}} \right) dF_Q(q)
$$

$$\leq F_Z\left(\frac{-\delta}{\sigma}\sqrt{x}\right) + \int_{(\bar{c}-\delta)x}^{\infty} dF_Q(q)$$

$$= F_Z\left(\frac{-\delta}{\sigma}\sqrt{x}\right) + \mathbb{P}\{Q > (\bar{c}-\delta)x\}.$$

Since Z converges to a standard Gaussian, and since $\int_{-\infty}^{-x} e^{-y^2/2}dy \sim \frac{1}{x}e^{-x^2/2}$ for large x [21], $F_Z\left(\frac{-\delta}{\sigma}\sqrt{x}\right)$ can be as small as $\frac{K_1}{\sqrt{x}}e^{-K_2 x}$ for some $K_1 > 0$ and $K_2 > 0$. Thus, for large x

$$F_Z\left(\frac{-\delta}{\sigma}\sqrt{x}\right) + \mathbb{P}\{Q > (\bar{c}-\delta)x\} \leq \frac{K_1}{\sqrt{x}}e^{-K_2 x} + \mathbb{P}\{Q_p > (\bar{c}-\delta)x\}.$$

Since $\lim_{x\to\infty} \frac{e^{-\alpha x}}{\mathbb{P}\{Q_p > x\}} = 0$ for any $\alpha > 0$ from the assumption, we have for any $\epsilon > 0$ that $\frac{K_1}{\sqrt{x}}e^{-K_2 x} \leq \epsilon \mathbb{P}\{Q_p > (\bar{c}-\delta)x\}$ for all large x. Hence,

$$\frac{K_1}{\sqrt{x}}e^{-K_2 x} + \mathbb{P}\{Q_p > (\bar{c}-\delta)x\} \leq (1+\epsilon)\mathbb{P}\{Q_p > (\bar{c}-\delta)x\}$$

for all sufficiently large x, and we have the right inequality.

■

II Resource Allocation and Admission Control

Price-Based Resource Allocation in Wireless Ad Hoc Networks*

Yuan Xue[1], Baochun Li[2], and Klara Nahrstedt[1]

[1] Department of Computer Science, University of Illinois at Urbana-Champaign.
{xue,klara}@cs.uiuc.edu
[2] Department of Electrical and Computer Engineering, University of Toronto.
bli@eecg.toronto.edu

Abstract. The shared-medium multi-hop nature of wireless ad hoc networks poses fundamental challenges to the design of an effective resource allocation algorithm to maximize the aggregated utility of flows, while maintaining basic fairness among multiple flows. When previously proposed scheduling algorithms have been shown to perform well in providing fair shares of bandwidth among *single-hop* wireless flows, they did not consider *multi-hop* flows with an end-to-end perspective. Moreover, the resource allocation strategies employed in the wireline network can not be applied directly in the context of ad hoc networks due to the unique characteristic of location dependent contention and spatial reuse of the shared wireless channel. In this paper, we propose a price-based resource allocation model to achieve maximized aggregated utility (*i.e.,* social welfare) of flows. Our original contributions are: First, we propose to use *maximal clique-associated* shadow prices for wireless channel access coordination, rather than *link-associated* price for wireline link access arbitration. Second, we present a new pricing policy for end-to-end multi-hop flow. Using this model, different fairness goals can be realized in ad hoc networks for end-to-end flows. With a two-tier distributed and iterative algorithm, scarce channel capacity is allocated fairly among multi-hop flows from an end-to-end perspective, using shadow prices as the mechanism to arbitrate channel access. Through extensive analysis and simulation results, we show that our proposed algorithm is able to fairly distribute resources among multi-hop flows, while simultaneously maximizing the aggregated utility of flows globally.

1 Introduction

A wireless ad hoc network consists of a collection of wireless nodes without a fixed infrastructure. Each node in the network serves as a router that forwards packets for other nodes. Each flow from the source to the destination traverses multiple hops of wireless links. Compared with wireline networks where flows contend only at the router with other simultaneous flows through the same router (contention in the time domain),

---

* This work was supported by the DoD Multi-disciplinary University Research Initiative (MURI) program administered by the Office of Naval Research under Grant NAVY CU 37515-6281, and the NSF EIA 99-72884 grant. Any opinions, findings, and conclusions are those of the authors and do not necessarily reflect the views of the above agencies.

K. Jeffay, I. Stoica, and K. Wehrle (Eds.): IWQoS 2003, LNCS 2707, pp. 79–96, 2003.
© Springer-Verlag Berlin Heidelberg 2003

the unique characteristics of multi-hop wireless networks show that, flows also compete for shared channel bandwidth if they are within the transmission ranges of each other (contention in the spatial domain). This presents the problem of designing an appropriate topology-aware resource allocation algorithm, such that contending multi-hop flows fairly share the scarce channel capacity, while the total aggregated utility of all flows is maximized.

In the context of wireline networks, *pricing* (*e.g.,* [1,2,3,4,5]) has been extensively used in the literature as a means to arbitrate resource allocation. In order to adopt a price-based approach, *utility functions* are used to characterize the resource requirements and the degree of satisfaction of individual users. The goal of the network is to appropriately allocate resources to maximize an objective function that depends on user utilities. For example, the total aggregated utility over all users may be maximized (called the social welfare) subject to certain resource constraints. Kelly *et al.* [3] have shown that, to achieve such a goal, the network may use price as a signal to reflect the traffic load on the wireline links, and users can choose a transmission rate to respond to such price so that their net benefit can be maximized. It is shown that at equilibrium, such a price-based resource allocation scheme maximizes the social welfare and achieves a (weighted) proportional fair rate allocation, if the logarithmic utility function is used.

Unfortunately, there exist fundamental differences in multi-hop wireless ad hoc networks compared with traditional wireline networks, preventing verbatim application of the existing pricing theories. First, in multi-hop wireless networks, flows that traverse the same geographical *vicinity* contend for the same wireless channel capacity. This is in sharp contrast with wireline networks, where the network resource is modeled as a set of links (or *edges* in the topological graph) connecting nodes, and only flows that traverse the same link contend for the capacity of this link. When it comes to pricing, we may conveniently associate *shadow prices* with individual links in wireline networks, such that the price of a flow is the aggregate of shadow prices of the links it traverses. However, we may not be able to accommodate such conveniences when pricing ad hoc networks. Second, as opposed to wireline networks, algorithms designed for wireless ad hoc networks may not rely on the convenience of any centralized management or authority. The search for a fully distributed algorithm further exacerbates the problem.

In this paper, we address these unique characteristics of wireless ad hoc networks, and follow a price-based approach to allocate channel bandwidth availability to competing multi-hop flows. The fundamental question we attempt to answer is: how much bandwidth should we allocate to each of the flows, so that the aggregated utilities over all users can be maximized? Towards this goal, our original contribution is the following: (1) We associate shadow prices with *maximal cliques* in the corresponding *wireless link contention graph* of the ad hoc network, rather than individual links as in wireline networks; (2) Based on this new model, we present a new pricing policy for end-to-end multi-hop flows. In this policy, the price of an end-to-end multi-hop flow is the aggregate of prices of all its subflows[1], while the price of each subflow is the sum of shadow prices of *all* maximal cliques that it belongs to. We present a distributed algorithm that determines shadow prices such that the aggregated utility of all flows is maximized.

---

[1] When each multi-hop flow is considered as multiple *single-hop flows*, each single-hop flow is referred to as a *subflow*.

We show that by choosing appropriate utility functions, different fairness models can be realized for multi-hop flows, including proportional fairness and max-min fairness. The algorithm consists of two tiers. The first tier constitutes an iterative algorithm to determine per-clique shadow prices. It can be shown that this algorithm converges to the unique system equilibrium. The second tier completes the details of the algorithm within the same maximal clique.

The remainder of this paper is organized as follows. Sec. 2 and Sec. 3 present related work and the network model, respectively. We propose our price-based resource allocation model in Sec. 4, and present our distributed algorithm in Sec. 5. Finally, we show simulation results in Sec. 6, and conclude in Sec. 7.

2   Related Work

Price-based resource allocation strategies, as well as the analysis of their fairness properties, have received much attention in recent years in the setting of wireline networks (*e.g.,* [1,2,3,4,5]). For example, in the work proposed in [1,3,2], a shadow price is associated with each wireline link. The network uses these prices as signals to users which reflect the traffic load on the links along their route, and users choose a transmission rate to optimize their net benefit. Nevertheless, the fundamental differences in contention models between ad hoc and wireline network deserve a fresh treatment to this topic. The resource allocation strategies employed in the wireline network can not be applied directly in the context of ad hoc networks due to the unique characteristic of location dependent contention and spatial reuse of the shared wireless channel. In this paper, we propose a new pricing model for wireless ad hoc networks to address such uniqueness. We propose using clique-associated shadow prices for channel access, rather than the traditional link-associated price for wireline link access arbitration. Based on this model, we present a new pricing policy with respect to end-to-end multi-hop flows.

In the setting of wireless LANs, the use of pricing has also been studied in the context of efficient power control (*e.g.,* [6]) and service differentiation [7]. These solutions focus on single-hop infrastructure wireless networks, while we consider multi-hop wireless networks.

There also exists work to use pricing as incentives to encourage packet relays in wireless ad hoc networks (*e.g.,* [8]). Our work is fundamentally different from these results in the following aspects. (1) In [8], a simplified ad hoc network model is used, where each node i in the network has a capacity of C_i, which is independent from other nodes. We will later show that such a network model can not correctly characterize the unique characteristics of location-dependent contention in ad hoc networks. (2) In [8], a user is assumed to have limited transmission resources. Thus, the user might not volunteer to forward packets for other users as this impacts the ability to transmit their own traffic. In light of this problem, the role of pricing is to provide adequate user incentives to forward packets for other users. The goal of optimal price setting at each node is to maximize its net benefit, which reflects its utility gain, its revenue from packet relays and its cost for paying other nodes to relay its own packets. In contrast, the role of pricing in our work is to regulate channel access and provide globally optimal resource allocation in the sense of maximizing aggregated utility. This goal is complementary to any incentives to packet relays.

Resource allocation, using MAC-layer fair scheduling for single-hop MAC layer flows, is also studied in ad hoc networks [9,10,11,12]. In comparison, we address end-to-end multi-hop flows. It can be shown with examples that, optimal resource allocation among single-hop flows may not be optimal for multi-hop flows, due to the unawareness of bottlenecks. Moreover, global optimal resource allocation among multi-hop flows can not be completely reached by MAC-layer scheduling, which is only based on local information. Pricing is needed as a signal to coordinate the global resource demand and supply.

3   Network Model and Resource Constraints

In this paper, we consider a *static* multi-hop wireless network with channel capacity C. In this network, only nodes that are within the transmission range of each other can communicate directly and form a *wireless link*. Data transmissions over a single wireless link are referred to as a *subflow*. Two subflows contend with each other if either the source or destination of one subflow is within the transmission range of the source or destination of the other[2]. Let l_{ij} denote the subflow from node i to j. For the example in Fig. 1(A), we may observe that l_{12} contends with l_{62}, l_{23} and l_{34}. The locality of wireless transmissions implies that the degree of contention for the shared medium is location-dependent.

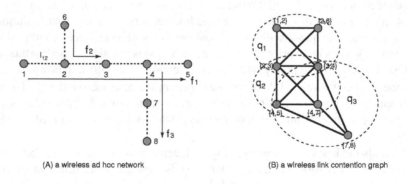

(A) a wireless ad hoc network   (B) a wireless link contention graph

Fig. 1. Location-dependent contention: an example.

We first illustrate resource constraints due to such location-dependent contention by using the example shown in Fig. 1, where there are three multi-hop flows f_1, f_2 and f_3, with data rates x_1, x_2 and x_3, respectively. Further, we use y_{ij} to denote the aggregated data rate of *all* subflows l_{ij} between node i and j. For example, $y_{12} = x_1$, $y_{23} = x_1 + x_2$. The channel capacity C gives the upper bound on the aggregated data rate of all

---

2 If we assume that the interference range is greater than the transmission range, the contention model can be straightforwardly extended.

mutually contending subflows. In this example, there are three contending subflow sets $\{l_{12}, l_{23}, l_{34}, l_{26}\}$, $\{l_{23}, l_{34}, l_{45}, l_{47}\}$ and $\{l_{34}, l_{45}, l_{47}, l_{78}\}$, where all subflows within a set contend with each other. We then have

$$y_{12} + y_{26} + y_{23} + y_{34} \leq C \tag{1}$$

$$y_{23} + y_{34} + y_{45} + y_{47} \leq C \tag{2}$$

$$y_{34} + y_{45} + y_{47} + y_{78} \leq C \tag{3}$$

This leads to $3x_1 + 2x_2 \leq C$, $3x_1 + x_2 + x_3 \leq C$ and $2x_1 + 2x_3 \leq C$, which show the resource constraints when it comes to end-to-end flow rate allocation.

Motivated by this example, we consider a static network topology modeled by a undirected graph $\mathcal{G}_T = (\mathcal{V}_T, \mathcal{E}_T)$, where $\mathcal{V}_T$ is the set of nodes in the network. A wireless link $\{i, j\} \in \mathcal{E}_T$, if nodes i and j are within the transmission range of each other.

We now introduce the concept of *wireless link contention graph*. In a wireless link contention graph, each vertex represents a wireless link. Each edge between two vertices denotes that subflows, if there exists any, on the wireless links corresponding to the two vertices contend with each other. A wireless link contention graph is different from a *flow contention graph* [11] in that each vertex in a flow contention graph represents a backlogged MAC layer flow, thus the topology of a flow contention graph depends on the traffic patterns and routes in the network. On the other hand, the wireless link contention graph only depends on the topology of the original network and is not related to the traffic patterns and routes of flows. As an example, Fig. 1(B) shows the wireless link contention graph of the ad hoc network in Fig. 1(A).

Formally, a graph $\mathcal{G}_C = (\mathcal{V}_C, \mathcal{E}_C)$ is a wireless link contention graph of network $\mathcal{G}_T$, if there exists a mapping function $\varphi : \mathcal{E}_T \to \mathcal{V}_C$ that satisfies

(1) $\varphi(l) \in \mathcal{V}_C$, *if and only if* $l \in \mathcal{E}_T$;

(2) $\{\varphi(l), \varphi(l')\} \in \mathcal{E}_C$, *if* for $l, l' \in \mathcal{E}_T$, $\exists l'' \in \mathcal{E}_T$, so that $l \cap l'' \neq \emptyset$ and $l' \cap l'' \neq \emptyset$.

In a graph, a complete subgraph is referred to as a *clique*. A *maximal clique* is referred as a clique that is not contained in any other cliques[3]. In a wireless link contention graph, the vertices in a maximal clique represent a maximal set of wireless links where subflows along any two links contend with each other. Intuitively, each maximal clique in a wireless link contention graph represents a "maximal distinct contention region", since at most one subflow in the clique can transmit at any time and adding any other flows into this clique will introduce the possibility of simultaneous transmissions. Formally, we denote a maximal clique of a wireless link contention graph $\mathcal{G}_C$ as $\mathcal{G}_q = (\mathcal{V}_q, \mathcal{E}_q)$, and the set of all maximal cliques in a wireless link contention graph as $\mathcal{Q}$. For simplicity, we use the vertices set $\mathcal{V}_q$ of a clique $\mathcal{G}_q$ to represent the clique, and sometimes simply denote it as q. For the example in Fig. 1, the set of maximal clique is $\mathcal{Q} = \{q_1, q_2, q_3\}$ where $q_1 = \{\{12\}, \{23\}, \{34\}, \{26\}\}$, $q_2 = \{\{23\}, \{34\}, \{45\}, \{47\}\}$ and $q_3 = \{\{34\}, \{45\}, \{47\}, \{78\}\}$. To this end, we show the role of maximal cliques in resource allocation in the following definition and lemma.

---

[3] Note that *maximal clique* has a different definition from *maximum clique* of a graph, which is the maximal clique with the largest number of vertices.

Definition 1 (feasibility). A wireless link bandwidth allocation $y = (y_l, l \in \mathcal{E}_T)$ is *feasible*, if there exists a collision-free transmission schedule that allocates bandwidth y_l to wireless link l.

Lemma 1. A wireless link bandwidth allocation $y = (y_l, l \in \mathcal{E}_T)$ is *feasible*, if and only if the following condition is satisfied:

$$\forall q \in \mathcal{Q}, \sum_{l \in q} y_l \leq C \qquad (4)$$

Proof: It is trivial to show that Eq. (4) is a *necessary* condition for feasible bandwidth allocation, as flows within a clique q can not transmit simultaneously. Now, we show that the condition Eq. (4) is also *sufficient* for a feasible bandwidth allocation. We assume the converse is true, *i.e.,* when Eq. (4) holds, there exists no feasible bandwidth allocation. This means that under any schedule, there always exists a set of mutually contending wireless links whose bandwidth allocation exceeds the channel capacity C. Naturally, this set of mutually contending wireless links constitutes a clique q' so that $\sum_{l \in q'} y_l > C$. If q' is a maximal clique, a contradiction exists. If q' is not a maximal clique, then there exists another maximal clique $q'' \in \mathcal{Q}$ that contains q'. It is obvious to see $\sum_{l \in q''} y_l > C$, which also leads to a contradiction. □

This lemma shows that each maximal clique can be regarded as an independent resource with capacity C. It motivates the use of a maximal clique as a basic resource unit for pricing.

We associate each user in the network with an end-to-end multi-hop flow (or simply *flow*) f, and denote the set of flows as $\mathcal{F}$. We assume each flow has a fixed path which passes a set of wireless links. We use this set of wireless links to represent the flow f (*i.e.,* $f \subset \mathcal{E}_T$). In the example shown in Fig. 1, $f_1 = \{\{1, 2\}, \{2, 3\}, \{3, 4\}, \{4, 5\}\}$, $f_2 = \{\{2, 6\}, \{2, 3\}\}$, and $f_3 = \{\{4, 7\}, \{7, 8\}\}$. We use the vector $\mathbf{x} = (x_f, f \in \mathcal{F})$ to denote the rate of flows in the set $\mathcal{F}$.

We now proceed to define a clique-flow matrix $\mathcal{R}$, where $\mathcal{R}_{qf} = |q \cap f|$ is the number of wireless links that flow f passes in clique q. If we treat a maximal clique as a singular resource, then the clique-flow matrix represents the "resource usage pattern" of each flow. In the example, the clique-flow matrix is shown in Fig. 2.

	f_1	f_2	f_3
q_1	3	2	0
q_2	3	1	1
q_3	2	0	2

$q_1 = \{\{1,2\},\{2,6\},\{2,3\},\{3,4\}\}$ $f_1 = \{\{1,2\},\{2,3\},\{3,4\},\{4,5\}\}$

$q_2 = \{\{2,3\},\{3,4\},\{4,5\},\{4,7\}\}$ $f_2 = \{\{2,6\},\{2,3\}\}$

$q_3 = \{\{3,4\},\{4,5\},\{4,7\},\{7,8\}\}$ $f_3 = \{\{4,7\},\{7,8\}\}$

Fig. 2. An example of the clique-flow matrix.

Finally, we use the vector $\mathcal{C} = (C_q, q \in \mathcal{Q})$ as the vector of channel capacities in each of the cliques, where C_qs are equal to the physical channel capacity C in the ideal case. Now, we give the constraints of resource allocation in an ad hoc network in the following theorem.

Theorem 1. In an ad hoc network $\mathcal{G}_T$, given the set of flows $\mathcal{F}$ that uses this network, there exists a feasible rate allocation $\mathbf{x} = (x_f, f \in \mathcal{F})$, if and only if $\mathcal{R}\mathbf{x} \le \mathcal{C}$, where $\mathcal{R}$ is the clique-flow matrix defined on the network $\mathcal{G}_T$ and the flow set $\mathcal{F}$.

Proof: It is obvious that $\mathcal{R}\mathbf{x} \le \mathcal{C} \Leftrightarrow \forall q \in \mathcal{Q}, \sum_{f \in \mathcal{F}} \mathcal{R}_{qf} x_f \le C$. By the definition of $\mathcal{R}$, we have $\sum_{f \in \mathcal{F}} \mathcal{R}_{qf} x_f = \sum_{l \in q} y_l$. The result follows naturally from Lemma 1.   □

4   Pricing Model in Wireless Ad Hoc Networks

4.1   Optimal Resource Allocation: Problem Formulation

We associate each flow $f \in \mathcal{F}$ with an *utility function* $U_f(x_f)$, where x_f is the rate of flow f. We make the following assumption regarding the utility function.

Assumption: For each flow $f \in \mathcal{F}$, the function $U_f : \mathfrak{R}_+ \to \mathfrak{R}_+$ satisfies the following conditions:

(1) On the interval $I_f = [m_f, M_f]$, the utility functions U_f are increasing, strictly concave and twice continuously differentiable.

(2) U_f is additive so that the aggregated utility of rate allocation $\mathbf{x} = (x_f, f \in \mathcal{F})$ is $\sum_{f \in \mathcal{F}} U_f(x_f)$.

(3) The curvatures of U_f are bounded away from zero on I_f.

Following the work of resource allocation in wireline networks [1,2], we investigate the optimal rate allocation in the sense of maximizing the aggregated utility function. As we will show in Sec. 4.2, by specifying appropriate utility functions, such an objective can enforce different fairness models, including proportional fairness and max-min fairness. We now formulate the problem of optimal resource allocation in wireless ad hoc networks as the following constrained non-linear optimization problem:

SYSTEM$(U, \mathcal{R}, \mathcal{C})$:

$$\textbf{maximize } \sum_{f \in F} U_f(x_f) \tag{5}$$

$$\textbf{subject to } \mathcal{R}\mathbf{x} \le \mathcal{C} \tag{6}$$

$$\textbf{over } \quad \mathbf{x} \ge 0 \tag{7}$$

We observe that the objective function in Eq. (5) of the optimization problem is differentiable and strictly concave, while the feasible region of Eq. (6) and (7) is compact. By non-linear optimization theory, there exists a maximizing value of argument $\mathbf{x}$ for the above optimization problem, and we can apply the Lagrangian method to solve such a problem. Let us consider the Lagrangian form of this optimization problem:

$$L(\mathbf{x}, z; \mu) = \sum_{f \in F} U_f(x_f) + \mu^T (\mathcal{C} - \mathcal{R}\mathbf{x} - \mathbf{z})$$

$$= \sum_{f \in F} \left(U_s(x_f) - x_f \sum_{q \in \mathcal{Q}} \mu_q \mathcal{R}_{qf} \right) + \sum_{q \in \mathcal{Q}} \mu_q \mathcal{C}_q - \sum_{q \in \mathcal{Q}} \mu_q z_q \tag{8}$$

where $\mu = (\mu_q, q \in \mathcal{Q})$ is a vector of Lagrange multipliers and $\mathbf{z} = (z_q, q \in \mathcal{Q})$ is a vector of slack variables. Hence, at a maximum of L over $\mathbf{x}, \mathbf{z} \geq 0$, the following conditions hold:

$$U_f'(x_f) = \sum_{q \in \mathcal{Q}} \mu_q \mathcal{R}_{qf}, \quad \text{if } x_f > 0$$

$$\leq \sum_{q \in \mathcal{Q}} \mu_q \mathcal{R}_{qf}, \quad \text{if } x_f = 0 \tag{9}$$

$$\sum_{q \in \mathcal{Q}} \mu_q = 0, \quad \text{if } z_q > 0$$

$$\geq 0, \quad \text{if } z_q = 0 \tag{10}$$

Thus, given that the system knows the utility functions U_f of all the flows, this optimization problem can be mathematically tractable through the above procedure. However, in practice, the system is not likely to know all the U_f, and it is also infeasible for an ad hoc network to compute and allocate resource in a centralized fashion.

In the Lagrange form shown in Eq. (8), the Lagrange multipliers μ_q can be regarded as the implied cost of unit flow accessing the channel within the maximal clique q. In other words, μ_q is the *shadow price* of clique q. Motivated by the concept of shadow price of cliques, we decompose the *SYSTEM* problem into the following two problems and seek a distributed solution where the ad hoc network does not need to know the utility functions of individual flows.

Suppose that each flow f is given the price per unit flow λ_f. Then f chooses an amount to pay per unit time w_f, and receives in return a rate x_f given by $x_f = \frac{w_f}{\lambda_f}$. The utility optimization problem for flow f becomes the following:
$FLOW_f(U_f; \lambda_f)$:

$$\textbf{maximize } U_f\left(\frac{w_f}{\lambda_f}\right) - w_f \tag{11}$$

$$\textbf{over } \quad w_f \geq 0 \tag{12}$$

The network, given the amounts that the flows are willing to pay, $w = (w_f, f \in \mathcal{F})$, attempts to maximize the function $\sum_{f \in \mathcal{F}} w_f \log(x_f)$. So the network's optimization problem can be formulated as follows:
$NETWORK(\mathcal{R}, \mathcal{C}; w)$:

$$\textbf{maximize } \sum_{f \in \mathcal{F}} w_f \log(x_f) \tag{13}$$

$$\textbf{subject to } \mathcal{R}x \leq C \tag{14}$$

$$\textbf{over } \quad \mathbf{x} \geq 0 \tag{15}$$

Note that in the *NETWORK* problem, the utility functions are not required to carry out the resource allocation computation. Similar to [3], we have the following results.

Theorem 2: There exist vectors $\lambda = (\lambda_f, f \in \mathcal{F})$, $w = (w_f, f \in \mathcal{F})$ and $\mathbf{x} = (x_f, f \in \mathcal{F})$ such that

(1) w_f solves $FLOW_f(U_f; \lambda_f)$, for $f \in \mathcal{F}$; (2) x solves $NETWORK(\mathcal{R}, \mathcal{C}; w)$; (3) $w_f = \lambda_f x_f$.

We omit the proofs due to space constraints. Refer to [13] for a detailed proof.

Corollary 1. The price λ_f of a flow f and the shadow price of channel clique μ_q satisfy the following relation:

$$\lambda_f = \sum_{q:f \cap q \neq \emptyset} \mu_q \mathcal{R}_{qf} \tag{16}$$

$$= \sum_{l:l \in f} \sum_{q:l \in q} \mu_q \tag{17}$$

This relation shows that the flow f needs to pay for *all the maximal cliques* that it traverses. For each clique, the price to pay is the product of the number of wireless links that f traverses in this clique and the shadow price of this clique as in Eq. (16). Alternatively, we can also explain the pricing model in the following way: (1) the price of a flow is *the aggregated price of its subflows*; (2) the price of a subflow is *the aggregated price of all the maximal cliques* that the subflow belongs to as in Eq. (17).

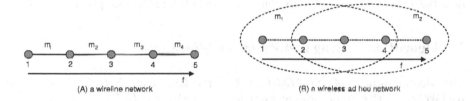

(A) a wireline network   (B) a wireless ad hoc network

Fig. 3. Wireline and wireless ad hoc networks: a comparison.

We now show an example to illustrate the difference between the proposed pricing model for wireless ad hoc networks and the existing model in wireline networks. In Fig. 3(A), the wireline network has a chain topology consisting of four links, which are associated with prices μ_i, $i = 1, \ldots, 4$. The price of flow f in this wireline network is $\lambda_f = \sum_{i=1}^{4} \mu_i$. On the other hand, although the wireless ad hoc network in Fig. 3(B) has the same topology as the wireline network, its resource is no longer "links". Instead, two maximal cliques $q_1 = \{l_{12}, l_{23}, l_{34}\}$ and $q_2 = \{l_{23}, l_{34}, l_{45}\}$ constitute the resources. Suppose that the shadow price of these two cliques are μ_1 and μ_2, respectively. Then the price of flow f in this ad hoc network is given by $\lambda_f = 3\mu_1 + 3\mu_2$, which is the number of subflows of f in this clique multiplied by the shadow price of this clique. Alternatively, the price can be written as $\lambda_f = \mu_1 + (\mu_1 + \mu_2) + (\mu_1 + \mu_2) + \mu_2$, which is the sum of its subflows' prices, with each subflow paying the aggregated price of all the maximal cliques that it belongs to.

4.2 Achieving Fairness among Multi-hop Flows

By choosing different utility functions for flows, the optimal resource allocation can enforce different fairness models among multi-hop flows in wireless ad hoc networks.

Definition 2 (proportional fairness). In a wireless ad hoc network, a vector of rates $\mathbf{x}^* = (x_f^*, f \in \mathcal{F})$ is *weighted proportionally fair* with weight vector w_f, if it is feasible, *i.e.*, $x_f^* \geq 0$ and $\mathcal{R}\mathbf{x}^* \leq \mathcal{C}$, and for any other feasible vector $\mathbf{x} = (x_f, f \in \mathcal{F})$, the aggregate of proportional change is zero or negative:

$$w_f \sum_{f \in \mathcal{F}} \frac{x_f - x_f^*}{x_f^*} \leq 0 \tag{18}$$

Proposition 1. A rate allocation $\mathbf{x}$ is weighted proportional fair with weight vector w_f in a wireless ad hoc network, if and only if it solves $SYSTEM(U, \mathcal{R}, \mathcal{C})$, with $U_f(x_f) = w_f \log x_f$ for $f \in \mathcal{F}$.

Definition 3 (max-min fairness). In a wireless ad hoc network, a vector of rates $\mathbf{x}^* = (x_f^*, f \in \mathcal{F})$ is *max-min fair*, if it is feasible, *i.e.*, $\mathbf{x}^* \geq 0$ and $\mathcal{R}\mathbf{x}^* \leq \mathcal{C}$, and if for any $f \in \mathcal{F}$, increasing x_f^* can not be done without decreasing the fair share $x_{f'}^*$ of another flow $f' \in \mathcal{F}$ which satisfies $x_f^* \geq x_{f'}^*$.

Proposition 2. A rate allocation $\mathbf{x}$ is max-min fair if and only if it solves $SYSTEM(U, \mathcal{R}, \mathcal{C})$, with $U_f(x_f) = -(-\log x_f)^\alpha$, $\alpha \to \infty$ for $f \in \mathcal{F}$.

These results straightforwardly follow its counterpart in wireline networks [3]. We omit the proofs due to space constraints. Refer to [13] for a detailed proof.

5   Algorithm: Pricing and Resource Allocation

The decomposition of $SYSTEM(U, \mathcal{R}, C)$ problem into $FLOW_f(U_f; \lambda_f)$ and $NETWORK(\mathcal{R}, C; w)$ problems suggests that solving $SYSTEM(U, \mathcal{R}, C)$ can be achieved by solving $FLOW_f(U_f; \lambda_f)$ and $NETWORK(\mathcal{R}, C; w)$ problems via an iterative algorithm. In each iteration, the source node of flow f individually solves its willingness to pay w_f in Eq. (11), adjusts its sending rate and notifies the network about this change. After the new sending rate is observed by the clique q, it updates its price μ_q accordingly and communicates the new prices to the flow, and the cycle repeats. To illustrate how flow f adjusts its willingness to pay, we define the demand function $D_f: \mathfrak{R}_+ \to \mathfrak{R}_+$ of flow f as follows. $D_f(\lambda_f)$ is the optimal solution w_f^* to the $FLOW(U_f; \lambda_f)$ problem. That is,

$$D_f(\lambda_f) = w_f^* = \arg \max_{w_f \geq 0} \{U_f(\frac{w_f}{\lambda_f}) - w_f\} \tag{19}$$

The iterative algorithm that computes the price and resource allocation is then given as follows.

Algorithm I (First Tier) – Per-clique Price Calculation and Resource Allocation

– *Clique q's algorithm at iteration k*
  (1) receives sending rate $x_f(k)$ from all flows f that go through clique q;
  (2) computes a new price according to the following formula

$$\mu_q(k + 1) = [\mu_q(k) + \alpha(\sum_{f: f \cap q \neq \emptyset} \mathcal{R}_{qf} x_f(k) - C)]^+ \tag{20}$$

where $\alpha > 0$ is a small step size parameter, and $[z]^+ = \max\{z, 0\}$. This algorithm is consistent with the law of supply and demand: if the demand for bandwidth at clique q exceeds the channel capacity supply C, which is the channel capacity, then the price μ_q is raised; otherwise, the price is reduced;
(3) communicates new price $\mu_q(k + 1)$ to all flows f that go through clique q.
– *Flow f's algorithm at iteration k*
    (1) receives from the network the path price $\lambda_f(k)$ along its path, where

$$\lambda_f(k) = \sum_{q: f \cap q \neq \emptyset} \mu_q(k) \mathcal{R}_{qf} \qquad (21)$$

(2) chooses a new willingness to pay $w_f(k + 1)$ to maximize its net benefit under the price $\lambda_f(k)$ according to

$$w_f(k + 1) = D_f(\lambda_f(k)) \qquad (22)$$

(3) calculates rate $x_f(k + 1)$ according to the following formula and transmits at rate $x_f(k + 1)$, where

$$x_f(k + 1) = \frac{w_f(k + 1)}{\lambda_f(k)}. \qquad (23)$$

We now show the convergence and the optimality of the above iterative algorithm through the following theorem.

Theorem 3 (Convergence). Provided that the stepsize α is sufficiently small, then Algorithm I has a unique equilibrium point $\mathbf{x}^*$, to which all trajectories converge.

Theorem 4 (Optimality). The equilibrium point $\mathbf{x}^*$ of Algorithm I is the optimal solution to the *SYSTEM* problem.

We omit the proofs due to space constraints. Refer to [13] for a detailed proof.

In the above iterative algorithm, a maximal clique is regarded as a network element that can carry out certain network functions. In particular, it assumes that a maximal clique q can perform the following tasks for price calculation and resource allocation: (1) obtain the aggregated bandwidth demand $\sum_{f: f \cap q \neq \emptyset} x_f \mathcal{R}_{qf}$ within the clique q; (2) calculate the per-clique shadow price μ_q; and (3) notify the price μ_q to the flows that pass through it.

However, a maximal clique is only a concept defined based on wireless link contention graph. To deploy the algorithm in an actual ad hoc network, the above tasks of a maximal clique need to be carried out by the nodes (hosts) that constitute the clique in a distributed fashion. To achieve this goal, the very first questions that need to be addressed are: (1) Which nodes constitute a maximal clique; (2) How many maximal cliques a node belongs to. The answer to these questions require an algorithm to find all maximal cliques in a graph. Although several such algorithms have been proposed in the existing literatures of graph theory [14], they can not be applied directly to our situation. This is because that these algorithms are all centralized and have high computational complexity, while the ad hoc network requires a full distributed solution.

Nevertheless, the unique graphical properties of the wireless link contention graph may have the potential to facilitate clique calculations. We proceed to propose a distributed maximal clique construction algorithm, in which the entire topology is decomposed into subgraphs. Maximal cliques can then be constructed only based on local topology information within each subgraph. Our algorithm can significantly reduce the communication and computational overhead. Using this algorithm, each node computes the maximal cliques it belongs to and carries out part of the tasks of these cliques. In particular, the tasks of maximal cliques are distributed among nodes in the following way.

- All nodes need to provide their local connectivity information to their neighborhood nodes.
- If a node i is sending packets to node j, then for all such j, i needs to
  (1) calculate *all cliques* q, which include link $\{i, j\}$;
  (2) collect rate information and calculate the price μ_q for all cliques q;
  (3) notify all the passing flows (for which node i forwards packets) of the updated price.

For example, in Fig. 1, node 2 needs to calculate all the cliques that contain link $\{2, 3\}$; node 4 needs to calculate all the cliques that contain link $\{4, 5\}$ and all the cliques that contain link $\{4, 7\}$, respectively.

First, we study the problem of how much information node i needs to know in order to construct *all maximal cliques* that contains wireless link $\{i, j\}$. To do that, we introduce the following definitions and denotations.

Definition 4 (neighbor sets).

(1) A neighbor set of link l, $N(l)$ is defined as $N(l) = \{l' | l \cap l' \neq \emptyset\}$;

(2) A neighbor set of link set L, $N(L)$, is defined as $N(L) = \cup_{l \in L} N(l)$;

(3) A k neighbor set of link l, denoted as $N^k(l)$, is defined by induction: (i) $N^1(l) = N(l)$, and (ii) $N^k(l) = N(N^{k-1}(l))$ for $k > 1$.

Lemma 2. Any clique that contains link l, denoted as $q_{<l>}$, satisfies condition $q_{<l>} \subseteq \mathcal{G}(N^2(l))$, where $\mathcal{G}(N^2(l))$ is a spanning subgraph of G_T whose edge set is $N^2(l)$.

By definitions of the *wireless link contention graph* and *clique*, Lemma 2 can be derived. This lemma shows that $\mathcal{G}(N^2(l))$ contains all the links to construct all maximal cliques $q_{<l>}$. As an example, in Fig. 1, $N^2(\{2, 3\}) = \{\{1, 2\}, \{2, 6\}, \{2, 3\}, \{3, 4\}, \{4, 5\}, \{4, 7\}\}$, which consists of all the links that are required to construct maximal cliques $q_{<2,3>}$.

In order to establish such a view of $\mathcal{G}(N^2(l))$ at node i, which sends packets along l, each node in the network distributes its connectivity and the traffic information to two hops away. Based on these information, node i constructs its local view of the network and uses the Bierstone algorithm [14] to find all maximal cliques that contain link $\{i, j\}$.

The iterative algorithm also requires communication between flows and the network. This is implemented via inbound signaling between the source nodes (in the role of flows) and the relaying nodes (in the role of network). In particular, there are two special fields in the packet header of each data packet. One field carries the sending rate of this flow; the other field carries the aggregated price of this flow along its path. The source of a flow fills in its sending rate x_f in the first field so that all the relaying nodes of flow f can distribute this rate to facilitate the price calculation. Similarly, each relaying node of f will fill in the price field of f's data packets. When the packets arrive at the destination, the destination node sends an acknowledgment packet to the source node to notify it about the possible price changes.

To summarize, each node i in an ad hoc network performs the following task locally in a cooperative manner to support global optimal resource allocation.

Algorithm II (Second Tier) - Per-node Price Calculation and Resource Allocation

- *Every node.* Every node i in the network sends its connectivity information $N(i) = \{j|\{i,j\} \in \mathcal{E}_T\}$ to two hops away.
- *Relaying node.* If node i transmits to node j, relaying packets for end-to-end flows $f_1, f_2, \ldots, f_m$, which means flow $f_k, k = 1, 2, \ldots, m$ is passing wireless link $\{i,j\}$, then i performs the following operations:
  (1) retrieves the sending rates x_k of flows $f_k, k = 1, 2, \ldots, m$, from their packet headers, calculates the aggregated rate $y_{ij} = \sum_{k=1}^{m} x_k$ and distributes the aggregated rate information;
  (2) collects connectivity information and constructs $G(N^2(\{i,j\}))$;
  (3) collects aggregated rate information $y_{l'}$, where $l' \in N^2(\{i,j\})$;
  (4) calculates all maximal cliques q, and their prices μ_q according to the iterative algorithm Eq. (20). Note that $\sum_{f:f \cap q \neq \emptyset} \mathcal{R}_{qf} x_f = \sum_{l' \in q} y_{l'}$.
  (5) updates the aggregated price $\lambda_f = \lambda_f + \lambda_{\{i,j\}}$, where $\lambda_{\{i,j\}} = \sum_{q:\{i,j\} \in q} \mu_q$, in the packet header for all flows f_k;
- *Destination node.* If node i is a destination node of an end-to-end flow f, then it observes the change of the aggregated price λ_f. If there is a change in λ_f, i sends a packet to the source to explicitly notify it about the change.
- *Source node.* If node i is a source node of an end-to-end flow f, then it
  (1) receives price update packets from the destination and retrieves path aggregated price λ_f from the packet.
  (2) calculates x_f according to Eq. (23);
  (3) updates its sending rate as x_f, and insert x_f into its packet header.

6   Simulation Results

In this section, we validate the performance of our price-based resource allocation algorithm through a detailed numerical study. In our simulation, the channel capacity of wireless networks and the bandwidth of wireline networks are both 1 Mbps. The utility function in use is $U_f(x_f) = \log(x_f)$, which will enforce the proportional fair resource allocation in both wireline and wireless ad hoc networks.

6.1   Resource Allocation in Wireline and Wireless Networks: A Comparison

We first compare the effects of resource allocations in wireless ad hoc networks with wireline networks, using identical topologies. We consider a simple example. The network topology is shown in Fig. 1(A), where the network is shared by three flows. The resulting rate allocation of two types of networks is listed in Table 1. The corresponding price vectors when the systems are converged are shown in Table 2.

From these results, we have the following observations: (1) In both networks, the price μ_j, at the bottleneck resource j (which is the clique q_2 in the ad hoc network,

Table 1. Rate allocation in the example topology shown in Fig. 1

	x_1	x_2	x_3
wireline network (Mbps)	0.5	0.5	1
wireless ad hoc network (Mbps)	0.111	0.333	0.333

Table 2. Equilibrium prices in the example topology shown in Fig. 1

	μ_1	μ_2	μ_3	μ_4	μ_5	μ_6	μ_7
wireline network	0	2	0	0	0	0	0
wireless ad hoc network	0	3	0	N/A	N/A	N/A	N/A

and the wireline link $\{2, 3\}$ in the wireline network) is larger than 0. In comparison, at non-bottleneck resources, they are equal to 0. This shows the role of shadow price to arbitrate resource allocation. When the demand (sending rate) exceeds the supply (channel capacity), which happens in the bottleneck resource, the shadow price, which reflects the marginal cost, is increased. When the demand is below supply, there is no such marginal cost, thus the price equals to 0. (2) Due to the contention in the spatial domain for the shared wireless medium, the rate allocation in the ad hoc network for each flow is less than the rate allocation for the corresponding flow in wireline networks.

We then proceed to show a more detailed comparison between the two types of networks using chain topologies, on which flows with different numbers of hops are sharing the resources. As shown in Fig. 4(A), a chain topology is shared among 5 flows. Four of them are single-hop flows, one of them is a flow with 4 hops. The rate allocation and the equilibrium prices for this scenario are given in Table 3 and Table 4. We also conduct simulations in a chain topology with 5 hops as shown in Fig. 4(B) for comparison purposes. The results are shown in Table 5 and Table 6.

Table 3. Rate allocation in the 4-hop chain topology shown in Fig. 4(A)

	x_1	x_2	x_3	x_4	x_5
wireline network (Mbps)	0.8	0.8	0.8	0.8	0.2
wireless ad hoc network (Mbps)	0.4	0.2	0.2	0.4	0.067

Table 4. Equilibrium prices in the 4-hop chain topology shown in Fig. 4(A)

	μ_1	μ_2	μ_3	μ_4
wireline network	1.25	1.25	1.25	1.25
wireless ad hoc network	2.5	2.5	N/A	N/A

From the above results, we have the following observations.

In the wireline network, the rates of all single hop flows are the same, *e.g.*, in the 4-hop chain topology, $x_1 = x_2 = x_3 = x_4 = 0.8$. In wireless ad hoc networks, however,

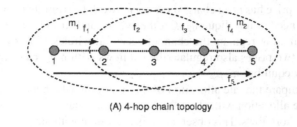

(A) 4-hop chain topology

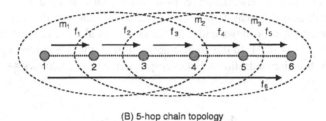

(B) 5-hop chain topology

Fig. 4. Two example chain topologies with 4 hops and 5 hops

Table 5. Rate allocation in the 5-hop chain topology shown in Fig. 4(B)

	x_1	x_2	x_3	x_4	x_5	x_6
wireline network (Mbps)	0.833	0.833	0.833	0.833	0.833	0.167
wireless ad hoc network (Mbps)	0.333	0.333	0.167	0.333	0.333	0.056

Table 6. Equilibrium prices in the 5-hop chain topology shown in Fig. 4(B)

	μ_1	μ_2	μ_3	μ_4	μ_5
wireline network	1.2	1.2	1.2	1.2	1.2
wireless ad hoc network	3.0	0.0	3.0	N/A	N/A

the rates of these flows are different. For example, in the 4-hop chain topology, $x_1 \neq x_2$. This is because, in wireline network flow $f_1 - f_4$ enjoy the same amount of resource in the network, while in the wireless ad hoc network, due to location-dependent contention, f_2 suffers higher contention than f_1. Alternatively, we can explain such resource allocation through the price that they need to pay. For f_1, the price is $\lambda_1 = \mu_1$, which is equal to 2.5 at equilibrium; while the price for f_2 is $\lambda_2 = \mu_1 + \mu_2$, which is equal to 5.0.

From the results in the 5-hop topology example, we can show another interesting observation in the ad hoc network scenario. In Table 5, we observe that $x_1 = x_2$, although it seems that these two flows suffer different degrees of contention. This result can be explained by the price of this flow, where $\lambda_1 = \mu_1 = 3$, and $\lambda_2 = \mu_1 + \mu_2 = 3$. Because the prices they need to pay are the same and they have the same utility function, they reach the same bandwidth allocation.

The reason why μ_2 is 0 in Table 6 can be intuitively explained as follows. The three cliques q_1, q_2 and q_3 have the same traffic demand. When q_1 and q_3 are appropriately priced, sufficient price has been charged on the network to arbitrate the resource usage, thus no price is needed for clique q_2. On the other hand, if only q_2 is priced, then a price is still required to regulate the channel access at wireless link $\{1,2\}$ and $\{5,6\}$. Moreover, these two prices also regulate the subflows within q_2, causing a decrease of μ_2. Eventually at equilibrium, $\mu_2 = 0$.

When we compare the rate allocation of the long flow which has a large number of hops and the rate allocation with short flows, we notice that the long flow is penalized compared to the short flows. This observation is consistent with the previously presented observations in wireline networks under proportional fairness model [4]. However, the degree of penalties is different in these two networks. In the wireline network, the ratio of rate allocation for short flows and long flows are equal, e.g., in the 4-hop topology, $\frac{x_1}{x_5} = \frac{x_2}{x_5} = \frac{x_3}{x_5} = \frac{x_4}{x_5} = 4$. In the ad hoc network with the 4-hop topology, such ratio depends on the location of the flows. For example, in the ad hoc network $\frac{x_1}{x_5} = 6, \frac{x_2}{x_5} = 3$.

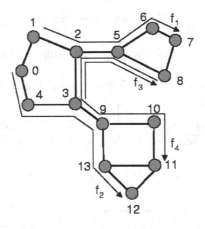

Fig. 5. A random topology

6.2   Convergence of the Iterative Algorithm

We now show the convergence behavior of our proposed algorithm using three example networks. They are the simple network in Fig. 1(A), the chain topology network shown in Fig. 4(B) and a random generated network shown in Fig. 5. For each example, we have plotted the time-varying values of the transmission rate of each flow and shadow price at each clique in Fig. 6, Fig. 7 and Fig. 8.

We note that the system converges to an equilibrium rate allocation and an equilibrium price vector within 800 iterations. This result is comparable to other relay-based pricing scheme in ad hoc networks [8]. In a mobile environment, such a convergence time will be orders of magnitude lower than the topology changing time.

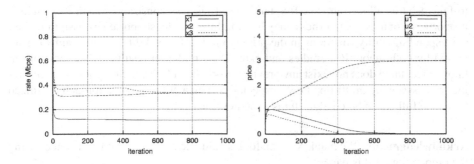

Fig. 6. Trajectories of the transmission rate and price of the network in Fig. 1(A)

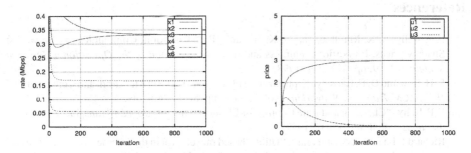

Fig. 7. Trajectories of transmission rate and price of the network in Fig. 4(B)

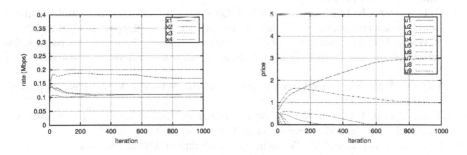

Fig. 8. Trajectories of transmission rate and price of the network in Fig. 5

7 Concluding Remarks

In this paper, we have presented a novel pricing-based resource allocation algorithm based on an analytical pricing model that is specifically designed for the unique characteristics of multi-hop wireless ad hoc networks. The original contribution incorporated in the pricing model is the association of shadow prices with the *maximal cliques* in the contention graph model, rather than with individual links as in wireline networks. Based on insights brought forth by such strategies, the algorithms proposed are fully distributed, and arbitrate the contention among end-to-end *multi-hop* flows with respect to fair resource allocation. The frequently used fairness constraints, such as weighted proportional or max-min fairness, may be straightforwardly supported by assigning their corresponding utility functions in the pricing model. The validity of our claims is supported by both theoretical studies and extensive simulation results. To the best of our knowledge, there does not exist any previous work that addresses the problem of enforcing fairness among multi-hop flows, especially when a pricie-based approach is utilized to design fully distributed algorithms to achieve this goal.

Acknowledgments. We thank Xue Liu for his valuable comments and assistance during the preparation of this paper.

References

1. F. P. Kelly, A. K. Maulloo, and D. K. H. Tan, "Rate Control in Communication Networks: Shadow prices, Proportional Fairness and Stability," *Journal of the Operational Research Society*, vol. 49, pp. 237–252, 1998.
2. S. H. Low and D. E. Lapsley, "Optimization Flow Control: Basic Algorithm and Convergence," *IEEE/ACM Trans. on Networking*, vol. 7, no. 6, pp. 861–874, 1999.
3. F. P. Kelly, "Charging and Rate Control for Elastic Traffic," *European Trans. on Telecommunications*, vol. 8, pp. 33–37, 1997.
4. Richard J. La and V. Anantharam, "Utility-based rate control in the Internet for elastic traffic," *IEEE/ACM Trans. on Networking*, vol. 10, no. 2, pp. 272–286, 2002.
5. L. Tassiulas K. Kar, S. Sarkar, "A simple rate control algorithm for maximizing total user utility," in *Proc. of INFOCOM*, 2001.
6. C. U. Saraydar, N. B. Mandayam, and D. J. Goodman, "Efficient power control via pricing in wireless data networks," *IEEE Trans. Commun.*, vol. 50, no. 2, pp. 291–303, Feb 2002.
7. R. Wouhaybi R. Liao and A. Campbell, "Incentive engineering in wireless lan based access networks," in *Proc. of 10th IEEE International Conference on Network Protocols (ICNP)*, Nov 2002.
8. Y. Qiu and P. Marbach, "Bandwith Allocation in Ad-Hoc Networks: A Price-Based Approach," in *Proc. of INFOCOM*, 2003.
9. T. Nandagopal, T.-E. Kim, X. Gao, and V. Bharghavan, "Achieving MAC Layer Fairness in Wireless Packet Networks," in *Proc. of ACM Mobicom*, 2000, pp. 87–98.
10. L. Tassiulas and S. Sarkar, "Maxmin fair scheduling in wireless networks," in *Proc. of INFOCOM*, 2002, pp. 763–772.
11. H. Luo, S. Lu, and V. Bharghavan, "A New Model For Packet Scheduling in Multihop Wireless Networks," in *Proc. of ACM Mobicom*, 2000, pp. 76–86.
12. X. L. Huang and B. Bensaou, "On Max-min Fairness and Scheduling in Wireless Ad-hoc Networks: Analytical Framework and Implementation," in *Proc. of ACM MobiHoc*, 2001, pp. 221–231.
13. B. Li Y. Xue and K. Nahrstedt, "Price-based resource allocation in wireless ad hoc networks," Tech. Rep. UIUCDCS-R-2003-2331, Univ. of Illinios at Urbana-Champaign, 2003.
14. J. G. Augustson and J. Minker, "An Analysis of Some Graph Theoretical Cluster Techniques," *Journal of the Association for Computing Machinery*, vol. 17, no. 4, pp. 571–586, 1970.

On Achieving Fairness in the Joint Allocation of Processing and Bandwidth Resources*

Yunkai Zhou and Harish Sethu

Department of Electrical and Computer Engineering
Drexel University
3141 Chestnut Street
Philadelphia, PA 19104-2875.
Tel: 215-895-5876; Fax: 215-895-1695.
{yunkai,sethu}@ece.drexel.edu

Abstract. The problem of achieving fairness in the allocation of the bandwidth resource on a link shared by multiple flows of traffic has been extensively researched over the last decade. However, with the increasing pervasiveness of optical networking and the occasional trend toward using over-provisioning as the solution to congestion, a router's processor also becomes a critical resource to which, ideally speaking, all competing flows should have fair access. For example, if the network is not fair in allocating processing resources, denial of service attacks based on an excessive use of the router processor (such as by using unnecessary optional headers) become possible. In this paper, we investigate the issue of achieving fairness in the joint allocation of the processing and bandwidth resources. We first present a simple but powerful general principle for defining fairness in such systems based on any of the classic notions of fairness such as max-min fairness, proportional fairness and utility max-min fairness defined for a single resource. We apply our principle to a system with a shared processor and a shared link with max-min fairness as the desired goal. We then propose a practical and provably fair packet-by-packet algorithm for the joint allocation of processing and bandwidth resources. We demonstrate the fairness achieved by our algorithm through simulation results using real gateway traffic traces. The principles and the algorithm detailed in this paper may also be applied in the allocation of other kinds of resources such as power, a critical resource in mobile systems.

1 Introduction

1.1 Introduction and Motivation

Fairness in the allocation of resources in a network shared amongst multiple users is not only an intuitively desirable goal but also one with many practical benefits. Fairness in traffic management can improve flow and user isolation, offer a more predictable performance and eliminate certain kinds of bottlenecks. In addition, strategies and algorithms for fair management of network traffic can serve as a critical component of

---

* This work was supported in part by NSF CAREER Award CCR-9984161 and U.S. Air Force Contract F30602-00-2-0501.

K. Jeffay, I. Stoica, and K. Wehrle (Eds.): IWQoS 2003, LNCS 2707, pp. 97–114, 2003.

Quality-of-Service (QoS) mechanisms to achieve certain guaranteed services such as delay bounds and minimum bandwidths. Various formal notions of fairness have been proposed in the literature to precisely define what is fair in the allocation of a resource amongst competing flows. These include, among others, max-min fairness [1, 2, 3, 4], proportional fairness [5], and utility max-min fairness [6].

Based on these notions of fairness—most commonly, based on the notion of max-min fairness—much research over the last decade or two has focused on the allocation of the bandwidth resource on a link [7, 2, 3, 8, 9, 10, 11]. It has also been shown that concepts and algorithms for achieving fairness in the allocation of a single resource can be extended to the case with multiple resources *of the same kind* [12]. However, as flows of traffic traverse a computer network, they share many different kinds of resources such as link bandwidth, buffer space, time on the router processors and also electrical power, a critical resource in mobile systems. The ultimate goal, therefore, should be the overall fairness in the *joint* allocation of all resources shared by the flows of traffic and not just one specific kind of resource such as the link bandwidth. For example, if the network is not fair in allocating processing resources, denial of service attacks based on an excessive use of the router processor (such as by using unnecessary optional headers) become possible.

The significance of considering the fair allocation of more than just the link bandwidth is increasingly becoming apparent today, since the link bandwidth is often not the only critical resource. With the current pervasiveness of optical networking in the Internet backbone, and with the occasional trend toward using over-provisioning as the solution to congestion in the edge networks, a router's processor is often also a critical resource to which, ideally speaking, all competing flows should have fair access. Given the fact that processing requirements of different packets vary widely, the issue of fairness in the allocation of the processing resources gains significance. In addition, besides the fact that packet lengths can vary widely, the presence of optional headers and the various kinds of control information carried by packets create a wide variation in the ratio of a packet's demand for bandwidth and its demand for processing cycles. Thus, packets of the same length cannot be guaranteed to have similar requirements for the processing resources on a router. In fact, the processing delay plotted as a function of the packet length shows that the processing requirements of packets vary across a wide range even for packets of the same length [13]. Thus, one cannot achieve overall fairness merely with the fair allocation of link bandwidth alone, or merely through the fair allocation of the processing resources alone, since different flows—and different packets within the same flow—may have very different demands for these two kinds of resources. Even if one of these resources is over-provisioned, not ensuring fairness in its allocation to the various flows exposes the network to denial-of-service attacks based on this resource. All of this begs the question that this paper seeks to address: how does one achieve fairness in the *joint* allocation of the processing and bandwidth resources?

The need for fairness in the joint allocation of multiple heterogeneous resources has also been recognized in other contexts besides the one discussed here. For example, it has been recognized that fair allocation of both the channel bandwidth and the power consumed needs to be achieved simultaneously in mobile networks where power and bandwidth are both critically important and scarce resources [14]. However, a rigorous theoretical framework that may be universally employed as a guide in the design of practical algorithmic strategies for the joint allocation of such heterogeneous sets of resources does not exist.

In this paper, we investigate the issue of fairness in such systems and develop a general principle that forms the foundation for the design of practical fair strategies for use in routers. We also present an evaluation of the practical strategies proposed in this paper using real gateway traces.

1.2 Contributions

In the joint allocation of the processor and bandwidth resources, if a certain resource is never the bottleneck, then the fair allocation strategy degenerates to the fair allocation of just the other resource. For example, if the available bandwidth is large enough that no flow experiences congestion due to lack of bandwidth alone, one only needs to worry about the allocation of the processing resources. Fair allocation of a single bottleneck resource has been studied extensively in the literature and has led to a large number of practical algorithms that are in use today in Internet routers, operating systems, and transport-level protocols. This paper, on the other hand, answers the question of what is a fair allocation when more than one resource is congested and extends the notions of fairness applied to a single resource to systems with multiple heterogeneous resources.

We define an *essential* resource as one for which a flow's demand does not reduce with an increase in the allocation of other resources to the flow. A number of resources such as the link bandwidth, processor or power, in most contexts, are essential resources. On the other hand, buffer resources in a network are often not essential resources as per the above definition; for example, in a system with a buffer and a link, a flow uses the buffer only if the link resource is currently unavailable to it, and thus a flow's demand for the buffer resource reduces as more of the link bandwidth is allocated to it. In the system model used in this paper, we assume that the flows are in competition for resources that are all essential. The issue of achieving fairness in a system where flows have to compete for a non-essential resource such as a buffer entails a different set of challenges than those considered here, and is addressed in some other recent works such as [15].

We define a pair of resources as *related* to each other if a flow's demand for one resource uniquely determines its demand for the other resource. Resources in a set are said to be *related* if each resource is related to every other resource in the set. Resources in real scenarios are almost always related since the demands of a flow for different individual resources are often related to each other. For example, since each packet is associated with certain processing and bandwidth requirements, a specific increase in a flow's demand for link bandwidth is typically associated with a specific increase in its demand for processing resources. A simpler example, involving multiple resources of the same kind, is a tandem network with multiple links where the demand of a flow for bandwidth is the same on all the links. In the system model used in this paper, we assume multiple resources that are related, although we make no assumptions on the specific nature of the relationship between a flow's demand for different resources. The existence of a relationship between the demands of a flow for various resources calls for the *joint* allocation of these resources, as opposed to an independent and separate allocation of the resources.

The primary contribution of this paper is a theoretical framework based on which one can define fairness in the joint allocation of multiple heterogeneous resources that are essential and related. We make no assumptions on the notion of fairness; in fact, our framework may be applied to any of several notions of fairness such as max-min fairness, proportional fairness or utility max-min. Through illustrative examples, we claim that, at each instant of time, it is the maximum of a flow's normalized demand for the various resources that should count in the decisions made by a fair resource allocation algorithm. We then develop the fundamental principles of fairness for systems with multiple essential and related heterogeneous resources and propose the *Principle of Fair Multiple Resource Allocation* or the *FMRA principle*, expressed within a rigorous theoretical framework.

Given the FMRA principle, we proceed to apply it to a system with a shared processor and a shared link, using max-min fairness as the notion of fairness. We propose an ideally fair policy, called the *Fluid-flow Processor and Link Sharing (FPLS)* algorithm, for the joint allocation of processing and bandwidth resources. We then develop a practical and *provably* fair packet-by-packet approximation of the FPLS algorithm, called *Packet-by-packet Processor and Link Sharing (PPLS)*. The PPLS algorithm, based on an extension of the Deficit Round Robin algorithm [9], has a per-packet work complexity of $O(1)$. We illustrate the fairness of the PPLS algorithm using real gateway traffic traces.

1.3 Organization

The rest of this paper is organized as follows. Section 2 introduces a generic notation to represent notions of fairness. This section also describes the general system model with multiple shared resources considered in this study, along with our notation. Section 3 presents the Principle of Fair Multiple Resource Allocation for the system model under consideration. Section 4 applies the FMRA principle to a system with a shared processor and a shared link, and proposes a practical and fair scheduling algorithm for the joint allocation of the processing and bandwidth resources, called the Packet-by-packet Processor and Link Sharing (PPLS) policy. The fairness properties of the PPLS strategy are demonstrated by simulation experiments using real gateway traffic in Section 5. Finally, Section 6 concludes the paper.

2   System Model and Notation

2.1   Notation for a Notion of Fairness

Consider a set of N flows, $1 \leq i \leq N$, competing for a single shared resource which may be consumed at a peak rate of R. Denote by w_i the weight of flow i, indicating the flow's relative rightful share of the resources. For a flow under a Differentiated Services framework [16], its weight is determined by its traffic class among the 64 possible classes; for a flow in a best-effort network, its weight is typically the same as that of all other flows.

Several different notions of fairness have been proposed in the research literature for the allocation of a single shared resource among a set of requesting entities. All of these notions specify a particular rate of consumption of the resource for each of the flows, given the consumption rate demanded by the flows. In this subsection, we develop a generic notation that can express any of these notions of fairness.

Without loss of generality, we assume that the entities competing for the single shared resource are traffic flows. Let d_i be the demand of flow i for the shared resource. Define the normalized demand of flow i, D_i, for the resource as follows:

$$D_i = \frac{d_i}{R}.$$

The normalized demand of flow i indicates the fractional share of the resource demanded by the flow. Denote by a_i the allocated resource consumption rate for flow i. Define the normalized allocation of flow i, A_i, as follows:

$$A_i = \frac{a_i}{R}.$$

The normalized allocation of flow i indicates the fractional share of the resource allocated to flow i. Any notion of fairness, thus, specifies how to distribute the fractional share of the resource allocated to each flow, given the desired share of this resource.

For the sake of convenience, throughout this paper we use vectors to indicate values corresponding to a set of flows. We denote a vector by the indexed value in a pair of square brackets. For instance, we denote the vector of normalized demands as $[D_i]$.

Therefore, given the normalized demand vector $[D_i]$ and the weight vector $[w_i]$, any given notion of fairness may be represented as a function as follows:

$$[A_i] = \mathcal{F}(C, [D_i], [w_i]) \tag{1}$$

where C is the constraint, described later in greater detail, imposed on the system. The function $\mathcal{F}$ is different for different notions of fairness such as max-min fairness, proportional fairness or utility max-min fairness.

The constraint C is used as a parameter in the function $\mathcal{F}$ because, given the same demand and weight vector, the fair allocation is different under different constraints imposed on the system. The constraint C can be used to indicate the performance level achieved by the allocation. For example, an allocation of no resource to any flow may also be considered a fair allocation by the max-min fair criterion albeit one that leads to very poor performance. In general, this parameter allows us to define the fairness of non-work-conserving allocation strategies by not imposing a specific level of performance achieved by the allocation in the definition of fairness. As a simple example, the constraint C can be just the sum of the utilities achieved by all flows.

Note that, in the research literature, notions of fairness have not been defined for multiple heterogeneous resources[1]. We use the above notation that specifies a notion of fairness for a single resource and extend the notion to multiple heterogeneous resources in subsequent sections.

---

[1] Some notions of fairness such as max-min fairness and proportional fairness can be defined for multiple resources of the same kind (e.g., a network of links), under the assumption that, if a flow receives allocations of several resources, the allocations it receives of these resources are identical [1,5]. However, it is not straightforward to extend these notions of fairness to systems with multiple heterogeneous resources. On the other hand, it can be readily verified that our framework is the same as these notions of fairness if the shared resources are of the same kind.

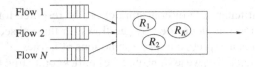

Fig. 1. A general system model.

2.2 System Model and Assumptions

In our system model, a set of N flows, $1 \leq i \leq N$, compete for a set of K related and essential resources, $1 \leq j \leq K$, as shown in Fig. 1. As also described in Section 1.2, we define an essential resource as one for which a flow's demand does not reduce with an increase in the allocation of other resources to it. Since a buffer is often not an essential resource, our assumption that flows only compete for essential resources implies that if there are buffers in the network shared by the flows, these buffers are of infinite capacity so that the flows never compete for the buffer resource. In developing our fundamental principles of fairness, we make no assumptions on the specific actions of the scheduler or the specific order in which the packets use the K resources.

Note that in this general model, we also make no assumptions on the internal architecture of the set of shared resources. It can be a simple sequence of resources such as in a tandem network with multiple links, a parallel structure such as the resources of electric power and bandwidth in a wireless sensor network, or a more complex hybrid.

Denote by R_j the peak rate at which resource j may be consumed. For example, in the case of a link resource L, R_L is the peak bandwidth available on the link. As before, denote by w_i the weight of flow i. Let $d_{i,j}$ be the consumption rate demanded by flow i for the shared resource j. Our assumption of related resources implies that, given $d_{i,k}$, one can determine $d_{i,j}$ for all $j \neq k$. Denote by $a_{i,j}^q$, the consumption rate of the shared resource j allocated to flow i under the allocation policy q.

3 The FMRA Principle

3.1 The Concept of the Prime Resource

We begin with a few preliminary definitions.

Definition 1. Define the normalized demand of flow i for resource j, $D_{i,j}$, as follows:

$$D_{i,j} = \frac{d_{i,j}}{R_j}.$$

Define the *largest normalized demand* of flow i, $\mathcal{D}_i$, as the maximum amongst the normalized demands of flow i for all resources. That is,

$$\mathcal{D}_i = \max_j D_{i,j}.$$

Definition 2.   Define $A^q_{i,j}$ as the normalized allocation of resource j to flow i under allocation policy q, i.e.,

$$A^q_{i,j} = \frac{a^q_{i,j}}{R_j}.$$

Definition 3.   The *largest normalized allocation* of a flow i under allocation policy q, denoted by $\mathcal{A}^q_i$, is defined as the maximum amongst the normalized allocations to flow i of all resources. That is,

$$\mathcal{A}^q_i = \max_j A^q_{i,j}.$$

Definition 4.   Under an allocation policy q, a resource is said to be a *prime resource* of flow i, denoted by $\mathcal{B}^q_i$, if and only if, the normalized allocation of this resource to flow i is its largest normalized allocation. In other words,

$$\mathcal{B}^q_i = \arg \max_j A^q_{i,j} = \arg \max_j \frac{a^q_{i,j}}{R_j}$$

where $\arg \max_x f(x)$ indicates the value of the argument x corresponding to the maximum value of function $f(x)$. In other words, we have

$$A^q_{i,\mathcal{B}^q_i} = \max_j A^q_{i,j} = \mathcal{A}^q_i$$

In networking terminology, a bottleneck resource is one that is the most congested resource. It is critical to note that neither the resource for which a flow has the largest normalized demand nor its prime resource under an allocation policy is necessarily the same as the bottleneck resource in the system.

Note that a flow may have more than one prime resource. The prime resource is defined based on the actual allocations and not on the demand of the flows for the resources.

3.2   The FMRA Principle

We introduce our principle with a few illustrative examples shown in Table 1. In these examples, two flows with equal weights, labeled as 1 and 2, share two different resources: a processor P for packet processing, and a link L. The system model in these examples is the same as the one we will discuss later in Fig. 2. The peak processing rate is 100 million processor cycles per second, i.e., 100 MHz, and the peak link rate is 100 Mbps. Let us assume linear utility functions and max-min as the notion of fairness. In addition, for the sake of convenience, we also assume in these examples a proportional relationship between a flow's demands for these resources and therefore, a proportional relationship between the allocations. In other words, the ratio of a flow's demand for one resource and its demand for another resource is always a constant.

In example A, assume that packets in flow 1 are all small, and therefore, its demand for bandwidth is small relative to its demand for processing time. In contrast, assume that packets in flow 2 are large, and therefore, its demand for bandwidth is large relative

Table 1. Examples illustrating what is a fair allocation in a system with a shared processor P and a shared link L. In all of these examples, the total amounts of the shared resources are, respectively, 100 MHz for P and 100 Mbps for L.

	Flow ID	Demand		Allocation	
		P (MHz)	L (Mbps)	P (MHz)	L (Mbps)
A	1	75	25	75	25
	2	25	75	25	75
B	1	225	75	75	25
	2	50	150	25	75
C	1	100	20	50	10
	2	100	10	50	5

to its demand for processing time. To better illustrate the concept, we exaggerate the difference between their demands as follows: Flow 1 has a demand of 75 MHz for processing time and 25 Mbps for bandwidth, while flow 2's demands are, respectively, 25 MHz and 75 Mbps. If a work-conserving allocation policy is used, there is enough of both resources to satisfy the demands of both the flows and so the allocations are exactly the same as the demands for each of the resources. Note that for flow 1, the prime resource is P, while for flow 2, it is L.

Next, consider what happens when both flows proportionally increase their demands for both resources. In example B, in comparison to example A, flow 1 increases its demands by a factor of three while flow 2 doubles its demands. Specifically, the demands for flow 1 become 225 MHz for P and 75 Mbps for L, while those for flow 2 become 50 MHz and 150 Mbps, respectively. A fundamental principle behind the max-min notion of fairness is that, given no additional resources, a flow should not be able to increase its allocation by merely demanding more. Thus, the fair allocation should be as shown in example B. Again, the prime resource for either flow remains the same as in the previous example.

We discuss example B further. Obviously, in this case, neither flow is satisfied by the allocated resources. Is the allocation actually fair?

One might argue that both flows should get equal bandwidth from a fair allocation, since ultimately both flows will depart from this system and the processor is only an intermediate resource before the flow's packets reach the link resource. Based on this notion, we can compute the allocations as follows:

$$\begin{cases} 3x + x/3 \le 100 \\ 2x \le 100 \end{cases}$$

where x is the bandwidth allocated to either flow, in units of Mbps. It can be readily verified that, under a work-conserving allocation policy, flow 1 gets 90 MHz of processing time and flow 2 gets only 10 MHz, while both flows get 30 Mbps of bandwidth. While this allocation underutilizes the link resources, that is not an argument against its fairness. The unfairness arises from the fact that it unnecessarily favors the flow whose prime resource is the "intermediate resource", which turns out to be flow 1 in this case.

Another argument against this notion is that, even though it is true that the processor in this case is positioned ahead of the link, it does not necessarily mean that the processing resource becomes less important, or less preferred, as compared to the link, which is positioned as the "final" resource.

Another allocation philosophy may be to allocate resources based on a fair allocation of the most congested resource as measured by the sum of the normalized demands for the resource. In this example, the processing resource P is the most congested resource. One may allocate resource P fairly as follows:

$$\begin{cases} 2y \leq 100 \\ y/3 + 3y \leq 100 \end{cases}$$

where y is the processing resources allocated to either flow, in units of MHz. Under a work-conserving allocation policy, flow 2 gets 90 Mbps of bandwidth and flow 1 gets only 10 Mbps, while both flows get 30 MHz of processing resources. Note that this allocation philosophy has a similar weakness as the one based on the fair allocation of the link resource. It unnecessarily favors the flow whose largest normalized demand is not for the most congested resource. A flow can trigger a change in the allocation policy by merely increasing its demand for a given resource, while that would actually be against the max-min notion of fairness.

One may suggest the following slight modification to the allocation strategy: to fairly allocate the most congested resource as measured by the sum of the normalized *allocations* for the resource. However, it can be shown that such an allocation may not exist. Assume a certain resource r is the most congested resource. Let α denote the flow with the smaller demand for resource r and let β denote the other flow. Assume that the normalized allocations of resource r are z_α and z_β for the two flows. It can be verified that the normalized allocations of the other resource are $3z_\alpha$ and $z_\beta/3$, independent of whether the resource r is the processing resource P or the bandwidth resource L. Since resource r is the most congested resource as measured by the sum of the normalized allocations, we have,

$$3z_\alpha + z_\beta/3 \leq z_\alpha + z_\beta$$

which leads to $3z_\alpha \leq z_\beta$. Since both flows have a high demand, under the max-min notion, this condition cannot lead to a fair allocation except for the trivial case where $z_\alpha = z_\beta = 0$. Thus, it may not be possible to achieve a fair allocation of the most congested resource as measured by the sum of the normalized allocations of the resource.

Based on the discussions above, we claim that in a network where no explicit preference of one resource over another exists (i.e., each resource is essential), fairness should not be defined based only on a single resource, no matter how this single resource is determined and whether it is determined before allocation (i.e., based on demand) or after allocation (i.e., based on allocation). Instead, the fairness in such a system should be defined with overall consideration of various resources involved in the system and the relationships between the demands for the various resources.

Given this observation, one may propose yet another scheme to define fairness: the sum of the normalized allocations of the resources computed for each flow should be max-min fair. In the previous example B, this leads to an allocation of 75 MHz of processing time and 25 Mbps of bandwidth for flow 1, and 25 MHz of processing time and 75 Mbps of bandwidth for flow 2. In this case, for both flows, the sum of the normalized allocations of the two resources is $75/100 + 25/100 = 1$. While this appears to be a reasonable strategy for fair allocation, this scheme of fairness cannot, in fact, be extended to other situations. This is illustrated by example C described below.

Assume that both flows have a demand of 100 MHz for resource P, while the demands for resource L are 20 Mbps and 10 Mbps for flows 1 and 2, respectively. Note that in this example, there is sufficient link bandwidth available for the demands of both flows, i.e., the flows are not in competition for resource L. In other words, the system regresses into an allocation of a single resource P. Applying the max-min notion of fairness on the single resource P, we know that the fair allocation would be 50 MHz of processing time for each flow, leading to 10 Mbps and 5 Mbps of bandwidth for flows 1 and 2, respectively. Thus, the ideally fair allocation leads to 0.6 and 0.55 as the sum of the normalized allocations. Clearly, if we were to be max-min fair in the sum of the normalized allocations of the resources to each flow, we would not get this result. This illustrates that the strategy of achieving max-min fair distribution in the sum of the normalized allocations fails to serve as the basis to define fairness in the allocation of multiple resources.

The fair allocation strategies in the three examples do have one property in common: the largest normalized allocations of the flows are distributed in a max-min fair manner among the flows. In our case with equal weights for the flows, the largest normalized allocations are equal for the two flows. In the first two examples in Table 1, resource P is the prime resource for flow 1, while the prime resource for flow 2 is resource L. In both examples, the largest normalized allocation equals 0.9. In the third example, the processor P is the prime resource for both flows, and this time the largest normalized allocation is 0.5 for both flows.

The observations from the above examples lead to the significance of incorporating the largest normalized allocation for each flow into a strategy for extending a notion of fairness to the allocation of multiple resources. In our examples, the fair allocation policy is to simply equalize the largest normalized allocations for different flows. In more general situations, different notions of fairness may be used and flows may have different weights and different largest normalized demands. We now present the *Principle of Fair Multiple Resource Allocation* or the *FMRA Principle*.

Principle of Fair Multiple Resource Allocation. In a system with multiple related and essential resources, an allocation policy q is said to be fair as per the notion of fairness $\mathcal{F}$, if and only if, the largest normalized allocations are distributed fairly, as per the notion of fairness $\mathcal{F}$, with respect to the largest normalized demands. In other words, allocation policy q is fair as per $\mathcal{F}$ if and only if,

$$[\mathcal{A}_i^q] = \mathcal{F}(C, [\mathcal{D}_i], [w_i])$$

where C is some constraint imposed on the system.

4   Fair Joint Allocation of Processing and Bandwidth Resources

In this section, we apply the framework established in the previous section into an important context of special interest: the fair joint allocation of a shared processor P and a shared link L under the max-min notion of fairness and linear utility functions.

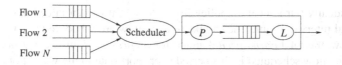

Fig. 2. The system model with a shared processor P and a shared link L.

4.1 System Model

In this system model, a set of N flows share a processor P and a link L, as shown in Fig. 2. Packets from each flow are processed by processor P first and then transmitted onto the output link L. Denote by R_L the peak bandwidth rate of link L and by R_P the peak processing rate of processor P. Packets of each flow await processing by the processor in an input buffer of infinite capacity, and then upon completion of the processing, await transmission on the output link in another buffer of infinite capacity. The joint allocation of the processing and bandwidth resources is accomplished by the scheduler which acts on the packets in the input buffers and appropriately orders them for processing by the processor. No scheduling action takes place after the processing; processed packets are received in the buffer between the processor and the link and are transmitted in a first-come-first-served fashion.

Denote by w_i the weight of flow i, $1 \leq i \leq N$, indicating the flow's relative rightful share of the resources.

4.2 Fluid-Flow Processor and Link Sharing

Denote by S the system illustrated in Fig. 2. We first consider fluid-flow traffic through system S, and describe an ideally fair allocation strategy called the *Fluid-flow Processor and Link Sharing (FPLS)* algorithm. FPLS is intended to serve the same purpose for system S as that served by GPS for a system with just a single shared link or a single shared processor [3, 4].

In GPS, it is assumed that traffic from each flow can be divided into infinitesimally small chunks, and each chunk has its demand for access to the link L depending on the size of the chunk. The GPS scheduler visits each active flow's queue in a round-robin fashion, and serves an infinitesimally small amount of data from each queue in such a way that during any infinitesimal interval of time, it can visit each queue at least once. In our study, this assumption is still valid, and we further assume that each infinitesimal chunk also has its demand for the processing time on the shared processor P.

At each time instant τ, the prime resource for each flow, according to Definition 4, can be determined based on its instantaneous demands for processing time and bandwidth. In addition, we assume that during each infinitesimal interval of time, $[\tau, \tau + \Delta\tau)$, the prime resource for each flow does not change.

Note that in GPS, it is guaranteed that during each infinitesimal interval of time, the chunks of each flow are scheduled in such a way that, for each flow, the total demand for bandwidth corresponding to the chunks of the flow scheduled in this period is proportional to the weight of the flow. Extending GPS to our case leads to the following:

Under the ideally fair allocation policy for system S, it is guaranteed that, during each infinitesimal interval of time, the chunks of each flow are scheduled in such a way that, for each flow, the total *normalized* demand for its *prime resource* corresponding to the chunks of the flow scheduled in this period is proportional to the weight of the flow. We refer to this as *Fluid-flow Processor and Link Sharing (FPLS)*. It can be readily verified that the FPLS strategy meets the FMRA principle described in Section 3.2.

4.3   Packet-by-Packet Processor and Link Sharing

It is apparent that FPLS is an ideally fair but unimplementable policy, in the same sense as GPS. In reality, network traffic is always packetized, and therefore, we next present a practical approximation of FPLS, called *Packet-by-packet Processor and Link Sharing (PPLS)*. The pseudo-code of PPLS is shown in Fig. 3.

The PPLS algorithm extends one of the most practical and simple scheduling strategies, Deficit Round Robin (DRR) [9], used in the allocation of bandwidth on a link. For each flow, the DRR algorithm maintains a *deficit counter (DC)*, which is incremented in each round by a predetermined quantity, *quantum*. When the scheduler visits one flow, it transmits the packets from this flow with a total length no more than the deficit counter associated with this flow. Upon the completion of a flow's service opportunity, its deficit counter is decremented by the total size of its packets scheduled in the round. It has been shown in [9] that, if the quantum of each flow is proportional to its weight, the relative fairness measure as defined in [8] can be bounded.

The PPLS algorithm approximates the ideal FPLS in a very similar fashion as DRR achieves an approximation of GPS. The PPLS scheduler maintains a linear list of the backlogged flows, *FlowList*. When the scheduler is initialized, *FlowList* is set to an empty list (line 2). For each flow, two variables, instead of one as in DRR, are maintained in the PPLS algorithm: a *processor deficit counter (PDC)* and a *link deficit counter (LDC)*. The link deficit counter is exactly the same as the deficit counter in DRR, which represents the deviation of the bandwidth received by the flow from its ideally fair share. The processor deficit counter, on the other hand, represents the deviation of the processing time allocated to the flow from its ideally fair share. Thus, each flow in PPLS is assigned two quantum values, a *processor quantum (PQ)* and a *link quantum (LQ)*.

When a new packet arrives, the *Enqueue* procedure is invoked (lines 3-10). If this packet comes from a new flow, the *Enqueue* procedure appends this flow to the end of the *FlowList* (line 7) and initializes both of its deficit counters to 0 (lines 8-9).

The *Dequeue* procedure (lines 11-38) functions as follows. It serves all flows in the *FlowList* in a round-robin fashion. When the scheduler visits flow i, it first increments each of the two deficit counters of this flow by the value of the corresponding quantum (lines 16-17). It then verifies whether or not these two deficit counters exceed their upper bounds respectively, and if they do, it resets them to the maximum possible values (lines 18-23). The rationale behind this bounding process will be discussed later in detail. After the deficit counters of flow i are updated, a sequence of packets from flow i are scheduled as long as the total length of these packets is smaller than the link deficit counter, and the total processing cost is smaller than the processing deficit counter, as in the **while** loop in lines 24-33. In the meantime, when a packet is scheduled, both deficit counters are decremented by the corresponding cost of this packet (lines 30-31). Finally, when the

```
1   Initialize:
2       FlowList ← NULL;

3   Enqueue: /* Invoked whenever a packet arrives */
4       p ← ArrivingPacket;
5       i ← Flow(p); /* Flow of packet p */
6       if (ExistsInFlowList(i) = FALSE) then
7           Append flow i to FlowList;
8           PDC_i ← 0;
9           LDC_i ← 0;
10      end if;

11  Dequeue: /* Always running */
12      while (TRUE) do
13          if (FlowList ≠ NULL) then
14          i ← HeadOfFlowList;
15          Remove i from FlowList;
16          PDC_i ← PDC_i + PQ_i;
17          LDC_i ← LDC_i + LQ_i;
18          if (PDC_i > maxPDC_i) then
19              PDC_i ← maxPDC_i;
20          end if;
21          if (LDC_i > maxLDC_i) then
22              LDC_i ← maxLDC_i;
23          end if;
24          while (QueueIsEmpty(i) = FALSE) do
25              p ← HeadOfLinePacketInQueue(i);
26              if (Size(p) > LDC_i OR
27                  ProcessingCost(p) > PDC_i) then
28                  break; /* escape from the inner while loop */
29              end if;
30              PDC_i ← PDC_i − ProcessingCost(p);
31              LDC_i ← LDC_i − Size(p);
32              Schedule p;
33          end while;
34          if (QueueIsEmpty(i) = FALSE) then
35              Append queue i to FlowList;
36          end if;
37          end if;
38      end while;
```

Fig. 3. Pseudo-code of the Packet-by-packet Processor and Link Sharing (PPLS) algorithm.

scheduler finishes serving a flow and the flow still remains backlogged, the scheduler places the flow back at the end of the *FlowList* (lines 34-36).

Recall that in DRR, for each flow, the quantum is set to be proportional to its weight, therefore, each flow receives in each round, on average, a service with total amount proportional to its weight. In this paper, the sum of a certain quantity over *all* flows is denoted by dropping the subscript for the flow in the notation. For example, w is the sum of the weights for all flows, i.e., $w = \sum_i w_i$. Therefore in DRR, we have,

$$\frac{Q_i}{w_i} = \frac{Q}{w}, \forall i.$$

Similarly, in PPLS, the quantum values of each flow are also proportional to its weight, i.e., $\forall i$,

$$\frac{PQ_i}{w_i} = \frac{PQ}{w} \tag{2}$$

$$\frac{LQ_i}{w_i} = \frac{LQ}{w} \tag{3}$$

Thus the amount of the shared resources each flow is entitled to utilize in each round is guaranteed to be, on average, proportional to its weight. In addition, the ratio of the sum of processing quanta for all flows, PQ, to the sum of link quanta for all flows, LQ, should also be equal to the ratio of the total amount of processing resource to the total amount of link resource in each round, i.e.,

$$\frac{PQ}{LQ} = \frac{R_P}{R_L}. \tag{4}$$

From (2), (3) and (4), it is apparent that,

$$\frac{PQ_i}{LQ_i} = \frac{R_P}{R_L}. \tag{5}$$

In other words, for each flow, the quantum value corresponding to a resource is proportional to the total amount of that resource.

Note that in PPLS, it is possible that the prime resource for flow i remains the same for a long period, and therefore, without the bounding procedure in lines 18-21, the deficit counter for the non-prime resource would reach a large value. For example, consider a case in which the prime resource for flow i has been the processing resource P for a long time and, as a result, the link deficit counter LDC_i is very large. Assume that at this point, the prime resource for flow i switches to the link resource L and, in addition, flow i now consumes almost no processing resource. In such a situation, flow i will be able to have a long sequence of packets scheduled because of its large link deficit counter LDC_i. This would significantly degrade the short-term fairness of the PPLS scheduler. For this reason, we choose to set a maximum threshold on the deficit counter for each resource, in case any specific resource has not been fully utilized for a long time. In cases where short-term fairness is not important, these thresholds may simply be set to infinity. A similar rationale may also be found in the context of fair scheduling in wireless networks where a maximum lag is applied when a flow has not fully utilized its share of the bandwidth [17].

It can be readily verified that if the processor resource P is sufficient for all flows, i.e., the processor resource P never becomes the prime resource for any flow, the PPLS strategy regresses into the DRR policy. It can also be readily verified that, like DRR, the per-packet computing complexity of the PPLS algorithm is $O(1)$, under the condition that for each flow i, $LQ_i > M_L$ and $PQ_i > M_P$ where M_L and M_P are the maximum packet size and the maximum packet processing cost, respectively. The proof of this work complexity is similar to that for DRR [9].

4.4   Fairness Analysis of PPLS

Our fairness analysis of PPLS is an extension of that in [9], and considers only the time intervals where all flows are backlogged.

The *cumulative processor allocation* of flow i during time interval (t_1, t_2), denoted by $CPA_i(t_1, t_2)$, is defined as the total amount of the processing resource allocated to flow i during interval (t_1, t_2), i.e., the sum of the processing costs associated with the packets scheduled during (t_1, t_2). The *normalized cumulative processor allocation*, $CPA_i^n(t_1, t_2)$, is defined as the cumulative processor allocation $CPA_i(t_1, t_2)$ normalized by the peak processing rate R_P, i.e.,

$$CPA_i^n(t_1, t_2) = \frac{CPA_i(t_1, t_2)}{R_P}.$$

The *cumulative link allocation* and the *normalized cumulative link allocation* of flow i during time interval (t_1, t_2), denoted by $CLA_i(t_1, t_2)$ and $CLA_i^n(t_1, t_2)$ respectively, are similarly defined, except that the resource considered is the link bandwidth.

Note that both the normalized cumulative link allocation and the normalized cumulative processor allocation are in units of time. Therefore, we are able to proceed to define the *normalized cumulative resource allocation* of flow i during time interval (t_1, t_2), denoted by $CRA_i^n(t_1, t_2)$, as the larger of the normalized cumulative processor and link allocations of flow i during (t_1, t_2). In other words,

$$CRA_i^n(t_1, t_2) = \max\{CPA_i^n(t_1, t_2), CLA_i^n(t_1, t_2)\}.$$

Now we can extend the definition of the fairness measure [8] as follows:

Definition 5. The *normalized fairness measure* $FM^n(t_1, t_2)$ is defined as the maximum value, amongst all pairs of flows (i, j) that are backlogged during time interval (t_1, t_2), of the normalized cumulative resource allocation $CRA_i^n(t_1, t_2)$. That is,

$$FM^n(t_1, t_2) = \max_{\forall (i,j)} \left| \frac{CRA_i^n(t_1, t_2)}{w_i} - \frac{CRA_j^n(t_1, t_2)}{w_j} \right|.$$

The *normalized fairness bound* FB^n is defined as the maximum value of the normalized fairness measure $FM^n(t_1, t_2)$ over all possible intervals (t_1, t_2).

Analogous to the case of a single shared resource, if a scheduling algorithm for the joint allocation of processing and bandwidth resources leads to a finite normalized fairness bound, one can conclude that this algorithm approximates the ideally fair allocation and achieves long-term fairness. The following theorem states this about the PPLS algorithm, the proof of which is omitted due to limited space.

Theorem 1. *The normalized fairness bound of PPLS is a finite constant.*

5   Simulation Results and Analysis

Our simulation model consists of 8 flows with equal weights sharing a processor P and a link L, as shown in Fig. 2. Five different scheduling policies including the PPLS algorithm are implemented.

- FCFS (First-Come First-Served): A simple FCFS scheme is used. The scheduling order is only determined by the packet timestamps.
- PPLS: When the PPLS algorithm is implemented, a FCFS strategy is used on the buffer between the processor P and the link L, since the order of the packets has already been determined by the PPLS algorithm.
- LDRR (Link Deficit Round Robin): A DRR algorithm in the allocation of only the link bandwidth is implemented (i.e., the original DRR).
- PDRR (Processor Deficit Round Robin): A DRR algorithm in the allocation of only the processing resources is implemented.
- DDRR (Double Deficit Round Robin): Two DRR schedulers are used. PDRR is used before the processor P and LDRR is used before the link L. Note that this is the only scheme in which a scheduler is implemented between the processor and the link.

In this study, we use real traffic recorded at an Internet gateway as the input traffic [13,18].[2] The traffic traces include the processing delay (in milliseconds) for each packet, along with the packet size (in bytes). For our experiments, we assume a fixed processing rate, and correspondingly convert the processing delay of each packet into processor cycles. For the sake of convenience and better comparison, we convert the processing delay of each packet in such a way that the average number of processor cycles needed per packet (in units of cycles) is numerically equal to the average size per packet (in units of bytes). For better illustration, the flows have been ordered in such way that the overall prime resource for flows 1 to 4 is the processor, and that for flows 5 to 8 is the link.

Fig. 4 shows the normalized cumulative resource allocation after a long run in the simulations. It is apparent that using the PPLS algorithm, in the time interval $(0, \tau)$ under consideration, the normalized cumulative resource allocation $\text{CRA}_i^n(0, \tau)$ for all flows i are very close, thus illustrating that fairness is achieved under the PPLS scheduling policy. Note that, as expected, the FCFS scheme has a very poor performance in terms of fairness. Regarding LDRR and PDRR, each can achieve fair distribution of the normalized cumulative allocation with respect to a certain resource, but not the overall normalized cumulative resource allocation. Take LDRR as an example. It achieves fair distribution of the normalized cumulative link allocation for all flows. Therefore, those flows with the processor as the prime resource, namely flows 2 to 4 in this case, result in a large value of the normalized cumulative processor allocation, thus failing to achieve fairness. PDRR functions exactly in the opposite way: it fairly distributes the normalized cumulative processor allocation among all flows, but those flows with the link as the

---

[2] Global Positioning System technology was used to precisely record the timestamp of each packet at each node. In the trace data, filtered IP headers were examined to track the same packet at different nodes. The difference between the timestamps of the same packet at adjacent nodes was computed as the delay. The link speed connecting these nodes was taken into consideration so that the transmission delay of each packet was removed from the recorded delay. Note that this delay was still the sum of the processing delay and the queueing delay. However, it was noticed that for traffic in a specific direction, the queue occupancy was never above 1 packet, and this eliminates the queueing delay and validates the use of this delay as the pure processing delay.

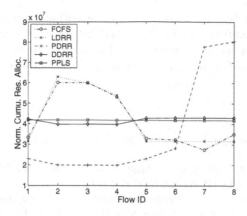

Fig. 4. The simulation results, using gateway traffic traces.

prime resource (flows 7 and 8) receive a large normalized cumulative link allocation, also failing to achieve fairness.

Note that in this study, the DDRR scheme performs close to the PPLS algorithm. This can be attributed to the fact that in these real traces, the demands of each flow for the processing and bandwidth resources are roughly balanced. However, it can be noticed that the DDRR scheme allocates resources fairly to all flows with the same prime resource, but favors the flows with the "final" resource as the prime resource. This difference becomes more apparent if a flow has a dominant demand for one resource in comparison to another, as might happen during a denial-of-service attack. In addition, the PPLS algorithm only needs one scheduler in real implementation while the DDRR needs two.

6 Concluding Remarks

Research in fair allocation of the bandwidth resource has been active for decades. Traffic flows, however, encounter multiple resources, including bandwidth, processor, buffer and power, when they traverse the network, and the bandwidth resource is not always the sole bottleneck causing network congestion. In this paper, we consider a set of shared resources which are *essential and related* and present the *Principle of Fair Multiple Resource Allocation*, or the FMRA principle, which defines what is fair in the joint allocation of these resources. We further apply the FMRA principle into a system consisting of a shared processor and a shared link, and propose a practical and *provably-fair* algorithm, the *Packet-by-packet Processor and Link Sharing (PPLS)*, for the joint allocation of the processor and bandwidth resources.

Even though we have focused on the joint allocation of the processing and bandwidth resources, the FMRA principle and the design of the PPLS algorithm can be similarly applied to systems with other kinds of essential and related resources, such as in a wireless system where processor, link and power are all shared. In this case, for each flow, three quanta and three deficit counters are needed. The basis of the algorithm, however, remains the same, i.e., a packet from a flow can be scheduled only if all three deficit counters of this flow are large enough. It is our hope that this paper will facilitate future research in the design of *provably* fair strategies for resource allocation in computer networks.

References

1. Bertsekas, D.P., Gallager, R.: Data Networks. 2nd edn. Prentice Hall, Upper Saddle River, NJ (1991)
2. Demers, A., Keshav, S., Shenker, S.: Analysis and simulation of a fair queueing algorithm. In: Proc. ACM SIGCOMM, Austin, TX (1989) 1–12
3. Parekh, A.K., Gallager, R.G.: A generalized processor sharing approach to flow control in integrated service networks – the single node case. In: Proc. IEEE INFOCOM, Florence, Italy (1992) 915–924
4. Keshav, S.: An Engineering Approach to Computer Networking: ATM Network, the Internet, and the Telephone Network. Addison-Wesley, Reading, MA (1997)
5. Kelly, F.: Charging and rate control for elastic traffic. Europ. Trans. Telecom. **8** (1997) 33–37
6. Cao, Z., Zegura, E.W.: Utility max-min: An application-oriented bandwidth allocation scheme. In: Proc. IEEE INFOCOM, New York, NY (1999) 793–801
7. Kleinrock, L.: Queueing System. Volume 2, Computer Applications. Wiley, New York, NY (1976)
8. Golestani, S.J.: A self-clocked fair queueing scheme for broadband applications. In: Proc. IEEE INFOCOM, Toronto, Canada (1994) 636–646
9. Shreedhar, M., Varghese, G.: Efficient fair queuing using deficit round-robin. IEEE/ACM Trans. Networking **4** (1996) 375–385
10. Bennett, J.C.R., Zhang, H.: WF^{2}Q: Worst-case fair weighted fair queueing. In: Proc. IEEE INFOCOM, San Francisco, CA (1996) 120–128
11. Kanhere, S.S., Sethu, H., Parekh, A.B.: Fair and efficient packet scheduling using elastic round robin. IEEE Trans. Parall. Distr. Syst. **13** (2002) 324–336
12. Blanquer, J.M., Özden, B.: Fair queuing for aggregated multiple links. In: Proc. ACM SIGCOMM, San Diego, CA (2001) 189–197
13. Mochalski, K., Micheel, J., Donnelly, S.: Packet delay and loss at the Auckland Internet access path. In: Proc. Passive Active Measure. Workshop, Fort Collins, CO (2002)
14. Raghunathan, V., Ganeriwal, S., Schurgers, C., Srivastava, M.: E^{2}WFQ: An energy efficient fair scheduling policy for wireless systems. In: Proc. Int. Symp. Low Power Electr. Design, Monterey, CA (2002) 30–35
15. Zhou, Y., Sethu, H.: Toward end-to-end fairness: A framework for the allocation of multiple prioritized resources. In: Proc. IEEE Perf. Comput. Commun. Conf., Phoenix, AZ (2003)
16. Blake, S., Black, D., Carlson, M., Davies, E., Wang, Z., Weiss, W.: An Architecture for Differentiated Services. (1998) IETF RFC 2475, http://www.ietf.org/rfc/rfc2475.txt
17. Lu, S., Bhargavan, V., Srikant, R.: Fair scheduling in wireless packet networks. IEEE/ACM Trans. Networking **7** (1999) 473–489
18. WAND Research Group: Auckland-VI trace data. http://pma.nlanr.net/Traces/long
19. Lu, S., Bharghavan, V., Srikant, R.: Fair scheduling in wireless packet networks. In: Proc. ACM SIGCOMM, Cannes, France (1997) 63–74

Distributed Admission Control for Heterogeneous Multicast with Bandwidth Guarantees

Sudeept Bhatnagar[1], Badri Nath[1], and Arup Acharya[2]

[1] Dept. of Computer Science,
Rutgers University
Piscataway, NJ 08854, USA,
{sbhatnag,badri}@cs.rutgers.edu
[2] IBM Thomas J.Watson Research Center
P.O.Box 704
Yorktown Heights, NY 10598, USA,
arup@us.ibm.com

Abstract. Many group communication applications have real-time constraints. Since multicast serves as a natural framework for such applications, it is desirable to support quality of service (QoS) guarantees for multicast. Limiting the amount of processing inside the network core has been recognized as a key for any QoS solution to be scalable and accordingly any QoS solution for multicast should not require core routers to perform extensive per-flow operations. We propose an architecture to implement distributed admission control for multicast flows with heterogeneous user requirements while not requiring core routers to perform any admission control. Our admission control framework guarantees that a request is only admitted if there is sufficient bandwidth available and only requires the edge routers of a domain to take admission decisions. An intra-domain signaling mechanism is used in conjunction with the admission control framework to install the forwarding state inside the network core. We show that using our architecture, the requirements for both installing and maintaining the forwarding state in core routers, are similar to that in a best-effort multicast, thus, providing the QoS control plane functionality with negligible additional complexity inside network core.

1 Introduction

Multicast is a natural framework for group communication. Since a number of applications with real-time constraints (e.g., streaming multimedia, network games) fall under the purview of group communications, supporting Quality of Service(QoS) for multicast traffic is desirable. Differentiated services [5] has emerged as a scalable paradigm to support QoS because it requires limited functions in core routers. Likewise, alleviating core routers of excessive operations is a key to having a scalable solution to provide QoS for multicast where end

K. Jeffay, I. Stoica, and K. Wehrle (Eds.): IWQoS 2003, LNCS 2707, pp. 115–134, 2003.

users might have heterogeneous requirements. However, no heterogeneous multicast QoS framework has gained universal acceptance because of the complexity introduced by user heterogeneity[19].

Admission control is a necessary component of any QoS framework in order to ensure that resources are not over-allocated. The existing admission control solutions for heterogeneous multicast have significant limitations because they either require per-flow state maintenance [7] or rely on centralized bandwidth broker [9]. A detailed discussion of existing solutions is given later (section 7 – Related Work).

In this paper, we propose a distributed admission control framework to support heterogeneous multicast. We aim at supporting a service akin to the *Virtual Leased Line Service* [12] of diffserv (also called premium service [18]) where an end user is assured of a fixed amount of bandwidth from ingress to egress points. To support such a service, it is mandatory that the admission control mechanism be able to *guarantee* that the bandwidth on any link in the domain is never over-allocated (i.e., it should guarantee *zero-false-positives*). Moreover, the architecture should be scalable in number of flows and routers, be robust and gracefully handle failures, and should allow a high network utilization.

To our knowledge, there is no distributed admission control framework which can support heterogeneous multicast and which does not require active participation of core routers in admission control process. We provide the first distributed solution to this problem and prove that our admission control mechanism, which does not require resource management or state maintenance at core routers, guarantees the zero-false-positives property. We provide two possible admission control solutions: one solution keeps the core entirely stateless but edge routers have to store more per-group information and the other solution requires core routers to keep the same amount of per-group state as for best-effort multicast (with the same amount of processing as best-effort multicast), while the edge router state requirements are simplified.

A very important implication of using our admission control architecture is that the scalability of the framework is inherently linked to that of the underlying multicast data forwarding framework. If the corresponding data dissemination mechanism requires rate information at forwarding interfaces, our architecture can provide that information. In such a case, the state maintenance requirements at the core routers are identical to that in best-effort multicast. In fact, the core routers could maintain soft-state QoS semantics by coupling the QoS-state with the multicast forwarding state, thus eliminating the need to process QoS-state refreshing messages. If the forwarding mechanism does not require forwarding rate information at the core, our architecture allows for an entirely core-stateless framework. In either case, the scalability of the multicast QoS framework is primarily determined by the data forwarding mechanism. Thus, using our architecture, any network domain which offers a best-effort multicast service, can provide multicast QoS with assured bandwidth at *almost no additional cost*.

2   Network Model

For the purpose of this paper, a network is assumed to be a collection of edge and core routers. Edge routers act as ingress and egress points for all traffic. Core routers switch the traffic between other routers of the domain. The edge nodes of the domain are assumed to be aware of the network topology. This information is available using the common routing protocols like OSPF [17]. It is noteworthy that this is not a valid assumption in the conventional end-to-end model because then it would entail knowing the entire Internet topology. Our solution is meant to operate on an *intra-domain edge-to-edge* basis. We aim at supporting a guaranteed bandwidth service for heterogeneous multicast traffic. Thus, our admission control algorithm is meant to guarantee the *zero-false-positive (ZFP)* property, i.e., a request is admitted only if there are enough resources to support its rate requirement.

For ease of exposition, we assume a single source multicast session instead of one having multiple senders. However, our admission control solution is equally applicable to multicast with shared tree like those in CBT [1] and PIM-SM [10].

An end user signals the rate requirement using some soft-state signaling mechanism like RSVP [7]. We assume a generic request signaling mechanism where the reservation message is termed Reserve(G,b) where G is the group to join and b is the amount of bandwidth that the user wants. Effectively, this decouples the intra-domain signaling from the inter-domain signaling. The domain processes Reserve message entirely on edge routers and the core routers use minimal intra-domain signaling for the purpose of installing QoS-state (if required). This approach of overlay-based reservation signaling has been used in [3,23] for unicast flows. However, in this paper, the intra-domain signaling for heterogeneous multicast is novel and has an important implication in alleviating the core routers from excessive processing.

Our admission control framework is independent of the underlying data-delivery mechanism. Similarly, routing a reservation request is an independent problem and any existing multicast QoS routing protocols like [14] can be used to route a request. This paper assumes a simple reverse shortest path forwarding technique to route requests in the domain. All requests are assumed to be forwarded toward the source and there is a single edge router through which the source could be reached.

3   Requirements for Admission Control

Before describing the admission control algorithm, we discuss the important properties that we want our solution to possess and the performance measures to evaluate the algorithm.

3.1   Essential Properties

The admission control framework is required to have the following properties:

- **Zero False Positives (ZFP):** If a request is admitted, there must be enough resources to support it. Thus, if an edge router decides to admit a request for b units of bandwidth on a path with links $l_1, l_2, \ldots, l_m$, then the available capacity (after accounting for existing reservations) on each of $l_1, l_2, \ldots, l_m$ must not be less than b.
- **Distributed Solution:** An admission control framework relying on a central server is neither robust nor scalable. In fact, even events as frequent as link failures and congestion could cause the server to be inaccessible from the edge routers even though the server might be working perfectly and when sufficient resources were available. Hence, we want a serverless solution, i.e., the edge routers should take the acceptance/rejection decisions *on their own* without intervention of a central server in any capacity.

3.2   Performance Criteria

While the above are the desired properties of an admission control framework, the e *ectiveness* of a solution is measured using the following criteria:

- **Response Time:** The response time to a request is defined as the duration between the instant the request arrives at an edge router of the domain and the instant an acceptance or rejection decision is taken for the request. Having a minimal response time is desirable from the perspective of the end user.
- **Utilization:** The solution should aim at maximizing the resource utilization of the system. Ideally a request must not be denied by an edge router if there is sufficient bandwidth on the path it would take. Note that, ZFP property in a serverless distributed system could be ensured by *denying all requests* while having a minimal response time. Utilization maximization criteria guards against such pessimism.

4   Admission Control Algorithm

We separate the intra-domain signaling involved in sending reservation request and installing forwarding entry at core router interfaces, from the actual decision of whether or not to admit a request. Thus, when an edge router receives a reservation request, it takes the admission decision for the entire domain, and then sends the signaling packets inside the domain where the core routers perform group management *without having to worry about admission control or resource management.* This keeps the core of the network simple while requiring operations similar to the control plane in best-effort multicast.

We first describe the resource management and admission control portion of our architecture and then the intra-domain signaling which installs multicast forwarding state inside the core routers.

4.1   Resource Management

The node taking an admission decision should know whether there are sufficient resources to admit a request or not. In prior work [2], we described a simple mechanism for distributed admission control for unicast flows in a core-stateless network. We treat edge routers as an *overlay token ring* residing on the border of the domain. For each link in the network, the edge routers pass around a token in the overlay ring and use it to partition the link bandwidth amongst themselves in fair proportion (determined by their traffic load using the link).[1] Effectively, we provide a *virtual network* view to each edge routers while guaranteeing that the sum of shares of all edge routers using a link does not exceed its capacity. The edge routers can independently take admission decisions on each link, based on their virtual network views.

Here we describe an improved version of the resource management portion described in [2]. The modifications and their original versions would be clear as we describe the algorithm.

Consider a single link l with capacity C_l and a set of N edge routers $E_1, \ldots, E_N$ which source some traffic passing through l. Let the amount of traffic from router E_j that uses l be t_j (ideally this should be t_{j_l}, however, we omit the subscript l for clarity). Let the aggregate traffic from all routers intended for l be T which is defined as $\sum_{i=1}^{N} t_i$. The routers use token passing to update their respective views of the aggregate traffic T with the token circulation starting at E_1 and going in order $E_2, E_3, \ldots, E_N, E_1, \ldots$. The time from the initiation of token circulation is divided into cycles where k^{th} cycle starts at the time when the token leaves E_1 and ends when E_1 receives that token after the circulation.

Let t_j^k represent the value reported by router E_j in the kth token circulation cycle. If E_j receives T' as the value in the token in the kth token cycle, then it updates it to $T' - t_j^{k-1} + t_j^k$. Let the last value of T seen in the token by user E_i be denoted as $\widetilde{T_i}$ and let $last_i$ represent the cycle number in which E_i last saw the token. Under these conditions we proved the following theorem in [2]:

Theorem 1. *If the share of link l that a router E_i gets, is not more than* $\dfrac{C_l . min(t_i^{last_i}, t_i^{last_i - 1})}{\widetilde{T_i}}$, *the ZFP property is satis e d.*

Using theorem 1 the routers can determine their *own* shares of the link bandwidth *without knowing the actual shares of other users*. Each router E_i maintains its current traffic load $Traffic_i$ using a link l. It has two variable t_i^{last} and t_i^{last-1} storing the values that it reported in the token during the last two token cycles and a third variable $\widetilde{T_i}$ which stores the last aggregate traffic value it saw in the token.

---

[1] In general, a single token can carry information for multiple links. Not all links need to be regulated by token-passing, e.g., an access link which is only going to be used by a particular router. There can be multiple overlay rings, potentially one ring per link with only the routers using a particular link being a part of the corresponding ring.

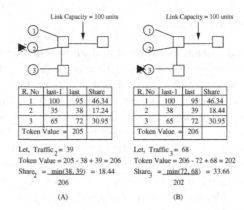

R. No	last-1	last	Share
1	100	95	46.34
2	35	38	17.24
3	65	72	30.95
Token Value =	205		

Let, $Traffic_2 = 39$
Token Value = 205 - 38 + 39 = 206
$Share_2 = \dfrac{min(38,39)}{206} = 18.44$

(A)

R. No	last-1	last	Share
1	100	95	46.34
2	38	39	18.44
3	65	72	30.95
Token Value =	206		

Let, $Traffic_3 = 68$
Token Value = 206 - 72 + 68 = 202
$Share_3 = \dfrac{min(72,68)}{202} = 33.66$

(B)

Fig. 1. Three edge routers 1,2,3 share a link with capacity 100 units among themselves. The black arrowhead represents the router which just received the token. The tables in the figure show the traffic values that the routers reported in last and (last-1) cycles. The *Share* column represents the share that the router receives at that instant. The token only carries the aggregate value denoted as Token Value. (A) Router 2 received the token. Till this point of time its share was $\frac{min(35,38)}{203}.100 = 17.24$ *units* (based on the token contents when it last sent the token). If its current traffic value ($Traffic_2$) is 39, it updates the token value to 205-38+39 = 206 units. Its new share is $\frac{min(38,39)}{206}.100 = 18.44$ *units*. (B) Router 3 receives the token with aggregate traffic 206. If its current traffic ($Traffic_3$) is 68 units, it updates token contents as 206-72+68=202 units. Its new share is $\frac{min(72,68)}{202}.100 = 33.66 units$

On receiving the token, edge router E_i updates the values of variables as follows:

$$
\begin{aligned}
token.T &\leftarrow token.T - t_i^{last} + Traffic_i \\
\tilde{T}_i &\leftarrow token.T \\
t_i^{last-1} &\leftarrow t_i^{last} \\
t_i^{last} &\leftarrow Traffic_i \\
Share_i &\leftarrow \frac{C_l \cdot min(t_i^{last-1}, t_i^{last})}{\tilde{T}_i}
\end{aligned}
$$

where $token.T$ is the aggregate traffic value stored in the token and $Share_i$ is the share of router i. An example of this bandwidth partitioning is shown in figure 1.

This algorithm partitions a link's bandwidth among the edge routers in proportion to their traffic loads on that link. It is easy to see that the solution imposes a notion of *delayed fairness*. The routers continue to use shares based on the *minimum* of their last two reported traffic values. Thus, if a routers traffic load has increased instantaneously, it may have to wait for two token cycles before it can claim its fair share according to the new traffic load.

Also, this mechanism is performed for all the links in the domain thus partitioning *each* link's bandwidth among the edge routers in proportion to their fair share. On receiving a request, the ingress router 1) Finds out the path it is going to take, 2) Determines how much additional bandwidth is to be reserved on each link on that path (taking into account the already reserved bandwidth) and 3) Takes an admission decision based on its own shares of the links and the bandwidth that it has already allocated from its share. Since the sum of shares of all routers can not be more than the link capacity (as per the theorem), the above mechanism *guarantees* that a reservation request is only admitted if there is enough bandwidth to support it.

4.2   Sharing Violation

The resource partitioning and admission control algorithms ensure that the ZFP property is not violated as long as routers limit their shares limited as above. However, the routers may not be able to limit their allocations to their shares in the following case:

Consider two edge routers E_1 and E_2 sharing a link l. E_1 senses that its share on the link should increase (due to increased traffic load) and accordingly increments the traffic value $token.T$ in the token. On receiving the token, user E_2 finds that its share $Share_2$ has reduced because of increase in $token.T$. If E_2's has already allocated more bandwidth than $Share_2$ to flows (based on its share during last token cycle), there is no way for E_2 to reduce its share unless it revokes some allocations. This is not a problem if the network policy allows for revocation of allocated resources [25]. However, the system cannot continue to operate as described above without violating ZFP property if the network policy does not allow pre-emption of allocated bandwidth.

In this situation, the router which sensed imminent over-allocation (E_2 in the above example), sets a *Mode Change Flag (MCF)* for the concerned link in the token. In the prior work, a set MCF was was used to shift to an alternate admission control strategy where token contents were changed to the *actual allocation* on the link and only the router which had the token could test its buffered requests before updating and passing token to the next router [2]. Effectively, the token was used as a semaphore among edge routers to control the common resource (link bandwidth). The disadvantage of that strategy was that the response time grew in proportion to the number of edge routers. Here we suggest an alternate strategy which can be used in case of imminent over-allocation.

A set MCF serves as an indication to *freeze* the current link shares. Thus, on seeing the MCF set, the routers fix their link shares to their current shares and are not allowed to increase it. However, if a router wishes to reduce its share (e.g., when its load on the corresponding link reduces), it is free to do so. If the traffic load on the link reduces below some threshold (x% of link capacity), then an edge router resets the MCF and the normal operation resumes (where routers can increase their traffic load values).

The gain in this strategy is in terms of response time. Using token as a semaphore (as in our prior work), linked the response time to the resource management framework that the token provides. The strategy described here *decou-*

ples the resource management framework entirely from the admission decision process.

Our prior work treated utilization as the key performance criterion and hence advocated request buffering and using token for controlling access to a link. Request buffering allows us to not reject requests unless the token contents indicate insufficient bandwidth. Thus, the only cases of false-negatives occur when a flow releases its allocated bandwidth and its edge router has not yet updated the token contents to show the additional bandwidth. Here, the response time is minimal, however, this gain comes at a cost in terms of utilization. It is easy to see that once the routers freeze their allocations, the partitioning becomes independent of future traffic profiles (until MCF is reset). Thus, if a sudden major deviation from the mean traffic loads causes the MCF to be set, it might lead to unfair bandwidth partitioning, thus causing false-negatives to occur at lower utilization.

In summary, in our prior work, we compromised on response time to attain a higher utilization when MCF was set. Here, we compromise on utilization while gaining in response time with an added benefit of decoupling the resource management framework from the admission decision process. Thus, the utilization achieved by this algorithm is significantly dependent on the effectiveness of the dynamics of the resource management algorithm. This is the key issue evaluated in our simulations later in the paper.

5   Signaling

For the following discussion we consider a single group G with a single source S. A reservation request Reserve(G,b) (reserve bandwidth b for group G), arrives at egress router E. The ingress router I through which all traffic from S enters the domain, is assumed as the root of the intra-domain distribution tree for G. The term *reservation tree* refers to the amount of bandwidth reserved for G on each of its distribution tree branches. The reserved bandwidth for G on an outgoing interface i of a router r is denoted as $B_{ri}(G)$ and the maximum reserved bandwidth over all outgoing interfaces at router r is denoted by $B_r(G)$. The headers of signaling packets are assumed to include IP router alert option [13] so as to allow intermediate routers to process them. The previous section tells us how to determine whether or not to admit a request on a link. However, there are two other important issues to be addressed: 1) Determining how much to reserve on which link and 2) how to install the correct forwarding state inside the network domain (if required).

5.1   Determining Bandwidth Requirements

There are two possible solutions to determine the amount of bandwidth to be reserved on each link, upon receiving a request:

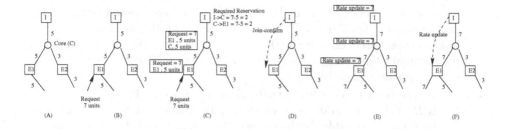

Fig. 2. A multicast group with ingress router I and one core router C. $E1$ and $E2$ are two egress routers which have some group members downstream. (A) Initial reservation tree. The numbers on links correspond to the forwarding reserved rates on the corresponding interfaces. (B) $E1$ receives a new request for 7 units. (C) $E1$ adds $(E1, 5$ units$)$ to the request packet. 5 units is the current rate that it receives. Similarly core router C adds $(C, 5$units$)$. I computes the extra reservation required to serve this request. (D) I sends a Join-confirm to $E1$. (E) $E1$ updates its interface rate and sends a Rate-update packet with 7 units bandwidth. C and I update their interface bandwidths using Rate-update. (F) I echoes back Rate-update packet to $E1$.

1. **Edge Routers Store the State:** In this case, the edge routers store the entire per-group reservation tree for each group rooted at themselves. Determining the bandwidth required on each link is straightforward. On receiving a reservation request Reserve(G,b), E tunnels the request to I, which looks up the reservation tree for G and determines the additional amount of bandwidth required on each of the links to satisfy the request. It could then take the admission decision based on its bandwidth share on each of those links and notify E of the decision.

   Storing per-group state at edge routers is an extra burden, but has two key benefits: 1) The response time to the reservation request is minimal and 2) State consistency requirements are significantly reduced (details in section 5.5).

   Lastly, in conjunction with a data dissemination mechanism like that described in [24], this type of storage architecture could provide an entirely core-stateless multicast framework with bandwidth guarantees.

2. **Core Routers Store the State:** An alternative to having edge routers store entire reservation tree, is to let the core routers store aggregate forwarding rate per group. As observed in [11], it is easy to store the pair (interface-id, forwarding rate) for each outgoing interface instead of just storing the interface-id without much increase in storage requirements. Since most data dissemination methods require each router to have information about the outgoing interfaces for each group, having the core routers store the forwarding rates does not put a heavy burden on them, if we ensure that they do not have to process or update the forwarding rate value too often.

   In such a model, determining the amount of bandwidth to be reserved on different links becomes somewhat complicated. The reason for this complication is that in heterogeneous multicast, a request for b units of bandwidth arriving at E *does not* mean that we need to reserve b units of bandwidth on the entire I to E path. The amount of bandwidth required on different links, varies based on the existing reservation tree. We use the following intra-domain signaling protocol to help I in determining the bandwidth requirements on the path:

- E receives a request `Reserve(G,b)` on interface i. (figure 2(B)).
- If $B_E(G) \geq b$, it adds interface-id, bandwidth pair (i, b) for the group to its forwarding table. It then drops the request packet (the tree further up is already established).
- Otherwise, it adds the tuple $(Request - id, E, B_E(G))$ to the request packet and forwards it towards I. $Request - id$ is a unique local sequence number generated by E. E stores $(Request - id, G, b, i)$ in a table of pending requests.(figure 2(C))
- Each core router c adds $(c, B_c(G))$ to the packet and forwards it towards I. (figure 2(C))
- When I receives the request packet, it knows how much is reserved on each distribution link along the request path and can determine the extra bandwidth to be reserved on each link. (figure 2(C))

5.2   Installing Forwarding State

If I decides not to admit the request, it sends a `Request-deny(Request-id,G,b)` message to E which clears the corresponding entry in its pending requests table and forwards the deny message downstream.

However, if I decides to admit a request with bandwidth requirement b, the correct forwarding state has to be installed in the network to allow the data forwarding mechanism to work properly. The kind of state required to be installed in the network is governed by both the requirements of the data dissemination technique and by the state storage techniques described above.

In case when the per-group reservation tree is stored at the edge routers and the data dissemination technique does not require any forwarding information in core, then no special signaling is required.

However, in case the core routers are required to store the forwarding rates at the interfaces, the following signaling protocol is used:

- I sends a `Join-confirm(Request-id, G,b)` message to E. The `Join-confirm` message encapsulates the `Reserve` message which already contains the path which it took from E to I. (figure 2(D))
- I looks-up the pending request table using $Request - id$, and updates its forwarding rate $B_{Ei}(G)$ on the corresponding interface i. If $B_{Ei}(G) > B_E(G)$, then it sets $B_E(G)$ to $B_{Ei}(G)$. It then sends a `Rate-update (G,b)` packet towards I along the path reported in `Join-confirm`. (figure 2(E))
- Each core router c on the path which receives a `Rate-update(G,b)` on interface i updates $B_{ci}(G)$ to b. If the new $B_{ci}(G) > B_c(G)$, then it updates $B_c(G)$ to $B_{ci}(G)$. It then forwards the `Rate-update(G,b)` packet upstream. (figure 2(E))

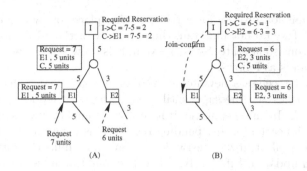

Fig. 3. A multicast group with ingress router I and one core router C. $E1$ and $E2$ are two egress routers which have some group members downstream. (A) Initial reservation tree. $E1$ receives a new request for 7 units, constructs Reserve packet as in figure 2 and sends it. I determines the extra reservation on $I \to C$ and $C \to E1$ links. Meanwhile another request for 6 units of bandwidth arrives at $E2$. (B) $E2$ adds ($E2$, 3 units) to the request packet; core router C adds (C, 5 units). I computes the extra reservation required to serve this request on $I \to C$ as 1 unit. Since the previous request with 7 unit bandwidth has already been accepted (only the interface rate has not yet been updated at C), this results in a spurious allocation of 1 unit of bandwidth on $I \to C$.

- On receiving `Rate-update(G,b)` message, I tunnels back the `Rate-update(G,b)` message to E. This allows E to be sure that the interface forwarding rates on all core routers have been properly set (that the `Rate-update(G,b)` message was not dropped) (figure 2(F)). If E does not receive `Rate-update(G,b)` as an acknowledgment, it resends the packet.

It is easy to see that for a single request arrival, the above process would correctly install the forwarding rates at all interfaces on the path of that request, irrespective of the original reservation tree. This follows directly from the processing of `Rate-update(G,b)` message. Moreover, the state maintenance operation at the core routers is of similar magnitude as in best-effort multicast and is updated only when a new request arrives/departs (corresponding to the group management activities for join/leave). Thus, the scalability of this architecture (with type of state storage semantics) is inherently similar to that of best-effort multicast.

5.3   Atomicity Problems

The signaling described above works correctly in case of a single request. However, the possible violation in "atomicity" of request admission needs to be handled by the signaling protocol. A request admission is complete in case the request is admitted only when 1)I sends a `Join-confirm` to E 2) E sends the corresponding `Rate-update` 3) All core routers receive and process `Rate-update` and 4) E gets back the echoed `Rate-update` message. If the request is denied the admission process is completed only when E receives the `Request-deny` message.

While the admission process for a request takes place, other requests to join G might arrive. If we do not maintain the atomicity of the admission process, we could have inconsistent state. Such an example is shown in figure 3. Our solution to this problem is as follows:

Whenever I receives a new Reserve(G,b) message and it decides to admit the flow, it caches the message until it gets the corresponding Rate-update message from E. In the meantime, if it receives a new request Reserve(G,b'), it first checks its cache for any pending reservations for group G. When it finds an entry to that effect, it can easily deduce on which links the forwarding rates have not been updated. Effectively, this is like maintaining a *partial reservation tree* for which state change is in progress. Thus, it could locally correct the required bandwidth on the path that the second request took. The cached entry is removed from the table once it gets the corresponding Rate-update message.

5.4   Leaving a Group

The signaling when a user leaves a group is as follows:

- On receiving a Leave(G,b) on an interface i, E checks if $B_E(G) > B_{Ei}(G)$. If so, it deletes the forwarding interface entry and drops the Leave(G,b) packet. (Because the upstream rate that it receives is required for other interfaces as well.)
- If $B_{Ei}(G) > B_{Ej}(G)$ for all other interfaces j, then it updates $B_E(G)$ to the maximum bandwidth $B_{Ej}(G)$ among other interfaces. It then deletes the forwarding entry for i, adds $(E, B_E(G))$ to the packet and forwards the Leave(G,b) message upstream.
- When a core router c receives Leave(G,b) on interface i, it does exactly the same as E.
- When I receives a Leave(G,b) message, the message contains the amount of bandwidth b that the Leave(G,b) request is freeing and the maximum amount required on links on its path after the removal. I can determine the extra bandwidth freed up on link to router r as $max\{0, b - B_r(G)\}$. It can then add that bandwidth to the available pool for new requests on those links.
- I sends a Leave-confirm(G,b) message to E.
- E sends a Rate-update(G,b) message towards E. All core routers receiving Rate-update(G,b) processes it identically as described for join.
- I tunnels back the Rate-update(G,b) message to I as an acknowledgment that all routers have updated their forwarding rates.
- If the group communication terminates, the egress routers could send an explicit Terminate(G) message towards I. All core routers along the path could eliminate group state.
- In case the group communication continues, but without QoS guarantees, then only the edge routers based overlay need to time out and remove QoS state. The QoS state in core router does not count towards the reservation anyway and thus could timeout as a normal multicast routing entry. In such

a case, to ensure that such a multicast session is serviced in a best-effort fashion, the ingress router has the responsibility of properly policing and marking the packets.

It is important to note that the atomicity problems described for two simultaneous request arrivals (Join-Join Conflict) could also occur with respect to Leave messages. In order to avoid such Join-Leave or Leave-Leave conflicts, the ingress router I is required to cache the Leave message as well until the leave transaction is complete. Such a cached entry serves to update the partial reservation tree that is in process of being updated. The cached entry is expunged once the router receives the Rate-update message.

5.5 Discussion

If the end-to-end reservation protocol is based on soft-state (e.g., RSVP), then the edge routers could just tunnel the refresh messages among themselves. The key advantage of using our approach is that the core routers *do not have to process refresh messages*. This eliminates the prime complexity introduced by soft-state reservation protocols in the core. Note that, processing required in initial state installation is approximately $1m\ sec$ (for RSVP) and the amount of time to process a RSVP refresh message is approximately $0.6m\ sec$ [21]. The savings in terms of not having to process refresh messages are significant when we consider that periodic refresh messages are issued by all receivers for all groups. Thus, inspite of having per-group forwarding state available at the core routers, avoiding request processing has its own benefits.

In case of group termination, having an edge router explicitly sending tear down message to notify the core routers to clear the forwarding state is beneficial with respect to state storage. However, it is not necessary from utilization point of view because the state inside the network core does not have any value from the perspective of resource management and it does not play an active part in admission decision. In fact, the forwarding entry could be maintained and timeout in exactly the same fashion as a normal multicast routing entry and not affect the admission decisions of flows. This allows us to retain the soft-state semantics despite not explicitly having to process QoS-state refresh messages in the core. This gives an additional robustness benefit in case of node failures where the explicit tear-down message could not reach all the intended routers.

The model requiring edge routers to maintain reservation trees has fewer consistency problems than one with reservation tree distributed across the network. This fundamental trade-off exists in any architecture which distributes state in order to share burden. Thus, if the relevant state is stored at only one node, then the consistency semantics with respect to that state could be locally handled. In case the edge router stores the entire reservation trees, on core router failure, it would automatically know which subtrees have become unusable and it could easily add the released bandwidth to the available bandwidth pool. On the other hand, if the reservation tree is distributed and the edge router only stores the currently active partial reservation trees, then a core router failure could lead

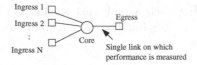

Fig. 4. The topology on which simulations are run. There are N ingress routers connected to one core router. The core router is connected to the egress router by a single link with 20000 units of bandwidth.

to unused and wasted bandwidth in all the subtrees unless a special consistency maintenance protocol is used. Such a protocol would have to notify the edge routers about the released bandwidth in different subtrees rooted at the failed node, corresponding to different groups. In fact, even if we allow core router to take local admission decision based on aggregate state, this consistency maintenance protocol is required. Due to this, we believe that the benefits of having simpler consistency maintenance are significant enough to allow edge routers to store entire reservation trees if the storage overhead is acceptable.

6   Simulation

In this section, we evaluate our admission control algorithm using simulations. Our simulations are aimed at testing the performance of the admission control algorithm with respect to link utilization that it can achieve. In case of heterogeneous multicast, utilization is also a function of the QoS routing algorithm. For example, if the routing algorithm just uses a shortest path tree, then there might be some links which remain under-utilized despite having sufficient capacity available on links on alternate paths (other than shortest path). Since our admission control algorithm is independent of the corresponding QoS routing algorithm, we evaluate the utilization that we could achieve on a single link assuming that the routing algorithm routes a sufficient number of requests through the link. The topology we use in our simulations (shown in figure 4) has a single link l connecting an edge router with a core router and having 20000 units of bandwidth. The edge routers contending for a share on l are all connected to the core router with links of 100000 units of bandwidth and a propagation delay of 1ms. The propagation delay is varied to get different token circulation delays in one simulation set. Since the contending edge routers form an overlay ring, the above simulation topology serves as a good representation of any link under contention because the algorithm is not dependent on their actual locations in the network.

All reservation requests are for 1 unit of bandwidth. The request arrival process is Poisson with the mean arrival rate varying across simulations. Each request is uniformly assigned to an ingress router except in one simulation where we consider biased traffic profile. Each simulation has 60000 request arrival events. The duration of a flow is exponentially distributed with mean 500 seconds. For

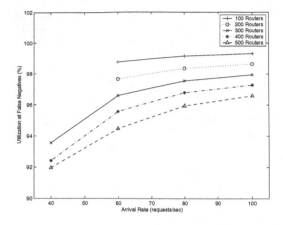

Fig. 5. Link utilization when false negatives occur at different request arrival rates for different number of contending routers.

purposes of simulation, we assume that each request carries with it the time at which it would terminate, so that, the simulator can compute expected traffic load at each instant as the sum of the number of active flows and the flows which would have been active if they were admitted. In practice, an exponential smoothing algorithm could be used to determine the load. The first 5000 requests are used to warm up the simulator and all the results are based on the subsequent requests. Each simulation was run 5 times (on traffic profiles generated with different seeds) and the points in the figures correspond to the means of these runs.

The performance measure that we use is the utilization level when false negatives occur, i.e., we keep track of the actual link utilization levels when a request was rejected when it could have been admitted. This serves as a better alternative than measuring link utilization because using actual link utilization itself does not give a means to identify where the algorithm under-performs as having x% link utilization at an instant does not tell us whether it could have been higher in case of better admission decisions. Moreover, not having any false-negatives is an indication of highest possible utilization. Thus, this metric serves the dual purpose of giving an indication of utilization as well as telling us the extent to which the algorithm's performance suffers whenever it does so.

Our first simulation result (figure 5) shows the effectiveness of our algorithm at relatively high and low request loads. The request load to saturate the link of bandwidth 20000 units and a holding time mean of 500 seconds, is nearly 40 requests per second. There are several observations that can be made in figure 5: 1) There are no points in the figure for an arrival rate of 40 request/sec for 100 or 200 edge routers because we did not have any false negatives in our simulations for these cases. However, at the same request load false negatives do occur when the number of contending routers is 300, 400 and 500. This

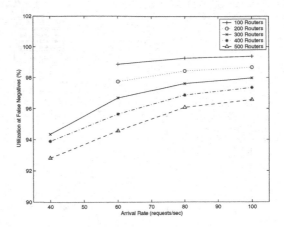

Fig. 6. Link utilization when false negatives occur at different request arrival rates for different number of contending routers when one edge router sources a traffic load 10 times the other routers.

is because each request is uniformly distributed across edge routers and the variance in request distribution with larger number of routers provides instances where the allocation has to be frozen at some time. The frozen shares are slightly unbalanced leading to the false negatives. 2) As the request arrival rate increases, the mean link utilization level when false-negatives occur, increases irrespective of the number of contending routers. This is because, even when the shares are frozen (in a possibly unbalanced way), the heavy request load serves to fill up the shares at each edge router. Thus, while we have unfairness, we do not have under-utilization in case of heavy request load. 3) Not having false negatives at a request load equal to the link capacity for 100 and 200 routers is also an indication that we won't have false negatives at lower arrival rates as well. In fact, we did not have any false negatives for the case with 500 routers when arrival rate was 38 requests/sec (a request load of 95% of link capacity).

The second simulation results is aimed at testing the utilization performance in case of biased traffic profile. In this case, while the requests arrive as a Poisson process, they are assigned to a particular edge router with a probability 10 times the others. Figure 6 shows the link utilization percentage when false negatives occur. We see that the figure is almost identical to the unbiased traffic profile case. In fact, there are very minor differences in the actual numbers (of the order of 0.2%-0.4%) and in all the cases, the system performs better in the biased case than the unbiased case. We have tested the system under different level of bias and found similar results. This is a good result because there is evidence that the traffic from different routers exhibits the "elephants and mice" phenomenon where there is a large difference in traffic loads between router pairs [4].

The third simulation is aimed at testing the impact of token circulation delay on the algorithm. For this simulation, the number of edge routers was fixed at

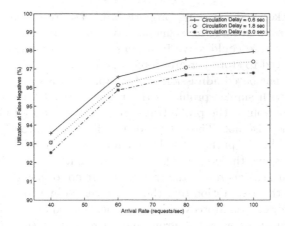

Fig. 7. Link utilization when false negatives occur at different request arrival rates for different token circulation delays.

300 and the propagation delay on the access links was set to 1ms, 3ms and 5ms for three sets of runs. Figure 7 shows the mean utilization percentage when false-negatives occur. We see that as the circulation delay increases, the false negatives start occurring at a lower utilization level. The increase in propagation delay leads to more requests arriving at each router during each token cycle. Thus, a router is more likely to have over-allocated its new share in this case. The shares are frozen at a lower utilization level resulting in a higher chance of unfair division.

One thing common in all the simulation results is the fact that false negatives occur at quite a high utilization level (90+%) even for reasonably large networks with around 500 edge routers. Note that, the number of backbone and core routers in large ISPs is of this order [22]. Thus, we expect our admission control algorithm to work well in the current backbones of large ISPs.

7   Related Work

Our prior work [2] provides a core-stateless distributed admission control framework for unicast flows. The approach we follow in this work is similar, however, there are significant modifications both in the underlying resource management framework and signaling due to the heterogeneous user requirements. RSVP [7] provides a stateful solution to resource reservation for heterogeneous multicast. We aim at eliminating the state maintenance requirements from the core routers.

A centralized bandwidth broker based approach is proposed in [9] where the edge routers forward each request to the broker which takes the admission decision. This approach is not scalable in number of requests and has a single point of failure. Another significant problem with any centralized broker based approach is that link failures or congestion could lead to service unavailability despite the broker node working properly and resources being available. Our solution is distributed and the signaling involving core routers is minimal. In fact, our architecture could serve in an entirely core-stateless way if the edge routers are allowed to store per-group reservation trees.

A measurement based admission control approach is proposed in [20] where a *probe* traffic with similar profile as the required bandwidth is sent from the source to destination. If the probe traffic receives the desired QoS, the request is admitted otherwise not. The key problem with this approach is that it relies on QoS received by the probes. The bursty nature of Internet traffic could cause the probes to receive the desired QoS while in reality the bandwidth might be insufficient. Thus, the *guarantee* that resources are not over-allocated can only be provided under the assumption that the QoS received by probe traffic represents the actual network state. Moreover, measurement-based approach only works for homogeneous multicast where all group members request *same* bandwidth. Our solution does not rely on probes and unconditionally guarantees that resources are never over-allocated and supports heterogeneous user requirements within the same multicast group.

Several solutions exist for forwarding multicast data to users with heterogeneous rate requirements. A couple of solutions involving router-based packet filtering require some per-group state. In [15], authors maintain the downstream rate information for each group. Packets are filtered based on the interface forwarding rate and the packet sequence numbers. An alternate filtering solution proposed in [8], maintains a tag value per interface and only forwards packets with a tag-value less than the stored tag on an interface. In [6] authors have proposed a method to provide normal IP multicast forwarding in differentiated services network. An alternate approach which puts an additional burden on edge routers is described in [24]. There the *entire* intra-domain multicast tree and the DSCP(DiffServ CodePoint) for each forwarding interface in the tree, is encoded in each packet header. The core routers use the encoded state in the packet header to determine the per-hop-behaviors for the packet on each of its interfaces.

8   Conclusion and Future Work

We described a dynamic bandwidth partitioning scheme and using that an admission control algorithm which does not require core routers to perform admission tests. We also described a signaling mechanism to enable admission control in heterogeneous multicast while maintaining a scalability equivalent to the best-effort multicast. The key advantage of our architecture is that we provide the QoS control at no additional cost in network core and still maintain the soft-state semantics. The simulations show that even for a reasonably large number of routers contending for a link, our simple admission control algorithm does not cause false-negatives at low utilization levels. Thus we have low response times and high utilization while not requiring core routers to perform resource management. In a larger perspective, dynamic bandwidth partitioning could be generalized as a solution to allow controlled concurrency for problems which have large amount of identical resources and for which the only existing solution was mutual exclusion based concurrency control. It is imperative to note that the resource partitioning scheme described in this paper is in its simplest form. There are lots of possible strategies using a similar technique which need theoretical and empirical validation. For example, instead of using one variable per link, we could use two variables where the first one is used as described in this paper. The routers could continue to update the second variable in case the first variable indicates that shares be frozen. In such a case, the second variable could be used as a *guide* by the routers to determine what their shares should be. Thus, even when their traffic load does not decrease, they could still reduce their traffic values and try to attain fairness. Another strategy to evaluate would be to look at a "partial freeze", i.e., only a subset of routers freeze their shares, depending on the available capacity in their shares. We believe that our scheme of dynamic bandwidth partitioning is just a preliminary step.

Furthermore, our algorithm provides an alternate way for *statistical admission control* as well. This is because an edge router has quite a leeway in deciding what is the aggregate traffic load of its flows. Thus, if it determines that a flow requiring b bandwidth is effectively using only $b'(\leq b)$ bandwidth, it could use b' as the share of traffic load for the flow, instead of b thus keeping a lower share of bandwidth. This aspect needs further investigation.

Our algorithm has an implicit notion of *delayed fairness* where a router has to wait for a token circulation cycle to use its current fair share. This has further implication in creating an extra avenue for optimization because a good partitioning is dependent upon how well the current traffic load is estimated. In fact, if a mechanism could predict future traffic loads (for example, expected load after one circulation cycle), better partitioning could be achieved.

Acknowledgement. We would like to thank the anonymous reviewers for their comments that improved the quality of this paper. Sudeept Bhatnagar and Badri Nath thank DARPA for their research support under contract number N-666001-00-1-8953.

References

1. A. Ballardie. Core Based Trees (CBT) Multicast Routing Architecture. *RFC 2201*, September 1997.
2. S. Bhatnagar and B. Nath. Distributed Admission Control to Support Guaranteed Services in Core-Stateless Networks. In *Proc. of IEEE Infocom*, May 2003.
3. S. Bhatnagar and B. Vickers. Providing Quality of Service Guarantees Using Only Edge Routers. In *Proc. of IEEE Globecom*, November 2001.
4. S. Bhattacharyya, C. Diot., J. Jetcheva, and N. Taft. Geographical and Temporal Characteristics of Inter-POP Flows: View from a Single POP. *European Transactions on Telecommunications*, 13(1):5–22, Feb. 2002.
5. S. Blake, D. Black, M. Carlson, E. Davies, Z. Wang, and W. Weiss. An Architecture for Differentiated Services. RFC 2475, IETF, December 1998.

6. R. Bless and K. Wehrle. IP Multicast in Differentiated Services Networks. *IETF Internet Draft*, March 2002. Work-in-progress.
7. R. Braden, L. Zhang, S. Berson, S. Herzog, and S. Jamin. Resource reSerVation Protocol (RSVP) version 1, Functional Specification. RFC 2205, IETF, September 1997.
8. A. Clerget. A Tag-based UDP Multicast Flow Control Protocol. Technical Report 3728, INRIA, July 1999.
9. J. Cui, A. Fei, M. Gerla, and M. Faloutsos. An Architecture for Scalable QoS Multicast Provisioning. Technical Report UCLA CSD TR 010030, Computer Science Department, University of California, Los Angeles, August 2001.
10. D. Estrin, D. Farinacci, A. Helmy, D. Thaler, S. Deering, M. Handley, V. Jacobson, C. Liu, P. Sharma, and L. Wei. Protocol Independent Multicast-Sparse Mode (PIM-SM): Protocol Specification. *RFC 2362*, June 1998.
11. M. Faloutsos, A. Banerjee, and R. Pankaj. Qosmic: Quality of Service Sensitive Multicast Internet Protocol. In *SIGCOMM*, pages 144–153, 1998.
12. V. Jacobson, K. Nichols, and K. Poduri. An Expedited Forwarding PHB. RFC 2598, IETF, June 1999.
13. D. Katz. IP Router Alert Option. RFC 2113, IETF, February 1997.
14. M. Kodialam, T. V. Lakshman, and S. Sengupta. Online Multicast Routing with Bandwidth Guarantees: A New Approach Using Multicast Network Flow. In *Proceedings of the ACM Sigmetrics Conference*, June 2000.
15. M. Luby, L. Vicisano, and T. Speakman. Heterogeneous Multicast Congestion Control Based on Router Packet Filtering. June 1999. Work in Progress, presented at RMRG meeting, Pisa.
16. N. A. Lynch. *Distributed Algorithms*. Morgan Kaufmann Publishers, San Mateo, CA, 1996.
17. J. Moy. OSPF Version 2. RFC 2178, IETF, April 1998.
18. K. Nichols, V. Jacobson, and L. Zhang. A Two-Bit Differentiated Services Architecture for the Internet. *RFC 2638*, July 1999.
19. D. Ooms, B. Sales, W. Livens, A. Acharya, F. Griffoul, and F. Ansari. Overview of IP Multicast in a Multi-Protocol Label Switching (MPLS) Environment. RFC 3353, IETF, August 2002.
20. E. Pagani and G. Rossi. Distributed Bandwidth Broker for QoS Multicast Traffic. In *Proc. of International Conference on Distributed Computing Systems*, July 2002.
21. P. Pan and H. Schulzrinne. YESSIR: A Simple Reservation Mechanism for the Internet. *ACM Computer Communication Review*, April 1999.
22. N. Spring, R. Mahajan, and D. Wetherall. Measuring ISP Topologies with Rocketfuel. *Proc. of ACM SIGCOMM*, August 2002.
23. I. Stoica and H. Zhang. Providing Guaranteed Services without Per-flow Management. In *Proc. of ACM SIGCOMM*, pages 81–94, September 1999.
24. A. Striegel and G. Manimaran. Dynamic DSCPs for Heterogeneous QoS in DiffServ Multicasting. In *Proc. of IEEE Globecom*, 2002.
25. R. Yavatkar, D. Pendarakis, and R. Guerin. A framework for Policy-based Admission Control. RFC 2753, IETF, January 2000.

III Multimedia
& Incentives

Subjective Impression of Variations in Layer Encoded Videos

Michael Zink, Oliver Künzel, Jens Schmitt, and Ralf Steinmetz

Multimedia Communications Lab, Darmstadt University of Technology
Merckstr. 25 • D-64283 Darmstadt • Germany
{Zink, Kuenzel, Schmitt, Steinmetz}@KOM.tu-darmstadt.de

Abstract. Layer encoded video is an elegant way to allow adaptive transmissions in the face of varying network conditions as well as it supports heterogeneity in networks and clients. As a drawback quality degradation can occur, caused by variations in the amount of transmitted layers. Recent work on reducing these variations makes assumptions about the perceived quality of those videos. The main goal of this paper respectively its motivation is to investigate the validity of these assumptions by subjective assessment. However, the paper is also an attempt to investigate fundamental issues for the human perception of layer encoded video with time-varying quality characteristics. For this purpose, we built a test environment for the subjective assessment of layer encoded video and conducted an empirical experiment in which 66 test candidates took part. The results of this subjective assessment are presented and discussed. To a large degree we were able to validate existing (unproven) assumptions about quality degradation caused by variations in layer encoded videos, however there were also some interesting, at first sight counterintuitive findings from our experiment.

1 Introduction

1.1 Motivation

In the area of video streaming layer encoded video is an elegant way to overcome the inelastic characteristics of traditional video encoding formats like MPEG-1 or H.261. Layer encoded video is particularly useful in today's Internet where a lack of Quality of Service (QoS) mechanisms might make an adaptation to existing network conditions necessary. In addition, it bears the capability to support a large variety of clients while only a single file has to be stored at a video server for each video object. The drawback of adaptive transmissions is the introduction of variations in the amount of transmitted layers during a streaming session. These variations affect the end-user's perceived quality and thus the acceptance of a service that is based on such technology.

Recent work that has focused on reducing those layer variations, either by employing intelligent buffering techniques at the client [3, 1, 4] or proxy caches [5, 6, 7] in the distribution network, made various assumptions about the perceived quality of videos with time-varying number of layers. To the best of our knowledge, these assumptions have not been verified by subjective assessment so far.

The lack of in-depth analysis about quality metrics for variations in layer encoded videos led us to conduct an empirical experiment based on subjective assessment to obtain results that can be used in classifying the perceived quality of such videos.

K. Jeffay, I. Stoica, and K. Wehrle (Eds.): IWQoS 2003, LNCS 2707, pp. 137–154, 2003.
© Springer-Verlag Berlin Heidelberg 2003

1.2   What Is the Relation between Objective and Subjective Quality?

The goal of this research work is to investigate if general assumptions made about the quality metrics of variations in layer encoded videos can be verified by subjective assessment. We use the following example to explain our intention in more detail: A layer encoded video that is transmitted adaptively to the client might have layer variations as shown in Figure 1. In Section 2.1, several quality metrics that allow the determination of the video's quality are presented. At first, we discuss the basics of these quality metrics. The most straightforward quality metric would be the total sum of all received segments (see Figure 1). However, common assumptions on the quality of a layer encoded video are that the quality is not only influenced by the total sum of received segments but also by the frequency of layer variations and the amplitude of those variations [1, 5, 7]. As shown in Figure 1, the amplitude specifies the height of a layer variation while the frequency determines the amount of layer variations.

All quality metrics we are aware of are based on these assumptions. Verifying all possible scenarios that are covered by those assumptions with an experiment based on subjective assessment is hard to achieve. Therefore, we decided to focus on basic scenarios that have the potential to answer the most fundamental questions, e.g., are the sequences on the left in Figure 1 ((a1) and (b1)) more annoying than sequences on the right ((a2) and (b2)) for an end-user who views a corresponding video sequence. In this example, the first scenario ((a1) and (a2)) is focused on the influence of the amplitude and the second ((b1) and (b2)) on the frequency of layer variations..

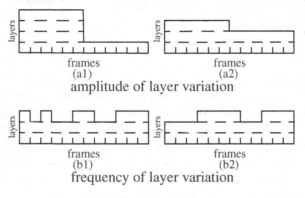

frames
(a1)

frames
(a2)

amplitude of layer variation

frames
(b1)

frames
(b2)

frequency of layer variation

Fig. 1. Quality criteria [1]

1.3   Outline

The paper is structured as follows. Section 2 reviews previous work on retransmission scheduling for layer encoded video and subjective assessment of video quality. The test environment and the subjective test method used for the experiment are described and discussed in Section 3. The details of the experimental setup are given in Section 4 and in Section 5 the results of the experiment are presented and discussed. Section 6 summarizes the major conclusions that can be drawn from the experiment.

2   Related Work

The related work section is split in two parts since our work is influenced by the two research areas briefly surveyed in the following.

2.1   Retransmission Scheduling

The work presented in this paper has been motivated by our own work on quality improvement for layer encoded videos. During our investigation of favorable retransmission scheduling algorithms which are supposed to improve the quality of layer encoded videos stored on a cache [7], we realized that in related work the quality metrics for layer encoded videos are based on somewhat speculative assumptions only. To the best of our knowledge none of these assumptions is based on a subjective assessment.

In [1], Nelakuditi et al. state that a good metric should capture the amount of detail per frame as well as its uniformity across frames. I.e., if we compare the sequences of layers in a video shown in Fig. 2 the quality of (a2) would be better than that of (a1) which is also valid for (b2) and (b1), according to their assumption. Their quality metric is based on the principle of giving a higher weight to lower layers and to longer runs of continuous frames in a layer.

The metric presented by the work of Rejaie et al. [5] is almost identical to the one advocated for in [1]. Completeness and continuity are the 2 parameters that are incorporated in this quality metric. Completeness of a layer is defined as the ratio of the layer size transmitted to its original (complete) size. E.g. the ratio of layer 2 in sequence (a2) in Fig. 2 would be 1 while the ratio for layer 3 would be 0.5. Continuity is the metric that covers the 'gaps' in a layer. It is defined as the average number of segments between two consecutive layer breaks (i.e., gaps). In contrast to the other metrics presented here, this metric is a per-layer metric.

In our previous work [7] we also made assumptions about the quality metrics for layer encoded videos. Similar to [1] we postulated that this metric should be based on a) the frequency of variations and b) the amplitude of variations.

2.2   Video Quality

There has been a substantial amount of research on methodologies for subjective assessment of video quality, e.g., [8] and [9], which contributed to form an ITU Recommendation on this issue [10]. This standard has been used as a basis for subjective assessment of encoders for digital video formats, in particular for MPEG-2 [11, 9] and MPEG-4 [12] but also on other standards like H.263+ [13]. The focus of interest for all these subjective assessment experiments was the quality of different coding and compression mechanisms. Our work, in contrast, is concerned with the quality degradation caused by variations in layer encoded videos. Like us, [14] is also concerned with layer encoded video and presents the results of an empirical evaluation of 4 hierarchical video encoding schemes. This is orthogonal to our work since the focus of their investigation is on the comparison between the different layered coding schemes and not on the human perception of layer variations.

In [15], a subjective quality assessment has been carried out in which the influence of the frame rate on the perceived quality is investigated. In contrast to our work elas-

ticity in the stream was achieved by frame rate variation and not by applying a layer encoded video format.

Effects of bit errors on the quality of MPEG-4 video were explored in [16] by subjective viewing measurements, but effects caused by layer variations were not examined.

Chen presents an investigation on an IP-based video conference system [17]. The focus in this work is mainly auditorium parameters like display size and viewing angle.
A layer encoded video format is not used in this investigation.

Probably closest to our work, Lavington et al. [18] used an H.263+ two layer video
format in their trial. In comparison to our approach, they were rather interested in the
quality assessment of longer sequences (e.g., 25 min.). Instead of using identical pre-
generated sequences that were presented to the test candidates, videos were streamed
via an IP network to the clients and the quality was influenced in a fairly uncontrolled
way by competing data originating from a traffic generator. The very specific goal of
this work was to examine if reserving some of the network's bandwidth for either the
base or the enhancement layer improves the perceived quality of the video, while we
are rather interested on the influence of variations in layer encoded videos and try to
verify some of the basic assumption made about the perceived quality in a subjective
assessment experiment. Furthermore, we try to conduct this experiment in a controlled
environment in order to achieve more significant and easier to interpret results.

3   Test Environment

In this section, we first present the layer encoded video format used for the experiment,
describe how we generated the test sequences, explain why we decided to use stimulus-
comparison as the assessment method, and shortly present our test application.

3.1   Layer Encoded Video Format – SPEG

SPEG (Scalable MPEG) [19] is a simple modification to MPEG-1 which introduces
scalability. In addition to the possibility of dropping complete frames (temporal scalability), which is already supported by MPEG-1 video, SNR scalability is introduced
through layered quantization of DCT data [19]. The extension to MPEG-1 was made
for two reasons. First, there are no freely available implementations of layered extensions for existing video standards (MPEG-2, MPEG-4), second, the granularity of scalability is improved by SPEG combining temporal and SNR scalability. As shown in
Figure 2, a priority (p_0(highest) - p_{11}(lowest)) can be mapped to each layer. The QoS

	I	B	P
Level 0	p_0	p_1	p_2
Level 1	p_3	p_4	p_5
Level 2	p_6	p_7	p_8
Level 3	p_9	p_{10}	p_{11}

Fig. 2. SPEG layer model

Mapper (see Figure 3, which depicts the SPEG pipeline and its components) uses the priority information to determine which layers are dropped and which are forwarded to the Net Streamer.

Our decision to use SPEG as a layer encoded video format is based on several reasons. SPEG is designed for a QoS-adaptive video-on-demand (VoD) approach, i.e., the data rate streamed to the client should be controlled by feedback from the network (e.g., congestion control information). In addition, the developers of SPEG also implemented a join function that re-transcodes SPEG into MPEG-1 [2] and therefore allows the use of standard MPEG-1 players, e.g., the Windows Media Player. We were not able to use scalable video encoders available as products (e.g., [20, 21]) because videos created by those can only be streamed to the corresponding clients which do neither allow the storage of the received data on a disk nor the creation of scheduled quality variations.

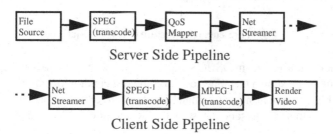

Server Side Pipeline

Client Side Pipeline

Fig. 3. Pipeline for SPEG [2]

3.2   Test Generation – Full Control

Since our test sequences must be created in a deterministic manner, we slightly modified the SPEG pipeline. The most important difference is, that in our case data belonging to a certain layer must be dropped intentionally and not by an unpredictable feedback from the network or the client. This modification was necessary, since identical sequences must be presented to the test candidates in the kind of subjective assessment method that is used in our experiment. Therefore, we modified the QoS Mapper in a way that layers are dropped at certain points in time specified by manually created input data. We also added a second output path to the MPEG-1 module that allows us to write the resulting MPEG-1 data in a file and eliminated the NetStreamer modules.

3.3   Measurement Method – Stimulus Comparison

The subjective assessment method is widely accepted for determining the perceived quality of images and videos. Research that was performed under the ITU-R lead to the development of a standard for such test methods [10]. The standard defines basically five different test methods double-stimulus impairment scale (DSIS), double-stimulus continuous quality-scale (DSCQS), single stimulus quality evaluation (SSCQE), simultaneous double stimulus for continuous evaluation (SDSCE), and stimulus-comparison (SC), respectively.

Since it was our goal to investigate the basic assumptions about the quality of layer encoded video, SSCQE and SDSCE are not the appropriate assessment method because comparisons between two videos are only possible on an identical time segment and not between certain intervals of the same video. In addition, SSCQE and SDSCE were designed to assess the quality of an encoder (e.g., MPEG-1) itself.

Two test methods which better suit the kind of investigations we want to perform are DSCQS and DSIS. Compared to SSCQE and SDSCE they allow to asses the quality of a codec in relation to data losses [8] and, therefore, are more suitable if the impairment caused by the transmission path is investigated.

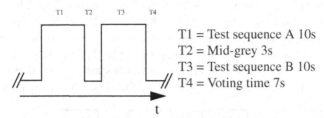

T1 = Test sequence A 10s
T2 = Mid-grey 3s
T3 = Test sequence B 10s
T4 = Voting time 7s

Fig. 4. Presentation structure of test material

The SC method differs from DSCQS and DSIS in a way that two test sequences with unequal qualities are shown (see Figure 4) and the test candidates can vote on a scale as shown in Table 1. Comparing two impaired videos directly with each other is our primary goal. Since this is represented best by the SC method we decided to use this method in our test.

Table 1. Comparison scale

Value	Compare
-3	much worse
-2	worse
-1	slightly worse
0	the same
1	slightly better
2	better
3	much better

Additionally, preliminary tests have shown us that test candidates with experience in watching videos on a computer are less sensitive to impairment. I.e., they recognize the impairment but do not judge it as annoying as candidates who are unexperienced. This effect is dampened since only impaired sequences have to be compared with each other in a single test that is based on the SC method. Our preliminary tests with the DSIS method, where always the original sequence and an impaired sequence are compared, delivered results with less significance compared to tests performed with the SC method.

3.4   Test Application – Enforcing Time Constraints

We created a small application[1] (see Figure 5) that allows an automated execution of the tests. Since we had to use a computer to present the videos anyway, we decided to let the candidates perform their voting also on the computer. Using this application has the advantage that we can easily enforce the time constraints demanded by the measurement method, because we allow voting only during a certain time interval. As a convenient side effect, the voting data is available in a machine readable format.

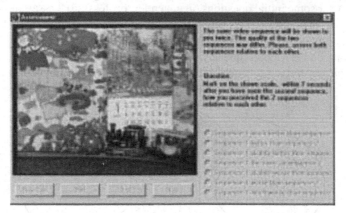

Fig. 5. Application for experiment

4   Experiment

4.1   Scenario

Since quality metrics for layer encoded video are very general, we have to focus on some basic test cases in order to keep the amount of tests that should be performed in the experiment feasible. We decided to investigate isolated effects, one-by-one at a time, which on one hand keeps the size of a test session reasonable and on the other hand still allows to draw conclusions for the general assumptions, as discussed above. That means we are rather interested in observing the quality ranking for isolated effects like frequency variations (as shown in sequences (b1) and (b2) in Fig. 2) than for combined effects (as shown in Fig. 1). This bears also the advantage that standardized test methods [10], which limit the sequence length to several seconds, can be applied. All patterns that were used for the experiment are shown in Fig. 8.

4.2   Candidates

The experiment was performed with 90 test candidates (62 males and 28 females), between the age of 14 and 64. 78 of them had experiences with watching videos on a computer.

---

1. A downloadable version of the test can be found at
    http://www.kom.e-technik.tu-darmstadt.de/video-assessment/

4.3   Procedure

Each candidate had to perform 15 different assessments, of which each single test lasted for 33 seconds. All 15 tests were executed according to the SC assessment method. The complete test session per candidate lasted for about 15 minutes[2], on average. We have chosen three video sequences for this experiment that have been frequently used for subjective assessment [22]. The order of the 15 video sequences was changed randomly from candidate to candidate as proposed in the ITU-R B.500-10 standard [10] (see also Figure 6). After some initial questions (age, gender, profession) 3 assessments were executed as a warm-up phase. This should avoid that the test candidates are distracted by the content of the video sequences as reported by Aldridge et al. [11]. In order to avoid that two consecutive video sequences (e.g., F_2 is following F_1 immediately) have the same content we defined a pattern for chronological order of the test sessions, as shown in Figure 6. F_x can be any video sequence from the F pool of sequences that has

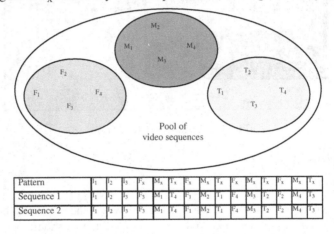

Pattern	I_1	I_2	I_3	F_x	M_x	T_x	F_x	M_x	T_x	F_x	M_x	T_x	F_x	M_x	T_x
Sequence 1	I_1	I_2	I_3	F_3	M_1	T_4	F_1	M_2	T_1	F_4	M_3	I_2	F_2	M_4	I_3
Sequence 2	I_1	I_2	I_3	F_3	M_1	T_4	F_1	M_2	T_1	F_4	M_3	I_2	F_2	M_4	I_3

F = Farm
M= Mobile & Calendar
T = Table Tennis

Fig. 6. Random generation of test sequence order

not been used in this specific test session, so far. Thus, a complete test session for a candidate could have a chronological order as shown in Figure 6.

4.4   Layer Patterns

Fig. 8 shows the layer patterns of each single sequence that was used in the experiment, except for the first 3 warm-up tests where the comparison is performed between the first sequence that consists of 4 layers and the second that consists of only one layer. Each of the 3 groups shows the patterns that were used with one type of content. Comparisons were always performed between patterns that are shown in a row (e.g., (a1) and (a2)).

---

2. Only watching the sequences and voting took less time, but the candidates had as much time as they wanted to read the questions and possible answers for each test ahead of each test.

As already mentioned in Section 1.2 it was our goal to examine fundamental assumptions about the influence of layer changes on perceived quality. This is also reflected by the kind of patterns we decided to use in the experiment. It must be mentioned that the single layers are not equal in size. The size of the nth layer is rather determined by the following expression: $s_n = 2s_{n-1}$. Thus, segments of different layers have different sizes. Preliminary experiments have shown that equal layer sizes are not appropriate to make layer changes perceivable. Since there exist layered schemes that produce layers with sizes similar to ours [23, 24], we regard this a realistic assumption.

In the experiment, we differentiate between two groups of tests, i.e., one group in which the amount of segments used by a pair of sequences is equal and one in which the amount differs (the latter has a shaded background in Fig. 8). We made this distinction because we are mainly interested in how the result of this experiment could be used to improve the retransmission scheduling technique (see Section 2.1) where it is necessary to compare the influence of additional segments that is added on different locations in a sequence.

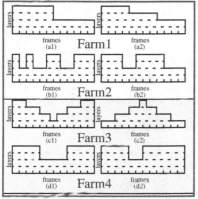

Patterns for Sequence "Farm" (F1-F4)

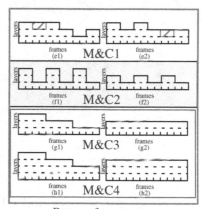

Patterns for sequence
"Mobile & Calendar" (M1-M4)

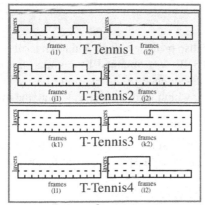

Patterns for sequence
"Table Tennis" (C1-C4)

Fig. 7. Segments that were compared in the experiment

Since segments from different layers are not equal in size, the amount of data for the compared sequences differs. However, somewhat surprisingly, as we discuss in Section 5.3, a larger amount of data (resulting in higher PSNR value) does not necessarily lead to a better perceived quality. Additional tests with different quantities of segments in between a pair were chosen to answer additional questions and make the experiment more consistent as we show in Section 5.2.

5   Results

In the following, we present the results of the experiment described in Section 4. Since we analyze the gathered data statistically it must clearly be mentioned that the presented results cannot prove an assumption but only make it less or more likely based on the gathered data. The overall results of all experiments are summarized in Figure 8 and are discussed in the following subsections. Next to the statistical results obtained from the

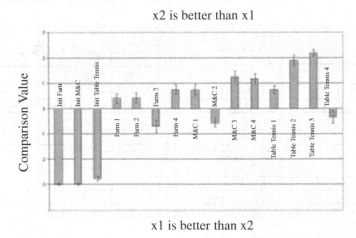

Fig. 8. Average and 95% confidence interval for the different tests of the experiment the comparison values

subjective assessment we also provide objective data in terms of the average PSNR per sequence. The average PSNR was obtained by comparing the original MPEG-1 sequence with the degraded sequence on a per frame basis. This results in 250 single PSNR values per sequence which were used to calculate the average PSNR.

5.1   Same Amount of Segments

In this section, we discuss the results for the assessments of tests in which the total sum of segments is equal. That means the space covered by the pattern of both sequences is identical.

5.1.1   Farm1: Amplitude

In this assessment the stepwise decrease was rated slightly better than one single but higher decrease. The result shows a tendency that the assumptions that were made about the amplitude of a layer change (as described in Section 2.1) are correct.

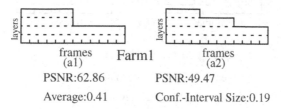

frames   Farm1   frames
(a1)   (a2)
PSNR:62.86   PSNR:49.47
Average:0.41   Conf.-Interval Size:0.19

Fig. 9. Farm1

5.1.2   Farm2: Frequency

The result of this test has a slightly increased likelihood that the second sequence has a better perceived quality than it is the case for *Farm1*. It tends to confirm the assumption that the frequency of layer changes influences the perceived quality, since, on average, test candidates ranked the quality of the sequence with lesser layer changes better.

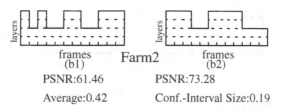

frames   Farm2   frames
(b1)   (b2)
PSNR:61.46   PSNR:73.28
Average:0.42   Conf.-Interval Size:0.19

Fig. 10. Farm2

5.1.3   M&C1: Closing the Gap

This test should try to answer the question, if it would be better to close a gap in a layer on a higher or lower level. The majority of the test candidates decided that filling the gap on a lower level results in a better quality than otherwise. This result tends to affirm our assumptions made for retransmission scheduling in [7].

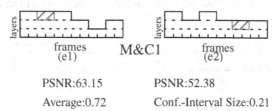

frames   M&C1   frames
(e1)   (e2)

PSNR:63.15   PSNR:52.38
Average:0.72   Conf.-Interval Size:0.21

Fig. 11. M&C1

5.1.4   M&C3: Constancy

Even more significant than in the preceding tests, the candidates favored the sequence with no layer changes as the one with the better quality. One may judge this a trivial and unnecessary test, but from our point of view the result is not that obvious, since (g1) starts with a higher amount of layers. The outcome of this test implies that it might be better, in terms of perceived quality, to transmit less but a constant amount of layers.

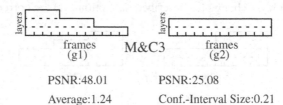

PSNR:48.01   PSNR:25.08

Average:1.24   Conf.-Interval Size:0.21

Fig. 12. M&C3

5.1.5   M&C4: Constancy at a Higher Level

This test was to examine if an increase of the overall level (in this case by comparison to the test in Section 5.1.4) has an influence on the perceived quality. Comparing the results of both tests (*M&C3* and *M&C4*) shows no significant change in the test candidates' assessment. 81% of the test candidates judge the second sequences ((g2) and (h2)) better (values 1-3 in Table 1 on page 6) in both cases which makes it likely that the overall level has no influence on the perceived quality.

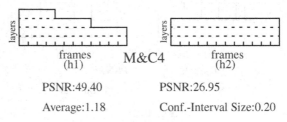

PSNR:49.40   PSNR:26.95

Average:1.18   Conf.-Interval Size:0.20

Fig. 13. M&C4

5.1.6   Tennis3: All Is Well That Ends Well

The result of this test shows the tendency that increasing the amount of layers in the end leads to a higher perceived quality. The result is remarkably strong (the highest bias of all tests). Future tests, that will be of longer duration and executed in a different order (first (k2) than (k1)), will show how the memory-effect [11] of the candidates influenced this test.

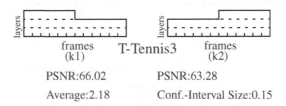

PSNR:66.02   PSNR:63.28

Average:2.18   Conf.-Interval Size:0.15

Fig. 14. Tennis3

5.1.7   Tennis4: The Exception Proves the Rule

As with the results for Farm2 and M&C3, the result of this test shows the same tendency. The sequence with no layer variations is assessed a better quality than the sequence with one variation. In all test that were related to the frequency of layer changes (Farrm2, M&C3, M&C4, and Tennis4) the sequence with lesser variations was assessed a better quality. Therefore, the results of the tests presented in this section strongly support the assumption that the frequency of layer variations should be kept as small as possible.

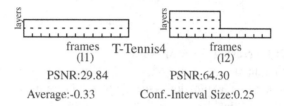

frames   T-Tennis4   frames
(l1)   (l2)

PSNR:29.84   PSNR:64.30

Average:-0.33   Conf.-Interval Size:0.25

Fig. 15. Tennis4

5.2   Different Amount of Segments

In the following 5 tests the total amount of segments per sequence differs. All 5 tests have in common that the perceived quality of the sequence consisting of a pattern that covers a larger number of segments were ranked better. This is obvious, but it makes the overall result more consistent, because test candidates mostly realized this quality difference.

5.2.1   Farm3: Decrease vs. Increase

Starting with a higher amount of layers, decreasing the amount of layers, and increasing the amount of layers in the end again seems to provide a better perceivable quality than starting with a low amount of layers, increasing this amount of layers, and going back to a low amount of layers at the end of the sequence. This might be caused by the fact that test candidates are very concentrated in the beginning and the end of the sequence and that, in the first case details become clear right in the beginning of the sequence.

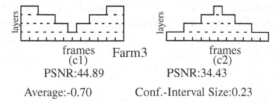

frames   Farm3   frames
(c1)   (c2)
PSNR:44.89   PSNR:34.43

Average:-0.70   Conf.-Interval Size:0.23

Fig. 16. Farm3

5.2.2   Farm4: Keep the Gap Small

In this test, it was our goal to investigate how the size of a gap may influence the perceived quality. The majority of test candidates (37 out of 90) judged the quality of the sequence with a smaller gap slightly better (Only 5 out of 90 judged the first sequence better). This indicates that filling a gap partly can be beneficial.

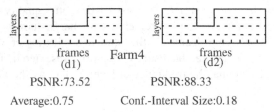

	Farm4	
frames (d1)		frames (d2)
PSNR:73.52		PSNR:88.33
Average:0.75		Conf.-Interval Size:0.18

Fig. 17. Farm4

5.2.3   M&C2: Increasing the Amplitude

The effect of the amplitude height should be investigated in this test. The result shows that, in contrast to existing assumptions (see Section 2.1), an increased amplitude can lead to a better perceived quality.

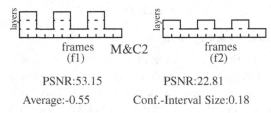

	M&C2	
frames (f1)		frames (f2)
PSNR:53.15		PSNR:22.81
Average:-0.55		Conf.-Interval Size:0.18

Fig. 18. M&C2

5.2.4   Tennis1: Closing All Gaps

In this test additional segments are used to close the existing gaps instead of increasing the amplitude of already better parts of the sequence (as it is the case for M&C2). This strategy decreases the frequency of layer changes. Test candidates, on average, judged the sequence without layer changes better. The result of this test reaffirms the tendency that was already noticed in Section 5.1.2, that the perceived quality is influenced by the frequency of layer changes. If we carefully compare the results of *M&C2* and *Tennis1*, a tendency towards filling the gaps and thus decreasing the frequency instead of increasing the amount of already increased parts of the sequence is recognizable. Definitely, further investigations are necessary to confirm this tendency, because, here, the results of tests with different contents are compared and we have not investigated the influence of the content on the perceived quality, so far.

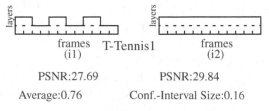

	T-Tennis1	
frames (i1)		frames (i2)
PSNR:27.69		PSNR:29.84
Average:0.76		Conf.-Interval Size:0.16

Fig. 19. Tennis1

5.2.5   Tennis2: Closing All Gaps at a Higher Level

In comparison to *Tennis1*, here, we were interested in how an overall increase of the layers (in this case by one layer) would influence the test candidates judgement. Again the sequence with no layer changes is judged better, even with a higher significance than for *Tennis1*. This might be caused by the fact that the amount of layer is higher in general in *Tennis2*.

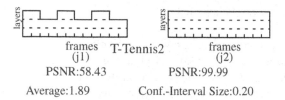

frames   T-Tennis2   frames
(j1)   (j2)

PSNR:58.43   PSNR:99.99

Average:1.89   Conf.-Interval Size:0.20

Fig. 20. Tennis1

5.3   Sequence Size and Quality

The PSNR is a popular metric to present the objective quality of video data. Therefore, we also computed the average PSNR of each sequence to investigate how subjective and objective quality are related. Since the determination of the objective quality can be performed with much less effort than a subjective assessment the result of this investigation could give hints if the determination of the average PSNR is sufficient in order to define the quality of a video sequence. Note, since the relation between subjective and objective quality is not the focus of the investigation presented in this paper this can only be seen as a by-product which certainly needs further elaboration. (The PSNR values for each sequence are given in Fig. 10 - Fig. 21.)

The results of the subjective assessments are contrary to the results of the PSNR in 8 of the 12 test cases. The obtained results for the test in which the sum of segments was equal for each sequence (Section 5.1) are even stronger. They do not indicate a positive correlation between both quality metrics (see Table 2). From the results in our tests we see a strong tendency that, in the case of layered video, the quality of a sequence is not well represented by the average PSNR.

Table 2. Comparison between spectrum, subjective and objective quality (same amount of segments)

Shape	Farm1	Farm2	M&C1	M&C3	M&C4	T-Tennis3	T-Tennis4
PSNR of shape 1	62.86	61.46	63.15	48.01	49.40	66.02	29.84
PSNR of shape 2	49.47	73.28	52.38	25.08	26.95	63.28	64.30
Average of assessment	0.35	0.55	0.73	1.18	1.02	2.18	-0.24

contrary to subjective assessment   in accordance with subjective assessment

6   Conclusion

In this paper, we presented the results of an empirical experiment based on subjective assessment of variations in layer encoded video. A statistical analysis of the experiment mostly validates assumptions that were made in relation to layer variations and the perceived quality of a video:

- The frequency of variations should be kept as small as possible.
- If a variation can not be avoided the amplitude of the variation should be kept as small as possible.

One basic conclusion from the results in Section 5.2 is: adding information to a layered video increases its average quality. But, as we already assumed in our work on retransmission scheduling, adding information at different locations can have a substantial effect on the perceived quality. Assumptions we made for our heuristics in retransmission scheduling (as well as others' assumptions) could be substantiated by this investigation (see Section 5.2). That means, it is more likely that the perceived quality of a layer encoded video is improved if

- the lowest quality level is increased, and
- gaps in lower layers are filled.

The results from Section 5.3 should be used to refine the retransmission scheduling heuristics in relation to the size of each single layer. Therefore, the metric that represents the quality improvement must also take into account that it might be more expensive to retransmit a segment of layer n+1 than of layer n. Another interesting outcome of the experiment is the fact that a quality improvement may be achieved by retransmitting less data, if a layered encoding scheme is used in which the layers are not of identical size. The obtained results can, in addition, be used to refine caching replacement policies that operate on a layer level [5] as well as layered multicast transmission schemes which try to offer heterogeneous services to different subscribers as, e.g., in the receiver-driven layered multicast RLM [25] scheme and its derivations.

The results of this investigation clearly strengthen the assumption that a differentiation between objective and subjective quality, in the case of variations in layer encoded video, must be made.

Nevertheless, it must be admitted that the presented work is only an initial investigation in the subjective impression of variations in layer encoded videos. In further work, we want to explore sequences with a longer duration (up to several minutes). In a next step, we will investigate if the shown sequences can be combined and if the subjective assessment is still consistent with the separated results. E.g., in this experiment sequences (e2) and (g2) were judged better than (e1) and (g1), will a sequence that combines (e2) and (g2) also be judged better than a sequence that combines (e1) and (g1)? We are also interested in how the content of a sequence influences the perceived quality.

Acknowledgments. The authors would like to thank Rico Tunk for creating the test application, Charles "Buck" Krasic for his support on SPEG, the test candidates for taking the time to perform the assessment, and RTL Television for providing the video sequences.

References

[1]   S. Nelakuditi, R. R. Harinath, E. Kusmierek, and Z.-L. Zhang. Providing Smoother Quality Layered Video Stream. In *Proceedings of the 10th International Workshop on Network and Operating System Support for Digital Audio and Video, Raleigh, NC, USA*, June 2000.

[2]   C. Krasic and J. Walpole. QoS Scalability for Streamed Media Delivery. Technical Report OGI CSE Technical Report CSE-99-011, Oregon Graduate Institute of Science & Technology, September 1999.

[3]   D. Saparilla and K. W. Ross. Optimal Streaming of Layered Video. In *Proceedings of the Nineteenth Annual Joint Conference of the IEEE Computer and Communications Societies 2000 (INFOCOM'00), Tel-Aviv, Israel*, pages 737–746, March 2000.

[4]   R. Rejaie, M. Handley, and D. Estrin. Quality Adaptation for Congestion Controlled Video Playback over the Internet. In *Proceedings of the ACM SIGCOMM '99 Conference on Applications, Technologies, Architectures, and Protocols for Computer Communication 1999, New York, NY, USA*, pages 189–200, August 1999.

[5]   R. Rejaie, H. Yu, M. Handley, and D. Estrin. Multimedia Proxy Caching for Quality Adaptive Streaming Applications in the Internet. In *Proceedings of the Nineteenth Annual Joint Conference of the IEEE Computer and Communications Societies 2000 (INFOCOM'00), Tel-Aviv, Israel*, pages 980–989, March 2000.

[6]   R. Rejaie and J. Kangasharju. Mocha: A Quality Adaptive Multimedia Proxy Cache for Internet Streaming. In *Proceedings of the 11th International Workshop on Network and Operating System Support for Digital Audio and Video, Port Jefferson, New York, USA*, pages 3–10, June 2001.

[7]   M. Zink, J. Schmitt, and R. Steinmetz. Retransmission Scheduling in Layered Video Caches, April 2002. Proceedings of the International Conference on Communications 2002, New York, New York, USA.

[8]   T. Alpert and J.-P. Evain. Subjective quality evaluation - The SSCQE and DSCQE methodologies. EBU Technical Review, February 1997.

[9]   R. Aldridge, D. Hands, D. Pearson, and N. Lodge. Continuous quality assessment of digitally-coded television pictures. *IEE Proceedings on Vision, Image and Signal Processing*, 145, 2:116–123, 1998.

[10] ITU-R: Methodology for the Subjective Assessment of the Quality of Television Picture. International Standard, 2000. ITU-R BT.500-10.

[11] R. Aldridge, J. Davidoff, M. Ghanbari, D. Hands, and D. Pearson. Measurement of scene-dependent quality variations in digitally coded television pictures. *IEE Proceedings on Vision, Image and Signal Processing*, 142, 3:149–154, 1995.

[12] F. Pereira and T. Alpert. MPEG-4 video subjective test procedures and results. *IEEE Transactions on Circuits and Systems for Video Technology*, 7, 1:32–51, 1997.

[13] M. Masry and S. Hemami. An analysis of subjective quality in low bit rate video. In *International Conference on Image Processing (ICIP), 2001, Thessaloniki, Greece*, pages 465–468. IEEE Computer Society Press, October 2001.

[14] C. Kuhmünch and C. Schremmer. Empirical Evaluation of Layered Video Coding Schemes. In *Proceedings of the IEEE International Conference on Image Processing (ICIP), Thessaloniki, Greece*, pages 1013–1016, October 2001.

[15] T. Hayashi, S. Yamasaki, N. Morita, H. Aida, M. Takeichi, and N. Doi. Effects of IP packet loss and picture frame reduction on MPEG1 subjective quality. In *3rd Workshop on Multimedia Signal Processing, Copenhagen, Denmark*, pages 515–520. IEEE Computer Society Press, September 1999.

[16] S. Gringeri, R. Egorov, K. Shuaib, A. Lewis, and B. Basch. Robust compression and transmission of MPEG-4 video. In *Proceedings of the ACM Multimedia Conference 1999, Orlando, Florida, USA*, pages 113–120, October 1999.

[17] M. Chen. Design of a virtual auditorium. In *Proceedings of the ACM Multimedia Conference 2001, Ottawa, Canada*, pages 19–28, September 2001.

[18] S. Lavington, N. Dewhurst, and M. Ghanbari. The Performance of Layered Video over an IP Network. *Signal Processing: Image Communication, Elsevier Science*, 16, 8:785–794, 2001.

[19] C. Krasic and J. Walpole. Priority-Progress Streaming for Quality-Adaptive Multimedia. In *ACM Multimedia Doctoral Symposium, Ottawa, Canada*, October 2001.

[20] Intel. Developers - What Intel Streaming Web Video Software Can Do For You, 2000. http://developer.intel.com/ial/swv/developer.htm.

[21] PacketVideo. Technical White Paper: PacketVideo Multimedia Technology Overview, 2001. http://www.packetvideo.com/pdf/pv_whitepaper.pdf.

[22] R. Neff and A. Zakhor. Matching Pursuit Video Coding–Part I: Dictionary Approximation. *IEEE Transactions on Circuits and Systems for Video Technology*, 12, 1:13–26, 2002.

[23] J. Hartung, A. Jacquin, J. Pawlyk, and K. Shipley. A Real-time Scalable Software Video Codec for Collaborative Applications over Packet Networks. In *Proceedings of the ACM Multimedia Conference 1998, Bristol, UK*, pages 419–426, September 1998.

[24] L. Vicisano, L. Rizzo, and J. Crowcroft. TCP-like congestion control for layered multicast data transfer. In *Proceedings of the 17th Annual Joint Conference of the IEEE Computer and Communications Societies (INFOCOM'98)*, pages 996–1003. IEEE Computer Society Press, March 1998.

[25] S. McCanne, M. Vetterli, and V. Jacobson. Receiver-driven layered multicast. In *Proceedings of ACM SIGCOMM'96*, Palo Alto, CA, August 1996.

A Moving Average Predictor for Playout Delay Control in VoIP

Víctor M. Ramos R.[1*], Chadi Barakat[2], and Eitan Altman[2]

[1] University of Nice-Sophia Antipolis, France. Victor.Ramos@ieee.org
[2] INRIA-Sophia Antipolis, France. {cbarakat,altman}@sophia.inria.fr

Abstract. Audio applications are now widely used in the Internet. Such applications require receiver playout buffers to smooth network delay variations and to reconstruct the periodic form of the transmitted packets. Packets arriving after their playout deadline are considered late and are not played out. Existing algorithms used in the Internet operate by adaptively adjusting the playout delay from talkspurt to talkspurt. There is an important tradeoff between loss percentage and average playout delay. Current algorithms fail to obtain a particular loss percentage. Controlling this parameter is a key characteristic for any playout adaptation algorithm. This paper presents a Moving Average algorithm for playout delay adaptation with tunable loss percentage. We show with trace-based simulations that, in most of the cases, our algorithm performs better than those implemented in popular audio tools, and this is for the range of loss rates of interest in interactive audio applications.

1 Introduction

Delay, jitter, and packet loss in packet-switched wide-area networks are the main factors impacting audio quality of interactive multimedia applications. Today's Internet still operates in a best-effort basis, and thus, the impact of jitter, delay, and packet loss must be alleviated by employing end-to-end control mechanisms.

Audio applications such as NeVoT [1] and Rat [2] generate packets spaced at regular time intervals. The traffic generated by an audio source is divided into periods of activity, called *talkspurts*, and periods of silence. Silence periods are periods where no audio packets are transmitted.

Audio packets encounter variable delay while crossing the Internet, which is mainly due to the variable queuing time in routers. This delay variability modifies the periodic form of the transmitted audio stream. To playout the received stream, an application must reduce or eliminate this delay variability, by buffering the received packets and playing them out after a certain deadline. Packets arriving after their corresponding deadline are considered late and are not played out. If the playout delay is increased, the probability that a packet will arrive before its scheduled playout time also increases. This reduces the number of packets artificially dropped in the playout buffer. However, very long playout delays have a negative impact on the interactivity of an audio session. Obviously, there

---

*Víctor Ramos is also with the Universidad Autónoma Metropolitana, Mexico.

K. Jeffay, I. Stoica, and K. Wehrle (Eds.): IWQoS 2003, LNCS 2707, pp. 155–173, 2003.
© Springer-Verlag Berlin Heidelberg 2003

exists a trade-off between delay and loss due to late packets. For interactive audio, packet delays up to 400 ms and loss rates up to 5% are considered adequate [3].

We focus in this paper on the tradeoff between loss and delay for playout delay control algorithms. Using measurements of packet end-to-end delay of audio sessions done with NeVoT, we present and validate a Moving Average (MA) algorithm that adjusts the playout delay at the beginning of each talkspurt. To prove the efficiency of our algorithm, we compare it with earlier work done by Ramjee et al. [4]. We present two versions of our algorithm: an offline algorithm and an online one. First, we explain the offline MA algorithm, which serves as a reference for our work. Then, we show how an online hybrid algorithm can be implemented by combining the ideas proposed by Ramjee et al. with the moving average algorithm we propose.

Moving average estimators have been used in different fields of research. For example, in [5] Zhang et al. show that moving average estimation is a good approach to predict end-to-end delay for TCP connections. We use a moving average technique not for predicting end-to-end delay, but rather for predicting an optimal value of the playout delay per-talkspurt in an audio session.

One characteristic that most of the playout delay adaptation algorithms lack is the ability to fix the loss percentage to some a priori value. By changing a measure of variability, the algorithms proposed by Ramjee et al. can achieve different loss percentages. However, there is no explicit relationship between the measure of variability that we can adapt in these algorithms and the average loss percentage. The average loss percentage can change from one audio session to another, even if this parameter is kept unchanged. Here lies the main contribution of our work. The moving average algorithm we propose adjusts the playout delay from talkspurt to talkspurt, given a desired target of average loss percentage p. Our algorithm ensures that the average loss percentage we obtain during the session is close, if not equal, to the target value. At the same time, and in most of the cases, our algorithm realizes this target with a smaller average playout delay than the one we need to obtain the same average loss percentage with the algorithms proposed by Ramjee et al. For practical loss percentages, we validate our algorithm and those of Ramjee et al. using real packet audio traces. By using collected audio traces we can compare the algorithms under the same network conditions.

The remainder of this paper is as follows. Section 2 provides some additional background and describes the packet delay traces used for validation, as well as the notation we use throughout the paper. In Sect. 3, we describe some related work on playout delay algorithms. Section 4 describes the performance measures we consider to validate our algorithm and to compare it with the algorithms of Ramjee et al. We present in Sect. 5 our moving average algorithm. Section 6 describes, based on results from Sect. 5, that it is better to predict a function of the delay rather than the optimal delay itself. Section 7 compares the performance of an online hybrid implementation of the moving average algorithm with the Ramjee et al. algorithms. Finally, Sect. 8 concludes the paper.

2   Some Background

Receivers use a playout buffer to smooth the stream of audio packets. This smoothing is done by delaying the playout of packets to compensate for variable network delay.

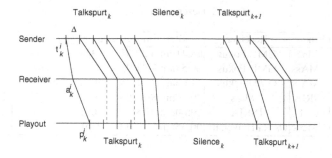

Fig. 1. The timings between the transmission, reception and playout of packets.

The playout delay can be either constant through the whole session, or can be adjusted between talkspurts. Moreover, in a recent work [6], it has been shown that by using a technique called *packet scaling*, it is possible to change the playout delay from packet to packet while keeping the resulting distortion within tolerable levels. In this paper we only focus on the per-talkspurt playout delay adaptation approach.

Figure 1 shows the different stages incurred in an audio session. The i-th packet of talkspurt k is sent at time t_k^i, it arrives at the receiver at time a_k^i, and is held in the smoothing receiver's playout buffer until time p_k^i, when it is played out. Inside a talkspurt, packets are equally spaced at the sender by time intervals of length Δ seconds.

By delaying the playout of packets and dropping those that arrive after their deadline, we are able to reconstruct the original periodic form of the stream. This adaptation results in a regenerated stream at having stretched or compressed silence periods compared to the original stream. These changes are not noticeable by the human ear if they are kept within tolerable small levels.

In Fig. 1, a dropped packet due to a late arrival is represented by a dashed line. A packet is artificially dropped if it arrives after its scheduled deadline p_i^k. The loss percentage can be reduced by increasing the amount of time that packets stay in the playout buffer. An efficient playout adaptation algorithm must take into account the trade-off between loss and delay in order to keep both parameters as low as possible.

Table 1. Definition of variables.

Param.	Meaning
L	The total number of packets arriving at the receiver during a session.
N	The total number of talkspurts in a session.
N_k	The number of packets in talkspurt k.
t_k^i	The time at which the i-th packet of talkspurt k is generated at the sender.
a_k^i	The time at which the i-th packet of talkspurt k is received.
d_k^i	The variable portion of the end-to-end delay of the i-th packet in talkspurt k. $d_k^i = a_k^i - t_k^i - \min_{\substack{1 \le k \le N \\ 1 \le i \le N_k}} (a_k^i - t_k^i).$
p_k^i	The time at which packet i of talkspurt k is played out.

Table 2. Description of the traces.

Trace	Sender	Receiver	Start time	Length [s]	Talkspurts	Packets
1	UMass	GMD Fokus	08:41pm 6/27/95	1348	818	56979
2	UMAss	GMD Fokus	09:58am 7/21/95	1323	406	24490
3	UMAss	GMD Fokus	11:05am 7/21/95	1040	536	37640
4	INRIA	UMass	09:20pm 8/26/93	580	252	27814
5	UCI	INRIA	09:00pm 9/18/93	1091	540	52836
6	UMass	Osaka University	00:35am 9/24/93	649	299	23293

Throughout the paper, we use the notation described in Table 1. For the validation of our algorithm, we consider the packet traces generated with the NeVoT audio tool that are described in [7]. NeVoT is an audio terminal program used to establish audio conversations in the Internet. The traces we use contain the sender and receiver timestamps of transmitted packets that are needed for the implementation of any playout adaptation algorithm. In these traces, one 160 byte audio packet is generated approximately every 20 ms when there is speech activity. A description of the traces (reproduced from [7]) is depicted in Table 2.

A typical sample of packet end-to-end delays is shown in Fig. 2. A packet is represented by a diamond and talkspurt boundaries by dashed rectangles. The x-axis represents the time elapsed at the receiver since the beginning of the audio session. Only the variable portion of the end-to-end delay (d_k^i) is represented on the y-axis of Fig. 2. To this end, the constant component of the end-to-end delay (mostly caused by the propagation delay) is removed by subtracting from packet delays their minimum over all the corresponding trace. By considering the variable portion of the end-to-end delay, synchronization between sender and receiver clocks can be avoided[1] [7].

We observe in Fig. 2 the presence of delay spikes. This phenomenon in end-to-end delay has been previously reported in the literature [4, 8]. Delay spikes represent a serious problem for audio applications since they affect the performance of playout delay adaptation algorithms. A *delay spike* is defined as a sudden large increase in the end-to-end delay followed by a series of packets arriving almost simultaneously, leading to the completion of the spike [4].

Delay spikes can be contained within a single talkspurt or can span over several talkspurts. Figure 2(a) shows a delay spike spanning through two consecutive talkspurts. Figure 2(b) shows a delay spike spanning over three talkspurts. Since the playout delay is generally changed between talkspurts, a playout algorithm behaves better when delay spikes span over more than one talkspurt. Only in this way, a playout algorithm can react adequately to the spike by setting the playout delay according to the experienced delay. If the spike vanishes before the end of a talkspurt, the playout algorithm will not have enough time to set the playout time accordingly.

In the next section, we briefly describe the algorithms proposed by Ramjee et al. Playout delay is adapted from talkspurt to talkspurt based on past statistics of the delay process. The playout delay of the first packet of each talkspurt is the basetime of the

---

[1] Later, when comparing the performance of different algorithms, all graphics consider the variable portion of end-to-end delays.

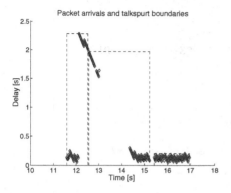
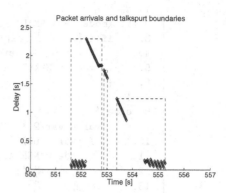

(a) A delay spike spanning through two consecutive talkspurts.

(b) A delay spike spanning through three consecutive talkspurts.

Fig. 2. Delay spikes in end-to-end delay measurements.

deadlines for subsequent packets in the same talkspurt. This principle is the basis for most of the existing playout adaptation algorithms [9,4,7,10].

3   Related Work

Extensive research work has been done in the area of adaptive playout mechanisms [11,9, 4,6,12,7,10]. In [4], Ramjee et al. propose four algorithms for playout delay. All the four algorithms proposed in [4] compute an estimate of the average end-to-end delay and a measure of variability of delay similarly to the computation of round-trip-time estimates by TCP for the retransmission timer. We denote them as $\hat{d}_k^i$ and $\hat{v}_k^i$ respectively. These statistics are used to set the playout time for a talkspurt.

The algorithms that perform better in [4] are 1 and 4. We rename these algorithms as A and B respectively, and refer to them as such throughout the rest of the paper.

To calculate $\hat{d}_k^i$ and $\hat{v}_k^i$, the packet's sender and receiver timestamps, t_k^i and a_k^i, are read from a trace file. Both algorithms differ only in the way they calculate $\hat{d}_k^i$ and $\hat{v}_k^i$. Algorithm A computes these statistics as follows:

$$\hat{d}_k^i = \alpha \hat{d}_k^{i-1} + (1-\alpha)d_k^i, \quad \text{and} \quad \hat{v}_k^i = \alpha \hat{v}_k^{i-1} + (1-\alpha)|\hat{d}_k^i - d_k^i|,$$

where $d_k^i = a_k^i - t_k^i$, and α has the default value of 0.998002.

Algorithm B is described in [4] but we also sketch it in Fig. 3 for completeness. It operates in two modes: normal mode and spike (or impulse) mode. In normal mode, it behaves like Algorithm A but with different coefficients. When the difference between two consecutive delay values exceeds a given threshold, algorithm B triggers the spike mode. During this mode, the variable var is updated with an exponentially decreasing

```
1.  d_k^i = a_k^i - t_k^i ;
2.  if (mode == NORMAL) {
3.      if (|d_k^i - d_k^i ^1| > 2|v̂_k^i| + 800) {
4.          var = 0; /* Detected beginning of spike */
5.          mode = SPIKE;
6.      }
7.  }
8.  else {
9.          var = var/2 + |(2d_k^i - d_k^i ^1 - d_k^i ^2)/8|;
10.         if (var ≤ 63) {
11.             mode = NORMAL; /* End of spike */
12.             d_k^i ^2 = d_k^i ^1 ;
13.             d_k^i ^1 = d_k^i ;
14.             return;
15.         }
16. }
17. if (mode == NORMAL)
18.     d̂_k^i = 0.125d_k^i + 0.875d̂_k^i ^1 ;
19. else
20.     d̂_k^i = d̂_k^i ^1 + d_k^i - d_k^i ^1 ;
21. v̂_k^i = 0.125|d_k^i - d̂_k^i| + 0.875v̂_k^i ^1 ;
22. d_k^i ^2 = d_k^i ^1 ;
23. d_k^i ^1 = d_k^i ;
24. return;
```

Fig. 3. Algorithm B

value that adjusts to the slope of the spike. The end of a delay spike is detected when var reaches an enough small value, and the algorithm returns to normal mode.

Once $\hat{d}_k^i$ and $\hat{v}_k^i$ are computed, the playout time of the i-th packet of talkspurt k is set by both algorithms as follows:

$$p_k^i = \begin{cases} t_k^i + \hat{d}_k^i + \beta \hat{v}_k^i, & \text{for } i = 1 . \\ p_k^1 + (t_k^i - t_k^1), & \text{for } 1 < i \le N_k . \end{cases} \tag{1}$$

These values are computed for each packet but the playout time is changed only at the beginning of a talkspurt. By varying β one is able to achieve different loss probabilities and different average playout delays. In [4], β is set equal to the constant value of 4. Larger values of β allow to obtain lower loss percentages due to late arrivals but at the cost of a longer average playout delay.

Algorithm A is slow in detecting delay spikes, but it maintains a good average playout delay over an audio session. Algorithm B reacts faster to delay spikes, but it underestimates the playout delay at the end of the spike [7].

To compare our moving average algorithm with algorithms A and B, we use the performance measures defined in [7]. For clarity of the presentation, we redefine these measures in Sect. 4.

4 Performance Measures

To assess the performance of a playout adaptation algorithm, we focus on the total number of packets that are played out during an audio session, as well as on the experienced average end-to-end delay. Suppose we are given a packet audio trace with the sender and receiver timestamps of audio packets. Let p_k^i, N, L, N_k, t_k^i, and a_k^i be defined as in Table 1. As in [7], we define r_k^i to be a variable indicating if packet i of talkspurt k is played out or not. So, r_k^i is defined as:

$$r_k^i = \begin{cases} 0, & \text{if } p_k^i < a_k^i \,. \\ 1, & \text{otherwise.} \end{cases}$$

The total number of packets, T, played out in an audio session is thus given by:

$$T = \sum_{k=1}^{N} \sum_{i=1}^{N_k} r_k^i. \tag{2}$$

The average playout delay, D_{avg}, is equal to :

$$D_{avg} = \frac{1}{T} \sum_{k=1}^{N} \sum_{i=1}^{N_k} r_k^i [p_k^i - t_k^i]. \tag{3}$$

Finally, the loss percentage, l, is equal to :

$$l = \frac{L - T}{L} \times 100. \tag{4}$$

5 Moving Average Prediction

Algorithms A and B are good in maintaining a low overall average playout delay and reacting to delay spikes. However, they lack a parameter allowing to have a direct control on the overall loss percentage during an audio session. It would be desirable to come up with an algorithm that sets the playout delay in a way to get a loss percentage p, given a trace of N talkspurts and L packets. By varying the parameter β in algorithms A and B, it is possible to obtain different loss percentages, but one is unable to have any particular control on this parameter. We describe in this section our moving average predictor (MA) for playout delay that takes as input the desired loss percentage per-session, p, and a packet delay trace. It returns a set of estimated playout delay values leading to an average loss percentage close, if not equal to the desired value p.

5.1 The Model

Let D_k be the optimal playout delay at the beginning of talkspurt k, and let p be the desired average loss percentage per-session. We mean by *optimal playout delay* the playout delay that makes the number of losses per talkspurt the closest to $p \times N_k$, N_k being the number of audio packets received during the k-th talkspurt. By controlling the loss percentage per-talkspurt to p, we are sure that the overall loss percentage during the whole audio session is also close to p. We compute D_k as follows, let d_k^j be the variable portion of the end-to-end delay of the j-th packet in talkspurt k. For each talkspurt, $1 \leq k \leq N$, we sort in ascending order the packet end-to-end delay values to obtain N new ordered sets $\{d_{k_{sort}}^j\}$, with $1 \leq j \leq N_k$. We set the optimal playout delay of the k-th talkspurt to the following value:

$$D_k = d_{k_{sort}}^i, \quad i \leq N_k, \tag{5}$$

with $i = \text{round}((1-p)N_k)$. Thus, if $d_k^i \leq D_k$, the i-th packet of talkspurt k is played out, otherwise the packet is dropped due to a late arrival.

We present now our moving average predictor. Consider that we have a set of optimal delay values in the past $\{D_k, D_{k-1}, D_{k-2}, \dots\}$, and that we want to predict the value of D_{k+1}. The predicted value of D_{k+1} is denoted by $\hat{D}_{k+1}$, and is taken as a weighted average of the last M values of the process $\{D_k\}$. Thus,

$$\hat{D}_{k+1} = \sum_{l=1}^{M} a_l D_{k-l+1}. \tag{6}$$

The coefficients a_l in (6) must be chosen in a way that minimizes the mean square error between $\hat{D}_k$ and D_k, i.e. $\mathbb{E}[(D_k - \hat{D}_k)^2]$. The desired coefficients are the solution of the set of the so-called normal equations [13]:

$$\sum_{m=0}^{M-1} a_{m+1} r_D(m-l) = r_D(l+1), \, l = 0, 1, \dots, M-1. \tag{7}$$

In (7), $r_D = \mathbb{E}[D_k D_{k+l}]$ is the lag-l autocorrelation function of the process $\{D_k\}$. The exact form of the autocorrelation function is unknown, but it can be estimated using the past values of the process $\{D_k\}$. Suppose we have K values in the past, we can thus write

$$r_D(r) \simeq \frac{1}{K-|r|} \sum_{k=1}^{K-|r|} D_k D_{k+|r|}, \quad r = 0, \pm 1, \pm 2, \dots, \pm(K-1). \tag{8}$$

The set of normal equations (7) can be solved using single matrix-vector operations. For large values of M (say $M > 100$), the well known Levinson-Durbin algorithm may be preferred [13].

M is called the *model's order*. Figure 4 illustrates how M is calculated. For a given packet trace, starting with $M = 1$, we compute all the values of $\{\hat{D}_k\}$ and estimate $\mathbb{E}[(D_k - \hat{D}_k)^2]$. Then, we increase M and we repeat the process. The model's order is taken equal to the lowest value of M preceding an increase in the mean square error. For example, for trace 1 the algorithm chooses M equal to 19, and for trace 3 it chooses M equal to 8. There exist different methods for selecting the model's order e.g. Double Sided t-test, Minimum Description Length, and Final Prediction Error; the reader is referred to [14].

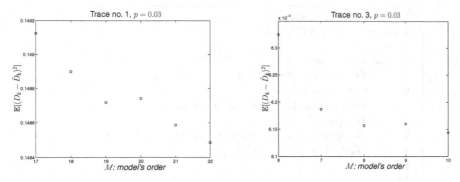

Fig. 4. Model order selection for the MA algorithm.

5.2   The Moving Average Algorithm

We describe now our moving average algorithm for playout delay. The algorithm takes as input a packet delay trace with sender and receiver timestamps, and looks for $\{\hat{D}_k\}$, the estimates of the optimal playout delays $\{D_k\}$. For each past talkspurt, the individual end-to-end delay values are sorted, and $\hat{D}_k$ is computed as in (6). $\hat{D}_k$ is calculated for each talkspurt as a weighted average of the last M talkspurts, for $k = M+1, M+2, \dots, N$. Later, when evaluating the average playout delay and the loss percentage per-session, we discard in the computation the first M talkspurts.

Figure 5 depicts a pseudo-code version of the MA algorithm. The getOptDelay() function takes as input the whole set of end-to-end delay values, d, and the desired loss percentage per-session p. Then, it applies (5) to return a set of optimal per-talkspurt delay values $\{D_k\}$. The first for loop solves the normal equations for a_l to compute $\hat{D}_{k+1}$ for each talkspurt, then it calculates $\mathbb{E}[(D_k - \hat{D}_k)^2]$ for different values of the model's order m, and holds the result in the vector $\overrightarrow{mse}$. Next, getOrder($\overrightarrow{mse}$) is called to find the model's order, M, by choosing the lowest value of M preceding an increase in $\overrightarrow{mse}$. Then, we compute the coefficients a_l with the value of M just found.

The last for loop computes $\hat{D}_{k+1}$ for each talkspurt and the playout times p_k^i. The playout time of the i-th packet of talkspurt k is set as follows:

$$p_k^i = \begin{cases} t_k^1 + \hat{D}_k, & \text{for } i = 1 \\ p_k^1 + (t_k^i - t_k^1), & \text{for } 1 < i \le N_k. \end{cases} \qquad (9)$$

The moving average algorithm requires the knowledge of the characteristics of the process $\{D_k\}$. Assuming the process $\{D_k\}$ is stationary during all the audio session, the best performance of this algorithm is obtained when it is run offline or after a large number of samples is collected.

5.3   The Problem with Low p

As our simulation results will show, the MA algorithm described in Sect. 5.2 deviates from the desired loss percentage p. See in (5) how the value of D_k depends on the talkspurt size N_k, and on the desired loss percentage p. For a given value of p, (5)

```
1.  D_k ← getOptDelay(d,p);
2.  R ← autocorr(D_k, N);
3.
4.  for m = 1 to N {
5.      /* Get the weights */
6.      a = solve(R, m);
7.      /* Compute D̂_{k+1} for each talkspurt */
8.      D̂_{k+1} = ∑_{l=1}^{m} a_l D_k l+1;
9.      /* Update the mse vector for this value of m */
10.     mse(m) = E[(D_k - D̂_k)^2];
11. }
12.
13. M = getOrder(mse⃗);
14. a = solve(R, M);
15.
16. for k = M to N - 1 {
17.     D̂_{k+1} = ∑_{l=1}^{M} a_l D_k l+1;
18.     p^1_{k+1} = t^1_{k+1} + D̂_{k+1};
19.     20. for j = 2 to N_{k+1}
21.             p^j_{k+1} = p^1_{k+1} + t^j_{k+1} - t^1_{k+1};
22. }
```

Fig. 5. The MA algorithm.

returns the delay value closest to $p \times N_k$. Thus, when computing $\hat{D}_k$, there will be a deviation of the overall perceived loss percentage from the one we desire. The highest deviation is for very low values of p. The algorithm leads to a loss percentage longer than the desired one. To deal with this deviation, for the range $0.005 \leq p \leq 0.02$, we allow our MA algorithm to slightly increase the playout delay by the following offset:

$$\Delta_{\hat{D}_k} = f(p)\sqrt{\mathbb{E}[(\hat{D}_k - D_k)^2]}. \tag{10}$$

In this way, the playout delay is increased as a function of the measured mean square error between D_k and $\hat{D}_k$, and as a function of p. Since the deviation of the measured loss percentage increases for small values of p, we set f to $f(p) = -\delta \times (\frac{p}{p_{max}} - 1)$, where δ is a constant controlling how much we increase the playout delay as a function of the square root of $\mathbb{E}[(D_k - \hat{D}_k)^2]$. So, as p increases in the range $(0, p_{max}]$, $\hat{D}_k$ converges to its original form (6), and if p decreases a longer offset is used. We set $p_{max} = 0.02$ and $\delta = 0.5$. This allows to reduce considerably the deviation of the measured loss percentage from p, without impacting much the delay.

The following lines must be added to the pseudo-code shown in Fig. 5 between lines 17 and 18:
  if $p \leq 0.02$
    $\hat{D}_{k+1} \leftarrow \hat{D}_{k+1} + \Delta_{\hat{D}_k}$.

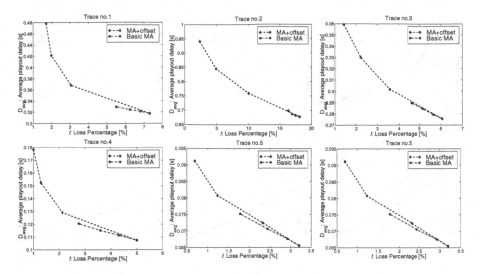

Fig. 6. Performance of the MA algorithm before and after adding the offset to $\hat{D}_k$ for $p \in [0.005, 0.02]$.

To see the gain obtained when applying (10), we plot in Fig. 6, for $p \in [0.005, 0.02]$ the performance of the original MA algorithm before and after this change. The x-axis represents the total measured loss percentage due to late losses, l, and the y-axis plots the average playout delay, D_{avg}, for discrete values of p from 0.005 to $p_{\text{max}} = 0.02$, with p increasing 0.005 at each step. We call this new algorithm *MA+offset*, and we refer to it as such during the rest of the paper.

The deviation of the loss percentage for the MA+offset algorithm is much lower, while keeping the average playout delay within reasonable values. The gain we get compared to the basic MA algorithm is very clear. For trace 1, the MA+offset algorithm reaches loss percentages of 1.7% compared to 5.4% in the basic MA algorithm. The MA+offset algorithm is beneficial for all traces, and the gain is higher for trace 2 and trace 6, where the deviation of the desired loss percentage is now much lower compared to the original case.

Section 5.4 compares the performance of our MA+offset algorithm with algorithms A and B.

5.4   Performance Comparison

To evaluate each of the three algorithms, we use a simulator that reads in an input file containing the sender and receiver timestamps of each packet of an audio session. Then, each algorithm is executed, and we use expressions (3) and (4) to compute the average playout delay and the loss percentage during an audio session.

As pointed out above, algorithms A and B are unable to get a particular target of loss percentage p. Thus, to obtain different loss percentages in Algorithms A and B we vary β in (1) from 1 to 20; larger values of β allow to get lower loss percentages, at the

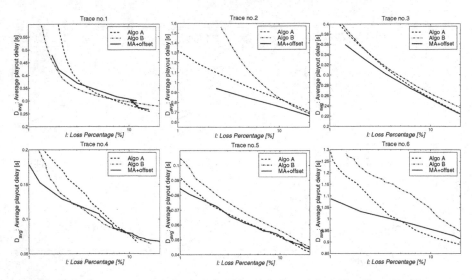

Fig. 7. Performance comparison of algorithms A, B, and the MA+offset algorithm.

expense of a higher average playout delay. We compare the performance of algorithms A and B with our MA+offset algorithm for $0.005 \leq p \leq 0.2$. Loss percentages smaller than 5% are rather desirable for interactive audio applications [3].

Figure 7 plots the corresponding results for each trace. The x-axis represents the perceived loss percentage per-session l, and the y-axis represents the average playout delay D_{avg}. Each execution of an algorithm gives a single point in the graphic. The plots in Fig. 7 were obtained by connecting the discrete points returned by each approach.

In trace 1, we see how for loss percentages greater than 5%, the performance of the three algorithms is quite similar, with algorithms A and B having a slightly better performance than the MA+offset algorithm for loss percentages between 5% and 11%. For loss percentages lower than 5%, the performance of algorithms B and MA+offset remains similar but they outperform algorithm A with a maximum gain on average playout delay of about 40% of the MA+offset algorithm compared to algorithm A. Trace 2 is the only multicast session and has a large network loss percentage of about 50%, it has also long inactivity periods of up to 2 minutes. The MA+offset algorithm clearly outperforms algorithms A and B for the whole range of loss percentage and average playout delay, with a maximum gain on playout delay of about 200% compared to algorithm B. In trace 3, algorithms A and B remain close to the MA+offset algorithm, with the MA+offset algorithm giving better performance for the whole range of loss percentage and average playout delay. For traces 4 to 6, algorithms A and MA+offset remain close in both, loss percentage and average playout delay, outperforming algorithm B. For loss percentages lower than 3%, the MA+offset algorithm performs better than algorithms A and B. This difference in performance is clearly seen in trace 6, where the MA+offset algorithm shows a considerable gain over algorithms A and B.

Deviations of loss percentage persist in the MA+offset algorithm. The highest deviations in Fig. 6 are for traces 2 and 6. Both are the shortest traces, they suffer from high variations on end-to-end delay, and high network loss due to congestion. Thus, the autocorrelation function does not have useful information about the process $\{D_k\}$, and consequently the estimated values $\{\hat{D}_k\}$ are inaccurate. Section 6 describes a transformation that can be done to reduce the deviations of the MA+offset algorithm.

6 Bias and Transformation

Our scheme is designed with the main objective to control the loss percentage to a certain value p, while minimizing the average playout delay. Here is the strength of our scheme compared to other schemes in the literature, where we do not have a direct control on the loss percentage. Our control on this parameter has been done till now by controlling the optimal playout delay per talkspurt D_k. But, the relationship between the playout delay and the loss percentage may not be linear. This may cause in a deviation of the perceived loss percentage from the desired one. Technically said, our predictor is unbiased with respect to D_k, however it may be biased with respect to the loss percentage per talkspurt. We illustrate this bias by the following analysis.

Our moving average predictor of D_k ensures that $\mathbb{E}\left[D_k\right] = \mathbb{E}[\hat{D}_k]$. Let d_k^i, $1 \leq i \leq N_k$, be the delay of the i-th packet of talkspurt k. The way we define D_k also ensures that $\mathbb{E}\left[1\{d_k^i > D_k\}\right] = p$, with $1\{A\}$ being the indicator function. But, the average loss percentage we experience during the audio conversation is not $\mathbb{E}\left[1\{d_k^i > D_k\}\right]$, but rather $\mathbb{E}[1\{d_k^i > \hat{D}_k\}]$. We explain next why this experienced average loss percentage can be different from p, when the relationship between loss and delay is non-linear.

Let $F(x)$ be the complementary CDF of packet end-to-end delay, i.e., $F(x) = \mathbb{P}\{d_k^i > x\}$. It is easy to see that for $x = \mathbb{E}\left[D_k\right]$, $F(x)$ is equal to p, since $\mathbb{P}\{d_k^i > D_k\} = \mathbb{E}\left[1\{d_k^i > D_k\}\right]$ is equal to p by definition.

The average packet loss percentage we obtain with our scheme is equal to $\hat{p} = \mathbb{E}[1\{d_k^i > \hat{D}_k\}]$. We condition on the value of D_k. This leads to

$$\hat{p} = \mathbb{E}\left[1\{d_k^i > \hat{D}_k\}\right] = \mathbb{E}\left[\mathbb{E}\left[1\{d_k^i > \hat{D}_k\}\right] \mid D_k\right] = \mathbb{E}\left[F(\mathbb{E}\left[D_k\right] + \hat{D}_k - D_k)\right].$$

The last equality results from the fact that

$$\mathbb{E}\left[1\{d_k^i > D_k + y\}\right] = \mathbb{E}\left[\mathbb{E}\left[1\{d_k^i > D_k + y\} \mid D_k\right]\right] = F(\mathbb{E}\left[D_k\right] + y). \quad (11)$$

The proof (11) is as follows. The objective is to compute the loss probability of a packet when the playout delay in a talkspurt is set y units far from the optimal playout delay D_k. In other words, we want to compute the loss probability of a packet, when the playout delay is set y units far from the playout delay that results in a packet loss percentage equal to p. But, the playout delay that results in a packet loss percentage equal to p (if we only look at the packet and not at the talkspurt to which the packet belongs) is simply $F(\mathbb{E}\left[D_k\right])$. Hence, the problem is equivalent to computing the loss probability of a random packet when the playout delay for this packet is set y units far from $\mathbb{E}\left[D_k\right]$, which is equal to $F(\mathbb{E}\left[D_k\right] + y)$.

Let ϵ_k be the prediction error for talkspurt k, i.e., $\epsilon_k = \hat{D}_k - D_k$. We write $\hat{p} = \mathbb{E}\left[F(\mathbb{E}\left[D_k\right] + \epsilon_k)\right]$. The bias of our predictor can be seen from this expression, when the function $F(x)$ in non-linear. $F(x)$ relates the packet loss probability of a packet to the playout delay. For example, if $F(x)$ is a convex function, we have by Jensen's inequality $\hat{p} > F(\mathbb{E}[D_k] + \mathbb{E}[\epsilon_k]) = F(\mathbb{E}[D_k]) = p$.

To correct this bias, some transformation of the process D_k can be used. Define $X_k = G(D_k)$. The prediction will be done on the process X_k instead of D_k, using a Moving Average predictor, i.e., $\hat{X}_{k+1} = \sum_{l=1}^{M} a_l X_{k-l+1}$. Once the estimate of X_k, denoted by $\hat{X}_k$ is obtained, we set the playout delay to $G^{-1}(\hat{X}_k)$. The average loss percentage becomes equal to $\hat{p} = \mathbb{E}\left[F(\mathbb{E}[D_k] + G^{-1}(\hat{X}_k) - G^{-1}(X_k))\right]$.

The function $G(x)$ must compensate for the non-linearity of the function $F(x)$. It must transform the error in setting the playout delay, so as to make $\hat{p}$ equal to p. Unfortunately, it is very difficult to find the expression of $G(x)$. Some approximations can be used. We give an example of a transformation that we use in this paper. Our measurements show that the function $F(x)$ is convex, and close to exponential. We consider then as transformation the exponential function, with a decay coefficient α, that is, we take $G(x) = e^{-\alpha x}$. Hence, we predict $X_k = e^{-\alpha D_k}$ instead of predicting D_k.

6.1 Performance Comparison

We apply the exponential transformation $G(x)$ to the process $\hat{D}_k$ in our MA algorithm. The MA algorithm remains the same, but we predict now the process $X_k = e^{-\alpha D_k}$ rather than directly predicting D_k. We call this new algorithm *transformed MA* algorithm.

When testing the transformed MA algorithm we found no significant differences for $10 < \alpha \leq 20$. For $\alpha < 10$ the performance degrades very slowly with decreasing α. We thus set empirically the value of α to 10, and we use it when comparing with algorithms A and B in the next section.

To further improve the performance of the transformed MA algorithm, when transforming back $\hat{D}_k$ from $\hat{X}_k$, we implement the procedure described in Sec. 5.3 to reduce the deviations for small values of p. We call this variant *transformed MA+offset*.

Figure 8 compares the performance of our two MA+offset algorithms with algorithms A and B. In the subsequent figures, the transformed MA+offset is denoted as MA+transf+offset. Observe how the transformation applied on D_k considerably improves the performance of the MA algorithm. For trace 1, the transformed MA+offset algorithm clearly outperforms algorithms A, B, and the original MA algorithm with a gain of up to 50% for the whole range of loss percentage and average playout delay. For trace 2, the transformed MA+offset algorithm does not reach loss percentages lower than 5%. This is still due to the high jitter and network loss present in trace 2 which does not provide the autocorrelation function with useful information about the process D_k. However, the transformed MA+offset algorithm largely outperforms algorithms A and B for other values of p. For traces 3 to 5, we see clearly the benefit of applying the transformation $G(x)$. The transformed MA+offset algorithm outperforms all the other algorithms with a maximum gain on average playout delay of up to 80% in trace 4 for low loss percentages, compared to algorithms A and B. We notice an interesting behavior of the transformed MA algorithm in trace 6. This is the only trace for which the MA+offset algorithm behaves better than the transformed MA+offset version. Like trace 2, trace 6

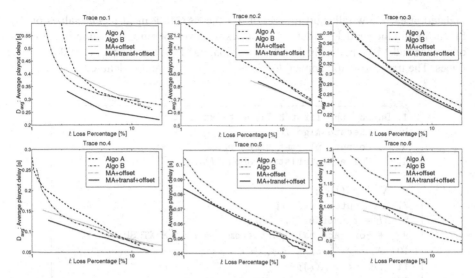

Fig. 8. Performance comparison of algorithms A, B, and the transformed MA+offset algorithm.

also has a high end-to-end delay and a high network loss percentage; besides, trace 6 is one of the shortest sessions (in number of talkspurts). Thus, the MA+offset algorithm should be preferred when there are long congestion periods in the network and very high jitter.

We conclude that a moving average scheme is an attractive approach for playout delay control. The algorithms studied till now are offline algorithms. Section 7 presents an online hybrid algorithm combining algorithm B and the transformed MA+offset algorithm which gives a very good performance for most of the scenarios.

7 A Hybrid Algorithm for Playout Delay

Moving average estimation has revealed to be an interesting approach for playout delay control. The transformed MA+offset algorithm described in the previous section gives in general better performance than any of the other algorithms we studied. This algorithm was run offline and the entire trace was used to compute the characteristics of $\{D_k\}$. We look now for an online version of the transformed MA+offset algorithm. During our simulations, the maximum model's order was never greater than 23. This means that we do not need a large number of samples to compute a good moving average estimation. We propose in this section a combination of the transformed MA+offset algorithm and algorithm B, that we call *hybrid algorithm*.

The idea is quite simple and is sketched as pseudo-code in Fig. 9. During the first talkspurts of an audio session, say MAXTKSP talkspurts, algorithm B is executed with $\beta = 4$. At the same time, we collect samples of $\{D_k\}$, we transform them to $\{X_k\}$, and we keep them in memory to be used later to compute the model's order and predictor coefficients. Then, starting from talkspurt MAXTKSP+1, the transformed MA+offset algorithm is executed and playout times are computed. The autocorrelation function is updated at each new talkspurt to account for the MAXTKSP most recent values of X_k. Since finding the model's order, M, is an exhaustive operation its value is computed only once and it is kept during the whole session. MAXTKSP is set equal to 100 for all the traces. The transformation applied to D_k is $X_k = e^{-\alpha D_k}$ and is denoted as $G(D_k)$.

```
1.  During the first MAXTKSP talkspurts {
2.      Execute Algo B;
3.      Compute playout times p_k^i;
4.      Collect statistics about D_k;
5.  }
6.  X_k ← G(D_k);
7.  R ← autocorr(X_k);
8.  M = findorder();
9.  /* For each talkspurt from k = 1 to MAXTKSP */
10. X̂_k = ∑_{l=1}^{M} a_l X_k l+1;
11. D̂_k = G^{-1}(X̂_k);
12.
13. for k = MAXTKSP to N − 1 {
14.     X̂_{k+1} = ∑_{l=1}^{M} a_l X_k l+1;
15.     D̂_{k+1} = G^{-1}(X̂_{k+1});
16.     if p ≤ 0.02
17.         D̂_{k+1} ← D̂_{k+1} + (0.5 − 25p)√(E[(D_k − D̂_k)²]);
18.
19.     p_{k+1}^1 = t_{k+1}^1 + D̂_{k+1};
20.     for j = 2 to N_{k+1}
21.         p_{k+1}^j = p_{k+1}^1 + t_{k+1}^j − t_{k+1}^1;
22.
23.     /* We recompute the autocorrelation function */
24.     /* for the MAXTKSP most recent values of X_k */
25.     R ← autocorr(X_k);
26. }
```

Fig. 9. The hybrid online algorithm for playout delay.

7.1 Performance Comparison

Figure 10 compares the performance of the hybrid algorithm with algorithms A and B. In trace 1, the hybrid algorithm outperforms algorithms A and B for almost all values of p. We observe an overall gain on playout delay of about 25% of the hybrid algorithm compared to algorithms A and B. We note again in trace 2 how the the hybrid algorithm does not reach loss percentages lower than 5%. In fact, since the number of D_k samples used to compute the autocorrelation functions is now small, the error introduced in $\hat{X}_k$, and consequently in $\hat{D}_k$, is larger in the hybrid algorithm than in the offline one. For traces 3 to 5, the performance of the hybrid algorithm and algorithms A and B is very

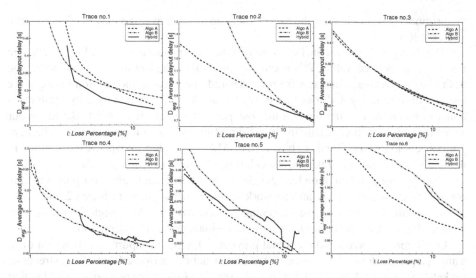

Fig. 10. Performance comparison of algorithms A, B, and the hybrid online algorithm.

similar, with the hybrid algorithm performing better than algorithm A for trace 4, and better than algorithm B for trace 5 in the loss range of interest ($p \leq 0.05$). Trace 6 has the highest session end-to-end delay and high network loss percentages (due to congestion), leading to a behavior similar to that of trace 2.

7.2 Delay Spikes

Algorithm B detects delay spikes; when a delay spike occurs, the algorithm switches to spike mode and follows the spike. When the end of the spike is detected, the algorithm switches back to normal mode. We executed the MA+offset algorithm employing the spike detection approach of Algorithm B. When comparing the performance with no spike detection we found no significant differences. The MA+offset algorithm computes the autocorrelation function of the process $\{D_k\}$ to solve the system of normal equations and to calculate $\{\hat{D}_{k+1}\}$. D_k is the optimal per-talkpsurt playout delay. When delay spikes occur, the autocorrelation functions of $\{D_k\}$ account for them by definition.

8 Conclusions

This paper describes a moving average algorithm that adaptively adjusts the playout delay at the beginning of talkspurts. To evaluate the performance of our algorithm, we compare it with existing schemes implemented in the NeVoT audio tool. Several variants of our moving average algorithm are studied. For small values of p, there is some deviation of the perceived loss percentage, and this deviation increases as p decreases. The MA+offset and the transformed MA+offset algorithms are proposed to reduce the deviation of the desired loss percentage. These variants allow to obtain a considerable gain compared to the original version while, at the same time, keeping the average playout delay within tolerable levels.

The strength of our scheme lies in the fact that we are able to tune the loss percentage p to a given desired value. When directly predicting the optimal playout delay, the desired loss percentage deviates from the desired one because the relation between the average playout delay and loss rate is not linear. We demonstrate that, by applying a transformation on D_k, the bias on the loss percentage can be reduced. Based on our measurements, we approximate this transformation by a negative exponential function. A mixture of algorithm B and our transformed MA+offset algorithm proves to be efficient in the loss percentages of interest. We call this algorithm *hybrid algorithm*.

Moving average estimation has revealed to be an efficient method for playout delay control. When network jitter and network loss are very high, as in traces 2 and 6, the MA algorithm do not reach loss percentages lower than 5%. Very high jitter decreases the correlation of the process D_k, leading to an inaccurate MA estimation.

Our algorithm predicts the optimal playout delay per-talkspurt, or a function of it, using the past history of the process. To reconstruct the periodic form of the stream of packets, the playout delay of packet in a talkspurt is based on the playout time of the first packet in the talkspurt. An interesting recent approach [6, 15] shows that it is possible to adapt the playout delay at each packet arrival, leading to a better performance than in a talkspurt basis. We are working on an extension of our MA approach that predicts the playout delay per-packet, allowing to change the playout delay during a talkspurt, and we expect our scheme to give better performance.

Acknowledgments.   We thank the CONACyT and the Universidad Autónoma Metropolitana at Mexico for supporting this work.

The authors also thank Sue Moon for making publicly available the traces we used in our simulations.

References

1. Schulzrinne, H.: Voice communication across the Internet: a network voice terminal. Technical report, University of Massachusetts, Amherst (1992)
2. Sasse, A.S., Hardman, V.: Multi-way multicast speech for multimedia conferencing over heterogeneous shared packet networks. RAT-robust audio tool. Technical report, EPSRC Project #GRIK72780 (February)
3. Jayant, N.: Effects of packet loss on waveform coded speech. In: Proceedings of the International Conference on Computer Communications. (1980) 275–280
4. Ramjee, R., Kurose, J., Towsley, D., Schulzrinne, H.: Adaptive playout mechanisms for packetized audio applications in wide-area networks. In: Proceedings of the IEEE Infocom. (1994) 680–688
5. Zhang, Y., Duffield, N., Paxson, V., Shenker, S.: On the constancy of Internet path properties. In: Internet Measurement Workshop (IMW), Marseille, France (2002)
6. Liang, Y.J., Farber, N., Girod, B.: Adaptive playout scheduling and loss concealment for voice communications over IP networks. IEEE Transactions on Multimedia (2001)
7. Moon, S.B., Kurose, J., Towsley, D.: Packet audio playout delay adjustment: Performance bounds and algorithms. ACM/Springer Multimedia Systems **6** (1998) 17–28

8. Bolot, J.: End-to-end packet delay and loss behavior in the Internet. In: Proceedings of the ACM SIGCOMM. (1993) 289–298
9. Kansar, A., Karandikar, A.: Jitter-free audio playout over best effort packet networks. In: ATM Forum International Symposium, New Delhi, India (2001)
10. Pinto, J., Christensen, K.J.: An algorithm for playout of packet voice based on adaptive adjustment of talkspurt silence periods. In: Proceedings of the IEEE Conference on Local Computer Networks. (1999) 224–231
11. Farber, N., Liang, Y., Girod, B., Prabhakar, B.: Adaptive playout and TCP window control for voice over IP in best-effort networks. Technical report, Stanford University, Information Systems Laboratory, Department of Electrical Engineering (2001)
12. Liu, F., Kim, J.W., Kuo, C.J.: Adaptive delay concealment for Internet voice applications with packet-based time-scale modification. In: Proceedings of the International Conference on Acoustics Speech and Signal Processing ICASSP, Salt Lake City (2001)
13. Proakis, J.G., Manolakis, D.G.: Digital Signal Processing: Principles, algorithms, and aplications. Prentice-Hall Inc. (1996)
14. Kleinbaum, D.G., Kupper, L.L., Muller, K.E.: Applied Regression Analysis and Other Multivariable Methods. PWS-Kent, Boston (1988)
15. Liang, Y.J., Farber, N., Girod, B.: Adaptive playout scheduling using time-scale modification in packet voice communications. In: Proceedings of the International Conference on Acoustics Speech and Signal Processing ICASSP. Volume 3. (2001) 1445–1448

To Play or to Control: A Game-Based Control-Theoretic Approach to Peer-to-Peer Incentive Engineering

Weihong Wang and Baochun Li

Department of Electrical and Computer Engineering
University of Toronto
{wwang,bli}@eecg.toronto.edu

Abstract. In peer-to-peer applications, we need to encourage selfish users to share and contribute local resources to the global resource pool that all peers may benefit from, by providing adequate *incentives*. If we assume that all users are non-cooperative and always attempt to maximize their own *net gains*, at the first glance, we could model such behavior as a non-cooperative game and derive the equilibrium that no users deviate from. However, two observations complicate the case. (1) In such a game, user valuation on the contribution amount fluctuates, due to the dynamic supply-demand relationship of the shared resources; and (2) desirable global system properties require payoff functions to be reasonably designed. In this paper, we model the peer-to-peer system as a *Cournot Oligopoly* game with dynamic payoff functions that incorporate system performance requirements, and propose a control-theoretic solution to the problem. Throughout the paper, we use a peer-to-peer global storage system as a running example and case study. Simulation results have shown that the control-theoretic solution may effectively adapt the user contributions to track system dynamics, maximize the local net gain, and achieve satisfactory global properties.

1 Introduction

In peer-to-peer networks, each peer host contributes its local resources to serve the common good, and may benefit from resources contributed by other peers in return. In peer-to-peer storage systems (*e.g.*, CFS [1], OceanStore [2], PAST [3]), peers contribute their local storage space and network bandwidth to the system, and are granted rights to store (or backup) data in the global storage pool. Similarly, other peer-to-peer applications may require peers to contribute network bandwidth (e.g., Resilient Overlay Networks [4]) or CPU cycles (e.g., the concept of Grid computing [5]). Based on such a fundamental design philosophy, peer-to-peer applications provide appealing features of enhanced system robustness, high service availability and scalability.

However, all is not rosy. The critical observation that users are generally *selfish* and *non-cooperative* may severely undermine the expected peer-to-peer structure. For example, the *free rider* phenomenon has been revealed [6,7] in peer-to-peer file sharing applications such as Gnutella: most users are selfish and never share any local files, such that the peer-to-peer system is only supported by a small group of *supernodes*, and degrades to a client-server-like centralized structure. The root cause of the problem is, obviously, there exist no *incentives* for users to be altruistic. Therefore, if we assume

K. Jeffay, I. Stoica, and K. Wehrle (Eds.): IWQoS 2003, LNCS 2707, pp. 174–192, 2003.

that all users are selfish and wish to maximize their own net gains at all times, engineering incentives is a must to encourage contribution and maintain the robustness and availability of peer-to-peer systems.

The question, now, turns to how incentives may be designed. We may naturally be led to game theory for two reasons. First, incentives and costs are natural components of the users' *net gains*, which may be easily modeled by *payoff functions* in game theory. Second, the selfishness of users guarantees that they seek to maximize their gains, which conforms with the fundamental assumptions in game theory as well. Game theory studies whether an equilibrium exists in a game, and if so, how to derive such an equilibrium. However, the question at hand leads to the issue of how we may *construct* (or *design*) the payoff functions in a game, such that *certain desired global properties* may be achieved once the users reach their respective equilibria. This is in the domain of *inverse game* (or *mechanism design* [8]), which is usually hard to solve.

Even if the payoff functions are designed, we need an adequate solution to drive the users toward the desirable equilibrium. In this case, system dynamics have to be incorporated into the incentives and costs that constitute such *time-varying* payoff functions. On one hand, user contributions dynamically affect the global system states (*e.g.*, total amount of resources contributed); on the other hand, to maintain acceptable system performance, their decisions on the amounts of contributed resources must be adjusted over time based on the observed and predicted system dynamics. In order to assist users to make such time-varying decisions with the presence of system uncertainties, a control-theoretic approach seems more adequate than game theory.

Towards peer-to-peer incentive engineering, should the users play games with specifically constructed payoff functions, or should they be controlled to make time-varying decisions? In this paper, we attempt to combine the benefits of both worlds. We design the payoff function in a game-theoretic perspective, such that it explicitly incorporates the desirable global system properties. We then use such designed payoff function as the *objective function* in an optimal control system deployed at every peer. The optimal control system makes decisions on the quantity of contribution to the global pool, such that the objective function is maximized, subject to certain constraints. Our game-based controller design may effectively adapt the user contributions to track system dynamics, maximize the local net gain, and achieve satisfactory global system performance. In simulation studies, we compare the optimal control based solution with the pure game-based solution. Throughout the paper, we use a peer-to-peer global storage system as a running example and case study.

The remainder of the paper is organized as follows. Sec. 2 presents preliminaries regarding our system models and objectives. A game-theoretic perspective of the system is illustrated in Sec. 3, which evolves into a control-theoretic approach presented in Sec. 4. The control performance of the proposed mechanisms is evaluated in Sec. 5. Related work is discussed in Sec. 6, and Sec. 7 concludes the paper.

2 Preliminaries

In this paper, we are concerned about engineering sufficient *incentives* for users in peer-to-peer systems, so that contribution of local resources to the common pool is encouraged.

We assume that all users are selfish, in the sense that they seek to maximize their net gains at all times once the incentives are provided. We believe that the *net gain* of a user is equivalent to the offered incentives subtracted by the *cost* in providing the resources.

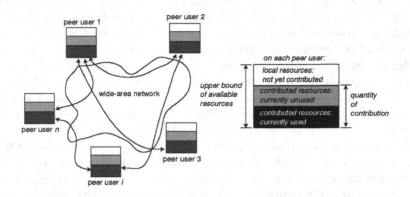

Fig. 1. Model of a peer-to-peer system: contributions, usage and bounds

Fig. 1 shows a detailed view of available resources on each of the peer users. The type of resource may be bandwidth, storage space or CPU cycles, depending on the features of the particular peer-to-peer application. On each peer user, there exists an *upper bound of available resources*, e.g., the maximum available storage space. The user makes one simple decision: what is the quantity of resource it should contribute to the globally shared pool? The contributed resource may not be utilized at all times, and may be further divided into used and unused portions.

Without loss of generality, we concentrate on the case study of a peer-to-peer storage system throughout the paper, where the local *storage space* is the resource to be contributed to the common pool. We proceed to present a brief description of such an application.

Peer-to-peer storage systems are designed to aggregate contributed storage space distributed over a network, in order to conserve the cost of proprietary high-capacity and centralized storage devices. A good motivating example of using such a system is off-site file system backups. A peer-to-peer storage system is by no means static: peer users join and leave the network freely, and may dynamically adjust the quantity of contributions. The size of the global pool of storage space varies over time, and such dynamic behavior has become the subject of extensive research (e.g., CFS [1]). In some of the existing proposals, user data files are stored in the granularity of *blocks*, which are scattered into the contributed storage of multiple peers. Such a strategy is beneficial to achieve load balancing, hotspot relief and robustness of data.

For our case study of peer-to-peer storage systems, we make the following reasonable assumptions on an abstract level:

(1) *Adaptive quantity of contribution.* Peer users are allowed to adjust the quantities of their contributed resources (*i.e.*, storage space), in order to maximize their own net gains at all times. In this case, the contributed resources may be reclaimed at a later time.

It is realistic to make such an assumption, since peer users are allowed to join or depart the system at will.

(2) *Hash-based location and lookup of data blocks.* We believe that the most effective peer-to-peer storage system utilizes *distributed hash tables* (DHTs) to hash data blocks into identifiers, and these identifiers are used to determine which peer users are going to store these blocks[1]. In this case, operations on data blocks in one peer user are obviously independent from other geographically nearby users.

(3) *Proportional usage of contributed capacity.* Effective peer-to-peer storage systems employ mechanisms to achieve almost ideal load balancing with respect to contributed but unused storage resources. For example, CFS employs *virtual servers* with approximately the same storage capacity, to guarantee that the usage of the contributed storage of every user is approximately in proportion to its amount of contribution.

3 Incentives: A Game-Theoretic Perspective

Since each selfish user seeks to maximize its own net gain, *i.e.,* the incentives minus the cost of contributions, it is natural to model the system from a game-theoretic perspective. Game theory addresses multi-person decision making problems, in which the *players* are autonomous and rational decision makers. Each player has a set of *strategies* at its disposal, and a *payoff function* (its valuation of each combination of strategies of all the players). Players choose strategies to maximize their own payoffs, with the consideration that their payoffs are affected by the decisions of all the players. Thus, information about others' strategy and payoff functions is critical in any game.

A *Nash equilibrium* identifies a stable state of the game, at which no player can improve its payoff by deviating from the state, if no other players do so. At the equilibrium, each player receives a payoff that is optimal with respect to the player's knowledge or belief about all other players' strategies. Formally, the condition of Nash equilibrium may be expressed as follows.

$$u_i(s^*_{-i}, s^*_i) \geq u_i(s^*_{-i}, s_i), \ \forall s_i \in S_i, \ \forall i \in N \tag{1}$$

where S_i is player i's strategy set, s^*_i is the strategy selected by player i at equilibrium, s^*_{-i} is the strategies selected by all the other players at equilibrium, and u_i is the payoff function for player i. Further, a *static game* characterizes the situation in which all players make decisions simultaneously without following any particular sequence of play, and decisions are made once for all. A *repeated static game* extends a static game in a stage by stage manner.

3.1 The Cournot Oligopoly Game

Assume that time is discretized, we model the decision-making procedure in the peer-to-peer system as a repeated static game, with each stage of the game corresponding to a time slot. In our case, the players correspond to the peer users, and the strategy space of each peer user i is represented by $S_i(k) = [0, C_i(k)]$, where $C_i(k)$ denotes the upper

---

[1] The reader is referred to the design of CFS [1] for further details.

bound of available resources for user i during the time slot k. When a peer user makes a decision on the quantity of contributed resource, it has selected a strategy within the strategy space $S_i(k)$.

Within each stage, the game closely resembles the *Cournot Oligopoly* game. In a Cournot Oligopoly game, n firms act as players, each rationally decide their own productions $\{q_i\}$ of a homogeneous product in the market. Let $Q = q_1 + \cdots + q_n$ denote the aggregate quantity on the market, and a denotes the total demand. The market-clearing price $P(Q)$ is given by the inverse demand relationship: $P(Q) = a - Q$ (assuming $Q < a$, otherwise $P = 0$). Assume all firms have the same marginal cost c (assume $c < a$), and no fixed costs exist.

Before exploring the Nash equilibrium of the *Cournot Oligopoly* game, we resort to the simpler case of a *Cournot Duopoly* game, where only *two* firms are present. In this case, the profit of either firm can be expressed by the following payoff function ($i, j = 1, 2$):

$$u_i(q_i, q_j) = q_i \cdot P(q_i + q_j) - q_i \cdot c = q_i[a - (q_i + q_j) - c] \tag{2}$$

The game assumes that both firms know that their rival has the same knowledge of the market-clearing price $P(Q)$ and produces at the same cost (in game theory, this case is referred to as a static game with perfect information), hence, either firm is able to decide their optimal quantities of production by solving the following equation array:

$$\begin{cases} \frac{du_1}{dq_1} = a - 2q_1 - q_2 - c = 0 \\ \frac{du_2}{dq_2} = a - 2q_2 - q_1 - c = 0 \end{cases} \tag{3}$$

And the derived Nash equilibrium is symmetric: $q_i = (a - c)/3$.

Fig. 2 (A) illustrates such an equilibrium. Similarly, it can be shown that the Nash equilibrium of the *Cournot Oligopoly* game is $q_i = (a - c)/(n + 1)$, where n is the number of firms as players. It is easy to see that, if n is sufficiently large, and c is relatively small compared with a, the total quantity of production on the market approaches a.

3.2   Designing the Payoff Function

In peer-to-peer systems under consideration, we aim to encourage appropriate user contributions, rather than *excessive* contributions. In this case, we need to reach a balanced trade-off between two objectives: to provision adequate total resources in order to accommodate unpredictable future service requirements with high probability, and to maintain high resource utilization levels. We therefore need to properly design the payoff function, so that the *incentive* a user receives for its quantity of contribution, as well as the associated *costs*, reflect the actual system dynamics.

In this paper, we model peer-to-peer resource contribution systems as a variant to the Cournot Oligopoly game due to the following reasons. First, in such peer-to-peer systems, each peer user i decides its quantity of contribution within the strategy space of $S_i(k) = [0, C_i(k)]$, with an incentive that is dependent on the contribution of all users. The semantics is identical to that of the Cournot Oligopoly game. Second, the market-clearing price in the Cournot Oligopoly game is based on the principle of reverse demand, and naturally regulates user behavior based on the supply-demand relationship.

Despite such similarities, we still need to tailor the definitions of a and c to the specific requirements of the context. The term a, in the expression of market-clearing price in the Cournot Oligopoly game, has been used to represent the maximum demand on the market, and thus regulates the maximum achievable total production in the game. In peer-to-peer systems, we let a reflect the *total desirable quantity of resource*. Then the market-clearing price is expressed as the difference between a and the *total contribution* of resources, according to the inverse demand principle as in the Cournot Oligopoly example. The *incentives* towards user contribution is thus the market-clearing price multiplied by the quantity of resource contribution.

It should be noted that it is hard to determine the total desirable quantity of resources off-line, since peers may join and leave the system at will, and usage in the shared resource pool is unpredictable. However, the quantity can be estimated based on the observed history, if it varies relatively slowly over time, which is the strategy we utilize.

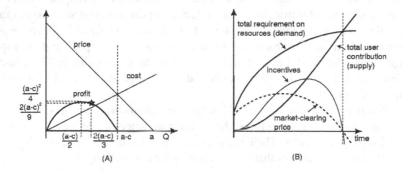

(A)   (B)

Fig. 2. (A) The Cournot Duopoly game. The star denotes the Nash equilibrium. $\frac{a-c}{2}$ is the optimal output quantity in the monopoly case. (B) The relationship among the total desirable quantity of resource (or demand), total resource contribution (or supply), the market-clearing prices and the engineered incentives (market-clearing price multiplied by the quantity of user contributions).

Fig. 2(B) shows that, when the market-clearing price and the user's quantity of contribution change over time, there exists a point, after which the incentives offered to the peer user start to decrease. This implies that when there are excessive resources available in the global pool, peers should no longer benefit further by contributing additional resources.

Beyond incentives, contributing valuable local resources to the global pool comes with costs. In designing the marginal cost c in the payoff function, a heuristic choice is to assume a constant cost per unit quantity, as in the original Cournot Oligopoly game. However, in realistic peer-to-peer resource sharing applications, such an assumption may not reflect the true associated costs. For example, in the case study of peer-to-peer storage systems, the overwhelming cost of sharing each unit of storage space may not be the local storage *per se*, the peer users may be much more concerned with the local *bandwidth* being consumed by other peers *accessing* data contained in the contributed storage space.

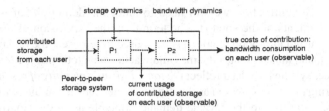

Fig. 3. The cause-effect relationship between the quantity of contribution, the contributed storage being used, and the bandwidth consumption due to such usage.

From a user's perspective, taking the quantity of contribution as the *cause*, the *effects* of the contribution may be reflected by the observable bandwidth consumption, as is shown by Fig. 3. Though both the cause and effects are locally observable, the system dynamics governing these parameters are, unfortunately, not known.

We now proceed to formally design the payoff function, which engineers appropriate incentives and models the true costs. With the peer-to-peer storage system as our example, we list all the important notations to be used in this paper in Table 1. Since we assume discrete time domain, the variables $s_i(k)$ and $b_i(k)$ in Table 1 represent their respective average values during slot k, and are observed at the end of slot k. The quantity of contribution $c_i(k)$, as well as the upper bounds $C_i(k)$ and $B_i(k)$, are determined at the beginning of slot k, however.

We design the term a as $\lambda \sum_j s_j(k)$, which represents the desirable quantity of total storage (or *system capacity*). λ is a system wide parameter that defines the desired level of global *storage utilization*. Then, market-clearing price is expressed by $\lambda \sum_j s_j(k) - \sum_j c_j(k)$, and the incentives that user i receives for contributing $c_i(k)$ is:

$$c_i(k) \cdot [\lambda \sum_j s_j(k) - \sum_j c_j(k)] \tag{4}$$

Since increased storage contribution results in increased bandwidth consumption by other peers, which is highly undesirable for the user, we model the user's reluctance towards further contributions as an exponentially increasing function of its bandwidth consumption: $[b_i(k)/B_i(k)] \cdot e^{b_i(k)/B_i(k)}$. Thus, the higher the relative bandwidth consumption $b_i(k)/B_i(k)$, the higher the marginal cost.

We now have finalized the payoff function, denoted by $u_i(k)$ for user i and in time slot k, as follows:

$$u_i(k) = c_i(k) \cdot \left\{ \lambda \sum_j s_j(k) - \sum_j c_j(k) - \frac{b_i(k)}{B_i(k)} \cdot e^{b_i(k)/B_i(k)} \right\}. \tag{5}$$

In the repeated static game we have defined, for each time slot k, every user i attempts to adjust $c_i(k)$, so as to maximize its payoff in the stage, based on the prescribed payoff function in Eq. (5). Comparing with Eq. (2), we may observe that the terms a and c are time-variant quantities, which are dependent on the actual system states. In addition, when the relative bandwidth consumption $b_i(k)/B_i(k)$ is sufficiently low, the marginal cost is negligible compared to the market-clearing price ($c \ll a$). Thus, the total storage

Table 1. Case study of peer-to-peer storage systems: notations

Symbols	Explanations
N	The total number of peer users
$c_i(k)$	The storage contribution of user i in slot k
$C_i(k)$	The upper bound of $c_i(k)$
$s_i(k)$	The amount of occupied storage contribution of user i in slot k
$b_i(k)$	The bandwidth consumption on user i in time slot k
$B_i(k)$	The upper bound of acceptable $b_i(k)$
$c^{\;i}(k)$	$\sum_{\substack{j \in N \\ j = i}} c_j(k)$
$s^{\;i}(k)$	$\sum_{\substack{j \in N \\ j = i}} s_j(k)$

contribution approximates $a \cdot N/(N+1) = \lambda \cdot N \sum_j s_j(k)/(N+1)$, which means that the desirable system storage utilization can be adjusted by tuning the value of λ. Assume an average storage utilization of $(66 \sim 80)\%$, the corresponding λ would be $(1.25 \sim 1.5)(N+1)/N$.

As a simple illustration, the functions of the aforementioned *incentives*, *costs* and *payoffs* are shown in Fig. 4.

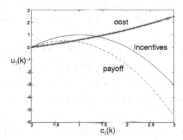

Fig. 4. The payoff function, including the incentives and costs.

4 Game-Based Optimal Control

Our process of engineering the incentives and the costs (that constitute the payoff function) is identical to that of *inverse game theory* (or *mechanism design*), where the payoff function is designed, so that certain desirable global properties are achieved at the Nash equilibrium. It may seem that we may now apply standard game theory and investigate the properties achievable at Nash equilibrium, once the equilibrium point is derived by solving a group of maximization problems.

However, there exist fundamental difficulties along this path. In the game we have designed, the payoff functions of Eq. (5) are not only heterogeneous for different users due to the user-specific parameter $B_i(k)$, but also time-varying: users locally estimate $b_i(k)$ and $s_i(k)$, based on their views of the global storage system updated on-the-fly.

Besides, each user makes its decision on $c_i(k)$ at the beginning of time slot k. However, at this time instant, $s_i(k)$ and $b_i(k)$, which denote their respective average value during slot k, are not yet obtainable. What we are able to obtain, instead, are their old values, $s_i(l)$ and $b_i(l)$, $l \leq k - 1$. A direct solution might be to use $s_i(k-1)$ and $b_i(k-1)$ in lieu of $s_i(k)$ and $b_i(k)$, respectively. However, considering the length of time slot k, such an estimation may be taken as a convenience at best.

In addition, from the game-theoretic perspective, the decision making procedure potentially requires each peer to know the parameters (*e.g.*, $s_i(k)$ and $b_i(k)$) of the payoff functions of all other peers before deciding their $c_i(k)$. However, such information cannot be exchanged beforehand, since $s_i(k)$ and $b_i(k)$ are still unavailable at the time of decision making. Therefore, the exact payoff function of any user remains unknown to all other users, which is different from the case of the Cournot Oligopoly example.

Despite these difficulties, what we do need to know is the relationship between (1) the optimal quantity of contribution $c_i(k)$, determined at the beginning of slot k; and (2) $s_i(k)$ and $b_i(k)$ to be observed during the same time slot. Such a relationship, apparently, is determined by the behavior of the external system that we have not investigated so far.

When deciding a new value of $c_i(k)$, it is possible for each user to dynamically identify a mathematical model for the external system based on its locally observed values of $s_i(k)$, $b_i(k)$ and $c_i(k)$. On one hand, given any $c_i(k)$, new values of $s_i(k)$ and $b_i(k)$ can be predicted, so that the objective function can be evaluated, and the optimal value of $c_i(k)$ can be calculated; on the other hand, since new decisions are made on the basis of the model, the user's strategy space is in fact restricted to a set that is closer to the probable system behavior. In this way, we are naturally led to a control-theoretic solution to the game.

Furthermore, due to the difficulty for users to promptly exchange information about their current payoff function, we propose that users determine new quantities of contributions based on other users' status (*i.e.*, $s_i(k)$, $c_i(k)$) in the previous time slot, so that they make decisions according to their observations on, rather than inference about, other users' behavior.

In this section, we propose a control-theoretic approach to address these problems. We design a decentralized optimal control system in the game setting, such that the payoff function Eq. (5), which has incorporated global system performance objectives — in the market-clearing price and marginal cost terms — are taken as the *objective function*. The control law, which is equivalent to the trajectory of contribution decisions, is derived as the maximizing solution to the objective, subject to constraints of the system model. Therefore, we utilize users' selfishness in maximizing their own payoff, and achieve the following goals simultaneously: (1) achieving sufficient total storage capacities; (2) maintaining high storage utilization; and (3) avoiding severe bandwidth stress at participating peers.

4.1 Design of the Optimal Control System

Towards our aforementioned objectives, the peer users rely on decentralized optimal controllers to locally adapt their decisions on their quantities of contribution. Fig. 5 shows the block diagram of the optimal control system design.

For the local control system at peer user i, the entire global peer-to-peer system is the *plant* to be controlled. However, any single peer user i acts only as a *port* to the plant, and $c_i(k)$ is the only control it may impose on the plant. $s_i(k)$ and $b_i(k)$ are affected not only by peer i's contribution quantity $c_i(k)$, but also by the quantities of contribution by other users, as well as unknown system dynamics that are beyond control of our model.

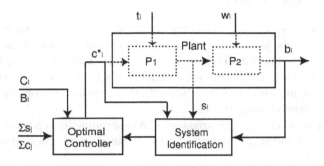

Fig. 5. The block diagram of the decentralized optimal control system.

More concretely, we consider the system seen by user i as a discrete time-varying linear system, with $c_i(k)$, $b_i(k)$, and $s_i(k)$ as the input, output, and state variables, respectively. System dynamics with regard to storage usage and bandwidth consumption, which are caused by the insertion, deletion and retrieval of data blocks, are modeled as random noises.

The problem can be further formulated as a decentralized optimal control task. each user i decides its optimal input trajectory $c_i(k)$ to the plant, which maximizes its playoff function as shown in Eq. (5), subject to the constraints given by Eq. (6):

$$c_i(k) = \arg\max u_i(c_i(k), c^{-i}(k))$$

$$\begin{cases} b_i(k) = F(c_i(k)) \\ c_i(k) \leq C_i(k) \\ b_i(k) \leq B_i(k) \end{cases} \tag{6}$$

where $b_i(k) = F(c_i(k))$ represents the stochastic model of the plant. As it becomes apparent, the correct identification of the plant is critical to the optimal control system.

4.2   The Plant: System Identification

From a control-theoretic perspective, we model the plant as a discrete-time stochastic linear system. A state space model can be formulated as follows:

$$\begin{cases} A(q^{-1})s_i(k) = B(q^{-1})c_i(k) \\ C(q^{-1})b_i(k) = D(q^{-1})s_i(k) \end{cases}$$

where $s_i(k)$ is the state variable, and the form $R(q)$ stands for a polynomial in the *forward shift operator* q, for instance, given $R(q^{-1}) = 1 + 2q^{-1} + q^{-2}$, $R(q^{-1})s_i(k) = s_i(k) + 2s_i(k-1) + s_i(k-2)$.

Further, we have assumed that at any time slot k, the block insertion rate at user i is roughly in proportion to its unused share of storage contribution (Sec. 2); the bandwidth consumption $b_i(k)$ is essentially dependent on the observed usages at user i (subject to uncertain factors). Therefore, the system model can be refined as:

$$\begin{cases} s_i(k) = s_i(k-1) + \alpha_i[c_i(k) - s_i(k-1)] - \beta_i s_i(k-1) + t_i(k) & (7.1) \\ b_i(k) = \gamma_i(q^{-1})s_i(k) + w_i(k) & (7.2) \end{cases} \quad (7)$$

where $\alpha_i[c_i(k) - s_i(k-1)]$ stands for the amount of inserted data at user i in slot k, $\beta_i s_i(k-1)$ is the amount of deleted data. Apparently, α_i and β_i are time-varying parameters, and the uncertainties in their variations are accounted for by the zero-mean *white noise* term $t_i(k)$. Similarly, the coefficients of $\gamma_i(q^{-1})$ also change over time, and the zero-mean white noise $w_i(k)$ represents the uncertain factors from the global system regarding bandwidth consumption at user i.

We adopt the *stochastic approximation* (SA) algorithm [9] to estimate the unknown parameters α_i, β_i and the coefficients of $\gamma_i(q^{-1})$, based on the observed values of $s_i(k)$, $c_i(k)$ and $b_i(k)$.

Consider Eq. (7.1) as an example. The equation can be written in the form of: $y(k) = \phi^T(k)\theta + t_i(k)$, where $y(k) = s_i(k)$, $\phi^T(k) = (s_i(k-1), c_i(k) - s_i(k-1))$, both consist of observable variables, $\theta(k) = (1 - \beta_i(k), \alpha_i(k))$ contains the parameters to be estimated, and $t_i(k)$ is the unknown noise.

The estimated parameter vector $\widehat{\theta}(k)$ is derived as the minimizing solution to the least-squares loss function $V(\theta, t) = \frac{1}{2}\sum_{i=1}^{t}(y(i) - \phi^T(i)\theta)^2$. A simplified recursive algorithm is given by

$$\widehat{\theta}(k) = \widehat{\theta}(k-1) + \epsilon P(k)\phi(k)(y(k) - \phi^T(k)\widehat{\theta}(k-1))$$

where

$$P(k) = \left(\sum_{i=1}^{k}\phi^T(i)\phi(i)\right)^{-1}$$

ϵ is the *adaptation gain* which tunes the adjustment step of the estimates.

For the sake of predicting system dynamics, it is advantageous to have the estimated model parameters update slower than system variables. We take the following averaging technique to achieve *smoother* parameter variations: $\widehat{\theta}(k) = \widehat{\theta}(k-1) + \epsilon E[P(i)\phi(i)(y(i) - \phi^T(i)\widehat{\theta}(i-1)]$, where the incremental term $\epsilon E[P(i)\phi(i)(y(i) - \phi^T(i)\widehat{\theta}(i-1))]$ is the arithmetic mean of previous corrections.

4.3   Optimization Objective: The Game-Based Objective Function

We have designed the payoff function following the principles of the Cournot Oligopoly game. We propose an optimal control solution to the game, which takes this payoff function as the *objective function* in the control system. Due to the unfeasibility for user i to observe $s^{-i}(k)$ and $c^{-i}(k)$ (defined previously in Table 1) at the time of decision making, the objective function (we again use $u_i(k)$ as a convenience) may be defined as follows, which is slightly different from the payoff function in Eq. (5):

$$u_i(k) = c_i(k) \cdot \{\lambda [\sum_{j \neq i} s_j(k-1) + s_i(k)] - [\sum_{j \neq i} c_j(k-1) + c_i(k)] - \frac{b_i(k)}{B_i(k)} \cdot e^{\frac{b_i(k)}{B_i(k)}} \}. \quad (8)$$

In Eq. (8), however, the terms $\sum_{j \neq i} s_j(k-1)$ and $\sum_{j \neq i} c_j(k-1)$ are global information and may not be conveniently known or observable to the peer users. Within a small-scale peer-to-peer group, if the decision updating period is sufficiently long, it is feasible for each peer user to constantly observe the $s_j(k)$, $c_j(k)$ and $b_j(k)$ values of all other peers. Thus, an arbitrary peer user i may directly use Eq. (8) as its decision making criterion. In this case, each peer user always attempts to form its best strategy based on the strategies selected by other peers in the previous stage, and users sequentially make their decisions in an iterative manner. If the iteration converges, it must converge to the Nash equilibrium.

As the network becomes larger, collecting complete information of all peers becomes infeasible. In such cases, certain characteristics of the peer-to-peer application may be of assistance in *estimating* such global information. In peer-to-peer storage systems, for example, if we assume that the location and lookup of data blocks are based on distributed hash [1,3], there is a high probability that ideal load balancing is achieved. In this case, if the user knows the total number of peers in the system (N), it may use $(N-1) \cdot s_i(k)$ to estimate $\sum_{j \neq i} s_j(k)$. Such an estimation is not as accurate, but it eliminates the message passing overhead of exchanging peer information.

As the network scales further up (*i.e.*, large-scale network), it is increasingly difficult for each peer user to even have the knowledge of the total number of users. In such cases, we modify the objective function as follows, so that users only rely on locally observable parameters to make the decision (note that this extension has deviated from the game setting):

$$u_i(k) = c_i(k) \cdot [\lambda s_i(k) - c_i(k) - \frac{b_i(k)}{B_i(k)} e^{b_i(k)/B_i(k)}] \quad (9)$$

4.4   The Optimal Control System

Our game-based optimal contribution mechanism periodically calculates $c_i(k)$ that maximizes $u_i(k)$, subject to the estimated system behavior (the identified plant model) and the upper bounds of $c_i(k)$ and $b_i(k)$.

Assume all users have the full knowledge of $c_i(k)$ and $s_i(k)$ of one another, the optimal control problem can be formulated as follows:

$$
\begin{cases}
c_i(k) = \arg\max c_i(k)\{\lambda[\sum_{j=i} s_j(k-1) + s_i(k)] - [\sum_{j=i} c_j(k-1) + c_i(k)] \\
\quad - \frac{b_i(k)}{B_i(k)} e^{b_i(k)/B_i(k)}\} & (10.1) \\
c_i(k) \leq C_i(k) & (10.2) \\
b_i(k) \leq B_i(k) & (10.3) \\
s_i(k) = [1 - \widehat{\beta}_i(k-1)]s_i(k-1) + \widehat{\alpha}_i(k-1)[c_i(k) - s_i(k-1)] + t_i(k) & (10.4) \\
b_i(k) = \sum_{j=0}^{n} \widehat{\gamma}_{i,j}(k-1)s_i(k-j) + w_i(k) & (10.5)
\end{cases}
$$
$$(10)$$

$t_i(k)$ and $w_i(k)$ are noises that may not be observed. We thus approximate them with the *estimation errors* of $s_i(k)$ and $b_i(k)$: $t_i(k) \doteq s_i(k) - \widehat{\alpha}_i(k-1)[c_i(k) - s_i(k-1)] +$

$[\widehat{\beta}_i(k-1)-1]s_i(k-1)$, $w_i(k) \doteq b_i(k) - \sum_{j=0}^{n} \widehat{\gamma}_i(k-1)s_i(k-j)$. Since they still cannot be evaluated as $c_i(k)$, $s_i(k)$ and $b_i(k)$ are unknown for the moment, we replace them with the average values of recent errors, i.e., $t_i(k) \doteq E(t_i)$, and $w_i(k) \doteq E(w_i)$.

Substitute (10.3) to (10.5), then substitute (10.5) to (10.4), we may obtain another upper bound on $c_i(k)$:

$$c_i(k) \leq \bar{c}_i(k) = \frac{1}{\widehat{\alpha}_i(k-1)}\{\frac{1}{\widehat{\gamma}_{i,0}(k-1)}[B_i(k) - w_i(k) - \sum_{j=1}^{n} \widehat{\gamma}_{i,j}(k-1)s_i(k-j)]$$
$$+[\widehat{\alpha}_i(k-1) + \widehat{\beta}_i(k-1) - 1]s_i(k-1) - t_i(k)\}$$

Combining it with (10.2), we obtain the tight upper bound on $c_i(k)$:
$c_i(k) \leq \min\{\bar{c}_i(k), C_i(k)\} = \widehat{c}_i(k)$.
Hence, the original problem is transformed to

$$\begin{cases} c_i^*(k) = \arg\max u_i(c_i(k)) = \arg\max c_i(k)\{\lambda[\sum_{j \neq i} s_j(k-1) + s_i(k)] \\ \quad -[\sum_{j \neq i} c_j(k-1) + c_i(k)] - \frac{b_i(k)}{B_i(k)}e^{b_i(k)/B_i(k)}\} \\ c_i(k) \leq \widehat{c}_i(k) \end{cases}$$

Similarly, in the case of large-scale networks, the optimal control problem is the following:

$$\begin{cases} c_i^*(k) = \arg\max u_i(c_i(k)) = \arg\max c_i(k)[\lambda s_i(k) - c_i(k) - \frac{b_i(k)}{B_i(k)}e^{\frac{b_i(k)}{B_i(k)}}] \\ c_i(k) \leq \widehat{c}_i(k) \end{cases}$$

It can be shown that, in both cases, $\frac{\partial^2 u_i(c_i(k))}{\partial c_i(k)^2}$ may not be negative definite (depending on the estimated parameters of the plant), thus, the solution to the above problem should be chosen as $c_i^*(k) = \arg\min u_i(c_i(k)), c_i(k) \in \{\widehat{c}_i(k), \{u_i(\widetilde{c}_i(k))\}\}$, where $\{u_i(\widetilde{c}_i(k))\}$ are the local maximums or minimums of $u_i(c_i(k))$ that satisfy the first order condition of the objective function.

By reforming the optimal control problem at every stage of the game, the best contribution strategy of user i with respect to other users' decisions can be derived as the *optimal control law* to the dynamic system. In the example of peer-to-peer storage systems, the local controller periodically performs the following tasks:

(1) *Local observations.* Before the control decision is made for the kth time slot, the upper bound of storage contribution $C_i(k)$ and the upper bound for bandwidth contribution $B_i(k)$ should be determined at the beginning of slot k. The actual usage of storage $s_i(k-1)$ and bandwidth consumption $b_i(k-1)$ must be measured and calculated at the end of time slot $(k-1)$.

(2) *Information exchange.* Depending on different assumptions with respect to the scale of the peer-to-peer network, peers may need to exchange their local observations $s_i(k-1)$ and $c_i(k-1)$ with other peers.

(3) *System identification.* Due to the time-variant and stochastic nature of the system view, the model of the plant needs to be periodically estimated based on the locally observed values of $c_i(k)$, $s_i(k)$, and $b_i(k)$.

(4) *Constrained optimization.* Besides the upper bounds on $c_i(k)$ and $b_i(k)$, the acceptable user strategies are further constrained by the system behavior predicted from the estimated system model. Thus, the decision drawn will be optimal in terms of actual system performance (*e.g.*, bandwidth consumption).

5 Performance Evaluation

We perform simulations to compare the performance of two categories of solutions to the incentive engineering problem in peer-to-peer systems: the proposed optimal control based solution (referred to as *solution* 1 henceforth) and the more primitive game-theoretic solution (referred to as *solution* 2). In the following presentation, emphasis is placed on revealing the fundamental differences between the two types of decision making processes. Again, we take the peer-to-peer storage system as a case study in all our evaluations.

5.1 Simulation Settings

In all the experiments, we take 50 peers with heterogeneous but constant upper bounds, C_i and B_i, on storage contributions and bandwidth consumptions. Periodically, new data insertion requests for the entire system are generated according to a sine function. At different peers, the amounts of insertion requests are approximately proportional to their contributed but unused storage space. Deletion operations are generated independently for individual peers, which are in approximate proportion to their contributed and used space.

The plant model is assumed as follows:

$$\begin{cases} s_i(k) = [1 - \beta_i(k)]s_i(k-1) + \alpha_i[c_i(k) - s_i(k-1)] + t_i(k) \\ b_i(k) = s_i(k) + 0.5 s_i(k-1) + w_i(k) \end{cases}$$

where $\beta_i(k)$ stands for the deletion rate that occurs at user i in slot k, which is a white noise with mean in $[0, 1]$ and variance 1; $\alpha_i(k)$ corresponds to the real insertion rate seen by peer i, which is affected by the total amount of data insertion requests and the total unused storage in the system, and the current contribution amount $c_i(k)$ of user i; $t_i(k)$ and $w_i(k)$ are zero-mean white noises, representing the uncertain factors in the external system, with regard to data insertion, deletion and bandwidth consumption.

We assume that the decision updating period is sufficiently long, so that peers exchange local observations on $s_i(k)$ and $c_i(k)$ to assist decision making. Thus, in both approaches to be evaluated, the objective function (in *solution* 1) and the payoff function (in *solution* 2) are periodically updated according to Eq. (8).

Solution 2 reaches the result by solving the following optimization problem:

$$\begin{cases} c_i^*(k) = \arg \max c_i(k)\{\lambda \sum_j s_j(k-1) - [\sum_{j \neq i} c_j(k-1) + c_i(k)] \\ \qquad - \frac{b_i(k-1)}{B_i(k)} e^{b_i(k-1)/B_i(k)}\} \\ c_i(k) \leq C_i(k) \end{cases} \tag{11}$$

where the old values of $s_i(k-1)$ and $b_i(k-1)$ are used to form the optimization goal, and a single scalar $c_i^*(k)$ is derived as the optimal decision on $c_i(k)$.

Solution 1, instead, relaxes $s_i(k)$ and $b_i(k)$ to be unknown, and employs three additional constraints (the estimated system equations and the bandwidth upper bound) to the optimization problem as in Eq. (10). Therefore, $c_i^*(k)$ is determined along with the estimates of $s_i(k)$ and $b_i(k)$.

5.2   Experimental Results

Since *solution* 1 relies on system identification to restrict the acceptable solution set (strategy space), the correctness of the estimated parameters directly affects the user's final decision. As Fig. 6 has shown, our parameter estimation procedure gives satisfactory estimates.

As will be evident in forthcoming results, in *solution* 2, user decisions fluctuate evidently under system dynamics, so does the entire system capacity (Fig. 7(A)). The reason is that, in *solution* 2, the cost term in the payoff function is evaluated at the bandwidth consumption for the previous time slot, thus, it forms a strong negative feedback for the contribution decision in the next slot. Since users make decisions based on their *static* views (*i.e.*, observed values of $s_i(k)$, $c_i(k)$, and $b_i(k)$) of the underlying dynamic system, without further knowledge of its future variations, they tend to make decisions that maximize the current payoff function, but stimulate higher bandwidth consumption, equivalently, higher costs in the payoff function, for the coming slot. Hence, the decision on contribution for the next slot may drop steeply, and further induce lower costs subsequently.

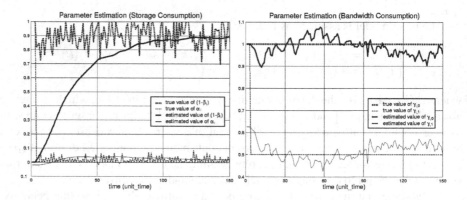

Fig. 6. Results of system identification. (A) Coefficients of the storage dynamic equation. (B) Coefficients of the bandwidth dynamic equation.

System Capacity. The total storage space provided by the system determines to a large extent the benefit a user can receive. We use the notion *equivalent data insertion requests*, which equals to the amount of insertion requests subtracted by the amount of deleted data, to depict the variation of storage requirement in the system. As Fig. 7 has shown, both solutions render adaptable system capacity in face of system dynamics (stimulated by the equivalent data insertion requests), but *solution* 2 reacts more sensitively to the system variations. Besides, although decisions in *solution* 2 fluctuate more heavily, the average system capacity is higher than that achieved in *solution* 1. Both the significant capacity fluctuation and the augmented capacity are results of strong feedbacks between the bandwidth consumption and the contribution decision, which come with remarkable costs.

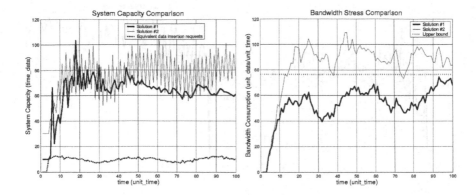

Fig. 7. Comparisons between the two solutions. (A) System capacity; (B) Bandwidth stress.

Bandwidth Stress. As Fig. 7(B) shows, bandwidth consumption in *solution* 2 may consistently exceed the prescribed upper bound; the quality of service that individual peer users receive from the system, and that provided to the other peer users, may be severely degraded as a result.

The reason is that, *solution* 2 does not explicitly consider the effects that each contribution decision has on the observable system status ($s_i(k)$ and $b_i(k)$), it tends to degrade network performance by more aggressively consuming user bandwidth. Primitive game-based strategies cannot avoid such phenomena, since the cost term in the payoff function only serves as a *virtual* penalty on the bandwidth consumption of the previous period: contribution quantities that may significantly increase future bandwidth consumption are still acceptable within the context, as long as the payoff function is maximized. On the contrary, the optimal control based solution effectively alleviates such deterioration on system performance, by restricting user strategy space with the estimated system model, so that the contribution decision is derived as an attempt to maximize the control objective, subject to the constraint of possible system behavior.

Storage Utilization. Fig. 8(A) shows the variations of storage usage for both solutions, and Fig. 8(B) illustrates the corresponding storage utilization factors. It can be seen that, the storage utilization is relatively stable for *solution* 1, due to its smoother contribution variations. In addition, we set λ to $1.25(N+1)/N$ in our simulation, which corresponds to an expected storage utilization of 80%, and it approximately agrees with our simulation results.

In summary, we have verified that, in peer-to-peer applications, primitive game-based strategies may not be readily applicable to manipulate real-time systems, due to their inherent restrictions of considering the underlying system with a static view. The limitation is alleviated when the physical rules governing the dynamic system behavior are explicitly incorporated into the decision making procedure. From an optimal control perspective, the user strategy space can be constrained by feasible system behavior, and incentives can be more adequately engineered by properly designing payoff functions. Therefore, distributed users may spontaneously make decisions to benefit themselves

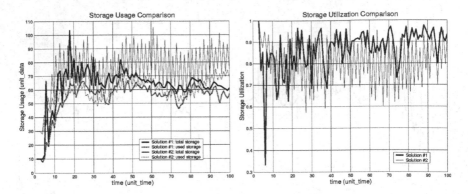

Fig. 8. Comparisons between the two solutions. (A) Contributed and used storage; (B) Capacity utilization.

and other users, unconsciously assisting the maintenance of optimal states in the global peer-to-peer system.

6   Related Work

We have resorted to two theoretical tools, game theory and control theory, to address the problem of incentive engineering. Both theories have been extensively employed in various network-related areas, but their applications to peer-to-peer system have only recently begun to be studied.

As a powerful tool in solving multi-person decision making problems, game theory has been applied in multiple channel access arbitration [10], optimal routing [11,12, 13], as well as flow and congestion control [14]. Some of the recent work has started to apply game theory in peer-to-peer applications. Golle *et al.* [15], for instance, have discussed game theory applications in peer-to-peer file sharing applications with centralized servers. In particular, they take into account the effect of users' levels of altruism on their behavior of contributing and receiving, and construct the user strategy space accordingly. Liao *et al.* [16] have focused on incentive provisioning for wireless access services, and constrained user strategy spaces with service purchasing power and price-service menu, so that only desirable cooperative behavior. Feigenbaum *et al.* [8] have studied the more general problem of mechanism design, which encourages users to behave in the way that leads to the system desirable outcome, by properly designing associated payoffs and specifications that are computationally tractable.

For the purpose of providing reasonable incentives and achieving desirable system performance in peer-to-peer applications, we believe that to investigate the relationship between user behavior and system performance, which closely depends on the mathematical model of the underlying system, is the primary task we should undertake. Only based on adequate knowledge about the relationship, can we proceed to design satisfactory mechanisms to control user behavior. Control theory, fortunately, provides the right concepts and techniques for modeling system dynamics, analyzing performance, and designing appropriate controllers to regulate system behavior. We believe that employing control-theoretic techniques in peer-to-peer networks will provide a solid basis for incentive engineering research, and will generate effective solutions. We have not been aware of any existing work that takes a control-theoretic approach to address problems in this aspect.

7 Conclusions

In this paper, we have investigated the issue of peer-to-peer incentive engineering from both the game-theoretic and the control-theoretic perspective. The original contributions of this paper are two-fold. First, we model the situation as a game and propose to *design* the payoff function such that, as the users maximize their own net gains, the desirable global system performance is obtained. Second, we propose an optimal control solution to regulate users' adaptive behavior of the game, by using the designed payoff function directly as the objective function that the controller optimizes. Our experimental results have demonstrated that the control solution behaves more stably in face of system dynamics, while the primitive game solution may also achieve acceptable performance in most cases. To the best of our knowledge, there do not exist previous studies in the area of incentive engineering based on either the design of payoff functions in a game (*i.e.,* the principles of inverse games) to achieve global properties, or the use of an optimal control system to adapt to system dynamics while catering to the selfishness of users.

References

1. F. Dabek, M. F. Kaashoek, D. Karger, R. Morris, and I. Stoica, "Wide-Area Cooperative Storage with CFS," in *18th ACM Symposium on Operating Systems Principles (SOSP 2001)*, October 2001.
2. J. Kubiatowicz, D. Binderl, Y. Chen, and S. Czerwinskl, "OceanStore: An Architecture for Global-Scale Persistent Storage," in *The Ninth International Conference on Architectural Support for Programming Languages and Operating Systems (ASPLOS)*, 2000.
3. A. Rowstron and R. Druschel, "Storage Management and Caching in PAST, a Large-Scale Persistent Peer-to-Peer Storage Utility," in *18th ACM Symposium on Operating Systems Principles (SOSP 2001)*, October 2001.
4. D. G. Andersen, H. Balakrishnan, M. Frans Kaashoek, and R. Morris, "Resilient Overlay Networks," in *18th ACM Symposium on Operating Systems Principles (SOSP 2001)*, October 2001.
5. I. Foster, "Internet Computing and the Emerging Grid," *Nature*, December 2000.
6. S. Saroiu, P. Gnummadi, and S. Gribble, "A Measurement Study of Peer-to-Peer File Sharing Systems," in *Proc. of SPIE/ACM Conference on Multimedia Computing and Networking (MMCN 2002)*, 2002.
7. E. Adar and B. Huberman, "Free Riding on Gnutella," *First Monday*, vol. 5, no. 10, 2000.
8. J. Feigenbaum and S. Shenker, "Distributed Algorithmic Mechanism Design: Recent Results and Future Directions," in *Sixth International Workshop on Discrete Algorithms and Methods for Mobile Computing and Communications (Dial'M 2002)*, September 2002.
9. K. J. Astrom and B. Wittenmark, *Adaptive Control, 2nd Edition*, Addison-Wesley Publishing Company, 1995.
10. A. B. MacKenzie and S. B. Wicker, "Selfish Users in Aloha: A Game-Theoretic Approach," in *Proceedings of IEEE Vehicular Technology Conference*, 2001.
11. A. Orda, R. Rom, and N. Shimkin, "Competitive Routing in Multi-User Communication Networks," *IEEE/ACM Transactions on Networking*, vol. 1, pp. 510–521, 1993.

12. Y. A. Korlis, A. A. Lazar, and A. Orda, "Architecting Noncooperative Networks," *IEEE Journal on Selected Areas in Communications*, vol. 13, no. 8, 1995.
13. R. J. La and V. Anantharam, "Optimal Routing Control: Game Theoretic Approach," in *Proceedings of the 36th Conference on Decision and Control*, 1997.
14. T. Alpcan and T. Basar, "A Utility-Based Congestion Control Scheme for Internet-Style Networks with Delay," submitted to IEEE Infocom 2003.
15. P. Golle, K. L. Brown, I. Mironov, and M. Lillibridge, "Incentives for Sharing in Peer-to-Peer Networks," in *Proceedings of the 2nd International Workshop on Electronic Commerce*, 2001.
16. R. R.-F. Liao, R. H. Wouhaybi, and A. T. Campbell, "Incentive Engineering in Wireless LAN Based Access Networks," in *Tenth International Conference on Network Protocols*, November 2002.

IV Dependability and Fault Tolerance

Improving Dependability of Real-Time Communication with Preplanned Backup Routes and Spare Resource Pool*

Songkuk Kim and Kang G. Shin

University of Michigan
Ann Arbor, MI 48109-2122
{songkuk,kgshin}@eecs.umich.edu

Abstract. Timely recovery from network component failures is essential to the applications that require guaranteed-performance communication services. To achieve dependable communication, there have been several proposals that can be classified into two categories: reactive and proactive.

The reactive approach tries to reroute traffic upon detection of a network link/node failure. This approach may suffer from contention and resource shortage when multiple connections need to be rerouted at the same time. The proactive approach, on the other hand, prepares a backup channel in advance that will be activated upon failure of the corresponding primary channel due to a broken link or node. The proactive approach, although it offers higher dependability, incurs higher routing overhead than the reactive approach.

We propose a hybrid approach that reduces signaling overhead by decoupling backup routing from resource provisioning. We also propose an efficient backup routing algorithm for the hybrid approach. Our in-depth simulation results show that the proposed approach can achieve the ability of failure recovery comparable to the proactive scheme without the need for broadcasting the routing information.

1   Introduction

Though the Internet has infiltrated into our everyday lives over the last couple of decades, its use has been limited to non-critical applications. Mission/safety-critical applications, which need real-time communication service, cannot use the Internet as their communication media. One chief reason for this is that the Internet cannot preserve real-time performance in case of link/router failures.

Paxson [1] measured the stability of routes between selected nodes, and reported that up to 2.2% of probes experienced connection outages. Labovitz *et al.* [2] showed that about 50% of routes were available for less than 99.9% of the time. This kind of route failures either fail the real-time applications or significantly degrade the performance of real-time communication.

---

* The work reported in this paper was supported in part by the Office of Naval Research under Grant No. N00014-99-1-0465.

K. Jeffay, I. Stoica, and K. Wehrle (Eds.): IWQoS 2003, LNCS 2707, pp. 195–214, 2003.

To achieve guaranteed performance, real-time communication schemes rely on off-line resource reservation and runtime traffic scheduling. Resources are reserved along a specific path before data packets are sent. If a failure occurs on the path, a new route should be found and resources need to be reserved along the new path. So, the instability of routes will disable the real-time communication service for a long time. According to Labovitz *et al.* [2], it may take tens of minutes for the intermediate routers to converge on a new topology. Furthermore, one link failure may disable many real-time connections, and their end systems will try to set up new channels at the same time. Because one real-time connection chooses a route without knowing others' choices, this re-establishment of real-time channels may experience severe contention. Many re-establishment attempts may result in signaling failures even when the network has sufficient resources.

Banerjea [3,4] explored use of the reactive scheme to provide dependable communication service. The reactive scheme deals with failures only after their occurrence. To restore a real-time connection affected by a failure, the connection's source node selects a detour path around the faulty component. The merit of the reactive scheme is that it requires no extra work in the absence of failures. However, the reactive scheme cannot guarantee success of recovery because it does not reserve resources *a priori* for backup channels. When the network load is high, most resources are consumed by primary channels, and it is difficult to find a path that has bandwidth available for an additional real-time channel.

Another drawback of the reactive scheme is that it may suffer from contention when the source node tries to set up a detour channel around the faulty link/node. Because each source node selects a detour path based on its *local* information that does not reflect other nodes' detour path choices, the decision may result in conflicts over a link that does not have enough available bandwidth. Banerjea showed that sequential signaling is effective to alleviate the contention. Sequential signaling means that connection setup requests are served one by one. However, it is practically impossible to coordinate the order of setup requests in a distributed manner, and the sequential signaling takes a long time to reroute the broken real-time channels.

To provide fast and guaranteed recovery, proactive schemes have been proposed [5,6,7,8]. In Han and Shin's scheme, a dependable (D-) connection consists of one primary channel and one or more backup channels. When a primary channel is established, a backup channel(s) is also set up with (spare) resource reservation. To reduce the amount of spare resources, they developed a backup multiplexing scheme. If primary channels do not share any network component, their backups can be multiplexed (and hence overbooked) over the same resources. Though the proactive scheme can guarantee dependability, it comes with high resource overhead. To establish a backup channel, the signaling procedure should be performed and the intermediate routers on the backup path should keep the information about backup channels for their multiplexing. Establishing a new backup channel can change the amount of available bandwidth for primaries because backups and primaries compete for same resources.

Thus, backup signaling hastens the broadcasting of link status. Furthermore, for backup multiplexing, the information on the amount of spare resource needs to be conveyed to other nodes, which incurs additional routing overhead.

To provide dependable communication service with low overhead, we propose a hybrid scheme in which a D-connection is composed of a *primary* channel and a preplanned *backup path*. To establish a detour channel immediately without contention upon failure of a link, we pre-select a backup route when we establish a primary channel. However, we do not perform any signaling along the backup route. When a failure occurs to a link, the disabled real-time connections try to reserve resources and set up backup channels along the pre-selected backup routes. To prevent bandwidth shortage, we set aside a certain amount of bandwidth on each link as spare resources. The spare resources can be used to deliver best-effort traffic until backup channels are activated. Because the amount of spare resources is fixed, we need not broadcast the information of spare resources.

2   Pool of Spare Resources

When almost all of the network resources are occupied by real-time channels, the network is said to be *saturated*. If a link is broken when the network is saturated, it will be impossible to find a detour path. Thus, dependability decreases dramatically as the network load increases. To cope with this problem, we need to set aside some resources. For the proactive approach, the backup channel establishment makes resource reservation, so it can prevent any drastic decrease of dependability. Because our proposed scheme does not reserve bandwidth for each connection, we need a separate mechanism to set aside some resources.

In general, the bandwidth of a link is divided into two parts when the network deploys a real-time service based on resource reservation. One part of bandwidth serves real-time traffic, and a proper amount of bandwidth needs to be reserved before the real-time data is delivered. The other part of bandwidth must be left unreserved to prevent best-effort traffic from starvation.

In our scheme, the bandwidth is divided into three parts. An additional, third part is reserved for backup channel traffic. In other words, we set aside a certain amount of bandwidth for an aggregate of backups. The spare resources of a link are used for best-effort traffic in the absence of failure.

This pre-reservation has several important differences from the per-channel-based resource reservation of the proactive scheme. Our proposed scheme does not require any complex signaling procedure for backups. Thus, our approach does not involve the intermediate routers on a backup path until the backup is activated, whereas the proactive approach demands the intermediate routers to maintain information about backup channels and to change the amount of spare resources as backup channels are added or released.

Another advantage of the hybrid scheme is that the backup preparation does not affect primary routing. As described in the previous section, the backup channel establishment under the proactive approach affects the primary channels

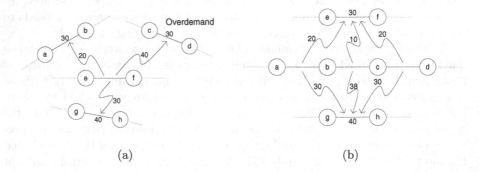

Fig. 1. The number next to each link is the amount of spare bandwidth and the number next to each arrow is the amount of backup bandwidth required to activate backups. The unit is Mbps.

that will be established later. The backup resource reservation of the proactive approach requires other nodes to update the link states, because it changes the amount of available link resources for real-time channels. This results in frequent exchanges of routing messages, which are usually expensive. Our proposed hybrid scheme does not incur these additional routing messages because it does not change the amount of spare resources.

The hybrid scheme affects the best-effort traffic only when backups are activated, whereas the proactive scheme changes the total available bandwidth for best-effort traffic whenever the spare resource changes. In fact, we can think of the backup channels as borrowing some bandwidth temporarily from the best-effort portion of bandwidth.

3   Selection of Backup Routes

The dependability of a D-connection is determined by its pre-selected backup route. When a link failure disables multiple primary channels, their backups that traverse a link without enough spare bandwidth will fail to be activated. To make the backup activation more likely to succeed, the backup routes should be chosen very carefully.

A link failure triggers activation of multiple backups that run through different links. If the demand of backup bandwidth on each of these links is smaller than the amount of spare bandwidth, all the activation will succeed. Let b_ℓ^k denote the bandwidth demand on link ℓ when link k fails. In other words, $b_\ell^k = \sum_{d \in \mathcal{D}_\ell^k} r_d$, where $\mathcal{D}_\ell^k$ is the set of D-connections whose primaries traverse link k with backups running through ℓ and r_d is the bandwidth requirement of D-connection d.

Figure 1 (a) shows an example of spare and backup bandwidth. The number next to a link is the amount of spare bandwidth and the number next to each arrow denotes the amount of backup bandwidth required to activate backups. When link (e,f) breaks down, backups will be activated along pre-selected routes. Because links (a,b) and (g,h) have enough spare bandwidths, the backups routed over them will be activated successfully. In link (c,d), the backups require more bandwidth than its spare bandwidth. So, some of the backups on the link may not be activated. Because the backups can use the primary portion of link bandwidth, if available, the overdemand of backup bandwidth does not always cause activation failures.

The goal of backup routing is to choose a route such that the new backup does not overdemand spare resources along its route. Because a D-connection prepares an end-to-end backup, we attempt to construct a backup route with links that does not overdemand resources from any link of the corresponding primary route. Figure 1 (b) shows an example of choosing the link of a backup route. We try to find a backup route for the primary channel that traverses links (a,b), (b,c), and (c,d). The new backup requires 5 Mbps. The backups, already routed, require bandwidth on each link as shown in the figure. Links (e,f) and (g,h) do not overdemand from links (a,b), (b,c), and (c,d).

If we select either link (e,f) or (g,h) to construct a backup route, each link of the primary route will demand more backup bandwidth on the selected link. If link (g,h) is selected, the backup bandwidth demand on link (b,c) will increase to 43 Mbps because the new backup requires 5 Mbps. This exceeds the spare bandwidth of 40 Mbps. If we choose link (e,f), however, we can avoid the overdemand because the spare bandwidth of link (e,f) is still larger than the increased demand of backup bandwidth of each link on the primary route. Thus, link (e,f) is a better choice than link (g,h) for the new backup.

As shown in the above example, when we choose a backup route for a D-connection d, link ℓ is an appropriate choice of the backup route if $s_\ell \geq b_\ell^k + r_d, \forall k \in PR_d$, where s_ℓ is the spare bandwidth of link ℓ and PR_d denotes the set of links of d's primary route. To maximize the probability of successful backup activation, a backup route should minimize the number of links that overdemand from its corresponding primary route. Also, a backup should be as disjoint as possible from its primary route. To find the shortest route among those that satisfy the requirements, we use Dijkstra's algorithm after assigning a cost, C_ℓ, to link ℓ:

$$
C_\ell = \begin{cases} M & \text{if } \ell \in PR_d, \\ m & \text{if } \exists k, \text{ such that } k \in PR_d \text{ and } s_\ell < b_\ell^k + r_d, \\ \varepsilon & \text{otherwise} \end{cases} \tag{1}
$$

where $M \gg m \gg \varepsilon$. Because the backup route is the least desirable when it overlaps with the primary, the largest cost is given to the link which belongs to the primary route. ε is given to a link to choose the shortest route when the other conditions are the same.

When a source node establishes a D-connection, the node selects a backup route after establishing a primary channel. So, the source node can easily check the first condition of the above equation. However, it is not trivial for the node to check the second condition because the node must know b_ℓ^k's. One possible way is that every node maintains all the b_ℓ^k's for every pair of links. However, this approach is not practical because it involves a huge amount of information exchange between nodes. To cope with this problem, we devised a new protocol that examines the second condition in a distributed manner.

4 The Protocol for a Hybrid Scheme

4.1 Notation and Data Structures

In a network $G(\mathcal{N}, \mathcal{L})$ with $|\mathcal{N}|$ nodes and $|\mathcal{L}|$ links, each link has a unique id between 1 and $|\mathcal{L}|$. Let l_i be the link whose id is i.

- SV (spare bandwidth vector): $|\mathcal{L}|$-dimensional integer vector whose i^{th} element denotes s_i, the amount of spare bandwidth of l_i. Every node keeps SV.
- BV_i (backup bandwidth vector): $|\mathcal{L}|$-dimensional vector whose j^{th} element is b_j^i. BV_i is maintained by node n if l_i is adjacent to n.
- APV (accumulated properness vector): $|\mathcal{L}|$-dimensional one-bit vector. This vector is calculated before selecting a backup route to check which link is appropriate to compose a backup route. If the ith bit is set to 1, l_i is suitable for the backup route.

4.2 Establishing a Primary Channel and Selecting a Backup Route

When a source node sets up a D-connection, the node establishes the primary path first. It can use any routing method for primary channels, because our backup routing is orthogonal to the primary routing. After selecting the primary path, the source node sends a QUERY message along the primary channel route.

When an intermediate node receives the QUERY message, it relays the message to the next node. When the QUERY message arrives at the destination node, the node prepares a RESULT message. The RESULT message has a field that contains APV. At the beginning, every bit of APV is set to 1. The destination node sends the confirmation message to the source node along the primary channel path in the reverse direction.

When an intermediate router receives the RESULT message through link l_i, it computes the links that overdemand resources on l_i and sets the corresponding bits of em APV to 0. In other words, if $b_j^i + r_d > s_j$, the jth element of APV is set to 0. Because this intermediate node maintains SV and BV_i, the node can easily update APV. After updating APV, the node relays the RESULT message to the next node.

When the RESULT message arrives at the source node, each bit of the APV in the RESULT message is as follows:

$$APV_i = \begin{cases} 0, & \text{if } \exists k, \text{ such that } k \text{ belongs to the primary links and } s_i < b_i^k + r_d, \\ 1, & \text{otherwise} \end{cases}$$

where APV^i denotes the ith element of APV. The above equation is equivalent to the second condition of Eq. (1). APV^i is 1 if and only if l_i has enough bandwidth to accommodate backups when any link on the corresponding primary route fails. The source node selects a backup route using Dijkstra's algorithm after assigning link cost C_l:

$$C_\ell = \begin{cases} M & \text{if } \ell \in PR_d, \\ m & \text{else if } APV^l = 0 \\ \varepsilon & \text{otherwise} \end{cases}$$

4.3   Maintaining BV

As described above, every router should maintain BV for each link attached to it to choose links suitable for a backup route and exchange BV during the signaling of the primary channel setup. BV_i represents the resource demand on each link to activate backups when link l_i is broken. More precisely, the jth element of BV_i is the sum of bandwidths required by all backups on l_j. If ℓ is link $(v1, v2)$, both $v1$ and $v2$ maintain BV_ℓ.

To keep BVs up-to-date, each node should know backup routes of D-connections whose primaries go through its links. After a source node chooses a backup route for a given primary channel, the source node informs nodes on the primary route of its decision. Also, when the backup route is no longer needed, the source node notifies the intermediate nodes to decrease BV. An intermediate node updates BV based on the data sent by the source node.

Because we cannot assume that the source node tears down the real-time connection gracefully, we take a soft state approach to maintaining BV. In the case of RSVP, the connection information is invalidated if it is not refreshed before a timer expires. However, maintaining BV as a soft state is more complex because BV is in summation form of information about backups, whereas RSVP keeps the information on a per-connection basis.

The basic idea is that a source node periodically sends Backup Bandwidth Demand (BBD) message carrying link ids of a backup route and its bandwidth requirement to intermediate nodes on the corresponding primary route. Intermediate nodes add the backup bandwidth requirements into a temporary BV when it receives BBD. An intermediate node updates BVs periodically by replacing them with temporary BVs in which the node has accumulated bandwidth demands of backups. To make this operation idempotent, we incorporate a version number into BV and BBD messages. The detailed procedure is given below.

1. A source node sends a BBD message along with the primary path. The BBD message constitutes the resource requirement of a backup route, the list of nodes that the message will visit, a version number for each router, and a backup route. All the version numbers are set to 0 when the end node sends the BBD message for a backup route for the first time.
2. When an intermediate router receives the BBD message, it compares the corresponding version number in the message with that of its BV. If the

version of the message is less than that of BV, the bandwidth requirement is added into both BV and temporary BV. If the two version numbers are equal, the resource requirement is added only into temporary BV. If the message has a higher version than BV, the bandwidth requirement is not added into either BV or temporary BV. The intermediate node relays this BBD message to the next node after increasing the corresponding version number in the message by one.

3. When the destination node receives the BBD message, it generates a BBD-ACK message that has updated version numbers and sends BBD-ACK to the source node along the primary route in reverse direction.
4. The intermediate nodes relay the BBD-ACK message until the message reaches the source node.
5. The end node records the version number in the real-time connection table and sets up a timer with interval T. When the timer expires the node resends the BBD message.
6. All the nodes have a timer with interval T. When the timer expires, the node replaces BVs with temporary BVs, resets temporary BV to 0, and increases the version number of BV by 1.

The above algorithm ensures two important features: (1) BV and temporary BV are not increased more than once during one period for the same real-time connection, even when the end node sends the BBD message more than once before the node's timer expires; (2) BV will be properly decreased within two periods even when the source node does not tear down the connection gracefully.

5   Scalability and Deployment

Every node maintains one BV per each link attached to the node and one SV. Because the vectors have as many elements as the number of links in the network, the space complexity is $O(|\mathcal{L}| \times (nd+1))$ where nd is the node degree. To set up a new D-connection, $O(|\mathcal{L}| \times h)$ messages need to be exchanged, where h is the hop count of the primary route. Because our scheme does not keep per-connection information in intermediate nodes and does not broadcast routing messages, it is highly scalable when the network has a limited number of links. Thus, overlay networks and VPNs are good candidates to deploy our scheme.

To deploy our scheme in the Internet, which has millions of links, we propose a hierarchical approach. The Internet is composed of Autonomous Systems (AS). Instead of an end-to-end backup, we can prepare an ingress-to-egress backup within an AS. ASs too are organized hierarchically. An AS is composed of POPs and a backbone. Recently, Spring et al. [9] measured ISP topologies. According to their results, an ISP has hundreds of backbone links, and each POP has less than one hundred routers. Thus, each POP can use our scheme to protect D-connections within the POP and an AS sets up ingress-to-egress backups in the backbone, which connects POPs, with a reasonable amount of storage and message overhead.

6   Performance Evaluation

We evaluated the proposed scheme by simulation. We implemented the reactive scheme, the proactive scheme, and the hybrid scheme using the network simulator **ns**. We generated scenario files where D-connection requests are listed. Each D-connection request consists of source node, destination node, bandwidth requirement, start and end times. The scenario files are fed to each simulator. Each simulator attempts to establish a D-connection based on the source node, the destination node, and the bandwidth requirement. If it succeeds, the simulator records the path taken by the primary and backup channels on a trace file, and terminates the D-connection at the specified end time. We analyzed the trace files thus generated, to derive performance metrics.

For simplicity, we assume that each D-connection requires 1 Mbps. The running time of a D-connection was uniformly distributed between 20 and 60 minutes so that the average running time may be 40 minutes. We conducted simulation with three network topologies: an 8×8 mesh, an 8×8 torus, and a random topology.

6.1   Load Index and Performance Metrics

To evaluate the performance of each scheme at various network loads, it is important to choose the load index that represents the load imposed on the network and the performance metrics to compare different schemes. For best-effort traffic, the overall resource usage or the amount of traffic can be a good load index. However, in real-time communication, the resource usage and the amount of traffic are the performance metrics because they can be affected by the routing and scheduling schemes. The path of a real-time channel is not always the shortest. Depending on the routing scheme used, a real-time channel traverses a different path, and the overall bandwidth consumption is different.

The amount of resources consumed by real-time channels can be expressed as:

$$\lambda' \times \overline{RT} \times \overline{h'} \times \overline{b'}$$

where λ' is the setup rate of real-time channels, $\overline{RT}$ is the average running time, $\overline{h'}$ is the average hop count of established real-time channels, and $\overline{b'}$ is the bandwidth requirement of established real-time channels. For our simulation, we assume that every real-time connection requires the same amount of bandwidth, b, so $\overline{b'} = b$. Because the network resources are limited, the setup rate has an upper limit:

$$\lambda' \leq \frac{B}{\overline{RT} \times \overline{h'} \times b} \leq \frac{B}{\overline{RT} \times \overline{D} \times b}$$

where B is the total amount of bandwidth of a network and $\overline{D}$ is the average hop count of the shortest paths between all pairs of nodes and $\overline{h'} \geq \overline{D}$. We

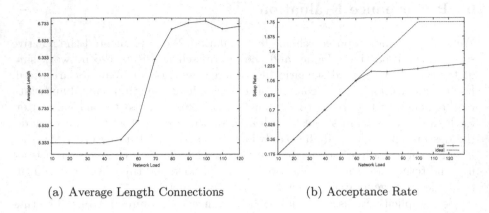

(a) Average Length Connections   (b) Acceptance Rate

Fig. 2. Example performance metrics and load index

define the maximum setup rate of real-time connections that the network can
accommodate as:

$$\lambda'_{max} = \frac{B}{\overline{RT} \times \overline{D} \times b}.$$

Because the network cannot accept the setup request at a rate higher than
λ'_{max}, we increase the request rate of real-time connections λ up to λ'_{max} to see
how each scheme performs. We defined *network load* as the ratio of λ to λ'_{max}:

$$NetworkLoad(\%) = \frac{\lambda}{\lambda'_{max}} \times 100.$$

As the network load increases, the bandwidths of some links are used up by
real-time channels. So, real-time channels traverse longer routes than the shortest
routes, i.e., $\overline{h'}$ becomes larger than $\overline{D}$. Thus, the network becomes saturated
before the network load reaches λ'_{max}.

Figure 2 shows how $\overline{h'}$ and λ change in a sample network. The average distance, $\overline{D}$, is 5.33 and the maximum setup rate, λ'_{max}, is 1.75. We established
real-time connections without backup channels. The line *real* represents the simulation results; in Figure (b), the line *ideal* shows the theoretical setup rate where
the $\overline{h'}$ remains equal to $\overline{D}$. After the network load reaches 80%, the network is
saturated and cannot accept more requests. When this happens, increasing the
network load does not make a considerable difference in the network.

$\overline{h'}$ is one of performance metrics. We use *normalized average hop count* $\overline{nh'}$,
defined as $\frac{\overline{h'}}{\overline{D}}$, to make the metric independent of the network characteristics. $\overline{nh'}$
of primaries shows the bandwidth each primary channel consumes, on average,
in proportion to bandwidth usage of the shortest path. Usually, $\overline{nh'}$ of backups
is longer than that of primaries. As $\overline{nh'}$ of backups becomes longer, the backups
consume more bandwidth when they are activated, and the end-to-end delay of
backups is increased.

The dependability is the probability that a D-connection can continue the service when a link on the primary channel of the D-connection is broken. To measure the dependability, we broke every link alternately and tried to activate the corresponding backups. We calculated the probability of successful backup activation of each link and computed the average over all links. More precisely, the dependability is defined as:

$$Dependability = \frac{\sum_{\ell \in \mathcal{L}} \frac{|\mathcal{S}_\ell|}{|\mathcal{D}_\ell|}}{|\mathcal{L}|}$$

where $\mathcal{S}_\ell$ is the set of backups successfully activated when link ℓ is broken, and $\mathcal{D}_\ell$ is the set of D-connections whose primaries traverse ℓ.

Another important metric is the *average acceptance rate*, $\alpha = \frac{\lambda'}{\lambda}$. Because the acceptance rate is closely related to bandwidth consumption, α implies a *capacity overhead*.

6.2 Topology Characteristics

As mentioned earlier, we used 8×8 mesh, 8×8 torus, and random network topologies. We generated the random topology using the Waxman 2 model with Georgia Tech Internetwork Topology Models (GT-ITM) [10]. Initially, we generated a network with 100 nodes and pruned nodes that have only one link to make every node have at least two links attached to it.

These three topologies have several different characteristics that affect the performance of fault-management schemes. Table 1 shows the characteristics of three topologies.

Though the torus and the mesh have the same number of nodes and similar numbers of links, the average distance of the torus network is only about $\frac{3}{4}$ of that of the mesh network. By "distance," we mean the length of the shortest path between two nodes. The random network has the shortest average distance although its node degree is the lowest.

Though the three topologies have a similar average node degree, the distribution of node degrees is different. Table 2 shows the distribution. In the torus, every node has the same node degree of 4. In the random topology, 28 nodes have only two links, so there are a small number of choices for detour routes.

Table 1. Characteristics of the topologies used for simulation

	8×8 mesh	8×8 torus	random
Nodes	64	64	78
Links	112	128	129
Avg. Dist.	$\frac{16}{3}$	$4 \times \frac{64}{63}$	3.706
Node Degree	3.5	4	3.308

Table 2. Distribution of node degrees

Node Degree	2	3	4	5	6	7
8×8 mesh		4	24	36		
8×8 torus			64			
random topology	28	21	13	12	1	3

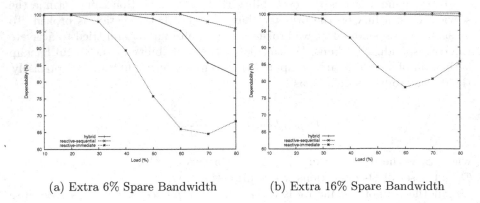

(a) Extra 6% Spare Bandwidth   (b) Extra 16% Spare Bandwidth

Fig. 3. Comparison with the reactive scheme on an 8× 8 mesh network.

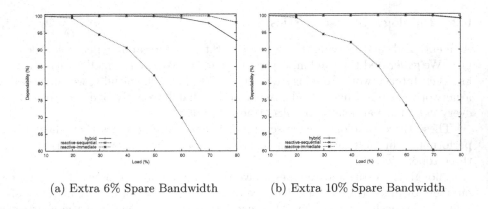

(a) Extra 6% Spare Bandwidth   (b) Extra 10% Spare Bandwidth

Fig. 4. Comparison with the reactive scheme on an 8×8 torus network

6.3   Comparison with the Reactive Schemes

Figure 3 shows the dependability of the two reactive schemes and the hybrid scheme. The reactive-immediate scheme tries to reroute all D-connections at the same time. The reactive-sequential scheme reroutes D-connections one by one.

The reactive schemes do not utilize spare resources and suffer from resource shortage when the network load is high. To make a fair comparison and to evaluate the effects of spare resources, we provisioned spare bandwidth for reactive schemes. In this simulation, the bandwidth for primary channels on each link is 100 Mbps, and we provisioned an additional spare bandwidth for backups. We changed the spare bandwidth to see how each scheme performs with various spare bandwidths.

As shown in Figure 3, the reactive-immediate scheme provides considerably low fault-tolerance. This scheme suffers from backup conflicts because each node tries to set up a backup channel independently without considering the backup route selection of other nodes. This is why the reactive-immediate scheme does not perform well with 16% spare bandwidth, with which the hybrid scheme and the sequential scheme provide 99% fault-recovery.

Both the hybrid scheme and the sequential scheme improve the dependability as the spare bandwidth increases. Because both schemes select backup routes avoiding backup conflicts by consideration of backup routes of other D-connections, they can take a full advantage of spare bandwidth.

The reactive-sequential scheme shows slightly better fault-tolerance than the hybrid scheme. The sequential scheme utilizes all the network resources excluding the broken link, whereas the hybrid scheme cannot use the entire primary path.

However, the sequential rerouting is practically impossible to implement and incurs a very long recovery delay. To reroute the D-connections one by one in a distributed manner, it is necessary to decide the order in which each node recovers. Moreover, each node, which wants to establish a backup channel, waits for the new link status that reflects the recently-established backups. Because fast recovery is one of the most important requirements for real-time communication, the sequential scheme is not applicable to real-time communication.

Figure 4 shows the performance of each scheme in the 8×8 torus network. Both the hybrid and the sequential schemes perform much better in this network compared to the 8×8 mesh network. As stated in the previous section, the torus has a shorter average distance between two nodes. The average length of backups is shorter in the torus than in the mesh and backups use less bandwidth. Thus, with less spare bandwidth the torus can accommodate more backups. To provide 99% dependability, the hybrid scheme needs only 10% extra bandwidth.

However, the reactive-immediate scheme performs worse in the torus than in the mesh topology. A shorter average distance means that the starting end nodes of the D-connections start are closer to the broken link. So, the end nodes that reroute D-connections are more closely located to each other in the torus and the end nodes are more likely to choose the same links for backup routes. The reactive-immediate scheme suffers from more contention in the torus.

As shown in this comparison with the reactive schemes, careful selection of backup routes improves dependability dramatically. To avoid contention, backups need to be distributed over a large area. With knowledge about backups of other D-connections, the hybrid scheme distributes backups and utilizes the spare bandwidth efficiently.

6.4 Comparison with the Proactive Scheme

We compared the hybrid scheme with the proactive scheme. Because the proactive scheme reserves spare bandwidth dynamically, it does not need separate spare bandwidths. To compare the two schemes under the same condition, we provided each link with 100 Mbps bandwidth for D-connections. Because the hybrid scheme requires separate spare bandwidth, we reserved a certain amount of bandwidth for backups out of the 100 Mbps bandwidth. To see the performance of the hybrid scheme with various amounts of spare bandwidth, we changed the spare bandwidth from 4 to 20% of the total bandwidth.

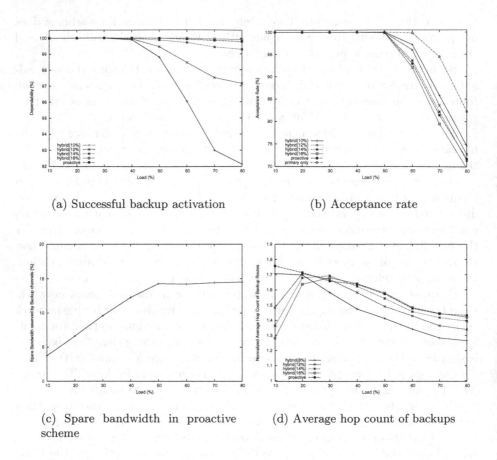

(a) Successful backup activation   (b) Acceptance rate

(c) Spare bandwidth in proactive   (d) Average hop count of backups
scheme

Fig. 5. Comparison with the proactive scheme on an 8×8 mesh network

Figure 5 shows the performance of the proactive and hybrid schemes. The hybrid scheme improves dependability as the spare bandwidth increases. When 16% of the total bandwidth is provisioned as spare bandwidth, the hybrid scheme shows dependability compatible to the proactive scheme.

However, as more bandwidth is reserved for backups, less bandwidth is available for primaries. Figure 5 (b) shows the acceptance rate of requests for D-connections. In the figure, the 'primary only' represents the acceptance rate when we establish real-time channels without backups. The difference between the primary only and each scheme is the *capacity overhead*.

The proactive scheme incurs a capacity overhead similar to that of the hybrid scheme with 14% spare bandwidth. We can find the reason from Figure 5 (c). The figure shows the amount of bandwidth reserved by backup channels in the proactive scheme. Because the proactive scheme reserves spare bandwidth according to the network load, more bandwidth is reserved for backups as the network load increases. After the network load reaches 50%, the spare bandwidth does not increase, because the primaries occupy the remaining bandwidth.

The proactive scheme reserves a maximum of about 14% bandwidth for backups. This is the reason why the proactive scheme shows an acceptance rate similar to the hybrid scheme with 14% spare bandwidth. However, the proactive scheme provides higher dependability than the hybrid scheme with 14% spare bandwidth. To match the dependability of the proactive scheme, the hybrid scheme requires a little more bandwidth. This is because the proactive scheme utilizes much more information when it selects backup routes.

Figure 5 (d) shows the average hop count of backups. When load is low, the backups of the proactive scheme is longer than those of the hybrid scheme with a similar amount of spare bandwidth. Because the hybrid scheme sets aside a certain amount of bandwidth in advance irrespective of the network load, the hybrid scheme has more room for backups and can find backup routes within a near area. The proactive scheme starts without any spare bandwidth and increases it. As the backup bandwidth increases, it can find a shorter route for a given D-connection using spare bandwidth reserved for other backups.

To see how the topology affects the performance of each scheme, we conducted simulation with the torus and the random topology. Figure 6 shows the performance in the 8×8 torus topology.

As described in Section 6.2, the torus has a shorter average distance between two nodes and a higher node degree. A shorter average distance means that each backup requires less backup bandwidth. As shown in Figure 6 (a), with 10% spare bandwidth, the hybrid scheme provides more than 99% dependability.

Figure 6 (c) shows the spare bandwidth reserved for backups in the proactive scheme. The maximum spare bandwidth is about 10%. In the torus, both the proactive and hybrid schemes need less spare bandwidth than in the mesh network. This is because the torus has more node degree in addition to a shorter average distance. A higher node degree means that there are more disjoint routes within a certain boundary between two nodes. So, backups are distributed over more routes without conflicts and less spare bandwidth accommodates more backups.

When the network load is 80%, the spare bandwidth of the proactive scheme decreases. Because the primary channel reserves the bandwidth before the backup channel, whenever the bandwidth is available, the free bandwidth is allocated to a primary channel and the corresponding backup channel squeezes into the spare bandwidth shared by other backups. This results in less allocation of bandwidth to backup channels and more backup conflicts. The contraction of the backup bandwidth accompanies the degradation of dependability. As the spare bandwidth of the proactive scheme decreases below 10%, the dependability of the proactive scheme also decreases.

Because less bandwidth is reserved for backups in the torus, more bandwidth is available for primaries. Figure 6 (b) shows the acceptance rate. Until the network load reaches 70%, the acceptance rate is 100%. Compared to the acceptance rate in the mesh topology, the torus improves the acceptance rate considerably.

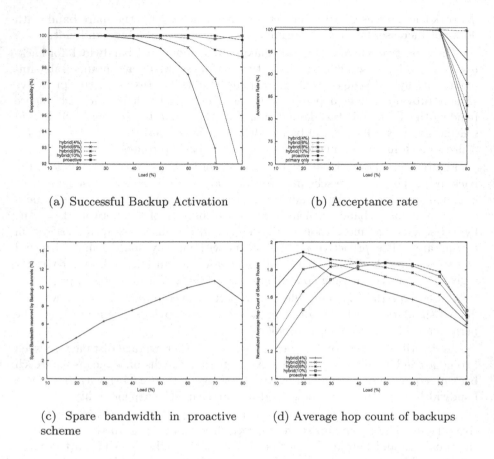

(a) Successful Backup Activation   (b) Acceptance rate

(c) Spare bandwidth in proactive   (d) Average hop count of backups
scheme

Fig. 6. Comparison with the proactive scheme on an 8×8 torus network

The average hop count of backups shows a similar pattern. As the network load increases, the hybrid scheme selects longer backup routes to avoid overdemands. After the network load reaches a certain point, it is impossible to build a route without links that do not overdemand. Then, the length of backup routes decreases because a shorter path incurs less conflicts and the routing algorithm selects the shortest path when several paths have the same number of conflicts.

The 8×8 torus has 16 more links than the 8×8 mesh. The additional 16 links improve the performance of D-connections dramatically. The torus uses 30% less spare bandwidth, provides higher dependability, and shows lower capacity overhead.

The random topology is similar to the torus in the average distance. However, in the node degree, the random topology is considerably different. On average, the node degree of the random topology is just a little smaller than the mesh. However, there is a large deviation in the node degree of the random topology.

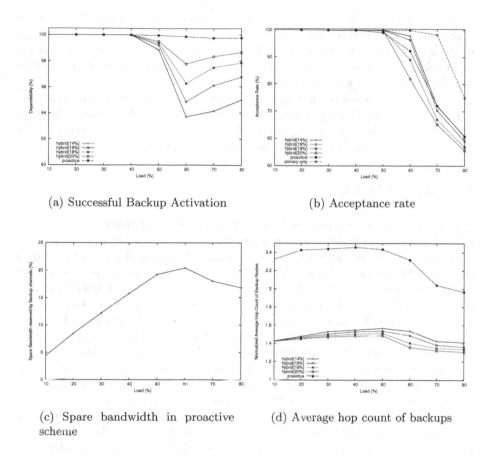

(a) Successful Backup Activation   (b) Acceptance rate

(c) Spare bandwidth in proactive   (d) Average hop count of backups
scheme

Fig. 7. Comparison with the proactive scheme on a random network

More than a half of the nodes have 2 or 3 links, whereas 4 nodes have 6 or 7
links.

The diverse node degrees introduce some disadvantages to the D-connections.
Because many nodes have a small number of links, there are fewer detour routes
and more backups conflicts occur. Though the average node degree is smaller,
the average distance of random topology is shorter than the mesh and the torus.
This is because a few nodes with many links act as crossroads. This results in
nonuniform traffic flows in the network.

Figure 7 (a) shows the dependability in the random topology. The hybrid
scheme provides a little lower dependability even with 20% spare bandwidth. As
shown in Figure 7 (c), the proactive scheme reserves a maximum of 20% spare
bandwidth. With a similar amount of spare bandwidth, the proactive scheme
provides higher dependability because the proactive scheme reserves different
amounts of spare bandwidth on each link according to network traffic, whereas
the hybrid scheme uses the same amount of spare bandwidth on each link.

The proactive scheme shows less capacity overhead in Figure 7 (b). When traffic is concentrated in some links, the proactive scheme reserves spare bandwidth in other links. So, the congested links have more bandwidth for primaries, and backups run through other less congested links. This improves dependability and decreases the capacity overhead.

Figure 7 (d) shows the average hop count of backup routes. The proactive scheme selects significantly longer routes than the hybrid scheme. The poor connectivity of the random topology affects more the backup routing of the proactive scheme because the proactive scheme uses less spare bandwidth.

7 Related Work

Since Han and Shin [6,7] proposed the backup multiplexing scheme, many proactive schemes have employed this idea. In the backup multiplexing scheme, the same spare resources can be shared by multiple backups, if the corresponding primaries do not traverse through same links. This approach needs to broadcast the information about spare bandwidth on each link to select backup routes. Also, it broadcasts the information about available bandwidth to select primary routes frequently, because changing the amount of spare bandwidth affects the amount of the available bandwidth. Our hybrid scheme is the first approach that does not broadcast the information about the shared spare bandwidth.

Though Han and Shin explored several routing heuristics for backup channels, they did not propose a distributed algorithm for backup routing. Kodialam *et al.* [11] developed a routing algorithm that selects a backup path based on the amount of the aggregate bandwidth used on each link by primary channels, the aggregate bandwidth used on each link by backup channels, and the link residual free bandwidth. The algorithm tries to minimize the amount of backup bandwidth increased by a new backup when selecting a route for a new backup. However, because the algorithm does not have any information about the paths of other backups, it overestimates the spare bandwidth by assuming that every disrupted D-connection has conflicts on the same link.

In [12], three routing schemes are proposed and evaluated. The algorithm with the best performance chooses a backup path based on *backup con icts* in addition to the amount of free bandwidth. Backup paths are said to have conflicts if they traverse the same link and their corresponding primaries share one or more links. Although this approach utilizes more information, backup paths are still selected without precise information.

Li *et al.* [13] recently proposed a distributed backup route selection algorithm for the proactive scheme. They use full information about spare resources as we do. Though their algorithm is similar to ours, there are several differences. First, their algorithm involves signaling for backup channels. Moreover, though it is not clearly stated, their scheme needs to broadcast information about the amount of spare resources, whereas our hybrid scheme does not need broadcasting.

Li *et al.* use the increment of spare resources as their metric to choose a backup route. In other words, they try to minimize the amount of spare resources.

Whereas, we select a backup route to minimize the number of links that do not have enough spare resources. Because two algorithms use different metrics for path selection, the information exchanged for backup selection is also different. In our algorithm, routers exchange a bit-vector that represents a list of links that are suitable for a backup route, while in Li's algorithm routers exchange an integer-vector representing the amount of spare resources that will be needed when a link fails. Because the size of the vector is the same as the number of links in the network, the integer-vector consumes more bandwidth than the bit-vector and may not be delivered in a single packet.

8   Conclusion

In this paper, we presented a hybrid scheme that pre-selects backup routes without reserving bandwidth for each backup channel. Because a certain amount of spare bandwidth is set aside *a priori* for backups, the hybrid scheme does not require global routing messages for spare bandwidth, thus eliminating one of the main drawbacks of the proactive scheme. Also, we devised a novel distributed routing algorithm that does not require nodes to keep information for each D-connection.

We evaluated and compared the effectiveness of the hybrid scheme by simulation. We compared the hybrid scheme with the proactive and reactive schemes for various network topologies. The hybrid scheme offers as high dependability as the proactive scheme without the need for broadcasting the information about spare bandwidth. When the network is homogeneous, the hybrid scheme is more effective. Using the hybrid scheme, we were able to reduce the overhead of the proactive scheme without degrading its performance.

References

1. Paxson, V.: End-to-end routing behavior in the internet. IEEE/ACM Transaction on Networking **5** (1997) 601–615
2. Labovitz, C., Ahuja, A., Jahanian, F.: Experimental study of internet stability and backbone failures. In: Proceedings of IEEE FTCS'99. (1999) 278–285
3. Banerjea, A., Parris, C., Ferrari, D.: Recovering guaranteed performance service connections from single and multiple faults. In: Proceedings of IEEE GLOBE-COM'94, San Francisco, CA (1994) 162–168
4. Banerjea, A.: Fault recovery for guaranteed performance communications connections. IEEE Transactions on Computer Systems **7** (1999) 653–668
5. Dovrolis, C., Ramanathan, P.: Resource aggregation for fault tolerance in integrated services networks. Computer Communication Review **28** (1998) 39–53
6. Han, S., Shin, K.G.: Efficient spare resource allocation for fast restoration of real-time channels from network component failures. In: Proceedings of IEEE RTSS'97. (1997) 99–108
7. Han, S., Shin, K.G.: Fast restoration of real-time communication service from component failures in multihop networks. In: Proceedings of ACM SIGCOMM'97. (1997) 77–88

8. Han, S., Shin, K.G.: A primary-backup channel approach to dependable real-time communication in multi-hop networks. IEEE Transactions on Computers **47** (1998)
9. Spring, N., Mahajan, R., Wetherall, D.: Measuring isp topologies with rocketfuel. In: Proceedings of ACM SIGCOMM 2002. (2002) 133–146
10. Calvert, K., Zegura, E.: Gt-itm: Georgia tech internetwork topology models. http://www.cc.gatech.edu/fac/Ellen.Zegura/gt-itm/gt-itm.tar.gz. (1996)
11. Kodialam, M., Lakshman, T.V.: Dynamic routing of bandwidth guaranteed tunnels with restoration. In: Proceedings of INFOCOM 2000. (2000) 902–911
12. Kim, S., Qiao, D., Kodase, S., Shin, K.G.: Design and evaluation of routing schemes for dependable real-time connections. In: Proceedings of DSN 2001. (2001) 285–294
13. Li, G., Wang, D., Kalmanek, C., Doverspike, R.: Efficient distributed path selection for shared restoration connections. In: Proceedings of INFOCOM 2002. (2002) 140–149

Fault Tolerance in Networks with an Advance Reservation Service

Lars-Olof Burchard and Marc Droste-Franke

Technische Universitaet Berlin
Franklinstrasse 28/29
10587 Berlin, GERMANY
{baron,mdf}@cs.tu-berlin.de

Abstract. Strategies for dealing with link failures in computer networks so far have only been discussed in the context of immediate reservations, i.e. reservations made immediately before the requested transmission commences. In contrast, advance reservation mechanisms provide the opportunity to reserve resources a longer time before a transmission starts. In such an environment, the requirement for defining strategies to deal with link failures exists, too. The differences between immediate and advance reservation mechanisms require to apply different and more complex mechanisms in order to implement fault tolerance. In this paper, we discuss the requirements for dealing with link failures in advance reservation environments. Based on these observations, in the second part of the paper strategies for handling link failures are developed and evaluated.

1   Introduction

Todays considerations about quality-of-service (QoS) usually deal with so-called *immediate reservations*, i.e. reservations that are made in a just-in-time manner directly before a given transmission is supposed to start. Mechanisms for dealing with link failures in such environments have already been widely discussed. The main focus of most recent work is on multi-protocol label switching (MPLS) and its functionality for rerouting flows in case of link failures. Once a failure is detected, this allows to switch flows to a different path. Especially when QoS guarantees for transmissions are required, it is necessary to carefully design the failure mechanisms in a way that prioritized flows can be rerouted without loss of QoS.

In contrast, *advance reservations* allow to allocate resources a longer time before the actual transmission commences. This results in a high admission probability for flows that are reserved sufficiently early. Applications for such advance reservation mechanisms are grid computing environments, where processing resources are allocated in advance and it is required to transmit large amounts of data between the different computers of the grid environment. Another example is the field of distributed media servers, where a requirement for the timely transmission of large media files exists. Such advance reservations also require

K. Jeffay, I. Stoica, and K. Wehrle (Eds.): IWQoS 2003, LNCS 2707, pp. 215–228, 2003.

the implementation of mechanisms in order to deal with link failures in a way that the admitted flows can be transmitted without loss of quality-of-service. In this paper, we show strategies to deal with link failures in network environments supporting advance reservations. Link failure in our notion means the breakdown of a link, i.e. no packets are transmitted over this link for a certain period of time[1].

In general, two types of strategies can be distinguished: pre-failure strategies are applied before a link failure occurs and determine how flows are distributed, i.e. routed, in the network. For that purpose, we use k-path algorithms which provide a set of paths for each two nodes of the network. Flows are then routed using these paths. The second type of strategy, called post-failure strategy, is applied after a link failure occurs. Post-failure strategies determine which of the affected flows are rerouted and to which paths these flows are switched. Generally, this is an NP-complete problem for which we present heuristics that determine the order in which flows are rerouted. These heuristics are based on different properties of the flows such as the remaining amount of data to be transmitted or the actual time the reservation was admitted.

Another aspect of our examinations is the question which flows are actually considered for rerouting. The reason is that in an advance reservation environment, flows can already be admitted but not started at the time a link failure occurs. Depending on the actual downtime of the link, such flows might also get affected by the link failure. We address this problem by introducing the *expected downtime* which is calculated for each link failure. Each flow supposed to start within the expected downtime is then considered for rerouting.

In the following sections, after discussing related work we describe the system environment for advance reservations. After that, we discuss how fault tolerance mechanisms can be applied in advance reservation scenarios in general. In Section 5 and 6, the pre- and post-failure strategies are described and evaluated. The paper concludes with some final remarks in Section 7.

2   Related Work

The general properties of advance reservation mechanisms in computer networks have been discussed in [6]. The authors examine fundamental properties and the difference compared to immediate reservations.

Applications for advance reservations can be found in the field of distributed computing where large amounts of data must be transferred between different computers. Examples are distributed media servers [4] and grid computing [7].

One of the fundamental requirements for an advance reservation service is to control the network especially in terms of routing. This can be achieved using an MPLS aware network infrastructure [9]. Our approach is to use MPLS together with a bandwidth broker as control component as described in [2].

---

[1] The failure of a node results in several link failures and therefore can be conceived as an identical problem

Fault tolerance for advance reservations has so far not been studied in detail. In [10], an advance reservation scenario is proposed using RSVP. Fault tolerance in this case is restricted to the corresponding mechanisms of the RSVP protocol, i.e. periodically repeated messages which take different paths in case of link failures and set up new reservations if possible. The order in which flows are rerouted is not part of their discussion.

We consider two pre-failure (routing) mechanisms in this document. The first makes use of the set of the k shortest paths between two nodes of the network. We use the algorithm described in [5] to compute these paths (EPP). For a given integer k, this algorithm computes the k shortest paths[2].

In [8], a load-balancing and fault tolerance mechanism for immediate reservations based on MPLS aware network infrastructure is discussed. The main idea is to distribute the flows or packets of a flow onto several *maximally disjoint paths* (MAXDIS) in order to more evenly balance the network load and reduce the impact of a link failure onto the flows. Therefore, a link failure affects only a part of the flow which is then rerouted using one of the other available paths. We implemented the maximally disjoint algorithm as the second pre-failure strategy using the flow-based approach described in [8], i.e. flows rather than packets between two network endpoints are distributed onto the available paths. In [8], the actual pre-failure strategy is not described. The implementations described in this paper use the shortest path with minimum average load to route admitted flows as described in [2].

Post-failure strategies so far have only been considered in terms of selecting a new path (rerouting) for interrupted flows. Examples for such strategies are path protection or link protection. A good overview about the different opportunities is given in [1], however the assumption in that paper is that sufficient bandwidth must be available on each of the alternative paths. This precondition must be checked at admission time and results in a waste of bandwidth. In contrast, our solution is to keep a number of k alternative paths without checking the available bandwidth and hence, no bandwidth is wasted in case of link failures.

To the authors knowledge, the properties of advance reservations and their implications for implementing fault tolerance mechanisms have not been considered so far.

3   Advance Reservation Model

Advance reservations in our case are requests for a certain bandwidth during a specified period of time. In general, a reservation can be made for a fixed period of time in the future called *book-ahead time* (see Figure 1). The book-ahead time is divided into *slots* of fixed size (e.g. minutes) and reservations can be issued for a consecutive number of slots. The time between issuing a request and the requests start time is called *reservation time*. In contrast to immediate reservations, advance reservations require to define the stop time

---

[2] Since paths can contain loops in the original version of the algorithm, we modified it such that paths with loops were removed.

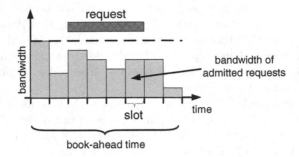

Fig. 1. Advance Reservation Environment

for a given request. This is required to reliably perform admission control, i.e. to determine whether or not sufficient bandwidth can be guaranteed for the requested transmission period. As depicted in Figure 1, this approach requires to keep the status of each link, i.e. information about future requests which are already admitted, for the whole book-ahead time. As proposed in [3], we use arrays for that purpose.

4   Issues of Implementing Fault Tolerance Mechanisms in Advance Reservation Environments

In this section, we analyze the requirements of advance reservation mechanisms with respect to fault tolerance and outline the general strategy used to compensate link failures.

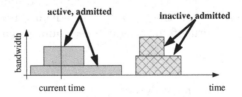

Fig. 2. Flows in Advance Reservation Environments

4.1   Properties

Advance reservations require a different approach for dealing with link failures. In immediate reservation environments, a link failure affects only the flows that are active at the time the failure occurs. Future flows are not affected, because they are not yet admitted by the network management system (i.e. bandwidth broker). In contrast, due to the nature of advance reservations, link failures in such environments do not only affect currently active flows but also those that have already been admitted but are not yet active (see Figure 2). Since a QoS guarantee has already been given for admitted flows, interruptions of these flows must be avoided.

Therefore the cancellation of flows admitted a long time ago should be avoided which leads to the question which flows are affected by a link failure. For that purpose, we introduce the notion of *expected downtime* which defines the assumed downtime period of a given link. Any flow which is active within this period is taken into account for rerouting. The expected downtime must be computed for each link failure, for example by using statistical data about the duration of former failures.

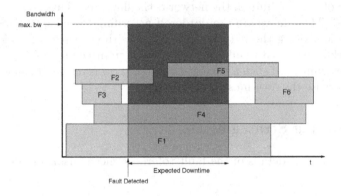

Fig. 3. Expected downtime and affected flows

An example for this procedure is given in Figure 3. The flows F1, F2, F4, and also F5 are affected by the link failure and are rerouted if possible. If F5 cannot be rerouted it will not be canceled but in case the link failure is still present at the start time of F5, the network management system will then again try to find an alternative path. F6 does not start within the expected downtime and therefore the network management system does not try to find another feasible route for F6.

The procedure previously described relies on the important assumption that the expected downtime can be reliably computed. The effects of incorrect downtime calculations are described in Section 6. In that section, the effect of not using the expected downtime, i.e. of not rerouting inactive but admitted flows, is also shown.

The other important difference between advance and immediate reservation scenarios is, that once an alternative path with sufficient bandwidth for a given flow is found at the time a link fails in an immediate reservation environment, this path can be used until the flow is finished. This means, no further computational effort is required. In an advance reservation scenario, such an approach is not feasible since future requests might block the available bandwidth. Hence, for any alternative path the whole transmission period of a given interrupted flow has to be checked for sufficient bandwidth.

4.2   Rerouting Process

As previously described, we distinguish two types of strategies for dealing with link errors: pre-failure and post-failure schemes. The pre-failure strategies use a set of k paths to perform load-balancing, i.e. trying to avoid that a single link failure affects too many flows. In contrast, the post-failure strategy which is applied after a failure occurred, determines which flows are rerouted the affected flows and selects paths. Both strategies are applied together in order to cope with link failures.

In case of a link failure in the network, the flows that have to be rerouted are determined. These flows are then ordered according to the strategies presented in Section 5.2. Using the path set associated with each pair of nodes, for each flow a backup path with sufficient bandwidth from the set of k pre-computed paths is determined. If such a path is found, the flow is rerouted using the backup path. Otherwise the flow must be terminated.

5   Rerouting Strategies

In this section, the details of the fault tolerance mechanisms are described.

5.1   Pre-failure Strategies

Fault tolerance in an environment as considered in this document is closely related to routing. The actual routing policy as enforced by the bandwidth broker determines how flows are mapped onto the network, i.e. which paths are used, and therefore influences the load that can be put onto the network. In [2], a number of routing strategies for advance reservations have been examined with respect to the suitability for advance reservations. The result was that k-path algorithms achieve the best performance. Therefore, in this paper we only consider k-path strategies, although the strategies presented here can also be applied using other routing algorithms.

Pre-failure mechanisms in our notion determine the routing strategy, i.e. in which way flows are routed within the network. Algorithms, that distribute the network load among several paths do have the potential to be less sensitive to link failures. The results from [2,8] show the superiority of k-path mechanisms concerning load balancing and therefore were used as the initial routing strategy here. In this paper, the load balancing is made on the flow level rather than packet level.

For that purpose, a set of k paths is computed. Two different k-path computation algorithms were used. The first determines the k shortest paths between two nodes of the network as described in [5] (EPP). Since this algorithm computes only shortest paths, the resulting paths usually have many links in common. The second algorithm presented in [8] tries to find *maximally disjoint* shortest paths (MAXDIS). This leads to paths that have fewer links in common but usually the size of the set of paths computed for two given nodes is smaller than that of EPP.

Using the k-path algorithms, the admission control procedure for a given request is to select one of the available paths. In [2], a combined SHORTEST/MINLOAD strategy is proposed for advance reservations. This means, initially the shortest among the available paths with sufficient bandwidth to satisfy the request is selected. In case, several paths with the same hop count are available, the one with the minimal load during the requested transmission period is chosen.

5.2   Post-failure Strategies

The task of the post-failure strategies is to determine which flows are rerouted. Formally, when having a number of i affected flows with bandwidth requirements b_i and a total capacity c on the alternative paths[3], the question which flows to reroute such that an optimal solution is achieved, i.e. that the amount of bytes transmitted by flows that can be successfully rerouted using the alternative paths is maximized, is a variant of the well-known KNAPSACK problem and hence NP-complete. In the following, we outline a number of heuristics to solve that problem.

Our strategy is to firstly order the flows and then try to find an alternative path for the flows in the computed order. In advance reservation environments, the key difference compared to immediate reservations is the availability of status information about the whole book-ahead time. Using this information allows to define a variety of post-failure strategies for ordering the affected flows. The additional amount of information available in advance reservation environments can be used to order the flows which leads to a large number of possible strategies. A selection of strategies considered to be sensible in the environment is described in the following.

First-Come First-Served (FCFS). This very simple and straightforward strategy prefers flows that have been requested early. This strategy provides a high degree of fairness as perceived by users in the sense that flows admitted at a very early stage are rerouted with a high probability, independent of other properties of the corresponding flow. This is the basic idea of advance reservations, where early requests for QoS result in a high probability that such requests will be admitted. This strategy however results in a rather unpredictable performance as can be observed in Section 6. In our experiments, FCFS nearly always ranged between the best and the worst.

---

[3] This is a simplification since the capacity c might be the combined capacity of several alternative paths

Largest Remaining Transmission Size (LRTS). The LRTS strategy prefers transmissions with a high amount of remaining bytes[4]. The strategy SRTS (*smallest remaining transmission size*) has the opposite effect, i.e. transmissions with few amount of bytes left to transfer are preferred.

Longest First (LF). This strategy prefers transmissions with the longest total duration. The counterpart of this strategy is *Shortest First* (SF), preferring flows with short duration.

Largest Request First (LRF). The last strategy uses the totally allocated bandwidth as a metric to order flows. LRF prefers flows transmitting a large amount of bytes and *SRF* prefers requests with a low amount of bytes.

Rerouting Duration. As described in Section 4, any flow which uses a broken link during its expected downtime is selected for rerouting. Two alternatives exist for how long these flows are rerouted: the first is trying to reroute a flow only during the expected downtime period (perhaps less if the link failures lasts shorter than expected) and then switch the flow back onto the original path. The other opportunity is trying to reroute flows during the whole remaining transmission period, independent of expected and real downtime. While the former has the potential to reroute a higher number of flows since rerouting is only required for a shorter period, the latter has the advantage of significantly reduced administrative overhead. The evaluations presented in Section 6 were made using the second strategy. The other strategy was also tested. However, the results did not significantly differ and therefore the reduced overhead in terms of switching flows justifies using the second approach.

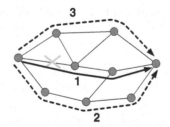

Fig. 4. Post-failure Strategy: Path Selection

---

[4] This strategy can be applied because in an advance reservation environment the stop time for each transmission is known.

Path Selection. When the previously described ordering of flows is finished, the set of k precomputed paths is used in order to select a new path for the affected flows.

The set of k paths (see Section 5.1) is used to implement a path protection approach where one of the remaining $k - 1$ paths of the set is used to reroute a flow. This is illustrated in Figure 4 with an example for $k = 3$: once the first path fails, the corresponding flow is rerouted using path 2 or 3 (if sufficient bandwidth is available). In this case, path 3 would be selected because it is shorter. In case, two paths with equal hop count exist, the one with the minimum average load during the transmission period is chosen. Obviously, any prospectively alternative path must be checked for sufficient bandwidth before a flow is rerouted.

6   Evaluation

In this section, the experimental setup and the results of the evaluations are described.

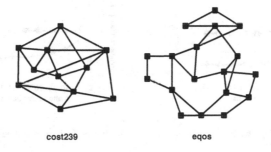

cost239   eqos

Fig. 5. Network topologies

6.1   Simulation Environment

The different strategies were evaluated using a simulation environment for advance reservations. Two network topologies representing ISP backbone networks as depicted in Figure 5 were used.

The source and destination nodes of flows were randomly chosen with the same probability for each node of the network. Table 1 shows the other parameters used to generate the network traffic and the link failures. The requests were generated using a uniform distribution for the duration and bandwidth requirement, and an exponentially distributed reservation time, i.e. the time between a request is made and the resources are used, with the given mean values.

The performance of the strategies was assessed using two metrics. Firstly, the *preemption rate* describes the impact of link failures on the flows and is defined as $preemption\_rate = \frac{|B|}{|A|}$, where B denotes the set of interrupted flows

Table 1. Simulation parameters

requests	avg. bandwidth requirement	100 kByte/s	uniform
	avg. duration	200 slots	exponential
	avg. reservation time	100 slots	exponential
failures	frequency	every 500 slots	
	duration	100 slots	
network	link capacity	100 MBit/s	
	book-ahead time	$2^{15} = 32768$ slots	

and A denotes the set of flows that was affected by the link failure as described in Section 4. The second metric is the bandwidth loss and is defined as $bandwidth\_loss = \frac{\sum_{i \in B} bandwidth(i)}{\sum_{i \in A} bandwidth(i)}$.

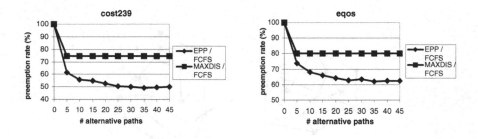

Fig. 6. Preemption rate for both pre-failure strategies

6.2   Performance of the Pre-failure Strategies

In order to assess the performance of the two pre-failure strategies, the preemption rate for different amounts of alternative paths is presented in Figure 6. The figures were generated using FCFS as post-failure strategy. It can be observed, that the preemption rate using the MAXDIS strategy reaches its minimum very early, i.e. approximately when $k = 5$.

Table 2. Average path set size for varying parameter k

$k =$	1	5	10	15	20	25	30	40	45
EPP	2.4	3.5	4.5	6.0	7.1	8.9	10.1	11.0	11.4
MAXDIS	1	2	2.5	2.5	2.5	2.5	2.5	2.5	2.5

Both k path algorithms do not compute exactly k paths. In case of EPP, this is due to the fact, that this algorithms also returns paths with loops which must be removed, and in case of MAXDIS, this is caused by the way the "maximally disjointedness" is determined by the algorithm. Table 2 shows the average size of the path set for two given end nodes of the cost239 topology which illustrates the general problem of the MAXDIS strategy: this algorithm only computes a very limited amount of alternative paths. For example, with a parameter of $k = 10$, the average path set consists of 4.5 paths for the EPP strategy whereas MAXDIS computes path sets with an average size of only 2.5. Hence, the amount of interrupted flows for which no alternative path can be found is higher than for the EPP strategy. This shows, that MAXDIS in general is less suited to be applied in an environment as considered here although its approach is to compute maximally disjoint paths and therefore to achieve a relatively even distribution of the network load. However, in a situation as discussed here, i.e. with high network load, the number of links with sufficient amount of free bandwidth for rerouting a flow is limited. Therefore, the MAXDIS strategy with only a few alternative paths cannot exploit the whole set of available paths and leads to increased termination of flows. For that reason, in the following sections only EPP is used as pre-failure strategy.

6.3   Performance of the Post-failure Strategies

The impact of the post-failure strategies on the network performance is presented in this section. Since the post-failure strategies must be seen in the context of the respective pre-failure mechanism, the most successful pre-failure strategy EPP was used for the evaluations presented in this section.

In order to assess the performance of the strategies, the preemption rate and the percentage of lost bandwidth were examined. Both parameters are computed relative to the number of affected flows (for the preemption rate) and the amount of bandwidth transmitted by affected flows (for the bandwidth loss) respectively. Bandwidth loss means the amount of bytes of admitted flows that could not be transmitted after to the link failure occurred. This figure does not include the amount of bandwidth already transmitted by terminated flows.

In Figure 7 the results of the simulations are presented. It can be seen, that considerable differences between the different strategies exist, especially regarding the preemption rate. Strategies which prefer requests with short remaining duration or requests with low remaining amount of bytes to be transfered (SRT,SRTS) perform well with respect to the preemption rate, and strategies which prefer flows with long duration respectively high remaining bandwidth requirement (LRT,LRTS) achieve a relatively low bandwidth loss. The FCFS strategy which prefers flows admitted the longest time ago, nearly always ranges between the best and the worst strategy, the same holds for LF and SF which do not allow to accurately predict their performance.

Although difficult to predict, the FCFS strategy can be used to implement preemption policies which prefer a certain class of flows, e.g. those admitted very early. This may positively influence the customer satisfaction and meet the clients expectations and therefore can also be of interest for network operators. For example, implementing FCFS is the strategy which implements an analogue

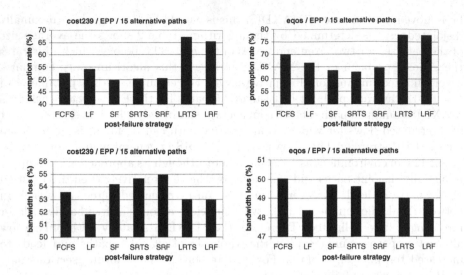

Fig. 7. Post-failure strategies: preemption rate and bandwidth loss

idea as the advance reservation service itself: requests issued at an early stage receive the requested QoS with the highest probability. Using the FCFS post-failure strategy, this holds not only for the admission probability but also for the probability of surviving link failures.

6.4   Influence of the Downtime Calculation

In the previous sections, it was assumed that the expected downtime was exactly calculated. In this section, we want to take a closer look on the impact of the calculation of the expected downtime onto the performance. In particular, it will be examined how wrong assumptions (i.e. over- or underestimations of the expected downtime) influence the preemption rate and the bandwidth loss.

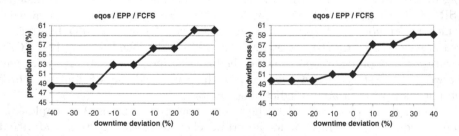

Fig. 8. Preemption rate and bandwidth loss depending on the downtime deviation

Two cases can be distinguished: the downtime might be calculated too conservatively which means the actual downtime of a link is shorter than expected. The second case is that the downtime is underestimated, i.e. the actual downtime is longer than expected.

In Figure 8, preemption rate and bandwidth loss of the eqos topology are shown as a function of the downtime deviation, i.e. the difference between estimated and actual downtime. The downtime remained constant, only the calculation of the expected downtime changed. A negative downtime deviation means that the actual downtime was shorter than expected. The results for the cost239 topology are similar but not given here due to the space limitation.

It can be observed that overestimating the actual downtime reduces the preemption rate and bandwidth loss. This is the expected behavior of the system since inactive flows that cannot be rerouted at the time of the failure will not be preempted. When the actual downtime is below the expected downtime, such flows are not affected at all by the failure. In contrast, underestimations of only a few percent lead to a significantly reduced performance concerning both metrics. Again, this is the expected result since in such a situation more than the expected flows are affected by the failure and are not rerouted. When these flows are started, the link failure still exists but newly admitted flows block the required bandwidth on alternative paths.

Figure 8 also shows what happens when the expected downtime calculation is omitted and only active flows are rerouted. Obviously, the result is similar to underestimating the expected downtime, i.e. the preemption rate and in particular the bandwidth loss increase significantly. This illustrates the requirement for rerouting not only active but also inactive but admitted flows.

7 Conclusion

In this paper, we examined how fault tolerance mechanisms for handling link failures can be implemented in networks with support for advance reservations and which properties of advance reservations have to be considered. Avoiding the preemption of admitted flows is most important in such an environment. For that purpose the expected downtime was introduced, which is computed when a link fails. Each flow which is active during the expected downtime is rerouted by the network management system. In this context, our examinations show that overestimating the expected downtime is not critical concerning the performance of the network. However, it introduces administrative overhead to reroute flows which are not affected. In contrast, an underestimation of the expected downtime leads to significantly increased preemption rate and bandwidth loss.

Additionally, we proposed a number of post-failure strategies. It could be shown, that the order in which flows are rerouted has a significant influence on the performance of the network. The most successful strategy in terms of performance may not always be the one which meets customers expectations. Hence, the FCFS strategy which prefers flows which were requested very early may be the best choice since it is based on the same idea as advance reservations:

early reservation guarantee a high admission probability and low preemption probability.

Among the pre-failure strategies, using the maximally disjoint algorithm (MAXDIS) turned out to perform worse than using the k shortest paths due to the reduced path set of the MAXDIS algorithm which cannot be compensated by the "disjointedness" of the paths. This is also a problem for the path selection process during the post-failure phase: MAXDIS provides only a few alternative paths which therefore leads to higher preemption rates.

References

1. A. Authenrieth and A. Kirstaedter. Engineering End-to-End IP Resilience Using Resilience-Differentiated QoS. *IEEE Communications Magazine*, 1(1):50–57, January 2002.
2. L.-O. Burchard. Source Routing Algorithms for Advance Reservation Mechanisms. Technical Report 2003-3, Technische Universitaet Berlin, 2003. ISSN 1436-9915.
3. L.-O. Burchard and H.-U. Heiss. Performance Evaluation of Data Structures for Admission Control in Bandwidth Brokers. In *Proceedings of the Intl. Symposium on Performance Evaluation of Computer and Telecommunication Systems (SPECTS)*, 2002.
4. L.-O. Burchard and R. Lüling. An Architecture for a Scalable Video-on-Demand Server Network with Quality-of-Service Guarantees. In *Proceedings of the 5th Intl. Workshop on Distributed Multimedia Systems and Applications (IDMS), Lecture Notes in Computer Science, Springer*, volume 1905, pages 132–143, 2000.
5. D. Eppstein. Finding the k Shortest Paths. *SIAM Journal on Computing*, 28(2), 1998.
6. D. Ferrari, A. Gupta, and G. Ventre. Distributed Advance Reservation of Real-Time Connections. In *Network and Operating System Support for Digital Audio and Video*, pages 16–27, 1995.
7. I. Foster, C. Kesselman, C. Lee, R. Lindell, K. Nahrstedt, and A. Roy. A Distributed Resource Management Architecture that Supports Advance Reservations and Co-Allocation. In *Proceedings of the 7th International Workshop on Quality of Service (IWQoS)*, 1999.
8. S. Lee and M. Gerla. Fault-Tolerance and Load Balancing in QoS Provisioning with Multiple MPLS Paths. In *Proceedings of IFIP Ninth International Workshop on Quality of Service (IWQoS)*, 2001.
9. E. Rosen, A. Viswanathan, and R. Callon. Multiprotocol Label Switching Architecture. ftp://ftp.isi.edu/in-notes/rfc3031.txt, January 2001. RFC 3031.
10. A. Schill, F. Breiter, and S. Kuhn. Design and evaluation of an advance reservation protocol on top of RSVP. In *4th International Conference Broadband Communications*, 1998.

V Routing

Routing and Grooming in Two-Tier Survivable Optical Mesh Networks

Somdip Datta[1], Subir Biswas, Sudipta Sengupta[2], and Debanjan Saha[3]

[1] Department of Electrical Engineering, Princeton University, NJ
[2] Bell Laboratories, Lucent Technologies, Holmdel, NJ
[3] IBM T.J. Watson Research Center, Hawthorne, NY

Abstract. While deploying the next generation of optical networks with a mesh topology, telecommunications carriers are being confronted with a choice between wavelength switches that can switch traffic at SONET STS-48 (2.5 Gbps) granularity and sub-wavelength grooming capable switches that can switch at STS-1 (51 Mbps) granularity. The former cannot switch circuits of capacity lower than STS-48 without the help of external grooming devices, and consumes high fragmented/unused capacity to support low capacity end to end circuits using high capacity STS-48 channels. The latter almost eliminates such capacity wastage by supporting STS-1 level switching, but involves larger switching delays leading to slower restoration and requires more complicated hardware design that decreases switch scalability with increasing port count.

This paper proposes an intelligent packing and routing algorithm in a network architecture which contains both kinds of switches configured in two tiers, and compares it with the other two network architectures - one with only wavelength switches with STS-48 granularity, and another with only grooming switches with STS-1 switching granularity. It is shown that the two-tier architecture with our routing scheme is comparable in capacity efficiency to the STS-1 only network, while its scalability and restoration delays are at par with the STS-48 only network.

Furthermore, we propose a partial two-tier network architecture where the functionality of STS-1 grooming is deployed at a subset of the network nodes. Our simulations show that the capacity efficiency of this architecture does not decrease significantly with reduction in the number of STS-1 switch equipped nodes.

1 Introduction

The rapid expansion of the Internet in the last decade has been made possible largely by optical backbone networks with high capacity and reliability. As capacity requirements continue to grow at healthy rates [1], mesh architecture [2, 4] has emerged as the solution for fast and efficient deployment of capacity in long-haul optical backbone networks. An optical mesh network consists of optical switches, interconnected by fiber links containing several optical channels. The basic service provided by the network is to setup high capacity circuits on demand, across the network connecting two access nodes.

K. Jeffay, I. Stoica, and K. Wehrle (Eds.): IWQoS 2003, LNCS 2707, pp. 231–248, 2003.
© Springer-Verlag Berlin Heidelberg 2003

As a consequence of the diversity in the nature and number of clients requesting circuits (e.g., IP routers, ATM switches), the backbone network has to support circuits of different capacities. While the usage of STS-48 (2.5Gbps) circuits is growing on heavier traffic routes, a large number of clients continue to use STS-1 (51 Mbps, usually carrying 45 Mbps DS3/T3), STS-3 (155 Mbps) and STS-12 (620 Mbps) circuits in line with their requirements, and will continue to do so in the near future.

As switching elements for such a network, the network designers may opt for switches with cross connects of smaller granularity (say, STS-1) as they are capable of making efficient use of the network transmission capacities while supporting a range of circuits of different capacities. On the other hand, they may use higher granularity switches (STS-48) to increase scalability, and reduce equipment cost and signaling delays during provisioning and more importantly, restoration. However, STS-48 granularity switches require end-to-end circuits of smaller capacities to be aggregated into STS-48 circuits before entering the switch, even if the full capacity of these STS-48 circuits may not be utilized, thus increasing inefficiencies of resource usage. Current requirements from telecommunications carriers for next generation network deployment have pointed towards a two-tier architecture [5] in which a lower tier of STS-1 granularity switches grooms smaller capacity circuits into STS-48 circuits at the source, destination, and possibly few intermediate nodes on the path. An upper tier of STS-48 granularity switches provisions and provides shared mesh restoration for the clients' (native) STS-48 circuits as well as the ones aggregated and groomed by the lower tier.

For such a network, we need a grooming strategy that would intelligently combine low capacity circuits on different end to end routes to as few STS-48 circuits as possible, while not using too many STS-1 switching ports either. We propose a packing scheme to solve this problem, and compare its performance with the two one-tier architectures - one with only STS-48 wavelength switches, and the other with only grooming switches with STS-1 switching granularity. Results obtained using different traffic mixes on two different networks shows that the two-tier architecture with our packing scheme is in capacity efficiency with the STS-1 only network, while its scalability and restoration delays are at par with the STS-48 only network.

A *full two-tier* architecture deploys both kinds of switches at each node for maximum grooming flexibility. In this paper, we also propose a *partial two-tier* architecture which has STS-48 switches at each node but STS-1 switches at selected strategic nodes only to reduce costs but still retain su cient grooming flexibility. We investigate the effect of changing the number of STS-1 switches deployed in a partial two-tier network architecture and thereby show that that the capacity efficiency of this architecture does not decrease significantly with reduction in the number of STS-1 switch equipped nodes.

The structure of the paper is as follows. Section 2 gives an overview of optical mesh networks and its basic components. Section 3 describes the salient features of the two one-tier network architectures and the full and partial two-tier architectures. Section 4 gives a detailed description of our routing strategy. Section 5 compares the full two-tier architecture with the one-tier architectures. It is followed by a comparison of partial two-tier networks with different number of STS-1 switch equipped nodes. We conclude in Section 6.

2   Optical Network Overview

2.1   STS-48 and STS-1 Switches

An STS-48 switch has a switch fabric that switches circuits at STS-48 granularity. The optical signal at an incoming OC-48 (optical equivalent of STS-48) port is switched to an outgoing OC-48 port, without any de-multiplexing of its constituent sub-channels. It can be an all-optical switch or an optical-electronic-optical switch without demultiplexing capability. In this paper we will assume that the switch has wavelength conversion capability.

An STS-1 switch can switch circuits at STS-1 granularity. In general, the input/output ports can be of any granularity but in our architecture they have been assumed to be OC-48 ports that connects to an OC-48 transmission channel. The incoming signal at an OC-48 port is de-modulated and de-multiplexed into STS-1 channels and fed to the STS-1 fabric. The outgoing channels of the fabric are multiplexed and modulated into OC-48 channels again. The sub-channels entering the switch as part of the same OC-48 channel may belong to different OC-48 channels when they leave the switch.

2.2   Transmission Links

In this paper we assume that all channels are OC-48 and each channel terminates in an OC-48 port of the switches at either end. As a result, link capacity is provisioned in increments of STS-48. We will refer to STS-48 circuits as *full-rate* circuits and all circuits of a smaller capacity than STS-48 as *sub-rate* circuits. Since a sub-rate circuit does not use the full capacity of an OC-48 channel, two or more of them can be multiplexed to use the same OC-48 channel. The advantage of an STS-1 switch lies in the fact that it allows such multiplexing anywhere in the network, while STS-48 switches allow multiplexing at the source and destination only, before they enter the network.

2.3   Restoration

Clients at the edge of the network send large amounts of data using these circuits, hence a restoration mechanism is needed to ensure reliable communication in the event of the failure of any network component. A common approach is to setup a *dedicated* backup path at the time of setting up the primary path of a circuit, and switch traffic to the backup path in the event of any failure in the primary path. An alternate approach is to setup sharable backup paths. Two or more backup paths can share the same channel in a link, if their corresponding primary paths are link disjoint. Since the same link failure would not affect disjoint primary paths simultaneously, their backups are assured of getting a channel without contention in the event of any single link failure. This method, called the *shared mesh protection* scheme [3,4], significantly reduces the extra capacity requirement for protection at the expense of (acceptable) increase in restoration latency (since cross-connects on the backup path need to be setup after failure). The routing mechanisms described in this paper are for shared mesh protected networks, but they can be applied to unprotected and dedicated protected networks as well with suitable simplifications.

3   Network Architectures

3.1   One-Tier STS-48 Network

A network of only STS-48 switches (Fig. 1 top left) is incapable of handling circuits other than STS-48. In our architecture, we will assume that all end to end traffic demands between the same node pair is aggregated into full-rate circuit requests, as many as necessary. Some of these circuits will only be partially filled, leading to an increase in the network capacity requirement. The advantages of a one-tier STS-48 network are:

1. The network is highly scalable.
2. Restoration is faster, as end to end STS-48 circuits only need to be switched to backup paths, and not its constituent sub-channels.

On the other hand, its main disadvantage is its higher capacity requirement stemming from fragmented capacitiy in STS-48 channels.

3.2   One-Tier STS-1 Network

A network of STS-1 switches (Fig. 1 top right) can switch sub-rate circuits from one OC-48 transmission channel to another, and therefore sub-rate circuits belonging to different end to end routes can use the same OC-48 transmission channel in a link that is common to both routes. In spite of their capacity efficiency, STS-1 switches pose other cost and performance disadvantages:

1. These switches need a much larger switching fabric for the same switching capacity, making the switch costlier and more difficult to scale.
2. The STS-1, STS-3 and STS-12 circuits need to be switched individually during setup and restoration, leading to higher switching delays (use of *dedicated* protection instead of *shared* will reduce delays but significantly increase the capacity requirement).

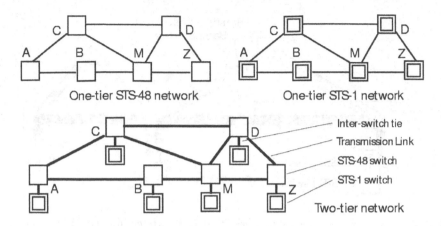

Fig. 1. One-tier and two-tier network architectures

3.3 Two-Tier Network

The way to get the best of both switches in capacity efficiency and scalability is a two-tier network (Fig. 1 bottom). The upper tier consists of STS-48 switches connected to each other with fiber links. The lower tier consists of STS-1 switches which are only connected to the STS-48 switches co-located at the same network node.

The STS-48 switches in the upper tier receive full-rate circuit requests from the clients directly. We will assume that if some of the sub-rate circuit requests between the *same* node pair can be aggregated to form *completely* filled full-rate circuits, then they have been aggregated and connected to the upper tier as well.

The STS-1 switches in the lower tier receive the remaining sub-rate circuit requests from the clients. These switches groom several of the sub-rate circuits into specially created full-rate circuits. To be groomed together, not all of these sub-rate circuits need to have the same final destination, but may only have a part of the route in common. The new full-rate circuit is only created for this common part, at the end of which the sub-rate circuits are de-multiplexed and rerouted towards their final destination by multiplexing into other STS-48 circuits, by another STS-1 switch. The STS-1 switches are not connected to each other, so the full-rate circuits they create are carried by the upper tier. The lower tier does not use any protection mechanism for the sub-rate circuits as they are groomed into full-rate circuits which are mesh protected by the upper tier.

We illustrate how intelligent grooming of sub-rate circuits (beyond simple aggregation into full-rate circuits) in a two-tier network can lead to increased utilization of network resources. In Fig. 2, consider 8 STS-3 (STS-24 equivalent) demands between each pair of nodes A, M, Z. Simple aggregation of sub-rate traffic requires one full-rate (STS-48) circuit to be provisioned between each pair of these nodes. This creates 3 full-rate circuits, each 50% utilized. In a more efficient sub-rate packing scenario, the STS-1 grooming switch at node M can

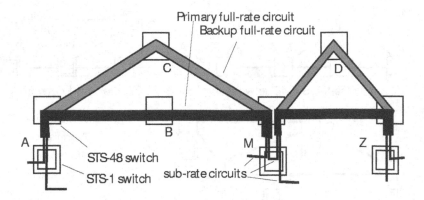

Fig. 2. Grooming in a two-tier network. Three sub-rate circuits (A-M, M-Z and A-Z) have been groomed into two full-rate circuits (A-M and M-Z). The full-rate circuits are physically routed in the upper tier with primary and shared backup paths. M acts as an intermediate grooming node for the sub-rate circuit A-Z.

be used to reduce the number of full-rate circuits in the upper-tier as follows – provision one full-rate circuit, P1, from A to M and another, P2, from M to Z. Circuits P1 and P2 carry the sub-rate traffic between their corresponding node pairs. Also, the sub-rate circuit from A to Z can ride on these two circuits with grooming at intermediate node M. This creates two full-rate circuits, each 100% utilized.

In Section 4.2, we propose an algorithm for efficient packing of sub-rate circuits into full-rate circuits that are routed in the upper tier. This intelligent sub-rate packing is crucial to realizing the full benefit of a two-tier architecture.

The advantages of the two-tier architecture, as validated in this paper, are:

1. Its capacity efficiency is comparable with the one-tier STS-1 architecture.
2. As most of the port usage is in the upper tier of STS-48 switches, large STS-1 switches are not required. Thus this network is as scalable as the one-tier STS-48 architecture.
3. As restoration switching is performed by the upper tier, restoration delays are at par with the one-tier STS-48 architecture.

Its principal disadvantage is that even though this architecture is economic in terms of the per-port cost component of installing switches, it incurs the cost of installing an additional switching fabric in each node. The partial two-tier network proposed in the next section adds the flexibility of deploying STS-1 switches at a subset of the nodes.

3.4   Partial Two-Tier Network

The full two-tier network described in the previous subsection offers grooming opportunity in every network node. It remains to be seen whether restricting this facility to a few selected nodes significantly affects the capacity efficiency. In our proposed partial two-tier network, the upper tier consists of STS-48 switches in every node and connected by a set of fiber links. The lower tier contains STS-1 switches in a selected subset of the nodes, connected to the STS-48 switch co-located at that node. If a node lacks an STS-1 switch, the sub-rate demands originating at that node are multiplexed at the client side into full-rate circuits terminating at another node containing an STS-1 switch, or the final destination. Note that two special cases of the partial two-tier network are - the one-tier STS-48 network (when none of the nodes contain STS-1 switches), and the full two-tier network (when all the nodes contain STS-1 switches).

The advantages of this architecture, as validated in this paper, are:

1. Its capacity efficiency does not decrease significantly with reduction in the number of STS-1 switch equipped nodes.
2. As most of the port usage is in the upper tier of STS-48 switches, large STS-1 switches are not required. Thus this network is as scalable as the full two-tier and one-tier STS-48 architecture.
3. As restoration switching is performed by the upper tier, restoration delays are at par with the full two-tier and one-tier STS-48 architecture.
4. The flexibility of deploying STS-1 switches at a subset of the nodes can lead to reduction in the cost of additional fabric for the lower tier.

4   Routing

In this section, we describe the basic stages of the routing algorithms for the different architectures. The one-tier STS-48 and the full two-tier architectures have not been separately described as they are special cases of the partial two-tier architecture.

4.1   Routing in One-Tier STS-1 Network

Initial routing. Route each circuit request (whether full-rate or sub-rate) one by one by finding the best primary-backup path pair. The problem of finding the least cost primary-backup pair with shared backup bandwidth is $\mathcal{NP}$-complete [7]. Section IV.D details out an heuristic (Algorithm PRIMARY_BACKUP) for this problem. In each network link, commission as many OC-48 channels as necessary to accommodate the total link traffic.

Improve link utilization by multiple passes. This applies to an offline planning scenario where the entire demand set is available at once. Try to decrease the cost of a previously routed circuit through better sharing of backup paths by rerouting it in the context of other already routed circuits. This multi-pass framework is also incorporated into Algorithm PRIMARY_BACKUP.

4.2 Routing in Partial Two-Tier Network

Packing of sub-rate circuits into STS-48 circuits. Create a *logical graph* (Fig. 3(b)), using those nodes from the physical graph (Fig. 3(a)) that have STS-1 switches and the source/destination nodes for the demand (the logical graph thus depends on the demand). Connect each node to every other node in the graph with a *logical link*, the cost of which is an *estimated* cost of the resources (ports and channels) required for setting up a shared mesh protected full-rate circuit in the physical graph, connecting the corresponding nodes. Each logical link represents a potential STS-48 circuit between two nodes formed by grooming together of several sub-rate circuits, like A-M and M-Z in Fig. 2. The nodes in the logical network represent potential grooming sites, e.g., node M in Fig. 2.

Route each sub-rate circuit on this graph one by one by finding the shortest (unprotected) path that does not include as an intermediate node any node where there is no STS-1 grooming capability. In each logical link, commission as many OC-48 channels as necessary for the total link traffic. In Section IV.C, we discuss in more detail Algorithm SUBRATE_PACKING for this problem.

Improve sub-rate packing by multiple passes. This applies to an offline planning scenario where the entire demand set is available at once. Try to de-commission under-utilized STS-48 circuits (logical links) by rerouting sub-rate circuits *away from* those logical links, and *towards* those logical links associated with higher utilized STS-48 circuits with sufficient remaining capacity to accommodate one or more additional sub-rate circuits. This multi-pass framework is also incorporated into Algorithm SUBRATE_PACKING.

Upper tier routing. For each logical link (i, j) in the graph used by Algorithm SUBRATE_PACKING, let u_{ij} be the capacity usage in STS-1 units. Compute the number of STS-48 circuits to be provisioned in the upper tier between nodes i and j as $\lceil u_{ij}/48 \rceil$. Note that in addition to full-rate circuits obtained from the lower tier through sub-rate packing as above, there are native (obtained directly from clients) full-rate demands. Route all full-rate circuits in the upper tier using Algorithm PRIMARY_BACKUP in Section IV.D. In each network link, commission as many OC-48 channels as necessary for the total link traffic.

4.3 Packing of Sub-rate Circuits

In this section, we propose an efficient algorithm for packing sub-rate circuits into full-rate (STS-48) circuits for routing in the upper STS-48 switched tier. Note that we have separated the overall problem of routing sub-rate circuits into two sub-problems – (i) packing sub-rate circuits into full-rate circuits (Algorithm SUBRATE_PACKING), and (ii) physical routing of full-rate circuits in the upper tier (Algorithm PRIMARY_BACKUP).

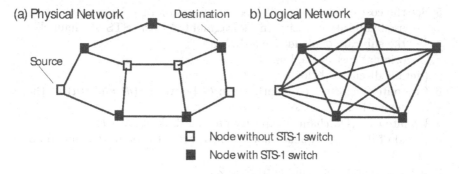

Fig. 3. A *logical graph* is created from the *physical graph* by connecting all nodes with STS-1 switches and source/destination nodes by a full mesh.

Each link of the graph on which the sub-rate packing algorithm is run corresponds to a physical layer STS-48 circuit, i.e., link (i, j) is representative of an STS-48 circuit between nodes i and j. Hence, for the packing sub-problem, we need an estimate of the cost of routing a full-rate circuit in the physical layer. The exact cost of such an STS-48 circuit cannot be determined without knowledge of the entire set of circuits to be routed at the upper tier because primary and backup paths may deviate from least cost disjoint routes in order to achieve better sharing of backup capacity. However, we can use an estimate of the cost of such a circuit by computing a dedicated (1+1) circuit and reducing the cost of the backup path by, say, 40%. This factor is taken from studies in the literature [8,12] which report substantial capacity savings of shared backup paths over dedicated (1+1) backup paths.

Note that if the underlying physical network is bi-connected, i.e., a diverse primary and backup path exists between every pair of nodes (which is usually the case), then the graph on which Algorithm SUBRATE_PACKING operates is a complete graph.

Algorithm SUBRATE_PACKING

Input: A (complete) graph $G = (N, E)$ with (logical) link costs, a sequence of sub-rate demands d between node pair $(s(d), t(d))$ and bandwidth $b(d) = 1, 3,$ or 12 (in STS-1 units).
Output: Path (sequence of full-rate circuits in upper tier) for routing each sub-rate demand.
Method:

1 Set iteration $i = 1$;
2 Set demand d to the first in the demand sequence ;
3 If $i > 1$, deallocate the channel capacity on each link of the current path for d.
4 For each non-grooming node (other than $s(d), t(d)$), set the cost of all its adjacent links to ∞ ;

5 Set the cost of each (logical) link as a function of
  − used sub-rate capacity on its fragmented (last) STS-48 channel,
  − the sub-rate demand size $b(d)$, and
  − original cost of the link
  (details discussed below)
6 Compute a shortest cost path P_d in G between $s(d)$ and $t(d)$ as the route for demand d;
7 Update the used channel capacity on each link of path P_d ;
8 If end of demand sequence not reached, set d to the next demand and goto Step 3 ;
9 If $i < 3$, increment i and goto Step 2 ;
10 Return the path for each sub-rate demand ;

Observe that a sub-rate circuit can be groomed only at nodes with STS-1 switching capability. Hence, the path computed for the circuit (representing the packing) cannot traverse intermediate non-grooming nodes. This fact is taken care of in Step 4 by setting the costs of all links adjacent to each non-grooming node (other than the source and destination of the demand) to ∞.

In Step 5, the original link cost L_{orig} is modified as follows:

$$x = T \cdot mod \cdot 48$$

$$L_{new} = L_{orig} \cdot P_i(x)$$

where T is the existing total traffic in that link expressed in STS-1 equivalents, and $P_i(x)$ is the multiplying factor used in the ith pass (Fig. 4).

$P_i(x)$ is explained as follows. While routing an STS-n circuit, if $x = 0, 48 - n + 1, 48 - n + 2, ...47$, allocating the new circuit in that link will lead to the requirement of an additional STS-48 channel. Also, if the link has low utilization in its fragmented (last) STS-48 channel ($x \leq W_i$), then rerouting a few more circuits away from that link may lead to the elimination of an OC-48 channel. To avoid using such links in the routing, $P_i(x)$ is set to a penalty value ($H_i \geq 1$), while for others it is set to 1.

Some demands can be moved from low utilization STS-48 channels to others without having to take a longer path, while others may take a longer path. As we intend to move the former kind in the earlier passes, and target the latter kind if necessary in the later passes, we increase the penalty H_i and reduce W_i in each subsequent pass.

4.4 Physical Routing of Primary and Backup Paths

In this section, we discuss the algorithm for physical routing of primary and shared backup paths. The optimization problem involves finding the primary and shared backup path for each circuit so as to minimize total network cost. The joint optimization of primary and shared backup path for even a single

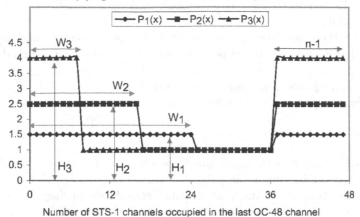

Fig. 4. Multiplying factor to adjust link costs for sub-rate packing while routing an STS-n circuit.

circuit is $\mathcal{NP}$-complete [7]. Algorithm PRIMARY_BACKUP outlined below is based on a framework [4,11] using enumeration of candidate primary paths and is described below.

Algorithm PRIMARY_BACKUP

Input: A graph $G = (N, E)$ with link costs, a sequence of demands d between node pair $(s(d), t(d))$ and bandwidth $b(d) = 1, 3, 12,$ or 48 (in STS-1 units).
Output: Primary and backup path for each demand.
Method:

1 Set iteration $i = 1$;
2 Set demand d to the first in the demand sequence ;
3 If $i > 1$, deallocate the channel capacity on each link of the current primary and backup path for d.
4 Compute a set $S = \{P_1, P_2, \ldots, P_k\}$ of k-shortest paths (between $s(d)$ and $t(d)$) in G where $cost(P_1) \leq cost(P_2) \leq \cdots \leq cost(P_k)$;
5 Set $j = 1$;
6 Set current primary path for demand d as $P_d = P_j$;
7 for each link e in G, set its cost to
   7a ∞ if edge e appears on P_d
   7b 0 (or small value ϵ_i times original cost) if edge e contains sharable backup channel bandwidth
   7c original cost otherwise
8 Compute the shortest path in G as the current backup path B_d for demand d ;
9 Save primary-backup path pair (P_d, B_d) if it has the least cost found so far ;

10 If $j < k$, increment j and goto Step 6 ;
11 Save the computed least cost primary and backup path pair $(\bar{P}_d, \bar{B}_d)$ for demand d ;
12 Update the used channel capacity on each link of paths $\bar{P}_d$ and $\bar{B}_d$;
13 If end of demand sequence not reached, set d to the next demand and goto Step 3 ;
14 If $i < num\_passes$, increment i and goto Step 2 ;
15 Return the primary and backup path for each demand ;

Yen's K-shortest path algorithm [6] can be used to generate the k-shortest paths in polynomial time in Step 4.

Determination of backup path channel sharability in Step 7b is based on the following rule: Two circuits can share channel bandwidth on any common link on their backup paths only if their primary paths are link disjoint. This guarantees complete recovery from single-link failures. The actual allocation of backup channel capacity can follow a (i) pool based, or (ii) channel assignment based reservation scheme as discussed in [9]. In (i), sufficient backup channel capacity is reserved on a link so as to recover from any single-link failure – the actual channel bandwidth slot within the link is assigned to the backup path only during restoration triggered by a failure of the primary path. In (ii), channel slots are assigned *apriori* to backup paths during circuit provisioning. For the results in Section V, we use the pool based backup bandwidth reservation scheme.

Note that the original link costs input to the algorithm represent the cost of an STS-48 channel on each link. The actual link cost model used in Algorithm PRIMARY_BACKUP needs to be modified when implemented for physical routing of primary and backup paths in an STS-1 switched network. For this case, if c is the cost of an OC-48 channel on a link, then the link cost used by the algorithm is $(c * b/48)$, where b is the bandwidth (in STS-1 units) of the current demand being routed. This quantity represents the amortized cost of using b STS-1 units of bandwidth on an STS-48 channel with cost c.

Finally, observe that the Algorithm PRIMARY_BACKUP accommodates an offline planning scenario where the entire set of demands is available at once. In this case, multiple passes can be made on the demand sequence (for a total of num_passes times) and during each such pass, the primary and backup path of each demand can be rerouted with progressively decreasing values of ϵ for the cost (ϵ times original cost) of a backup link containing sharable bandwidth. Before we explain this, note that increased backup capacity sharing leads to longer backup paths as has been explored in [8].

The motivation for a decreasing ϵ_i over subsequent passes i is as follows: in the first pass, since later demands in the sequence have not been routed, a higher ϵ provides a tradeoff between shorter hop backup paths and longer backup paths with increased capacity sharing. Over subsequent passes, since all demands have associated (initial) routes, more opportunities for backup sharing open up and a lower ϵ favors longer backup paths with increased capacity sharing.

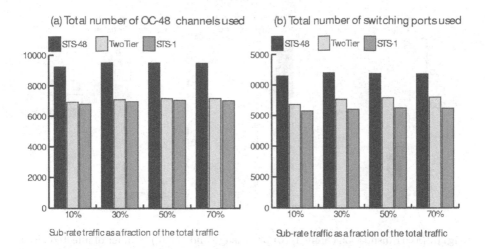

Fig. 5. Transmission channel and port usage for one-tier and full two-tier networks for the 38-node topology, and four different traffic mixes.

4.5 Selection of Grooming Nodes in Partial Two-Tier Network

In a partial two-tier network where a given number of nodes are to be installed with STS-1 switches, the selection of nodes is an important consideration. In our simulations, we performed the selection using the following criteria:

1. Nodes with higher degree are more deserving candidates for STS-1 switch deployment, because they offer more opportunity for sub-rate circuits to go different ways. Removing STS-1 switches from degree two nodes have the least effect on performance.
2. Nodes in the interior are more deserving than the nodes in corner or periphery of the network.
3. The nodes which have a higher sub-rate traffic component passing through them in a full two-tier version of the network also deserve STS-1 switches more than others.
4. STS-1 switches should be adequately dispersed around the network rather than clustered together.

5   Performance Comparison

For evaluating the performance of the network architectures, we use a 38-node network with 60 bidirectional links and a 16-node network with 27 bidirectional links. The total traffic demand is about 1100 OC-48 equivalent for the 38-node network and 100 OC-48 equivalent for the 16-node network. For the 38-node network, four different traffic sets (with same total traffic) were created for diversity in traffic mix. In each set, the total number of full-rate and sub-rate

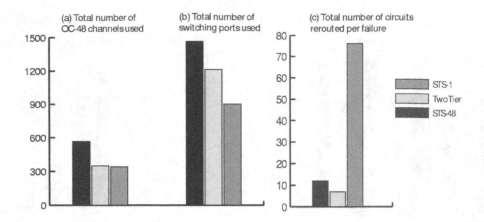

Fig. 6. (a) Transmission channel, (b) port usage and the (c) number of affected circuits per failure in the one-tier and full two-tier networks for the 16-node topology. The sub-rate traffic is 45% of the total traffic.

circuit requests were changed to set the traffic contribution of the sub-rate circuits to 10%, 30%, 50% and 70% of the total traffic respectively. In all the four sets, the fraction of sub-rate traffic contributed by STS-12, STS-3, and STS-1 circuits were 50%, 25%, and 25% respectively. In other words, the number of STS-48, STS-12, STS-3, and STS-1 circuits in the four sets were in the ratio 9:2:4:12, 9:6:12:36, 9:10:20:60, and 9:14:28:84. For the 16-node network, we have used one set with sub-rate traffic accounting for 45% of the total traffic. The topology and traffic data are representative of US nationwide backbone carrier networks but have been desensitized for confidentiality.

The given sets of circuit requests for each network were routed with *shared mesh protection* with the objective of minimizing the total cost of the network. We have used an additive cost model where the total network cost for routing a set of demands is the sum of the costs of bandwidth deployed on each link and the cost of ports used in each node. For the graph on which our routing algorithms operate, each link has a cost representative of an STS-48 channel on that link, which was obtained in an amortized fashion by taking into account the following parameters associated with deploying the fiber link: fiber miles, optical amplifiers, DWDM common equipment, DWDM channel capacity, Transmit/Receive (TR) switch port at each endpoint, and regenerating transponders. Representative industry list pricing has been used for all of the above components. These numbers vary from vendor to vendor and our results are fairly insensitive to small/moderate changes in the pricing model. Hence, instead of reporting a total network cost based on them, we are reporting the number of OC-48 transmission channels and the number of OC-48 switching ports separately.

Section 5.1 compares the one-tier and full two-tier architectures. Section 5.2 describes the effect of changing the number of STS-1 switches in a partial two-tier architecture.

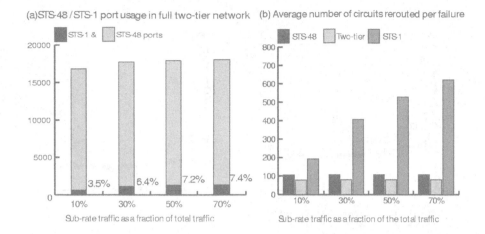

Fig. 7. (a)STS-1 and STS-48 switch port usage in full two-tier network (b) Number of affected circuits per failure for one-tier and full two-tier networks, for the 38-node topology.

5.1   One-Tier vs. Full Two-Tier Network

Transmission channel and port usage. In Fig. 5(a) and 6(a) the total number of OC-48 transmission channels used in the one-tier STS-48, one-tier STS-1 and full two-tier network architectures are shown, for the two networks.

In all the scenarios the one-tier STS-48 network appears to use a larger number of channels owing to its inability to use the sub-channels of the same OC-48 channel for different sub-rate circuits. In comparison, the two-tier network uses only a few channels more than the one-tier STS-1 network.

In Fig. 5(b) and 6(b), the total number of OC-48 switching ports used in the network are shown. The STS-48 network again uses a larger number of ports than the STS-1 network. The relative gap in port usage between the two-tier and the STS-1 network is more than the corresponding gap in transmission channel usage because the circuits in a two-tier network sometimes pass through more than one switch in the same node (when being groomed). While comparing with the STS-1 network, it should be observed that most of the ports used in a two-tier network are STS-48 switch ports, which are more easily scalable (Fig. 7(a)).

These results demonstrate that the two-tier architecture with our sub-rate packing algorithm is almost as capacity efficient as the one-tier STS-1 architecture. Furthermore, it has lower restoration latencies than the STS-1 architecture (described in the next subsection), and it does not require large capacity STS-1 switches.

Restoration latency. When any link in the network fails, all affected circuits are switched to their backups. The delay in completing the restoration of all services through the backup depends on the number of cross-connect configurations

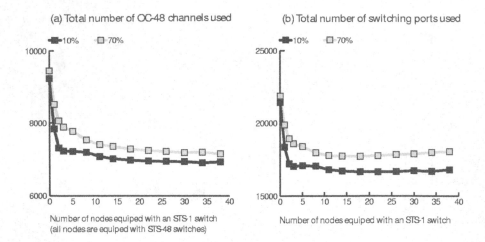

Fig. 8. Effect of reducing STS-1 switches in partial two-tier networks based on the 38-node topology.

that need to be changed as a result of the failure. In an STS-1 switch, switching an STS-48 circuit involves changing 48 such configurations, in contrast with an STS-48 switch which needs just one. However, we will assume that the STS-1 switch implements some kind of grouping scheme so that any single circuit, whether STS-48, STS-12, STS-3 or STS-1, can be switched with one operation per node.

In Fig. 7(b) and 6(c), we show the average number of circuits that are affected by a single failure in each network. These numbers give an indication of how the restoration delays in the three network architectures would compare. In the one-tier STS-48 and the two-tier architecture (where restoration is provided by the upper tier), these circuits are all STS-48. In the one-tier STS-1 architecture however, there are STS-1, STS-3 and STS-12 circuits as well that need to be switched, and this increases the number of affected circuits, leading to greater delays compared to the two-tier or one-tier STS-48 architecture.

5.2   Partial Two-Tier Network

In Fig. 8(a-b) and 9(a-b) we show the effect of changing the number of STS-1 switches in the partial two tier architecture, for two traffic mix scenarios (10% and 70%) for the 38-node topology and one for the 16-node topology. The nodes for STS-1 switch deployment were chosen in accordance with the rules outlined in Section 4.5. Note that the two extreme points in each curve correspond to the one-tier STS-48 (left most) and the full two-tier architecture (rightmost).

It is interesting to note that the partial two-tier architecture is comparable in capacity efficiency to the full two-tier architecture with only about 10 and 6 nodes equipped with STS-1 switches for the 38-node and 16-node networks respectively.

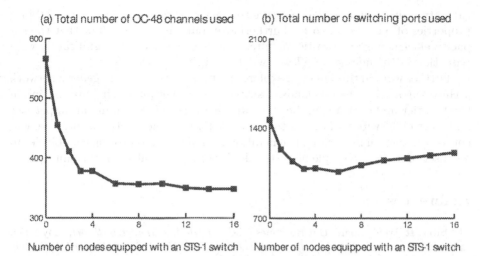

Fig. 9. Effect of reducing STS-1 switches in partial two-tier networks based on the 16-node topology.

Furthermore, when STS-1 switches are deployed at the above number of nodes, the number of ports used is also slightly less than the full two-tier network. This is because a full two-tier network tends to use more STS-1 ports for grooming, thereby reducing the number of transmission channels used, which are costlier than ports.

Since reducing the number of STS-1 switches reduces the fixed cost component of installing switches at the lower tier, the partial two-tier architecture adds the flexibility of deploying STS-1 switches at a subset of the nodes without significant reduction in capacity efficiency in terms of the number of transmission channels and ports. In [10], we further investigate the effect of sub-wavelength grooming at the lower tier and present an upper bound analysis (for arbitrary traffic scenarios) of how the fragmented/unused capacity in STS-48 channels (fragmentation loss) varies with the number of nodes equipped with STS-1 switches.

6   Conclusion

The selection of the appropriate architecture for the design of any optical mesh network will most certainly depend upon the cost structures of the individual switching and transmission components available to the state of the art. Furthermore, the relative merits of the architectures will also be sensitive to the particular network topology and traffic characteristics. However, we have successfully showed that for the representative network topologies and range of reasonable traffic mixes considered in the paper, the two-tier architecture with our routing strategy can approach the efficiency of one-tier STS-1 networks in capacity utilization as well as preserve the fast restoration and switch scalability properties of STS-48 networks. Furthermore, our simulations show that the capacity efficiency of the two-tier architecture does not decrease significantly with reduction in the number of STS-1 switch equipped nodes.

Further work in this area will explore the possibilities of more generic network architectures using the two kinds of switches. Another interesting application of the two-tier architecture can be with *all-optical switches* forming an upper tier and electronic switches forming the lower tier where the electronic switches will contribute their multiplexing, regeneration and quality monitoring capabilities in a subset of nodes to complement their high throughput all-optical counterparts.

References

1. Internet Traffic Soars, But Revenues Glide. *RHK Inc. Industry Report*, May 2002.
2. T. E. Stern and K. Bala. *Multiwavelength Optical Networks: A Layered Approach*. Prentice Hall, May 1999.
3. G. Mohan and C. Siva Ram Murthy. Lightpath Restoration in WDM Optical Mesh Networks. *IEEE Network Magazine*, Vol.14, No.6, November/December 2000.
4. Sudipta Sengupta and Ramu Ramamurthy. From Network Design to Dynamic Provisioning and Restoration in Optical Cross-Connect Mesh Networks: An Architectural and Algorithmic Overview. *IEEE Network Magazine*, Vol. 15, No. 4, July/August 2001.
5. AT&T Points the Way to Intelligent Optical Networking. *Business Week 2001 Special Section on The Future of Broadband*. http://www.businessweek.com/ adsections/broadband/innovation/publicnet/nec.htm.
6. J. Y. Yen. Finding the K Shortest Loopless Paths in a Network. *Management Science*, Vol. 17, No. 11, July 1971.
7. B. T. Doshi, S. Dravida, P.Harshavardhana, O. Hauser and Y. Wang. Optical Network Design and Restoration. *Bell Labs Technical Journal*, Vol. 4, No. 1, Jan-Mar 1999.
8. Ramu Ramamurthy, et al. Capacity Performance of Dynamic Provisioning in Optical Networks. *IEEE Journal of Lightwave Technology*, Vol. 19, No. 1, January 2001.
9. Somdip Datta, Sudipta Sengupta, Subir Biswas and Samir Datta. Efficient Channel Reservation for Backups Paths in Optical Mesh Networks. *IEEE Globecom 2001*, November 2001, San Antonio, TX.
10. Somdip Datta, Sudipta Sengupta, Subir Biswas, Debanjan Saha and Hisashi Kobayashi. Analysis of Sub-wavelength Traffic Grooming Efficiency in Optical Mesh Networks. *Submitted for publication*.
11. Chunsheng Xin, Yinghua Ye, Sudhir Dixit and Chunming Qiao. A Joint Working and Protection Path Selection Approach in WDM Mesh Networks. *IEEE Globecom 2001*, November 2001, San Antonio, TX.
12. Sudipta Sengupta and Ramu Ramamurthy. Capacity Efficient Distributed Routing of Mesh-Restored Lightpaths in Optical Networks. *IEEE Globecom 2001*, November 2001, San Antonio, TX.

Fast Network Re-optimization Schemes for MPLS and Optical Networks

Randeep Bhatia, Murali Kodialam, and T.V. Lakshman

Bell Labs, Lucent Technologies,
{randeep,lakshman}@research.bell-labs.com., muralik@dnrc.bell-labs.com.

Abstract. This paper presents algorithms for re-optimizing network routing in connection-oriented networks such as Multi-Protocol Label Switched (MPLS) networks. The objective in re-optimization is to allow the network to carry more traffic without adding capacity. The need for re-optimization arises because of dynamic connection routing where connections, such as bandwidth guaranteed Label Switched Paths (LSPs) in MPLS networks, are routed as they arrive one-by-one to the network. Continual dynamic routing leads to network inefficiencies due to the limited information available for routing and due to simple path selection algorithms often used to satisfy connection set-up time constraints. We present a re-optimization scheme, where the reoptimizer constantly monitors the network to determine if re-optimization will lead to sufficient network efficiency benefits. When sufficient benefits can be obtained, the re-optimizer computes the least cost set of connections which must be re-routed to attain the necessary network efficiency and then computes the routes for the connections to be re-routed. We develop efficient re-optimization algorithms and demonstrate by simulations that several network performance metrics are significantly improved by re-optimization.

1 Introduction

We consider efficient network routing in connection oriented networks such as MPLS, Optical, and ATM networks. Efficient network routing with QoS guarantees has been well studied in both offline (where all connections to be routed are known ahead of time) and online (where connections arrive to the network one-at-a-time) contexts [3,6,7]. However, the hybrid scenario where the network dynamically routes most connections in an on-line fashion and occasionally re-optimizes the network routing has not been studied extensively. This paper considers network re-optimization in dynamically routed connection oriented networks.

Online connection routing is used in networks for quick set-up of connections. An example is the set-up of bandwidth guaranteed LSPs in MPLS networks [4]. Here, LSP set-up requests arrive to edge routers which route the LSP using a quick path selection scheme such as min-hop or shortest path with a priori fixed weights. The routing algorithm uses the OSPF link-state database to obtain

K. Jeffay, I. Stoica, and K. Wehrle (Eds.): IWQoS 2003, LNCS 2707, pp. 249–265, 2003.
© Springer-Verlag Berlin Heidelberg 2003

topology and link-bandwidth usage (made possible by traffic engineering extensions to OSPF). The simple path selection scheme and the limited information available for online routing can cause network capacity to be inefficiently used. It is possible that LSP requests between certain ingress-egress pair are rejected due to lack of capacity whereas a more efficient network routing would allow successful LSP routing. The objective of network re-optimization is to offset the inefficiencies of online dynamic routing by occasional re-routing of LSPs.

We develop a re-optimization scheme where the re-optimizer monitors the network by keeping track of the aggregate routed traffic between the network ingresses and egresses. It also obtains the network topology by passive peering to the network routing protocol or by periodically obtaining the routing protocol's link state data base from one the routers (or switches) in the network. Knowing the currently routed aggregate traffic, the re-optimizer computes the potential benefit from re-optimization. This is done by comparing the amount of additional traffic that can be accommodated in the current network, if the traffic were to scale proportionally to the current load, to that which can be accommodated if the the network were to be re-optimized. If this re-optimization benefit is considered sufficient (exceeds a set threshold), then the re-optimizer computes the set of connections which need to be re-routed so as to incur the minimum re-routing cost. Re-routing costs are determined using a re-routing penalty associated with every connection. The new routes for the set of connections to be re-routed is also computed by the re-optimizer. A key feature of our scheme is the ability to keep the network well balanced by ensuring sufficient available capacity between all ingress-egress pairs so that connections arriving to specific ingress-egress pairs are not all rejected. Note that since the re-optimization algorithms do not run on the network elements and re-optimization is infrequent, the re-optimization algorithms do not have to be restricted to very simple computations as is the case for online routing. Nevertheless, for large networks it is desirable to find computationally efficient re-optimization schemes.

Overall, our scheme has the following characteristics:

1. Use of limited network knowledge to compute re-optimization benefit.
2. Use of a network efficiency measure that ensures better network performance for online routing and the admission of more connections to the network.
3. Minimal re-routing to achieve high efficiency.
4. Computationally efficient

2   Outline and Assumptions

For illustrative purposes, consider an MPLS network where bandwidth guaranteed LSPs are provisioned between edge routers. (We use the terms LSPs and connections synonymously in the rest of the paper.) Requests for new LSPs arrive to the network over time. When an LSP set-up request arrives to an edge router, if the network has enough capacity to accommodate the request, the request causes an LSP set-up using a signaling protocol such as RSVP-TE or CR-LDP. Otherwise the request is rejected. Requests for tear-down of existing

LSPs also arrive over time leading to the network freeing up resources for the removed LSPs. Thus at any given time the network may have LSPs provisioned between certain pair of edge routers. However, the chosen network routing may not be efficient in the sense that the network may have insufficient capacity between certain ingress-egress pairs to accommodate new LSP requests, whereas a different allocation of routes to LSPs would permit it. The networks routing optimality may be restored by occasional re-optimization that re-routes some of the LSPs. Note that features such as the make-before-break feature in RSVP-TE [1] are usable for LSP re-routing. The paper presents an efficient scheme for re-optimization that can dramatically improve the performance of the network in terms of its ability to accommodate new LSPs.

The network is to be re-optimized to maximize its ability to accommodate the future demands. Even though demands (connection or LSP set-up requests) arrive in an online fashion, we will assume that the long term average traffic between ingress-egress pairs remain in proportion to what the network is currently carrying (i,e., in the absence of traffic forecasts, we take the current network traffic to be indicative of the long term to within a scaling factor). Here a demand for a source sink (ingess-egress) edge router pair represents the aggregate bandwidth of all the LSPs to be provisioned between the source sink pair.

We define a "Network Efficiency Measure" for measuring the instantaneous routing efficiency with respect to performance metrics of interest. Informally this measures the fraction or multiple of the traffic demand matrix that can be accommodated by the network. In general the network may be able to accommodate a bigger fraction (or multiple) of the demand between a given source sink pair but at the expense of other source sink pairs. However we are interested in a fair network efficiency measure that tries to maximize the minimum fraction of demands that can be accommodated for any given source sink pair. In the spirit of max-min fairness we can generalize this measure to first maximize the minimum fraction of demands that can be accommodated for any given source sink pair. Then for the source sink pairs that can still accommodate more demands we maximize the minimum fraction of demands that can be accommodated for these source sink pairs and so on. We use a Network Efficiency Measure where we maximize the minimum fraction of demands accommodated for every source sink pair.

For a fixed demand matrix and for a particular Network Efficiency Measure the re-optimization algorithm works as follows. Given the network with some currently provisioned LSPs we measure the efficiency of the network, assuming that the currently provisioned LSPs stay as they are. Next we compute the maximum possible gain in the efficiency of the network that can be obtained by re-routing the provisioned LSPs. If this gain in network efficiency is significant then we proceed with the re-routing of the LSPs. Finally among all the re-routings that result in the same improvement in the network efficiency the algorithm chooses the one which minimizes the cost of re-routing. The algorithm allows the operator to assign a cost-benefit measure down to the level of individual LSPs to guide the algorithm in picking the solution of minimum cost.

We now describe our scheme in more detail. We will start out by assuming the demand matrix is scaled from the currently provisioned traffic demands between

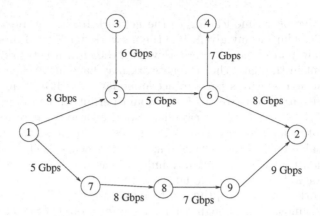

Fig. 1. Illustrative Example

source sink pairs and we will use the Network Efficiency Measure to maximize the minimum fraction of demands accommodated for every source sink pair.

3   Key Ideas for the Re-optimization Scheme

In this section, we give an informal description of the key ideas used for the re-optimization scheme. The next section presents a more formal mathematical description.

3.1   Illustrative Example

Connection oriented networks that use online routing tend to get unbalanced over time resulting in uneven load distribution. This may lead to some links getting congested that are "critical" for carrying some future demands. Re-optimization involves balancing the load on the links such that network congestion is alleviated. We illustrate this with a simple example. Figure 1 shows a network of 9 nodes. Associated with each link is its capacity as shown in the figure. Nodes 1 and 3 are ingress routers and nodes 2 and 4 are egress routers. Demands for connections arrive between two pair of nodes $(1,2)$ and $(3,4)$. We assume that the network uses min-hop routing. For illustrative purposes we make the assumption that all connections require 1Mbps of bandwidth. We also assume that connections last for a long time, thus a connection once provisioned stays provisioned in the network permanently.

Let the first demand be for a connection from node 1 to node 2 of bandwidth 1Mbps. Note that this will be routed over the path $1, 5, 6, 2$ since this is the min-hop path between node pair $(1,2)$. In fact all connections for node pair $(1,2)$ will be routed over the path $1, 5, 6, 2$ until some link on this path runs out of available capacity. Subsequently additional connections for node pair $(1,2)$ will be routed over path $1, 7, 8, 9, 2$. The connections for the node pair $(3,4)$ have only one choice: they can only be routed over path $3, 5, 6, 4$. Note that link $(5, 6)$ is one of the critical links for the connections for node pair $(3, 4)$ and as long this link has available capacity all the newly arrived connections, for both node pairs, will be routed over this link. At the same time the other links such as those on path $1, 7, 8, 9, 2$ remain unloaded. Thus assuming a uniform mix of connections for the two node pairs, over time the network would get unbalanced.

Now consider the scenario where the network is to support 5000 connections for each of the node pairs. Let us say at some time t_1 2500 connections for each of the node pair $(3, 4)$ and $(1, 2)$ have arrived and been provisioned in the network. Note that connections for node pair $(3, 4)$ are routed over path $3, 5, 6, 4$ while those for node pair $(1, 2)$ are routed over path $1, 5, 6, 2$. At this point the link $(5, 6)$ is loaded to its full capacity and no more connections can be accommodated in the network for node pair $(3, 4)$. Note that this is not due to the network not having enough capacity to admit any more connections for node pair $(3, 4)$. But it is due to the load imbalance which results in some capacity getting stranded in the network. This stranded capacity can be recovered by re-balancing the network. One possible re-optimization involves migrating the connections for node pair $(1, 2)$ from the path $1, 5, 6, 2$ to the path $1, 7, 8, 9, 2$, thus alleviating the congestion on the link $(5, 6)$. Note that this creates enough capacity in the network to accommodate 2500 more connections for node pair $(3, 4)$. Let this re-optimization be performed at time t_1 and then subsequently at some time t_2 let 1000 additional connections for each of the node pair $(3, 4)$ and $(1, 2)$ have arrived and been provisioned in the network. Note that the additional connections for node pair $(3, 4)$ are routed over path $3, 5, 6, 4$ while those for node pair $(1, 2)$ are routed over path $1, 5, 6, 2$. At this point the network can only admit 500 more connections for node pair $(3, 4)$. However by doing another re-optimization where all of the $(1, 2)$ connections are migrated from the path $1, 5, 6, 2$ to the path $1, 7, 8, 9, 2$, we create enough capacity to accommodate 1500 additional connections for node pair $(3, 4)$.

The example shows that periodic re-optimization of these connection oriented networks helps recover the stranded capacity and keeps the network re-balanced. However re-optimization has a cost associated with it in terms of the disruption of provisioned connections possibly resulting in traffic hits. Thus re-optimization has to be carefully planned to maximize the benefits gained in terms of the recovered stranded capacity. To do this we need some quantification of how useful re-optimization is for a given state of the network. To this end we define a "network efficiency" measure. We compute the network efficiency before and after (a potential) re-optimization. If re-optimization can lead to a significant gain in the network efficiency we proceed with re-optimization otherwise we continue with the current state of the network.

In the example above the "network efficiency" of the network is computed at time t_1 as follows. Given the state of the network at time t_1 we ask the question what fraction of the demand matrix (5000 connections for each of the node pairs) can be accommodated by the network. Note the network has already accommodated 2500 connections for each node pair and the network cannot accommodate any more connections for the node pair $(3, 4)$. Thus this fraction is $2500/5000 = 0.5$. Thus the network efficiency of the network at time t_1 is 0.5. However if we were to re-reroute all the connections provisioned on the path $1, 5, 6, 2$ to the path $1, 7, 8, 9, 2$ then the network can accommodate a total of 5000 connections for each of the node pairs (assuming an optimal routing algorithm is used for routing the additional connections), with all the connections for node pair $(1, 2)$ routed on the path $1, 7, 8, 9, 2$, and all the connections for node pair routed on the path $3, 5, 6, 4$. Thus the network efficiency after re-optimization is $5000/5000 = 1.0$ a gain of 100%. Similarly at time t_2 the network can only admit a total of 3500 connections for node pair $(3, 4)$, giving a network efficiency of $3500/5000 = 0.7$. Also note that the network can admit 5000 connections for each node pair after re-optimization giving a network efficiency of 1.0 subsequent to re-optimization. Thus re-optimization at time t_2 will result in a gain of about 43%.

4   Basic Re-optimization Scheme

4.1   Network Model

In the following we describe the network model that we use in the rest of the paper. We assume we are given a network with N routers (also called nodes) and M links between them. The network supports demands between n source sink router pairs (i, j) where each source and sink router is an edge router. These source sink pairs are numbered 1 to n and for the k-th source sink pair (i, j) there is currently d_k amount of end to end demand provisioned in the network. This demand for a source sink pair is measured by the aggregate bandwidth allocated to all the LSPs between the source sink pair. We also denote this currently provisioned demand between source sink pair (i, j) by $d_{(i,j)}$. In addition we denote by $D_{(i,j)}$ or D_k the total desired demand to be supported for the k-th source sink pair (i, j) as defined by a demand matrix D. For each link e in the network $c(e)$ and $b(e)$ denote its current residual capacity and its total capacity respectively.

In this section we assume that the demand matrix is defined by the currently provisioned demands between source sink pairs and we will use the Network Efficiency Measure to maximize the minimum fraction of demands accommodated for every source sink pair. Thus $D_{(i,j)} = d_{(i,j)}$ and the Network Efficiency Measure is the largest value for λ such that at least $\lambda d_{(i,j)}$ demand can be accommodated between source sink pair (i, j). Our results extend to the the more general demand matrix and the more general Network Efficiency Measure. However for lack of space we omit these results from this paper.

4.2   Solution Approach

In this section we outline our approach to re-optimization. We first present our ideas for quantifying the usefulness of re-optimization for a given network. To this end we define a natural "network efficiency" measure. We compute the network efficiency before and after (a potential) re-optimization, which in conjunction with a network re-optimization benefit threshold help us determine the benefit of re-optimization. Having determined that re-optimization is beneficial, we determine a re-optimization solution that involves minimal amount of disruption to the network. All these ideas are formally presented in the following sections.

4.3   Network Efficiency Measure before Re-optimization

We now formally define the Network Efficiency Measure for a network with currently provisioned demands $d_{(i,j)}$ between source sink pairs (i,j). Here we are interested in the Network Efficiency Measure before re-routing. Thus we assume that the currently provisioned flows stay as they are and we want to compute the additional flow that can be routed between each source sink pair. Here we measure the efficiency of the network by the maximum value of $\lambda + 1$ where there exist a multi-commodity flow between every source sink pair such that the flow assigned in this multi-commodity flow to source sink pair (i,j) is $d_{(i,j)}\lambda$ and the total flow through any link e is at most $c(e)$. Thus if r is the efficiency then we can increase the flow between every source sink pair by a factor of $r - 1$. Note also that $r \geq 1$ and the larger r is the more "efficient" the network is in admitting new connections between any source sink pair. Intuitively we are taking the currently provisioned demand matrix as a measure for the expected demand in the future to within a multiplicative factor such that we expect the demand ratios for future demands to follow the ratios in the current demand matrix.

We take the total traffic demand between a source-sink router pair to be a single commodity. We denote by $f^k(P)$ the flow for commodity k for the k-th source sink pair on path P. Then λ can be obtained as a solution to the following multi-commodity concurrent flow problem.

$$\max \lambda \tag{1}$$

$$\sum_{k=1}^{n} \sum_{P:e \in P} f^k(P) \leq c(e) \quad \forall e \in E \tag{2}$$

$$\sum_{P} f^k(P) = \lambda \, d_k \quad \forall k \tag{3}$$

$$f^k(P) \geq 0 \quad \forall P \quad \forall k \tag{4}$$

4.4   Network Re-optimization Benefit Measure

This measures the maximum network efficiency that can be obtained by re-routing the existing demands in the network.

The Network Re-optimization Benefit Measure is thus the maximum value of λ where there exist a multi-commodity flow between every source sink pair such that the flow assigned in this multi-commodity flow to source sink pair (i,j) is $d_{(i,j)}\lambda$ and the total flow through any link e is at most $b(e)$. Thus if b is the network re-optimization benefit then note that $b/r \geq 1$ and that by re-routing the existing demands the efficiency of the network can be increased to b.

Note that $b = \lambda$ can be obtained as a solution to the following multi-commodity concurrent flow problem.

$$\max \lambda \tag{5}$$

$$\sum_{k=1}^{n} \sum_{P:e \in P} f^k(P) \leq b(e) \quad \forall e \in E \tag{6}$$

$$\sum_{P} f^k(P) = \lambda\, d_k \quad \forall k \tag{7}$$

$$f^k(P) \geq 0 \quad \forall P \quad \forall k \tag{8}$$

4.5   Network Re-optimization Benefit Threshold

A threshold α is used which is used to determine if network re-optimization is beneficial. In other words we say that it is beneficial to do network optimization if the ratio of the network benefit measure b and the network efficiency measure r exceeds α. Our goal would be to do re-routing so that after re-routing the efficiency of the new network is $r\alpha$.

4.6   Minimum Cost Re-routing

As mentioned in the introduction our goal is not just to improve the network efficiency but to do this with re-routing of minimum cost. Note that these are contradictory goals since minimum cost re-routing would imply least network efficiency and vice versa. However in order to achieve a balance we strive to increase the efficiency of the network to $r\alpha$ yet at the same time find the minimum cost re-routing that achieves this network efficiency. Here we outline a scheme for just this.

The algorithm allows the operator to assign a cost-benefit measure down to the level of individual LSPs to guide it in picking the re-routing solution of minimum cost. Let $x^k(P)$ denote the amount of commodity k currently provisioned on path P. Let LSP_k denote the set $\{(P, k) : x^k(P) > 0)\}$. We assume that LSP_k is some operator specified splitting of the flow for commodity k in the existing network. We will assume an ordering of the elements of LSP_k such that the i-th element is denoted by tuple $(k, f_k(i))$ and would correspond to flow for commodity k on path $P_{f_k(i)}$, for some function f_k. For convenience we will write f_k as f whenever the dependence on k is obvious from the context. Thus we will denote the i-th tuple as $(k, f(i))$. Let LSP denote the union of the n sets LSP_k. We assume that the operator has associated a cost $c^k(P)$ for the flow of commodity k that is not routed on path P in any re-routing. Let $(k, f(i)) \in LSP_k$. Let P denote the path $P_{f(i)}$. Thus commodity k has $x_P^k > 0$ flow provisioned on path P. Let after re-routing only a fraction f of this flow stay on path P.

Then a cost of $(1-f)c^k(P)$ is incurred for the commodity k for this path in the re-routing solution.

We now present a scheme for determining the re-routing solution of minimal cost that achieves the required re-optimization benefit. This scheme is based on solving a budgeted version of the maximum concurrent flow problem. First we split each commodity k into $|LSP_k|+1$ commodities such that the i-th commodity among the first $|LSP_k|$ commodity corresponds to the i-th tuple $(k, f(i)) \in LSP_k$. We set the demand for the i-th commodity among the first $|LSP_k|$ commodity, which we denote by (k, i), to $x^k(P_{f(i)})/(r\alpha)$. We set the demand for the $|LSP_k|+1$-th commodity, denoted by $(k, |LSP_k|+1)$, to

$$d_k - \sum_{(k,i)} x^k(P_{f(i)})/(r\alpha) = d_k(1 - 1/(r\alpha)).$$

For sake of simplicity we will use the notation P_i for $P_f(i)$ in the following description.

The i-th commodity denoted by (k, i), for $i \leq |LSP_k|$ can be routed on any path, however for any flow not routed on path P_i a cost per unit flow of $c^k(P_i)/x^k(P_i)$ is incurred. We solve a maximum concurrent multi-commodity flow problem for these commodities subject to the constraint that the total cost incurred is some budget B. Our aim is to find the smallest value for B such that the solution to this maximum concurrent flow problem is $\lambda = r\alpha$. Putting this together we get the following budgeted maximum concurrent flow problem:

$$\max \lambda \tag{9}$$

$$\sum_{k=1}^{n} \sum_{i=1}^{|LSP_k|+1} \sum_{P:e\in P} f^{(k,i)}(P) \leq b(e) \quad \forall e \in E \tag{10}$$

$$\sum_{P} f^{(k,i)}(P) = \lambda\, d_{(k,i)} \quad \forall k \; 1 \leq i \leq |LSP_k|+1 \tag{11}$$

$$f^{(k,i)}(P) \geq 0 \quad \forall P \; \forall k \; 1 \leq i \leq |LSP_k|+1 \tag{12}$$

$$\sum_{k=1}^{n} \sum_{i=1}^{|LSP_k|} \frac{c^k(P_i)}{x^k(P_i)} \sum_{P\neq P_i} f^{(k,i)}(P) \leq B \tag{13}$$

Here $f^{(k,i)}(P)$ denotes the flow for commodity (k, i) on path P and $d_{(k,i)}$ denotes the demand for commodity (k, i). Note that here $c^k(P_i)f$ is the cost incurred for routing a fraction $1-f$ of the currently provisioned flow on path P_i for commodity k.

Claim 1. There exists a choice of B for which the optimal solution to this LP $\lambda^* = r\alpha$.

Proof. Let $\lambda = g(B)$ denote the optimal solution to the budgeted LP for a given value B of the budget constraint. Note $g(B)$ is monotonically non-decreasing in B. In addition $g(B)$ is a continuous function of B, since from a flow scaling argument it follows that for $B' \leq B$, $g(B') \geq g(B)B'/B$. Note that if B is set to the value

$$\sum_{k=1}^{n} \sum_{i=1}^{|LSP_k|} c^k(P_i)$$

then $\lambda = r\alpha$ is a feasible solution to the budgeted LP. Thus for this choice of B we have $g(B) \geq r\alpha$. Also if B is set to 0 then $\lambda = r\alpha$ is not a feasible solution to the budgeted LP, since then even without re-routing we will have a network efficiency of $r\alpha$. Thus for this choice of B we have $g(B) < r\alpha$. Thus by continuity of $g(B)$ there exists a B for which $g(B) = r\alpha$. □

Corollary 2. The choice of B for which $\lambda^* = r\alpha$ can be found to within a factor of $(1 + \epsilon)$ by performing a binary search for an additional running time factor of $\log_{1+\epsilon} \sum_{k=1}^{n} \sum_{i=1}^{|LSP_k|} c^k(P_i)$.

4.7   LSP Rerouting

Note that so far we have looked at the flows for a commodity at the granularity of the paths which define the set LSP_k. In general for each path P such that $(P, k) \in LSP_k$ we may have multiple LSPs (connections) for commodity k provisioned on it, and our goal is to find a re-routing for these individual connections so as to maximize the total profit. We use the solution of the linear program given by the constraints (9) to (13) as a starting point for computing a re-routing solution for the individual connections.

The overall algorithm for the re-routing of the connections uses at most four phases. The first phase involves solving the multi-commodity flow problems as described in previous sections. In the second phase we find a set of connections that do not need to be re-routed, since they are currently routed over a path on which sufficient flow is routed by the multicommodity solution. The connections are selected in a priority order which can be modified by the operator. As connections are assigned to path the flows on the paths are updated to reflect the capacity that is used up by the assigned connections. The third phase is a re-routing phase where connections unassigned in phase two are assigned to paths on which positive flow was routed in the multicommodity solution (and as updated by phase two). Here again the algorithm selects the connections to be re-routed in an order defined by their priorities and it tries to assign selected connections to the first path in which they can fit i.e. the path has enough flow associated with it, for the source sink pair of the connection, to accommodate the connection. As connections are assigned to path the flows on the paths are updated to reflect the capacity that is used up by the assigned connections. The fourth phase is required if some connections remain un-assigned after the three phases. In our simulations this phase was rarely invoked. This phase involves re-routing the leftover connections by using constrained shortest path first (CSPF) over the residual graph resulting from phase three.

Note that the re-routing scheme described above requires the knowledge of the currently provisioned connections on each path for each commodity. This knowledge is available on the edge routers corresponding to the source sink pair for each of the commodity k. The edge router for commodity k just needs to know the flows f_P^k for each $(P, k) \in LSP_k$. Therefore a natural place to implement such a scheme would be in the edge routers. This means that the route server need not have information about all the connections that are provisioned in the network and thus it can gather all the information it needs to solve the three linear programs by passively peering with OSPF-TE and/or looking into the network mib elements.

4.8   Overall Scheme

We now describe the overall re-optimization algorithm.

Phase I
  $r =$ solution of LP defined by equations (1) to (4)
  $b =$ solution of LP defined by equations (5) to (8)
  If $\frac{b}{r} < \alpha$ **then** Stop; /* Re-optimization is not useful */
  $B^* =$ value of B in LP defined by equations (9) to (13) for which $\lambda = r\alpha$
  $f^{(k,i)}(P) =$ solution of LP defined by equations (9) to (13) for $B = B^*, \forall k, i, P$
  $f^k(P) = \sum_i f^{(k,i)}(P) \; \forall k, P$

Phase II /* Find connections that are not to be re-routed */
  For $k = 1$ to n
    For connection $s_i = s_1, s_2 \ldots$ of k-th source sink pair
      Let P be the path for s_i.
      If Bandwidth b_i for connection s_i is $\leq f^k(P)$.
        s_i stays routed on P.
        $f^k(P) = f^k(P) - b_i$.
      EndIf
    end For
  end For

Phase III /* Re-route remaining connections */
  For $k = 1$ to n
    For connection $s_i = s_1, s_2, \ldots$ of k-th source sink pair
      For paths $P_j = P_1, P_2, \ldots$ between k-th source sink pair
        If Bandwidth b_i for connection s_i is $\leq f^k(P_j)$.
          Route s_i on P_j.
          $f^k(P_j) = f^k(P_j) - b_i$.
        EndIf
      end For
    end For
  end For

Phase IV /* CSPF to re-route un-assigned connections */
  Let $s_1, s_2, \ldots s_r$ be the set of un-assigned connections
  For $i = 1$ to r
    Use CSPF to route connection s_i over the residual network
    Update residual network
  end For

---

5   Efficient Implementation

Note that our scheme relies heavily on solving linear programs for certain multi-commodity flow problems. Use of linear program solvers is computationally prohibitive if the schemes are to run on devices with limited computational capabilities such as edge routers. We therefore seek fast and efficient algorithms for solving these linear programs while trading off optimality of the found solutions. We use the machinery developed by Garg et. al. [2,5] for this purpose.

Note that the results in [2,5] can be directly applied to solve linear program given by equations (1) to (4) and to solve linear program given by equations (5) to (8) to obtain the network efficiency r to within any specified error ϵ of the optimal value and to to obtain the network re-computation benefit measure b to within any specified error ϵ. The techniques presented in [2,5] rely only on shortest path computations on a suitable network and hence are computationally efficient. More formally the running time is given by:

Claim 3. ([5]) There is a Fully Polynomial Time Approximation Scheme for solving the maximum concurrent multicommodity flow problem whose running time for a connected network with M edges is $O(\epsilon^{-2}M^2\log^{O(1)}M)$.

Our budgeted version of the maximum concurrent flow problem as defined by equations (9) to (13) differs from the same problem defined in [2], where costs are associated with flows over edges and not with paths for the flows. Hence the results in [2] are not directly applicable. However we can modify the results in [2] to show:

Claim 4. There is a Fully Polynomial Time Approximation Scheme for solving the budgeted version of the maximum concurrent multicommodity flow problem that runs in time $O(2n\log n+M)C_2T_{sp}$, where $C_2\log n = O(\log M(\epsilon^{-2}+\log n))$ and $T_{sp} = O(N\log N+M)$ is the running time of a shortest path algorithm such as Dijkstra. Here n is the number of source sink pairs, N and M are the number of nodes and edges respectively in the network.

To find the smallest value of the budget for which a network efficiency of $r\alpha$ is achieved we need an additional running time factor of $\log_{1+\epsilon}\sum_{k=1}^{n}\sum_{i=1}^{|LSP_k|}c^k(P_i)$, as established in Corollary 4.6.

The running time of Phase II and III of the algorithm is dependent on the number of tuples (P,k) for which $f^k(P) > 0$, and the number of currently provisioned connections in the network. The former is at most $O(2n\log n+M)C_2$, where C_2 is as defined in Claim 5, since there are these many iterations of the algorithm for solving the budgeted maximum concurrent flow problem each potentially routing the flow on a distinct path.

Finally the running time of Phase IV is dependent on the number of unassigned connections which is bounded by the number of currently provisioned connections in the network.

6   Simulation

In this section we present our simulation results for the basic re-optimization scheme. For our simulation we used a network of 20 nodes which is shown

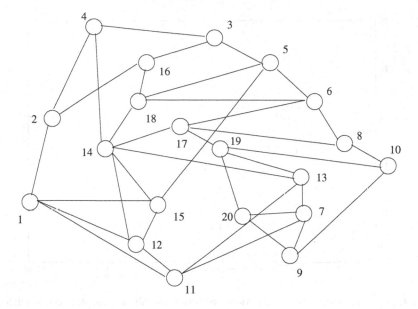

Fig. 2. Graph used for simulations

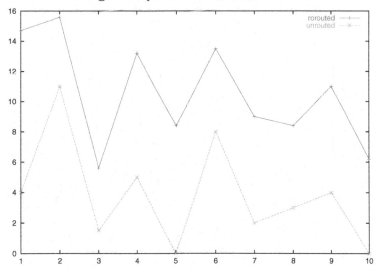

Fig. 3. Minimum of maximum number of connections that can be accommodated for all source sink pairs

in Fig. 2. All links in the network are bi-directional and have 15 Gbps of total available bandwidth in each direction. This network has 6 ingress routers: 1, 3, 4, 5, 10, 11 and 6 egress routers: 6, 7, 8, 9, 12, 18. The network has 36 source sink node pairs one for each ingress egress router pairs.

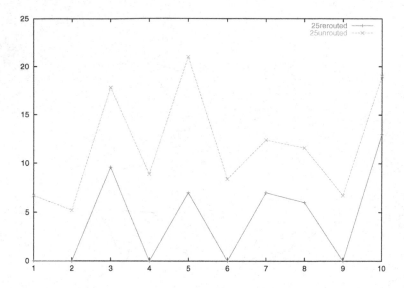

Fig. 4. Max percentage of connections rejected for all source sink pairs with 25% additional loading

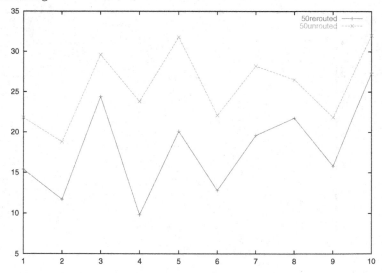

Fig. 5. Max percentage of connections rejected for all source sink pairs with 50% additional loading

Our basic simulation setup is as follows. We generate a demand matrix at random for the source sink pairs. Then we load the network with connections that arrive for node pairs at rate proportional to the demand for the node pairs in the demand matrix. Each connection is an LSP of bandwidth 1Mbps. We route these connections using min-hop routing. As the network is getting loaded

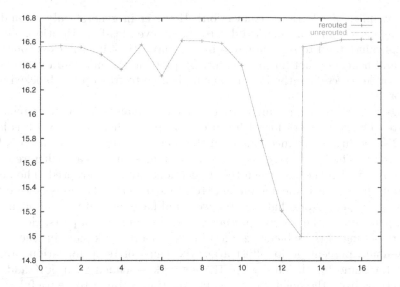

Fig. 6. Normalized network efficiency before and after re-routing

we continuously monitor the network efficiency. When the network efficiency of the loaded network falls below approximately 10% of the network efficiency of a network obtained by re-routing the provisioned connections we invoke re-optimization. We then measure the re-optimization gain in terms of the load that can be handled by the re-optimized network versus the load that can be handled by the network if no re-optimization was performed. We measure this gain in terms of two quantities. First we compute the maximum number of additional connections that the network can accommodate for each source sink pair just before re-optimization and we compare it to the same quantity immediately after doing the re-optimization. Second after re-optimization we load the network with 25% additional connections (proportional to the demand for the node pairs in the demand matrix). We count the number of connections that are rejected for each source sink pair. We then do the same for the network without performing re-optimization and compare the two quantities. We also do this before and after comparison after loading the network with 50% additional connections. Finally we also compute the network efficiency for different loading of the network for a particular demand matrix both with and without re-optimization.

In our simulations the number of connections provisioned in the network ranged from 150000 to 250000. Our simulations were performed with 10 different demand matrices.

Figure 3 shows the minimum over all source sink pair of the maximum number of additional connections that can be accommodated by the network for each source sink pair both before re-routing and after re-routing. The number shown in the Y-axis is this quantity expressed in units of 1000 connections. The values are plotted for 10 different demand matrices. Note that we could have plotted instead of the minimum the average value for all source sink pairs of the maximum number of additional connections. However in general only a handful of the source sink pairs are blocked due to the un-even load distribution. Thus the average values tend to be dominated by the majority of non-blocked source sink pairs and hence are not much different. By plotting the minimum value instead we are able to see how the load balancing is able to free up the blocked source sink pairs.

Figure 4 shows the maximum percentage of demands that cannot be accommodated by the network for each source sink pair, when the network is loaded with 25% additional connections from the point where re-optimization is found to be useful. The figure compares these percentages for the case when re-routing is performed with the case when the connections are not re-routed. The number shown in the Y-axis is the maximum percentage of demands and is plotted for 10 different matrices. Note that here too we could have plotted instead of the maximum percentages the average percentages for all source sink pairs. However the same reasoning of there being very few blocked source sink pairs justifies the use of minimum percentage for illustrating the gains of re-optimization. Figure 5 shows the same for the case when the network is loaded with 50% additional connections from the point where re-optimization is found to be useful.

Finally Figure 6 shows the variation in network efficiency as the network is loaded with connections, both when re-optimization is performed and when the network is not re-optimized. For this simulation we fixed a single demand matrix and then we loaded the network with connections that arrive for node pairs at rate proportional to the demand for the node pairs in the demand matrix. This helps us calibrate the network efficiency in terms of a loading factor of the demand matrix. The X-axis represents the various loading of the network (in terms of the demand matrix) and the Y-axis plots the network efficiency in terms of a loading factor of the demand matrix. At a loading of 13 times the demand matrix re-optimization is useful since here the network efficiency of the un-optimized network is less than 15 while by re-optimizing the network efficiency is raised to 16.6. Also note that if re-optimization is not performed the network starts rejecting connections at a loading of approximately 15 times the demand matrix. However if re-optimization is performed the first time the network starts rejecting connections is at a loading of 16.5 times the demand matrix.

7   Concluding Remarks

Even though much research attention has been focused on efficient network routing of bandwidth guaranteed connections, the issue of network re-optimization has not been extensively studied. Network re-optimization introduces new constraints such as minimizing the re-routing cost, working with limited network information (in comparison to offline routing), and using network efficiency measures different from those used for offline routing. We presented efficient network reoptimization algorithms that use limited aggregate information to continually monitor the network for re-optimization opportunities. The algorithm needs more detailed connection specific information only when connection re-routing is to be done. The algorithms are computationally efficient and can be implemented in network management systems for connection oriented data (MPLS, ATM) networks or optical networks.

References

1. A. Awduche, L. Berger, D. Gan, T. Li, V Srinivasan, G. Swallow, "RSVP-TE: Extensions to RSVP for LSP Tunnels", IETF RFC 3209, December 2001.
2. N. Garg and J. Könemann, "Faster and Simpler Algorithms for Multi-commodity Flow and other Fractional Packing Problems", *Proceedings of the 39th Annual Symposium on Foundations of Computer Science*, pp. 300–309, 1998.
3. R. Guerin, D. Williams, A. Orda, "QoS Routing Mechanisms and OSPF Extensions", *Proceedings of IEEE Globecom 1997*.
4. B. Davie, Y. Rekhter, "MPLS Technology and Applications", Morgan Kaufman Publishers, 2000.
5. G. Karakostas, "Faster approximation schemes for fractional multicommodity flow problems", *Proceedings of the thirteenth annual ACM-SIAM symposium on Discrete algorithms*, pp. 166–173, 2002.
6. K. Kar, M. Kodialam, T. V. Lakshman, "Minimum Interference Routing of Bandwidth Guaranteed Tunnels with Applications to MPLS Traffic Engineering", *IEEE Journal on Selected Areas in Communications: Special Issue on Quality of Service in the Internet*, December 2000.
7. S. Plotkin, Competitive Routing of Virtual Circuits in ATM Networks, *IEEE J. Selected Areas in Comm.*, 1995 pp. 1128–1136. Special Issue on Advances in the Fundamentals of Networking.

HMP: Hotspot Mitigation Protocol for Mobile Ad hoc Networks

Seoung-Bum Lee and Andrew T. Campbell

COMET Group, Department of Electrical Engineering,
Columbia University, New York, NY 10027
{sbl, campbell}@comet.columbia.edu

Abstract. "Hotspots" represent transient but highly congested regions in wireless ad hoc networks that result in increased packet loss, end-to-end delay, and out-of-order packets delivery. We present a simple, effective, and scalable Hotspot Mitigation Protocol (HMP) where mobile nodes independently monitor local buffer occupancy, packet loss, and MAC contention and delay conditions, and take local actions in response to the emergence of hotspots, such as, suppressing new route requests and rate controlling TCP flows. HMP balances resource consumption among neighboring nodes, and improves end-to-end throughput, delay, and packet loss. Our results indicate that HMP can also improve the network connectivity preventing premature network partitions. We present analysis of hotspots, and detail the design of HMP. We evaluate the protocol's ability to effectively mitigate hotspots in mobile ad hoc networks that are based on best effort on-demand routing protocols, such as, AODV and DSR.

1 Introduction

Hotspots are often created in regions of mobile ad hoc networks (MANETs) where flows converge and intersect with each other. We define hotspots as nodes that experience flash congestion conditions or excessive contention over longer time-scales (i.e., order of seconds). Under such conditions nodes typically consume more resources (e.g., energy) and attempt to receive, process, and forward packets but the performance of the packet forwarding and signaling functions is considerably diminished and limited during the duration of hotspots. This is the result of excessive contention of the shared media wireless access, and due to flash loading at hotspot nodes, and importantly, at neighboring nodes that are in the region of hotspots. Hotspots are often transient in nature because the mobility of nodes in the network continuously creates, removes, and to some degree, migrates hotspots because node mobility changes the network topology and causes flows to be rerouted. Hotspots are characterized by excessive contention, congestion, and resource exhaustion in these networks. In other words, hotspots appear when excessive contention exists, prompting congestion when insufficient resources are available to handle the increased traffic load.

Hotspots are intrinsic to many on-demand MANET routing protocols because most on-demand routing protocols [4][5][8] utilize shortest path (or hop count) as their

K. Jeffay, I. Stoica, and K. Wehrle (Eds.): IWQoS 2003, LNCS 2707, pp. 266–283, 2003.

primary route creation metric. Most on-demand routing protocols allow an intermediate node to reply to a route query from cached route information, causing traffic loads to concentrate at certain nodes. We observe from our analysis of hotspots presented in this paper that although many on-demand routing protocols prove to be effect in routing packets in these networks they also have a propensity to create hotspots. Other researchers have also made such observations [1][3][7]. We also observe that hotspot nodes consume a disproportionate amount of resources (e.g., energy).

In this paper, we present a simple, effective, and scalable *Hotspot Mitigation Protocol (HMP)*, which seamlessly operates with existing ad hoc routing protocols, such as AODV [8] and DSR [4]. HMP balances resource consumption among neighboring nodes and improves end-to-end throughput, delay, and packet loss. Our results indicate that HMP can also improve network connectivity preventing premature network partitions. Ideally, establishing routes through non-congested areas of the network and rerouting active flows away from congested areas to non-congested areas would be the best approach to hotspot mitigation. However, this would require extensive collaborations between nodes to establish load-aware routes and sophisticated algorithms to update time-varying loading conditions. Such an approach is unscalable and not practical in mobile ad hoc networks.

HMP represents a fully distributed, localized, and scalable protocol where nodes independently monitor local conditions, and take local actions:

- *to declare* a node to be a hotspot if a combination of MAC contention/delays, packet loss, buffer occupancy, and energy reserves exceed certain predefined system thresholds;
- *to suppress* new route requests at hotspots to ensure that routed traffic does not compound the hotspot's congestion problems; and
- *to throttle* traffic locally at hotspots to force TCP flows to slow down.

HMP also seeks to decrease the energy consumption of nodes via use of these mechanisms.

This paper is structured as follows. In Section 2, we first analyze the behavior of hotspots using existing on-demand MANET routing protocols. Observations from this evaluation show that hotspots are evident even under relatively lightly loaded conditions, motivating the need for HMP. Related work is discussed in Section 3, followed by the design of the protocol in Section 4. We present a detailed analysis of HMP in Section 5 using AODV and DSR. In Section 6, we present some concluding remarks.

2   Hotspots

2.1   Hotspot Observations

Figure 1 illustrates some typical hotspot conditions found in mobile ad hoc networks. Hotspots are generally created where traffic loads converge to a node or small cluster of nodes. Flows traversing multiple wireless hops from various locations intersect with each other and create transient hotspot conditions. We observe that hotspot nodes and nodes in the vicinity of the hotspots (i.e., in hotspot regions) are prone to consume more resources than others. Left unchecked such unbalanced resource consumption is detrimental to mobile ad hoc networks because overtaxed nodes would prematurely exhaust their energy reserves before other nodes. As a consequence the network connectivity can be unnecessarily impacted. In addition, we observe that hotspot nodes are often responsible for generating a large amount of routing overhead. In general, as the traffic load increases more hotspots appear and conditions in hotspot regions become aggravated.

In what follows, we make a number of observations about hotspots using ns-2 [9] and AODV [1]. Note that that the observations we make in this section are common to other on-demand protocols such as DSR [4]. Our simulation consists of 100 mobile nodes in a 1200m by 1200m network with moderate mobility conditions (i.e., pause time of 80 seconds using the random waypoint mobility model with maximum speed of 10 m/sec). Thirty CBR/UDP and 10 TCP flows are used to produce an offered load of approximately 480 Kbps. We detect hotspots through a combination of MAC-delay measurements of unicast packets, packet loss, buffer occupancy, and by optionally considering the remaining energy resources at a node. While the thresholds for these hotspot metrics are configurable, we considers a node to be a hotspot in our current implementation (which is based on IEEE 802.11), when the node consecutively measures *i)* MAC delays that exceed a predefined value, *ii)* packet loss during the RTS-CTS-DATA-ACK cycle, and *iii)* buffer overflow; we discuss these metrics and their configuration in Section 5.1 on hotspot detection.

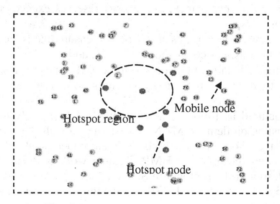

Fig. 1. Illustrative Snapshot of Hotspots

Note that hotspots are often transient because of the mobility of nodes changes the topology and continuously varies the traffic load in the network causing hotspots to migrate. We observe in our simulations that nodes are rarely in a permanent hotspot state. As a rule of thumb once a node is declared a hotspot, it is marked as a hotspot for the next 5 seconds. Thus, under simulation, nodes could be declared a hotspot a number of times (e.g., 20 times) during the lifetime of the simulation run. Using this time-scale, we observe an average of 816 congestion hotspot incidents during the simulation runs (i.e., 300 seconds) described above where the offered load is 480 Kbps. Note, that 816 hotspots instances corresponds to 4080 seconds of hotspot conditions, or, an average of 40.8 seconds of hotspot conditions per node. Results are from 5 simulation runs.

2.2   Traffic Load

Figure 2 shows the packet delivery ratio (PDR), number of hotspots, and offered load for the simulation. The packet delivery ratio is defined as the total number of packets received out of the total number of packets sent. The offered load is varied from 50 Kbps to 963 Kbps for moderate mobility involving 4831 link changes and 39830 route changes. The y-axis represents the packet delivery ratio and x-axis the offered load. In Figure 3, we also show the corresponding number of hotspot instances.

As expected, the number of hotspots increases with offered load, while the packet delivery ratio decreases with increasing load. When the offered load is light, only few hotspots are detected where the network encounters few problems in routing packets. For example, when the traffic load is 72.2 Kbps, approximately 98% of packets are delivered correctly, and only 22 hotspot instances are detected during the simulation. This means that mobile nodes in the network encounter 110 seconds of congested conditions that in turn represents an average of 1.1 seconds/node of congestion. Note that link/route errors can occasionally be interpreted as congestion conditions because packet loss due to congestion is indiscernible from packet loss due to route failure.

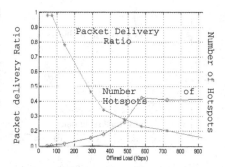

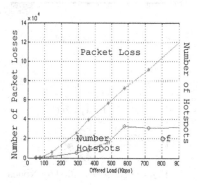

Fig. 2. Packet Delivery Ratio and Number of Hotspots

Fig. 3. Packet Loss and the Number of Hotspots

In contrast, when the offered load is increases to 963 Kbps then only 15 % of the data packets are correctly delivered with 1566 hotspots instances observed. The difference is more than 70-fold when compared to an offered load of 72.2 Kbps. One interesting observation shown in Figure 3 is that number of hotspots levels-off when the offered load exceeds 580 Kbps. We identified that the reason for this anomaly is mainly due to the failure of congestion detection. All types of packets continuously fail to complete the collision avoidance cycle of IEEE 802.11, and as a consequence, they are considered to be route errors while our hotspot detection mechanism, which relies on the measurement of the RTS-CTS-DATA-ACK cycle, fails to capture the congestion implications. The corresponding packet loss count observed during the simulation clearly supports this.

2.3   Overhead

Figure 4 illustrates the total number of packets transported when offered load is 290 Kbps. The x-axis represents the node IDs and y-axis the number of packets handled by each node. Figure 4 also shows the number of data packets handled or forwarded by each node. One interesting observation is that most of the packets handled in the system are routing-related packets and only a small portion of the total transit traffic are data packets. For example, mobile node 2 handles 20103 packets in total during the simulation but only 1076 are data packets while 19027 are routing packets. Such observations are consistently observed in the network with the result that the ratio of signaling to data packets grows with the offered load.

The increase in the offered load aggravates congested conditions and as a consequence more packet loss is observed. Consecutive packet loss is often treated as route failures by ADOV triggering route recovery procedures that entail additional route requests, route errors, and route reply packet exchanges. It is observed that the routing overhead and number of hotspots increases with the offered load but begins to decrease beyond a certain load (e.g., 700 Kbps in this simulation set) due to substantial packet loss, as discussed earlier (i.e., route request packets continuously fails to be forwarded and rarely reach destination nodes, route replies are rarely generated, with the result that routes are seldom successfully established).

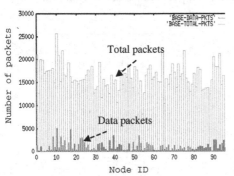

Fig. 4. Packets Handled by Nodes

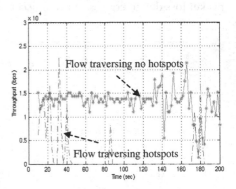

Fig. 5. Throughput Traces of Two Monitored Flows

2.4   Hotspot Regions

Figure 5 shows the throughput traces of two similar flows under the simulation configuration discussed previously. We selected a flow traversing multiple hotspots and a flow encountering no hotspots (from our simulation results) and compare their throughput performance. The trace intuitively demonstrates how hotspots impact flow performance. Among 100 mobile nodes, 11 nodes are identified as 'severe' hotspots where they experience congestion for more than 110 seconds out of 200 seconds (monitoring period). We identified 59 nodes as immediate neighbors of the 11 severe hotspots. We observed the packet loss of these 70 nodes (i.e., 11 severe hotspots and their 59 neighbors) that resided in hotspot regions, and compared their performance to other nodes in the rest of the network. We observed that nodes residing close to hotspot nodes also experience degradation in performance. For example, when the offered load is 290 Kbps, hotspot regions are responsible for 94.9 % of total packet loss while rest of network contributed only 5.1 % to the total packet loss. Moreover, nodes in hotspot regions have an average congestion time of 94 seconds while the rest of the network nodes only experience 36 seconds of congestion time. Based on these observations we argue that there is a need to study, design, and evaluate mechanisms that can seamlessly interwork with existing routing protocols to mitigate the impact of hotspots in MANETs.

3   Related Work

MANET [2] routing protocols can be simply classified into best effort routing protocols that have no built in mechanisms to provide better than best effort service [1] [3], QoS-based routing protocols [10][11][12][13], and multipath routing protocols [14][15][16]. While HMP is not a routing protocol it is designed to interwork with the existing best effort routing protocols (e.g., on-demand and proactive protocols) to provide hotspot mitigation support.

Currently, none of the existing on-demand best effort routing protocols [4][8][18][19] take hotspots into account in their routing decisions. As shown in the last section this allows hotspots to quickly emerge and build up in the network under normal operating conditions. There is a clear need to propose new mechanisms that can interwork with, or be directly incorporated into, these best effort routing protocols, hence enhancing the network's performance. HMP is designed as a separate mechanism and is therefore capable of being used in combination with any of the existing best effort routing schemes.

HMP incorporates measures of congestion and contention as well as resource shortages (e.g., energy) into its definition of hotspots. We believe that this is a more realistic definition for wireless mobile networks than one that only considers the buffer occupancy statistics at intermediate nodes. Using buffer occupancy as an indication of congestion has been widely used by a number of Internet congestion control/ hotspot management schemes. HMP manages these hotspots locally (i.e., at the point of interest) in a fully distributed fashion as opposed to traditional end-to-end approach for managing congestion.

The simple goal of HMP is to disperse new flows away from being routed through hotspots and congestion-prone areas, avoiding the further build up of traffic load at hotspots or in hotspot regions. HMP distinguishes itself from the various QoS routing approaches, which in practice are complex to implement, in that HMP does not attempt to provide QoS support nor QoS routes. However, the deployment of QoS routing and multipath routing algorithms would also minimize the likelihood of hotspots, but not eradicate them. QoS routing algorithms require accurate link state (e.g., available bandwidth, packet loss rate, estimated delay, etc.) but due to the time-varying capacity of wireless links, limited resources and mobility, maintaining accurate routing information is very difficult if not impossible in mobile ad hoc networks. Finding a feasible route with just two independent path constraints is an NP-complete problem [17]. Moreover, finding a QoS satisfying path is merely the first part of the problem because it is more challenging to maintain QoS routes when the network topology changes [11]. Because QoS routing relies on this distributed but global review of resources in the network the likelihood of stale state and traffic fluctuations beyond the anticipated load also calls for localized reactive mechanisms such as HMP to help alleviate transient hotspots. We therefore consider that HMP would also be useful in QoS routed networks.

Alternate path routing and multipath routing protocols can outperform single path routing protocols. A common feature of these protocols is that they utilize backup or alternate routes when primary routes fail. Some multipath routing protocols are designed to distribute traffic among multiple paths and reassemble the traffic at the destination nodes. However, reassembling traffic at destination node in this manner can be problematic because it leads to out-of-sequence delivery and extra re-sequencing delays [12]. Moreover, maintaining additional path information requires additional routing and computational overhead. Alternate paths should be comprised of disjoint-paths [15] in order to be effective. Such alternate paths often do not exist, particularly in single channel mobile ad hoc networks (e.g., based on IEEE 802.11).

In summary, HMP is designed as a localized node mechanism that takes local actions to prevent the build up of hotspots, which we believe will be very likely in MANETs. While HMP is targeted to interwork with the existing best effort routing protocols it could also provide efficient support for hotspot mitigation in MANET networks based on QoS routing and multipath routing. This is the subject of future work.

4   Hotspot Mitigation Protocol

4.1 Protocol Operations

The simple goal of HMP is to redirect new "routes" away from hotspots. HMP disperses new flows away from being routed through hotspots and congestion-prone areas, avoiding the further build up of traffic load in hotspot regions. HMP effectively mitigates hotspot conditions and reduces congestion-related problems. Mitigating hotspot in this manner also helps to balance resource consumption among neighboring nodes, and can extend the lifetime of certain overtaxed nodes.

HMP utilizes MAC-delay measurements, buffer occupancy information, neighbor status information and other resource monitoring mechanisms (i.e., buffer, energy) to detect hotspots. HMP does not limit the scope of monitoring and detection mechanisms, however. Operators are free to introduce additional mechanisms and algorithms according to their needs. In fact, we envision that a HMP network would embody diverse mechanisms operating concurrently. HMP utilizes monitored and measured information to respond to conditions by executing the most appropriate algorithms to alleviate the condition at hand. The measured conditions are explicitly expressed by a multimetric parameter called STATUS, which consists of two components: *symptom* and *severity*. Symptom describes the dominant condition a node is experiencing while severity expresses the degree of the symptom. For example, a node may declare its status as $Y_{CONGESTION}$ while another node may declare its status as R_{ENERGY}. This status is analogous to traffic lights, where green (denoted by G) indicates a good condition, yellow (Y) represents a marginal condition, and red (R) represents a critical condition. Therefore, $Y_{CONGESTION}$ indicates marginal congestion and

R_{ENERGY} indicates critically low energy reserves. Users/operators are free to introduce more granularity if needed. HMP piggybacks this status information in the IP option field and neighboring nodes operating in promiscuous mode learn the status of transmitters by eavesdropping their packets. The eavesdropped information is used to create and update a *Neighborhood Status Table (NST)*. This cached information is locally maintained and updated at each node.

An NST caches a list of immediate neighbors and their status. It is primarily used to manipulate new-route-creation decisions at nodes. In other words, a node refers to its NST to ensure that it is not aggravating the conditions of neighboring nodes by creating additional routes through them. We assume a finite number of neighboring nodes surrounding any node, which in effect defines the size of the NST at a node.

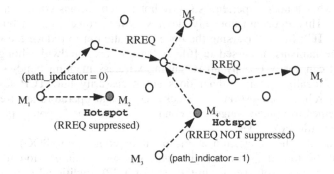

Fig. 6. Hotspot Mitigation Protocol Illustration

The naïve suppression of new route creation may prevent the use of the only possible path between two hosts and may yield poor connectivity in the network, or even cause network partitions. To avoid this, a new-route-suppression mechanism is used, if and only if, there exists a sufficient number of non-hotspot neighbors within its transmission range. HMP also makes sure that preceding nodes en-route also have enough non-hotspot neighbors. The notion of 'enough neighbors' is defined by the enough_nh_neighbor parameter (i.e., currently set at 6 in our implementation). The value of this parameter has a direct impact on the network connectivity, as discussed in Section 5.5. If enough_nh_neighbor is too small, (e.g., 2), then HMP manifests low connectivity among mobile nodes and often fails to provide useful routes. HMP also ensures that it is not inadvertently denying the only possible path between two end hosts by utilizing an indicator called the path_indicator, which is carried in the IP option field of Route Request (RREQ) messages. A node that has only a few neighbors sets this indicator (path_indicator = 1) and upstream nodes that receive the RREQ (with IP option that includes path_indicator) check this indicator and avoid suppressing new routes if it is set. This is illustrated in Figure 6 where hotspot M_4 forwards RREQ toward M_5 because the source node M_3 has set its path indicator whereas hotspot M_2 suppresses RREQ from M_1 because its path_indicator is not set in the IP option field of the RREQ.

4.2 Congestion Levels

The main objective of congestion avoidance algorithms is preventing the further build up of traffic at hotspots. HMP distinguishes two levels of congestion (i.e., levels 1 and 2) and adopts two corresponding algorithms to support this view. The first algorithm is activated when HMP determines the current status of a node is in a moderately congested condition (i.e., level 1), denoted by $Y_{CONGESTION-1}$. This algorithm simply suppresses the creation of additional routes at hotspots by discarding new route request packets. As mentioned previously, HMP ensures not to deny the 'only route' between two hosts.

The second algorithm is more aggressive and executes when nodes encounter substantial congestion (i.e., level 2), denoted by $Y_{CONGESTION-2}$. This algorithm is executed when a node experiences severe hotspot conditions without any non-hotspot neighbors. This algorithm not only suppresses new route creation but also throttles best effort TCP flows traversing the node in an attempt to reduce the load using rate control mechanisms discussed in [6]. TCP flows are bandwidth hungry and unless controlled can easily occupy all remaining wireless medium bandwidth. Throttling TCP rates locally in this manner does not necessarily hurt TCP sessions but can effectively relieve congestion bottlenecks. Users and operators are free to introduce other schemes to relieve congestion conditions. One simple policy is dropping TCP packets at bottleneck nodes.

HMP attacks the congestion at the point of congestion (POC) as opposed to a traditional end-to-end approach. Although congestion is an end-to-end issue where it is detected and controlled (e.g., in the case of TCP), traditional remedies for end-to-end congestion control are not effective in mobile ad hoc networks. In fact, such traditional control mechanisms may limit the utilization of the wireless medium that is constrained by hotspots. We argue that we can avoid such shortcomings if we tackle the problem at the point of congestion rather than responding on end-to-end basis.

4.3 Energy Conservation

Mobile ad hoc networks are essentially energy-limited networks and are likely to be comprised of heterogeneous nodes with diverse energy constraints. Some mobile devices will have large energy reserves in comparison to others. There exist various energy-aware power-conserving protocols for mobile ad hoc networks [20]. The common objective these protocols lie in conserving energy as much as possible to prolong the lifetime of the network or extend the lifetime of individual nodes.

Although energy conservation is not a primary function of HMP, the protocol provides a simple mechanism to conserve energy through its status declaration mechanism. A node with limited energy reserves can declare itself a hotspot by setting its status to Y_{ENERGY} or R_{ENERGY} when its energy reserves are marginally or critically low, respectively. The triggering thresholds are $P_{YELLOW-THRESH}$ and $P_{RED-THRESH}$. In our current implementation, $P_{YELLOW-THRESH}$ is set to 50% of node's initial (or maximum) energy reserves and $P_{RED-THRESH}$ is fixed at 1.00 joule. The latter value represents the amount of energy needed for a node to sustain a CBR flow for approximately 300 packets in most of our simulation sets. However, we note that operators and users are free to set these values according to their own needs, based on the characteristics of the targeted network. A node with energy concerns is acknowledged by neighboring nodes and new route creation through the node is avoided if possible. On the other hand, a node with critical energy (i.e., R_{ENERGY} status) immediately relinquishes its role as a router and functions strictly as an end host in order to conserve energy (maximize its lifetime) unless it is identified as the only intermediate node between two communicating end hosts.

5   Performance Evaluation

In what follows, we evaluate HMP through simulation and discuss the performance improvements that the protocol offers. Simulation metrics such as packet delivery ratio, packet loss, throughput, end-to-end delay, per-hop delays, and energy consumption are used in our evaluation. We also discuss the impact of various parameters on the performance of HMP.

In the initial part of the evaluation we use the AODV [1] [8] routing protocol with HMP, and in the latter part, DSR [4] with HMP. We implemented HMP using the ns-2 simulator and its wireless extension. The HMP implementation includes monitoring modules, measurement mechanisms, an NST module, and the HMP algorithms discussed in Section 4. The simulated network size is 1200 meters by 1200 meters where 100 mobile nodes create 10 TCP and 30 CBR/UDP flows that arbitrarily last for 60 to 280 seconds. Moderate mobility is assumed with a pause time of 80 second using the random way point mobility model [1] [4] unless specified otherwise. All data packets are of fixed size of 128 bytes, each simulation run lasts for 300 seconds, and each data point represents an average of 5 simulation runs with the identical traffic model but different mobility scenarios. Each mobile node has a transmission range of 250 meters and shares a 2 Mbps radio channel with its neighboring nodes. The simulations also include a two-ray ground reflection model, finite energy module, and IEEE 802.11 MAC protocol. Throughout the evaluation section we use the terms 'HMP system' and 'baseline system' to refer to wireless ad-hoc networks with and without the HMP mechanisms, respectively.

5.1   Hotspot Detection

Accurate and timely hotspot detection is one of most crucial aspect of HMP. To determine hotspots, the protocol relies on MAC-delay measurements, packet loss detection in RTS-CTS-DATA-ACK exchanges, buffer occupancy, and residual node energy. Among the measurements we have observed that the MAC-delay measurement is the most useful since a hotspot always manifest increased delays in the RTS-CTS-DATA-ACK cycle. Surprisingly, relying solely on the buffer occupancy is rather inaccurate. We often witnessed that hotspot conditions are created without any buffer occupancy problems. Such events are due to excessive contention among neighboring nodes and not buffer overflow. Therefore, in order to minimize the margin of error in hotspot detection, we utilize both buffer information and MAC-delay measurements together with some other additional system parameters discussed later.

Figure 7 shows a typical trace of the MAC-delay measurement of a node. The x-axis represents the simulation time and y-axis represents the MAC-delay measurements of a randomly selected mobile node. As shown in the figure, MAC-delay measurements continuously fluctuate throughout the simulation. Spikes in the delay trace typically represent congested conditions, while zero delay measurements are observed when the node is not participating in the RTS-CTS-DATA-ACK activity. Note that detection of a hotspot is dependent on two key parameters: (i) MAC-delay threshold (i.e., denoted by cong_thresh), which determines when a packet is considered a delayed packet; and (ii) num_thresh, which determines when a node is considered a hotspot. Specifically, a node is considered a hotspot when the measured MAC-delay measurements exceed a predetermined threshold (i.e., cong_thresh) for more than num_thresh times consecutively. These two parameters have an impact on how many hotspots are detected by HMP. When cong_thresh and num_thresh are configured as large values, HMP is too conservative and only detects a small number of hotspots rendering the protocol to be less effective against moderate congestion. In contrast, when cong_thresh and num_thresh are configured with small values, HMP is aggressive and detects too many hotspots too hastily. Therefore, the appropriate choice of these parameters is important for HMP to function properly. The use of the num_thresh parameter also prevents HMP from premature detection of a hotspot when experiencing a momentary increase in the MAC-delay measurement. It was observed that the MAC-delay measurements intermittently "spike" without any noticeable congestion conditions (e.g., during rerouting). To avoid reacting to such transient behavior and to increase the accuracy of hotspot detection, HMP marks a node as a hotspot, if and only if, the MAC-delay measurements are violated (i.e., exceeds cong_thresh) more than num_thresh times 'consecutively'. Currently, cong_thresh is set to 20 msec and num_thresh is set to 4. In Section 5.5, we evaluate a number of different configurations of the protocol based on these parameters and study the sensitivity of the parameter settings to HMP's ability to efficiently and accurately detect and mitigate hotspots in MANETs.

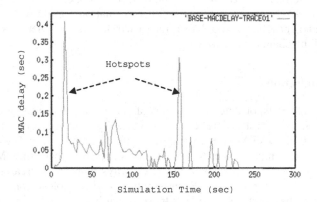

Fig. 7. Trace of MAC-delay Measurements

5.2   Throughput Analysis

We first observe how the HMP system performs in comparison to the baseline system in terms of the packet delivery ratio (PDR). Figure 8 shows a comparison of the packet delivery ratio against increasing load for two different HMP system configurations (discussed below) and the baseline system. The two HMP systems are simply called HMP-P and HMP-R where HMP-R is more aggressive than HMP-P in its route suppression mechanism. HMP-P stands for HMP-POC where HMP mechanisms are executed only at points of congestion (POC). On the other hand, HMP-R represents HMP-Regional signifying the regional execution of hotspot mitigation algorithms. In other words, when a hotspot is detected HMP-P executes hotspot mitigation algorithms at the point of hotspots whereas HMP-R executes its mechanisms across a hotspot region. A node belongs to a hotspot region if it is a hotspot or it is an immediate neighbor of a hotspot. We note that both enough_nh_neighbor and path_indicator are always considered in all hotspot mitigation decisions.

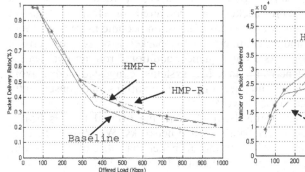
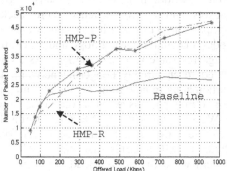

Fig. 8. Comparison of PDR against network load

Fig. 9. Number of Data Packets Delivered

As observed in Figure 8, HMP-P and HMP-R have little impact on lightly loaded networks, (e.g., below 100 Kbps). This is because the baseline system already achieves more than 90 % PDR and HMP has little room to make any improvements. However, as the offered load increases, and congestion builds up, HMP begins to provide improvements, as shown in the figure. Both HMP-P and HMP-R provide substantial improvements in the PDR. Specifically, HMP-P and HMP-R provide up to a 43% and 46% increase in the packet delivery ratio when compared to the baseline system performance. From Figure 8, we also observe the behavior of HMP-R is more aggressive than that of HMP-P. When the offered load is moderately high, HMP-R often outperforms HMP-P and the baseline systems but becomes less effective when the offered load is light, (e.g., below 250 Kbps). The performance of HMP-R varies with different loads, as shown in Figure 8. We conclude that HMP-R is too aggressive for lightly loaded networks rendering it only useful in heavily loaded networks.

Further analysis of the HMP-P, HMP-R and baseline systems can be seen by inspecting the number of delivered packets, as shown in Figure 9. One interesting observation is that number of packets delivered by the baseline system levels-off around 2.3 x 10^4 delivered packets but in the HMP-P and HMP-R systems the number of delivered packets continuously increases with increasing offered load. There are two major reasons for this improvement. First, HMP creates routes through non-congested nodes whenever possible allowing networks to utilize more distributed routes in the network even if these routes are not the shortest path. Creating routes at non-hotspot nodes helps traversing flows to encounter fewer problems, and as consequence, more packets are delivered. Secondly, HMP generates less routing overhead through suppression executed at hotspots. Many hotspot nodes rebroadcast route request packets and these route request packets often flood large areas of the network or even the entire network. However, many of these rebroadcast route request packets are lost before reaching destination nodes. We observed that a considerable amount of route request packets are just wasted in the network without successful route creation in heavily loaded networks.

In the HMP systems, routing packets (i.e., route request) are pre-filtered at hotspot nodes/regions. This not only prevents new routes being created through hotspots but also helps reduces the number of 'wasted' new route requested packets (that rely on broadcast/flooding), which are likely to be lost. This opens up room for more data packets and as consequence more packets are delivered in HMP systems in comparison to the baseline system. Moreover, as congestion become more sever more nodes encounter packet loss and often interpret this packet loss as route errors, triggering route recovery routines. As a consequence, additional routing overhead is added to an already congested network. In HMP systems, congested nodes avoid participating in new route creation to mitigate congested conditions, and consequently less routing packets are observed in the network.

We observe that HMP-R outperforms HMP-P when the offered load is heavy. However, HMP-R is too aggressive for lightly loaded networks. We observe that the PDR of HMP-R is less than that of HMP-P and no better than that of the baseline system when the offered load is less than 150 Kbps. However, both HMP systems outperform the baseline system. Hereafter, we refer to HMP-P when we discuss HMP unless specified otherwise.

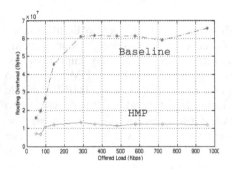

Fig. 10. Comparison of Routing Overhead

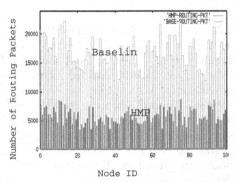

Fig. 11. Routing Overhead Compared

5.3   Routing Overhead Analysis

Figure 10 shows the routing overhead of the HMP and baseline systems accumulated over 300 seconds of simulation. The advantage of the HMP system over the baseline system in terms of the routing overhead is shown in the figure. It is observed that the HMP system provides up to a 75.7 % reduction in the routing overhead over the baseline system because of better route selection and routing packet suppression in hotspot regions. For example, when the offered load is 722 Kbps, the baseline system generates approximately 59 x 10^6 bytes of routing overhead while the HMP system only generates 13.3 x 10^6 bytes of routing overhead.

Figure 11 compares the total number of routing packets transported by the HMP and baseline systems when the offered load is 577 Kbps. As expected there is a substantial difference between the two systems. It is observed that the HMP system always carries less routing load in comparison to the baseline system. This implies that HMP is not over-suppressing routes because if connectivity were limited, the number of route request packets would quickly increase and be reflected in the routing overhead. Therefore, it is safe to say that HMP provides sufficient connectivity in all the simulated scenarios. The HMP system outperforms the baseline system in terms of the PDR, number of packet delivered, and routing overhead. These improvements are mainly due to effective hotspot mitigation through implicit route dispersal and suppression of new route request packets. HMP is prudent in route suppression decisions while ensuring sufficient connectivity when the configuration of the system (i.e., cong_thresh, num_thresh, enough_nh_neighbor and path_indicator) is enforced.

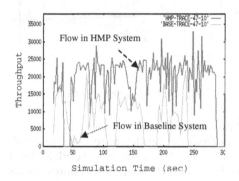

Fig. 12. Throughput Trace Comparisons

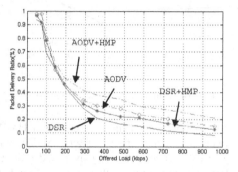

Fig. 13. Impact of HMP on DSR and AODV

Next, we compare throughput traces of a flow in the two systems. Figure 12 shows a monitored flow between node 47 and node 10. The monitored flow in the HMP system shows substantial improvements over the baseline system. More importantly, it is observed that the monitored flow traverses different routes in the two systems. Specifically, flow 47-10 traverses nodes 16, 18, 43, 51, 78 and 83 in the baseline system and traverses 16, 21, 38, 65, 78 and 83 in HMP system, during the monitored period of 50 seconds. Nodes 18 and 43 are identified as hotspots and consequently flow 47-10 avoided these two hotspots when using HMP. Such characteristics are consistently observed throughout the simulation, and as a consequence, the HMP system provides better throughput performance.

The previous evaluation of HMP considered AODV routing only. In what follows, we describe how HMP performs with DSR [4]. First, we observe the PDR traces of the baseline DSR system in comparison to the HMP+DSR system. Figure 13 shows the PDR trace for increasing offered load with moderate mobility for these systems. The figure also includes the PDR trace for the baseline AODV system and the AODV+HMP system (taken from Section 5.2) for comparison purposes.

As expected, the DSR+HMP system provides improvements over the baseline DSR system. From Figure 13, it is observed that all the systems demonstrate similar performances under lightly loaded conditions but they begin to diverge as the offered load increases. One interesting observation is that DSR and AODV display different performances against increasing offered load. They show similar results only in lightly loaded conditions. As congestion intensifies AODV begins to outperform DSR. This observation coincides with the results reported in [1]. Moreover, the HMP is seen to be more effective with AODV than DSR. The main reason for this is related to the amount of routing load reduction.

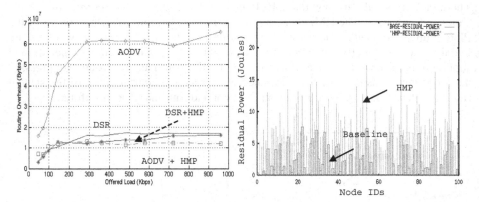

Fig. 14. Routing Overhead Compared   **Fig. 15.** Residual Energy Compared

It is observed from Figure 14 that HMP provides substantial reductions in routing overheads when operating with AODV but demonstrates different results with DSR. The difference in routing overhead reduction is directly reflected in the PDR traces (or when we compare the number of packets delivered). HMP provides improvements with AODV mainly through the reduction in the routing overhead, and route diversions away from hotspots. In contrast, in the DSR system the dominant reason for the improvement is mainly due to route diversion from hotspots. It is also observed that DSR's aggressive use of route-cache limits its performance. Under harsh conditions (i.e., increased mobility, increased load), it is observed that DSR maintains stale routes, generating a large amount of route-error messages. This observation is also reported in [1]. HMP successfully routes traffic through non-hotspot nodes but DSR's route-optimization scheme [4] utilizes cached routes, which often introduce new hotspots. Figure 14 reflects this observation. The bottom line is that HMP can provide improvements for both AODV and DSR.

5.4   Energy Analysis

We note that energy consumption is concentrated in hotspot regions and nodes. Figure 15 shows measurements of residual energy for nodes at the end of the simulation run. We assign a uniform energy of 25 joules to each node and conducted simulation for 100 seconds with AODV. The x-axis represents node IDs and y-axis represents the residual energy in joules. Bars represent the residual energy measurements of baseline system and the superimposed impulses represent the corresponding measurements of the HMP system. As shown in the plot, the energy conservation provided by HMP for nodes in hotspot regions is significant. The baseline system exhibits 21 energy-depleted nodes (i.e., remaining energy is less than 0.01 joule such that it can no longer participate in communications) while there is not even one depleted node in the HMP system at $t = 100$ sec. Note that HMP improves packet delivery ratio, delay measurements, and reduces routing overheads, while providing energy conservation in hotspot regions.

5.5 Parameterization Sensitivity

In what follows, we describe four different HMP system configurations to study the responsiveness of the protocol to detect and mitigate hotspots. Four key parameters govern the HMP system control mechanisms; these are, cong_thresh, num_thresh, enough_nh_neighbor and path_indicator. For example, if the cong_thresh value is too small HMP may become too aggressive and declare too many hotspots. A small increase in the MAC-delay threshold measurement (or jitter) may falsely be recognized as congestion with many nodes being claimed as hotspots. In contrast, if the cong_thresh value is too large HMP may not identify any hotspots in the network and relegate itself to the baseline system. The second parameter num_thresh is used to prevent HMP from reacting to transient behavior. A momentary increase in the MAC-delay measurement and buffer occupancy are not necessarily a product of congestion or excessive contention. Delay may be observed for a very short period due to the rerouting of flows or a small burst of route query packets. Reacting to such transitory phenomenon is not beneficial because real hotspots cannot be distinguished from transient events. The third parameter is the path_indicator, which indicate that insufficient conditions exist for new route suppression. Nodes receiving packets with this indicator set know that at least one preceding node explicitly requested 'no new-route-suppression'. This is a valuable HMP feature because it provides a safeguard against potential over-suppression of new route creation that may result in limited connectivity. The fourth parameter is the enough_nh_neighbor that prevents the HMP algorithm from being too aggressive.

Figure 16 shows the PDR traces of the four different HMP systems under discussion. HMP-P and HMP-R are described in Section 5.2 while HMP-C and HMP-A represent HMP-Conservative and HMP-Aggressive HMP system configurations, respectively. HMP-A is literally an aggressive version of HMP-P that quickly determines hotspots (i.e., num_thresh = 3, cong_thresh = 10 msec, enough_nh_neighbor = 4) and without utilization of the path_indicator. HMP-A is equally effective as HMP-P when the network is heavily loaded but results in limited connectivity when lightly loaded. As a consequence of its aggressiveness, HMP-A supports only 91 % PDR even when the offered load is only 72 Kbps. At the slightest indication of congestion, HMP-A suppresses new route creations and limited connectivity among mobile nodes.

HMP-C is a conservative version of HMP-P that utilizes the path_indicator and configures num_thresh = 8, cong_thresh = 100 msec, enough_nh_neighbor = 8. As shown in Figure 16, HMP-C closely resembles the baseline system with slight improvements. In other words, if the HMP protocol is too aggressive it is deemed to limit connectivity. On the other hand, if HMP is too conservative, it rarely detects hotspots and degrades to the baseline system performance.

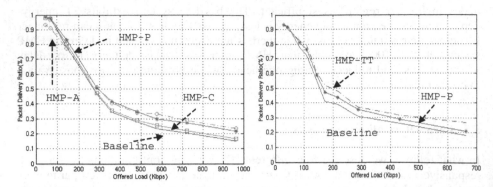

Fig. 16. PDR Trace of HMP-A, HMP-C, HMP-P and Baseline System Compared

Fig. 17. PDR of HMP-P, HMP-TT and Baseline system Compared

As mentioned in Section 2.2 HMP relies on TCP throttling when severe congestion persists. As observed in Figure 17, HMP-TT (for HMP-TCP-Throttle) can selectively throttle TCP flows to relieve hotspots. TCP throttling is meaningful in the presence of congestion since TCP flows are typically transported as a best effort service where traffic rates are often transparent to higher layers (i.e., applications). In contrast, CBR/UDP traffic often requires better than best effort service. However, details on these issues are not immediately related to HMP and considered outside the scope of our initial research.

6 Conclusion

In this paper, we have presented a protocol that works with existing best effort routing protocols to mitigate hotspots in mobile ad hoc networks. We have demonstrated through simulation that hotspots exist in mobile ad hoc networks and can limit the performance of these networks. HMP tackles the congestion problem at the point of congestion as opposed to traditional end-to-end approaches. We argue that traditional remedies such as end-to-end congestion control are often not effective in mobile ad hoc networks and can limit the utilization of the wireless network in the face of hotspots. We are currently working on a testbed implementation of HMP and studying a more comprehensive set of simulation scenarios with larger numbers of nodes, a wider variety of offered traffic, and other routing schemes, (e.g., proactive schemes).

Acknowledgements. This work is supported in part by the Army Research Office (ARO) under Award DAAD19-99-1-0287 and with support from COMET Group industrial sponsors. The authors would like to thank Jiyoung Cho for her comments on this paper.

References

1. Samir R. Das, Charles E. Perkins, and Elizabeth M. Royer. "Performance Comparison of Two On-demand Routing Protocols for Ad Hoc Networks." Proceedings of the IEEE Conference on Computer Communications (INFOCOM), Tel Aviv, Israel, March 2000
2. MANET Working Group, http://www.ietf.org/html.charters/manet-charter.html
3. S.B Lee, G.S. Ahn, and A.T. Campbell, "Improving UDP and TCP Performance in Mobile Ad Hoc Networks with INSIGNIA", June 2001, IEEE Communication Magazine.
4. David B. Johnson, David A. Maltz, and Josh Broch. "DSR: The Dynamic Source Routing Protocol for Multi-Hop Wireless Ad Hoc Networks", in Ad Hoc Networking, edited by Charles E. Perkins, Chapter 5, pp. 139-172, Addison-Wesley, 2001
5. V. Park and S. Corson "A Highly Adaptive Distributed Routing Algorithm for Mobile Wireless Networks, Proc. IEEE Infocom 1997, Kobe, Japan
6. G.S. Ahn, A.T. Campbell, A. Veres and L-H Sun, "SWAN: Service Differentiation in Stateless Wireless Ad Hoc Networks", Proc. IEEE Infocom 2002, New York, New York, June 2002
7. S.J. Lee and M. Gerla "Dynamic Load-Aware Routing in Ad hoc Networks" Proceedings of IEEE ICC 2001, Helsinki, Finland, June 2001
8. C. Perkins and E. Royer. "Ad hoc On-Demand Distance Vector Routing." Proc. of the 2nd IEEE Workshop on Mobile Computing Systems and Applications, New Orleans, LA, February 1999, pp. 90–100
9. The NS-2 Simulator, http://www.isi.edu/nsnam/
10. Chunhung Richard Lin, "On-demand QoS Routing in Multihop Mobile Networks", Proc. IEEE Infocom 2001, Anchorage, April 22–26, 2001
11. S. Chen and K. Nahrstedt, "Distributed Quality of Service Routing in Ad Hoc Networks", IEEE Journal on Selected Areas in Communications", vol. 17, No. 8, Aug 1999.
12. C. R. Lin and C-C Liu, "On-Demand QoS Routing for Mobile Ad Hoc Networks", IEEE International Conference on Networks (ICON'00), September 5–8, 2000, Singapore
13. W.H. Liao, Y.C. Tseng, S.L. Wang, and J.P. Sheu, "A Multi-path QoS Routing Protocol in a Wireless Mobile Ad Hoc Network," Telecommunication Systems Vol. 19, No. 3-4, pp. 329–347, 2002
14. S. Guo and O.W. Yang, " Performance of Backup Source Routing in mobile ad hoc networks", in Proc. 2002 IEEE Wireless Networking Conference
15. A. Nasipuri and S. Das, "On-demand multipath routing for mobile ad hoc networks," in Proc. IEEE ICCCN '99, Oct. 1999
16. M.R. Pearlman, Z.J. Haas, P. Scholander, and S.S. Tabrizi, "Alternate Path Routing in Mobile Ad Hoc Networks," IEEE MILCOM'2000, Los Angeles, CA, October 22-25, 2000
17. M. Garey and D. Johnson, Computer and Intractability: A Guide to Theory of NP-Completeness: W.H. Freeman, 1979
18. D. Johnson, D. Maltz, Y-C Hu and J. Jetcheva, "The Dynamic Source Routing Protocol for Mobile Ad'Hoc Networks", Internet Draft, draft-ietf-manet-dsr-07.txt, work in progress, Feb 2002.
19. C. Perkins, E. Royer and S. Das, "Ad Hoc On-demand Distance Vector Routing", Internet Draft, draft-ietf-manet-aodv-12.txt, work in progress Nov 2002.
20. Christine E. Price, Krishna M. Sivalingam, Prathima Agarwal and Jyh-Cheng Chen, "A Survey of Energy Efficient Network Protocols for Wireless and Mobile Networks", in ACM/Baltzer Journal on Wireless Networks, vol. 7, No. 4, pp. 343–358, 2001

VI Availability and Dependability

Failure Insensitive Routing for Ensuring Service Availability*

Srihari Nelakuditi[1], Sanghwan Lee[2], Yinzhe Yu[2], and Zhi-Li Zhang[2]

[1] Dept. of Computer Science & Engineering,
University of South Carolina,
Columbia, SC 29201, USA
srihari@cse.sc.edu

[2] Dept. of Computer Science & Engineering,
University of Minnesota,
Minneapolis, MN 55414, USA
{sanghwan,yyu,zhzhang}@cs.umn.edu

Abstract. Intra-domain routing protocols employed in the Internet route around failed links by having routers detect adjacent link failures, exchange link state changes, and recompute their routing tables. Due to several delays in detection, propagation and recomputation, it may take tens of seconds to minutes after a link failure to resume forwarding of packets to the affected destinations. This discontinuity in destination reachability adversely affects the quality of continuous media applications such as Voice over IP. Moreover, the resulting service unavailability for even a short duration could be catastrophic in the world of e-commerce. Though careful tuning of the various parameters of the routing protocols can accelerate convergence, it may cause instability when the majority of the failures are transient. To improve the failure resiliency without jeopardizing the routing stability, we propose a *local rerouting* based approach called *failure insensitive routing*. Under this approach, upon a link failure, adjacent router *suppresses* global updating and instead initiates local rerouting. All other routers *infer* potential link failures from the packet's incoming interface, *precompute* interface specific forwarding tables and route around failed links *without explicit* link state updates. We demonstrate that the proposed approach provides higher service availability than the existing routing schemes.

1 Introduction

Link state routing protocols such as OSPF and IS-IS are the most widely used protocols for intra-domain routing in today's Internet. Using these protocols, routers exchange changes in link state, recompute their routing tables, and thus respond to link and node failures in the network by routing around them. However, several recent studies [1,5,7] have reported that rerouting after a link failure takes tens of seconds to minutes. During

---

* This work is partly supported by National Science Foundation Grants CAREER Award ANI-9734428, ANI-0073819, and ITR ANI-0085824. Any opinions, findings, and conclusions or recommendations expressed in this paper are those of the authors and do not necessarily reflect the views of the National Science Foundation.

K. Jeffay, I. Stoica, and K. Wehrle (Eds.): IWQoS 2003, LNCS 2707, pp. 287–304, 2003.

this period, some destinations would be unreachable and the corresponding services unavailable. This discontinuity in routing adversely affects the quality of continuous media applications such as Voice over IP. Furthermore, downtime of even a few seconds could significantly impact the reputation and the profitability of a company in the world of e-commerce. Moreover, it has been observed [7] that link failures are fairly common in the day to day operation of a network due to various causes such as maintenance, faulty interfaces, and accidental fiber cuts. Hence, there is a growing demand for ensuring destination reachability and thus service continuity even in the presence of link failures.

There have been some modifications proposed [1,2] for accelerating the convergence of link state routing protocols. But the recipe involves tuning several delays associated with link failure detection, link state propagation and routing table recomputation. Furthermore, it is not a suitable solution for handling transient failures. It has been found [7] that majority of the link failures are short-lived with around half of the failures lasting less than a minute. In such a scenario, it is not prudent to disseminate these link state changes globally and recompute routing tables at each router in the network. Instead, it is much more appropriate to perform local rerouting and trigger global updating and recomputation only if the link failure persists for a longer duration. Such a local rerouting approach can recover promptly from failures trading off optimality of routing for continuity of forwarding. Our objective is to devise a stable and robust routing scheme that ensures continuous loop-free forwarding of packets to their destinations regardless of the various delays in link state propagation and routing table recomputation.

We propose a local rerouting based approach for failure resiliency which we refer to as *failure insensitive routing* (FIR). Under FIR, when a link fails, adjacent nodes suppress global updating and instead initiate local rerouting of packets that were to be forwarded through the failed link. Though other nodes are not explicitly notified of the failure, they *infer* it from the packet's *flight*. When a packet arrives at a node through an *unusual* interface (through which it would never arrive had there been no failure), corresponding potential failures can be inferred and the next hop chosen avoiding those links. This way under FIR, the next hop for a packet is determined based on not only the destination address but also the incoming interface. Note that such *interface specific forwarding* is very much feasible with current router architectures as they anyway maintain a forwarding table at each line card of an interface for lookup efficiency. These interface specific forwarding tables can be *precomputed* since inferences about the link failures can be made in advance. Thus with the FIR approach, when a link fails, only the nodes adjacent to it locally reroute packets to the affected destinations and all the other nodes simply forward packets according to their precomputed interface specific forwarding tables without being explicitly aware of the failure. Once the failed link comes up again, original forwarding tables are locally restored and forwarding resumes over the recovered link as if nothing ever happened. This approach decouples destination reachability and routing stability by handling transient failures locally and notifying only persistent failures globally. Essentially with FIR, in the presence of link failures, packets get locally rerouted (possibly along suboptimal paths) without getting caught in a loop or dropped till the new shortest paths are globally recomputed.

There are several benefits in employing FIR. First, it can be deployed without altering the destination based forwarding paradigm used in the current Internet. Only the traditional interface independent routing table computation algorithm needs to be replaced with an FIR algorithm for computing interface dependent forwarding tables. Second, reachability of destinations does not depend on tuning of the various parameters associated with link failure propagation and routing table recomputation. Thus FIR improves the service availability without jeopardizing the routing stability. Third, under FIR approach local rerouting happens only during the time a link failure is suppressed, i.e., not reflected globally. But once all the routers have the same consistent view of the network, forwarding under FIR would be no different from traditional routing. So FIR can be used in conjunction with any other mechanism for engineering traffic. Finally, FIR increases network reliability and obviates the need for expensive and complex layer 2 protection schemes. Essentially, the FIR approach is about preparing for failures instead of reacting to them.

We make the following contributions in this paper. We propose a mechanism for facilitating prompt local rerouting. We present an efficient algorithm that computes interface specific forwarding tables for dealing with single link failures in $O(|\mathcal{E}| \log^2 |\mathcal{V}|)$ time, where $\mathcal{V}$ is the set of nodes and $\mathcal{E}$ is the set of edges. We demonstrate that by preparing for single link failures, most of the simultaneous failures can also be handled and the service availability can be improved by an order of magnitude. We describe an incremental algorithm for forwarding table computation that requires $O(D^2|\mathcal{V}|)$ space, where D is the network diameter, for remembering the intermediate steps of the previous computation but takes on average less than $O(|\mathcal{E}| \log |\mathcal{V}|)$ time. We argue that with its resiliency and stability, FIR is a better alternative to the existing routing schemes.

The rest of the paper is organized as follows. Section 2 introduces our FIR approach for failure resiliency. Efficient algorithms for computing interface specific forwarding tables are described in Section 3. Section 4 presents the results of our evaluation of the performance of FIR. The related work is discussed in Section 5. Finally, Section 6 concludes the paper.

2   Failure Insensitive Routing

The fundamental issue in designing a local rerouting scheme is the avoidance of forwarding loops. A straightforward local recomputation of new shortest paths without the failed link by the adjacent node could result in a loop since other nodes are not aware of the failure and their routing tables do not reflect the failure. We propose to address this looping problem by forwarding a packet based on its incoming interface. This enables a router to *infer* failures when a packet arrives through an *unusual* interface due to local rerouting. These inferences about link failures can be made in advance and interface specific forwarding tables can be *precomputed* avoiding the potentially failed links. This way when a link fails, only the adjacent nodes reroute packets that were to be forwarded through the failed link. All other nodes simply forward packets according to their precomputed interface specific forwarding tables without being explicitly aware of the failure. We refer to this approach as *failure insensitive routing* (FIR). In the following, using an example topology, we illustrate how packets get forwarded under FIR and how these forwarding tables are computed.

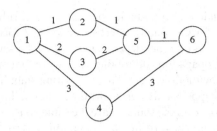

Fig. 1. Topology used for the illustration of the FIR approach

2.1 Forwarding under FIR

Consider the topology shown in Figure 1 where each link is labeled with its weight. The corresponding shortest path routing entries at each node to destination node 6 are shown in Figure 2. First, we point out the problem with the conventional routing in case of a link failure. Suppose link 2–5 is down. When node 2 recomputes its routing table, it will have 1 as the next hop to reach 6 as shown in Figure 2. If only node 2 recomputes its entries while others are not notified or still in the process of recomputing their entries, then packets from 1 to 6 get forwarded back and forth between nodes 2 and 1. This shows that using conventional forwarding tables, local rerouting is not viable as it causes forwarding loops.

node	1	2	3	4	5	node	1	2	3	4	5
next	2	5	5	6	6	next hop	2	1	5	6	6

Fig. 2. Routing entries: *before* and *after* local recomputation by node 2

Under FIR, forwarding loops are avoided by inferring link failures from the packet's incoming interface. When a packet with destination 6 arrives at 1 from 2, node 1 can sense that some link must have failed. Otherwise, based on shortest path routing, node 2 should never forward to 1, a packet destined for 6. Node 2 would forward packets for 6 to node 1 if the link 2–5 is down. Same is true even when 5–6 is down. So when a packet for 6 arrives at 1 from 2, node 1 can infer that one or both of these links are down. Since node 1 is not explicitly notified of the failures, it can ensure that the packet reaches 6 by forwarding it to 4 avoiding both the potentially failed links 2–5 and 5–6. That is why in Figure 3, a packet arriving at node 1 with destination 6 through neighbor node 2 is forwarded to 4 while it is forwarded to 2 if it arrives through the other two neighbors. Such interface specific forwarding makes it possible to perform local rerouting.

Let us again consider the case of link 2–5 going down. Node 2 recomputes its forwarding table entries as shown in Figure 3. So a packet from 2 to 6 takes the route 2→1→4→6 when the link 2–5 is down. Since node 1 is not aware of the failure, a packet from 1 to 6 gets forwarded to 2 which reroutes it back to 1. Node 1 then forwards the

node	1			2		3		4		5		node	1			2		3		4		5	
prev	2	3	4	1	5	1	5	1	6	2	3	6	prev	2	3	4	1	5	1	5	1	6	2	3	6
next	4	2	2	5	1	5	1	6	-	6	6	-	next	4	2	2	1	-	5	1	6	-	6	6	-

Fig. 3. Interface specific forwarding entries: *before* and *after* local recomputation by node 2

packet to 4 according to its entry at the interface with previous hop 2. This way, packets from 1 to 6 traverse the path $1\to2\to1\to4\to6$. Note that though node 1 appears twice in the path, it doesn't constitute a loop. With interface specific forwarding, a packet would loop only if it traverses the same link in the same direction twice. Thus using interface specific forwarding tables, FIR avoids looping and provides local rerouting.

It should be noted that FIR adheres to conventional destination based forwarding paradigm though it has different forwarding table at each interface. While FIR requires that the next hop for a packet is determined based on its previous hop, it is very much feasible with the current router architectures as they anyway maintain a forwarding table at each line card of an interface for lookup efficiency. The only deviation is that unlike in the current routers with the same forwarding table at each interface, with the FIR approach these tables are different. However, the forwarding process remains the same — when a packet arrives at an incoming interface, the corresponding forwarding table is looked up to determine the next hop and the outgoing interface.

2.2   Forwarding Table Computation

The forwarding process under FIR is essentially the same as it is under the conventional routing. The key difference is in the way interface specific forwarding tables are computed. The computation of the forwarding table entries of an interface involves identifying a set of links whose individual or combined failure causes a packet to arrive at the node through that interface. We refer to these links as *key links* and denote by $\mathcal{K}^d_{j\to i}$ the set of links which when one or more down cause packets with destination d to arrive at node i from node j. Note that this key link set is empty, i.e., $\mathcal{K}^d_{j\to i} = \emptyset$ if node i is anyway the next hop along the shortest path from j to d without any link failures. For the topology in 1, $\mathcal{K}^6_{2\to1} = \{2\text{--}5, 5\text{--}6\}$ and $\mathcal{K}^6_{3\to1} = \{3\text{--}5\}$ while $\mathcal{K}^6_{1\to2} = \emptyset$ as explained below.

Consider the node 1. The next hop along the shortest path from node 1 to reach 6 is 2, i.e., $\mathcal{K}^6_{1\to2} = \emptyset$. So if all the links are up, node 1 should never receive from 2 a packet destined for 6. However, if the link 2–5 is down, node 2 would forward packets with destination 6 to node 1. Similarly when the link 5–6 is down, packets from 5 to 6 would traverse the path $5\to2\to1\to4\to6$. So from the arrival of a packet with destination 6 from neighbor node 2, node 1 can infer that one or both of the links 2–5 and 5–6 are down, i.e., $\mathcal{K}^6_{2\to1} = \{2\text{--}5, 5\text{--}6\}$. Similarly, node 1 would receive a packet for the destination 6 through 3 when the link 3–5 is down. In the other case when link 5–6 is down, packets arrive at node 1 through 2 and not through 3 since from 5 to 6 the (recomputed) shortest path would be $5 \rightarrow 2 \rightarrow 1 \rightarrow 4 \rightarrow 6$. Hence from arrival of packets with destination 6 through node 3, node 1 infers that only link 3–5 is down, i.e., $\mathcal{K}^6_{3 \rightarrow 1} = \{3\text{–}5\}$.

	$2 \rightarrow 1$				
dest	2	3	4	5	6
next hops	-	3	4	3	4

	$3 \rightarrow 1$				
dest	2	3	4	5	6
next hops	2	-	4	2	2

	$4 \rightarrow 1$				
dest	2	3	4	5	6
next hops	2	3	-	2	2

Fig. 4. Forwarding tables at node 1

Once the key links are determined, it is straightforward to compute the interface specific forwarding tables. Let $\mathcal{E}$ be the set of all links in the network. Suppose $\mathcal{R}^d_i(\mathcal{X})$ represents the set of next hops from i to d given the set of links $\mathcal{X}$. Let $\mathcal{F}^d_{j \rightarrow i}$ denote the forwarding table entry, i.e., the set of next hops to d for packets arriving at i through the interface associated with neighbor j. This entry can be computed using Dijkstra's Shortest Path First (SPF) algorithm after excluding the links in the set $\mathcal{K}^d_{j \rightarrow i}$ from the set of all links $\mathcal{E}$. Thus,

$$\mathcal{F}^d_{j \rightarrow i} = \mathcal{R}^d_i(\mathcal{E} \setminus \mathcal{K}^d_{j \rightarrow i})$$

The forwarding tables corresponding to node 1 of Figure 1 are shown in Figure 4. Given that $\mathcal{K}^6_{2 \rightarrow 1} = \{2\text{–}5, 5\text{–}6\}$, the shortest path from 1 to 6 without those links be $1 \rightarrow 4 \rightarrow 6$. Therefore, packets destined for 6 arriving at 1 through 2 are forwarded to next hop 4. On the other hand, the next hop for packets to destination 5 arriving through 2 is set to 3 since $\mathcal{K}^5_{2 \rightarrow 1} = \{2\text{–}5\}$. The other entries are also determined similarly. Once the forwarding tables are computed, packets arriving through an interface are forwarded in the usual manner by looking up the table corresponding to that interface.

We reiterate that these inferences about potential link failures are made *not on the fly* but in advance and forwarding tables are precomputed according to these inferences. Furthermore, packets are forwarded according to their destination addresses only. In other words, FIR does not require any changes to the existing forwarding plane, making it amenable for ready deployment.

2.3   Local Recomputation of Forwarding Tables

The forwarding tables computed as explained above help perform local rerouting without any global recomputation of routing and forwarding tables. Only the nodes adjacent to a failed link have to recompute their entries. However, if the local recomputation takes significant time, then there would not be substantial savings due to this approach over conventional global updating based approach. Fortunately, we do not have to compute these tables from scratch. It is possible to locally recompute the forwarding tables in negligible amount of time by maintaining what we refer to as *backwarding table* for each interface.

When an interface is down, its backwarding table can be used to reroute packets that were to be forwarded through that interface. The entries in this table, denoted by $\mathcal{B}^d_{i \rightarrow j}$,

1 → 2					
dest	2	3	4	5	6
back hops	3	4	3	3	3

1 → 3					
dest	2	3	4	5	6
back hops	4	2	-	4	4

1 → 4					
dest	2	3	4	5	6
back hops	-	-	2	-	-

Fig. 5. Backwarding tables at node 1

give the set of alternate next hops, referred to as *back hops*, from node i for forwarding a packet with destination d when the interface or the link to the usual next hop node j is down. The backwarding table entries can also be precomputed similar to forwarding table entries once the key links are identified as follows:

$$\mathcal{B}_{i \mapsto j}^{d} \Leftarrow \mathcal{R}_{i}^{d}(\mathcal{E} \setminus \mathcal{K}_{i \mapsto j}^{d} \setminus i\text{--}j)$$

Essentially we exclude all the links that would cause the packet to exit from the interface of i to j and also the link i–j itself in computing the back hops. When preparing for at most single link failures, this amounts to

$$\mathcal{B}_{i \mapsto j}^{d} \Leftarrow \mathcal{R}_{i}^{d}(\mathcal{E} \setminus i\text{--}j)$$

The backwarding table entries for node 1 of the topology in Figure 1 are shown in Figure 5. Let us look at the entries for the interface $1 \rightarrow 2$. It is clear that when the link 1–2 is down, packets to destinations 2, 5 and 6 be rerouted to 3 since the shortest path to these nodes without 1–2 is through 3. But, it may not be obvious why the next hops for destinations 3 and 4 are 4 and 3 respectively. Consider the entry of 3. The corresponding set of key links $\mathcal{K}_{1 \mapsto 2}^{3}$ is $\{1\text{--}3\}$, i.e., a packet with destination 3 is forwarded from 1 to 2 only if $\{1\text{--}3\}$ is down. So when $\{1\text{--}2\}$ is also down, the next best path is through 4. Similarly $\mathcal{B}_{1 \mapsto 2}^{4}$ is 3. Now let us turn our attention to the backwarding table in Figure 5 for the interface 1–4. According to these entries, when link 1–4 is down, packets to 4 get rerouted to 2 and packets to any other destination are simply discarded as they are not reachable. This is because packets to other destinations are forwarded to 4 only when certain other links are also down. For example, $\mathcal{K}_{1 \mapsto 4}^{6} = \{2\text{--}5, 5\text{--}6\}$ and when link 1–4 also fails, node 6 becomes unreachable from node 1.

By employing interface specific forwarding and backwarding tables, we can eliminate the delay due to any dynamic recomputation and reroute packets without any interruption even in the presence of link failures. The downside is that the deployment of backwarding tables requires changes to the forwarding plane. When an interface is down, the corresponding backwarding table needs to be looked up to reroute the packet through another interface. This necessitates change in the router architecture, the cost of which we are not in a position to assess. To avoid altering the forwarding plane, we propose to maintain the backwarding tables in the control plane and recompute the forwarding tables as follows. Suppose the failed link is i–k and the new forwarding tables are denoted by $\tilde{\mathcal{F}}$. Then the forwarding table entry of destination d for $j \rightarrow i$ interface, where $j \neq k$, is computed as follows:

$$\tilde{\mathcal{F}}_{j \mapsto i}^{d} = \begin{array}{l} \mathcal{F}_{j \mapsto i}^{d} \setminus k \cup \mathcal{B}_{i \mapsto k}^{d} \text{ if } k \in \mathcal{F}_{j \mapsto i}^{d} \\ \mathcal{F}_{j \mapsto i}^{d} \qquad\qquad \text{otherwise} \end{array}$$

The above expression takes into account the possibility of multiple next hops along equal cost paths to a destination. A simplified expression for single path routing would be

$$\tilde{\mathcal{F}}_{j\rightarrow i}^{d} = \frac{\mathcal{B}_{i\rightarrow k}^{d} \text{ if } \mathcal{F}_{j\rightarrow i}^{d} = k}{\mathcal{F}_{j\rightarrow i}^{d} \text{ otherwise}}$$

Essentially, only those entries in the forwarding tables that have k as the next hop are reset according to the backwarding table associated with k. Thus, using the backwarding tables, in case of an adjacent link failure, a node quickly recomputes the forwarding tables locally and promptly resumes forwarding.

2.4   Summary of the FIR Scheme

We now summarize the operation of the FIR scheme. Each node i under FIR maintains a forwarding table $\mathcal{F}_{j\rightarrow i}$ per each neighbor j, and a backwarding table $\mathcal{B}_{i\rightarrow j}$ per each neighbor j. $\mathcal{F}_{j\rightarrow i}$ is used to forward packets arriving at i through neighbor j. $\mathcal{B}_{i\rightarrow j}$ is needed for locally recomputing the forwarding tables of i when the link i–j is down.

Suppose the failure of the link i–j is detected by node i at time t_{down}. Then node i locally recomputes its forwarding tables and performs local rerouting of the packets that were to be forwarded to j. If the failure persists for a preset duration T_{down}, then a global link state update is triggered at $t_{down} + T_{down}$ and forwarding tables at all routers are recomputed. During the time period between t_{down} and $t_{down} + T_{down}$, the link failure update is said to be *suppressed* since all the nodes other than the adjacent nodes i and j are not aware of the failure. Local rerouting is in effect when and only when there exists a suppressed failure event.

After sometime, suppose at time t_{up}, link i–j comes up. Then the action taken by node i depends on whether the failure event is being suppressed or not. If the failure event is being suppressed, original forwarding tables are locally restored and forwarding resumes over the recovered link as if nothing ever happened. Otherwise, the link is observed for a preset period T_{up} and if it stays up, then at time $t_{up} + T_{up}$, a global update is triggered announcing that the link is up. This way, failures of short duration are handled locally while persistent failures are updated globally. When the failures are transient, FIR not only improves reachability but also reduces overhead.

3   Efficient FIR Algorithms

The process of forwarding and backwarding table computation, as explained in the previous section, involves determining a set of key links for each interface of a node. In this section, we develop efficient algorithms for identifying key links. We show that by saving some intermediate steps of the previous computation, forwarding and backwarding tables can be obtained incrementally in time less than an SPF computation.

The algorithms described here assume that all the links are point to point, and bidirectional with equal weight in both directions, which is generally true for the backbone networks. It is also assumed that no more than one link fails simultaneously. There are several reasons for concentrating on singe link failures. First, it has been observed [13] that failure of a single link is more common than simultaneous multiple link failures. Second, under FIR a failure is *suppressed* for a certain duration and if it persists beyond that time, a global update is triggered. Only simultaneous suppressed failures could pose problem for FIR. The possibility of multiple simultaneous suppressed failures happening in the network is rare considering that suppress interval would be in the order of a minute. Third, as we demonstrate in the next section, by preparing just for single link failures, FIR can deal with the majority of the multiple simultaneous failures also.

3.1 Available Shortest Path First

We now present an algorithm for determining key links and computing forwarding and backwarding tables. We refer to this procedure as *available shortest path first* (ASPF) since it computes shortest paths excluding the unavailable (potentially failed) links. The notation used here and the rest of the paper is listed in a table along with all the algorithms. A straightforward method for determining key links would be to invoke Dijkstra's SPF procedure once per each link in the network. Its time complexity would be $O(|\mathcal{E}|^2 \log |\mathcal{V}|)$, which is too high to be practical. Fortunately, it is possible to compute key links more efficiently for single link failures in $O(|\mathcal{E}| \log^2 |\mathcal{V}|)$ time based on the following observations:

- Only the failure of a link along the shortest path from node i to a destination d may require *unusual* forwarding of packets to d arriving at i. Otherwise packets are forwarded simply along the usual shortest path. As per this *revised* definition of key links, for the topology in Figure 1, $\mathcal{K}^6_{3\rightarrow1} = \emptyset$ instead of the original set $\{3\text{--}5\}$ since 3–5 is not along the shortest path from 1 to 6. This new interpretation limits the search space for key links to links in SPT rooted at i. Given that the number of links in a tree would be $O(|\mathcal{V}|)$, search space is reduced from $O(|\mathcal{E}|)$ to $O(|\mathcal{V}|)$.
- A packet needs to be forwarded to an unusual next hop only when it arrives back from a usual next hop. In other words, an edge e is included in $\mathcal{K}^d_{j\rightarrow i}$ only if j *is a next hop from i to d with e*, and i *is a next hop from j to d without e*. This helps segregate nodes and links based on the next hops from i, i.e., $\mathcal{K}^d_{j\rightarrow i}$ is $\emptyset$ if j is not a usual next hop from i to d. Also, an edge e is not a member of $\mathcal{K}^d_{j\rightarrow i}$ if e is not in the subtree below j of the SPT of i. Therefore, the key links of all the interfaces together can be determined within $O(|\mathcal{V}|)$ SPT computations.
- Incremental SPF (ISPF) procedure can be used for efficiently figuring out the effect of a link failure. ISPF adjusts an existing shortest path tree instead of constructing it from scratch. The complexity of the ISPF is proportional to the number of nodes affected by the link failure which on the average is much smaller than $|\mathcal{V}|$.

The ASPF procedure based on the above observations is shown in Algorithm 1. It uses ISPF procedure (not shown here but can be found in [12]), for incrementally building a new SPT from an existing SPT. The arguments to ISPF include the tree $\mathcal{T}$ corresponding to the edge set $\mathcal{E}$, the set $\mathcal{E}'$ of (failed) edges to be removed and the set $\mathcal{V}'$ of interested destinations. It returns a new tree consisting of nodes in $\mathcal{V}'$ without the links in $\mathcal{E}'$. In ASPF procedure, the sets of key links are first initialized to $\emptyset$ (lines 1–3). Then the

Notation	
$\mathcal{V}$	set of all vertices
$\mathcal{E}$	set of all edges
$\mathcal{N}_i$	set of neighbors of node i
W_e	weight of edge e
$|\mathcal{N}|$	avg no. of neighbors of a node
D	diameter of the network
$\mathcal{R}_i^d$	set of next hops from i to d
$\mathcal{F}_{j\rightarrow i}^d$	set of next hops from $j\rightarrow i$ to d.
$\mathcal{B}_{j\rightarrow i}^d$	set of back hops from $i\rightarrow j$ to d.
$\mathcal{K}_{j\rightarrow i}^d$	key links from $j\rightarrow i$ to d.
$\mathcal{T}_i$	shortest path tree rooted at i
$\mathcal{T}_i^e$	SPT of i without edge e
$C(k,\mathcal{T})$	cost to node k from root of $\mathcal{T}$
$P(k,\mathcal{T})$	parents of node k in tree $\mathcal{T}$
$N(k,\mathcal{T})$	next hops to k from root of $\mathcal{T}$
$S(k,\mathcal{T})$	subtree below k in tree $\mathcal{T}$
$V(\mathcal{T})$	set of all vertices in tree $\mathcal{T}$
$E(\mathcal{T})$	set of all edges in tree $\mathcal{T}$
$\mathcal{Q}$	priority queue

Algorithm 1 : ASPF(i)

1: **for all** $j \in \mathcal{N}_i$ **do**
2:   **for all** $d \in \mathcal{V}$ **do**
3:     $\mathcal{K}_j^d{}_i \Leftarrow \emptyset$
4:
5: $\mathcal{T}_i \Leftarrow \text{SPF}(i, \mathcal{V}, \mathcal{E})$
6: **for all** $j \in \mathcal{N}_i$ and $j \in N(j, \mathcal{T}_i)$ **do**
7:   $\mathcal{T}_j \Leftarrow \text{SPF}(j, \mathcal{V}, \mathcal{E})$
8:   $\mathcal{E} \Leftarrow E(S(j, \mathcal{T}_i))$
9:   **for all** $u\rightarrow v \in \mathcal{E}$ **do**
10:     $\mathcal{V} \Leftarrow V(S(v, \mathcal{T}_i))$
11:     $\mathcal{T}_j^{u\ v} = \text{ISPF}(\mathcal{T}_j, \mathcal{V}, \{u-v\})$
12:     **for all** $d \in \mathcal{V}$ **do**
13:       **if** $i \in N(d, \mathcal{T}_j^{u\ v})$ **then**
14:         $\mathcal{K}_j^d{}_i \Leftarrow \mathcal{K}_j^d{}_i \cup \{u-v\}$
15:
16: **return** TABLES(i)

Algorithm 2 : TABLES(i)

1: **for all** $j \in \mathcal{V}$ **do**
2:   $\mathcal{T}_i^{i\ j} \Leftarrow \text{ISPF}(\mathcal{T}_i, \mathcal{V}, \{i-j\})$
3:   **for all** $d \in \mathcal{V}$ **do**
4:     $\mathcal{B}_i^d{}_j \Leftarrow N(d, \mathcal{T}_i^{i\ j})$
5:     **if** not exists $\mathcal{T}_i^{\mathcal{K}_{j\rightarrow i}^d}$ **then**
6:       $\mathcal{T}_i^{\mathcal{K}_{j\rightarrow i}^d} \Leftarrow \text{ISPF}(\mathcal{T}_i, \mathcal{V}, \mathcal{K}_j^d{}_i)$
7:       $\mathcal{F}_j^d{}_i \Leftarrow N(d, \mathcal{T}_i^{\mathcal{K}_{j\rightarrow i}^d})$
8: **return** $\mathcal{F}_j{}_i, \mathcal{B}_i{}_j \ \forall j \in \mathcal{N}_i$

Algorithm 3 : IASPF1(i, f)

1: $\tilde{\mathcal{T}}_i \Leftarrow \text{ISPF}(\mathcal{T}_i, \mathcal{V}, \{f\})$
2: **for all** $j \in \mathcal{N}_i$ and $j \in N(j, \mathcal{T}_i)$ **do**
3:   $\tilde{\mathcal{T}}_j \Leftarrow \text{ISPF}(\mathcal{T}_j, \mathcal{V}, \{f\})$
4:   $\mathcal{E} \Leftarrow E(S(j, \tilde{\mathcal{T}}_i))$
5:   **for all** $u\rightarrow v \in \mathcal{E}$ **do**
6:     $\mathcal{V} \Leftarrow V(S(v, \tilde{\mathcal{T}}_i))$
7:     $\tilde{\mathcal{T}}_j^{u\ v} = \text{ISPF}(\tilde{\mathcal{T}}_j, \mathcal{V}, \{u-v\})$
8:     **for all** $d \in \mathcal{V}$ **do**
9:       **if** $i \in N(d, \tilde{\mathcal{T}}_j^{u\ v})$ **then**
10:         $\mathcal{K}_j^d{}_i \Leftarrow \mathcal{K}_j^d{}_i \cup \{u-v\}$
11:
12: **return** TABLES(i)

Algorithm 4 : IASPF2(i, f)

1: $\tilde{\mathcal{T}}_i \Leftarrow \text{ISPF}(\mathcal{T}_i, \mathcal{V}, \{f\})$
2: **for all** $j \in \mathcal{N}_i$ and $j \in N(j, \mathcal{T}_i)$ **do**
3:   $\tilde{\mathcal{T}}_j \Leftarrow \text{ISPF}(\mathcal{T}_j, \mathcal{V}, \{f\})$
4:   $\mathcal{E} \Leftarrow E(S(j, \tilde{\mathcal{T}}_i))$
5:   **for all** $u\rightarrow v \in \mathcal{E}$ **do**
6:     $\mathcal{V} \Leftarrow V(S(v, \tilde{\mathcal{T}}_i))$
7:     **if** $\not\exists \mathcal{T}_j^{u\ v}$ or $\mathcal{V} \not\subseteq V(\mathcal{T}_j^{u\ v})$ or $f \in E(\mathcal{T}_j^{u\ v})$ **then**
8:       $\tilde{\mathcal{T}}_j^{u\ v} \Leftarrow \text{ISPF}(\tilde{\mathcal{T}}_j, \mathcal{V}, \{u-v\})$
9:     **else**
10:       $\tilde{\mathcal{T}}_j^{u\ v} \Leftarrow \mathcal{T}_j^{u\ v}$
11:     **for all** $d \in \mathcal{V}$ **do**
12:       **if** $i \in N(d, \tilde{\mathcal{T}}_j^{u\ v})$ **then**
13:         $\mathcal{K}_j^d{}_i \Leftarrow \mathcal{K}_j^d{}_i \cup \{u-v\}$
14:
15: **return** TABLES(i)

shortest path tree $\mathcal{T}_i$ rooted at i is computed using SPF procedure (line 5). Each neighbor j that is a next hop to some destination is considered in turn (line 6). If not, the key links for the corresponding interface $j\to i$ remain $\emptyset$. Otherwise, j is the next hop to all the nodes in the subtree below j. Only the links $E(S(j,\mathcal{T}_i))$ in this subtree $S(j,\mathcal{T}_i)$ could be key links for the nodes $V(S(j,\mathcal{T}_i))$. So the search for key links is restricted only to $E(S(j,\mathcal{T}_i))$ (lines 8−9). A SPT $\mathcal{T}_j^{u-v}$ without each of these edges u–v is incrementally computed using ISPF (line 11) from $\mathcal{T}_j$ which was computed earlier using SPF (line 7). These SPTs are partial trees computed to span only the affected nodes below u–v in tree $\mathcal{T}_i$ (lines 10−11). Finally, a link u–v is included in $\mathcal{K}_{j\to i}^d$ for all d in $V(S(v,\mathcal{T}_i))$ if i is a next hop to d from j in tree $\mathcal{T}_j^{u-v}$ rooted at j without edge u–v (lines 12−14). We can prove that with key links computed thus, when no more than one link fails, FIR always finds a loop-free path to a destination if such a path exists. The proof is given in [12].

Once key links are determined, forwarding and backwarding tables are computed using TABLES procedure shown in Algorithm 2. Since we are preparing the forwarding tables for handling single link failures, the backwarding table for an interface $i\to j$ contains the next hops without only the edge i–j. These entries are obtained using ISPF on $\mathcal{T}_i$ (lines 2–4). The forwarding table entry for destination of $j\to i$ interface is computed by excluding the links in the set $\mathcal{K}_{j\to i}^d$. A tree $\mathcal{T}_i^{\mathcal{K}_{j\to i}^d}$ corresponding to key link set $\mathcal{K}_{j\to i}^d$ is computed only if it wasn't previously computed (lines 5−6). In particular, when the key link set is empty, existing tree $\mathcal{T}_i$ can be reused. Essentially, a shortest path tree is computed only once for each distinct set of key links.

We now analyze the complexity of the ASPF procedure. There are $|\mathcal{N}|+1$ invocations of SPF (lines 5 and 7) and $O(|\mathcal{V}|)$ of ISPF invocations (line 11). The running time of an incremental algorithm such as ISPF depends on the number of nodes affected (requiring recomputation of paths) by the changes in the edge set. So let us measure the complexity in terms of the affected nodes. Each link e in the tree $\mathcal{T}_i$ is pulled down in turn to see its impact on the next hops from a neighbor j. Only those nodes that are below the link e are affected by the removal of e. A node is affected by the removal of any of the links along the path to it from the root. The number of link removals (the ISPF computations) affecting a node in the worst case would be the diameter of the network D. So the total number of affected nodes due to $O(|\mathcal{V}|)$ ISPF invocations would be $O(D|\mathcal{V}|)$. Since regular SPF computation has to start from scratch, we can say that the affected nodes are $O(|\mathcal{V}|)$. So the complexity of key link computation is then $O(D+|\mathcal{N}|+1)$ times regular SPF computation. The time taken by TABLES depends on the sets of key links and it is found to be dominated by the time for key link computation. Therefore, considering that D can be approximated by $\log|\mathcal{V}|$ and SPF takes $O(|\mathcal{E}|\log|\mathcal{V}|)$, the complexity of ASPF is $O(|\mathcal{E}|\log^2|\mathcal{V}|)$.

3.2   Incremental ASPF Algorithms

The ASPF procedure described above computes forwarding tables efficiently and thus makes the deployment of FIR feasible. Its running time can be further improved by saving the intermediate steps of the previous computation of these tables (corresponding to the previous global update) instead of obtaining them from scratch. We devised two incremental versions IASPF1 and IASPF2 that take advantage of the saved information in determining new key links and tables when an update is received notifying the failure of a link. These two versions differ in the amount of memory usage. IASPF1 remembers $\mathcal{T}_i$ rooted at i, $\mathcal{T}_j$ and $\mathcal{T}_i^{i-j}$ for each neighbor j. So the total space required for IASPF1 is $O((2|\mathcal{N}|+1)|\mathcal{V}|)$. In addition to this, IASPF2 saves partial trees $\mathcal{T}_j^{u-v}$ for each edge $u-v$ in $\mathcal{T}_i$. The additional space required for IASPF2 is $O(D^2|\mathcal{V}|)$.

The procedure IASPF1 shown in Algorithm 3 is quite similar to ASPF with changes only in lines 5 and 7 (renumbered 1 and 3 respectively in IASPF1). Suppose the failed link is f. While ASPF uses SPF (line 5), IASPF1 invokes ISPF to compute new $\tilde{\mathcal{T}}_i$ without link f based on the saved old $\mathcal{T}_i$ (line 1). Similarly $\tilde{\mathcal{T}}_j$ is computed for each j using old $\mathcal{T}_j$ (line 3). The backwarding table computation time can also be improved by using the saved $\mathcal{T}_i^{i-j}$. The rest of the IASPF1 procedure is no different from ASPF. With only minor changes, using $O((2|\mathcal{N}|+1)|\mathcal{V}|)$ space, IASPF1 reduces approximately $|\mathcal{N}|+2$ SPF computations. These procedures are shown only for a link down event. A link up event can also be treated analogously.

The IASPF2 procedure shown in Algorithm 4 further improves the running time by avoiding unnecessary computations of the partial trees $\mathcal{T}_j^{u-v}$ for each edge $u-v$ in $\mathcal{T}_i$. This procedure is similar to IASPF1 except for lines $7-10$. A tree $\mathcal{T}_j^{u-v}$ is reused if it exists and spans all the nodes affected when $u-v$ is down without including the failed link f. Otherwise, a new such tree is constructed by invoking IASPF. Since these trees are partial trees and a link is not part of many such trees, a large fraction of IASPF invocations can be avoided. In the next section, we show that the average running time of IASPF2 is less than even a single SPF computation. Now let us look at the additional space required for storing these partial trees. As mentioned earlier, a node is affected by all the links along its path from the root and their count in the worst case would be the network diameter D. So a node would be a member of at most D partial trees. The space needed for a partial tree in the worst case would be D times the number of affected nodes in it. So the total space for all the partial trees put together would be less than $D^2|\mathcal{V}|$ which is only linear in terms of the number of nodes in the network.

4   Evaluation of the FIR Scheme

We now evaluate the performance of the FIR scheme and demonstrate its failure resiliency and forwarding efficiency. We first describe how link failures in random topologies are modeled. Then, we show how service downtime is reduced substantially by employing FIR. It is also shown that compared to the optimal shortest path routing the extent of path elongation due to local rerouting by FIR is not significant. Finally, the relative computational complexity of ASPF and incremental ASPF algorithms w.r.t. Dijkstra's SPF algorithm is presented to affirm that FIR is viable.

4.1   Link Failure Model

The pattern of link failures in large operational networks is yet to be characterized very well. In [7], some detailed measurements and analysis on the link failure events in the Sprint's IP backbone network are reported. They presented a histogram of the mean time between failure of links and the cumulative distribution of failure durations. Their

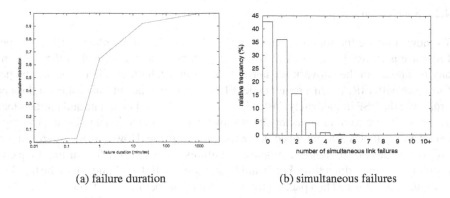

(a) failure duration   (b) simultaneous failures

Fig. 6. Distribution of failures

findings are used in this paper as the basis for inducing failures on random topologies generated using the BRITE topology generator [9] with link weights chosen randomly from the range 100 to 300. We modeled the mean time between failures (MTBF) of links with a heavy tailed distribution, with the distribution function obtained by curve fitting on the histogram reported in [7]. The MTBF values generated in this way vary from several hours to tens of days. Our model of failure events duration was based on the cumulative distribution reported in [7]. We partitioned that distribution function into several segments and use straight lines to approximate each segment as shown in Figure 6(a). Histograms on the relative frequency of the number of simultaneous failures is shown in Figure 6(b) for 50 node topology with average degree 4.

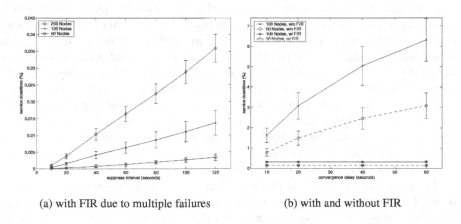

(a) with FIR due to multiple failures   (b) with and without FIR

Fig. 7. Performance evaluation in terms of service downtime

4.2 Service Downtime

We now compare the routing performance with and without employing FIR. The performance is measured in terms of *service downtime* which is defined as the total time any two nodes in the network are unreachable from each other. First consider the performance with FIR. When a router under FIR detects an adjacent link failure, it does not propagate the LSP immediately. Instead it *suppresses* the global update and initiates local rerouting. There would not be any delay between failure detection and local rerouting if backwarding tables are employed in the forwarding plane. However, local rerouting by different nodes due to multiple suppressed failures can result in a forwarding loop contributing to service downtime. For example, suppose the links 2-5 and 4-6 of the topology in Figure 1 are down. Then packets from 1 to 6 take the path $1\to2\to1\to4\to1\to2\to1\cdots$, thus keep looping even though 6 is reachable through $1\to3\to5\to6$. Nevertheless, since failures are suppressed only for a certain *suppress interval*, it is less likely that multiple links fail simultaneously within a short duration. Moreover, only a specific scenario of failures of links along the shortest path and the alternate path can cause looping.

To demonstrate the ability of FIR in handling simultaneous failures, the downtime with FIR is plotted as a function of the suppress interval in Figure 7(a). The results are shown for network topologies of different size (50, 100, and 200 nodes) and average degree of 4. Every point in the plot is the average of 5 simulation runs, with the vertical bars reporting 95% confidence intervals. When the suppress interval is 60 seconds, the fraction of the time some destination is unreachable due to loop-causing simultaneous multiple suppressed failures is less than 0.02%. Even when the suppress interval is made 2 minutes to further reduce the global link state update overhead, all nodes are reachable 99.95% of the time. These results suggest that by preparing for single link failures, FIR can also handle most of the simultaneous link failures.

The discussion above assumed that local rerouting does not incur any delay. But when the backwarding tables are not employed in the forwarding plane there would be some delay in locally sensing the failure, recomputing the forwarding tables and updating FIBs. The time to detect a link failure would be much shorter with local rerouting than with global rerouting. For example, a link can be considered failed and local rerouting is triggered with the loss of single hello packet, while the failure event is notified globally only after the loss of 5 hello packets. Essentially, local rerouting enables swift response to failures without causing routing instability. Using the backwarding tables stored in the control plane, the forwarding tables can be recomputed in negligible amount of time. Then, the time to update FIBs depends on the number of entries changed. Assuming that the total local rerouting delay is 2 seconds, the service downtime with FIR is contrasted with downtime without FIR in Figure 7(b).

Let us look at the downtime without FIR. Suppose a link fails at time t and after a period T all routers reconverge and forwarding to the affected destinations is resumed. We refer to this time T as the convergence delay which is the sum of all the delays due to several contributing factors such as *lsp-generation* interval, and *spf-interval* as explained in [7]. During this period certain node pairs that have shortest paths through the failed link are not reachable. Figure 7(b) shows the service downtime without FIR as a function of the convergence delay. It also shows the downtime with FIR assuming local rerouting delay of 2 seconds and suppress interval of 1 minute. It is clear that by employing FIR, service downtime can be improved by at least an order of magnitude. In addition, by suppressing the update of failures that last less than a minute, majority of the failures are handled without global updating and recomputation. These results indicate that FIR not only increases failure resiliency but also ensures routing stability while reducing update overhead.

4.3   Path Length Stretch

Under FIR, only the node adjacent to a failed link is aware of the failure and all other nodes are not. So, a packet takes the usual shortest path till the point of failure and then gets rerouted along the alternate path. Consequently, in the presence of link failures, FIR may forward packets along longer paths compared to the globally recomputed optimal paths based on the link state updates. For example in the topology of Figure 1, when the link 2–5 is down, packets from 1 to 6 are forwarded along the path $1\rightarrow2\rightarrow1\rightarrow4\rightarrow6$. Had node 1 been made aware of the link failure, packets would be forwarded along the shorter path $1\rightarrow3\rightarrow5\rightarrow6$. However, we found that on realistic large topologies the extent of this elongation is not significant. Let *stretch* of a path between a pair of nodes be the ratio of the lengths of the path under FIR and the optimal shortest path. When the weights of all the links are not same, path length is said to be the sum of the weights of its links. Without any link failures, there is no difference between the FIR paths and the optimal shortest paths. So the stretch is 1. We have measured the stretch under link failures due to FIR for random topologies of various sizes. Across all topologies the average stretch is less than 1.2 and in most cases it is close to 1.

4.4   Forwarding Table Computation Complexity

As explained before, the main change required in the control plane for the deployment of FIR is the replacement of traditional interface independent routing table computation algorithm with an algorithm for computing interface dependent forwarding tables. This algorithm is invoked only when a link failure lasts longer than a suppress interval and a global update is triggered. This computation is done while packets to the affected destinations are locally rerouted. Therefore, unlike in the existing routing schemes, the running time of the FIR algorithms does not affect the reachability of destinations. Nevertheless, it is desirable to reduce the computational overhead on a router. Here we evaluate the running time of the FIR algorithms and show that the forwarding tables can be incrementally computed in less than a SPF computation time.

We measured the time complexity of all these SPF based algorithms in terms of the number of distance comparisons made as was done in [10]. The distances of two nodes are compared for updating distance of one of them or for readjusting the priority queue after an extract or enque operation. The running time of ASPF and its incremental versions IASPF1 and IASPF2 are shown in Figure 8. We show the relative performance of these algorithms w.r.t. well known Dijkstra's SPF algorithm. Since Dijkstra's algorithm is widely deployed, using it as a reference helps in assessing the running time of these algorithms. The memoryless ASPF procedure takes around 10 times longer than SPF for computing forwarding tables from scratch. The incremental procedure IASPF1 remembers $2|\mathcal{N}|+1$ shortest path trees and improves the running time to less than 5 times SPF.

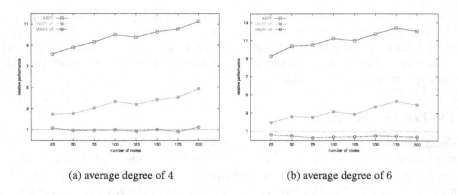

(a) average degree of 4   (b) average degree of 6

Fig. 8. Comparison of run time complexity of FIR algorithms

Using an additional space of less than $D^2|\mathcal{V}|$, IASPF2 takes no more than a single SPF computation. Its relative performance gets better as the connectedness increases. Apart from the modest space requirement, IASPF2 does not add any additional processing burden on routers that currently employ Dijkstra's SPF algorithm for computing routes.

These results establish that FIR is feasible, reliable, and stable. Furthermore, it requires minimal changes in control plane only and also reduces communication overhead. These features make FIR an attractive alternative to the existing routing schemes.

5   Related Work

The nature of link failures in a network and their impact on the traffic has received a great deal of attention recently. The frequency and the duration of link failures in a backbone network has been studied and reported in [5,7]. They observe that link failures are part of everyday operation of a network due to various causes such as maintenance, accidental fiber cuts, and misconfigurations. It is also found that the majority of the failures are transient lasting less than a minute warranting local rerouting. The impact of link failures on Voice-over-IP is assessed in [4]. They noticed that link failures may be followed by routing instabilities that last for tens of minutes resulting in the loss of reachability of large sets of end hosts. Since the level of congestion in a backbone is almost negligible, offering high availability of service is identified as the major concern for VoIP. These findings about the link failures and their debilitating effect on the network services provide a strong motivation for schemes such as FIR that focus on ensuring service continuity.

There have been several proposals for mitigating the impact of link failures on network performance. [6] and [13] address the issue of assigning weights to links such that the traffic is balanced across the network even in the presence of link failures. These schemes can be thought of as preparing for link failures in terms of reducing overload while FIR is concerned with increasing availability. As mentioned earlier, guaranteeing reachability is found to be an overriding concern than avoiding congestion in a backbone network. Moreover, these schemes can be used in conjunction with FIR. A detailed analysis of the sources of delay in routing reconvergence after a link failure is provided in [1, 2]. They suggest tuning various parameters related to link state propagation and routing table computation for accelerating the convergence and reducing the downtime. This may not be the best recipe for handling common transient link failures. The objective of FIR is to make forwarding insensitive to the parameter values chosen for accelerating convergence and insuring stability.

A recent work closely related to FIR is the deflection routing proposed in [8]. The basic idea underlying their approach is to select a next hop node based on strictly decreasing cost criterion. While deflection routing guarantees loop-free paths, it may not always find such a path even if one exists. For example, in a simple triangle topology when a link with the smallest cost goes down, the corresponding pair of nodes are not reachable. Apart from this last hop problem, deflecting routing requires that the weights of links satisfy a certain condition. FIR imposes no such restrictions on weight assignment and assures loop-free forwarding to any reachable destinations in case of single link failures. An algorithm proposed in [11] performs local restoration by informing only the routers in the neighborhood about link failure events instead of all routers. FIR achieves similar effect without requiring any changes to link state propagation mechanism. An application layer solution is proposed in [3] for detecting and recovering from path outages using a resilient overlay network. While RON is an attempt to overcome the slow convergence of BGP based inter-domain routing, FIR is a remedy for outages in intra-domain routing. Nevertheless, we believe network layer schemes such as FIR obviate the need for application layer approaches like RON.

6   Conclusions and Future Work

In this paper, we addressed the problem of ensuring destination reachability in the presence of link failures. We proposed a *failure insensitive routing* approach where routers infer link failures from the packet's flight and precompute interface specific forwarding tables avoiding the potentially failed links. When a link fails, only adjacent nodes locally reroute packets while all other nodes simply forward them according to their precomputed interface specific forwarding tables without being explicitly aware of the failure. We presented an *available shortest path first* algorithm that computes interface specific forwarding tables for dealing with single link failures in $O(|\mathcal{E}| \log^2 |\mathcal{V}|)$ time. We have also described an incremental ASPF algorithm that requires $O(D^2|\mathcal{V}|)$ space for remembering intermediate steps of the previous computation but runs in less time than a SPF computation. We have demonstrated that FIR handles simultaneous multiple failures also and reduces service downtime by an order of magnitude. Essentially FIR approach improves failure resiliency without jeopardizing routing stability. It does so without altering the forwarding plane while reducing communication overhead. Hence, we believe that FIR is an attractive alternative to the existing routing schemes. We are currently in the process of conducting packet level simulations to assess the utility of FIR in terms of throughput received by TCP flows and quality experienced by VoIP flows. Also, we plan to actually implement FIR and evaluate its performance to make its case more compelling.

References

1. C. Alattinoglu, V. Jacobson, and H. Yu, "Towards Milli-Second IGP Convergence," draft-alaettinoglu-ISIS-convergence-00.txt, November 2000.
2. C. Alattinoglu, and S. Casner, "ISIS routing on the Qwest backbone: A recipe for subsecond ISIS convergence," NANOG 24, 2/2002.
3. D. Anderson, H. Balakrishnan, F. Kaashoek, and R. Morris, "Resilient Overlay Networks," SOSP, 2001.
4. C. Boutremans, G. Iannaccone, and C. Diot, "Impact of Link Failures on VoIP Performance," NOSSDAV, 2002.
5. C.-N. Chuah, S. Bhattacharyya, G. Iannaccone, C. Diot, "Studying failures & their impact on traffic within a tier-1 IP backbone", CCW, 2002.
6. B. Fortz, "Optimizing OSPF/IS-IS weights in a changing world", IEEE JSAC Special Issue on Advances in Fundamentals of Network Management, Spring 2002.
7. G. Iannaccone, C.-N. Chuah, R. Mortier, S. Bhattacharyya, C. Diot, "Analysis of link failures in an IP backbone", IMW 2002.
8. S. Iyer, S. Bhattacharyya, N. Taft, N. McKeown, and C. Diot, "An approach to alleviate link overload as observed on an IP backbone," INFOCOM, 2003.
9. A. Medina, A. Lakhina, I. Matta, and J. Byers, "BRITE: An Approach to Universal Topology Generation", Proceedings of MASCOTS 2001, Cincinnati, August 2001.
10. P. Narvaez, "Routing reconfiguration in IP networks", Ph.D. Dissertation, MIT, June 2000.
11. P. Narvaez, K.-Y. Siu, and H.-Y. Tzeng, "Local Restoration Algorithms for Link-State Routing Protocols", ICCCN, 1999.
12. S. Nelakuditi, S. Lee, Y. Yu, and Z.-L. Zhang, "Failure Insensitive Routing for Ensuring Service Availability," Technical Report, University of South Carolina, Columbia, February 2003.
13. A. Nucci, B. Schroeder, S. Bhattacharyya, N. Taft, C. Diot, "IS-IS link weight assignment for transient link failures," SPRINT ATL Technical Report TR02-ATL-071000.

Network Availability Based Service Differentiation

Mathilde Durvy[1], Christophe Diot[2], Nina Taft[2], and Patrick Thiran[1]

[1] ***EPFL (Inst. of Communication Systems), CH-1015 Lausanne, Switzerland
[2] Sprint Advanced Technology Labs, Burlingame CA-94010, USA
{mathilde.durvy,patrick.thiran}@epfl.ch, {nina,cdiot}@sprintlabs.com

Abstract. Numerous approaches have been proposed to manage Quality of Service in the Internet. However, none of them was successfully deployed in a commercial IP backbone, mostly because of their complexity. In this paper, we take advantage of the excess network bandwidth to offer a degraded class of traffic. We identify and analyze the impact of link failures on such a service and show that under certain circumstances they provide the main vector to service differentiation. We simulate our QoS scheme on a real IP backbone topology and derive Service Level Agreements for the new degraded service. We find that by adding a degraded class of traffic in the network, we can at least double the link utilization with no impact on the current backbone traffic.

1 Introduction

Although link failures occur everyday in backbone networks [1], providers are able to guarantee impressive performance at the price of an appropriate dimensioning of their network. In other words, enough spare bandwidth must be made available to reroute the traffic without degradation of performance in case of link failures. In the absence of failure, the excess bandwidth is unused. This is a major concern for providers who are always looking for new ways to maximize the return on investment from their network infrastructure. The target of this work is to provide a mean to increase the network traffic load without any penalty on the current backbone traffic (identified here as legacy traffic).

We propose to take advantage of the unused bandwidth to offer a degraded class of service. The legacy traffic remains served with an absolute priority. Degraded traffic is added if bandwidth is available, in such a way that it does not affect the performance of the legacy traffic. Its performance will thus be very sensitive to the total link load and to link failures. More specifically, if there is no link failure and if the links are not overloaded (which translates in a link utilization below 80% [2]), the performance of the two traffic classes should be very similar. Instead, in the event of a link failure, the degraded service can be

---

*** The part of this work carried out at EPFL was supported by a grant of Sprint, and by grant DICS 1830 of the Hasler Foundation

K. Jeffay, I. Stoica, and K. Wehrle (Eds.): IWQoS 2003, LNCS 2707, pp. 305–325, 2003.

dropped to accommodate the legacy traffic that should suffer last from network outages.

The contribution of this work is threefold:

1. This is the first time the impact of link failures is taken into consideration in the definition and evaluation of a QoS scheme in backbone networks.
2. We analyze by simulation the performance of the degraded service for a real IP backbone network topology.
3. We identify and define a new SLA metric, i.e., service availability, in order to capture the service uptime as perceived by the users.

In today's IP backbone networks, failures are a potential cause of congestion and packet losses and are thus a main problem in maintaining high quality services. Therefore, failure events should be included in any study relative to the deployment of a QoS scheme. We define *network availability* to be the percentage of the total network bandwidth available to route the traffic. When averaged over time, network availability effectively reflects the frequency and impact of failures in a given network. We perform a thorough analysis of the relative performance of the two traffic classes based on realistic failure patterns.

Despite the multitude of existing QoS models, none was successfully deployed in the Internet. It is too easy to blame the conservatism of network engineers. In fact most of the proposed schemes involve a significant increase in complexity while providing no explicit, or difficult to guarantee, end-to-end performance. In response to these issues, our two-class scheme is solely based on local, and very simple decisions. We run an extensive set of *ns-2* simulations using the Sprint domestic backbone topology and its observed failure patterns. We study the range of Service Level Agreements that can be offered to the degraded class of traffic. We introduce a new SLA metric named *service availability*. We define service availability as the fraction of time the service is available to a customer. In failure prone environment, packet loss and delay may reach level where most applications are unable to function properly. In such cases we consider the service to be unavailable to the customer. We believe that service availability is an important parameter in the quality of a service perceived by the user, and should thus be included in the SLAs.

The degraded class of traffic proposed in this work is in line with the strategy of some ISPs that recently started to provide a "no SLA" service (even though this service is not proposed in conjunction with a high quality class of traffic). We also believe that our solution is of special interest for networks with very volatile bandwidth such as wireless networks. In such environments, it might be difficult to predict what resource will be available at the time it is needed and a very simple QoS mechanism that provides absolute priority to a subset of the traffic may ultimately be the only feasible approach. However, we choose to validate our approach on the Sprint IP backbone network that represents a more complex and demanding environment in terms of traffic performance and network availability.

The rest of the paper is organized as follows. Section 2 defines the two classes of service and discuss implementation related issues. In Section 3, we introduce important characteristics of IP backbones including current network engineering practices and recent data on failure patterns. Section 4 explains the role of Service Level Agreements in commercial networks and provide an enhanced definition. In Sections 5 and 6 we present experimental settings and results. We discuss related work and conclude in Sections 7 and 8 respectively.

2   Service Definition and Implementation

We now give an overview of the two service classes and discuss implementation related issues.

2.1   Legacy Service: Fully Available (FA)

The Fully Available traffic corresponds to the existing (legacy) traffic in backbone networks. Its performance is defined by traffic engineering rules. Only unlikely events could visibly affect its performance. The network is designed in such a way that the FA service is available 99.999% of the time, end-to-end delays are close to the propagation delays and loss are below 0.3%. FA traffic is currently the default service available on major Tier-1 backbone networks.

2.2   Degraded Service: Partially Available (PA)

The Partially Available (or degraded) traffic is designed to have *no* impact on the existing traffic. PA is a low priority traffic that runs exclusively on the bandwidth unused by the FA traffic. PA traffic does not affect network engineering rules. The performance of the PA traffic will thus depend on the network traffic load and on the occurrence of failures. As a consequence, the PA service can occasionally become unavailable to its users. Introducing the PA traffic in backbone networks allows carriers to reduce the amount of unused bandwidth while providing a cheaper service to their customers.

2.3   Implementation Issues

One of the main concerns is that a QoS scheme must be easy to deploy. Our goal is not to derive a new scheduling policy but instead to introduce a simple (possibly already available) scheduler in network routers, and to evaluate the resulting traffic performance.

   To satisfy the FA traffic performance requirements we isolate the two classes of traffic in two separate queues. The FA queue has an absolute priority over the PA queue. Note that giving a strict priority to the FA traffic may lead to starvation of the PA traffic. This is part of the PA service definition. In practice however, the link overprovisioning is such that we will seldom observe a complete starvation of the PA traffic.

   This scheme conforms to strict priority scheduling with two drop tail queues. It can be implemented in most of the current routers and does not imply modification in the routing infrastructure. The only additional requirement is that

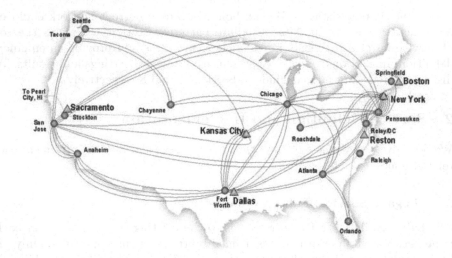

Fig. 1. Simplified view of the Sprint U.S IP domestic backbone (circles represent PoPs)

the two classes of traffic need to be identified by a single bit marking in the IP header. In particular, this QoS scheme does not require signaling, known to account for most of the complexity in QoS architectures.

3   Backbones: Design and Engineering Principles

Backbone networks appear as a black box delivering high quality service. However, to understand the rationales behind the proposed QoS scheme, and to measure the impact of such a scheme, it is necessary to understand some backbone design and engineering practices.

3.1   Network Topology

At the logical level, a backbone network can be represented as a graph whose vertices are *Point-of-Presence (PoPs)* and edges are *inter-PoP links* (Fig.1).

A PoP is a collection of access and core routers collocated in the same site. Clients connect to the network via access routers, which are in turn connected to at least two core routers. The number of core routers per PoP can vary. However, core routers are typically fully meshed with each other.

A pair of neighboring PoPs is connected by multiple, high capacity links (OC-48 and OC-192); each of these parallel links initiates and terminates on different backbone routers (Fig. 2(a)). Having numerous parallel inter-PoP links between two given PoPs increases the robustness of the network. It also increases the opportunities for load balancing.

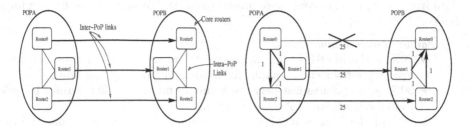

(a) 2 PoPs (with 3 core routers each), interconnected by 3 inter-PoP links

(b) Single-hop rerouting in case of partial failure (top link is down). The numbers attached to the links are IS-IS weights

Fig. 2. 2-PoP topology

3.2   Network Engineering

Today, the majority of large backbones use IP over DWDM technology. SONET protection has been removed because of its high cost, although SONET framing is kept for failure detection purpose. Protection and restoration are thus provided at the IP layer only.

Link state protocols such as OSPF or IS-IS are used for intra-domain routing. When a link fails, the traffic is rerouted on the path with the smallest weight sum. In networks with multiple parallel inter-PoP links we differentiate between two types of rerouting events:

- *Single-hop rerouting*. The traffic of the failed link is load balanced on the n remaining links (Fig. 2(b)). The result is an implicit link protection scheme similar in concept to a $1 : n$ protection scheme at the optical level. Single-hop rerouting is possible if the parallel inter-PoP links have equal weights (in Fig. 2(b) the three inter-PoP links have an IS-IS weight of 25 while the intra-PoP links have an IS-IS weight of 1) and enough excess bandwidth to support the rerouted traffic. The main advantage of single-hop rerouting is to limit the geographical impact of failures and thus the additional propagation delay incurred by the rerouted traffic.
- *Multi-hop rerouting*. The traffic is rerouted through an additional PoP. Multi-hop rerouting only happens when all the links between two PoPs fail at the same time (e.g. if all the links between San Jose and Anaheim fail, the traffic is rerouted through Relay DC, Atlanta and Fort Worth).

We include both types of rerouting events in our simulations.

3.3   Failures in Backbone Networks

To the best of our knowledge a complete characterization of failures in backbone networks is not available. However some preliminary results, based on monitoring data from the Sprint network, were presented in [1]. We summarize their findings below.

- *Failure duration and causes.*
  - 20% of the inter-PoP link failures last longer than 10 minutes. Possible causes are fiber cuts, equipment failures and/or link upgrades.
  - 30% of the failures last between 1 and 10 minutes. Likely causes include router reboots and software problems.
  - 50% of the failures last less than 1 minute. These failures could be the result of oscillatory effects when a router mistakenly considers the adjacency to be down or could be due to optical equipment.
- The *mean time between successive failure events* is of the order of 30 minutes.
- The *failure distribution across the links* is far from uniform. Some links hardly fail while three links account for 25% of the failures.
- *Failures can be strongly correlated.* Depending on the mapping of the logical topology on the optical topology, a single fiber cut may bring down several logical links. Failures of logical links mapped on disjoint fiber path are, on the other hand, mostly independent.

The knowledge of failure characteristics is an important step toward a model of failure in backbone networks. It is also mandatory to provide pragmatic evaluations of QoS models. We use these observations to include realistic failure patterns in our evaluation of the degraded traffic performance.

4   Service Level Agreements

A Service Level Agreement (SLA) specifies a contractual service target between a provider and its customers. The tradeoff between the SLA and the service pricing is often a significant factor in the success of an offered service.

4.1   SLAs in Commercial Networks

The SLAs offered by Tier-1 provider typically include packet loss, packet delay and port availability. The first two metrics are computed network wide and usually averaged over a one month period. The loss metric reports the average percentage of packet lost in a transmission while the delay metric (or latency) reports the round-trip transmission time averaged over all PoP pairs in the ISP backbone network. Contrary to the other SLA metrics, port availability does not capture the performance of the traffic inside the backbone. Instead, port availability measures the fraction of time a customer's physical connectivity to the ISP's network is up. The notion of port availability may differ between providers.

Table 1 reports SLA values inside the continental USA for some Tier-1 providers. For comparison purposes, Table 2 presents the actual measured traffic performance for the Sprint U.S domestic backbone. Port availability cannot be included as it is measured per customer. We observe no SLA violation during the observation period (the second half of year 2002).

Table 1. Intra-US SLAs[1]: packet loss and latency metric (12/2002)

	AT&T	C&W	Genuity	Sprint	UUNET
Latency (ms)	60	50	55	55	55
Loss (%)	0.7	0.5	0.5	0.3	0.5
Port Availability (%)	95	99.97	99.97	99.9	100.0

Table 2. Sprint measured performance for the last six months of 2002

	July	Aug	Sept	Oct	Nov	Dec
Latency (ms)	45.68	46.36	46.76	46.76	47.08	47.68
Loss (%)	0.01	0.06	0.06	0.01	0.00	0.00

4.2   SLA: Enhanced Definition

For the purpose of this work we slightly modify the SLA metric definition. Our aim is to better capture the behavior of each class of traffic and to provide a network wide counterpart to port availability. To make the number of simulations manageable, we also reduce the SLA computation period to 10 days rather than the conventional one month. However, we use a measurement granularity of one minute which is much lower than the one used in commercial networks. As a result, the number of samples averaged to compute our SLA is greater than for a commercial SLA despite the shorter SLA computation period. We now provide a high-level definition of our three SLA metrics:

- *Packet loss*: the loss rate averaged over all inter-PoP links.
- *Packet delay*: the packet delays averaged over all inter-PoP links.
- *Service availability*: the fraction of time the service is available. The service is available if the following conditions are verified:
  - All possible source-destination pairs are connected by at least one route.
  - No traffic transmission experiences persistent (10 consecutive minutes or more) high (above 50%) loss rates.

At this point of the paper it is not possible to provide a more detailed description of the SLA metrics, since their computation is closely related to the simulation environment. The exact methodology used to compute the value of each SLA metric will be explained in Sect. 6.2.

We believe that these three metrics capture accurately the performance of a service while being easier to compute than their commercial equivalent. In particular, we consider service availability to be a good measure of the service quality as perceived by the user and thus a valuable addition to the SLA metrics.

---

[1] http://ipnetwork.bgtmo.ip.att.net/averages.html,
http://www.sprintbiz.com/business/network/slas.html,
http://netperformance.genuity.com/ourdata.htm,
http://www.worldcom.com/global/about/network/latency/,
http://sla.cw.net/sla/Help.jsp

5   Capturing Backbone Properties

The target of this work is to derive quantitative SLAs for the degraded service. To do so we perform *ns-2* simulations on the Sprint U.S. backbone topology. Performing realistic simulations on a backbone network is a challenge. The generation of traffic matrices and failure patterns are two research topics by themselves. Our approach was thus to use known models or available monitoring data. In addition, we had to make several assumptions to make the simulations computationally tractable. We provide hereafter a pragmatic and experimental justification of these assumptions and show that they do not impact our observations.

5.1   Topology

To analyze the degraded service SLA, we use the exact topology of the IP Sprint domestic backbone (not shown here for confidentiality issues). For each of the 91 inter-PoP links, we specify the propagation delay, the bandwidth and the IS-IS weight. The intra-PoP topology is fully meshed in all the PoPs.

The typical bandwidth of inter-PoP links in backbone networks is 2.5 or 10 Gb/s. To reduce the simulation complexity we set the bandwidth of inter-PoP links to 10Mb/s . Such a huge reduction of the link capacities might appear to be a rather severe simplification. However, we expect the two classes of traffic to react in similar ways. Section 5.4 shows that the relative performance of FA and PA traffic are indeed maintained.

5.2   Traffic

It is not possible today to obtain an exact PoP-to-PoP traffic matrix for an ISP backbone via direct measurement, and techniques for inferring traffic matrices are still under development. Some recent studies [3] have shown the gravity models can capture reasonably well properties of PoP-to-PoP flow volumes. The basic idea behind the gravity models is that the flow between a pair of PoPs is proportional to the product of two factors, one which is a metric of the ingress node and one a metric of the egress node. These metrics should capture key features of the total volume flowing from a PoP into (or out of) the backbone of the ISP. We generated an FA traffic matrix according to these principals and checked that the resulting link loads matched actual Sprint backbone link loads closely on most links. Using the FA traffic matrix we then create approximately 900 router-to-router data flows.

We made an attempt to run the simulations on the Sprint network with TCP traffic but the requirements in terms of memory and time exceeded the capacity of our simulation platform. Therefore, the simulations presented in this paper use UDP constant rate traffic with exponentially distributed On and Off periods. The results for the 2-PoP topology (Sect. 5.4) show that the UDP performance provide an appropriate lower bound for the performance of TCP traffic. In addition, UDP offers a simple and convenient way to look at service availability as it does not adapt its sending rate in case of network congestion.

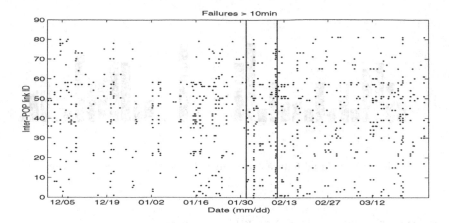

Fig. 3. Failure distribution in the Sprint network. Each dot corresponds to a link failure lasting at least 10 minutes. The two vertical lines indicate the 10-day period selected to run our simulations

5.3 Failure Scenario

As we explained earlier, a probabilistic model of failure in backbone networks is not yet available. Therefore, we decided to replay failure sequences as they appear in the Sprint backbone in an attempt to reproduce the failure characteristics observed in Sect. 3.3. Figure 3 shows the distribution of link failures in the Sprint network between December 2001 and March 2002. We use a 10-day period from February 1st to February 11th to run our simulations. This time interval was chosen because it is representative of an heavily perturbated period.

We isolate each failure event by grouping simultaneous, equal length, failures together, this leads to 15 multi-link failure events. Figure 4 shows the length of the failure and the number of links involved in each of the failure event. Up to 12 links can fail simultaneously and the longest failure event lasted for 8 hours. Half of the failure events result in multi-hop rerouting of the traffic.

Based on the failure events we construct our failure scenario. We define a failure scenario as a sequence of failure events separated by time intervals where the network is not in a failure state. The failure scenario used to run our simulation corresponds to a 10-day snapshot of the network, with a total cumulative failure event time of approximately 2 days.

We made two minor assumptions relative to the failure patterns. First we do not consider intra-PoP failures. The main reason is that intra-PoP link failures have a much smaller impact on traffic since core routers are fully meshed. Second, we only replicate failure events that last more than 10 minutes. Even if those failure events represent only a minority of the total number of failures, they are the ones that significantly affect the traffic performances, and as a consequence the SLA of the degraded class of traffic.

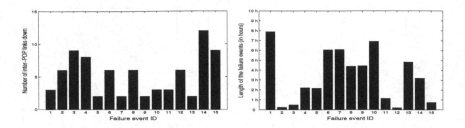

Fig. 4. Individual failure events included in the SLA computation

5.4   Proof of Concept and Validation of Assumptions

We use the 2-PoP topology shown in Fig. 2 to validate our assumptions and provide an initial intuition of the PA performance. The three inter-PoP links have a 10 ms propagation delay and a bandwidth of either 10Mb/s (the link bandwidth chosen for our simulations on the Sprint network) or 2Gb/s ($\simeq$ OC-48). All the inter-PoP links have the same IS-IS weight. When a link fails, the traffic is thus load balanced on the remaining links. The queue size is set equal to the bandwidth-delay product of the link. Each router in PoP A (see Fig. 2) generates the same total amount of traffic. The FA traffic load is fixed and occupies approximately 27% of the link bandwidth in the no-failure case. The amount of FA traffic generated was chosen to yield a 80% FA link utilization in the most severe failure event (i.e., when two inter-PoP links are down). The PA traffic is added progressively until we reach a link utilization close to 100%. The packet size is set to 500 bytes for both UDP and TCP traffic.

General Observations. The goal of the 2-PoP topology is not to provide quantitative traffic performance, as it could be very different on a large network, but to verify that the two classes of traffic behave as expected. First, we notice that FA traffic is not affected by the addition of the PA traffic (as shown by the flat curves of Fig. 5(a)). As a direct consequence, the FA service will have the same SLA as the current backbone traffic. Second, we observe that after a short and sharp increase the PA delay stabilizes (see one-failure curves in Fig. 5(b)). At this point the PA traffic occupies all the bandwidth unused by the FA traffic, i.e., the link utilization is 100%. Its performance are then dictated only by the amount of spare bandwidth unused by FA traffic (60% in the one-failure case and 20% in the two-failure case). In general, the PA performance will thus depend on the total traffic load (FA load and PA load), and on the quantity of failures. Indeed, Fig. 5(d) clearly shows that, as long as there is no failure and the link utilization remains under 80%, the two classes of traffic have very similar performance.

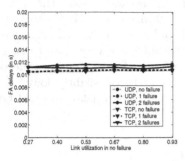

(a) UDP and TCP packet delays for the FA traffic vs. the total link utilization

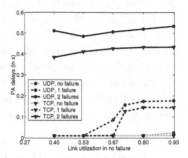

(b) UDP and TCP packet delays for the PA traffic vs. the total link utilization

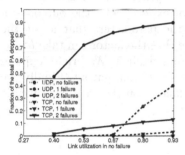

(c) UDP and TCP packet loss rate for PA traffic vs. the total link utilization

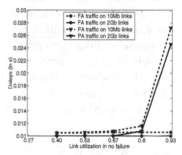

(d) UDP packet delays for FA and PA traffic in the no-failure case. The link bandwidth is 10Mb/s or 2Gb/s

Fig. 5. Experimental results on 2-PoP topology

Experimental Justification of Our Assumptions

UDP performance provides a lower bound to TCP performance. Figures 5(a), 5(b) and 5(c) compare packet delay and packet loss performance for UDP and TCP traffic. The link bandwidth is set to 10Mb/s. We did not report the packet loss metric for the FA traffic since its value is null by design. The curves of Fig. 5(a) and 5(b) show that delays for UDP traffic are only slightly higher than delays for TCP traffic and follow the same trend. UDP delays thus provide a good approximation of TCP delay performance. However, the PA packet losses for UDP traffic are substantially larger than the corresponding TCP loss rates. Contrary to TCP, UDP does not adapt its sending rate to the amount of congestion in the network. A high level of UDP loss thus reflects a poor availability of the service. Although our decision to use UDP traffic for our simulations on the Sprint network was mainly motivated by complexity considerations for large-scale network simulations, UDP loss rate happens to be a convenient metric to measure service availability.

Simulated link bandwidth has a limited impact. Figure 5(d) shows the delay performance of the PA and FA service on links of 10 Mb/s and 2Gb/s capacity. The traffic type is UDP and the three inter-PoP links are up. We observe that the traffic performance on the different bandwidth links are very close to each other and that the relative performance of the FA and PA service are indeed maintained. Note however, that queuing delays tend to be slightly lower on high bandwidth links. This is due essentially to transmission delay and will be neglected in the remaining of the study.

6   Experimental Design and Results

Experimental design is an area of statistics used to maximize the information gain obtained from a finite set of simulations and to provide an accurate analysis of the simulation results. In statistical design of experiments, the outcome of an experiment is called the *response variable*, the parameters that affect the response variable are called *factors* and the value that the factor can take *levels*. In this section we first present the different factors studied. We briefly explain how the response variable is computed from the simulation output. Finally, we analyze the effect of factors and combination of factors on the response variable and discuss SLA for the degraded class of traffic.

6.1   Factors Evaluated

We identify three important factors which could potentially affect the performance of the degraded traffic.

The PA Traffic Generation Strategy. In order to consider a variety of demand scenarios for the degraded traffic class we have chosen two different strategies to generate the PA traffic:

- *PA-fraction.* The PA traffic matrix is a fraction of the FA traffic matrix. The justification for this approach is simply that the demand for the new traffic class is likely to be proportional to the existing demand (this is also in agreement with the gravity model [3]). The PA-fraction generation strategy may, however, yield poor PA traffic performance since links with an already high utilization receive the largest PA traffic load. Non-uniformity in the traffic distribution across the links will thus be amplified rather than attenuated.
- *PA-optimal.* This strategy is meant to reproduce an 'optimal' placement of the PA traffic. We compute the PA traffic matrix to yield an equal link utilization on all inter-PoP links. If the utilization of FA traffic alone on a link is already larger than the target average utilization, we do not add any PA traffic on the link. Although such a distribution of the PA traffic is unlikely to arise in reality, it represents the best case and thus allows us to assess the best possible SLA this traffic class could receive.

The PA Load. The main goal of this study is to determine how much PA traffic can be added to the network before too much degradation in the SLA occurs. The FA load in the network is constant and is determined by the FA traffic matrix. The average FA link utilization (i.e., the total FA load divided by the sum of the link capacities) is approximately 16%. The PA traffic load is variable and is added as a multiple of the FA traffic load in the network. In the context of this work we run simulation for PA load equals to up to four times the FA load. This corresponds to an average link utilization between 16% and 80%.

Network Availability. To take into account the variation of failure rates in backbone network, we derive the SLAs for different levels of *network availability*, α. We define network availability as the percentage of the total bandwidth available to carry the backbone traffic. Network availability is averaged over time. For the 10-day failure scenario described in Section 5.3 we can compute the network availability as follows:

$$\alpha = \frac{1}{\sum_{i=0}^{15} t_i}(t_0 + t_1\alpha_1 + t_2\alpha_2 + ... + t_{15}\alpha_{15}) = 0.99$$

where t_i is the length of the ith failure event (as reported by Fig. 4), t_0 is the time spent in the no-failure state and α_i the percentage of links up during the ith failure event. The actual level of network availability in the Sprint network is 0.99. We vary the network availability by scaling the time spent in failure events (t_i, $0 < i \leq 15$), versus the time spent in the no-failure state (t_0) and were thus able to run simulations for $\alpha \in [0.95, 1.00]$ (α=0.95 corresponds to $t_0 = 0$, i.e., the Sprint network is permanently in one of the failure state).

6.2   Computation of the Response Variable

We are interested in multiple response variables, namely the packet loss (p_l), the packet delay (p_d) and the availability (s_{avail}) of a service. As we have seen previously we can group those three metrics together under the notion of SLA. To compute the response variables we simulate each of the 15 multi-link failure events and record the average performance of the two classes of traffic. The simulation time is 1min per failure event. It was not necessary to run the simulations longer since the performance become stable after a couple of seconds. The simulation output for the ith failure event can thus be described as the tuple ($p_{l_i}, p_{d_i}, s_{\text{avail}_i}$). We calculate a response variable by performing a weighted average of the metric of interest observed during each failure event:

$$
\begin{cases}
p_{\mathrm{l}} &= \frac{1}{\sum_{i=0}^{15} t_i}(t_0 p_{\mathrm{l}_0} + t_1 p_{\mathrm{l}_1} + t_2 p_{\mathrm{l}_2} + \ldots + t_{15} p_{\mathrm{l}_{15}}) \\
p_{\mathrm{d}} &= \frac{1}{\sum_{i=0}^{15} t_i}(t_0 p_{\mathrm{d}_0} + t_1 p_{\mathrm{d}_1} + t_2 p_{\mathrm{d}_2} + \ldots + t_{15} p_{\mathrm{d}_{15}}) \\
s_{\mathrm{avail}} &= \frac{1}{\sum_{i=0}^{15} t_i}(t_0 s_{\mathrm{avail}_0} + t_1 s_{\mathrm{avail}_1} + \ldots + t_{15} s_{\mathrm{avail}_{15}})
\end{cases}
$$

The resulting SLA is then the tuple $(p_{\mathrm{l}}, p_{\mathrm{d}}, s_{\mathrm{avail}})$ rounded up with a suitable granularity.

6.3   Impact of the Different Factors on the Response Variable

We now apply the experimental design methodology to study the impact of each factor, and each combination of factors, on the response variables, and to identify factors with the highest influence on the traffic SLAs. The importance of each factor, is measured by the proportion of the total variation in the response that is explained by the factor. Several types of experimental design are available, we use the very popular 2^k *factorial design* [4,5]. A 2^k factorial design is used to determine the effect of k factors each of which have two alternatives or levels. In our experiment $k = 3$ and the two level selected are the maximum and the minimum values for each of the factor. To make our analysis more precise we perform two distinct 2^3 factorial designs. In the first factorial design, we assume that the amount of PA traffic added to the network is lower than the current FA traffic load (i.e PA load level ≤ 1). In the second one, we relax this assumption and move to PA load above one where FA and PA traffic performance are different even in the no-failure case.

Network Availability Based Service Differentiation. Table 3 summarizes the impact of each factor and combination of factors on the different SLA metrics (values under 1% are omitted). For example, the first cell of the table tells us that the increase in PA load from zero to one is responsible for 4.3% of the variation in the PA loss performance. Results in terms of FA service availability are undefined since there is no variation in the response (i.e. the FA service availability is uniformly equal to 100% across all factor levels). The output of the first 2^k factorial design (PA load ≤ 1) is reported in the left most column for each SLA metric. It shows that at low PA traffic load the network availability accounts for the major variation in the traffic performance. Since the two classes of service have initially the same performance we can thus conclude that, for PA load ≤ 1, the difference of performance between the FA and PA service will be essentially a function of the frequency of failures in the network. Notice though that PA delay are sensitive to all factors and combination of factors.

Link Load as a Main Factor in Service Differentiation. The second 2^k factorial design (Table 3, columns labeled > 1) reports the impact of the different factors on the SLA metrics for PA load above 1. At high traffic load,

Table 3. Impact of each factor on the SLA metrics (values under 1% are omitted, NaN stands for Not a Number)

%	PA loss		FA loss		PA delay		FA delay		PA service availability		FA service availability	
	≤ 1	> 1	≤ 1	> 1	≤ 1	> 1	≤ 1	> 1	≤ 1	> 1	≤ 1	> 1
PA load (Ld)	4.3	**52.6**			17.4	**63.7**					NaN	
Network Availability (NAv)	**71.1**	22.6	**98.4**	**98.9**	**17.6**	18.9	**99.5**	**99.7**	**100.0**	**68.2**	NaN	
PA generation Strategy (St)	5.9	18.3			12.2	16.5				15.8	NaN	
Ld,NAv	4.3	1.8			14.7						NaN	
Ld,St	4.2	4.0			13.0						NaN	
NAv,St	5.9				13.5					15.8	NaN	
Ld,NAv,St	4.2				11.7						NaN	
Ld+NAv+St	81.3	93.4	99.2	99.4	47.2	99.0	99.8	99.9	100.0	84.1	NaN	

the PA load becomes the dominant factor affecting the delay and loss of the PA traffic. However, the FA traffic remains only influenced by the level of network availability; the PA generation strategy and the amount of PA traffic in the network have no impact on its performance. This confirms the immunity of the legacy traffic SLA to the adjunction of the degraded traffic in the Sprint network. Table 3 also shows that, contrary to other PA performance metrics, the PA service availability is mainly affected by the network availability. We conclude that even for large PA loads the service availability could remain high as long as there are few failures in the network (i.e. the network availability is high). Yet, in the event of failures, PA customers should expect a severe reduction in the availability of their service. Finally, we observe that contrary to low PA loads the interactions between the different factors are small and can thus be neglected.

Discussion – Implication of the Results. Figure 6 illustrates the results of the 2^k factorial designs in terms of network availability. For PA delay and loss (Fig. 6(a) and 6(b)) we observe essentially a vertical translation of the performance curves as additional PA load is added to the network. On the other hand, for the PA service availability (Fig. 6(c)) we mainly notice an increased inclination of the curves when the average link utilization becomes higher. The "translation" phenomenon reflects the impact of the PA load on the PA performance while the "inclination" or the slope of the curves shows the influence of the network availability factor.

As expected, the impact of the network availability on the delay and loss rate is significant, but still acceptable by most non interactive applications. However, service availability seems to suffer severely from a reduced network availability. A 5% reduction in the level of network availability can cause a 50% drop in the level of PA service availability. This result is surprising and is likely to limit

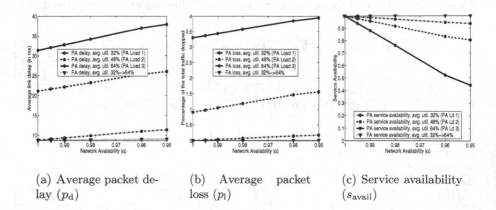

(a) Average packet delay (p_d)

(b) Average packet loss (p_l)

(c) Service availability (s_{avail})

Fig. 6. Impact of the network availability on the different SLA parameters. Three sets of curves, for low, medium and high PA load. The PA-fraction generation strategy was used and FA traffic performance are shown for reference

the introduction of the degraded traffic in a failure prone environment. Suppose that we target a PA service available 75% of the time (that would correspond to the service being unavailable during peak hours and in case of major failure events). Only networks with high level of network availability (above 98%) could potentially admit a PA load of three. Yet, at the same time service availability appears to provide a natural distinction between the FA and the PA service quality. As a consequence, customers with high service availability requirements have a strong incentive to remain in the FA service class.

6.4   Analysis of the SLA for the Degraded Class of Service

To conclude our analysis, we provide upper and lower "bounds" on the degraded traffic performance, and present SLAs for the current level of network availability in the Sprint network. Please note that we do not intend to use the term "bound" in its mathematical sense. The bounds provided in this section are found by simulations and represent a favorable (respectively an unfavorable) setting for the introduction of degraded traffic in the network.

Figures 7(a), 7(b) and 7(c) show performance intervals for packet delay, packet loss and service availability, as a function of the PA load. To compute the lower bound we measured the traffic performance under the PA-fraction generation strategy and a network availability of 95%. The upper bound corresponds to the traffic performance observed when we set the traffic generation strategy to PA-optimal and the network availability to the level of 100%. The tight bounds on the FA traffic performance are a good indication that the Sprint network is carefully provisioned to support the current backbone traffic. They demonstrate that even at high levels of failures the performance

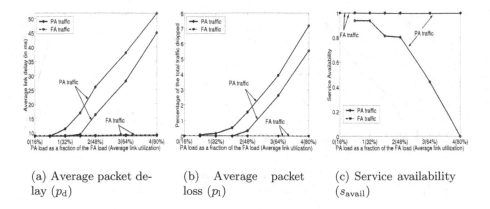

(a) Average packet delay (p_d)

(b) Average packet loss (p_l)

(c) Service availability (s_{avail})

Fig. 7. Performance interval for the FA and PA class of traffic. Two extreme cases are shown: 1) The PA-fraction generation strategy combined with a network availability of 95%; 2) The PA-optimal generation strategy with a network availability of 100%

of the FA traffic remains stable. They also show that the addition of the PA traffic has no impact on the FA traffic as demonstrated earlier by our factorial design analysis. In the case of PA traffic delays and losses, we observe a small performance interval at low PA loads which increases until the PA load in the network is twice the FA load. It is interesting to notice though that for high PA loads the PA performance interval stops expanding. The PA service availability exhibits different properties. Its performance interval keeps increasing as more traffic is added to the network while in the best case the service availability stays equal to 100%. It reflects the fact that even for large traffic loads the service availability can remain high as long as the network availability is high too and the PA traffic distribution is homogeneous.

Figure 8 depicts SLAs for the current level of network availability ($\alpha = 0.99$) in the Sprint backbone. The reported SLAs are based on measured traffic performance rounded up to the nearest ms for delay, the nearest 0.01% for loss and the nearest 0.5% for service availability. For each PA load, we present the worst performance observed among the two PA traffic generation strategies. Based on the results presented in Fig. 8 we can extract SLAs for different PA loads.

We observe that if the amount of added PA traffic is 50% of the FA traffic, then the PA will experience the same SLA as FA traffic. Moreover, we can add an amount of PA traffic equal to the amount of FA traffic, and still leave PA's SLA only marginally degraded. If more PA is added, the PA SLA begins to degrade monotonically as the load increases. In particular, the sharp decrease in service availability between PA loads of 3 and 4 indicates that we could at most quadruple the traffic load carried by the network. Nevertheless, these results are encouraging for carriers. Depending on the quality of the degraded service they

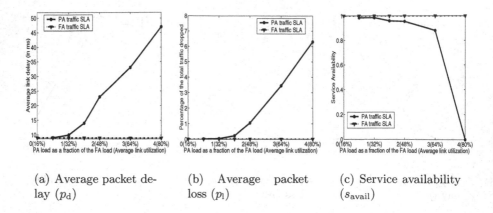

(a) Average packet de-   (b) Average packet   (c) Service availability
lay (p_d)   loss (p_l)   (s_{avail})

Fig. 8. FA and PA SLAs for the current level of network availability in the Sprint network

want to sell, they can at least double the total traffic load in their networks. The corresponding increase in revenue should then be determined through marketing studies and is outside the scope of this work.

7   Related Work

QoS is a very prolific area of research. A multitude of QoS models exist, but to date none was successfully deployed in the Internet. There is a common belief that QoS can help manage resources at no cost. This is wrong. QoS has a cost in terms of complexity, management and network robustness. This is especially true of stateful schemes such as Intserv [6]. Schemes which are almost stateless, such as Diffserv [7], seem a priori better suited for backbone deployment. Nevertheless, most of those schemes greatly increase the complexity of edge routers, while offering no explicit guarantees.

Our service differentiation technique does not require complex admission control schemes or traffic profiles. A simple one bit marking at the ingress router and a strict priority scheduler with two drop tail queues are all we need to provide service differentiation.

Backbone networks have their own characteristics. Due to the large amount of overprovisioning all users experience a very high QoS. It is thus difficult to create a Class of Service (CoS) with improved performance. Instead we decided to provide a degraded class of service. The idea of a degraded service, though not new (Internet drafts [8,9]), is especially appropriate for backbone networks. The first Internet draft [8], describes a Lower than Best Effort (LBE) Per-Hop Behavior (PHB). The primary goal is to separate the LBE traffic from best-effort traffic in congestion situations. LBE packets are discarded more aggressively than best-effort packets but nevertheless LBE traffic is guaranteed a minimal share of the bandwidth. Our proposal is, however, closer to the ideas presented in [9]. We believe that the creation of a new PHB is not required since existing PHB can be configured to forward packet of the degraded traffic only when the output link would otherwise be idle. Note that both Internet drafts are now expired. QBone Scavenger Service (QBSS) and Alternative Best Effort (ABE) are two other examples of non-elevated services and are currently under investigation by QBone [10]. QBSS is similar to the PA service we investigate in this paper but it uses different queuing disciplines. Introducing the QBSS would not allow us to maintain the SLAs of the current backbone traffic.

Packet losses in backbone network are almost always the result of failures [1]. The notion of service differentiation as a function of failures was first proposed in [11]. However, in [11], the two classes of service were protected at two different layers, one at the WDM layer and one at the IP layer. In this paper we consider that both classes are protected at the IP layer. This reflects an important reality because many carriers find protection at the optical layer to be too costly.

To the best of our knowledge, none of the previous works provides quantitative SLAs for a degraded service class in a large scale commercial backbone. We also appear to be the first to introduce real failure patterns in our analysis.

8   Conclusion

In this paper we introduce the idea of a new class of service intended to be a degraded service relative to the existing service offered by today's Internet. Our solution has three major advantages; first, it reduces the amount of unused bandwidth in the IP backbone thus improving resource utilization; second, it offers ISPs a way to increase their revenue; and third, it offers users a cheaper service which quality is sufficient for most non real-time applications. We show that, by introducing a very simple scheduling mechanism in backbone routers, it is possible to add a degraded class of traffic and still maintain the impressive performance of the legacy traffic.

The objective of this work was to evaluate the Service Level Agreements which could be offered to the customers of the degraded traffic. To do so we carry out large-scale simulations that mimic the topology, traffic matrices and failure patterns of a commercial IP backbone (i.e., the Sprint U.S domestic backbone). Although we had to make several simplifications to make our simulations tractable, we claim that our evaluation is realistic enough to prove the feasibility of our QoS scheme.

In particular, this work contains two major innovations in the area of QoS management:

- This is the first time network availability is used in the evaluation of a QoS scheme in a wired environment. Network availability effectively captures the impact of link failures on the network infrastructure.
- We introduce a new SLA metric, the service availability, in order to reflect the ability of a customer to successfully use its network connectivity at any time, independently of the destination end-point.

We demonstrate that when the amount of degraded traffic added to the network is lower than the load of the legacy traffic, the level of network availability is the primary factor affecting the degraded service quality. However, when higher loads of degraded traffic are added to the network, the average link utilization becomes the dominant factor influencing the delay and loss performance of the degraded traffic. Yet we noticed that across all traffic loads the service availability metric remains mainly affected by the level of network availability. The distribution of the degraded traffic across the links was shown to have a limited impact on its overall performance.

Our results demonstrate that it is possible to double the utilization of the network resources and still guarantee decent performance to the degraded service customers. In the context of a non-real time traffic such as web or peer-to-peer, carriers can even expect to triple or quadruple the existing traffic load depending on the level of network availability in their backbones.

The current evaluation environment has some limitation, mostly due to the simulation setting. A statistical model of resource failures in IP backbone is mandatory to provide a more accurate estimate of the degraded traffic performance and to refine the notion of network availability. In addition, the definition of service availability could be adjusted to target the needs of specific applications which are likely to generate a large share of the degraded traffic load. These subjects will form the basis of future work.

References

1. G. Iannaccone, C.-N. Chuah, R. Mortier, S. Bhattacharyya, and C. Diot, "Analysis of link failures in an IP backbone," in *ACM SIGCOMM* Internet Measurement Workshop, Marseille, France, November 2002.
2. C. Fraleigh, F. Tobagi, and C. Diot, "Provisioning IP Backbone Networks to Support Latency Sensitive Traffic," in *IEEE Infocom,* San Francisco, March 2003.
3. A. Medina, N. Taft, K. Salamatian, S. Bhattacharyya, and C. Diot, "Traffic Matrix Estimation: Existing Techniques and New Directions," in *ACM SIGCOMM,* Pittsburgh, USA, August 2002.
4. R. Jain, *The art of Computer Systems Performance analysis: techniques for experimental design, measurement, simulation, and modeling.* New York: Jon Wiley, 1991, no. 0-471-50336-3.
5. P.W.M. John, *Statistical Design and Analysis of Experiments.* 3600 University City Science Center, Philadelphia, PA 19104-2688: Society for Industrial and applied Mathematics, 1998, no. 0-89871-427-3.
6. R. Braden, D. Clark, and S. Shenker, *Integrated Services in the Internet Architecture: An Overview,* IETF RFC 1633, June 1994.
7. Y. Bernet *et al., A Framework for Differentiated Services,* IETF Internet Draft, February 1999.
8. R. Bless and K. Wehrle, *A lower Than Best-Effort Per-Hop Behavior,* IETF Internet Draft, Expired.
9. B. Carpenter and K. Nichols, *A Bulk Handling Per-Domain Behavior for Differentiated Service,* IETF Internet Draft, Expired.
10. "http://qbone.internet2.edu/."

Quality of Availability: Replica Placement
for Widely Distributed Systems

Giwon On, Jens Schmitt, and Ralf Steinmetz

Multimedia Communications Lab (KOM), Department of Electrical Engineering and
Information Technology, Darmstadt University of Technology, Germany
Tel.: +49-6151-166150, Fax: +49-6151-166152
{Giwon.On,Jens.Schmitt,Ralf.Steinmetz}@KOM.tu-darmstadt.de
http://www.kom.e-technik.tu-darmstadt.de/

Abstract. In this paper, we take an availability-centric view on Quality of Service
(QoS) and focus on the issues of providing availability guarantees for widely distributed systems such as web servers and peer-to-peer (P2P) file sharing systems.
We propose a concept called *Quality of Availability* (QoA) in which the availability is treated as a new controllable QoS parameter. The newly refined fine-
grained availability definitions and QoA metrics enable the specification and
evaluation of the different level of availability for different users and applications. We tackle specifically the replica placement (RP) problem where our focus
is on choosing the number and location of replicas while (1) meeting *different*
availability QoS requirement levels for all individual users and (2) taking the
intermittent connectivity of system nodes explicitly into account. We decompose
the RP problem into two sub-problems: (1) *improving* QoA and (2) *guaranteeing*
QoA. We investigate a number of simulations - for *full* and *partial* replication
models and *static* and *dynamic* placements - to compare and evaluate the
achieved availability QoS of the developed RP algorithms. Our proposed QoA
concept and model can be used as a base mechanism for further study on the
effectiveness of realistic replication schemes on both availability and performance QoS for widely distributed systems.

1 Introduction

Even though there are many significant research results, technology advances and
solutions in *Quality of Service* (QoS) in the last 20 years [1,2], their application to
commercial products or systems has not been so successful in comparison with their
attention in the research arena. One probable critical reason is that, as pointed out in
[3], the main research focus for QoS was to control transmission characteristics like
bandwidth, delay, and loss. This is because Internet applications which typically
assumed the need for QoS support, such as video-on-demand (VoD) and Internet
telephony, strongly motivated the development of QoS technologies. While for these
the control of the transmission characteristics is certainly important it seems likely by
now that, on the one hand, for them this may not be the most pressing need with regard
to QoS requirements, and on the other hand that there are other applications having
quite different requirements. Indeed, the perceived QoS may be much more influenced
by how available a certain service and its data are. In the context of QoS, availability
as an issue has so far seldom been mentioned, and there is no work known to us which
tries to treat availability as a controllable QoS parameter.

Concerning (service) availability support, while most research efforts in high
availability and fault-tolerant systems areas focus on achieving the so-called 'five

K. Jeffay, I. Stoica, and K. Wehrle (Eds.): IWQoS 2003, LNCS 2707, pp. 325–342, 2003.

nines' (99.999%) availability [4], there is a demand for service differentiation from service consumers and providers due to costs and competitive nature of the market space, which derives for the mechanisms that support different levels of services and their availability.

The work in this paper is strongly motivated by the two aspects mentioned above - importance of *service availability* and *differentiation* of service classes and availability requirements. As a consequence, we take an availability-centric view on QoS and focus on the issues of providing availability guarantees in widely distributed systems and services. For this purpose, we propose a concept called *quality of availability* (QoA) where the availability is treated as a new controllable QoS parameter. Based on the QoA concept, service providers and consumers can specify and check the target levels of service availability that they offer and require, respectively, in a fine-grained form. To enable these features, we first refine the traditional availability definitions which are limited to reasonably quantify achieved availability of widely distributed systems. This is because the traditional definitions are mostly used to specify the service uptime of tightly-coupled or clustered distributed systems. Thus they are neither suited to explicitly capture the supplying availability of individual system components nor to cover failures of communication links between peers.

We then tackle the replica placement (RP) problem where the main goal is to choose the number and location of replicas to satisfy (and eventually guarantee if required) *different* level of availability QoS requirement for all individual users while taking the intermittent connectivity of system nodes explicitly into account. We decompose the RP problem into two sub-problems: (1) *improving* QoA and (2) *guaranteeing* QoA. For improve QoA, we take simple ranking-based heuristics which calculate the supplying availability for all service hosting nodes and select the nodes with higher (or highest) availability values as replica nodes on which the replicas are placed. To guarantee QoA, we develop an exact method *state enumeration* which enumerates all possible placements without skipping any solution case. The algorithm can actually guarantee QoA but has exponential run-time complexity. Thus, we develop an additional algorithm called *admission-controlled placement* which also offers a QoA guarantee but has significantly low run-time complexity.

To quantitatively study the effectiveness of the proposed placement algorithms, we run and analyse a number of simulations - for *full* and *partial* replication models and *static* and *dynamic* placements. For the dynamic placement we develop an event-driven simulation model which captures the data access model as well as systems' dynamic behaviour. Simulation results show that (1) even simple heuristics can achieve reasonably high availability QoS, but they cannot give any guarantee for their achieved availability QoS, (2) the state enumeration algorithm guarantees the availability QoS with its placement results, but the run-time complexity is exponential, and (3) satisfying availability QoS requires more replicas than only increasing the performance, e.g., increasing hit rate.

The rest of this paper is organized as follows. In Section 2, we describe the proposed refinements of availability definitions, the QoA concept and its metrics which are used for specifying and evaluating the quality of replication. Section 3 presents the replica placement problem. We details our target system and replica placement model and the proposed algorithms. In Section 4, we present the simulation study and results. Section 5 discusses related work and Section 6 concludes the paper.

2 Availability Refinement and QoA Metrics

2.1 Traditional Definitions

Availability is one of the most important issues in distributed systems. Traditional definitions of availability are typically based on (a) how reliable the underlying system is, (b) whether the system has any built-in features of failure detection and recovery, and (c) whether the system has any redundancy for its individual system components ([5]). In traditional distributed systems, service availability is usually defined as the percentage of time during which the service is available (Equation 1).

$$Availability = \frac{MTTF}{MTTF + MTTR} \quad \text{where} \tag{1}$$

```
MTBF = MTTF + MTTR
failure means no distributed service
MTBF is the mean time between failure
MTTF is the mean time to failure
MTTR is the mean time to repair
```

However, these traditional availability definitions cannot explicitly capture the availability of individual system components or the reachability of any data required by the system, in particular when all these individual system components which affect the quality of supplying service availability have different failure levels. For example, an availability value of 99% does not indicate whether it is due to the failures of any disks or system nodes. Furthermore, since these definitions are mostly used to specify the availability values for tightly-coupled or clustered distributed systems, especially when they are applied to widely distributed systems, they do not cover failures of communication links between system nodes. In Section 2.2 we propose three availability refinements, *fine-grained*, *decoupled* and *differentiated* availability.

2.2 Refining Availability Definition

While we keep the traditional availability definitions as a basis for our availability study, we refine them to enable the specification of all the individual availability requirement levels between different users, as well as to quantitatively evaluate the reached availability of widely distributed systems.

2.2.1 Fine-Grained Availability

We refine the traditional availability definition as follows:

$$Avail_{Service} = Avail_{Data} \times Avail_{System} \quad \text{with} \tag{2}$$

$$Avail_{System} = Avail_{Node} \times Avail_{Link} \quad \text{and} \tag{3}$$

$$Avail_{Node} = Avail_{NodeDynamics} \times Avail_{NodeIntrinsics} \tag{4}$$

This fine-grained availability definition captures the following:

- a service is available when both its data and the system on which the service is running are available.
- a data is available when it is reachable at access time.
- a system is available, when both nodes and communication links are available.
- a link is available when it does not fail and there are enough resources which can be allocated for transmitting the requested data for the demanding application.

- a node is available when it is up, i.e. not disconnected from the network, and its intrinsics can be allocated for processing the service request. Resources such as memory, CPU cycle, and storage spaces are examples of such intrinsics.

2.2.2 Decoupled Availability: Demand versus Supply

We distinguish between availability levels which the service (or the underlying system) supplies from the availability levels which users (or applications) request and perceive. This refinement enables one to check whether the service system maximizes availability, as well as whether the service system satisfies the requested availability.

For specifying demand availability, we re-use the availability definition where availability is defined as a ratio of successful accesses to totally requested accesses. For example, demand service availability of 99.99% means that a user expects to have an availability level of at least 99.99 % of the whole successful service access requests. The demand availability levels can be specified directly by users at service access time or by means of Service Level Agreements (SLAs) which may be a service contract between users and service providers. In comparison to the demand availability, the supply service availability can be calculated by using Equation (2)-(4).

2.2.3 Differentiated Availability

In widely distributed systems where several multiple applications are hosted, the availability levels required by different applications may usually vary, i.e. not all applications require the highest availability level of 'five nines', but instead an appropriate level which satisfies the application specific requirements. A similar phenomenon can be observed within a single application in which individual users demand different levels of availability due to resource or cost limitations. We now summarize some selected motivations for differentiating availability levels:

- Different users require different availability levels.
- Different services and contents have different importance priority levels.
- Availability levels are affected by the time of day.

Figure 1 shows the three refined availability definitions proposed above.

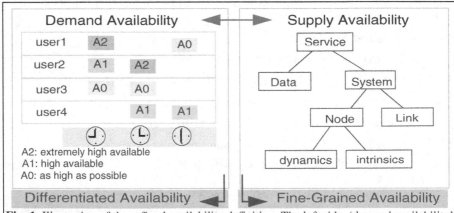

Fig. 1. Illustration of the refined availability definition. The left side, 'demand availability' can be easily mapped to a single service usage scenario in which the different availability levels (A0 - A2) are affected by the time of day (9 am, 3 pm and 6 pm).

2.3 The Concept of Quality of Availability (QoA)

2.3.1 Basic Idea and Goals

The basic idea of the QoA concept is that the availability can be defined as *a new controllable, observable QoS parameter*. Indeed, we move the focus of the objective function for the resource and performance optimization problems of the QoS field from satisfying transmission-dependent characteristics such as minimizing transmission delay, jitter, and/or loss to satisfying the availability requirements such as minimizing failure time of service systems and their components and to maximizing the total time in which the required service functions as expected and its data are reachable.

The goal of our work is to understand and satisfy quality of availability (QoA), i.e. to maximize service systems' requested service time and to control and guarantee QoA. Given a set of different levels of availability requirements and a network topology with a finite number of possible replica locations, we are then interested in how many replicas are needed, where should they be placed, whether their placement on the given topology satisfies the individually required availability QoS and how they affect the overall service availability quality. In the following section we define QoA metrics.

2.3.2 QoA Metrics

To compare and evaluate the achieved availability among the proposed replication strategies in this work, we define and use the following QoA metrics (see Table 1):

- *satisfiedQoA* - this indicates for each demanding peer how much the availability requirement has been fulfilled by the selected placement R. For example, if the required and supplied availability values are 95% and 94%, respectively, the *satisfiedQoA* is 0.99.
- *guaranteedQoA* - it indicates for how many demanding nodes the selected placement R satisfies the QoA requirement.

Table 1. QoA Metrics: V is set of entire system nodes of a widely distributed system and R is set of replica nodes (i.e. a placement) where $R \subseteq V$. |V| and |R| are cardinality of the node sets V and R, respectively.

Parameter	Notation	Definition	E.g.
satisfiedQoA	$QoA_{sat}(v)$	the ratio of supplied availability to demanding availability for node v	0.95, 1.05
minSatQoA	QoA_{min}	min $\{ QoA_{sat}(v) : \forall v \in V \backslash R \}$	0.9
avgSatQoA	QoA_{avg}	$1/n(\sum QoA_{sat}(v)), \forall v \in V \backslash R$ where $n = (|V| - |R|)$	0.95
guaranteed-QoA(v)	$QoA_{gua}(v)$	for each demanding node v, availability guarantee: $A_R(v) = 1$, if $QoA_{sat}(v) \geq 1$	1 or 0
guaranteed-QoA	QoA_{gua}	the ratio of $|V_{sat}|$ to $|V|$, where V_{sat} = set of nodes with $QoA_{sat}(v) \geq 1$	0.9

3 Replica Placement in Widely Distributed Systems

3.1 System Model

3.1.1 Target System Features and Basic Assumptions

We take peer-to-peer (P2P) systems as the target distributed system of this work. Some selected characteristics of the P2P systems, which are considered in this paper are:

- Peers go up/down independently of each other. They are connected to a P2P network for a while and become disconnected after doing some service-related operations, e.g., downloading or uploading contents.
- Peers demand and supply *different levels* of service availability. The fact, whether a peer has launched the P2P program and whether the peer has still enough storage capacity or access link bandwidth, affect strongly the supplied availability.
- The availability level, that peers demand at service access time, differs between peers; some peers may expect extremely high available access, while others may be happy with '*best-effort*' QoA level.

We assume that the P2P system runs over an overlay network where each peer's physical connection link can be mapped to a logical link in the overlay network. Furthermore, each peer, like a single Autonomous System (AS) and BGP router of the Internet, has the ability to manage multiple routing paths to any destination peer to access service contents, either the original or replicas. Thus, when the destination peer or any peer among the path crashes or the (sub)path goes down, it can see other operational paths and choose the best one to continue its service access.

3.1.2 Modelling P2P Service Systems as Stochastic Graphs

P2P systems that consist of peer nodes and interconnection links between them can be modelled as an *undirected graph, G(V,E)*, where V is the set of nodes and E the set of connection links. This graph is *dynamic* if the members and the cardinality (|V| and |E|) of V and E change else it is *static*. The graph is said to be *stochastic* when each node and link are parameterized, statistically independently of each other, with known availability or failure probabilities. For all of our simulation, we model the target P2P system as a *undirected stochastic* graph where the placement can be made in both *static* and *dynamic* modes.

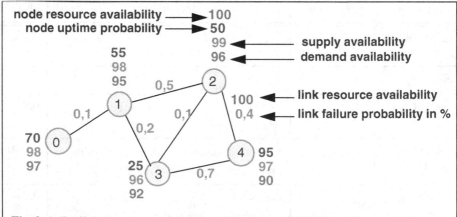

Fig. 2. A distributed service modeled as a stochastic graph G(V,E), with example figures.

In this graph, we assign the availability values to every node of the graph, where the demand and the supply availability are decoupled for each node: the demanding availability value is assigned at the graph creation time, while the supplying availability value is calculated by Equation (4). Furthermore, in a dynamic graph, the nodes change their state between up and down according to the given probability distribution function. The scope of dynamics that we capture in this work are peers' state (up/down) which causes the change of the number of total peers being up, their connectivity and their available storage capacity. Concerning a peer's state and the availability of contents located on the peer, we can assume that the contents on the nodes are unavailable, when the peer goes down. In our P2P model, we treat the up/down probability of each peer as (a) given as a prior knowledge or (b) unknown. Figure 2 illustrates an example stochastic graph that models a distributed system such as P2P system.

3.1.3 Replication Model

Replication is a proven concept for increasing the availability for distributed systems. Replicating services and data from the origin system to multiple networked computers increases the redundancy of the target service system, and thus the availability of the service is increased. In this paper we capture both *full* and *partial* replication models. In the full replication model, the entire data of an origin (server) system is replicated to other nodes located within the same network. *Mirroring* is a typical case of the full replication model. In the partial replication model, the individual data is replicated from its original system location to other systems, independently of each other. Important decisions for these replication models, which affect strongly the achieved QoA are:

- *what to replicate?* - replica selection. Selecting target replicas depends on the popularity and importance of content, which can be gained by tracing users' access history. To build a realistic access model, the *Uniform* and *Zipf*-like query distributions [6,7] are adopted for our simulation study of the dynamic placement mode. As content access type we assume read-only access. This is generally the case in P2P file-sharing systems such as Gnutella [8] and KaZaA [9]. In this case, we *do not address the consistency issue*.
- *how many to replicate?* - replica number. In addition to the popularity and importance of contents, the storage capacity and access bandwidth of peers affect strongly the decision of the number of replicas. In this work, we also capture the number of replicas under replication, i.e. the number of peers that have a particular content. To fix the number of replicas during the initial placement phase of our simulation runs, we will use the static replica distributions, *Uniform* and *Proportional*, as given in [6].
- *where to place the replicas?* - replica location. As [10] shows, the location of replicas is a more relevant factor than the number of replicas for achieving high QoA. Furthermore, to find a 'good' placement we should take not only contents' popularity or peers' storage/link capacity into account, but also the availability of individual peers, e.g. the number of up peers which may have the original content or its replicas to be accessed. Our replica placement model consists of two phases, *proactive* and *on-demand* placement. The proactive placement is done at service initialization time before any content access query is issued, while the on-demand placement occurs during service run time. We model the proactive placement to be performed with/without *a prior* knowledge about the content popularity and

the network topology. In case of the on-demand placement, some new replicas are created if the set of currently reachable replicas (including the original content, if available) does not satisfy the demanding availability value of the querying peer. Additionally, some existing replicas may be replaced by new replicas, if there is a storage capacity problem at peers on which the created replicas should be placed.

3.2 Problem Statement

We formulate replica placement as an optimization problem as follows. Consider a P2P system which aims to increase its service availability by pushing its content or replicating the content to other peers. The problem is to (dynamically) decide where content is to be placed so that some objective function is optimized under the given access model and resource constraints. The objective function can either minimize the total number of replicas on the whole peer systems or satisfy all individual peers' QoA requirement levels. For example, we have a stochastic graph $G(V, E)$ as input and eventually a positive integer number k as a maximum number of replicas for each content.

The objective of this problem is to place the k replicas on the nodes of V, i.e. find R such that a given target condition $O(|R|, R, QoA\_condition)$ is optimized for given availability requirements of the service demanding nodes. How well the target condition is optimized depends on the size of $|R|$ and the topological placement R. Because the main goal associated with placing replicas on a given network in our work is satisfying QoA which can be required in different levels, we take the availability and failure parameters as our key optimization target, i.e. $O(|R|, R, satisfiedQoA)$ or $O(|R|, R, guaranteedQoA)$ for the two RP sub-problems, *improving* QoA and *guaranteeing* QoA, respectively.

3.3 Replica Placement Algorithms

The RP problem can be classified as NP-hard discrete location problem [11]. In literature, many similar location problems are introduced and algorithms are proposed to solve the problems in this category. In this section we propose two algorithms that can be classified according to the two conditions described in Section 3.2.

3.3.1 Ranking-Based Heuristics for Improving QoA

To improve QoA, we take some basic heuristic algorithms. We note however not different variants of these heuristics and improvement techniques can be used with small modifications to enhance the efficiency and performance of our basic heuristics. A short description of each of the used heuristics is as follows:

- *Random (RA)*. By using a random generator, we pick a node v with uniform probability, but without considering the node's supplying availability value and up probability, and put it into the replica set. If the node already exists in the replica set, we pick a new node, until the given number reaches k.
- *HighlyUpFirst (UP)*. The basic principle of the *UP* heuristic is that nodes with the highest up probability can potentially be reached by more nodes. So we place replicas on nodes of V in descending order of up probability.
- *HighlyAvailableFirst (HA)*. For each node v, we calculate its actual supply availability value by taking all the availability values of its data, intrinsics and of all its adjacent edges into account. The nodes are then sorted in decreasing order of their actual availability values, and we finally put the best k nodes into the replica set.

The use of the UP and HA heuristics assumes that we have a prior knowledge about the network topology.

- *HighlyAvailableFirst with HighestTransitNode (HA+TR)*. This method is a combination of the *HA* algorithm with *TransitNode* concept. The basic principle of the *TransitNode* concept is that nodes with the highest (in/out) degrees, i.e., the number of connection links to adjacent nodes, can potentially reach more nodes with smaller latency. So we place replicas on nodes of V in descending order of (in/out) degree.
- *Combined (HA+UP)*. This method is a combination of the *HA* and *UP* algorithms. For this algorithm, we first calculate the average values of uptime probability and supplying availability for all peers. We then select those nodes as replica nodes for which both values are greater than the average values: we first check the uptime probability value and then the availability probability value.
- *Local*. To create or replace a new replica during service runtime (i.e., simulation runtime), the peer places a new replica on its local storage. The replica replacement policy bases either on *least recently used* (LRU) or on *most frequently used* (MFU) concept.

3.3.2 Exact Method - *State Enumeration* for Guaranteeing QoA

Guaranteeing QoA is likely to satisfy a certain, required QoA value with a guarantee. This means we have to always offer a replica set which fulfils the given QoA requirements for all demanding nodes in any case. In comparison to the problem of improving QoA described above in Section 3.3.1, this problem requires a solution which exactly tests all possible placements and finds the optimum, i.e. a placement that offers a QoA guarantee with a minimal number of replica nodes. Some similar work is described in the literature, which are devoted to the problem of *network reliability* [12]. The methods that provide an exact reliability are called exact methods, in contrast to the heuristic methods which provide an approximate result. From some exact methods we adopt the *state enumeration* method [12] and modified it for our problem.

In the state enumeration method, the state of each node and each edge are enumerated: the state value is either *1* when it functions or *0* when it fails. Indeed, there are $2^{|V|+|E|}$ states for a graph $G = (V,E)$, i.e., $2^{|V|+|E|}$ partial graphs for G. We then check the QoA for all partial graphs with all instances of replica sets.

4 Simulation

4.1 Simulation Methodology

We built an experimental environment to perform an event-driven simulation study for the replica placement problem addressed in Section 3. For our availability evaluation, we conducted simulations on random network topologies. By using the LEDA library [13] several random topologies in different sizes can be generated at run time. The simulation program was written in C/C++ and tested under Linux and Sun Solaris.

We ran a number of simulations - both for *full* and *partial* replication models and *static* and *dynamic* placement approaches. The dynamic placement consists of the proactive and on-demand placement phases, while the static placement considers only the proactive placement. We then compared and evaluated the achieved QoA of the developed RP algorithms using topologies of different sizes as well as parameter values shown in Tables 2 (for the static approach) and 3 (for the dynamic approach).

The demanding and initial data availability values of the nodes, as well as the up probability values of the nodes are assigned randomly, from a uniform distribution. To evaluate the QoA offered by our replication schemes, we used the QoA metrics defined in Table 1 of Section 2.3.2.

Table 2. Simulation parameters and their value ranges: these values are used for the simulation runs in the static placement mode in Sections 4.2 and 4.3. The data availability for a given node is 1, if the node contains the original data or its replica.

Type	Parameter	Value
Graph	node and edge size	G1(20:30), G2(100:300)
Edge	edges' failure probability	1 ~ 10%, 0%
Node	nodes' demanding availability	90~99%, 50~99%, 50-90-99%
Data	data availability	1 or 0

4.2 Improving QoA - Static Approach

In this simulation study, we evaluate the achieved QoA by our simple heuristics. As replication model, we assumed *full replication*. We further assumed that the failure probabilities of nodes and links are known. To calculate the supplying service availability, we considered only the system's availability and assumed that the data is available when the system is available. The baseline for our experiment is an initial placement R_0 which is obtained by randomly selecting k nodes from V. We then compare the achieved QoA of each heuristic to this baseline and present the relative QoA improvement obtained with each heuristic.

4.2.1 Effects of Number (|R|) and Location (R) of Replicas on Achieved QoA

We experimented to find good locations of a replica set R with |R| = k for given graphs G with maximal replica number k. The conditions that we assumed for this problem were: (1) *minSatQoA* > 0.9, 0.95, and 0.99, respectively, and (2) *avgSatQoA* > 1.0. In this case, there was no constraints on the topological location of the replicas and replicas may be placed at any node v in G.

Figure 3 shows the results from this experiment with *G2*. We plot the number of k on the x-axis and the reached QoA on the y-axis. In each graph, we plot different curves for different heuristics and different ranges for required availability values. From Figure 3, we can see that the heuristics *HA* and *HA+TR*, although they are very simple, reach significantly higher QoA in comparison to the baseline placement. For example, at the placement with 10 replicas, our both heuristics achieved ca. 100% higher satisfied QoA in average than the Random method. On the other hand, even though the improvement of 12% QoA guarantee rate with replicas 5 to 25 (totally, 20% of the whole nodes are replicas) may not seem much, it is important to note that the number of replicas is really a relevant factor for improving QoA: the lager the replica number is, the better is the reached QoA.

4.3 Guaranteeing QoA - Static Approach

The goal of this second simulation study is to find optimal selection with a guaranteed QoA for all demanding nodes. We take the same assumptions to the simulation study of Section 4.2: *full replication* model, the failure probabilities of nodes and links known as a prior information, and the same service availability scope for supplying availability.

Avg. Satisfied QoA: demand QoA: 50-99%, link failure probability: 0-10%

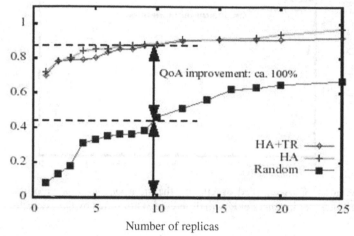

Number of replicas

Fig. 3. Achieved QoA values by our heuristics. y-axis means the satisfied QoA in average.

In this experiment, we used the *state enumeration* algorithm. Due to the exponential growing run-time complexity and the memory requirements with growing graph sizes, we limited our experiments for the *state enumeration* to a small graph, the test graph *G1* with $|V| = 20$ and $|E| = 30$. We started the routine with a replica degree of 1, i.e., $k=|R| = 1$, and selected each node as replica node. We then incremented the replica degree, until we reached the *guaranteedQoA* = 1.0 (a QoA with guarantee). Table 3 shows the achieved QoA values at each k $(k-1,2,3)$. Figure 4 plots the reached QoA that the *state enumeration* algorithm calculated exactly with each instance for the given k. Figure 4 shows significantly how the achieved QoA varies, and how big the gap between good and bad QoA rates reached by the instances is.

Table 3. A test result from state enumeration algorithm with G1, failure probability: 0%, and req. availability range: 90-99%. 'QoA value' means the guaranteed QoA value in average.

$|R|$	Best QoA value	Worst QoA value	Mean QoA value	Instances achieved the best QoA value
1	0.80	0.10	0.3345	{0},{8}
2	0.95	0.15	0.8078	{0,11},{0,18},{8,11},{8,18}, {11,13},{12,16},{13,16}
3	1.00			{0,11,16},{0,16,18},{8,11,16}, {8,16,18},{11,12,16},{11,13,16}

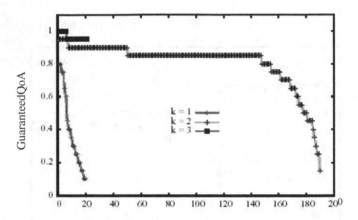

Fig. 4. Achieved QoA checked exactly by the *state enumeration* algorithm. x-axis means the number of instances of R with different $k = |R|$: sorted by QoA decreasing order.

4.4 Improving QoA - Dynamic Approach

The main goal of this simulation study is to choose dynamically a 'good' placement which increase/maximize the satisfied QoA for a given replica number. We developed an event-driven simulation model which captures the data access model as well as peers' dynamic behaviour, e.g., going up or down, etc. As replication model, we assumed the *partial replication*. However, we did not assume any a prior knowledge more for the failure probabilities of nodes and links. Furthermore, we used the whole scope of the service availability definition (Equation 4) to calculate the supplying service availability. We modelled the dynamic placement in two phases: *proactive* and *on-demand*. The proactive placement is likely the static placement of Sections 4.2 and 4.3, while the on-demand placement means a replica replacement that is done by each demanding peers, i.e., content access query issuing peers, when the supplying QoA does not satisfy the demanding QoA. Thus, the dynamic placement is a decentralized and on-line placement. As placement algorithms, we used Random, HA, UP, combined HA+UP and Local-LRU. Table 4 summarizes the simulation parameters with their values used for the simulation study in this Section. The simulation starts by placing k distinct contents randomly into the graph without considering peers' up probability. Then the query event generator starts to generate events according to the *Uniform* process with average generating rate at 10 queries per simulation time slot. For each query event, a peer is randomly chosen to issue the query. As search method, we use a multi-path search algorithm which finds all redundant paths from the querying peer to all peers that have the target content (either the original or a replica).

4.4.1 Effects of Initial Replica Selection on Satisfied QoA

In the first experiment we compared the two replica selection schemes - *Uniform* and *Proportional* which decide, for a given fixed number of k, the target replicas among original contents at the service initialization phase. In this experiment we placed the k replicas on randomly chosen peers which do not contain the original content of the corresponding replica. Furthermore, the peer contains only one replica for each

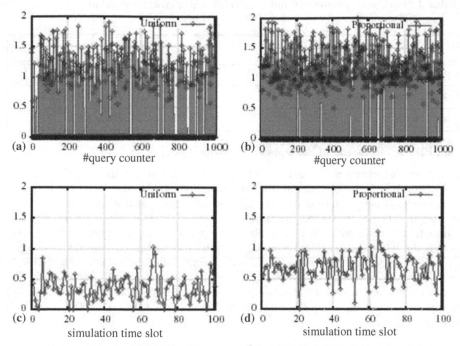

Fig. 5. Effects of initial replica selection schemes on satisfied QoA with proactive placement: *Random*, #peers=1000, peers' up probability=0.3, and query model: *Zipf*. y-axis means the satisfied QoA in average. For (a) and (b) x-axis means the number of query counter, while for (c) and (d) it means simulation time slot.

original content. As Figure 5 shows, the *Proportional* scheme offers higher satisfied QoA than the *Uniform* scheme for the *Zipf*-like access query model.

Table 4. Simulation parameters and their value ranges for the simulation runs with the dynamic placement.

Parameters	Values
peer up probability	0.0 - 0.9
content popularity	.01 - .99
number of peers	100, 1000
number of origin contents	1000
number of query events	1000
number of simulation time slots	100
range of demand availability values	.50 - 0.99
range of supply data availability	.50 - 0.99
query distribution	Uniform, Zipf

Table 4. Simulation parameters and their value ranges for the simulation runs with the dynamic placement.

Parameters	Values
proactive placement heuristics	Random, UP, HA, HA+UP
on-demand placement heuristics	Local-LRU, UP, HA, HA+UP
test graphs	G1(100,300), G2(1K,5K)

4.4.2 Effects of Placement Schemes on Satisfied QoA

In the second experiment we took different on-demand schemes that create new replicas during the simulation run when the supplied QoA with existing replicas from the up peers at the given time slot does not satisfy the demanding QoA. In addition to the *Local* scheme, we tested the three heuristics *UP, HA,* and *UP+HA* with the assumption that we have knowledge about the peers' state. As Figure 6 shows, even though the heuristic algorithms are very simple, they achieved considerably higher satisfied QoA than the *Local* scheme. For example, the QoA improvement of the replication ratio range 10-50 is about 30-70%. Figure 6(b) shows that this improvement pattern is observable independent of the graph size: Peer100 and Peer1K in Figure (b) are equal to the nodes size 100 (graph G1) and 100 (graph G2), respectively.

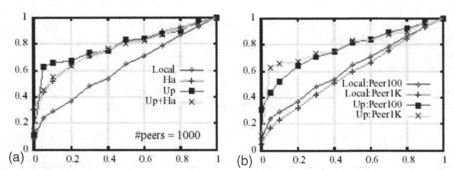

Fig. 6. Effect of placement strategies
on satisfied QoA where proactive placement: *Random* and peers' up probability=0.3. (a) average satisfied QoA from all four heuristics used. #peers=1000, (b) a comparison of the average satisfied QoA between *Local-LRU* and *UP* heuristic with different graph sizes. The number of peers of Peer100 and Peer1K is100 and 1000, respectively. X-axis means replication ratio, 0-100%, while y-axis means the satsfied QoA

4.4.3 Satisfied QoA versus Hit Probability

Maximizing hit probability is one frequently used goal for content replication [13]. In Figure 7 we show a comparison between the two replication goals, i.e. satisfying required QoA and maximizing hit probability. In this comparison the hit probability is increased when the querying peer finds the target content, while for satisfying QoA the peer should additionally check the supplied QoA by calculating all the reachable paths to the peers containing the target content (or replica). We run the simulation on the test graphs G1 and G2. The average up probability of peers is fixed again at 0.3 and we used *Random* and *UP* placement schemes for proactive and on-demand phase respectively. As Figure 7 shows, satisfying required QoA incurs higher cost, i.e. more number of replicas than just maximizing hit probability. For example, when the replica rate is 0.2, the gap between *sqoa* (satisfied QoA) and *Found* (hit probability reached) is about 20% of achieved rate. And, to achieve the same rate of 80%, for satisfying QoA, we need a 30% higher replication ratio.

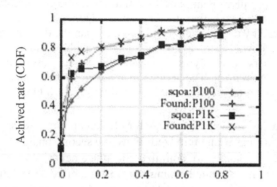

Fig. 7. Comparison of replication cost for different replication goals: satisfying QoA vs. maximizing hit probability. P100 and P1K mean 100 and 1000 nodes, respectively. X-axis means replication ratio.

4.5 Discussion

4.5.1 Summary of Simulation Results

The following observations could be identified from our experiment results:

- The location of replicas is a relevant factor for the availability QoS. Even though the QoA improvement could be achieved by increasing replica numbers, replicas' placement and their dependability affected the QoA more significantly.
- Using a heuristic method is more efficient than the exact method, at least in terms of the runtime complexity, to find a good placement for large graphs. But, the replica degree of their placement results are in most cases higher than those of exact methods. Furthermore, the heuristics give no guarantee for availability QoS.
- In opposite to the heuristic method, the exact method can exactly find the optimum and give QoA guarantee with its placement results, although the runtime complexity is very high: to find the optimum, we need to call the state enumeration method $2^{|V|}$ times, i.e., for all the possible replica solution sets. The algorithm complexity is then $O(2^{|V|} \cdot 2^{|V|+|E|})$ to find the optimum with all possible instances.
- Satisfying availability QoS requires more replicas than only improving performance, e.g. increasing hit rate.

4.5.2 Algorithm Improvement: Admission Controlled Placement for Guaranteeing QoA

We investigate for new placement algorithms which reduce the exponential runtime complexity while guaranteeing QoA. One of possible solution algorithms is using the admission control technique [2] where the placement is controlled based on available resources of the system nodes and links: each system node (peer) checks its current (node and intrinsics) availability and either accepts or rejects the new request based on the check result. For this purpose, we take additional constraints on resource capacities, e.g. storage space, load and access bandwidth capacity. We further assume that there may be at least one replica or its original data available at any access time. In the new placement algorithm which we call *admission-controlled placement*, the replica placement can be performed in two (or more) phases: *Base placement* and *Optimization*. In the base placement phase, we find the highest available path for each of demanding nodes and test whether the path gives a QoA guarantee, i.e. whether the supplied QoA achieved by the selected path is greater than the demanding QoA for the node. If the test fails, we select a node along the path, which is closest to the destination node (i.e. service supplying node) and has enough resource to be allocated and fulfils the QoA requirement. The node is then added to the replica node set. After the first placement phase, this replica node set will then give a QoA guarantee for all demanding nodes.

The resulting replica set R guarantees QoA for all demanding nodes. However, R is neither the optimum nor has been optimized. Thus, the second phase of our admission-controlled placement is mainly to optimize the placement. We try to reduce |R| determined in the first phase, while keeping the QoA guarantee. One simple approach is to delete the replicas with lower supply QoA values. For example, each replica node of R is taken (or hidden). We then check for the demanding nodes which are assigned to the hidden node whether their demand QoA values can be fulfilled by supply QoA of all other replica nodes in R. If yes, the hidden node can be deleted. This test is repeated for all the replica nodes of R. We call this phase as *Optimization* phase.

The optimized placement R2, which is determined in the second phase of the admission-controlled algorithm, offers also QoA guarantee for all demanding nodes. However, it may still not be the optimum. Therefore, one may adopt additional optimization techniques such as '*Move and Update*' [21]. We used the admission-controlled algorithm for both static and dynamic replication modes. Currently, we are collecting simulation results of the algorithm. [19] shows a pseudo-code the base placement module of the admission-controlled algorithm.

5 Related Work

The key ideas on which our work on QoA concept in this paper bases are (i) an availability-centric view on QoS and (ii) satisfying different levels of QoA values required by individual users. Since the common goals associated with replica placement problems in existing studies are reducing clients' download time and alleviating server load, the main feature of the problem solving approaches for this problem category is that they usually addressed the cost and resource minimization issues, but not the question how to guarantee the required availability.

Kangasharju et al [14] studied the problem of optimally replicating objects in content distribution network (CDN) servers. As with other studies [15-17], the goal of their work is to minimize object lookup time/cost, i.e., minimize average number of nodes visited to find the requested object. Furthermore, they assumed that all of the objects are always available in their origin server, regardless of the replica placement.

In [18] Kangasharju et al. also studied the problem of optimally replicating objects in P2P communities. The goal of their work is to replicate content in order to maximize hit probability. They especially tackled the replica replacement problem where they proposed *LRU* (least recently used) and *MFU* (most frequently used) based local placement schemes to dynamically replicate new contents in a P2P community. As we have shown in Figure 5, maximizing hit probability does not satisfy the required QoA and, furthermore the two different goals lead to different results.

Lv et al. [6] and Cohen and Shenker [7] have recently addressed replication strategies in unstructured P2P networks. The goal of their work is to replicate in order to reduce random search times. Yu and Vahdat [20] have recently addressed the costs and limits of replication for availability. The goal of their work is to solve the minimal replication cost problem for a given target availability requirements, thus they tried to find optimal availability for given constraint on replication cost where the replication cost was defined to be the sum of the cost of replica creation, replica tear down and replica usage. Our work differs in that our goal is to replicate content in order to satisfy different levels of QoA values required by individual users. Furthermore, their work does not address an availability guarantee (guaranteedQoA = 1 at least), whereas finding the optimum in an exact way is one of the focus of this paper.

6 Conclusion

We took an availability-centric view on QoS and focused on the issues of providing models and mechanisms to satisfy availability requirement for widely distributed systems such as P2P systems. We developed a concept called *quality of availability (QoA)* in which the availability is treated as a new controllable QoS parameter. Based on the QoA concept, we modelled widely distributed systems as a stochastic graph where all nodes and edges are parameterized with known availability and failure probabilities.

We tackled specifically the replica placement problem in which we specified different placement problems with different QoA metrics such as *satisfiedQoA* and *guaranteedQoA*. Our goal was choosing the number and location of replicas to satisfy the availability QoS requirement for all individual peers, while taking intermittent connectivity of service systems explicitly into account.

From simulation studies, we have learned that

- heuristics cannot give any guarantee on their achieved availability QoS, even when hey achieve reasonably high availability QoS,
- the location of replica is a more relevant factor than its number for satisfying the required QoA,
- in opposite to the heuristic method, the exact state enumeration algorithm guarantees the availability QoS with its placement results, although the algorithm has an exponential runtime complexity, and
- satisfying availability QoS requires more replicas than for only increasing the performance.

Our proposed QoA concept and simulation model can be used for further study on the dual availability and performance QoS for dynamically changing, large-scale P2P systems, as well as on the dynamic replica placement for availability QoS guarantees. Furthermore, for a practical use of our proposed model, one can adopt a service and resource monitor located in each peer, which gathers periodically the necessary availability-related information such as total service launch time and percentage of freely available storage space.

References

[1]   Zheng Wang. *Internet QoS: Architectures and Mechanisms for Quality of Service*. Lucent Technologies, 2001.

[2]   J. Schmitt. *Heterogeneous Network QoS Systems*. Kluwer Academic Pub., June 2001. ISBN 0-793-7410-X.

[3]   H. Schulzrinne. "QoS over 20 Years". Invited Talk in *IWQoS'01*. Karlsruhe, Germany, 2001.

[4]   HP Forum. *Providing Open Architecture High Availability Solutions*, Revision 1.0, Feb. 2001. document available at <http://www.mcg.mot.com/us/products/solutions/ha_solutions.pdf>

[5]   G. Coulouris, J. Dollimore and T. Kindberg. *Distributed Systems*, 3rd Ed., Addison-Wesley, 2001.

[6]   Q. Lv, P. Cao, E. Cohen, K. Li, and S. Shenker. "Search and replication in unstructured peer-to-peer networks." In *Proc. of the 16th annual ACM International Conf. on Supercomputing (ICS'02)*, New York, USA, June 2002.

[7]   E. Cohen and S. Shenker. Replication Strategies in unstructured peer-to-peer networks. In *Proc. of ACM SIGCOMM'02*, Pittsburgh, USA, Aug. 2002.

[8]   Gnutella. http://www.gnutella.com/.

[9]   KaZaA. http://www.kazaa.com/.

[10] G. On, J. Schmitt and R. Steinmetz. "On Availability QoS for Replicated Multimedia Service and Content." in *LNCS 2515 (IDMS-PROMS'02)*, pp. 313-326, Portugal, Nov. 2002.

[11] Christos H. Papadimitrio and Kenneth Steiglitz. *Combinatorial Optimization: Algorithms and Complexity*. Prentice-Hall, ISBN 0-13-152462-3, 1982.

[12] C. Lucet and J.-F. Manouvrier. "Exact Methods to compute Network Reliability". In *Proc. of 1st International Conf. on Mathematical Methods in Reliability*, Bucharest, Roumanie, Sep. 1997.

[13] LEDA - the library of efficient data types and algorithms. Algorithmic Solutions Software GmbH. software available at <http://www.algorithmic-solutions.com/>

[14] J. Kangasharju, J. Roberts and K.W. Ross. "Object Replication Strategies in Content Distribution Networks", *Computer Communications*, Vol.25 (4), pp. 376-383, March 2002.

[15] S. Jamin, C. Jin, Y. Jin, D. Raz, Y. Shavitt and L. Zhang. "On the Placement of Internet Instrumentation", In *Proc. of IEEE INFOCOM'00*, Mar. 2000.

[16] S. Jamin, C. Jin, A. R. Kurc, D. Raz, Y. Shavitt. "Constrained Mirror Placement on the Internet", In *Proc. of IEEE INFOCOM'01*, pp. 31-40, 2001.

[17] P. Krishnan, D. Raz and Y. Shavitt. "The Cache Location Problem", In *IEEE/ACM Transactions on Networking, 8(5)*, pp. 568-582, Oct. 2000.

[18] J. Kangasharju, K.W. Ross, and D. Turner. Optimal Content Replication in P2P Communities. Manuscript. 2002.

[19] G. On, J. Schmitt and R. Steinmetz. "Admission Controlled Replica Placement algorithms." Technical Report KOM-TR-2003-7, April. 2003.

[20] Haifeng Yu and Amin Vahdat. "Minimal Replication Cost for Availability" In *Proc. of the 21th ACM Symposium on Principles of Distributed Computing (PODC)*, July 2002.

[21] N. Mladenovic, M. Labbe and P. Hansen. "Solving the p-Center Problem with Tabu Search and Variable Neighbourhood Search" July 2000. paper available at <http://www.crt.umontreal.ca/>

VII Web Services

Using Latency Quantiles to Engineer QoS Guarantees for Web Services

Ulrich Fiedler and Bernhard Plattner

Compute Engineering and Networks Laboratory
Swiss Federal Institute of Technology
ETH-Zentrum, Gloriastrasse 35
CH-8092 Zurich, Switzerland
{fiedler, plattner}@tik.ee.ethz.ch

Abstract. Simulations with web traffic usually generate input by sampling a heavy-tailed object size distribution. As a consequence these simulations remain in transient state over all periods of time, i.e. all statistics that depend on moments of this distribution, such as the average object size or the average user-perceived latency of downloads, do not converge within periods practically feasible for simulations. We therefore investigate whether the 95-th, 98-th, and 99-th latency percentiles, which do not depend on the extreme tail of the latency distribution, are more suitable statistics for the performance evaluation. We exploit that corresponding object size percentiles in samples from a heavy-tailed distribution converge to normal distributions during periods feasible for simulations. Conducting a simulation study with ns-2, we find a similar convergence for network latency percentiles. We explain this finding with probability theory and propose a method to reliably test for this convergence.

1 Introduction

Evaluating performance of web services for QoS purposes is a difficult problem due to the great variability of web traffic. An important characteristic of web traffic is that it usually shows bursts within a wide range of times scales [1]. This characteristic is called self-similarity and has been shown to be a consequence of a related observation, the heavy-tail in the size distribution of downloaded objects [2]. Modeling self-similarity in simulations with web traffic is important given that it has been shown that self-similarity has a significant negative impact on network performance [3] [4]. However, generating the input to self-similar web traffic in simulations by sampling a heavy-tailed object size distribution with infinite variance has severe implications on stability. Crovella and Lipsky [5] report that the convergence of the average object size of a sample to the average of the heavy-tailed object size distribution used to generate this sample requires simulation periods that are magnitudes too long to be practically feasible. Also, the distribution of output statistics that depend on all moments of the heavy-tailed object size distribution does not converge during practically feasible simulation periods. Therefore, the simulation remains in transient state for all practically

K. Jeffay, I. Stoica, and K. Wehrle (Eds.): IWQoS 2003, LNCS 2707, pp. 345–362, 2003.

feasible simulation periods. A similar statement can be made, considering the fact that heavy-tails are always finite in any physical or simulation environment, as long as the tail is "sufficiently long", e.g. several orders of magnitude beyond the average. Hence, to enable performance evaluation with simulation, there is a need to investigate meaningful output statistics that do not inherently have this dependency on moments of the object size distribution and thus can converge within feasible simulation periods.

In this paper, we take a end-user's perspective in a client/server scenario for web services. We propose a performance analysis method for simulations with web traffic which is based on the latency quantiles of system components such as network, server/cache, client. The latencies of these components essentially sum up to the user-perceived latency of web downloads. We exploit (i) that latency quantiles are naturally suited to describe QoS and (ii) that quantiles of interest do not depend on the extreme tail of a distribution and hence not on the moments of the distribution. (i) can be explained with the fact that the p-th quantile of user-perceived latency of web downloads equating to t_0 seconds means that a p fraction of downloads is faster than t_0. If p is represented by a percentage value, we call the pth quantile a *percentile*. Thus we argue that it is meaningful to characterize system performance for web traffic with high percentiles of the user-perceived latency such as the 95-th, 98-th, or 99-th percentile (see [6] for further details). A similar statement holds for the performance characterization of system components.

Therefore, in this paper, we explore the convergence of network latency quantiles. We exploit the fact that, if network utilization is not too high the relation between network latency and object size can be approximated as linear around latency quantiles of interest. In this case, a network latency quantile can converge when the corresponding object size quantile converges. From probability theory we know that the corresponding object size quantile converges to a normal distribution at rate $n^{-1/2}$ where n is the sample size. This convergence is fundamentally different from the convergence of the sample's average object size to an α-stable distribution at rate $n^{1/\alpha-1}$ where α is the tail index of the heavy-tailed object size distribution. As a consequence, the amount of time required to converge object size quantiles of interest and thus latency quantiles is magnitudes smaller than the amount of time required to converge the average object size which is a minimum requirement to converge the whole system. This large difference in time to converge continues to hold under the assumption of realistic limits to the object size distribution inherent to common operating systems. Under higher utilization probability theory let us still expect convergence of latency quantiles to normal although the rate will be slower than $n^{-1/2}$. The sample size required to converge an object size quantile can then be viewed as an estimation of the inital phase of the convergence of the corresponding latency quantile.

Conducting a simulation study with ns-2, we find the expected convergence of the 95-th, 98-th, and 99-th network latency percentiles for both low and high utilization. With low utilization we mean utilizations that are reported average to private networks (see [7]). With high utilization we mean utilizations that are known as an upper limit to what is acceptable during the busiest period (see [8] on provisioning procedures). We therefore propose a method that enables us to reliably test for convergence. In case of convergence the method additionally provides accurate estimates of the p-th network latency quantile which can be exploited to engineer QoS guarantees.

Finally, we argue that both, the estimation of the initial phase of the convergence, as well as the test method can also be applied to evaluate latency quantiles which are associated with system components other than the network.

Hence, the main research contributions of this paper are:

1. We give evidence that quantiles of user-perceived latencies are suitable statistics to evaluate performance of web services for QoS purposes.
2. We give evidence that latency quantiles, in contrast to other statistics such as the average latency, converge within an amount of time which is practically feasible for simulations. As a consequence, engineering QoS guarantees for latency quantiles of web services becomes feasible.
3. We provide lower bounds that estimate the initial phase required to converge latency quantiles.

The rest of this paper is structured as follows: In section 2 we review workload modeling with respect to convergence. In section 3 we determine sample sizes required to estimate object size quantiles in simulation. In section 4 we propose a method to test for convergence of network latency quantiles. In section 5 we apply this method to simulation results of a client/server scenario. Finally, we conclude in section 6.

2   Web Workload Modeling

In this section, we shortly review web workload modeling with respect to convergence.

For our analysis of convergence, we assume that the web traffic in the simulation is generated with a SURGE [9] type of model. We follow [10] and assume that the model accounts for probability distributions for the following user/session attributes:

- inter-session time between sessions from different users
- pages per session to quantify the number of web pages accessed within a session by the same user
- think time to quantify the time between completion of a download and initiation of the next request
- number of embedded objects per page
- inter-object time to quantify time between requests of embedded objects
- object size.

With respect to convergence, the probability distributions of interest are the object size distribution and the think time distribution since it is the heavy-tails of these distributions that are the essential cause for the great variability and the self-similarity of web traffic [11] [4]. We say here that a distribution with cumulative density function (CDF) F is *heavy-tailed* with *tail index* α if

$$1 - F(x) \sim x^{-\alpha} \quad for \quad n \to \infty \quad with \quad \alpha \in (0, 2] \tag{1}$$

where $a(x) \sim b(x)$ means

$$\lim_{n \to \infty} \frac{a(x)}{b(x)} = 1.$$

We note that more general definitions are possible (see e.g. [12]). Effects from the heavy-tail in the object size distribution clearly dominate the effects from the heavy-tail in the think time distribution [4]. We therefore focus our analysis of simulation input on the object size distribution. We follow the approach of [10] and model the object size distribution with a *ParetoII* [13] distribution with CDF

$$F(x) = 1 - \frac{1}{(1 + \frac{x}{s})^\alpha} \quad x \in [0, \infty[\tag{2}$$

This ParetoII distribution has two free parameters: the average a, and the shape parameter α which equals to its tail index. $s = a * (\alpha - 1)$ is a dependent parameter.

3   Characterization of Simulation Input

In this section, we characterize object size quantiles in simulation input with respect to convergence to determine minimal simulation durations. We follow [5] and assume that for any dependent parameter in simulation output to converge, the corresponding parameter in simulation input has to converge. Thus, presumably for the 95-th, 98-th, or 99-th network latency quantile in simulation output to converge, the corresponding object size quantile in simulation input has to converge. Of course, much more input may be necessary to converge the 95-th, 98-th, or 99-th network latency percentiles. We employ quantile estimation techniques in statistics to estimate minimal sample sizes required to converge object size quantiles of interest from a ParetoII distribution.

3.1   Distribution of the Sample's Quantile

Under assumption of independent sampling, the expected value of the p-th sample's quantile is given by $x_p = F^{-1}(p)$. The probability density distribution of the p-th quantile of a random variable can then be derived as follows (see e.g. [14], section 3.7, p. 101).

Let $X_{(1)}, .., X_{(n)}$ be the ordered observations from a i.i.d random variable. Let $X_{(k)}$ be the p-th quantile where $k = np$ if np is an integer, and $k = \lfloor np+1 \rfloor$ if np is not an integer. The event $x \leq X_{(k)} \leq x+dx$ occurs if $k-1$ observations are less than x, one observation is in the interval $[x, x + dx]$, and $n - k$ observations are greater than $x + dx$. The probability of any particular arrangement of this type is $F^{k-1}(x)f(x)[1 - F(x)]^{n-k}dx$. By the multinomial theorem, there are $n\binom{n-1}{k-1}$ such arrangements. Thus, the probability density distribution of the sample's p-th quantile is given by:

$$f_k(x) = n\binom{n-1}{k-1}(F(x))^{k-1}(1 - F(x))^{n-k}f(x) \tag{3}$$

The corresponding distribution $F_k(x)$ from which we can infer confidence intervals at a given sample size can be obtained by numerical integration. Moreover, it is of interest to denote that this distribution $F_k(x)$ converges to a normal distribution at rate $n^{-1/2}$. This follows from the following theorem:

Theorem 1 (Limit Theorem for Sample's Quantiles).
Let $X_1, .., X_n$ be n independent observations on a random variable X with CDF F. Let $X_{(k)}$ be the p-th quantile where $k = np$ if np is an integer, and $k = \lfloor np + 1 \rfloor$ if np is not an integer. Let (i) $F(x)$ admit a continuous PDF $f(x)$ for all x. Further let (ii) the p-th quantile x_p of F be unique and $f(x_p) > 0$. Then the distribution of the sample s p-quantile $X_{(k)}$ converges to a normal distribution:

$$\sqrt{n}(X_{(k)} - x_p) \to \mathcal{N}(0, \sigma^2) \quad for \quad n \to \infty \quad with \quad \sigma = \frac{\sqrt{p(1-p)}}{f(x_p)}$$

For a proof of this limit theorem, which is the quantile's equivalent to the more commonly kown central limit theorem (CLT) for the sample's average, refer to Rao [15], section 6f.2, p.423. The proof is essentially straightforward from Equation 3.

Both, Equation 3 and Theorem 1 can now be applied to evaluate the convergence of object size quantiles in simulation input. Theorem 1 applies for a heavy-tailed ParetoII distribution (see Equation 2 for CDF) since the ParetoII distribution fulfills the required regularity condition specified in the theorem. In detail, $f(x) = F'(x)$ of a ParetoII distribution is continuous for all $x \in [0, \infty)$ and all quantiles x_p of a ParetoII distribution are unique with $f(x_p) > 0$ since the CDF is strictly monotonous. This is although the ParetoII distribution does not fulfill the regularity condition of the central limit theorem (see [5]).

This leads to the following fundamental implications:

3.2 Implications

Object size quantiles obtained by sampling a heavy-tailed ParetoII distribution behave completely different than the average object size in the sample. The distribution of the p-th sample object size quantile converges to a normal distribution at rate $n^{-1/2}$ for sample size $n \to \infty$. Thus the p-th object size quantile can be estimated from relatively small samples since (i) the normal distribution is symmetric and has fast decaying exponential tails which lead to relatively small confidence intervals and (ii) the rate $n^{-1/2}$ is "fast". The distribution of the average object size quantile converges to a α-stable distribution at a rate $n^{1/\alpha-1} < n^{-1/2}$ where $\alpha < 2$ is the tail index of the object size distribution (see [5]). Thus estimating the average object size requires extremely large samples since (i) the α-stable distribution is usually skewed and has itself heavy-tails, which, particularly for α close to 1, leads to very large confidence intervals and (ii) the rate $n^{1/\alpha-1}$ get extremely slow for $\alpha \to 1$.

To evaluate sample sizes required to estimate object size quantiles, we can now iterate the sample size n and determine the corresponding confidence intervals and expected values. We can perform this evaluation by numerical integration of the probability density given in Equation 3 (method 1) or employ Theorem 1 as a large sample approximation (method 2). Method 2 is computationally very cheap since approximations for the confidence interval immediately follow from evaluating the variance of the approximated normally distributed sample's quantiles:

$$s_n^2 = \frac{p(1-p)}{n * f^2(x_p)} \tag{4}$$

Table 1. Sample Size Required to Estimate the 99-th Object Size Percentile

Accuracy of the 99-th Percentile	Sample Size
1%	$2.8 \cdot 10^6$
2%	$7.2 \cdot 10^5$
3%	$3.2 \cdot 10^5$
5%	$1.2 \cdot 10^5$
10%	$3.1 \cdot 10^4$

Table 2. Sample Size Required to Estimate other Object Size Percentiles

Percentile (5% Acc.)	Sample Size
95-th	$2.6 \cdot 10^4$
98-th	$6.0 \cdot 10^4$
99-th	$1.2 \cdot 10^5$
99.9-th	$1.2 \cdot 10^6$
99.99-th	$1.1 \cdot 10^7$
Average	10^8

To perform a numerical evaluation we define the *accuracy* with which we can estimate a random variable such as the object size from a samples of size n as:

$$Accuracy = max\{|\frac{L_n - E_n}{E_n}|, |\frac{U_n - E_n}{E_n}|\} \tag{5}$$

Here E_n is the expected value and L_n, U_n are the lower and upper bound of the confidence interval. We denote that evaluations in this paper are at confidence level 95%. To produce numerical values we assume that the average in the ParetoII object size distribution is 12KB and that the shape parameter $\alpha = 1.2$. These are the same values as in [10]. The exact values obtained with method 1 are listed in Table 1 and Table 2. The approximation to these values obtained with method 2 maximally differ by ± 0.2 in the mantissa.

We refer to Crovella and Lipsky [5] to compare these sample sizes to the sample sizes required to estimate the average object size from a sample. They analyze convergence to α-stable and roughly approximate the sample size required to estimate the average with a k digit accuracy as

$$n \geq c_2 * (10^{-k})^{-\frac{1}{1-1/\alpha}} \tag{6}$$

where $c_2 \approx 1$. This can be applied to estimate the average object size in the sample. Setting $10^{-k} = 0.05$ leads to the value of comparison which we added to Table 2.

This value of comparison shows that object size quantiles which are of interest to engineer guarantees on the response times of web downloads, converge at sample sizes which are magnitudes smaller than the samples sizes required to converge the average object size. This difference also holds at the presence of realistic bounds to the object size distribution inherent to common operating systems such as a 2.1GB or 4.2GB upper bound. A 2.1GB upper bound to the object size distribution leads to a required sample size of approximately 10^7 instead of 10^8 in Table 2 which can be calculated with the standard formulae based on the CLT.

Moreover, we can show that the difference between the sample size required to estimate quantiles and the sample size required to estimate the sample's average gets more pronounced when the tail index $\alpha \to 1$ (see Table 3). We denote that Table 3 lists estimates with 5% accuracy.

Table 3. Sample Size Required for Estimation of 99-th Quantile and Average

Tail Index α	99-th Percentile	Average (w/o bound)	Average (2.1GB bound)
1.1	$1.3 \cdot 10^5$	10^{14}	10^{12}
1.2	$1.2 \cdot 10^5$	10^8	10^7
1.3	$9.1 \cdot 10^4$	10^6	10^6

We summarize the findings of this section as follows: We have analyzed the convergence of object size quantiles in simulation input which is necessary that we can see convergence of latency quantiles in simulation output. We have applied quantile estimation techniques to derive this convergence which is to normal at a rate $n^{-1/2}$. This fundamentally differs from the convergence of the average object size to a α-stable distribution at a rate $n^{1/\alpha-1}$. As a consequence, the sample size required to converge the 95-th, 98-th, and 99-th object size quantile is several orders of magnitudes smaller than the sample size required to converge the average object size for α close to 1.

4   Characterization of Simulation Output

In this section, we analyze latency quantiles in simulation output with respect to convergence. We refer to probability theory to show that latency quantiles can be expected to converge to normal. We show how to reliably test for this convergence. We then conduct a simulation study to show that latency quantiles converge within periods which are practically feasible to simulations. As a consequence it becomes feasible to engineer QoS guarantees for network latency quantiles of web downloads.

Formally, convergence of latency quantiles cannot be treated in the same way as the convergence of object size quantiles. The initial assumption in Theorem 1, that the observations are independent, does not hold for the latency quantiles given that concurrent downloads can be from the same server or can share the bottleneck link on the network. Hence, the observed latencies are correlated. Literature on probability theory ([16] section 8.3) indicates that quantiles of correlated observations continue to converge to a normal distribution at a rate $n^{-1/2}$, where n is the sample size, if two conditions are fulfilled. First, a regularity condition on the distribution like (i) and (ii) in Theorem 1 is required. We think it is reasonable to assume such regularity for a latency distribution. In detail, this regularity means (i) to assume that the latency distribution F can for any latency be arbitrarily closely approximated with a differentiable function, (ii-a) that the latency associated with the quantile occurs in the simulation and (ii-b) that latencies very close to the quantile do also occur. Second, dependence of the observations must be sufficiently weak. Sufficiently weak dependence of observations means that autocorrelations of the observations decay so fast that that the convergence to normality at a $n^{-1/2}$ is not perturbed. This is e.g. the case when dependencies that depend on the lag only lead to autocorrelations which are summable over all lags (for details refer to [17]). We expect this to apply if network utilization is low. At higher utilization we expect that latency quantiles also convergence to a normal distribution. However, this convergence is at a rate slower than $n^{-1/2}$ since the observations of latencies are known to be long-range dependent. The expectation can be justified with Theorem 8.2 in [17] since quantiles can be written as M-estimators.

4.1   Testing for Convergence to Normality

We propose to (i) produce and (ii) analyze normal plots for increasing sample sizes n to test when and whether latency quantiles become convergent. We (i) apply the frequently used normal plot[1] method (see e.g. Rice[14] p. 321–328) to

---

[1] sometimes also called normal probability plot or Q-Q plot

a set of latency quantiles obtained from simulation runs with different seeds to the random number generator. This method only leads to qualitative results. We therefore (ii) enhance this method with a fully fledged statistical test to obtain quantitative results (see [14]) which can be successively monitored for increasing sample size n. We call this analyzing the normal plot. Moreover, we propose to (iii) monitor the rate of convergence. We call this consistency check.

The normal plot is produced as follows: Let $Y_{(k),j}$ be the latency quantile $Y_{(k)}$ estimated from a sample with index j which was obtained from a simulation run with a specific seed to the random number generator. Hence,

Simulation run $1 \rightarrow Y_{1,1} \leq \, .. \, \leq Y_{(k),1} .. \leq Y_{max,1}$

...

Simulation run $m \rightarrow Y_{1,m} \leq \, .. \, \leq Y_{(k),m} .. \leq Y_{max,m}$

To produce the normal plot, we arrange the estimated latency quantiles $Y_{(k),1} \ldots Y_{(k),m}$ in ascending order:

$$Y_{(k),1} \ldots Y_{(k),m} \rightarrow Y_{(k),(1)} \ldots Y_{(k),(m)}.$$

Then we exploit that if this ordered set is consistent with normality, the expected value of $Y_{(k),(i)}$ is the $\frac{i}{m+1}$ quantile of a normal distribution with unknown parameters μ and σ:

$$E(Y_{(k),(i))}) = \mathcal{N}^{-1}(\mu, \sigma^2)(\frac{i}{m+1}) \tag{7}$$

Not knowing the parameters μ and σ of the normal distribution $\mathcal{N}(\mu, \sigma^2)$, we can exploit that any quantile of a normal distribution can be closely approximated with the corresponding quantile of the standard normal distribution $\mathcal{N}(0, 1)$. The approximation relation is (see [14]):

$$\mathcal{N}^{-1}(\mu, \sigma^2)(\frac{i}{m+1}) \approx \sigma * \mathcal{N}^{-1}(0, 1)(\frac{i}{m+1}) + \mu \tag{8}$$

Therefore a *normal plot* plots the $Y_{(k),(i)}$ against the $\frac{i}{m+1}$ quantile of the standard normal distribution. If the data in the set is close to normal distributed, the result of the plot is close to a straight line. Any deviation in the data from normality such as skewness or subexponential tails can be visually inspected. However, care needs to be taken in classifying a set as representing data which is consistent with a normal distribution. Due to the ordering process $Y_{(k),1} \ldots Y_{(k),m} \rightarrow Y_{(k),(1)} \ldots Y_{(k),(m)}$ normal plots always tend to look somewhat linear.

To be reliable, we need to extend this qualitative test of visual inspection to a hypothesis test which produces quantitative results. Moreover, we want this test to provide accurate estimates of the parameters σ and μ of the normal distribution which can be exploited to engineer QoS guarantees for latencies. Therefore, we apply linear regression between the set and its expected values.

The correlation coefficient of the linear regression, which quantifies the deviation from linearity, can now be exploited to test the hypotheses that the data in the ordered set is consistent with normality. For $i = 30$ data points [14] reports that, if the data is consistent with normality, 10% of plots have a correlation coefficient below 0.9707, 5%, have a coefficient below 0.9639, and 1% have a coefficient below 0.9490. Values for $i = 40$ are 0.9767, 0.9715, and 0.9597. These values for coefficients can thus be used in a hypothesis test as critical values at desired significance level. This hypothesis test should have sufficient power to distinguish a set consistent with a normal distribution from a set consistent with a heavy-tailed α-stable distribution given that the correlation is sensitive to outliers at the extremes of the ordered set. Moreover, the slope and intercept of the linear regression provide accurate estimates of the parameters μ and σ of the normal distribution.

To enhance the robustness of the test, we additionally monitor the rate of convergence, i.e. check the consistency. We take the estimate for the standard deviation from the linear regression and check whether this estimate is consistent with a $n^{-1/2}$ rate of convergence. We do this by plotting the estimated standard deviation times $\sqrt{n}$ and check whether this is constant.

5   Results

We now apply this test method to investigate the convergence of network latency quantiles from a ns-2 (network simulator version 2) [18] simulation study of a client server scenario for web services. To perform this study we have extended ns-2 version ns-2.1b9a with our own implementation of the hyper text transfer protocol HTTP/1.1[19] on top of ns-2's FullTCP. The implementation is available via the ns-2 contributed code web page. The implementation explicitly models the HTTP interactions and includes HTTP/1.1 features like pipelining of requests for embedded pages and persistent connections between client and servers. To facilitate analysis, we limit user/session attributes in workload generation to the minimum set which is relevant to study convergence properties. This set includes the think time to quantify the time between completion of a download and initiation of the next request, the number of embedded objects per page, and object sizes. What we do not account for are session-related attributes which have distributions with fast converging tails. We also do not account for the effects of server and client latencies on the network. We also randomly chose the web server where a request goes to. We follow [10] with the choice of parameters for the think time, object size, and number of embedded objects per page distributions. We work with two models (see Table 4): The first model ("coarse model") allows us to directly associate object sizes and download times to enable a in-depth analysis. The second set ("accurate model") removes this simplification and models web workload at its full complexity. To keep results with both models comparable, we adjusted the think time in the first model such that the resulting average utilization of both workload model is equal. This means that we have kept the ratio between *average number of objects times average object size* and *average think time* constant.

Table 4. Probability Distributions for Web Traffic Generation

Workload Model	Object Size Distribution	Embedded Objects. Per Page Distribution.	Think Time Distribution
Coarse Model	ParetoII Average 12 KB Shape 1.2	None	ParetoII Average 10s Shape 2.0
Accurate Model	ParetoII Average 12 KB Shape 1.2	ParetoII Average 3 Shape 1.5	ParetoII Average 40s Shape 2.0

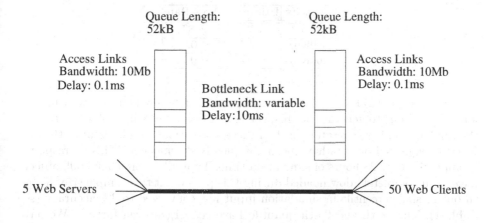

Fig. 1. Validation Topology

We then start with a simulating the dumbbell topology of Figure 1 which essentially models a bottleneck link. This bottleneck link can be viewed as an abstraction of a transoceanic link or a critical backbone link in private network. We assign a 10ms propagation delay to this bottleneck link which may also be viewed in a more general sense, since it has been argued that there is always a single bottleneck link on any network path which is usually not fast moving[20]. Access links to the bottleneck have a capacity of 10 Mb/s and a propagation delay of 0.1ms. Clients and servers are attached to the access links. Queue sizes are set to 52KB.

5.1   Simulation Study

We start our investigation of convergence of network latency quantiles with the coarse model for web traffic generation (see Table 4 for parameters). We vary the capacity at the bottleneck link to obtain samples at different network utilizations. We define *link utilization* as the amount of traffic transported over the link per time unit in proportion to the link capacity. We consider three cases for the link capacity: 6400Kb/s, 2560Kb/s, and 640Kb/s. The 6400Kb/s case leads to a utilization of slightly more than 7% (see Table 5) which is roughly equivalent to what [7] reports as average in private networks. We then gradually increase utilization up to 64% which is known as an upper limit to what's acceptable during the busiest period (see [8] on provisioning procedures). We refer to the 6400Kb/s case as low utilization, to the 2560Kb/s case as medium utilization, to the 640KB/s case as high utilization.

Table 5. Bottleneck Link: Utilization and Loss Rate

Capacity	Utilization	Loss Rate
640Kb/s	64%	0.8%
2560Kb/s	17%	$\leq 0.1\%$
6400Kb/s	7.0%	$\leq 0.1\%$

Since our goal is to investigate convergence of latency quantiles we run very long simulations to generate 30, respectively 40, samples with different seeds to the random number generator. Each of these simulations terminate after the first 500,000 requested objects have been completely downloaded. This corresponds to approximately 28 hours of simulation time. Typically more than 500k objects have been completely downloaded during this period. At this sample size the 99-th object size percentile in simulation input has converged to 3% accuracy (see Table 1). The 98-th and 95-th quantile have converged even further. We have verified that the largest object size over all simulations runs at each utilization investigated is larger than 2.1GB, i.e. very close to the object size limit inherent to ns-2. We have also verified that neither the average object size nor the average network latency converge in our simulations.

At low utilization we find convergence which is consistent with a $n^{-1/2}$ rate for all latency quantiles investigated. Therefore, we investigate whether our findings about convergence of network latency percentiles under low utilization continue to hold when we model the full variability of the structure inherent to web pages. We thus repeat the simulations for low utilization with the accurate model for web traffic generation. We run simulation with 30 different seeds to obtain samples. Each of these simulations terminate after the first 120,000 requested web pages have been completely downloaded. We successively apply the convergence test and find that the 95-th, 98-th, and 99-th network latency percentile converge to normality at a $n^{-1/2}$ rate. Figure 2 depicts that the correlation coefficient from the normality test remains above all critical values after

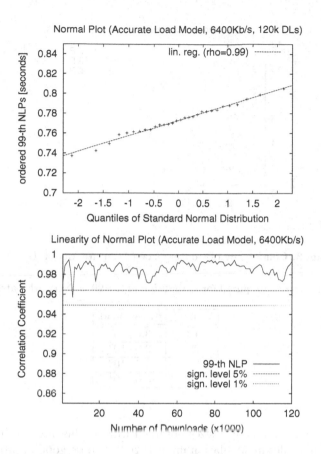

Fig. 2. Normal Plot and Linearity (99-th NLP, Accurate Model, Low Util.)

some initial phase. The same finding can be reported for the 95-th and 98-th network latency quantile. For all quantiles investigated, i.e. the 95-th, 98-th and 99-th percentile, the convergence is at a $n^{-1/2}$ rate (see Figure 3) given that deviations from constant are not larger than in the corresponding consistency check for object size quantiles in simulation input (not depicted).

Table 6 lists the sample sizes required to estimate the 99-th network latency quantile in simulation output at 5% accuracy. The listed sample sizes, which base on the accuracy definition given with equation 5, have been obtained as follows: The expected latency quantile has been estimated from the normality plot at 120k downloads. The confidence interval radius has been approximated with $1.96 * s_n$ where s_n^2 is the quantile's sample variance which has been evaluated with $s_n^2 = \sigma^2/n$. σ in turn has been estimated from the data of Figure 3. The values listed in Table 6 are slightly larger than in Table 1 which lists sample sizes required to converge object size quantiles in simulation input. A similar observation can be made for the 95-th and 98-th network latency quantile. Thus,

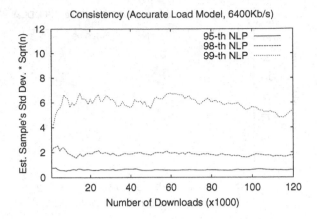

Fig. 3. Consistency of Convergence (Accurate Model, Low Util.)

Table 6. Sample Size Required for Estimation of the 99-th Network Latency Percentile

Accuracy	#Downloads
1%	$3.6 \cdot 10^6$
2%	$9.0 \cdot 10^5$
5%	$1.5 \cdot 10^5$
10%	$3.6 \cdot 10^4$

under low utilization sample sizes obtained from evaluating the convergence of object size quantiles in simulation input turn out to be good approximations for sample sizes required to estimate latency quantiles from simulation output.

At medium utilization we do not find convergence for any of the latency quantiles investigated within samples sizes we have analyzed. We explain this finding with the fact that the latency distribution in the "estimated confidence interval" around the quantiles of interest does not exhibit sufficient regularity which is required for convergence. Presumably this comes from discontinuities in TCP's reaction to minimal packet loss.

For the simulations with the coarse workload model we find that the 99-th and 98-th latency percentiles converge to a normal distribution at high utilization (see Figure 4 for results obtained with applying the test method described in section 4.1 to 40 simulation runs). The estimated confidence intervals for these latency quantiles after 500,000 downloads are: 7.35 ± 0.92 seconds for the 99-th percentile and 5.08 ± 1.37 seconds for the 98-th percentile. The 95-th latency quantile does not converge within sample sizes that we have analyzed. However, the convergence of the 99-th and 98-th latency percentile is not consistent with a $n^{-1/2}$ rate (see Figure 5 for a log-log plot of sample variance vs. sample size). Such convergence at a $n^{-1/2}$ rate would result in a line parallel to the reference line entitled with Hurst parameter $H = 0.5$. The convergence is also not com-

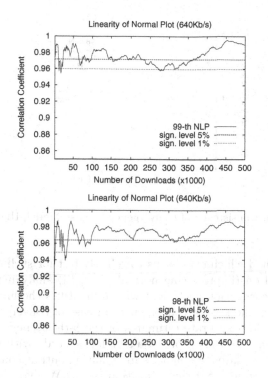

Fig. 4. Linearity of Normal Plot (Coarse Model, High Util.)

pletely consistent with a slower rate $n^{-\beta}$ with $\beta < 1/2$ which is expected for a long-range dependent correlation structure among observations of latency quantiles. Such a correlation structure would result in a straight line with smaller slope (see e.g. the reference line for Hurst parameter $H = 0.9$ which is to be expected for the corresponding on/off process (see [11])). Moreover, the 99-th and the 98-th latency percentiles converge at different rates which is to be explained with the fact that the simulation has not yet reached stability. Nevertheless, we argue that it is possible to give guarantees for these latency quantiles based on estimating an upper bound of the confidence intervals to the variance of latency quantiles at sample size n. Such an estimation can be obtained by grouping simulations and evaluating the variance of latency quantiles at sample size n for each group. In our case this implies to perform e.g. 20 times 40 simulation runs instead of 40 to estimate the confidence interval bounds. However, for practical applications some rough approximation from Figure 5 may already be sufficient.

We summarize the findings of this sections as follows: We have referred to probability theory to explain that the sample's p-th latency quantile can converge to normal at a $n^{-1/2}$ rate, where n is the sample size, if utilizaiton is low. If utilization is high, the sample's p-th latency quantile can continue to converge to normal. However, the rate will be slower than $n^{-1/2}$. Hence, we have

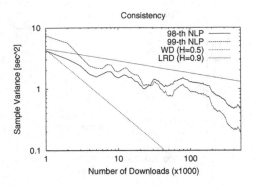

Fig. 5. Consistency of Convergence (Coarse Model, High Util.)

proposed a method which enables us to reliably test for such convergence. This method is based on (i) producing normal plots, (ii) analyzing normal plots by monitoring the correlation coefficient which quantifies the linearity of the plot, and (iii) checking the rate of convergence. In case of convergence this methods additionally provides accurate estimates of the p-th latency quantile. We have applied this method to the output of a simulation study with ns-2. We have observed that network latency quantiles in simultion output converge to a normal distribution at rate $n^{-1/2}$ if the utilization is low. We have also observed that network latency quantiles continue to converge to normal with a slower rate if utilization is high.

6   Summary and Conclusion

In this paper, we have investigated whether the 95-th, 98-th, or 99-th percentile of user-perceived latencies are suitable statistics to measure performance of web services and hence to engineer QoS guarantees for web services. We have exploited that (i) latency quantiles have a natural interpretation in evaluating QoS, (ii) quantiles do not depend on the extreme tail of the distribution and thus not on moments of the distribution, and (iii) user-perceived latency is a sum of the latencies of system components, which essentially are network, server/cache, and client. We have analyzed the convergence of simulation input to determine minimal simulation durations necessary to estimate the latency quantiles of interest from simulations. We have applied quantile estimation techniques to derive the convergence of the p-th object size quantile which is to a normal distribution at a rate $n^{-1/2}$ where n is the sample size. This convergence is fundamentally different from the convergence of the average object size to a α-stable distribution at a rate $n^{1/\alpha-1}$. As a consequence, the sample size required to converge the 95-th, 98-th, and 99-th object size quantile is several orders of magnitudes smaller than the sample size required to converge the average object size. The large difference in amount of time to converge continues to hold under the assumption of realistic limits to the object size distribution inherent to common operating systems.

We have referred to probability theory to explain that latency quantiles under low utilization converge to a normal distribution at a $n^{-1/2}$ rate. We have proposed a method to reliably test for such convergence. We have validated the test method in a simulation study with ns-2. Moreover, we have found that network latency quantiles converge to normal distributions under high load which we also explain with probability theory.

As a consequence engineering QoS guarantees for web services based on latency quantiles becomes feasible since we argue that the proposed method can as well accurately estimate latency quantiles associated with server/cache and client. In order to further clarify this issue, we plan to explore the impact of network topology and document popularity on our results.

Acknowledgements. We would like to thank many people for helpful discussions particularly Martin Maechler, Polly Huang, and Samarjit Chakraborty.

References

1. W.E.Leland, M.S. Taqqu, W. Wilinger, and D.V. Wilson, "On the Self-Similar Nature of Ethernet Traffic (Extended Version)," *IEEE/ACM Transactions on Networking*, vol. 2, no. 1, pp. 1–15, Dec. 1994.
2. M. Crovella and A. Bestavros, "Self-Similarity in World Wide Web Traffic: Evidence and Possible Causes," *IEEE/ACM Transactions on Networking*, vol. 5, no. 6, pp. 835–846, Dec. 1997.
3. A. Erramilli, O. Narayan, and W. Willinger, "Experimental Queueing Analysis with Long-Range Dependent Packet Traffic," *IEEE/ACM Transactions on Networking*, vol. 4, no. 2, pp. 209–223, Apr. 1996.
4. K. Park, G. T. Kim, and M. E. Crovella, "On the Relationship between File Sizes, Transport Protocols, and Self-Similar Network Traffic," in *Proceedings of the Fourth International Conference on Network Protocols (ICNP'96)*, Columbus, Ohio, USA, Oct. 1996, pp. 171–180.
5. M. Crovella and L. Lipsky, "Simulations with Heavy-Tailed Workloads," in *Self-Similar Network Traffic and Performance Evaluation*, K.Park and W. Willinger, Eds., chapter 3, pp. 89–100. Wiley-Interscience, NY, 2000.
6. U. Fiedler, P. Huang, and B.Plattner, "Towards Provisioning Diffserv Intra-Nets," in *Proceedings of IWQoS'01*, Karlsruhe, Germany, June 2001, pp. 27–43, Springer.
7. A. M. Odlyzko, "The Internet and other Networks: Utilization Rates and their Implications," *Information Economics and Policy*, vol. 12, pp. 341–365, 2000.
8. S. Ben Fredj et. al., "Statistical Bandwidth Sharing: A Study of Congestion at Flow Level," in *Proceedings of SIGCOMM'01*, San Diego, California, USA, Aug. 2001, pp. 111–122, ACM.
9. P. Barford and M. Crovella, "Generating Representative Web Workloads for Network and Server Performance Evaluation," in *Proceedings of Performance '98/ACM SIGMETRICS '98*, Madison, Wisconsin, USA, June 1998, pp. 151–160.
10. A. Feldmann et. al., "Dynamics of IP traffic: A Study of the Role of Variability and the Impact of Control," in *Proceedings of SIGCOMM'99*, Cambridge, Massachusetts, USA, Sept. 1999, ACM.

11. Walter Willinger, Murad S. Taqqu, Robert Sherman, and Daniel V. Wilson, "Self-Similarity through High-Variability: Statistical Analysis of Ethernet LAN Traffic at the Source Level," *IEEE/ACM Transactions on Networking*, vol. 5, no. 1, pp. 71–86, 1997.

12. C. Goldie and C. Kluppelberg, "Subexponential Distributions," in *A Practical Guide to Heavy Tails: Statistical Techniques for Analysing Heavy Tails*, R. Feldman R. Adler and M.S. Taqqu, Eds., pp. 435–460. Birkhauser, Basel (CH), 1997.

13. Norman L. Johnson, Samuel Kotz, and N. Balakrishnan, *Continuous Univariate Distributions*, vol. 1 of *Wiley Series in Probability and Mathematical Statistics*, Wiley, NY, 2 edition, 1994.

14. J. Rice, *Mathematical Statistics and Data Analysis, 2nd edition*, Duxbury Press, 1995.

15. C. Radhakrishna Rao, *Linear Statistical Inference and Its Applications*, Wiley, New York, 2 edition, 1973.

16. Frank R. Hampel, Elvezio M. Ronchetti, Peter J. Rousseeuw, and Werner A. Stahel, *Robust Statistics: The Approach Based on Influence Functions*, Wiley, NY, 1986.

17. Jan Beran, *Statistics for Long-Memory Processes*, Chapman & Hall, NY, 1994.

18. L. Breslau et. al., "Advances in Network Simulations," *IEEE Computer*, May 2000.

19. R. Fielding et. al., "Hypertext Transfer Protocol – HTTP/1.1," RFC 2616, Internet Request For Comments, June 1999.

20. S. Bajaj et. al., "Is Service Priority Useful in Networks?," in *Proceedings of the ACM Sigmetrics '98*, Madison, Wisconsin USA, June 1998.

DotQoS – A QoS Extension for .NET Remoting

Andreas Ulbrich[1], Torben Weis[1], Kurt Geihs[1], and Christian Becker[2]

[1] Berlin University of Technology, iVS[***]
Einsteinufer 17
D-10587 Berlin, Germany
{ulbi,weis,geihs}@ivs.tu-berlin.de
[2] University of Stuttgart, IPVS
Breitwiesenstr. 20-22
D-70565 Stuttgart, Germany
becker@informatik.uni-stuttgart.de

Abstract. The concern for Quality of Service (QoS) management in middleware has been an area of active research for many years. We present a novel QoS management framework for .NET, called DotQoS, which adds generic QoS management to .NET in an architecturally conforming way. It is shown how built-in .NET features such as reflection, interception, and custom meta-data facilitate the QoS integration. Throughout the paper we compare the design and implementation of DotQoS to a CORBA-based QoS framework that we developed in a previous project. Our experience with the two frameworks reveals general insights into the principles of middleware QoS engineering.

1 Introduction

Middleware facilitates the development and operation of distributed applications. The concern for Quality of Service (QoS) management in middleware has been an area of active research for many years. This research focuses on the support for non-functional properties of a service or application component. While the underlying general principle of middleware development has been distribution transparency that hides the complexity of the networked environment, QoS management explicitly deals with the effects caused by the nature of distributed systems, such as partial failures, dynamic changes in resource supply, load fluctuations and the like. In addition to such network-related effects users may be concerned about application-level QoS issues such as the level of security for a remote interaction or the precision of a computational service. Thus, our focus is on application-layer QoS and how it can be supported by the middleware layer. Clearly, application-layer QoS management is an end-to-end issue that may involve all layers on the path from the client to the server. Therefore, the support for QoS automatically becomes an issue for middleware architects, and there

[***] The work presented in this paper is partially funded by the European QCCS project, IST-1999-20122, the German DFG project GE 776/4, and the Discourse project.

K. Jeffay, I. Stoica, and K. Wehrle (Eds.): IWQoS 2003, LNCS 2707, pp. 363–380, 2003.
© Springer-Verlag Berlin Heidelberg 2003

have been many attempts to integrate QoS management in popular middleware architectures.

QoS management involves different activities in the lifecycle of a QoS-enabled distributed application. Application developers need to specify the required QoS categories along with their associated QoS parameters and their dimensions. Appropriate QoS mechanisms have to be integrated into the middleware that realize the QoS management. Once the client and server component are connected, a QoS level needs to be negotiated between the components. This leads to a QoS contract which implies an initial resource allocation as well as potential configuration changes in the middleware. During application run-time the QoS needs to be monitored in order to maintain the contractually guaranteed QoS. If necessary, QoS control activities are initiated to compensate or adapt to dynamic resource fluctuations. QoS-based service accounting and billing complete the QoS management picture.

In this paper we will show how QoS can be supported elegantly in the middleware of Microsoft's .NET framework, which is called .NET Remoting [1]. Our resulting QoS management platform is called DotQoS. It adds QoS specification, negotiation and provision to .NET by using the built-in reflection, interception, and custom meta-data features. One of the design goals for DotQoS was to avoid incompatible changes to the underlying system architecture. Our approach is based on our earlier experience with a CORBA QoS management framework called MAQS [2]. There we had to modify the internals of the platform in order to support QoS handling.

We present the design and implementation of DotQoS, as well as experiences with the new framework. Throughout the paper we will compare QoS in .NET to QoS in CORBA and thereby highlight general middleware and programming environment features that substantially ease the engineering of QoS in middleware and distributed applications. The paper is structured as follows. Section 2 contains a discussion of requirements and related work. In Section 3 we review relevant features of .NET and in particular of .NET Remoting, which stands in the center of the DotQoS work. Section 4 presents the architecture and implementation of DotQoS, while Sections 5 and 6 comment on application experiences and performance measurements. Section 7 contains our conclusions and outlines our future activities in this research area.

2   Requirements and Related Work

The demand for explicit QoS handling has increased with the emergence of new application requirements and the commercial usage of innovative services. For reasons of compatibility with QoS-agnostic applications and to foster general user acceptance QoS extensions to middleware platforms should be integrated in a "non-invasive" way that conforms to the underlying middleware architecture. An important requirement for our DotQoS approach was that QoS management should be provided as a non-conflicting add-on to the standard platform. Thus, besides QoS-enabled applications existing applications would continue to run on the same platform. One consequence of this objective was that we did not want to bother the application developer by introducing an additional QoS specification language, e.g. a modified IDL as in MAQS [3] or an aspect language as in QuO [4].

Another requirement of QoS management is that the framework configuration must be able to adapt to a changing environment during run-time, e.g. to load new transport modules or other relevant QoS mechanisms. Generally this can be achieved elegantly by the use of reflection, as was shown in [5,6,7]. DotQoS also relies on reflection, however, compared to earlier work with CORBA, the .NET framework makes our life easier in this respect due to its powerful built-in reflection mechanisms. In Section 3 we will come back to this issue.

We consider it important that a QoS-enabled middleware can handle several QoS categories at the same time, e.g. for an application scenario that requires fault-tolerance as well as security. Therefore, in contrast to many single QoS category systems, DotQoS is designed to support multi-category QoS. Conceptually, our framework is capable to handle all kinds of QoS categories. However, QoS categories that would require very specialized middleware modifications, e.g. hard real-time [8], are not our primary target, as we do not want to replace the underlying system infrastructure.

Adaptation, reflection, monitoring, logging etc. are often useful for in-process components, too [9]. Thus, handling cross-component calls inside a single process in a similar fashion as cross-process calls was also an objective of the DotQoS design.

2.1   Related Work

Previous work on middleware QoS management can be coarsely classified into *single-category* and *multi-category* QoS architectures. Several approaches provide single-category QoS management. Due to its popularity CORBA [10] has been a predominant target for middleware QoS research. Real-time control (TAO [11]) and fault-tolerance (Eternal [12], Electra [13]) were added to CORBA. These approaches start with standard CORBA and extend the architecture in order to integrate the required QoS specifications and mechanisms. Some of these proposals have found their way into the CORBA standard, e.g. most prominently the real-time CORBA specification [14] has benefited directly from the TAO project.

However, the usage of single-category QoS management platforms is likely to lead to a mix of platforms when more than one QoS category is required by complex application scenarios. Multi-category QoS management frameworks aim at generic QoS support that can be configured for arbitrary QoS demands. Such QoS engineering attempts need to provide generic means for the specification of QoS categories, abstractions for their usage at implementation time, as well as support for the integration of QoS mechanisms and their run-time configuration. This results in two general problems: The integration of QoS specifications into applications – primarily a software engineering problem, and the integration and re-configuration of corresponding QoS mechanisms into the middleware – primarily a systems programming and engineering problem.

Generic QoS specifications and their integration into a programming model is a challenge from a software engineering point of view, since QoS represents an *aspect* in the sense of the aspect-oriented programming paradigm [15], [16]. Several aspect languages have been proposed for QoS specifications and their integration into applications by aspect weaving. Examples are QuO [4], MAQS [2], and AspectiX [17]. Obviously, a drawback of such approaches is the introduction of an additional language for the specification of QoS attributes which increases the complexity of the application development environment.

The integration of QoS mechanisms in generic QoS management middleware is typically done by adding reflection support to the middleware. Such reflective middleware allows the dynamic extension and reconfiguration of QoS mechanisms, e.g. specialized transport protocols or new encryption modules, at run-time. Examples are TAO [11], Meta-Spaces [5], or MAQS [18]. Approaches such as [7] and [6] focus on run-time adaptation based on reflection mechanisms.

The availability of middleware platforms[1] that have built-in reflection support, facilitates the required extensibility of the middleware with respect to the QoS mechanism integration. But still the mapping and integration of arbitrary QoS specifications into the application remain to be solved. Composition Filters [20] or Meta-Spaces [5] offer a general concept here.

In the following sections we will show how the concepts needed for generic multi-category QoS management can be integrated into .NET without new specification languages or architectural modifications to the platform. It will become clear that .NET features such as meta-data attributes in the common type system and the modular design of the .NET Remoting middleware facilitate considerably the integration of generic QoS management.

3   Overview of .NET

The Microsoft .NET framework contains a number of interesting features that foster the integration of QoS. This section provides an overview of the most important features used for DotQoS.

3.1   The .NET Framework

The .NET framework is a (theoretically platform-independent) execution environment for applications. Just like in Java applications are compiled to byte-code. This byte-code is executed by the .NET CLR [21] (Common Language Runtime). In contrast to Java many different languages (e.g. C#, managed C++, J#, VB.NET, etc.) can be used to create CLR compatible byte-code. It is possible to use classes implemented in many different languages seamlessly in one application. Hence, applications may be implemented in a different language than the QoS mechanisms that realize the application's QoS requirements.

---

[1] In contrast to [19] we also view homogenous remoting platforms, e.g. Java/RMI or .NET, as middleware.

3.2   Custom Meta-data

A very powerful feature of .NET is the support for custom meta-data. The type system of the CLR allows so called custom attributes as annotations to classes, interfaces, or fields. Most .NET languages, especially C# [22], provide language constructs for assigning custom attributes. At run-time the reflection API provides access to custom meta-data in the same manner as to conventional type meta-data. DotQoS uses custom attributes for adding QoS-specific information to classes, fields, and QoS mechanisms (see Section 4.1).

3.3   .NET Remoting

A key element of .NET is the .NET Remoting framework. Remoting is .NET's object oriented distribution platform. Its core functionality is comparable to CORBA or Java RMI.

Invocations in an object-oriented middleware such as .NET Remoting travel through a chain of software modules, generally called *sinks*, that together form the message path (see Figure 1). Conceptually, the message path consists of a *request-level* (above dashed line) and a *message-level* (below dashed line). Sinks on the request-level work with unserialized invocations. They have full access to an invocation's parameters, e.g. the method name and arguments. Message-level sinks work with serialized messages, i.e. octet sequences. The sinks that implement the message protocol separate the request-level from the message-level. They are responsible for serialization and de-serialization.

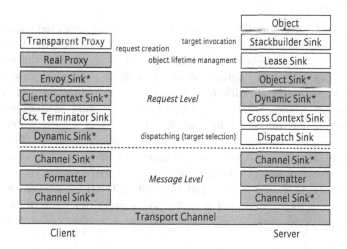

Fig. 1. .NET Remoting message path; sinks marked with ∗ can have multiple different incarnations

DotQoS uses two kinds of request-level sinks. An *envoy sink* (client side) is associated with a specific proxy and processes all messages emitted from and received by this proxy. The server side counterpart of an envoy sink is the *object sink*, which is associated with one specific object.

Message-level sinks belong to the channels that are used for message transport. A channel contains the *message formatter* (for example SOAP) and the message transport protocol (for example HTTP). The channel specific preprocessing and post-processing of messages, for example encryption or compression in DotQoS, is handled by channel sinks.

Sinks can flexibly be added to or exchanged in the sink chain. Hence, request creation, message transport, and processing can be instrumented for the needs of QoS provisioning. DotQoS and its QoS mechanisms have been implemented using these elementary building blocks.

As a similar concept CORBA supports interceptors and pluggable protocols in recent versions of the architecture. However, the use of portable interceptors for QoS provisioning is unsatisfactory. For example, client side interceptors don't necessarily execute in the same thread as the invoking application. Thus, mechanisms that require invocation tracing are hard to implement. Furthermore, an implementation of a transport protocol for a Java ORB cannot be used with a C++ ORB. This makes distribution and installation of QoS mechanisms difficult. The problem of distribution and installation could be solved using Java RMI. However, in contrast to CORBA, Java RMI does not provide the ability to configure its message path. .NET combines and improves the advantages of CORBA, which offers a partially adaptable message path, and Java, which offers portability due to its platform independence.

3.4   Contexts

In the .NET execution model methods of an object are executed within a *context*. Once an invocation crosses a context boundary, it is intercepted by the request-level sinks described above. In case the invocation is remote, the message-level sink intercepts it, too. A context boundary will be crossed in case the invoked object has been bound to a different context than the calling one. At instantiation time it can be decided whether an object will be bound to the current or to a new context. A custom attribute that is attached to the object's class controls this selection. Most objects are not bound to a specific context. They are called *context-agile*. However, a QoS-aware component in DotQoS is always context-bound to enforce interception even for in-process invocations.

.NET contexts should not be confused with CORBA's *service context*, which is a mechanism to pass context specific parameters, for example a transaction state, with an invocation. .NET Remoting has a similar concept called *logical call context*.

4   DotQoS Architecture and Implementation

This section explores how DotQoS uses the features described above. We explain how QoS categories can be specified, attached to components, and realized at run-time.

4.1   QoS Specification in DotQoS

In CORBA, QoS specification requires either IDL extensions or reserved keywords in IDL, or an additional aspect language. Consequently, modified IDL compilers or additional aspect weavers are needed. With reflective execution environments and type systems supporting custom meta-data, precompilers are no longer necessary and developers can use existing tools and standard APIs.

In DotQoS, a QoS category is represented by a class inheriting from QoSCategorySchemeBase. Category specialization can simply be achieved using class inheritance. At run-time, instances of such category classes are used to hold the actual parameters that define a certain level of QoS.

A dimension of a QoS category can be declared as a public property of a simple type (i.e. int, double, enum, string, etc.). Dimension properties have to be *decorated* with the QoSDimension meta-attribute to mark them as such. QoSDimension is a custom meta-attribute defined by DotQoS. This meta-attribute can be configured in order to define the unit of measurement (QoSUnit) and whether higher values mean better quality or vice versa (QoSDirection).

The following example shows a simple definition for a Performance QoS category with one dimension. The Throughput property is marked as a QoS dimension. Its unit of measurement is s^{-1} (per second) where higher values denote a better quality of service. The getter and setter methods have to be implemented by the QoS mechanism developer. An instance of Performance holds a value for the Throughput dimension specifying a certain QoS level.

```
public class Performance : QoSCategorySchemeBase
{
  // custom meta-attribute for the definition of a QoS dimension
  [QoSDimension(QoSUnit.PerSec, QoSDirection.Ascending)]
  public int Throughput {
    // definition of a property
    // getter and setter implementation omitted
    get { ... } set { ... }
  }
}
```

This definition of QoS categories has the same expressive power as QIDL [3] or QML [23]. However, it is directly written for the type system used by the application. No language specific mapping is necessary.

4.2   Defining QoS-Enabled Components

Apart from defining QoS categories, DotQoS also provides a means to declare which QoS category a certain component supports. DotQoS uses the notion of components having *ports* [24]. Each port of a component can support a distinct set of QoS categories.

A class implementing interfaces realizes a component. The implemented interfaces are its provided ports. The custom meta-attribute QoSContractClass defines which QoS category is attached to a port. A class definition can be decorated with this meta-attribute and thus features a certain QoS category. A QoS category is specified by its corresponding category class. The following example shows a component that is marked to support **Performance** category on the port that is provided via the **IQuery** interface.

```
public interface IQuery {
  ArrayList FindByName(string name);
}

// custom meta-attribute for a QoS category
[QoSContractClass(typeof(Performance), typeof(IQuery))]
public abtract class SearchComponent : DotQoS.RemoteObject, IQuery
{
  ...
}
```

It is worth noting that decorating the class with the **QoSContractClass** meta-attribte does not prescribe the actual QoS mechanism that will be used. For example, the throughput of some component could be increased by adjusting the server thread's priority, or by balancing the load on several servers. It is the task of the QoS mechanism developer to configure DotQoS in such a way that it can enforce the specified contract (see Section 4.7).

A class can have more than one contract class attribute, hence, multi-category QoS can be declared. Again, it is the task of the mechanism developer to specify the necessary QoS mechanisms and how they interact. A generic framework cannot resolve all potential dependencies automatically. However, some QoS mechanisms can be combined automatically, as will be explained in Section 4.8.

4.3   Handling Contracts in DotQoS

A vital piece of all QoS platforms is contract negotiation, i.e. reaching agreement between client and server about the level of QoS that shall be provided. The concrete negotiation protocol is not discussed here because its design is not that much affected by the kind of run-time system and middleware used. Nevertheless, it is worthwhile explaining what happens to contracts after client and server have negotiated successfully. In DotQoS every QoS-aware component implementation has to inherit from **DotQoS.RemoteObject**, which provides an interface for contract negotiation. After the negotiation protocol is finished, the client activates the contract and receives a transcript of the negotiated contract. This call is intercepted on client and server side in order to store the transcript in internal tables.

Thereafter, DotQoS ensures that the negotiated contracts are obeyed in the relevant situations. If the client invokes a call on an object for which it has negotiated a contract, the request-level sink of DotQoS will fetch the contract from the internal table by the URI of the invoked component. Section 4.7 explains how a QoS contract is processed. Furthermore, DotQoS places the unique ID of the contract in the transport headers of the request message sent to the server. If, for example, a HTTP channel is used, this data is placed as a key-value pair in the HTTP header. Sinks along the message path can use the contract identifier to fetch the contract from the internal tables. Upon reception of a message on the server side, DotQoS places the contract identifier in the logical call context. The application implementation can use it to retrieve the QoS parameters of the ongoing invocation if necessary.

The contract negotiation protocal itself is encapsulated in a special server-side *frame contract*. By deriving from the `FrameContract` class, special negotiation protocols can be implemented. The frame contract object, which belong to the client/server connection, is also responsible for driving the resource control.

4.4 Scope of Contracts

Contracts in real-life have at least two contracting parties. Obviously, the server side component is one contracting party. On the client side, the candidates are client object, client process and client context. The first solution (client object) is problematic, because delegation is extremely restricted. Only one object could make use of the negotiated contract. The client process is not a suitable candidate either, because it would not solve the problem for the in-process case. Furthermore, two components in one process could not negotiate different contracts with the same service.

In DotQoS the contracting parties are the server object, which acts as component, and the client context. This means that every object in a certain context can make use of the negotiated contract. A process can host more than one context, hence, in-process QoS management between two components is possible. Additionally, every client component can negotiate contracts independently of other components in the same process.

4.5 DotQoS Request-Level Sinks

Using a highly reflective system makes it comparatively easy to install sinks on all relevant server side objects. A special meta-attribute on the class can describe the sinks that have to be installed. During every instantiation the system can use reflection to find out about the appropriate sinks and install them. The advantage is that this happens automatically. Therefore, the application developer cannot, by mistake, forget to install the appropriate sinks. Fortunately, .NET supports a comparable concept already. Application developers just need to attach a meta-attribute to a QoS-aware component as shown below.

```
[DotQoS.QoSContextAttribute("Query")]
public class SearchComponentImpl : SearchComponent
{
   // implementation detail omitted
}
```

This attribute will be evaluated by the run-time system during every object instantiation. It will create a new context called Query in which the created object will reside. At the same time, a sink is hooked into the server object. This sink will receive all cross-context calls but none of the in-context calls. This is very important, because if the class or one of its utility classes make calls to the object, they will not be subject to QoS handling. Therefore, this sink will not act as a performance drain for in-context calls.

The next problem we had to tackle was the installation of sinks on the relevant proxies on the client side. Whenever someone wants to transfer a reference to some object across the boundaries of a context or process, an object reference will be created. This is the same in almost every middleware platform. .NET allows us to easily add information about the proxy sinks in the object reference. When the .NET Remoting infrastructure creates a proxy from such an object reference on client-side, it will add the required client-side sinks automatically as described in the object reference. Hence, no special hooks on the client side are needed. The only requirement is that the client side is provided with the assembly, i.e. a .NET run-time component (for example a DLL), implementing the required sinks.

Fortunately, the additional information required for the object references will be contributed indirectly by the DotQoS.QoSContextAttribute shown above. This means that the application developer just needs to add this single line to his code and DotQoS, based on the .NET run-time mechanisms, will manage to install the appropriate sinks and context on server and client side.

4.6   DotQoS Message-Level Sinks and Transport Channels

The sinks discussed in the previous section work on the application layer. This means they can inspect, modify, redirect or reject any in-coming or out-going message. However, a QoS framework needs to take care of the transportation, too. Perhaps you may want to use a transport channel with bandwidth reservation or you may want to encrypt or compress all messages after they have been serialized but before they are put on the wire. These tasks can be handled by channel sinks in .NET. Channels are only used for cross-process calls. Channels exist independently of the objects which may receive messages via the channel. This means a different way of hooking QoS mechanisms into the channel is required. Two cases have to be distinguished:

1. pre and post processing of messages sent over a channel
2. implementing a new transport channel

At first, DotQoS installs a channel sink on client and server side for every possible channel. This is straightforward in .NET since the channels are configured in a XML file. An excerpt is shown below.

```
<channel ref="http">
 <clientProviders>
```

```
<formatter ref="soap" />
<provider type="DotQoS.QoSChannelSinkProvider, Framework"/>
</clientProviders>
</channel>
```

During the creation of the channel the DotQoS sink provider is asked to add a sink for the channel.

The second case above is addressed in the same way. Using the XML file we can install an alternative channel, e.g. implementing bandwidth reservation. Alternatively, it is possible to do the same programmatically during run-time, but using XML files is more convenient and allows for configuration after the build process.

4.7 QoS Mechanisms in DotQoS

The previous sections described how to define QoS categories and which classes of mechanisms, i.e. message-level and request-level, are supported in DotQoS. This section covers how the QoS mechanisms, which enforce a contract, are installed. QoS mechanisms may be replaced or added during run-time in order to adapt to changing QoS requirements or resource availability. Unfortunately, sinks cannot be exchanged once .NET Remoting has set up the message path. Hence, DotQoS introduces a special sink at message-level and request-level in order to evaluate a QoS contract and invoke the necessary QoS mechanisms.

The communication path of DotQoS is depicted in Figure 2. At object creation corresponding sinks are installed at the client and the server side. As long as no QoS contract is negotiated the communication just passes through the envoy $(1 \rightarrow 4)$, the client channel $(4 \rightarrow 7)$, the server channel $(8 \rightarrow 11)$ and eventually the object sink $(11 \rightarrow 14)$. These sinks check whether a contract has been negotiated and associated with the current call. In this case reflection is used to determine the port on which the method is to be invoked. The messages are forwarded through the relevant mechanism sinks according to the QoS parameters negotiated for the port in the contract under which the invocation is executed. Hence, the mechanism sinks realize a chain of responsibility patterns [25].

A QoS mechanism in DotQoS is a collection of several sinks and possibly a transport channel. Hence, we managed to encapsulate the implementation of QoS mechanisms in a set of classes. Due to the well-known cross-cutting nature of QoS aspects [18] this is in general a difficult task. Without a highly reflective, modular, and open framework this would hardly work. Aspect-oriented programming could be another solution to overcome the problem of cross-cutting. However, using an AOP-based approach such as AspectJ would tie us to one programming language. Especially the QoS mechanism and the application code would have to be implemented using the same language. Thanks to the language independence of the CLR [21] (Common Language Runtime of .NET) we are able to implement the mechanisms and the application in different languages. Hence, the language-independence achieved with DotQoS is superior to that of CORBA-based solutions.

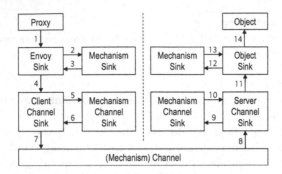

Fig. 2. Hooking mechanisms in DotQoS

Sinks can be used to implement mechanisms that work on the request-level, such as caching, authentication, access control, logging or licensing. Message-level mechanisms such as encryption or compression can be realized as channel sinks. Mechanisms requiring special message transport protocols, for example protocols using UDP or raw sockets, as well as connections with bandwidth control can be implemented as transport channels.

4.8   Compostion of QoS Mechanisms

As mentioned above, DotQoS supports multi-category QoS. In order to enforce QoS of multiple categories, several mechanisms have to be used in combination. Furthermore, some QoS mechanisms may consist of several other mechanisms, which have to be integrated in the message path. However, the system cannot always automatically combine the appropriate QoS mechanisms.

The QoS developer has to provide a specification of how QoS mechanisms have to be arranged for a multi-category contract, for example by defining the order of the mechanism sinks in the sink chain. Hence, sink implementations can be decorated with *ordering hints*:

- **head:** sink must be passed before any other sink in the chain
- **tail:** sink must be passed after any other sink in the chain
- **arbitrary:** sink can take any position in the chain

Furthermore, dependency parameters can be defined:

- **after:** sink must be passed after the sink specified by the parameter
- **before:** sink must be passed before the sink specified by the parameter
- **counterpart:** sink requires the specified sink as a counterpart in the client-/server-side message path

These hints are specified by decorating a sink's implementation with the `QoSInterceptor` meta-attribute. The DotQoS sinks can use these hints to establish an order among several QoS mechanism sinks.

For example, authorized access to a component requires authentication of the client component. The identity of the client is approved before the access right can be determined. Hence, a sink for authorization has to be placed after the authentication sink in the server-side message path. The server-side authentication sink requires a client-side counterpart that inserts the credentials required for authentication in the message.

However, combining QoS mechanisms may fail, for example, when two sinks are required to be at the head of the same sink chain. In this case the negotiation of a QoS contract is not possible as no compatible QoS mechanisms could be installed.

In cases where no simple combination of mechanisms is sufficient, the QoS developer can provide new mechanisms that serve multiple QoS categories. Such mechanisms can in turn aggregate existing mechanisms. A discussion of reuse of QoS mechanisms is provided in [18].

5   Performance

DotQoS is not targeted at hard real-time systems. Nevertheless, it is interesting to know the computational overhead introduced by such a middleware extension. DotQoS extends the .NET Remoting message path in several aspects. In respect to potential performance penalties the most important ones are:

- the envoy sink on client side and
- the corresponding object sink on server side,
- the channel sinks on client and server side,
- the mechanism sinks (request-level),
- the mechanism channel sinks (message-level),
- the lookup of active contracts for each call, and
- the dynamic selection of mechanism sinks for each call.

Most of these enhancements make heavy use of reflection. Figure 2 shows how the sinks are related to each others. We conducted four experiments to determine how much time these enhancements consume. We connected two machines with a switched 100 MBit Ethernet. Each machine was equipped with a Pentium IV 2.2 GHz CPU, 1 GB RAM and Windows XP with .NET SDK 1.0. .NET Remoting has been configured to use a binary encoding on the transport channel. Using SOAP instead would have resulted in larger messages and a more complex marshaling and unmarshaling procedure. The results of our measurements are shown in Figure 3.

Throughout all experiments we invoked a method that did neither have parameters nor a return value because we are not interested in the marshaling and unmarshaling capabilities of .NET Remoting. For each experiment we conducted 20 runs, each run executed 100,000 calls. The systematic error due to imprecise time measurement is 1 %. The statistical error is small in comparison to the systematic error and can be neglected.

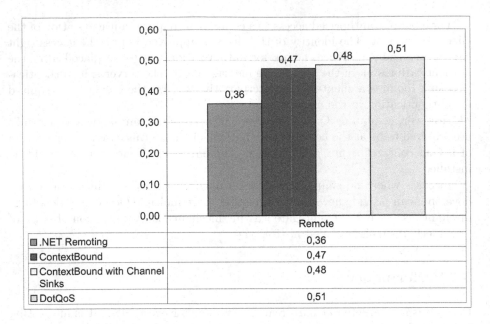

Fig. 3. Measurement of DotQoS' computational overhead (average time to complete one invocation in milliseconds)

The first experiment used vanilla .NET Remoting to perform the remote invocations. The second experiment added the object sink and the envoy sink. Therefore, the remote object was derived from the .NET class `ContextBound-Object` instead of `MarshalByRefObject`. These sinks simply passed each message to the next sink. Hence, this measurement shows how much computational overhead the context boundness of objects introduces in .NET. The third experiment added special channel sinks on client and server side to investigate the cost of intercepting message before and after they are handled by the transport channel. Finally, we measured the entire DotQoS message path. Before the time measurement started the client negotiated a QoS contract with the server. However, the mechanism sinks used for this QoS contract just forwarded all messages without any further processing.

It is conspicuous that the context boundness of objects is responsible for 73 % of the overhead. Adding the channel sinks to the message path is comparably cheap. The introduced run-time penalty is around 0.01 ms. Finally, the lookup of contracts and the selection of the corresponding mechanism sinks introduced an average overhead of 0.03 ms.

Especially the small performance penalty of the contract lookup and mechanism selection is worth noting. As explained before, DotQoS uses the reflection capabilities of .NET to determine the contracts that apply to each method call. In this respect (among others) DotQoS differs substantially from CORBA. Obviously, the costs introduced by reflection are small when compared to the costs of intercepting messages in the .NET Remoting message path.

The average overhead introduced by the DotQoS framework is approximately 0.15 ms. Even a method call with simple parameters and a return value takes substantially longer due to the increased message size and marshaling overhead. If more complex objects such as hash tables, arrays etc. are passed along with a method call, this additional time for QoS management can be neglected.

6 Experience

When comparing DotQoS with our CORBA-based approach MAQS from the perspective of an application programmer, we can claim that the use of a modern run-time environment and an open distribution framework allows a more seamless integration of QoS. Application developers do not have to adapt their tool chain since no additional tools such as IDL compilers or precompilers are needed. The QoS concepts integrate almost seamlessly in the programming model. This ease of use is especially important since we use DotQoS not only for academic research but also in the European QCCS project [26] with industrial applications. For our industry partners it would be a major drawback if they had to significantly modify their tool chain to integrate QoS support in their applications. Furthermore, our industrial partners consider QoS as an add-on to their platform. DotQoS runs out of the box on a .NET compatible system. For MAQS we had to make fundamental changes to the ORB itself in order to adapt the message path.

From the perspective of the framework implementers the creation of DotQoS has been much easier compared to the development of MAQS. The development of new tools such as interface compilers or aspect weavers was not necessary due to the extensibility and reflection mechanisms built into the run-time. We can even use parts of the DotQoS framework for in-process calls, for example for license checking, synchronization and logging issues.

The DotQoS framework can adapt itself to a changing environment on the fly by exchanging sinks and channels at run-time. This was not possible with MAQS because it uses aspect weavers during implementation time. The strict separation between business logic and QoS-related code is lost after aspect weaving. DotQoS keeps up the separation even during run-time. Combined with the extensive reflection capabilities it is possible to inspect and adapt the framework at run-time.

To prove that the framework can actually deliver QoS we implemented several QoS mechanisms based on our experience with MAQS. On the message layer we realized compression and encryption of messages (as opposed to the encryption of the transport channel such as SSL). On the request layer we implemented a load balancer to test the redirection of messages. Furthermore, we realized a server-side access control mechanism using request-level sinks. Finally, we worked on a license checker that limits the number of concurrent calls made by a client to a component depending on the provided license key.

However, .NET also causes some annoyances. For example, there is no way to configure object dispatching as the dispatch sink is hard-wired into the server's message path. Instead, object dispatching can only be influenced by modifying a message's target URI. This can only be done on the message-level before the message reaches the dispatch sink, although it is clearly a request-level issue. CORBA's concept of object adapters is superior here. Thus, a configurable dispatch sink would benefit .NET and DotQoS.

7   Conclusions and Outlook

DotQoS is an extension for .NET Remoting that provides a component container with configurable and adaptive provision of QoS properties. Comparing the DotQoS architecture with the CORBA-based MAQS has shown that using a modern reflective middleware such as .NET significantly fosters QoS integration. Modern language and platform features enable application developers to stay with their well-known programming model throughout the entire development process. No IDL compiler or aspect weaver is necessary to specify contracts or to integrate QoS support in the application. Our experiments have revealed that the overhead incurred by DotQoS is neglectable.

Multi-category QoS has proven to be quite useful in real-life applications. For example, demanding security and load balancing for the same object is no extraordinary requirement. DotQoS provides category definition, contract negotiation and QoS management for such applications. However, conflicts arising from non-orthogonal QoS categories may not be solved automatically. In such cases the application developer must provide a specially tailored QoS mechanism that supports the category mix. Whether the DotQoS ordering hints for QoS mechanisms are appropriate for complex cases, does require more experiments as well as a more formal investigation.

We are currently working on QoS support for entity components (as known from Enterprise JavaBeans [27]). Obviously it is not feasible to negotiate QoS with every entity component since there may be thousands of them in one application. Instead, DotQoS will support QoS negotiation with the component's *home*. The negotiated QoS contracts are then applied to all entity components managed by the QoS. Additionally, new QoS mechanisms are currently added to DotQoS, especially bandwidth reservation and multicast groups.

Adaptation strategies and policies currently have to be implemented as part of the frame contract. This is unsatisfactory as it has to be repeated for each application. Thus, we are investigating more generic ways of specifying adaptation strategies and policies in order to automatically drive run-time adaptation.

References

1. Rammer, I.: Advanced .NET Remoting. Apress (2002)
2. Becker, C., Geihs, K.: Generic QoS-support for CORBA. In: International Symposium on Computers and Communications (ISCC'00), Antibes, France (2000)

3. Becker, C., Geihs, K.: Generic QoS specification for CORBA. In: Kommunikation in verteilten Systemen (KiVS'99), Darmstadt, Germany (1999)
4. Loyall, J.P., Bakken, D.D., Schantz, R.E., Zinky, J.A., Karr, D.A., Vanegas, R., Anderson, K.R.: QoS aspect languages and their runtime integration. In: 4th Workshop on Languages, Compilers, and Run-time Systems for Scalable Computers (LCR). (1998)
5. Blair, G.S., Andersen, A., Blair, L., Coulson, G.: The role of reflection in supporting dynamic QoS management functions. In: International Workshop on Quality of Service (IWQoS'99), London, UK (1999)
6. Kon, F., Costa, F., Blair, G.S., Campbell, R.H.: The case for reflective middleware. Communications of the ACM **45** (2002)
7. Wang, N., Schmidt, D.C., Kircher, M., Prameswaran, K.: Adaptive and reflective middleware for QoS-enabled CCM applications. Distributed Systems Online **2** (2001)
8. Schmidt, D.C.: Middleware for real-time and embedded systems. Communications of the ACM **45** (2002)
9. Weis, T., Geihs, K.: Components on the desktop. In: Technology of Object-Oriented Languages and Systems (TOOLS Europe'00). (2000)
10. OMG: The Common Object Request Broker: Architecture and specification. Specification 02-06-33, Object Management Group, Inc., Needham, USA (2002)
11. Schmidt, D.C., Levine, D.L., Mungee, S.: The design of the TAO real–time object request broker. Computer Communications Journal **21** (1998)
12. Moser, L.E., Melliar-Smith, P., Narasimhan, P.: The Eternal System. In: Workshop on Dependable Distributed Object Systems (OOPSLA'97), Atlanta, USA (1997)
13. Maffeis, S.: Adding group communication and fault–tolerance to CORBA. In: Conference on Object-Oriented Technologies and Systems (COOTS'95). (1995)
14. OMG: Real-time CORBA specification. Specification 02-08-02, Object Management Group, Inc., Needham, USA (2002)
15. Kizcales, G.: Aspect-Oriented Programming. Technical Report SPL97-008P971-0042, Xerox Palo Alto Research Center (1997)
16. Becker, C., Geihs, K.: Quality of service – aspects of distributed programs. In: Aspect-Oriented Programming Workshop (ICSE'98). (1998)
17. Hauck, F.J., Becker, U., Geier, M., Meier, E., Rastofer, U., Steckermeier, M.: AspectiX: A quality-aware object-based middleware architecture. In: Distributed Applications and Interoperable Systems (DAIS'01), Krakow, Poland (2001)
18. Geihs, K., Becker, C.: A framework for re-use and maintenance of quality of service mechanisms in distributed object systems. In: IEEE International Conference on Software Maintenance (ICSM'01), Florence, Italy (2001)
19. Waldo, J.: Remote procedure calls and Java Remote Method invocation. IEEE Concurrency **July-September, 5-7** (1998)
20. Bergmans, L.M.J., Aksit, M.: Aspects and crosscutting in layered middleware systems. In: Reflective Middleware Workshop (RM'00), New York, USA (2000)
21. ECMA: Common Language Infrastructure. ECMA Standard 335, European Computer Manufacturers Association, Geneva, Switzerland (2001)
22. ECMA: C# language specification. ECMA Standard 334, European Computer Manufacturers Association, Geneva, Switzerland (2001)
23. Frølund, S., Koistinen, J.: Quality of service specification in distributed object system design. In: Conference on Object-Oriented Technologies and Systems (COOTS'98), Santa Fee, USA (1998)
24. Weis, T., Becker, C., Geihs, K., Plouzeau, N.: An UML meta-model for contract aware components. In: UML 2001, Toronto, Canada (2001)

380   A. Ulbrich et al.

25. Gamma, E., Helm, R., Johnson, R., Vlissides, J.: Design Patterns. Addison Wesley Publishing Company (1995)
26. QCCS: QCCS Homepage http://www.qccs.org (2002)
27. Sun: Java 2 Platform – Enterprise Edition Specification, v1.3. Technical Report 7/27/01, Sun Microsystems, Inc. (2001)

Dynamic Resource Allocation for Shared Data Centers Using Online Measurements*

Abhishek Chandra[1], Weibo Gong[2], and Prashant Shenoy[1]

[1] Department of Computer Science
University of Massachusetts Amherst
{abhishek,shenoy}@cs.umass.edu
[2] Department of Electrical and Computer Engineering
University of Massachusetts Amherst
gong@ecs.umass.edu

Abstract. Since web workloads are known to vary dynamically with time, in this paper, we argue that dynamic resource allocation techniques are necessary to provide guarantees to web applications running on shared data centers. To address this issue, we use a system architecture that combines online measurements with prediction and resource allocation techniques. To capture the transient behavior of the application workloads, we model a server resource using a time-domain description of a generalized processor sharing (GPS) server. This model relates application resource requirements to their dynamically changing workload characteristics. The parameters of this model are continuously updated using an online monitoring and prediction framework. This framework uses time series analysis techniques to predict expected workload parameters from measured system metrics. We then employ a constrained non-linear optimization technique to dynamically allocate the server resources based on the estimated application requirements. The main advantage of our techniques is that they capture the transient behavior of applications while incorporating nonlinearity in the system model. We evaluate our techniques using simulations with synthetic as well as real-world web workloads. Our results show that these techniques can judiciously allocate system resources, especially under transient overload conditions.

1 Introduction

1.1 Motivation

The growing popularity of the World Wide Web has led to the advent of Internet data centers that host third-party web applications and services. A typical web application consists of a front-end web server that services HTTP requests, a Java application server that contains the application logic, and a backend database server. In many cases, such applications are housed on managed data centers where the application owner pays for (rents) server resources, and in return, the application is provided guarantees on resource availability and performance. To provide such guarantees, the data center—typically a cluster of servers—must provision sufficient resources to meet application needs. Such

---

* This research was supported in part by NSF grants CCR-9984030 and EIA-0080119.

K. Jeffay, I. Stoica, and K. Wehrle (Eds.): IWQoS 2003, LNCS 2707, pp. 381–398, 2003.

provisioning can be based either on a dedicated or a shared model. In the dedicated model, some number of cluster nodes are dedicated to each application and the provisioning technique must determine how many nodes to allocate to the application. In the shared model, which we consider in this paper, an application can share node resources with other applications and the provisioning technique needs to determine how to partition resources on each node among competing applications.[1]

Since node resources are shared, providing guarantees to applications in the shared data center model is more complex. Typically such guarantees are provided by reserving a certain fraction of node resources (CPU, network, disk) for each application. The fraction of the resources allocated to each application depends on the expected workload and the QoS requirements of the application. The workload of web applications is known to vary dynamically over multiple time scales [14] and it is challenging to estimate such workloads a priori (since the workload can be influenced by unanticipated external events—such as a breaking news story—that can cause a surge in the number of requests accessing a web site). Consequently, static allocation of resources to applications is problematic—while over-provisioning resources based on worst case workload estimates can result in potential underutilization of resources, under-provisioning resources can result in violation of guarantees. An alternate approach is to allocate resources to applications dynamically based on the variations in their workloads. In this approach, each application is given a certain minimum share based on coarse-grain estimates of its resource needs; the remaining server capacity is dynamically shared among various applications based on their instantaneous needs. To illustrate, consider two applications that share a server and are allocated 30% of the server resources each; the remaining 40% is then dynamically shared at run-time so as to meet the guarantees provided to each application. Such dynamic resource sharing can yield potential multiplexing gains, while allowing the system to react to unanticipated increases in application load and thereby meet QoS guarantees. Dynamic resource allocation techniques that can handle changing application workloads in shared data centers is the focus of this paper.

1.2   Research Contributions

In this paper, we present techniques for dynamic resource allocation in shared web servers. We model various server resources using *generalized processor sharing (GPS)* [29] and assume that each application is allocated a certain fraction of a resource. Using a combination of online measurement, prediction and adaptation, our techniques can dynamically determine the resource share of each application based on (i) its QoS (response time) needs and (ii) the observed workload. The main goal of our techniques is to react to transient system overloads by incorporating online system measurements.

We make three specific contributions in this paper. First, in order to capture the transient behavior of application workloads, we model the server resource using a *time-domain queuing model*. This model dynamically relates the resource requirements of each application to its workload characteristics. The advantage of this model is that it

---

[1] This requirement is true even in a dedicated model where service differentiation between different customers for the same application may be desirable.

does not make steady-state assumptions about the system (unlike some previous approaches [10,24]) and adapts to changing application behavior. To achieve a feasible resource allocation even in the presence of transient overloads, we employ a *non-linear optimization* technique that employs the proposed queuing model. An important feature of our optimization-based approach is that it can handle non-linearity in system behavior unlike some approaches that assume linearity [1,25].

Determining resource shares of applications using such an online approach is crucially dependent on an accurate estimation of the application workload characteristics. A second contribution of our work is a *prediction algorithm* that estimates the workload parameters of applications in the near future using online measurements. Our prediction algorithm uses time series analysis techniques for workload estimation.

Third, we use both synthetic workloads and real-world web traces to evaluate the effectiveness of our online prediction and allocation techniques. Our evaluation shows that our techniques adapt to changing workloads fairly effectively, especially under transient overload conditions.

The rest of the paper is structured as follows. We formulate the problem of dynamic resource allocation in shared web servers in Section 2. In Section 3, we present a time-domain description of a resource queuing model, and describe our online prediction and optimization-based techniques for dynamic resource allocation. Results from our experimental evaluation are presented in Section 4. We discuss related work in Section 5 and present our conclusions and future work in Section 6.

2   Problem Formulation and System Model

In this section, we first present an abstract GPS-based model for a server resource and then formulate the problem of dynamic resource allocation in such a GPS-based system.

2.1   Resource Model

We model a server resource using a system of n queues, where each queue corresponds to a particular application (or a class of applications) running on the server. Requests within each queue are assumed to be served in FIFO order and the resource capacity C is shared among the queues using GPS. To do so, each queue is assigned a weight and is allocated a resource share in proportion to its weight. Specifically, a queue with a weight w_i is allocated a share $\phi_i = \frac{w_i}{\sum_j w_j}$ (i.e., allocated $(\phi_i \cdot C)$ units of the resource capacity when all queues are backlogged). Several practical instantiations of GPS exist—such as weighted fair queuing (WFQ) [15], self-clocked fair queuing [18], and start-time fair queuing [19]—and any such scheduling algorithm suffices for our purpose. We note that these GPS schedulers are work-conserving—in the event a queue does not utilize its allocated share, the unused capacity is allocated fairly among backlogged queues. Our abstract model is applicable to many hardware and software resources found on a server; hardware resources include the network interface bandwidth, the CPU and in some cases, the disk bandwidth, while software resource include socket accept queues in a web server servicing multiple virtual domains [25,30].

2.2 Problem Definition

Consider a shared server that runs multiple third-party applications. Each such application is assumed to specify a desired quality of service (QoS) requirement; here we assume that the QoS requirements are specified in terms of a target response time. The goal of the system is to ensure that the mean response time (or some percentile of the response time) seen by application requests is no greater than the desired target response. In general, each incoming request is serviced by multiple hardware and software resources on the server, such as the CPU, NIC, disk, etc. We assume that the specified target response time is split up into multiple resource-specific response times, one for each such resource. Thus, if each request spends no more than the allocated target on each resource, then the overall target response time for the server will be met.[2]

Since each resource is assumed to be scheduled using GPS, the target response time of each application can be met by allocating a certain share to each application. The resource share of an application will depend not only on the target response time but also on the load in each application. As the workload of an application varies dynamically, so will its resource share. In particular, we assume that each application is allocated a certain minimum share ϕ_i^{min} of the resource capacity; the remaining capacity $(1 - \sum_j \phi_j^{min})$ is dynamically allocated to various applications depending on their current workloads (such that their target response time will be met). Formally, if d_i denotes the target response time of application i and $\bar{T}_i$ is its observed mean response time, then the application should be allocated a share ϕ_i, $\phi_i \geq \phi_i^{min}$, such that $\bar{T}_i \leq d_i$.

Since each resource has a finite capacity and the application workloads can exceed capacity during periods of heavy transient overloads, the above goal can not always be met. To achieve feasible allocation during overload scenarios, we use the notion of utility functions to represent the satisfaction of an application based on its current allocation. While different kinds of utility functions can be employed, we define utility in the following manner.[3] We assume that an application remains satisfied so long as its allocation ϕ_i yields a mean response time $\bar{T}_i$ no greater than the target d_i (i.e., $\bar{T}_i \leq d_i$). But the discontent of an application grows as its response time deviates from the target d_i. This discontent function can be represented as follows:

$$D_i(\bar{T}_i) = (\bar{T}_i - d_i)^+, \tag{1}$$

where x^+ represents $\max(0, x)$. In this scenario, the discontent grows linearly when the observed response time exceeds the specified target d_i. The overall system goal then is to assign a share ϕ_i to each application, $\phi_i \geq \phi_i^{min}$, such that the total system-wide discontent, i.e., the quantity $D = \sum_{i=1}^n D_i(\bar{T}_i)$ is minimized.

We use this problem definition to derive our dynamic resource allocation mechanism, which is described next.

---

[2] The problem of how to split the specified server response time into resource-specific response times is beyond the scope of this paper. In this paper, we assume that such resource-specific target response times are given to us.

[3] Different kinds of utility functions can be employed to achieve different goals during overload, such as fairness, isolation, etc.

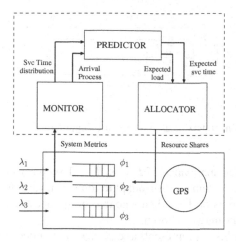

Fig. 1. Dynamic Resource Allocation

3   Dynamic Resource Allocation

To perform dynamic resource allocation based on the above formulation, each GPS-scheduled resource on the shared server will need to employ three components: (i) a *monitoring* module that measures the workload and the performance metrics of each application (such as its request arrival rate, average response time $\bar{T}_i$, etc.), (ii) a *prediction* module that uses the measurements from the monitoring module to estimate the workload characteristics in the near future, and (iii) an *allocation* module that uses these workload estimates to determine resource shares such that the overall system-wide discontent is minimized. Figure 1 depicts these three components.

In what follows, we first present an overview of the monitoring module that is responsible for performing online measurements. We follow this with a time-domain description of the resource queuing model, and formulation of a non-linear optimization problem to perform resource allocation using this model. Finally, we present the prediction techniques used to estimate the parameters for this model dynamically.

3.1   Online Monitoring and Measurement

The online monitoring module is responsible for measuring various system and application metrics. These metrics are used to estimate the system model parameters and workload characteristics. These measurements are based on the following time intervals (see Figure 2):

– *Measurement interval (I): I* is the interval over which various parameters of interest are sampled. For instance, the monitoring module tracks the number of request arrivals (n_i) in each interval I and records this value.
  The choice of a particular measurement interval depends on the desired responsiveness from the system. If the system needs to react to workload changes on a fine

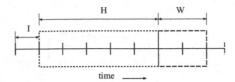

Fig. 2. Time intervals used for monitoring, prediction and allocation

time-scale, then a small value of I (e.g., $I = 1$ second) should be chosen. On the other hand, if the system needs to adapt to long term variations in the workload over time scales of hours or days, then a coarse-grain measurement interval of minutes or tens of minutes may be chosen.

- *History (H):* The history represents a sequence of recorded values for each parameter of interest. Our monitoring module maintains a finite history consisting of the most recent H values for each such parameter; these measurements form the basis for predicting the future values of these parameters.
- *Adaptation Window (W):* The adaptation window is the time interval between two successive invocations of the adaptation algorithm. Thus the past measurements are used to predict the workload for the next W time units, and the system adapts over this time interval. As we would see in the next section, our time-domain queuing model description considers a time period equal to the adaptation window to estimate the average response time $\bar{T}_i$ of an application, and this model is updated every W time units.

The history and the adaptation window are implemented as sliding windows.

3.2 Allocating Resource Shares to Applications

The allocation module is invoked periodically (every adaptation window) to dynamically partition the resource capacity among the various applications running on the shared server. To capture the transient behavior of application workloads, we first present a time-domain description of a resource queuing model. This model is used to determine the resource requirements of an application based on its expected workload and response time goal.

Time-domain Queuing Model. As described above, the adaptation algorithm is invoked every W time units. Let q_i^0 denote the queue length at the beginning of an adaptation window. Let $\hat{\lambda}_i$ denote the estimated request arrival rate and $\hat{\mu}_i$ denote the estimated service rate in the next adaptation window (i.e., over the next W time units). We would show later how these values are estimated. Then, assuming the values of $\hat{\lambda}_i$ and $\hat{\mu}_i$ are constant, the length of the queue at any instant t within the next adaptation window is given by

$$q_i(t) = \left[q_i^0 + \left(\hat{\lambda}_i - \hat{\mu}_i \right) \cdot t \right]^+, \tag{2}$$

Intuitively, the amount of work queued up at instant t is the sum of the initial queue length and the amount of work arriving in this interval minus the amount of work serviced in this duration. Further, the queue length cannot be negative.

Since the resource is modeled as a GPS server, the service rate of an application is effectively $(\phi_i \cdot C)$, where ϕ_i is the resource share of the application and C is the resource capacity, and this rate is continuously available to a backlogged application in any GPS system. Hence, the request service rate is

$$\hat{\mu}_i = \frac{\phi_i \cdot C}{\hat{s}_i},\tag{3}$$

where $\hat{s}_i$ is the estimated mean service demand per request (such as number of bytes per packet, or CPU cycles per CPU request, etc.).

Note that, due to the work conserving nature of GPS, if some applications do not utilize their allocated shares, then the utilized capacity is fairly redistributed among backlogged applications. Consequently, the queue length computed in Equation 2 assumes a worst-case scenario where all applications are backlogged and each application receives no more than its allocated share (the queue would be smaller if the application received additional unutilized share from other applications).

Given Equation 2, the average queue length over the adaptation window is given by:

$$\bar{q}_i = \frac{1}{W} \int_0^W q_i(t)dt \tag{4}$$

Depending on the particular values of q_i^0, the arrival rate $\hat{\lambda}_i$ and the service rate $\hat{\mu}_i$, the queue may become empty one or more times during an adaptation window. To include only the non-empty periods of the queue when computing $\bar{q}_i$, we consider the following scenarios, based on the assumption of constant $\hat{\mu}_i$ and $\hat{\lambda}_i$.

1. *Queue growth:* If $\hat{\mu}_i < \hat{\lambda}_i$, then the application queue will grow during the adaptation window and the queue will remain non-empty throughout the adaptation window.
2. *Queue depletion:* If $\hat{\mu}_i > \hat{\lambda}_i$, then the queue starts depleting during the adaptation window. The instant t_0 at which the queue becomes empty is given by $t_0 = \frac{q_i^0}{\hat{\mu}_i - \hat{\lambda}_i}$. If $t_0 < W$, then the queue becomes empty within the adaptation window, otherwise the queue continues to deplete but remains non-empty throughout the window (and is projected to become empty in a subsequent window).
3. *Constant queue length:* If $\hat{\mu}_i = \hat{\lambda}_i$, then the queue length remains fixed ($= q_i^0$) throughout the adaptation window. Hence, the non-empty queue period is either 0 or W depending on the value of q_i^0.

Let us denote the duration within the adaptation window for which the queue is non-empty by W_i (W_i equals either W or t_0 depending on the various scenarios). Then, Equation 4 can be rewritten as

$$\bar{q}_i = \frac{1}{W} \int_0^{W_i} q_i(t)dt \tag{5}$$

$$= \left(\frac{W_i}{W}\right)\left[q_i^0 + \frac{W_i}{2}\left(\hat{\lambda}_i - \hat{\mu}_i\right)\right] \tag{6}$$

Having determined the average queue length over the next adaptation interval, we derive the average response time $\bar{T}_i$ over the same interval. Here, we are interested in the average response time in the near future. Other metrics such as a long term average response time could also be considered. $\bar{T}_i$ is estimated as the sum of the mean queuing delay and the request service time over the next adaptation interval. We use Little's law to derive the queuing delay from the mean queue length.[4] Thus,

$$\bar{T}_i = \frac{(\bar{q}_i + 1)}{\hat{\mu}_i} \tag{7}$$

Substituting Equation 3 in this expression, we get

$$\bar{T}_i = \left(\frac{\hat{s}_i}{\phi_i \cdot C}\right) \cdot (\bar{q}_i + 1), \tag{8}$$

where $\bar{q}_i$ is given by equation 6. The values of q_i^0, $\hat{\mu}_i$, $\hat{\lambda}_i$ and $\hat{s}_i$ are obtained using measurement and prediction techniques discussed in the next section.

This time-domain model description has the following salient features:

- The parameters of the model depend on its current workload characteristics ($\hat{\lambda}_i$, $\hat{s}_i$) and the current system state (q_i^0). Consequently, this model is applicable in an *online* setting for reacting to dynamic changes in the workload, and does not make any steady state assumptions.
- As shown in Equation 8, the model assumes a non-linear relationship between the response time $\bar{T}_i$ and the resource share ϕ_i. This assumption is more general than linear system assumption made in some scenarios.

Next we describe how this model is used in dynamic resource allocation.

Optimization-based Resource Allocation. As explained earlier, the share allocated to an application depends on its specified target response time and the estimated workload. We now present an online optimization-based approach to determine resource shares dynamically.

As described in section 2, the allocation module needs to determine the resource share ϕ_i for each application such that the total *discontent* $D = \sum_{i=1}^{n} D_i(\bar{T}_i)$ is minimized. This problem translates to the following constrained optimization problem:

$$\min_{\{\phi_i\}} \sum_{i=1}^{n} D_i(\bar{T}_i)$$

subject to the constraints

$$\sum_{i=1}^{n} \phi_i \leq 1,$$

$$\phi_i^{min} \leq \phi_i \leq 1, \ 1 \leq i \leq n.$$

---

[4] Note that the application of Little's Law in this scenario is an approximation, that is more accurate when the size of the adaptation window is large compared to the average request service time.

Here, D_i is a function that represents the discontent of a class based on its current response time $\bar{T}_i$. The two constraints specify that (i) the total allocation across all applications should not exceed the resource capacity, and (ii) the share of each application can be no smaller than its minimum allocation ϕ_i^{min} and no greater than the resource capacity.

In general, the nature of the discontent function D_i has an impact on the allocations ϕ_i for each application. As shown in Equation 1, a simple discontent function is one where the discontent grows linearly as the response time $\bar{T}_i$ exceeds the target d_i. Such a D_i, shown in Figure 3, however, is non-differentiable. To make our constrained optimization problem mathematically tractable, we approximate this piece-wise linear D_i by a continuously differentiable function:

$$D_i(\bar{T}_i) = \frac{1}{2}[(\bar{T}_i - d_i) + \sqrt{(\bar{T}_i - d_i)^2 + k}],$$

where $k > 0$ is a constant. Essentially, the above function is a hyperbola with the two piece-wise linear portions as its asymptotes and the constant k governs how closely this hyperbola approximates the piece-wise linear function. Figure 3 depicts the nature of the above function.

We note that the optimization is with respect to the resource shares $\{\phi_i\}$, while the discontent function is represented in terms of the response times $\{\bar{T}_i\}$. We use the relation between $\bar{T}_i$ and ϕ_i from Equation 8 to obtain the discontent function in terms of the resource shares $\{\phi_i\}$.

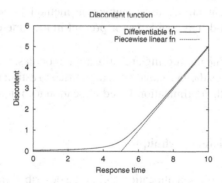

Fig. 3. Two different variants of the discontent function. A piecewise linear function and a continuously differentiable convex functions are shown. The target response time is assumed to be $d_i = 5$.

The resulting optimization problem can be solved using the Lagrange multiplier method [9]. In this technique, the constrained optimization problem is transformed into an unconstrained optimization problem where the original discontent function is replaced by the objective function:

$$L(\{\phi_i\}, \beta) = \sum_{i=1}^{n} D_i(\bar{T}_i) - \beta \cdot (\sum_{i=1}^{n} \phi_i - 1). \tag{9}$$

The objective function L is then minimized subject to the bound constraints on ϕ_i. Here β is called the Lagrange multiplier and it denotes the shadow price for the resource. Intuitively, each application is charged a price of β per unit resource it uses. Thus, each application attempts to minimize the price it pays for its resource share, while maximizing the utility it derives from that share. This leads to the minimization of the original discontent function subject to the satisfaction of the resource constraint.

Minimization of the objective function L in the Lagrange multiplier method leads to solving the following system of algebraic equations.

$$\frac{\partial D_i}{\partial \phi_i} = \beta, \quad \forall i = 1, \dots, n \tag{10}$$

and

$$\frac{\partial L}{\partial \beta} = 0 \tag{11}$$

Equation 10 determines the optimal solution, as it corresponds to the equilibrium point where all applications have the same value of diminishing returns (or β). Equation 11 satisfies the resource constraint.

The solution to this system of equations, derived either using analytical or numerical methods, yields the shares ϕ_i that should be allocated to each application to minimize the system-wide discontent. We use a numerical method for solving these equations to account for the non-differentiable factor present in the time-domain queuing model (Equation 2).

Having described the monitoring and allocation modules, we now describe the prediction module that uses the measured system metrics to estimate the workload parameters that are used by the optimization-based allocation technique.

3.3   Workload Prediction Techniques

The online optimization-based allocation technique described in the previous section is crucially dependent on an accurate estimation of the workload likely to appear in each application class. In this section, we present techniques that use past observations to estimate the future workload for an application.

The workload seen by an application can be characterized by two complementary distributions: the *request arrival process* and the *service demand distribution*. Together these distributions enable us to capture the workload intensity and its variability. Our technique measures the various parameters governing these distributions over a certain time period and uses these measurements to predict the workload for the next adaptation window.

Estimating the Arrival Rate. The request arrival process corresponds to the workload intensity for an application. The crucial parameter of interest that characterizes the arrival process is the request arrival rate λ_i. An accurate estimate of λ_i allows the time-domain queuing model to estimate the average queue length for the next adaptation window.

To estimate λ_i, the monitoring module measures the number of request arrivals a_i in each measurement interval I. The sequence of these values $\{a_i^m\}$ forms a time series. Using this time series to represent a stochastic process A_i, our prediction module attempts to predict the number of arrivals $\hat{n}_i$ for the next adaptation window. The arrival rate for the window, $\hat{\lambda}_i$ is then approximated as $\left(\dfrac{\hat{n}_i}{W}\right)$ where W is the window length. We represent A_i at any time by the sequence $\{a_i^1, \ldots, a_i^H\}$ of values from the measurement history.

To predict $\hat{n}_i$, we model the process as an AR(1) process [7] (*autoregressive* of order 1). This is a simple linear regression model in which a sample value is predicted based on the previous sample value

Using the AR(1) model, a sample value of A_i is estimated as

$$\hat{a}_i^{j+1} = \bar{a}_i + \rho_i(1) \cdot (a_i^j - \bar{a}_i) + e_i^j, \tag{12}$$

where, ρ_i and $\bar{a}_i$ are the autocorrelation function and mean of A_i respectively, and e_i^j is a white noise component. We assume e_i^j to be 0, and a_i^j to be estimated values $\hat{a}_i^j$ for $j \geq H + 1$. The autocorrelation function ρ_i is defined as

$$\rho_i(l) = \frac{E[(a_i^j - \bar{a}_i) \cdot (a_i^{j+l} - \bar{a}_i)]}{\sigma_{a_i}^2}, 0 \leq l \leq H - 1,$$

where, σ_{a_i} is the standard deviation of A_i and l is the *lag* between sample values for which the autocorrelation is computed.

Thus, if the adaptation window size is M intervals (i.e., $M = W/I$), then, we first estimate $\hat{a}_i^{H+1}, \ldots, \hat{a}_i^{H+M}$ using equation 12. Then, the estimated number of arrivals in the adaptation window is given by $\hat{n}_i = \sum_{j=H+1}^{H+M} \hat{a}_i^j$ and finally, the estimated arrival rate, $\hat{\lambda}_i = \dfrac{\hat{n}_i}{W}$.

Estimating the Service Demand. The service demand of each incoming request represents the load imposed by that request on the resource. Two applications with similar arrival rates but different service demands (e.g., different packet sizes, different per-request CPU demand, etc.) will need to be allocated different resource shares.

To estimate the service demand for an application, the prediction module computes the probability distribution of the per-request service demands. This distribution is represented by a histogram of the per-request service demands. Upon the completion of each request, this histogram is updated with the service demand of that request. The distribution is used to determine the expected request service demand $\hat{s}_i$ for requests in the next adaptation window. $\hat{s}_i$ could be computed as the mean, the median, or a percentile of the distribution obtained from the histogram. For our experiments, we use the mean of the distribution to represent the service demand of application requests.

Measuring the Queue Length. A final parameter required by the allocation model is the queue length of each application at the beginning of each adaptation window. Since we are only interested in the instantaneous queue length q_i^0 and not mean values, measuring this parameter is trivial—the monitoring module simply records the number of outstanding requests in each application queue at the beginning of each adaptation window.

4   Experimental Evaluation

We demonstrate the efficacy of our dynamic resource allocation techniques using a simulation study. In what follows, we first present our simulation setup and then our experimental results.

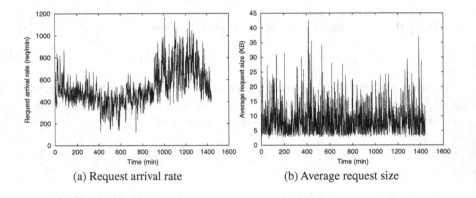

(a) Request arrival rate   (b) Average request size

Fig. 4. 24-hour portion of the World Cup 98 trace

4.1   Simulation Setup and Workload Characteristics

Our simulator models a server resource with multiple application-specific queues; the experiments reported in this paper specifically model the network interface on a shared server. Requests across various queues are scheduled using weighted fair queuing [15]—a practical instantiation of GPS. Our simulator is based on the *NetSim* library [22] and *DASSF* simulation package [23]; together these components support network elements such as queues, traffic sources, etc., and provide us the necessary abstractions for implementing our simulator. The adaptation and the prediction algorithms are implemented using the *Matlab* package [28] (which provides various statistical routines and numerical non-linear optimization algorithms); the Matlab code is invoked directly from the simulator for prediction and adaptation.

We use two types of workloads in our study—synthetic and trace-driven. Our synthetic workloads use Poisson request arrivals and deterministic request sizes. Our trace-driven workload is based on the World Cup Soccer '98 server logs [4]—a publicly available web server trace. Here, we present results based on a 24-hour long portion of the trace that contains a total of 755,705 requests at a mean request arrival rate of 8.7 requests/sec, and a mean request size of 8.47 KB. Figures 4 (a) and (b) show the request arrival rate and the average request size respectively for this portion of the trace. We use this trace workload to evaluate the efficacy of our prediction and allocation techniques. Due to space constraints, we omit results related to our prediction technique and those based on longer portions of the trace. More detailed results can be found in a technical report [11].

4.2   Dynamic Resource Allocation

In this section, we evaluate our dynamic resource allocation techniques. We conduct two experiments, one with a synthetic web workload and the other with the trace workload and examine the effectiveness of dynamic resource allocation. For purposes of comparison, we repeat each experiment using a static resource allocation scheme and compare the behavior of the two systems.

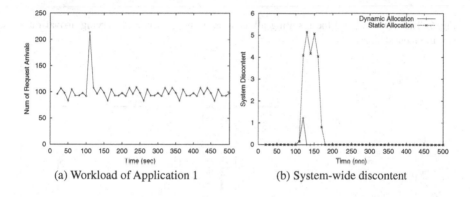

(a) Workload of Application 1   (b) System-wide discontent

Fig. 5. Comparison of static and dynamic resource allocations for a synthetic web workload.

Synthetic Web Workload. To demonstrate the behavior of our system, we consider two web applications that share a server. The benefits of dynamic resource allocation accrue when the workload temporarily exceeds the allocation of an application (resulting in a transient overload). In such a scenario, the dynamic resource allocation technique is able to allocate unused capacity to the overloaded application, and thereby meet its QoS requirements. To demonstrate this property, we conducted a controlled experiment using synthetic web workloads. The workload for each application was generated using Poisson arrivals. The mean request rate for the two applications were set to 100 requests/s and 200 requests/s. Between time t=100 and 110 sec, we introduced a transient overload for the first application as shown in Figure 5(a). The two applications were initially allocated resources in the proportion 1:2, which corresponds to the average request rates of the two applications. ϕ_{min} was set to 20% of the capacity for both applications and the target delays were set to 2 and 10s, respectively. Figure 5(b) depicts the total discontent of the two applications in the presence of dynamic and static resource allocations. As can be seen from the figure, the dynamic resource allocation technique provides better utility to the two applications when compared to static resource allocation and also recovers faster from the transient overload.

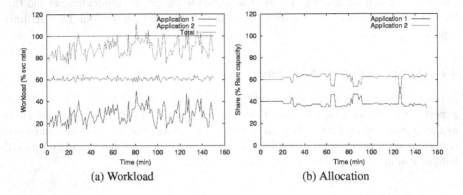

(a) Workload   (b) Allocation

Fig. 6. The workload and the resulting allocations in the presence of varying arrival rates and varying request sizes.

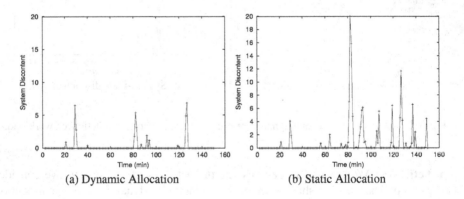

(a) Dynamic Allocation   (b) Static Allocation

Fig. 7. Comparison of static and dynamic resource allocations in the presence of heavy-tailed request sizes and varying arrival rates.

Trace-driven Web Workloads. Our second experiment considered two web applications. In this case, we use the World Cup trace to generate requests for the first web application. The second application represents a background load for the experiment; its workload was generated using Poisson arrivals and deterministic request sizes. For this experiment, ϕ_{min} was chosen to be 30% for both applications and the initial allocations are set to 30% and 70% for the two applications (the allocations remain fixed for the static case and tend to vary for the dynamic case). We present results from only that part of the experiment where transient overloads occur in the system and result in behavior of interest.

Figure 6(a) shows the workload arrival rate (as a percentage of the resource service rate) for the two applications, and also the total load on the system. As can be seen from the figure, there are brief periods of overload in the system. Figure 6(b) plots the resource shares allocated to the two applications by our allocation technique, while Figures 7(a) and (b) show the system discontent values for the dynamic and the static resource allocation scenarios. As can be seen from the figures, transient overloads result in temporary deviations from the desired response times in both cases. However, the dynamic resource allocation technique yields a smaller system-wide discontent, indicating that it is able to use the system capacity more judiciously among the two applications.

Together these experiments demonstrate the effectiveness of our dynamic resource allocation technique in meeting the QoS requirements of applications in the presence of varying workloads.

5 Related Work

Several research efforts have focused on the design of adaptive systems that can react to workload changes in the context of storage systems [3,26], general operating systems [32], network services [8], web servers [6,10,13,21,25,30] and Internet data centers [2,31]. In this paper, we focused on an abstract model of a server resource with multiple class-specific queues and presented techniques for dynamic resource allocation; our model and allocation techniques are applicable to many scenarios where the underlying system or resource can be abstracted using a GPS server.

Some adaptive systems employ a control-theoretic adaptation technique [1,25,27, 34]. Most of these systems (with the exception of [27]) use a pre-identified system model. In contrast, our technique is based on online workload characterization and prediction. Further, these techniques use a linear relationship between the QoS parameter (like target delay) and the control parameter (such as resource share) that does not change with time. This is in contrast to our technique that employs a non-linear model derived using the queuing dynamics of the system, and further, we update the model parameters with changing workload.

Other approaches for resource sharing in web servers [10] and e-business environments [24] have used a queuing model with non-linear optimization. The primary difference between these approaches and our work is that they use *steady-state queue behavior* to drive the optimization, whereas we use *transient* queue dynamics to control the resource shares of applications. Thus, our goal is to devise a system that can react to transient changes in workload, while the queuing theoretic approach attempts to schedule requests based on the steady-state workload. A model-based resource provisioning scheme has been proposed recently [16] that performs resource allocation based on the performance modeling of the server. This effort is similar to our approach of modeling the resource to relate the QoS metrics and resource shares.

Other techniques for dynamic resource allocation have also been proposed in [5,12]. Our work differs from these techniques in some significant ways. First of all, we define an explicit model to derive the relation between the QoS metric and resource requirements, while a linear relation has been assumed in these approaches. The approach in [5] uses a modified scheduling scheme to achieve dynamic resource allocation, while our scheme achieves the same goal with existing schedulers using high-level parameterization. The approach described in [12] uses an economic model similar to our utility-based approach. This approach employs a greedy algorithm coupled with a linear system model for resource allocation, while we employ a non-linear optimization approach coupled with a non-linear queuing model for resource allocation.

Prediction techniques have been proposed that incorporate time-of-day effects along with time-series analysis models into their prediction [20,33]. While these techniques work well for online prediction at coarse time-granularities of several minutes to hours, the goal of our prediction techniques is to predict workloads at short time granularities of upto a few minutes and to respond quickly to transient overloads.

Two recent efforts have focused on workload-driven allocation in *dedicated* data centers [17,31]. In these efforts, each application is assumed to run on some number of dedicated servers and the goal is to dynamically allocate and deallocate (entire) servers to applications to handle workload fluctuations. These efforts focus on issues such as how many servers to allocate to an application, and how to migrate applications and data, and thus are complementary to our present work on *shared* data centers.

6   Conclusions

In this paper, we argued that dynamic resource allocation techniques are necessary in the presence of dynamically varying workloads to provide guarantees to web applications running on shared data centers. To address this issue, we used a system architecture that combines online measurements with prediction and resource allocation techniques. To capture the transient behavior of the application workloads, we modeled a server resource using a time-domain description of a generalized processor sharing (GPS) server. The parameters of this model were continuously updated using an online monitoring and prediction framework. This framework used time series analysis techniques to predict expected workload parameters from measured system metrics. We then employed a constrained non-linear optimization technique to dynamically allocate the server resources based on the estimated application requirements. The main advantage of our techniques is that they capture the transient behavior of applications while incorporating nonlinearity in the system model. We evaluated our techniques using simulations with synthetic as well as real-world web workloads. Our results showed that these techniques can judiciously allocate system resources, especially under transient overload conditions.

In future, we plan to evaluate the accuracy-efficiency tradeoff of using more sophisticated time series analysis models for prediction. In addition, we plan to investigate the utility of our adaptation techniques for systems employing other types of schedulers (e.g., non-GPS schedulers such as reservation-based). We would also like to explore optimization techniques using different utility functions and QoS goals. We also plan to evaluate these techniques with different kinds of workloads and traces. Finally, we intend to compare our allocation techniques with other dynamic allocation techniques to evaluate their relative effectiveness.

References

1. T. Abdelzaher, K. G. Shin, and N. Bhatti. Performance Guarantees for Web Server End-Systems: A Control-Theoretical Approach. *IEEE Transactions on Parallel and Distributed Systems*, 13(1), January 2002.
2. J. Aman, C.K. Eilert, D. Emmes, P Yocom, and D. Dillenberger. Adaptive algorithms for managing a distributed data processing workload. *IBM Sytems Journal*, 36(2):242–283, 1997.
3. E. Anderson, M. Hobbs, K. Keeton, S. Spence, M. Uysal, and A. Veitch. Hippodrome: Running Circles around Storage Administration. In *Proceedings of the Conference on File and Storage Technologies*, January 2002.
4. M. Arlitt and T. Jin. Workload Characterization of the 1998 World Cup Web Site. Technical Report HPL-1999-35R1, HP Labs, 1999.
5. M. Aron, P. Druschel, and S. Iyer. A Resource Management Framework for Predictable Quality of Service in Web Servers, 2001.
   http://www.cs.rice.edu/~druschel/publications/mbqos.pdf.
6. N. Bhatti and R. Friedrich. Web server support for tiered services. *IEEE Network*, 13(5), September 1999.
7. G. Box and G. Jenkins. *Time Series Analysis: Forecasting and Control*. Holden-Day, 1976.
8. A. Brown, D. Oppenheimer, K. Keeton, R. Thomas, J. Kubiatowicz, and D. Patterson. IS-TORE: Introspective Storage for Data-Intensive Network Services. In *Proceedings of the Workshop on Hot Topics in Operating Systems*, March 1999.
9. A. Bryson and Y. Ho. *Applied Optimal Control*. Ginn and Company, 1969.
10. J. Carlström and R. Rom. Application-Aware Admission Control and Scheduling in Web Servers. In *Proceedings of the IEEE Infocom 2002*, June 2002.
11. A. Chandra, W. Gong, and P. Shenoy. Dynamic resource allocation for shared data centers using online measurements. Technical Report TR02-30, Department of Computer Science, University of Massachusetts, 2002.
12. J. Chase, D. Anderson, P. Thakar, A. Vahdat, and R. Doyle. Managing energy and server resources in hosting centers. In *Proceedings of the Eighteenth ACM Symposium on Operating Systems Principles (SOSP)*, pages 103–116, October 2001.
13. H. Chen and P. Mohapatra. The content and access dynamics of a busy web site: findings and implications. In *Proceedings of the IEEE Infocom 2002*, June 2002.
14. M R. Crovella and A. Bestavros. Self-Similarity in World Wide Web Traffic: Evidence and Possible Causes. *IEEE/ACM Transactions on Networking*, 5(6):835–846, December 1997.
15. A. Demers, S. Keshav, and S. Shenker. Analysis and simulation of a fair queueing algorithm. In *Proceedings of ACM SIGCOMM*, pages 1–12, September 1989.
16. R. Doyle, J. Chase, O. Asad, W. Jin, and Amin Vahdat. Model-Based Resource Provisioning in a Web Service Utility. In *Proceedings of USITS'03*, March 2003.
17. K Appleby et. al. Oceano - sla-based management of a computing utility. In *Proceedings of the IFIP/IEEE Symposium on Integrated Network Management*, May 2001.
18. S.J. Golestani. A self-clocked fair queueing scheme for high speed applications. In *Proceedings of INFOCOM'94*, pages 636–646, April 1994.
19. P. Goyal, H. Vin, and H. Cheng. Start-time Fair Queuing: A Scheduling Algorithm for Integrated Services Packet Switching Networks. In *Proceedings of the ACM SIGCOMM '96 Conference on Applications, Technologies, Architectures, and Protocols for Computer Communication*, pages 157–168, August 1996.
20. J. Hellerstein, F. Zhang, and P. Shahabuddin. A Statistical Approach to Predictive Detection. *Computer Networks*, January 2000.

21. S. Lee, J. Lui, and D. Yau. Admission control and dynamic adaptation for a proportional-delay diffserv-enabled web server. In *Proceedings of SIGMETRICS*, 2002.
22. B. Liu and D. Figueiredo. Queuing Network Library for SSF Simulator, January 2002. http://www-net.cs.umass.edu/fluidsim/archive.html.
23. J. Liu and D. M. Nicol. DaSSF 3.0 User's Manual, January 2001. http://www.cs.dartmouth.edu/~jasonliu/projects/ssf/docs.html.
24. Z. Liu, M. Squillante, and J. Wolf. On Maximizing Service-Level-Agreement Profits. In *Proceedings of the 3rd ACM conference on Electronic Commerce*, 2001.
25. C. Lu, T. Abdelzaher, J. Stankovic, and S. Son. A Feedback Control Approach for Guaranteeing Relative Delays in Web Servers. In *Proceedings of the IEEE Real-Time Technology and Applications Symposium*, June 2001.
26. C. Lu, G. Alvarez, and J. Wilkes. Aqueduct: Online Data Migration with Performance Guarantees. In *Proceedings of the Conference on File and Storage Technologies*, January 2002.
27. Y. Lu, T. Abdelzaher, C. Lu, and G. Tao. An Adaptive Control Framework for QoS Guarantees and its Application to Differentiated Caching Services. In *Proceedings of the Tenth International Workshop on Quality of Service (IWQoS 2002)*, May 2002.
28. Using MATLAB. MathWork, Inc., 1997.
29. A. Parekh and R. Gallager. A generalized processor sharing approach to flow control in integrated services networks – the single node case. In *Proceedings of IEEE INFOCOM '92*, pages 915–924, May 1992.
30. P. Pradhan, R. Tewari, S. Sahu, A. Chandra, and P. Shenoy. An Observation-based Approach Towards Self-Managing Web Servers. In *Proceedings of the Tenth International Workshop on Quality of Service (IWQoS 2002)*, May 2002.
31. S. Ranjan, J. Rolia, and E. Knightly H. Fu. QoS-Driven Server Migration for Internet Data Centers. In *Proceedings of the Tenth International Workshop on Quality of Service (IWQoS 2002)*, May 2002.
32. M. Seltzer and C. Small. Self-Monitoring and Self-Adapting Systems. In *Proceedings of the Workshop on Hot Topics in Operating Systems*, May 1997.
33. F. Zhang and J. L. Hellerstein. An approach to on-line predictive detection. In *Proceedings of MASCOTS 2000*, August 2000.
34. R. Zhong, C. Lu, T. F. Abdelzaher, and J. A. Stankovic. Controlware: A middleware architecture for feedback control of software performance. In *Proceedings of ICDCS*, July 2002.

VIII Rate-Based QoS

Providing Deterministic End-to-End Fairness Guarantees in Core-Stateless Networks

Jasleen Kaur[1] and Harrick Vin[2]

[1] Department of Computer Science
University of North Carolina at Chapel Hill
[2] Department of Computer Sciences
University of Texas at Austin

Abstract. End-to-end fairness guarantee is an important service semantics that network providers would like to offer to their customers. A network provider can offer such service semantics by deploying a network where each router employs a fair packet scheduling algorithm. Unfortunately, these scheduling algorithms require every router to maintain per-flow state and perform per-packet flow classification; these requirements limit the scalability of the routers. In this paper, we propose the *Core-stateless Guaranteed Fair (CSGF)* network architecture—the first work-conserving architecture that, without maintaining per-flow state or performing per-packet flow classification in core routers, provides to flows fairness guarantees similar to those provided by a network of core-stateful fair routers.

1 Introduction

With the commercialization of the Internet, there is a significant incentive for network service providers to offer value-added services to customers. An opportunity for adding value comes with the emergence of wide-area real-time and mission-critical applications; these applications benefit from network services that provide guarantees, on a per-flow basis, on the end-to-end delay, jitter, loss, and throughput. Over the past decade, several link scheduling algorithms that enable networks to provide such guarantees—by arbitrating access to shared link bandwidth at routers by packets of different flows—have been proposed [3,4,9,10,11,19,23,24]. In this paper, we address the problem of designing a *work-conserving, core-stateless* network architecture that can provide *fairness* guarantees to flows. In what follows, we first justify the need for fairness as well as core-stateless and work-conserving network architectures, and then summarize our contributions.

Why Fairness? *Fairness* of bandwidth allocation is an important guarantee provided by link scheduling algorithms. Using a fair scheduling algorithm, routers provide throughput guarantees to backlogged flows at short time-scales (independent of their past usage of link bandwidth), and allocate idle link capacity to competing flows in proportion to their weights (or reserved rates).

The property of providing throughput guarantees at short time-scales independent of the past bandwidth usage by the flow is important for two reasons. First, in many

K. Jeffay, I. Stoica, and K. Wehrle (Eds.): IWQoS 2003, LNCS 2707, pp. 401–421, 2003.

applications, sources may not be able to predict precisely their bandwidth requirements at short time-scales (consider, for instance, the problem of transmitting variable bit-rate encoded live video stream). To support these applications effectively, a network should allow flows to utilize occasionally more than their reserved bandwidth if such over-usage does not come at the expense of violating the bandwidth guarantees provided to other flows. Second, it is in the best interest of a network to allow sources to transmit data in bursts; bursty transmissions allow a network to benefit from statistical multiplexing of the available network bandwidth among competing traffic. If a network were to penalize a flow for using idle bandwidth, then the source would have no incentive to transmit bursts into the network; this, in turn, would reduce the statistical multiplexing gains and thereby reduce the overall utilization of network resources.

The property of fair scheduling algorithms of allocating available bandwidth to flows in proportion to their reserved rates is desirable from an economic perspective. Consider, for instance, the case when a network provider charges its customers based on their reserved bandwidth. In such a network, if a user A pays twice as much as user B, then A expects the network to allocate bandwidth in the ratio 2:1 to users A and B; any other allocation would be considered unfair. Fair scheduling algorithms allow a network to ensure this proportionate allocation property independent of the amount of available bandwidth.

Why Core-stateless? The design of next-generation networks is faced with the challenge that link capacities and traffic demands are increasing rapidly [8,12], whereas processor speeds are increasing at only about half the rate [1]. This implies that the per-packet processing and computation performed by next-generation routers must be simplified to enable them to operate at high link speeds. Link scheduling algorithms proposed in the last decade to enable networks to provide fairness guarantees to flows [3, 4,9,10,11,19], on the other hand, require routers to maintain and use per-flow state, and perform packet classification to identify the flow to which an incoming packet belongs. The complexity of these operations grows as the number of flows increase. Thus, routers in such fair networks may not be able to operate at high link speeds, especially routers in the core of the network that aggregate a large number of flows originating from different edges of the network.

In order to alleviate this issue, over the past few years, several core-stateless networks have been designed to provide end-to-end service guarantees without maintaining or using any per-flow state at the core routers of a network [6,7,13,16,18,20,21,25]; this property improves the scalability of the core routers to large number of flows and high-speed links. Existing proposals for providing fairness in core-stateless networks, however, only provide *approximate* fairness in the end-to-end throughput achieved by flows over large time-scales [6,7,18,20]. In particular, due to the statistical nature of these guarantees, such schemes can not provide fairness guarantees to short-lived flows or for specific durations of interest in the lifespan of long-lived flows.

Why Work-conserving? Throughput and proportionate allocation guarantees can be ensured in networks that are *non work-conserving*, in which flows are allocated no more than their reserved rates at any time. In fact, the only known core-stateless networks that guarantee deterministically, that flows would receive throughput in proportion to their reserved rates, are non work-conserving [21]. Non work-conserving networks shape the rate of incoming traffic to a maximum of the reserved rate for a flow; sources are not allowed to achieve larger transmission rates, even if network bandwidth is idle. This property results in high average delays [22] and limits the ability of the network to utilize resource efficiently. With the predicted growth in traffic demands [12], this is undesirable. To the best of our knowledge, the only kind of deterministic guarantees provided by work-conserving core-stateless networks proposed in the literature, are on delay and throughput [13,16,17,25].

Research Contributions. In this paper, we propose the *first* work-conserving core-stateless network that provides deterministic fairness guarantees. We argue that an end-to-end notion of proportionate allocation in fair networks is meaningful only when defined across flows that share the same end-to-end network path. We show that networks that provide throughput guarantees are a crucial building block for networks that provide proportionate allocation guarantees. We then use a set of two simple mechanisms— namely, aggregation and fair-ingress—to enable a core-stateless network that provides throughput guarantees (previously proposed) to also guarantee proportionate allocation. We show that the resultant network, referred to as a Core-stateless Guaranteed Fair (CSGF) network, provides deterministic fairness guarantees similar to those provided by core-stateful networks.

The rest of this paper is organized as follows. In Section 3, we formulate the problem of end-to-end fairness. In Section 4, we present the key insights and mechanisms used to design CSGF networks. We derive properties of CSGF networks in Section 5. Deployment considerations are discussed in Section 6. We summarize related work in Section 7 and our conclusions in Section 8.

2   Notation and Assumptions

Throughout this paper, we use the following symbols and notation.

p_f^k	: the kth packet of flow f
$a_{f,j}^k$	: arrival time of p_f^k at node j on its path
$d_{f,j}^k$	: departure time of p_f^k from node j
l_f^k	: length of packet p_f^k
r_f	: rate reserved for flow f
π_j	: upper bound on propagation delay of the link connecting node j and $(j+1)$
C_j	: outgoing link capacity at node j
$W_{f,j}(t_1, t_2)$	: throughput of flow f at server j during $[t_1, t_2]$
$\gamma_{f,j},\ U_{j,\{f,m\}},\ I_{j,m,f}$	: constants associated with service guarantees

H denotes the number of routers along the path of flow f. The source of flow f is connected to router 1 and the destination is connected to router H. A source is said to transmit packets *at least at its reserved rate* r_f, if $a_{f,1}^k \leq a_{f,1}^{k-1} + \frac{l_f^{k-1}}{r_f}$. The kth packet,

p_f^k, transmitted from the source, is said to have a *sequence number* of k. The *throughput*, $W_{f,j}(t_1, t_2)$, received by flow f at server j during a time interval $[t_1, t_2]$, is defined as the number of bits of flow f that depart server j during the time interval $[t_1, t_2]$. Also, a flow f is said to be *continuously backlogged* at server j in a time interval $[t_1, t_2]$ if, at all instances within this interval, there is at least one packet belonging to flow f in the server queue. Throughout our analysis, we use the terms *server* and *router* interchangeably; further, we assume that the sum of rates reserved for flows at any server does not exceed the server capacity (i.e., the link bandwidth).

3   Problem Formulation

Background. Networks can provide fairness guarantees by employing *fair schedul- ing algorithms* at all routers [3,4,9,10,11,19]. The fairness guarantee provided by fair scheduling algorithms at a *single* node can be formalized[1] as follows:

Definition 1. *The scheduling algorithm at node j is said to provide a fairness guar- antee if in any time interval $[t_1, t_2]$ during which two flows f and m are continuously backlogged, the number of bits of flows f and m transmitted by the server, $W_{f,j}(t_1, t_2)$ and $W_{m,j}(t_1, t_2)$ respectively, satisfy:*

$$\left| \frac{W_{f,j}(t_1, t_2)}{r_f} - \frac{W_{m,j}(t_1, t_2)}{r_m} \right| \leq U_{j,\{f,m\}} \tag{1}$$

where r_f and r_m are the rates reserved for flows f and m respectively, and $U_{j,\{f,m\}}$ is an unfairness measure—a constant that depends on the scheduling algorithm and traffic characteristics at server j. Further, if the sum of reserved rates of all flows at node j does not exceed the outgoing link capacity, then in any time interval $[t_1, t_2]$, during which the source of a flow f transmits packets at least at its reserved rate r_f, the server guarantees a minimum throughput to flow f:

$$W_{f,j}(t_1, t_2) > r_f(t_2 - t_1) - r_f \gamma_{f,j} \tag{2}$$

where $\gamma_{f,j}$ is an error term — a constant that also depends on traffic and server char- acteristics.

Fair scheduling algorithms are capable of providing a proportionate allocation guarantee slightly stronger than given in (1): if flow m is continuously backlogged during $[t_1, t_2]$, then the throughput of any other flow f, whether backlogged or not, is given by [15]:

$$\frac{W_{f,j}(t_1, t_2)}{r_f} \leq \frac{W_{m,j}(t_1, t_2)}{r_m} + I_{j,m,f} \tag{3}$$

where $I_{j,m,f}$ is a constant that also depends on the server and traffic characteristics. Different fair scheduling algorithms differ in the values of $U_{j,\{f,m\}}$, $I_{j,m,f}$, and $\gamma_{f,j}$ [3, 4,10,11,19]. The smaller is the value of these constants, the better is the corresponding throughput or proportionate allocation guarantee. Table 1 lists known values for several algorithms.

---

[1] Fairness of a link scheduling algorithm can be defined equivalently in terms of a bound on its deviation from an idealized fluid model of fairness [3]. In terms of describing network properties perceivable by end-users, however, Definition 1 is more useful.

Table 1. Unfairness measures for some fair algorithms

	$U_{j,\{f,m\}}$	$I_{j,m,f}$	$\gamma_{f,j}$
GPS	0	0	0
SCFQ	$\frac{l_f^{max}}{r_f} + \frac{l_m^{max}}{r_m}$	$\frac{l_f^{max}}{r_f} + \frac{l_m^{max}}{r_m}$	-
SFQ	$\frac{l_f^{max}}{r_f} + \frac{l_m^{max}}{r_m}$	$\frac{l_f^{max}}{r_f} + \frac{l_m^{max}}{r_m}$	$\sum_n F\{\ f\}\frac{l_n^{max}}{C_j} + \frac{l_f^{max}}{r_f}$
WF²Q	$l^{max}(\frac{1}{r_f} + \frac{1}{r_m} - \frac{1}{C})$	$\frac{l^{max}}{r_m} + l_f^{max}(\frac{1}{r_f} - \frac{1}{C})$	$\frac{l_f^{max}}{r_f} + \frac{(l^{max} - l_f^{max})}{C_j}$

The literature contains analyses that extend these single-server guarantees on throughput and proportionate allocation to *end-to-end* guarantees provided by a network of fair scheduling servers [2,14,15]. Specifically, a network of fair servers (1) guarantees a minimum end-to-end throughput to flows with an associated error term, $\gamma_{f,H}^{net}$, and (2) guarantees proportionate allocation of end-to-end throughput to flows that share the same path, with an unfairness measure, $U_{H,\{f,m\}}^{net}$, where these constants are given by [2,14,15]:

$$\gamma_{f,H}^{net} = (H + 1)\frac{l_f^{max}}{r_f} + \sum_{j=1}^{H-1} \pi_j + \sum_{j=1}^{H} \gamma_{f,j} \qquad (4)$$

$$U_{H,\{f,m\}}^{net} = U_{1,\{f,m\}} + \sum_{h=2}^{H} (I_{h,f,m} + I_{h,m,f}) \qquad (5)$$

Unfortunately, to provide fairness guarantees, fair scheduling algorithms require routers to maintain per-flow state. It is especially challenging to design networks that provide fairness without maintaining per-flow state in core routers because unlike delay guarantees (that can be characterized entirely in terms of the intrinsic properties of a flow such as its reserved rate), a fairness guarantee is inherently a function of the state (throughput) of all other flows sharing a resource (Definition 1). Prior attempts at designing core-stateless fair networks have realized this constraint; hence, prior designs of core-stateless fair networks provide only *statistical* (or approximate) fairness over large time-scales and for long-lived flows [6,7,18,20]. In this paper, we attempt to design a core-stateless network architecture that can provide deterministic end-to-end fairness guarantees to flows.

Our Approach. To derive a work-conserving, core-stateless network architecture that can provide deterministic fairness guarantees, we observe that a core-stateful network of fair routers provide to flows two types of guarantees: (1) throughput guarantee, and (2) a per-link proportionate bandwidth allocation guarantee.

Recently, we have proposed CSGT—a Core-stateless Guaranteed Throughput network architecture—that can provide end-to-end throughput guarantees to flows [16]. CSGT can provide, at all time-scales, a throughput guarantee that is within a constant of what is provided by a core-stateful network of fair scheduling routers. Thus, CSGT provides part of the functionality offered by a core-stateful network of fair routers. Unfortunately, since core routers in CSGT networks do not maintain any per-flow state, they can not ensure per-link proportionate allocation of bandwidth to flows.

In what follows, we argue that the per-link proportionate bandwidth allocation offered by fair scheduling algorithms translates to meaningful end-to-end guarantees only when flows share the *entire* end-to-end paths. To support this argument, observe that the end-to-end bandwidth allocated to a flow depends on the flow's share of the bottleneck[2] link bandwidth. Flows that share the entire end-to-end network path also share the bottleneck link; hence, the allocation of bandwidth on the bottleneck link governs the relative end-to-end bandwidth allocation to these flows. On the other hand, flows that do not share the entire end-to-end network paths may not share the bottleneck link. Further, since the bottleneck link for each flow may change continuously with fluctuations in traffic conditions, even when the bottleneck link is shared between such flows, the sharing is likely to be transient (or short-lived).[3] Hence, in networks where each router employs a fair scheduling algorithm to allocate spare bandwidth proportionally among competing flows on a per-link basis, it is difficult to relate, in a consistent manner, the end-to-end bandwidth allocated to two flows that do not share the complete end-to-end path. Consequently, core-stateful networks can not provide any strong consistent *guarantees* with respect to the relative bandwidth allocated to flows that do not share complete path.

From the above arguments, we conclude that, from the perspective of a network provider, an architecture that only supports *end-to-end* proportionate bandwidth allocation (a weaker guarantee) is likely to be indistinguishable from a core-stateful fair network architecture that supports proportionate allocation on a per-link basis. Hence, in this paper, we explore the design of networks that can provide end-to-end throughput guarantees and proportionate allocation guarantees to flows that share the same *end-to-end* path. Our design proceeds in two steps. First, we show that a network that provides throughput guarantees is a crucial building block for designing one that provides fairness guarantees. Second, we explore mechanisms that, when integrated with a work-conserving core-stateless network that provides throughput guarantees, lead to the design of the *Core-stateless Guaranteed Fair* (CSGF) network architecture—the *first* work-conserving core-stateless architecture that provides deterministic fairness guarantees.

---

[2] In this paper, the bottleneck link for a flow refers to the link with the least share of *available bandwidth* for the flow, rather than the link with the least link capacity. Depending on the cross traffic load, the link with the least share of available bandwidth for a flow may be different from the link with the least link capacity.

[3] For some flows, such as those that originate from a common source behind a slow modem line, the access link may be the non-transient bottleneck link due to its limited capacity. However, such links lie outside the scope of the network provider architectures we consider in this paper. The edge and core routers that we consider belong to the provider's network, which does not include slow access links.

4   The Design of Core-Stateless Guaranteed Fair Networks

4.1   Providing Fairness Guarantees: Key Insights

Our objective is to design a *work-conserving, core-stateless* network architecture that can provide *fairness* guarantees to flows. Specifically, we want to provide two types of guarantees: (1) an end-to-end throughput guarantee to each flow, and (2) a proportionate bandwidth allocation guarantee to flows that share the same end-to-end path. In what follows, we show that by *decoupling* the objectives of providing these two guarantees, and by using the following two observations, we can design core-stateless networks that provide both kinds of guarantees.

Observation 1. As the following theorem indicates, providing a throughput guarantee is necessary for providing a proportionate allocation guarantee.

Theorem 1. *A work-conserving server that provides proportionate allocation guarantees to a continuously-backlogged flow* m *of the form:*[4]

$$\frac{W_{f,j}(t_1, t_2)}{r_f} \leq \frac{W_{m,j}(t_1, t_2)}{r_m} + I_{j,m,f} \qquad (6)$$

where f *is any other flow, also provides to flow* m *a throughput guarantee of the form:*

$$W_{m,j}(t_1, t_2) \geq r_m(t_2 - t_1) - r_m * \gamma_{m,j}$$

where $\gamma_{m,j} = \frac{l^{max}}{C_j} + \frac{\sum_{f \in F} r_f I_{j,m,f}}{C_j}$, *and* C_j *is the total capacity of the server.*

Proof: See Appendix A. □

The converse of the above theorem indicates that *a server that does not provide throughput guarantees can not provide proportionate allocation guarantees.* A core-stateless network that provides throughput guarantees is, therefore, a crucial building block for the design of one that provides proportionate allocation.

Observation 2. A network that is capable of providing throughput guarantees, can additionally provide end-to-end proportionate bandwidth allocation to flows that share the same path, by employing a set of three mechanisms:

1. Treat the aggregate traffic between a pair of edge nodes as a single flow and provide throughput guarantees to it,
2. Employ a fair scheduling algorithm at the *ingress edge node*, that allocates a proportionate share of the aggregate throughput (at the ingress) to individual flows within the aggregate, and
3. Ensure that the network preserves the order in which packets are transmitted within the aggregate at the ingress node.

---

[4] Note that this notion of proportionate allocation is slightly different from that in Definition 1, which requires *both* flows to be backlogged. It can be shown that fair scheduling algorithms provide this stronger notion of proportionate allocation as well [15].

The third mechanism implies that the sequence in which packets depart at the last node in any time interval $[t_1, t_2]$—and hence the *relative* number of packets of two flows that depart in this time interval—can be equated to the sequence of packet departures at the ingress node in some other time interval $[t'_1, t'_2]$. The end-to-end proportionate allocation guarantee provided by the network is, therefore, exactly the same as the one provided by the ingress server. The second mechanism ensures that the ingress server does provide such a guarantee. The first mechanism ensures that the aggregate traffic on the end-to-end path is guaranteed a minimum throughput; since the individual flows are allocated a proportionate share of this aggregate throughput, it follows that individual flows are provided minimum throughput guarantees as well. A network that employs the above three mechanisms, therefore, provides throughput as well as proportionate allocation guarantees to individual flows.

Note that any core-stateless network that employs the three mechanisms described above can provide fairness guarantees. Below, we present one specific instantiation of such a network, called the Core-stateless Guaranteed Fair (CSGF) network.

4.2   Realization: A CSGF Network

As discussed above, a core-stateless network that provides throughput guarantees is a crucial building block for the design of one that provides fairness guarantees. In [16], we have proposed the Core-stateless Guaranteed Throughput (CSGT) network architecture, a work-conserving core-stateless architecture that enables a network to provide throughput guarantees. We briefly describe this architecture below.

A CSGT Network. A number of work-conserving core-stateless networks that provide delay guarantees have been proposed in the literature [13,17,25]. These networks, however, do not provide throughput guarantees to flows at short time-scales. This is a consequence of a central property of these networks to let packet deadlines grow ahead of current time for flows that use idle bandwidth to transmit packets at more than their reserved rates. Such flows may be penalized during a subsequent time interval by being denied throughput at even their reserved rate. To avoid this, a CSGT network *re-uses* deadlines of packets that depart the network much earlier than their deadlines, for new packets within the same flow. Formally, a CSGT network is defined as follows [16].

The Definition of a CSGT Network. A CSGT network consists of two types of routers: *edge routers* and *core routers* (see Figure 1). The ingress edge router, in addition to maintaining per-flow state, maintains a sorted-list $\mathcal{R}$ of re-usable deadline vectors. On receiving a packet p_f^k of flow f, the ingress router assigns to it a *deadline vector*[5] $[F_1(p_f^k), F_2(p_f^k), ..., F_H(p_f^k)]$ where H is the number of servers along the path of flow f, and $F_j(p_f^k)$ is the deadline of packet p_f^k at server j. The assignment of the deadline

---

[5] In practice, the ingress router computes only $F_1(p_f^k)$—the other values are computed at the respective routers by adding appropriate constants to $F_1(p_f^k)$.

vector to packet p_f^k proceeds as follows: If $\mathcal{R} \neq \emptyset$, an incoming packet is assigned the smallest deadline vector from $\mathcal{R}$. Otherwise, a new deadline vector is created as follows:

$$F_1(p_f^k) = \max\left(a_{f,1}^k, \widehat{F}(a_{f,1}^k)\right) + \frac{l_f^k}{r_f} \tag{7}$$

$$F_j(p_f^k) = F_1(p_f^k) + \sum_{h=1}^{j-1}(\beta_{f,h} + \pi_h) + (j-1)\max_{1 \leq i \leq k} \frac{l_f^i}{r_f}, \ j > 1 \tag{8}$$

where $\beta_{f,h} = \frac{l_h^{max}}{C_h}$, π_h is the propagation latency on the link connecting node j and $j+1$, and $\widehat{F}(t)$ is the maximum deadline at server 1 assigned to any packet by time t. All servers in the CSGT network transmit packets in the increasing order of their deadlines at that server. The egress server notifies the ingress server, using acknowledgment packets, whenever packets depart much earlier than their deadlines.

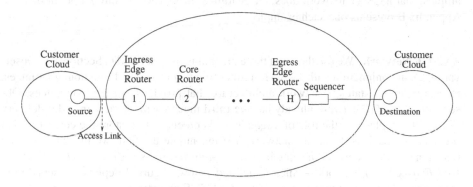

Fig. 1. The CSGT Network Architecture

When deadlines get re-used as described above, packets of a flow f may depart the egress router out-of-order. This is because packets transmitted later by the source may be assigned smaller deadlines than packets transmitted earlier, and may overtake the latter inside the network. To provide in-order delivery semantics to applications, a CSGT network employs an entity, referred to as the *sequencer*, to buffer packets of a flow that arrive out-of-sequence at the egress router, and restore packet order before delivering them to the destination. In order to bound the buffer space occupancy at the sequencer, the maximum number of deadlines simultaneously in use by packets of a given flow is maintained within an upper bound, W.

The following theorem from [16] derives the throughput guarantee provided by a CSGT network.

Theorem 2. *If the source of flow f transmits packets at least at its reserved rate, and D^{max} is an upper bound on the latency after which an acknowledgment packet transmitted by the egress node reaches the ingress node, then a CSGT network guarantees a minimum throughput in any time interval $[t_1, t_2]$, $W_{f,H}(t_1, t_2)$, given by:*

$$W_{f,H}(t_1, t_2) > r_f(t_2 - t_1) - r_f * D^{max} - W * l_f$$
$$-r_f \left((H+1)\frac{l_f}{r_f} + \sum_{j=1}^{H-1} \pi_j + \sum_{j=1}^{H} \beta_{f,j} \right)$$

where $\beta_{f,j}$ is a constant that depends on the server and traffic characteristics at node j.

Recall that fair networks provide two kinds of guarantees: a minimum throughput guarantee at the reserved rate and a proportionate allocation guarantee. Theorem 4 indicates that networks that guarantee proportionate allocation, also provide throughput guarantees. A network that provides throughput guarantees, however, need not guarantee proportionate throughput allocation to different flows. For instance, a network may provide throughput exactly at the reserved rate to one flow, but may allow another flow to use significantly more than its reserved rate. In fact, it can be shown, through examples, that a CSGT network does not guarantee proportionate throughput allocation. Appendix B presents one such example.

A CSGF Network. We use the set of three mechanisms described in Section 4.1 (Observation 2), in conjunction with a CSGT architecture that provides throughput guarantees, to design a core-stateless network architecture that provides fairness guarantees. Observe that a CSGT network already has the third mechanism, namely in-order delivery of packets, in place — the role of a *sequencer* is precisely to restore the correct packet order before packets depart the network. We instantiate the first two mechanisms in a CSGT network to derive a new architecture—referred to as a *Core-stateless Guaranteed Fair (CSGF)* network—which is defined below. Figure 2 depicts the scheduling framework deployed at the ingress router of a CSGF network.

Definition of a CSGF network: The ingress router for F, a set of flows sharing the same end-to-end path in a CSGF network, has two logical components:

- **Deadline Assignment:** A packet that belongs to an "aggregate" flow F is assigned a tag-vector exactly as in a CSGT network; new tag-vectors are computed using a reserved rate of $R = \sum_{f \in F} r_f$.
- **Packet Selection:** The next packet to be assigned a deadline within an aggregate flow F, is selected according to a fair schedule of transmission across individual flows in F. Since the bandwidth available to the aggregate F can fluctuate over time due to variations in cross-traffic, it is desirable to use a scheduler that achieves fair allocation even with fluctuating capacity. We use the Start-time Fair Queuing (SFQ) [11] scheduler, which has this property, to determine the next flow to select a packet from.[6]

---

[6] Note that *any* fair scheduling algorithm that guarantees proportionate allocation despite fluctuating capacity can be used at the ingress. SFQ has one of the best known unfairness measures, $U_{j,\{f,m\}}$, among such algorithms (see Table 1).

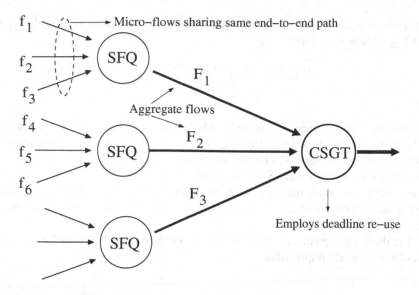

Fig. 2. Scheduling in a CSGF Ingress Router

The core routers and the egress router in a CSGF network function in the same manner as in a CSGT network. At the egress, a sequencer re-orders packets within the "aggregate" before they are split into micro-flows.

Properties of a CSGF network: We now formally derive the proportionate allocation and throughput guarantees provided to individual flows by a CSGF network. We assume that all flows between the same pair of edge routers transmit packets of the same size l.[7]

Proportionate Allocation Guarantees. Our objective is to compute: $\left(\frac{W_{f,H}(t_1,t_2)}{r_f} - \frac{W_{m,H}(t_1,t_2)}{r_m} \right)$, the difference in the normalized number of bits of two backlogged flows f and m, that depart the sequencer during a time interval $[t_1, t_2]$.

Let F be the aggregate flow containing packets of micro-flows f and m. Let p_1 and p_2, respectively, be the first and last bits belonging to the aggregate F, that depart the sequencer during $[t_1, t_2]$. Then, since packets belonging to F depart the sequencer in the same order as their transmission from the SFQ server at the ingress node, all (and only) bits that are transmitted between p_1 and p_2 at the ingress SFQ server, depart the sequencer during $[t_1, t_2]$. If p_1 and p_2 are transmitted from the ingress SFQ server at t'_1 and t'_2, respectively, then the throughput of flow f and flow m at the sequencer during $[t_1, t_2]$ is exactly the same as their throughput at the ingress server during $[t'_1, t'_2]$. That is, $\frac{W_{f,H}(t_1,t_2)}{r_f} = \frac{W_{f,1}(t'_1,t'_2)}{r_f}$, and $\frac{W_{m,H}(t_1,t_2)}{r_m} = \frac{W_{m,1}(t'_1,t'_2)}{r_m}$. The unfairness measure guaranteed to flows for the end-to-end throughput during $[t_1, t_2]$ in a CSGF network

---

[7] If l^{max} is the maximum allowed packet size, it is reasonable to expect a source that is backlogged with data to transmit, to use packets of size l^{max}.

is, therefore, *equal* to that of the SFQ server at the ingress node during $[t'_1, t'_2]$. For a backlogged flow m, it follows that:

$$\frac{W_{f,H}(t_1, t_2)}{r_f} \leq \frac{W_{m,H}(t_1, t_2)}{r_m} + U_{f,m}^{SFQ} \tag{9}$$

Throughput Guarantees. Theorem 2, which states the throughput guarantees of a CSGT network, indicates that the *aggregate* traffic between the pair of edge routers in a CSGF network is guaranteed a minimum throughput characterized by $R = \sum_{f \in F} r_f$, the cumulative reserved rate. Since each flow gets a fair share of this throughput, it follows (using the same reasoning as used to prove Theorem 4), that each micro-flow is provided a throughput guarantee as well. We formally derive this guarantee for a backlogged flow m below.

The throughput guarantee of a CSGT network derived in Theorem 2, when applied to a CSGF network, implies that

$$W_{F,H}(t_1, t_2) > R(t_2 - t_1) - Wl - R\left((H+1)\frac{l}{R} + \sum_{j=1}^{H-1} \pi_j + \sum_{j=1}^{H} \beta_{f,j} + D^{max}\right) \tag{10}$$

Let $a = \frac{W_{m,H}(t_1, t_2)}{r_m}$. From (10) and (9), it follows that:

$$R(t_2 - t_1) - W * l - R\left((H+1)\frac{l}{R} + \sum_{j=1}^{H-1} \pi_j + \sum_{j=1}^{H} \beta_{f,j} + D^{max}\right)$$

$$\leq \sum_{f \in F} W_{f,H}(t_1, t_2)$$

$$\leq \sum_{f \in F} a * r_f + r_f * U_{f,m}^{SFQ}$$

$$\leq a * R + \sum_{f \in F} r_f\left(\frac{l}{r_m} + \frac{l}{r_f}\right)$$

$$\leq a * R + \frac{l}{r_m} R + \sum_{f \in F} l$$

This implies that a CSGF network provides a per-flow throughput guarantee given by:

$$W_{m,H}(t_1, t_2) \geq r_m(t_2 - t_1) - \frac{r_m}{R}(W+1)l - \frac{r_m}{R}\sum_{f \in F} l$$

$$-r_m\left((H+1)\frac{l}{R} + \sum_{j=1}^{H-1} \pi_j + \sum_{j=1}^{H} \beta_{f,j} + D^{max}\right) \tag{11}$$

5   Evaluation of a CSGF Network

The CSGF is the *first* work-conserving core-stateless network architecture that provides deterministic end-to-end throughput and proportionate allocation guarantees. We next address the question: *how do the end-to-end fairness guarantees of a CSGF network compare to those provided by core-stateful fair networks?* We answer these questions below by comparing the error terms ($\gamma_{f,H}^{net}$) and unfairness measures ($U_{H,\{f,m\}}^{net}$), associated with the end-to-end throughput and proportionate allocation guarantees respectively (Section 3), of CSGF and core-stateful networks. For our computations, we consider example network topologies in which link capacities are $100Mbps$ and the propagation latency on each link is $1ms$.

5.1   Proportionate Allocation Guarantees

Observe that the proportionate allocation guarantee in a CSGF network (Inequality (9)) is even better than that provided by a core-stateful network of SFQ servers (see (5)). The reason for this is that while packets of different flows depart the sequencer in a CSGF network exactly in the same order as transmitted by the fair ingress server, packets from different flows that share the same end-to-end path in a core-stateful network may not depart the network in the same order. The end-to-end fairness guarantee of a core-stateful network, therefore, can not be equated to that of its ingress server. We compute the unfairness measures provided by CSGF and a core-stateful networks of SFQ servers[8] for the example topology described above ($C = 100Mbps$ and single-link propagation latency = $1ms$).

Observe that the difference in the unfairness measures provided by CSGF and a core-stateful network of SFQ servers is directly proportional to H, the path length, and inversely proportional to r_f, the reserved rates of the concerned flows. Figure 3(a) plots the unfairness measures provided by both network architectures, as a function of the reserved rates of individual flows (assuming $r_f = r_m$) and the path length (varied from 1 to 10). We observe that, for large-scale network topologies, the unfairness measure in a core-stateful architecture can be an order of magnitude higher than in a CSGF architecture.

Figure 3(a) indicates that the throughput received in a CSGF network by two flows f and m, during any given time interval, may differ by an amount worth playing out for a few milli-seconds. To put this observation in perspective, we plot the reserved rate multiplied by the unfairness measure, in Figure 3(b). We observe that, during a given time interval, a CSGF network may deliver only a few kilo-bytes of more data for one flow, in comparison to other flows. In large-scale core-stateful networks, on the other hand, the difference in throughput could be of the order of tens of kilo-bytes.

5.2   Throughput Guarantees

We next compute and compare $\gamma_{f,H}^{net}$—the minimum timescale at which non-zero throughput is guaranteed to an application—in a CSGF , CSGT, and core-stateful net-

---

[8] SFQ provides one of the smallest unfairness measures among known stateful fair scheduling algorithms.

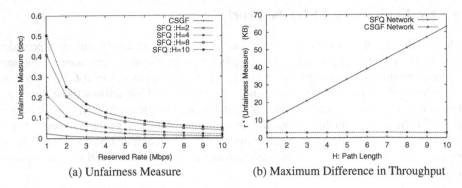

(a) Unfairness Measure   (b) Maximum Difference in Throughput

Fig. 3. Proportionate Allocation of Throughput in a CSGF Network

work of WF^{2}Q+ [4] servers.[9] The smaller is the value of $\gamma_{f,H}^{net}$ for a network, the better is its throughput guarantee [16]. The difference in $\gamma_{f,H}^{net}$ for the three network architectures is governed mainly by the quantities (see (4), (11), and Theorem 2): r_f, the reserved rate of a flow, R, the aggregate reserved rate between a pair of edge routers, H, the number of hops in the path, D^{max}, the maximum latency experienced by feedback messages, and R^{max}, the maximum rate a flow in a CSGT or CSGF network is allowed to achieve.[10] We use the topology described initially ($C = 100Mbps$ and single-link propagation latency = $1ms$), to compute $\gamma_{f,H}^{net}$ for different settings of these quantities.

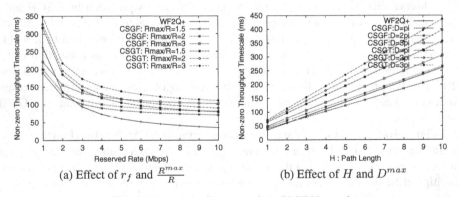

(a) Effect of r_f and $\frac{R^{max}}{R}$ (b) Effect of H and D^{max}

Fig. 4. Throughput Guarantee in a CSGF Network

Figure 4(a) plots for the three network architectures, the value of $\gamma_{f,H}^{net}$ as a function of r_f, the reserved rate for a flow, for different values of R^{max}/R, when the flow traverses

---

[9] A WF^{2}Q+ network guarantees the smallest $\gamma_{f,H}^{net}$ among known stateful fair scheduling algorithms. For networks with uniform packet sizes, the single-node throughput guarantee of a WF^{2}Q+ server is characterized by $\gamma_{f,j} = \frac{l}{r_f}$ [4].

[10] R^{max} governs the value of W, the maximum number of deadlines used simultaneously in CSGT and CSGF networks [16].

a 10-hop path. We assume D^{max} is equal to the sum of link propagation latencies on the reverse network path. We observe the following:

1. For flows with small reserved rates, the per-flow throughput guarantee provided by a CSGF network may be better than that of a CSGT network. The reason for this can be understood by observing that $\gamma_{f,H}^{net}$ for a flow f is inversely related to r_f, its reserved rate (see (11) and Theorem 2). The throughput guarantee provided to the "aggregate" flow (larger reserved rate) in a CSGF network is, therefore, better than that provided to a micro-flow (smaller reserved rate) in a CSGT network. When combined with the fact that the unfairness measure of a CSGF network is small, this implies that the throughput guarantee provided to a micro-flow in a CSGF network may be better than in a CSGT network. The difference between the two networks is less for flows with large bit-rates.
2. The throughput guarantee of a CSGF network may be better than that of a core-stateful network for flows with small reserved rates. This is because although $\gamma_{f,H}^{net}$ is inversely related to r_f for both CSGF and core-stateful networks, the inverse relation is much stronger for flows that traverse multi-hop paths in core-stateful networks (see (4) and (11)). For flows with large reserved rates, however, the additional terms in (11), as compared to (4), dominate the value of $\gamma_{f,H}^{net}$.

Figure 4(b) plots for the three network architectures, the value of $\gamma_{f,H}^{net}$ for a $1 Mbps$ flow as a function of H, for D^{max} ranging from a multiple of 1 to 3 times the sum of link propagation latencies. Flows in the CSGT and CSGF networks are allowed to achieve a maximum rate of up to 3 times their reserved rates ($R^{max}/R = 3$). We observe the following:

1. $\gamma_{f,H}^{net}$ increases linearly with the number of hops traversed by a flow in all three network architectures. In CSGT and CSGF networks, $\gamma_{f,H}^{net}$ also increases with D^{max}: these networks, therefore, benefit from the provisioning of low-delay feedback channels between edge routers.
2. The throughput guarantee provided by a CSGF network is comparable to that provided by core-stateful networks (even when D^{max} is two times the sum of propagation latencies). Perhaps more importantly, we find that a CSGF network can guarantee non-zero throughput to flows, including flows with small reserved rates, at short time-scales of hundreds of milliseconds.

Our observations illustrate that a CSGF network is capable of providing throughput guarantees to individual flows at small time-scales. Large-scale CSGF networks provisioned with low-delay feedback channels may provide even better throughput guarantees to flows with small reserved rates, than core-stateful networks.

5.3 Discussion

Our observations in this section reveal that the end-to-end proportionate allocation guarantee of a CSGF network is better than that provided by core-stateful fair networks. Note that because a CSGF network does not maintain per-flow state in core routers, it, unlike core-stateful networks, does not guarantee the stronger notion of single-link (bottleneck) proportionate allocation. It may seem tempting to conclude that this stronger guarantee is useful to relate the throughput of flows that share their paths only *partially*. However, as argued in Section 3, two such flows may not share their bottleneck links, which govern the allocation of end-to-end throughput. Further, even if the flows share their bottleneck links, the sharing may be short-lived. Hence, it is difficult to relate, in a consistent manner, the end-to-end bandwidth attained by the two flows whose paths overlap only partially. Hence, we believe that our weaker notion of end-to-end proportionate allocation across flows that share the same *end-to-end* path, is adequate for the purposes of defining meaningful end-to-end service semantics.

We also find that it is possible to design CSGF networks that provide throughput guarantees similar to core-stateful networks by provisioning low-delay feedback channels between edge routers. However, the ability to provide comparable guarantees, without maintaining per-flow state in core routers, does not come for free. We discuss some of these issues in the next section.

6   Deployment Considerations

Use of a Sequencer. A CSGF network uses a sequencer to provide in-order delivery of packets to applications. It has been shown in [16] that sequencer buffer requirements are modest even in large-scale networks.

It may seem that due to re-sequencing delays, end-to-end delay guarantees provided to flows in a CSGT or a CSGF network are weaker than those provided in core-stateful fair networks. This is, however, not the case, as is evident from the following two facts. First, despite deadline re-use, the transmission deadlines assigned to a given packet at routers in a CSGT or a CSGF network are never larger than the deadlines assigned to it without deadline re-use [13], or in a corresponding core-stateful network (we omit a detailed proof of this assertion). Second, a CSGT network provides deadline guarantees (see Lemma 2 of [16]). Together, these two facts imply that the delay guarantees provided in CSGT or CSGF networks are no worse than those provided by a core-stateful network of fair servers.

Feedback Channels. The CSGF proportionate allocation guarantee does not depend on the delay or losses experienced by feedback messages on the reverse network path—it merely depends on the proportionate allocation guarantee of the ingress server. The throughput guarantee, on the other hand, depends on the maximum delay experienced in the feedback channels—the larger are the delays and losses on the reverse path, the weaker is the throughput guarantee. Note that delays or losses, though only those that occur on the forward path, can weaken the throughput guarantee of even core-stateful networks. Nevertheless, adequately provisioned feedback channels between the edge routers are an essential component of a CSGF or a CSGT architecture.

Overhead Due to Feedback Messages. The transmission of feedback messages from the egress routers to the ingress routers in a CSGT or CSGF network raises some concern about the overhead introduced by this traffic. This overhead can be reduced for flows with bi-directional data transmission; the acknowledgments from the egress router can be *piggy-backed* on to data packets on the reverse path. In general, this overhead is a price paid for eliminating per-flow state and computation in the core of the network. It is, however, worthwhile to note that feedback messages are transmitted on the reverse path only when packets depart *much* earlier than their deadlines. This, in turn, happens only when sufficient idle bandwidth is available on the forward path. The feedback messages enable the efficient and fair use of such idle bandwidth on the forward path.

Complexity of Edge Routers. Edge routers in a CSGF network are more complex than in core-stateful networks—the additional complexity is in terms of both extra per-aggregate state (set of reusable deadlines), as well as the use of two schedulers instead of one. Note, however, that the scheduler complexity is associated mainly with maintaining priority queues. In a CSGF network, priority queue operations incur a complexity of $O(\log N_A + \log N_F)$, where N_A is the number of aggregates and N_F is the average number of flows within an aggregate. In a corresponding core-stateful network, the priority queue complexity is $O(\log(N_A * N_F))$, which is the same as above. Therefore, processing complexity of ingress routers in CSGF networks is similar to those in core-stateful networks. Since edge routers are likely to process lower volumes of traffic, the extra state maintenance may not affect the performance of the network.

The egress edge router does not maintain any extra per-flow or per-aggregate state information; the sequencer does buffer packets that arrive out of sequence and maintains them in a sorted order of their sequence number. However, as mentioned before, the sequencer buffer space requirement is modest even in large-scale networks. This also implies that the size of the priority queue is bounded and small; the priority queue maintenance, therefore, does not introduce significant costs.

Admission Control. In this paper, we have addressed the issue of providing fairness guarantees without maintaining per-flow state in the data path of core routers. Note, however, that we still need to ensure that the sum of reserved rates of flows at any router does not exceed its outgoing link capacity. One way to ensure this is to maintain and use per-flow state only in the control plane of core routers; since the control plane is accessed at a much lower frequency than the data plane, this may not affect the scalability and performance of the core routers. Recently, admission control frameworks have been proposed, that, instead of maintaining state at all routers, either use one or more *bandwidth brokers* or the edge routers to perform admission control [5,26].

7   Related Work

The Core-Jitter Virtual Clock (CJVC) [21] network provides the same end-to-end delay guarantees as a corresponding core-stateful Jitter Virtual Clock network. A CJVC network, however, is non work-conserving, which limits network utilization and results in higher average delays, as discussed before. A number of work-conserving core-stateless networks that provide end-to-end delay guarantees similar to core-stateful networks have been proposed recently [13,17,25]. However, these networks do not provide throughput guarantees at short time-scales (they may penalize flows that use idle capacity to transmit at more than their reserved rates). The first core-stateless network that provides through-put guarantees at short time-scales has been proposed recently [16]. This architecture, however, does not guarantee proportionate allocation of throughput across flows sharing the same end-to-end path. Core-stateless schemes proposed to provide fairness, provide only approximate fairness in the long-term throughput achieved by flows. In particular, these schemes do not provide guarantees for short-lived flows or for specific durations of interest in the lifespan of long-lived flows [6,7,20].

8 Summary

In this paper, we present the Core-stateless Guaranteed Fair (CSGF) network architecture—the *first* work-conserving core-stateless architecture that provides deter-ministic end-to-end fairness guarantees at short time-scales. We decouple the throughput and proportionate allocation guarantees provided by a fair network and use a number of insights to develop a core-stateless network that provides both guarantees. First, we argue that an *end-to-end* notion of proportionate allocation is meaningful only when defined across flows that share the same end-to-end path. Second, we show that for a network to guarantee proportionate allocation, it must also provide throughput guarantees. Third, we show that a set of three mechanisms—fair access at the ingress, aggregation of micro-flows in the core, and re-sequencing at the egress—when used in conjunction with a network that provides throughput guarantees, leads to a network that guarantees proportionate allocation as well. We use these insights, and the previously proposed CSGT network architecture, to design a CSGF network that provides deterministic fair-ness guarantees at short time-scales. The end-to-end proportionate allocation guarantee of a CSGF network is better than that or a core-stateful fair network. The end-to-end throughput guarantees of CSGF networks provisioned with low-delay feedback chan-nels are comparable to core-stateful networks, and may even be better for flows with small bit-rate requirements.

References

1. V. Agarwal, M.S. Hrishikesh, S.W. Keckler, and D.C. Burger. Clock Rate Versus IPC: The End of the Road for Conventional Microarchitectures. In *27th International Symposium on Computer Architecture (ISCA)*, June 2000.
2. J.C.R. Bennett, K. Benson, A. Charny, W.F.Courtney, and J.Y. LeBoudec. Delay Jitter Bounds and Packet Scale Rate Guarantee for Expedited Forwarding. to appear in IEEE/ACM Trans-actions on Networking.
3. J.C.R. Bennett and H. Zhang. WF²Q: Worst-case Fair Weighted Fair Queuing. In *Proceedings of INFOCOM'96*, pages 120–127, March 1996.
4. J.C.R. Bennett and H. Zhang. Hierarchical Packet Fair Queueing Algorithms. In *IEEE/ACM Transactions on Networking*, volume 5, pages 675–689, October 1997.
5. S. Bhatnagar and B.R. Badrinath. Distributed Admission Control to Support Guaranteed Services in Core-stateless Networks. In *Proceedings of IEEE INFOCOM*, April 2003.
6. Z. Cao, Z. Wang, and E. Zegura. Rainbow Fair Queueing: Fair Bandwidth Sharing Without Per-Flow State. In *Proceedings of IEEE INFOCOM*, March 2000.

7. A. Clerget and W. Dabbous. TUF: Tag-based Unified Fairness. In *Proceedings of IEEE INFOCOM*, April 2001.

8. K. Coffman and A. Odlyzko. The Size and Growth Rate of the Internet. March 2001. http://www.firstmoday.dk/issues/issue3_10/ coffman/.

9. A. Demers, S. Keshav, and S. Shenker. Analysis and Simulation of a Fair Queueing Algorithm. In *Proceedings of ACM SIGCOMM*, pages 1–12, September 1989.

10. S.J. Golestani. A Self-Clocked Fair Queueing Scheme for High Speed Applications. In *Proceedings of INFOCOM'94*, 1994.

11. P. Goyal, H. Vin, and H. Cheng. Start-time Fair Queuing: A Scheduling Algorithm for Integrated Services Packet Switching Networks. In *Proceedings of ACM SIGCOMM'96*, pages 157–168, August 1996.

12. P. Kaiser. A (R)evolutionary Technology Roadmap Beyond Today's OE Industry. *NSF Workshop on The Future Revolution in Optical Communications & Networking*, December 2000.

13. J. Kaur and H. Vin. Core-stateless Guaranteed Rate Scheduling Algorithms. In *Proceedings of IEEE INFOCOM*, volume 3, pages 1484–1492, April 2001.

14. J. Kaur and H. Vin. Core-stateless Guaranteed Throughput Networks. *Technical Report TR-01-47, Department of Computer Sciences, University of Texas at Austin*, November 2001.

15. J. Kaur and H. Vin. End-to-end Fairness Analysis of Fair Queuing Networks. In *Proceedings of the 23rd IEEE International Real-time Systems Symposium (RTSS)*, December 2002.

16. J. Kaur and H. Vin. Core-stateless Guaranteed Throughput Networks. In *Proceedings of IEEE INFOCOM*, volume 3, April 2003.

17. C. Li and E. Knightly. Coordinated Network Scheduling: A Framework for End-to-end Services. In *IEEE ICNP*, November 2000.

18. R. Pan, B. Prabhakar, and K. Psounis. CHOKE, A Stateless Active Queue Management Scheme for Approximating Fair Bandwidth Allocation. In *Proceedings of IEEE INFOCOM*, March 2000.

19. A.K. Parekh. *A Generalized Processor Sharing Approach to Flow Control in Integrated Services Networks*. PhD thesis, Department of Electrical Engineering and Computer Science, MIT, 1992.

20. I. Stoica, S. Shenker, and H. Zhang. Core-Stateless Fair Queueing: Achieving Approximately Fair Bandwidth Allocations in High Speed Networks. In *Proceedings of ACM SIGCOMM*, September 1998.

21. I. Stoica and H. Zhang. Providing Guaranteed Services Without Per Flow Management. In *Proceedings of ACM SIGCOMM*, September 1999.

22. H. Zhang. Service Disciplines For Guaranteed Performance Service in Packet-Switching Networks. *Proceedings of the IEEE*, 83(10), October 1995.

23. H. Zhang and S. Keshav. Comparison of Rate-Based Service Disciplines. In *Proceedings of ACM SIGCOMM*, pages 113–121, August 1991.

24. L. Zhang. VirtualClock: A New Traffic Control Algorithm for Packet Switching Networks. In *Proceedings of ACM SIGCOMM'90*, pages 19–29, August 1990.

25. Z.L. Zhang, Z. Duan, and Y.T. Hou. Virtual Time Reference System: A Unifying Scheduling Framework for Scalable Support of Guarantees Services. *IEEE Journal on Selected Areas in Communication, Special Issue on Internet QoS*, December 2000.

26. Z.L. Zhang, Z. Duan, Y.T. Hou, and L. Gao. Decoupling QoS Control from Core Routers: A Novel Bandwidth Broker Arcitecture for Scalable Support of Guaranteed Services. In *Proceedings of ACM SIGCOMM, Sweden*, August 2000.

A   Proof of Theorem 1

A work-conserving server that has at least one continuously backlogged flow in $[t_1, t_2]$ would satisfy: $\sum_{f \in F} W_{f,j}(t_1, t_2) \geq C_j(t_2 - t_1) - l^{max}$, where the l^{max} term appears due to packetization effects. Consider a particular interval $[t_1, t_2]$. Let $a = \frac{W_{m,j}(t_2 - t_1)}{r_m}$. From (6), for any other flow f (whether continuously backlogged or not), we have: $W_{f,j}(t_2 - t_1) \leq r_f * a + r_f * I_{j,m,f}$. Since we assume that the sum of reserved rates at any server does not exceed its capacity (Section 2), we have:

$$C_j(t_2 - t_1) - l^{max} \leq \sum_{f \in F} W_{f,j}(t_1, t_2)$$

$$\leq a * \sum_{f \in F} r_f + \sum_{f \in F} r_f I_{j,m,f}$$

$$\leq a * C_j + \sum_{f \in F} r_f I_{j,m,f}$$

This implies: $a \geq (t_2 - t_1) - \frac{l^{max}}{C_j} - \frac{\sum_{f \in F} r_f I_{j,m,f}}{C_j}$. Therefore, $W_{m,j}(t_1, t_2) \geq r_m(t_2 - t_1) - r_m \gamma_{m,j}$, where $\gamma_{m,j} = \frac{l^{max}}{C_j} + \frac{\sum_{f \in F} r_f I_{j,m,f}}{C_j}$.

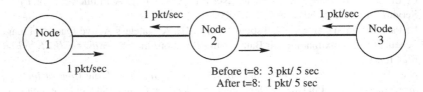

1 pkt/sec
1 pkt/sec

Node 1   Node 2   Node 3

1 pkt/sec

Before t=8: 3 pkt/ 5 sec
After t=8: 1 pkt/ 5 sec

Fig. 5. Topology for the Example

B   CSGT Networks Do Not Guarantee Proportionate Allocation: An Example

At time $t = 0$, let flow f be created, and at time $t = 0.1$, let flow m be created. Let both flows traverse the 3-hop network depicted in Figure 5. Let the reserved rate of each of the flows at all nodes be 1 packet every 10 seconds. Let the CSGT parameter, W, for flows f and m be 2—this implies that by any time t, no packet (from either flow f or flow m) with a deadline greater than $t + 2 * 10$ has been transmitted from the first (ingress) node.

Let the transmission capacity on all outgoing links, except the link from node 2 to node 3, be 1 packet every second, and let there be no other flows sharing these links. Let the capacity available to flows f and m on the link from node 2 to node 3 (which is shared with other flows) be 3 packets every 5 seconds before $t = 8$, and 1 packet every 5 seconds after $t = 8$. Let the link propagation latencies be 0.

Since $W = 2$ for both flows, at $t = 1$, the first node transmits the following sequence of packets starting at $t = 0$: at $t = 1$, the first flow f packet with a deadline of 10; at $t = 2$, the first flow m packet with deadline of 10.1; at $t = 3$, the second flow f packet with deadline of 20; and at $t = 4$, the second flow m packet with deadline of 20.1.

The acknowledgment for the second flow f packet (deadline=20) arrives at the first node at $t = 9$, at which time, the first node *re-uses* it for the third flow f packet, which gets transmitted by $t = 10$. Further, since $W = 2$, the fourth flow f packet gets transmitted immediately after that, with a deadline of 30.

The acknowledgment for the second flow m packet does not arrive in time for deadline 20.1 to get re-used. The third blue packet is therefore assigned a deadline of 30.1, and gets transmitted after the fourth flow f packet, by $t = 12$. By $t = 12$, therefore, flow f has transmitted 4 packets, whereas flow m has transmitted only 3.

The acknowledgment for the fourth flow f packet (deadline=30) arrives at the first node at $t = 19$, at which time, the first node re-uses it for the fifth flow f packet, which gets transmitted by $t = 20$. Further, since $W = 2$, the sixth flow f packet gets transmitted immediately after that, with a deadline of 40.

The acknowledgment for the third flow m packet does not arrive in time for deadline 30.1 to get re-used. The fourth flow m packet is, therefore, assigned a deadline of 40.1 and is transmitted after the sixth flow f packet. By $t = 22$, therefore, flow f has transmitted 6 packets, whereas flow m has transmitted only 4.

It is easy to examine further time intervals to see that the difference between number of flow f packets transmitted and the number of flow m packets transmitted, grows with time. Specifically, the difference at time t is given by: $|(t-2) \bmod 10|$. It follows that the difference $\left| \frac{W_{f,j}(t_1,t_2)}{r_f} - \frac{W_{m,j}(t_1,t_2)}{r_m} \right|$ is not bounded, and grows approximately linearly with the length of the time interval $[t_1, t_2]$.

Per-domain Packet Scale Rate Guarantee for Expedited Forwarding

Yuming Jiang

Institute for Infocomm Research
#2-34/37 TeleTech Park, Singapore Science Park II, 117674 Singapore
ymjiang@ieee.org

Abstract. The Expedited Forwarding Per-hop Behavior (EF PHB) was recently replaced by a new definition, called Packet Scale Rate Guarantee (PSRG), under the Differentiated Services (DiffServ) framework. This replacement raises two challenges. One is the implementation of PSRG server. Another is the provision of per-domain PSRG. To address the first challenge, we introduce a new concept called Latency-Rate Worst-case Service Guarantee (LR-WSG). We prove that if a server provides LR-WSG, it also provides PSRG. We show that many well-known schedulers support LR-WSG, which include not only one-level schedulers but also their hierarchical versions. To address the second challenge, we first prove that PSRG can be extended from per-node to per-domain if no flow aggregation is performed. The proof is notable in that it depends solely on the concept of PSRG itself. We then investigate the provision of per-domain PSRG in presence of flow aggregation. We propose to use Packet Scale Fair Aggregator (PSFA) to aggregate flows. We show that with PSFA, per-domain PSRG can be provided in spite of flow aggregation. We finally provide a brief discuss on the viability of using PSFA in DiffServ networks and define an Expedited Forwarding Per-domain Behavior (EF PDB).

1   Introduction

In a Differentiated Services (DiffServ) network [5], packets are classified into a small number of behavior aggregates, such as Expedited Forwarding (EF) [10] and Assured Forwarding (AF). Within each class, flows with similar performance requirements are aggregated. The IETF DiffServ Working Group (WG) has defined two Per-Hop Behaviors (PHBs), namely EF PHB and AF PHB, to provide local per-node quality of service (QoS) guarantees. An undergoing effort of the WG is to define Per-Domain Behaviors (PDBs) to describe edge-to-edge (e2e) QoS guarantees provided by a DiffServ domain [19].

In this paper, we focus on the EF class. EF PHB was initially defined in RFC 2598 [14]. In essence, RFC 2598 defined a service for EF aggregate, with which the EF aggregate should receive on all time scales at least its configured rate. Unfortunately, in a recent work [2], it was identified that the schedulers and configuration rates on which the EF definition in RFC 2598 can be implemented are

K. Jeffay, I. Stoica, and K. Wehrle (Eds.): IWQoS 2003, LNCS 2707, pp. 422–439, 2003.
© Springer-Verlag Berlin Heidelberg 2003

very limited. It was also showed in [2] that these difficulties cannot be corrected with simple incremental fixes. Due to these, an alternative EF definition was recently proposed in [2] and the new definition for the EF PHB, called Packet Scale Rate Guarantee (PSRG), has been adopted by IETF as RFC 3246 [10].

In contrast to the definition in RFC 2598 where the configured rate for EF aggregate is provided on all time scales ranging, it is provided to EF aggregate only down to packet scale in RFC 3246. Under the new definition, an EF-compliant node on an output link must provide to the EF aggregate PSRG [2]:

Definition 1. *A server s is said to o er a (possibly aggregate) ow f Packet Scale Rate Guarantee (PSRG) with rate R_s^f and error term E_s^f, if the departure time $d_s^{f,i}$ of its ith packet $p^{f,i}$ satis es the following condition for all $i \geq 0$:*

$$d_s^{f,i} \leq F_s^{f,i} + E_s^f \tag{1}$$

where $F_s^{f,i}$ is iteratively de ne d by

$$F_s^{f,i} = max[a_s^{f,i}, min(d_s^{f,i-1}, F_s^{f,i-1})] + \frac{l^{f,i}}{R_s^f} \tag{2}$$

with $F_s^{f,0} = 0$, $d_s^{f,0} = 0$. Here, $F_s^{f,i}$, called PSRG virtual nish time function, is the target departure time for the ith packet of ow f; $a_s^{f,i}$ is the arrival time of the packet and $l^{f,i}$ is the length of the packet.

Note that an EF-compliant node may have multiple inputs and complex internal scheduling and hence the ith EF packet to arrive at the node destined for a certain output interface may not be the ith EF packet to depart from the interface. To deal with this, in the new EF PHB definition, equations (1) and (2) are defined as both the "aggregate behavior" set and the "packet-identity-aware" set [10]. For the former, the ith EF packet in (1) and (2) refers to the ith EF departure from the interface. For the latter, the ith EF packet in (1) and (2) refers to the ith EF arrival destined to the interface via any input.

If FIFO aggregation is adopted, the "aggregate behavior" EF PHB is the same as the "packet-identity-aware" EF PHB. In addition, a one-level scheduler, such as Strict Priority, can be used to implement the new EF PHB, i.e. PSRG. Clearly, FIFO aggregation results in a very simple implementation of PSRG. However, the ability of appropriately provisioning a network domain with FIFO aggregation to provide edge-to-edge delay guarantee has been questioned. In several recent works by Charny and Le Boudec [7], Jiang [15], and Zhang, Duan and Hou [23], it has been shown that to provide guaranteed delay service using FIFO aggregation, the overall network utilization level must be limited to a small fraction of its link capacities or configured rates.

If, however, other aggregation methods are used, not only is the "aggregate behavior" EF PHB different from the "packet-identity-aware" EF PHB, but also a hierarchical scheduler is needed [16]. Consequently, for this case, to determine the "packet-identity-aware" EF PHB, it is highly desirable to study the PSRG provided by a hierarchical scheduler. On the other hand, while the provision of PSRG by one-level scheduler has been studied in [2], whether a hierarchical scheduler can provide PSRG leaves as an open challenge.

In addition, while PSRG has been well-defined for the per-hop case as presented in above, whether such a guarantee can be provided for the per-domain case remains as another challenge. Since PSRG implies delay guarantee, if a network domain, such as a DiffServ domain, provides PSRG, it will also provide e2e delay guarantee. Note that per-hop guarantee does not necessarily result in per-domain guarantee and consequently end-to-end guarantee. On the other hand, from the end-user's point of view, a service guarantee such as PSRG makes more sense end-to-end than per-hop. In this sense, the challenge of providing per-domain PSRG becomes more critical.

These two challenges motivate the work of this paper. We show through analysis that a wide family of schedulers including their hierarchical versions provide PSRG, and by adopting a new flow aggregation approach, we can extend PSRG from per-node to per-domain and consequently define EF PDB for DiffServ. In particular, in Section 2, we investigate a wide family of scheduling disciplines that provide Latency-Rate Worst-case Service Guarantee (LR-WSG) which has its root in Strong Service Guarantee (SSG) [1] and Bit Worst-case Fair Index (B-WFI) [4]. We prove that if a scheduler provides LR-WSG, it also provides PSRG. An appealing implication of LR-WSG is that since many well-known schedulers and their hierarchical versions belong to the LR-WSG family, they can hence be used to implement both the "aggregate behavior" EF PHB and the "packet-identity-aware" EF PHB. In Section 3, we study the provision of PSRG in a network implementing per-flow PSRG scheduling. By extending PSRG virtual finish time function from per-node to per-domain, we show that per-domain PSRG is implicitly offered by such networks. We then in Section 4 investigate the provision of per-domain PSRG in a network where aggregate scheduling is implemented as required by the DiffServ architecture. We propose to use Packet Scale Fair Aggregator (PSFA) to aggregate flows. We present a theoretic basis for the implementation of PSFAs. We also prove that with PSFA, per-domain PSRG can be provided in spite of flow aggregation. Moreover, we discuss the viability of using PSFA approach in DiffServ networks and introduce a definition of EF PDB. In Section 5, we summarize our results.

2   Packet Scale Rate Guarantee Servers

2.1   Previous Work

In [2], it was showed that if a scheduler s provides Adaptive Service Guarantee (ASG) [1] of the latency-rate type to a flow f, then it is PSRG server to the flow. Clearly, this result can be used to find PSRG servers. However, due to heavy formalism of ASG, it was used primarily to derive the concatenation property of PSRG in [2].

To find PSRG servers, another general approach was proposed in [2], which is based on the relationship shown by (3). Inequality (3) describes the accuracy of a scheduler s with respect to its reference Generalized Process Sharing (GPS) fluid scheduler by two error terms E_1 and E_2.

$$G_s^{f,i} - E_1 \le d_s^{f,i} \le G_s^{f,i} + E_2, \tag{3}$$

where $d_s^{f,i}$ denotes the ith departure time of flow f under scheduler s while $G_s^{f,i}$ denotes the ith departure under the reference GPS scheduler with rate R_s^f allocated to the flow. In [2], it was proved that if a scheduler satisfies (3), then it is PSRG server to the flow f with rate R_s^f and error term $E_s^f = E_1 + E_2$.

While the two approaches proposed in [2] can be used to find PSRG servers and determine their error terms, more effort is required. First, the approach based on (3) applies only to schedulers approximating GPS. For other types of PSRG servers, e.g. Strict Priority, separate proof is needed. Second, although the approach based on (3) has provided a basis for finding PSRG servers, the E_1 and E_2 values are known for only a few schedulers and a systematic collection of the error terms for all known schedulers is needed [2] [6]. Third, it is difficult to apply these two approaches to hierarchical schedulers. Indeed, it is not clear whether a hierarchical scheduler made of servers satisfying (3) still satisfies (3) and if so, what are the error terms, E_1 and E_2, for the hierarchical scheduler.

2.2   Definition of LR-WSG

In the following, we define a family of scheduling disciplines that provide Latency-Rate Worst-case Service Guarantee (LR-WSG). We shall prove that if a scheduler is LR-WSG server, it also is PSRG server. Hence, LR-WSG PSRG servers are a subset of PSRG servers. While LR-WSG is more stringent than PSRG, many well-known scheduling disciplines can be proved to provide LR-WSG. More appealingly, hierarchical versions of them also belong to the LR-WSG server family.

Let $A_s^f(t_1, t_2)$ denote the amount (number of bits) of arrivals from flow f to server s during interval $[t_1, t_2]$, and $A_s(t_1, t_2)$ denote the amount (number of bits) of arrivals from all input flows to the server during the same interval. Denote by $W_s^f(t_1, t_2)$ the amount (number of bits) of service received by the flow from the server and by $W_s(t_1, t_2)$ the amount (number of bits) of service offered by the server to all its inputs during the same interval. Here, we adopt the convention that a packet is said to have arrived to a server when and only when its last bit has been received by the server and is said to have been serviced by the server when and only when its last bit has left the server. As such, $A_s^f(t_1, t_2)$ and $A_s(t_1, t_2)$ increase only when the last bit of a packet has arrived to the server; likewise, $W_s^f(t_1, t_2)$ and $W_s(t_1, t_2)$ increase only when the last bit of the packet in service leaves the server. In addition, a packet is said to be backlogged in a server if it has arrived to but not left the server.

Let R_s be the guaranteed service rate of server s and R_s^f be the guaranteed service rate to flow f by the server. Denote by L the maximum packet length in the network. For ease of exposition, throughout the paper, we assume that each queue in a server is serviced in the FIFO manner, the buffer size for the queue is large enough to ensure no packet loss, and there is no propagation delay between any two consecutive servers.

Definition 2. *A server s is said to be WSG server with Worst-case Service Curve (WSC) $S^*(\cdot)$ to a ow f, if for any $d_s^{f,i}$ and for all intervals $[t_1, d_s^{f,i}]$ ($t_1 < d_s^{f,i}$) during which f is continuously backlogged, $W_s^f(t_1, d_s^{f,i}) \geq S^*(d_s^{f,i} - t_1)$.*

Definition 3. *A server s is said to be Latency-Rate WSG (LR-WSG) server to a ow f with rate R_s^f and latency E_s^f, if s is WSG server with WSC $S^*(\cdot)$ to the ow, and $S^*(\cdot)$ has the latency-rate service curve type, i.e. for any interval $[t_1, d_s^{f,i}]$, $W_s^f(t_1, d_s^{f,i}) \geq R_s^f(d_s^{f,i} - t_1 - E_s^f)^+$, where $(x)^+ \equiv max\{x, 0\}$.*

2.3   PSRG by LR-WSG Server

Theorem 1. *If a server s is LR-WSG server with rate R_s^f and latency E_s^f to a ow f, it is PSRG server with rate R_s^f and error term E_s^f to the ow.*

Proof. Consider any backlogged period of f at server s, $[a_s^{j_0}, d_s^{j_e}]$, where j_0 is the first f packet arriving to the server in the period and j_e is the last f packet arriving to and hence leaving (due to FIFO assumption) the server in the period. For the backlogged period, we must have

$$a_s^{f,j_0} > d_s^{f,j_0-1} \tag{4}$$

$$a_s^{f,j} \leq d_s^{f,j-1}, \quad \text{for } j_0 < j \leq j_e. \tag{5}$$

Otherwise, if $a_s^{f,j_0} \leq d_s^{f,j_0-1}$, the server is still busy with serving flow f packet $j_0 - 1$ when packet j_0 arrives and hence packet $j_0 - 1$ should be in the same backlogged period as packet j_0; if $a_s^{f,j} > d_s^{f,j-1}$ for $j_0 < j \leq j_e$, the server has no backlogged packet from flow f in the period $(d_s^{f,j-1}, a_s^{f,j})$.

Consequently,

$$F_s^{f,j_0} = a_s^{f,j_0} + \frac{l^{f,j_0}}{R_s^f}, \quad \text{for } j = j_0 \tag{6}$$

$$F_s^{f,j} \geq \begin{cases} d_s^{f,j-1} + \frac{l^{f,j}}{R_s^f} & \text{if } d_s^{f,j-1} \leq F_s^{f,j-1} \\ F_s^{f,j-1} + \frac{l^{f,j}}{R_s^f} & \text{if } d_s^{f,j-1} > F_s^{f,j-1}. \end{cases} \quad \text{for } j_0 < j \leq j_e \tag{7}$$

For any packet j, $(j_0 \leq j \leq j_e)$, from the definition of LR-WSG, we have for any time $(a_s^{f,j_0} \leq)t_1 \leq d_s^{f,j}$

$$W_s^f(t_1, d_s^{f,j}) \geq R_s^f(d_s^{f,j} - t_1 - E_s^f)^+, \tag{8}$$

based on which, we shall prove

$$F_s^{f,j} \geq d_s^{f,j} - E_s^f, \tag{9}$$

from which, the theorem follows.

Specifically, let $t_1 = a_s^{f,j_0} + \epsilon, d_s^{f,j_0} + \epsilon, d_s^{f,j_0+1} + \epsilon, \cdots$ in (8) with $\epsilon \to 0$. We then get for any j, and any k satisfying $j_0 \leq k < j$,

$$a_s^{f,j_0} + \frac{\sum_{m=j_0}^{j} l^{f,m}}{R_s^f} \geq d_s^{f,j} - E_s^f, \quad \text{and,} \tag{10}$$

$$d_s^{f,k} + \frac{\sum_{m=k+1}^{j} l^{f,m}}{R_s^f} \geq d_s^{f,j} - E_s^f. \tag{11}$$

Based on (10) and (11), we now prove (9). For $j = j_0$, with (10), we can get $a^{f,j_0} + \frac{l^{f,j_0}}{R_s^f} \geq d_s^{f,j_0} - E_s^f$. Then, with (6), (9) is obtained for the $j = j_0$ case.

For $j > j_0$, continuously applying the condition between the departure time and virtual finish time, the righthand side of (7) becomes

$$
\begin{cases}
d_s^{f,j-1} + \frac{l^{f,j}}{R_s^f} & \text{if } d_s^{f,j-1} \leq F_s^{f,j-1}; \\
\cdots & \\
d_s^{f,k} + \frac{\sum_{m=k+1}^{j} l^{f,m}}{R_s^f} & \text{if } d_s^{f,j-1} > F_s^{f,j-1}, ..., d_s^{f,k+1} > F_s^{f,k+1}, d_s^{f,k} \leq F_s^{f,k}; \quad (12) \\
\cdots & \\
a^{f,j_0} + \frac{\sum_{m=j_0}^{j} l^{f,m}}{R_s^f} & \text{if for all } k = j-1, ..., j_0,\ d_s^{f,k} > F_s^{f,k}.
\end{cases}
$$

With (10) and (11), it is easy to verify that for all cases, (12) is greater than or equal to $d_s^{f,j} - E_s^f$ and hence (9) is proved for $j > j_0$. This ends the proof.

2.4 LR-WSG Schedulers

One-Level Schedulers We first prove that many well-known one-level schedulers provide LR-WSG. Their proofs can be found in [16].

Theorem 2. *A nonpreemptive SP scheduler s provides LR-WSG to ow f at the highest priority level with rate $R_s^f = C$ and error term $E_s^f = \frac{L}{C}$, where C is the total output rate of the server.*

Theorem 3. *A Sart-time Fair Queueing (SFQ) scheduler s [13] is LR-WSG server to ow f with rate $R_s^f = \frac{\phi_f}{\phi_s} C$ and error term $E_s^f = \frac{QL}{C} + \frac{L}{R_s^f}$ where ϕ_f is the weight of ow f, Q is the set of ows served by the scheduler and $\phi_s = \sum_Q \phi_f$.*

In [4], many fair queueing algorithms approximating GPS have been proved to guarantee B-WFI [4], which include Weighted Fair Queueing (WFQ) [20], Worst-case Fair Weighted Fair Queueing (WF^{2}Q) [3] and WF^{2}Q+ [4].

Definition 4. *A server s is said to guarantee a Bit Worst-case Fair Index (B-WFI) of α_s^f to a ow f, if for any packet $p^{f,i}$ of the ow, there holds*

$$
W_s^f(t_1, d_s^{f,i}) \geq \frac{\phi_f}{\phi_s} W_s(t_1, d_s^{f,i}) - \alpha_s^f, \tag{13}
$$

where $d_s^{f,i}$ is the departure time of the packet, t_1 is any time such that $t_1 < d_s^{f,i}$ and the ow is continuously backlogged during $[t_1, d_s^{f,i}]$, and $\frac{\phi_f}{\phi_s}$ is the service share guaranteed to the ow by the server.

The following theorem shows that if a scheduler provides B-WFI guarantee, it also provides LR-WSG and hence is PSRG server.

Theorem 4. *If a one-level scheduler s guarantees a B-WFI of α_s^f to a ow f, then the server is LR-WSG server to the ow with rate $R_s^f = \frac{\phi_f}{\phi_s}C$ and error term $E_s^f = \frac{\alpha_s^f}{R_s^f}$.*

Finally, we consider another class of schedulers that provide Strong Service guarantee [1]. Many well-known schedulers have been proved to belong to this class, which include SFQ, DRR, URR, SRR, etc.

Theorem 5. *If a one-level scheduler s provides Strong Service Guarantee of latency-rate type to ow f with rate R_s^f and latency E_s^f, i.e. for any interval $[t_1, t_2]$ in a backlogged period of f, $W_s^f(t_1, t_2) \geq R_s^f(t_2 - t_1 - E_s^f)^+$, then the server is LR-WSG server to the ow with rate R_s^f and error term E_s^f.*

From the above results, it is clear that LR-WSG can be used as another basis in addition to (3) for determining the PSRG error term for a known scheduler.

Hierarchical Schedulers We next focus on hierarchical schedulers. Particularly, we consider a class of hierarchical schedulers, called Hierarchical Worst-case Service Guarantee (H-WSG) schedulers. An H-WSG scheduler is formed of one-level LR-WSG schedulers organized in a hierarchical structure and each server node s in the scheduling hierarchy guarantees that for its input flow f, there holds

$$\frac{W_s^f(t_1, d_s^{f,i})}{R_s^f} \geq \frac{W_s(t_1, d_s^{f,i})}{R_s} - E_s^f, \tag{14}$$

where R_s denotes the guaranteed rate of server node s; R_s^f denotes the guaranteed rate to flow f by server node s; $[t_1, d_s^{f,i}]$ is a period as defined in Definition 4.

Comparing with (13), it can be found that (14) is indeed re-written from (13) by letting $R_s^f = \frac{\phi_f}{\phi_s}R_s$ and $E_s^f = \frac{\alpha_s^f}{R_s^f}$. Nevertheless, (14) makes some sense in defining H-WSG. This is because in [4], (13) is mainly used for studying packet fair queueing (PFQ) algorithms that approximate GPS and their hierarchical versions (H-PFQ). On the other hand, Definition 4 itself is very general and (13) can be used to characterize other types of scheduling algorithms. Hence, to distinguish from H-PFQ, we define H-WSG based on (14).

It is easy to verify that a one-level scheduler satisfying (14) is LR-WSG server with rate R_s^f and error term E_s^f. In addition, we have the following result for H-WSG server, which is similar to that for H-PFQ server [4].

Theorem 6. *For a ow f with A ancestors in an H-WSG server, it is guaranteed an LR-WSC with rate R_{H-WSG}^f and error term $\sum_{a=0}^{A-1} E_{a+1}^a$, where E_{a+1}^a is the error term for the logical queue at node a by its server node $a+1$; R_{H-WSG}^f is the guaranteed rate to ow f by the corresponding leaf server node.*

It can be shown that all schedulers studied in the previous subsection satisfy (14). Hence, with Theorem 6, we could use them to implement hierarchical schedulers providing PSRG.

2.5   An Example of PSRGs for EF PHB

To demonstrate the use of above results for H-WSG schedulers, let us consider a simple example, in which per-hop PSRGs are determined for EF PHB in a DiffServ node. Suppose the EF aggregate is given (non-preemptive) priority over all other types of aggregates. Some route pinning mechanism such as Multi-Protocol Label Switching (MPLS) [21] is assumed to ensure that the forwarding path along which a flow traverses the DiffServ network keeps unchanged. Note that the flow in a forwarding path can itself be an aggregated one. Assume that in the DiffServ node, SFQ is adopted to aggregate EF flows from different EF forwarding paths to form the EF aggregate.

Clearly, these assumptions result in a two-level hierarchical scheduler for EF traffic, in which the root is SP and the leaf is SFQ [16]. Suppose the corresponding output link has capacity C and there are Q number of forwarding paths equally sharing C with allocated rate $R = \frac{C}{Q}$. Then, based on Theorem 2, it is clear that the node provides to the EF aggregate the "aggregate behavior" PSRG with rate C and error term $\frac{L}{C}$. Furthermore, based on Theorems 6, 3, and 2, we can prove that the node provides to the EF aggregate the "packet-identity-aware" PSRG with rate R and error term $\frac{L}{C} + \frac{2L}{R}$. The proof can be found in [16].

3   Per-domain PSRG without Flow Aggregation

Before proceeding to the investigation of per-domain PSRG in presence of flow aggregation, we study per-domain PSRG in a network where every flow is provided PSRG by each server along its path and no other flows are aggregated with the flow along the path.

3.1   Network Model

Consider the path of a flow across a network domain as shown in Fig. 1. Along the path is the concatenation of servers numbered 1 to h, where the output of s is the input of $s + 1$ for $s \geq 1$. Let f be the flow. Assume that each server $s(= 1, \ldots, h)$ is PSRG server to the flow with rate R_s^f and error term E_s^f. For ease of exposition, assume that there is no propagation delay between any s and $s + 1$. Hence, for any packet $p^{f,i}$, $d_s^{f,i} = a_{s+1}^{f,i}$. Note that for any server $s(= 1, \ldots, h)$, since it is PSRG server to f, then from (2) and (1), we get $F_s^{f,i} = max[a_s^{f,i}, min(d_s^{f,i-1}, F_s^{f,i-1})] + \frac{l^{f,i}}{R_s^f}$ and $d_s^{f,i} \leq F_s^{f,i} + E_s^f$.

For per-domain PSRG, we introduce the following definition. For the edge-to-edge path with h servers, we iteratively define for $i \geq 1$,

$$\widetilde{F}_h^{f,i} = max[a_1^{f,i}, min(d_h^{f,i-1}, \widetilde{F}_h^{f,i-1})] + \frac{l^{f,i}}{R^f} \qquad (15)$$

with $\widetilde{F}_h^{f,0} = 0$ and $d_h^{f,0} = 0$, and $R^f = min_{s=1,\ldots,h} R_s^f$.

Comparing (2) and (15), we can view the latter as a generalization of the former. Particularly, if we view the global system of the edge-to-edge path as a

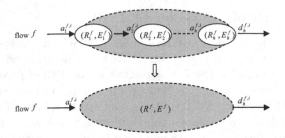

Fig. 1. Per-domain PSRG without flow aggregation

blackbox as shown by Fig. 1, definition (15) is indeed the PSRG virtual finish time function for the global concatenation system with h servers, where $a_1^{f,i}$ is the arrival time of packet $p^{f,i}$ to the blackbox and $d_h^{f,i}$ is the departure time of the packet leaving the blackbox. To distinguish from (2), we call (15) the *domain PSRG virtual nish time function* for the global concatenation system while (2) the *nodal PSRG virtual nish time function* for server s. Similar to nodal PSRG (1), the provision of per-domain PSRG is to guarantee that there exists some constant E^f, called error term for the per-domain PSRG, such that

$$d_h^{f,i} \le \widetilde{F}_h^{f,i} + E^f. \tag{16}$$

3.2   Per-domain PSRG

We now prove that the global concatenation system, or the blackbox, provides edge-to-edge PSRG (16) and hence can be treated as a PSRG server as shown in Fig. 1. The proof follows easily from the definitions of PSRG. In particular, the definition of domain PSRG virtual finish time function (15) helps the proof, which, to the best of our knowledge, has not been explicitly defined in the literature. We begin with a lemma.

Lemma 1. *Consider the concatenation of two PSRG servers, s and t, where the output of s is the input of t. Suppose s and t respectively o er PSRG to   ow f with rate R_s^f and error term E_s^f, and rate R_t^f and error term E_t^f. Then, there holds*

$$F_t^{f,i} \le \widetilde{F}_t^{f,i} + E_s^f + \frac{L}{R^f}, \tag{17}$$

where $\widetilde{F}_t^{f,i}$ is iteratively de ne d to be

$$\widetilde{F}_t^{f,i} = max[a_s^{f,i}, min(d_t^{f,i-1}, \widetilde{F}_t^{f,i-1})] + \frac{l^{f,i}}{R^f} \tag{18}$$

with $\widetilde{F}_t^{f,0} = 0$ and $d_t^{f,0} = 0$, and $R^f = min\{R_s^f, R_t^f\}$.

Proof. It is easy to verify that, since $d_s^{f,i} \leq d_t^{f,i}$, we have for any $i \geq 1$, $F_s^{f,i} \leq \widetilde{F}_t^{f,i}$.

We now prove (17) by induction on i. For the base case, let $i = 1$. Then, $F_s^{f,1} \leq \widetilde{F}_t^{f,1}(= a_s^{f,1} + \frac{l^{f,1}}{R_t^f})$ and $F_t^{f,1} = a_t^{f,1} + \frac{l^{f,1}}{R_t^f}$. Since $a_t^{f,1} = d_s^{f,1} \leq F_s^{f,1} + E_s^f$, $F_t^{f,1} \leq F_s^{f,1} + E_s^f + \frac{l^{f,1}}{R_t^f} \leq \widetilde{F}_t^{f,1} + E_s^f + \frac{L}{R_t^f}$. Hence, (17) is proved for the base case.

For induction, let us assume (17) holds for all $1 < i \leq j$. We need to prove (17) holds for $j + 1$. There are two cases:

1. If $a_t^{f,j+1} \geq min(d_t^{f,j}, F_t^{f,j})$, we have from the definition of $F_t^{f,j+1}$,

$$F_t^{f,j+1} = a_t^{f,j+1} + \frac{l^{f,j+1}}{R_t^f} \leq F_s^{f,j+1} + E_s^f + \frac{l^{f,j+1}}{R_t^f} \leq \widetilde{F}^{f,j+1} + E_s^f + \frac{L}{R^f}. \quad (19)$$

2. If $a_t^{f,j+1} < min(d_t^{f,j}, F_t^{f,j})$, we have

$$F_t^{f,j+1} = min(d_t^{f,j}, F_t^{f,j}) + \frac{l^{f,j+1}}{R_t^f}. \quad (20)$$

For this case, let us further consider two conditions:
2.1 If $d_t^{f,j} \leq \widetilde{F}_l^{f,j}$, from (18), we have

$$\widetilde{F}^{f,j+1} \geq min(d_t^{f,j}, F_t^{f,j}) + \frac{l^{f,j+1}}{R_t^f} = F_t^{f,j+1}. \quad (21)$$

2.2 Otherwise, if $d_t^{f,j} > \widetilde{F}_t^{f,j}$, together with the induction assumption $F_t^{f,j} \leq \widetilde{F}_t^{f,j} + E_s^f + \frac{L}{R^f}$, we get from (20),

$$\widetilde{F}_t^{f,j+1} \geq \widetilde{F}_t^{f,j} + \frac{l^{f,j+1}}{R^f} \geq F_t^{f,j} - E_s^f - \frac{L}{R^f} + \frac{l^{f,j+1}}{R^f} \geq F_l^{f,j+1} - E_s^f - \frac{L}{R^f}. \quad (22)$$

Finally, we conclude from (19), (20), (21) and (22) that (17) holds for $j + 1$ for the induction case. This ends the proof of Lemma 1.

Lemma 1 implies that the concatenation of two PSRG servers can be treated as a single PSRG server with rate $R^f(= min\{R_s^f, R_t^f\})$ and error term $E_s^f + E_t^f + \frac{L}{R^f}$. With this implication, by iteratively applying Lemma 1 to the considered network shown in Fig. 1, we can conclude:

Lemma 2. *For the concatenation of $h(\geq 1)$ PSRG servers, there holds*

$$F_h^{f,i} \leq \widetilde{F}_h^{f,i} + \sum_{s=1}^{h-1}(E_s^f + \frac{L}{R^f}). \quad (23)$$

Consequently, with Lemma 2 and the assumption that server h is PSRG server, we get $d_h^{f,i} \leq \widetilde{F}_h^{f,i} + \sum_{s=1}^{h-1}(E_s^f + \frac{L}{R^f}) + E_h^f$, with which, the following result is obtained:

Theorem 7. *For a network domain where ow f passes through, if along its path each server s provides to the ow PSRG with rate R_s^f and error term E_s^f, then the network domain guarantees the ow PSRG with rate R^f and error term E^f where $R^f = min_{s=1,...,h} R_s^f$, and $E^f = \sum_{s=1}^{h-1}(E_s^f + \frac{L}{R^f}) + E_h^f$.*

3.3   Delay Bounds

With Theorem 7, we can further obtain e2e delay guarantees for the network in Fig. 1. We consider two types of traffic source. One is the so-called leaky bucket constrained source; another is generalized Stochastically Bounded Bursty source defined in [22]. While the former is usually used to derive deterministic delay bound, the latter can be used to determine statistical delay guarantee.

Definition 5. *Flow f is said to be leaky bucket (σ^f, r^f)-constrained, if for all $t_1 \geq 0$ and $\tau \geq 0$, the amount of tra c satis es $A^f(t_1, t_1 + \tau) \leq r^f \tau + \sigma^f$.*

Definition 6. *Flow f is said to have gSBB (generalized Stochastically Bounded Burstiness) with rate r^f and bounding function $\mathcal{F}(\cdot)$, if for all $t_2 \geq 0$, $Pr\{\hat{A}(t_2; r^f) \geq \sigma^f\} \leq \mathcal{F}(\sigma^f)$, where $\hat{A}(t_2; r^f) \equiv max_{0 \leq t_1 \leq t_2}\{A^f(t_1, t_2) - r^f(t_2 - t_1)\}$.*

For these two types of traffic source, we can derive their corresponding delay bounds based on Theorem 7 and analytical results for Guaranteed Rate (GR) servers [12]. Comparing definitions of PSRG and GR, we can see that the former is stronger than the latter. Hence, we can apply results derived for GR servers to PSRG servers. Specifically, we have the following results where Corollary 1 corresponds to deterministic delay guarantee and Corollary 2 could be used as a basis for statistical delay guarantee. Their proofs can be found in [16].

Corollary 1. *With the same assumption as for Theorem 7, if ow f is (σ^f, r^f)-constrained before entering the network and $r^f \leq R^f$, the e2e delay of any packet in the ow is bounded by: $D^f \leq \frac{\sigma^f}{R^f} + E^f$.*

Corollary 2. *With the same assumption as for Theorem 7, if ow f has gSBB with rate r^f and bounding function $\mathcal{F}$ before entering the network and $r^f \leq R^f$, the e2e delay of any packet in the ow satis es: $Pr\left(D^f \geq \frac{\sigma^f}{R^f} + E^f\right) \leq \mathcal{F}(\sigma^f)$.*

4   Per-domain PSRG with Flow Aggregation

Now that we have studied per-domain PSRG in a network implementing per-flow scheduling, the focus of this section is to investigate the provision of per-domain PSRG in presence of flow aggregation. Specifically for Expedited Forwarding service, while nodal PSRG has been defined and studied for EF PHB, it is not clear whether such a guarantee can be extended to per-domain under DiffServ.

4.1   Impact of Flow Aggregation

The major difference between a DiffServ network and the network studied in Section 3 is that the DiffServ network adopts aggregate scheduling. In such networks, flow aggregation is natural. For the discussion, we adopt the following concepts as by [8]. An *aggregator* or *multiplexer* is defined to be a scheduler that receives a set of flows as input and produces a single aggregate flow as output whose constituents are these input flows. This set of input flows are called *immediate constituents* of the output aggregate flow. Note that each one of the input flows can be a microflow or aggregate flow. A flow g is said to be the *root* of another flow f at some point in the network if g is not a constituent of any other flow while f is a constituent of g. A scheduler is said to be *aggregating server* to an input flow if the flow is aggregated with other flows to form the output aggregate flow, and *non-aggregating server*, if the output flow is the input flow. A *separator* or *demultiplexer* is defined to be a process that receives an aggregate flow as input and produces the constituent flows of the aggregate as output. Throughout the rest of this paper, we assume that a separator does not introduce additional packet delay.

As for packet scheduling, there are possibly infinite methods to aggregate flows, since each scheduler is itself an aggregator. Similar to scheduling, FIFO is the simplest approach. However, FIFO aggregator can be very unfair for flow aggregation in the sense that the delay of a packet is affected not only by packets from the same flow but also by packets from other flows. If the burstiness of other flows is extremely high, this packet can be delayed excessively even though its own flow is smooth. As a result, to have a meaningful edge-to-edge delay bound for a network domain with FIFO flow aggregation, recent studies [7] [15] [23] have shown that the amount of traffic must be limited to a (possibly very) small fraction of its guaranteed rate. In addition, it is not clear what is the PSRG provided by a network domain with FIFO aggregation.

From the concatenation property of PSRG servers studied in Section 3, it seems reasonable to use PSRG scheduler to aggregate flows. However, similar to the discussion in [8] for aggregating flows with GR scheduler, the example in [16] shows that aggregating flows with PSRG scheduler is not sufficient to guarantee a bounded edge-to-edge delay or a per-domain PSRG. The burstiness of other flows can affect the delay performance of a flow significantly.

4.2   Packet Scale Fair Aggregator

To avoid the problem with FIFO aggregation and the simple PSRG aggregation, other methods are needed for flow aggregation. In the following, we propose to use Packet Scale Fair Aggregator to aggregate flows.

Definition 7. *An aggregator s is said to be Packet Scale Fair Aggregator (PSFA), if for every input flow f, it provides PSRG, and for all packets $p^{f,i}$, $i(\geq 1)$, there exists a constant $\mathcal{E}_s^f$, called the aggregation parameter, such that*

$$G_s^{g,j} \leq F_s^{f,i} + \mathcal{E}_s^f, \tag{24}$$

where g is the corresponding output aggregate flow of f, $p^{g,j} = p^{f,i}$ and $G_s^{g,j}$ is iteratively defined as

$$G_s^{g,j} = max[d_s^{g,j}, G_s^{g,j-1}] + \frac{l^{g,j}}{R_s^g} \tag{25}$$

with $G_s^{g,0} = 0$ and R_s^g defined to be $R_s^g \equiv \sum_{f \in g} R_s^f$.

Compared with the PSRG virtual finish time function defined in (2), the virtual time function $G_s^{g,j}$ can be treated as both the finish time function and the PSRG virtual finish time function of a virtual server. The virtual server has rate R_s^g and its input is g. The name of PSFA in some sense borrows the name of Fair Aggregator (FA) in [8]. This is similar to the definition extension of PSRG server from GR server [12]. The differences between PSFA and FA are similar to those between PSRG and GR which have been extensively discussed in [2] [17]. The discussion can be traced back to [3] and [4].

To construct PSFAs, we can rely on Maximum Service Curve (MSC) [9]. In particular, we are interested in a specific MSC type, called Latency-Rate MSC.

Definition 8. *A server s is said to guarantee a Latency-Rate Maximum Server Curve (LR-MSC) with rate R_s^g and error term $\beta_s^g(\geq 0)$ to a ow g, if for all t_2 and all $0 \leq t_1 \leq t_2$,*

$$W_s^g(t_1, t_2) \leq R_s^g(t_2 - t_1 + \beta_s^g). \tag{26}$$

The following lemma shows that a PSFA can be formed from a server with LR-MSC. The proof is given in [16].

Lemma 3. *If server s guarantees ow g an LR-MSC with rate R_s^g and error term $\beta_s^g(\geq \frac{L}{R_s^g})$, then for all $j \geq 1$, $G_s^{g,j} \leq d_s^{g,j} + \beta_s^g$.*

With Lemma 3, if the server also provides LR-WSG to every input flow f, then the server is PSFA to the flow. Since in this case, the server is PSRG server to f from Theorem 1 and hence for any packet $p^{f,i}$ of f, $d_s^{f,i} \leq F_s^{f,i} + E_s^f$. Supposing in flow g, of which f is an immediate constituent, $p^{g,j} = p^{f,i}$, we must have $d_s^{g,j} = d_s^{f,i}$ and hence $d_s^{g,j} \leq F_s^{f,i} + E_s^f$. On the other hand, from Lemma 3, $G_s^{g,j} \leq d_s^{g,j} + \beta_s^g$. Consequently, $G_s^{g,j} \leq F_s^{f,i} + E_s^f + \beta_s^g$, with which and the definition of PSFA, we get:

Theorem 8. *If a server s guarantees a ow g an LR-MSC with rate R_s^g and error term β_s^g, and for every immediate constituent ow f of g, the server guarantees an LR-WSC with rate R_s^f and latency E_s^f, then the server s is PSFA to the ow f with aggregation parameter $\mathcal{E}_s^f = E_s^f + \beta_s^g$.*

Theorem 9 provides a theoretical basis for constructing PSFA. Note that we have shown in Section 2.4 that a wide family of well-known schedulers provide LR-WSG and hence are PSRG servers. Also note that an LR-MSC can be realized through a token bucket controller. Hence, a PSFA is formed by using a token bucket controller to limit the service rate offered to the aggregator that provides PSRG to all its inputs.

4.3   Per-domain PSRG in Presence of Flow Aggregation

Consider the path of a flow f crossing a network domain, which is a tandem system of servers as illustrated in Fig. 2. The network, while similar to that discussed in Section 3, allows flow aggregation along the path. We assume that

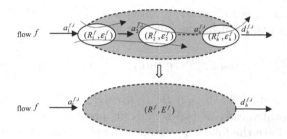

Fig. 2. Per-domain PSRG with flow aggregation

all servers along the path are PSRG servers and if one is an aggregating server, it also is a PSFA.

Suppose each server $s(= 1, \ldots, h)$ provides PSRG with rate $R_s^{f_s}$ and error term $E_s^{f_s}$ to input flow f_s, the root aggregate of flow f at server s. Let g_s denote the output flow of which f_s is its immediate constituent flow. If s is aggregating server to f_s, we use $\mathcal{E}_s^{f_s}$ to denote the aggregation parameter to flow f_s by the PSFA. If s is non-aggregating server to f_s, then for ease of exposition, we define $\mathcal{E}_s^{f_s} \equiv E_s^{f_s} + \frac{L}{R_s^{f_s}}$ for this server.

If there is no separator between servers s and $s + 1$, then it is clear that $f_{s+1} = g_s$. If, however, there is one or more separators between them, f_{s+1} is a subset of g_s. Nevertheless, each packet of f_{s+1} will arrive to server $s + 1$ at the same time as it would arrive when no separation had happened to flow g_s, since we have assumed no packet delay is introduced by a separator. This also implies the order of packets in f_{s+1} remains the same as that in g_s. Assume that for all $s = 1, \ldots, h$, the reserved rate for f_{s+1} at server $s + 1$ is not less than the reserved rate for g_s at server s, i.e. $R_{s+1}^{f_{s+1}} \geq R_s^{g_s}$.

As for the per-domain PSRG without flow aggregation case, we define the following *domain* virtual finish time function for the edge-to-edge path with h servers. Specifically, for any $i \geq 1$, define

$$\widetilde{F}_h^{f,i} = max[a_1^{f,i}, min(d_h^{f,i-1}, \widetilde{F}_h^{f,i-1})] + \frac{l^{f,i}}{R^f} \qquad (27)$$

with $\widetilde{F}_h^{f,0} = 0$ and $d_h^{f,0} = 0$, and $R^f = min_{s=1,\ldots,h} R_s^{f_s}$. Here, the flow f denotes the sequence of packets traversing the path edge-to-edge. In other words, f represents the common set of packets of flows f_s, $s = 1, \ldots, h$. Similarly, if we treat the global system of the edge-to-edge path as a blackbox, (27) defines the nodal PSRG virtual finish time function for the blackbox. As shown in Fig. 2, $a_1^{f,i}$ is the arrival time of packet $p^{f,i}$ to the blackbox while $d_h^{f,i}$ is the departure time of the packet leaving the blackbox.

We now prove per-domain PSRG for the considered system. We begin with studying the concatenation of two servers s and t with flow aggregation. Let f_s be the sequence of packets that arrive to server s and depart from server t, g_s be the corresponding aggregate output flow of f_s, and f_t be the aggregate flow to server t, of which f_s is a constituent. Similar to (27), we define the edge-to-edge domain PSRG virtual finish time function for the two-server system as follows

$$\widetilde{F}_t^{f_s,i_s} = max[a_s^{f_s,i_s}, min(d_t^{f_s,i_s-1}, \widetilde{F}_t^{f_s,i_s-1})] + \frac{l^{f_s,i_s}}{R^{f_s}} \qquad (28)$$

with $\widetilde{F}_t^{f_s,0} = 0$ and $d_s^{f_s,0} = 0$, and $R^{f_s} = min(R_s^{f_s}, R_t^{f_t})$.

For the concatenation of two servers in presence of flow aggregation and separation, we have the following results. The proof can be found from [16].

Lemma 4. *For any two consecutive PSRG servers s and t, no matter whether there are separators in between, if $R_s^{g_s} \leq R_t^{f_t}$, we have for any packet p^{f_s,i_s},*
i) if t is non-aggregating server,

$$F_t^{f_s,i_s} \leq \widetilde{F}_t^{f_s,i_s} + \mathcal{E}_s^{f_s}; \qquad (29)$$

ii) otherwise, if t is aggregating PSFA,

$$F_t^{f_s,i_s} \leq \widetilde{F}_t^{f_s,i_s} + \mathcal{E}_s^{f_s} \quad and \qquad (30)$$
$$G_t^{f_s,i_s} \leq \widetilde{F}_t^{f_s,i_s} + \mathcal{E}_s^{f_s} + \mathcal{E}_t^{f_t}. \qquad (31)$$

Here if s is non-aggregating server, $\mathcal{E}_s^{f_s}$ is de ned to be $\mathcal{E}_s^{f_s} \equiv E_s^{f_s} + \frac{L}{R^{f_s}}$, otherwise s is assumed to be PSFA with aggregation parameter $\mathcal{E}_s^{f_s}$.

Lemma 4 has two important implications. One is that the concatenation system provides PSRG to the flow of packets traversing them, no matter whether the second server is PSFA. Hence, we can treat the system as a single conceptual PSRG server with virtual finish time function $\widetilde{F}_t$ and error term $\mathcal{E}_s^{f_s} + E_t^{f_t}$. Another is that, if the second server is PSFA, the system can further be treated as PSFA with aggregation parameter $\mathcal{E}_s^{f_s} + \mathcal{E}_t^{f_t}$. In consequence, if a network as shown by Fig. 2 includes more than two PSRG/PSFA servers, we can iteratively apply Lemma 4 and get the following result.

Lemma 5. *For the network shown by Fig. 2, we have for any packet $p^{f,i}$*

$$F_h^{f,i} \leq \widetilde{F}_h^{f,i} + \sum_{s=1}^{h-1} \mathcal{E}_s^{f_s}. \qquad (32)$$

Note that h is PSRG server with error term $E_h^{f_h}$. Hence, $d_h^{f,i} \leq F_h^{f,i} + E_h^{f_h}$. With this and (32), $d_h^{f,i} \leq \widetilde{F}_h^{f,i} + \sum_{s=1}^{h-1} \mathcal{E}_s^{f_s} + E_h^{f_h}$. Since $\widetilde{F}_h^{f,i}$ defines the domain PSRG virtual finish time function, the following theorem is proved.

Theorem 9. *For the network shown by Fig. 2, it o ers to ow f PSRG with rate R^f and error term E^f where $R^f = min_{s=1,\ldots,h} R_s^{f_s}$ and $E^f = \sum_{s=1}^{h-1} \mathcal{E}_s^{f_s} + E_h^{f_h}$.*

Comparing Theorem 9 with Theorem 7, it is easy to verify that Theorem 7 is a special case of Theorem 9 in which all servers are non-aggregating PSRG servers with $\mathcal{E}_s^{f_s} = E_s^{f_s} + \frac{L}{R}$ and $f_s = f$ for all $s = 1, \ldots, h$. Similarly, we can derive e2e delay bounds for the network shown by Fig. 2.

Corollary 3. *For the network shown by Fig. 2, if ow f is constrained by a leaky bucket* (σ^f, r^f) *before entering the network and* $r^f \leq R^f$, *the e2e delay of any packet in the ow is bounded by:* $D^f \leq \frac{\sigma^f}{R^f} + E^f$.

Corollary 4. *For the network shown by Fig. 2, if ow f has gSBB with upper rate* r^f *and bounding function* $\mathcal{F}$ *before entering the network and* $r^f \leq R^f$, *then the e2e delay of any packet in the ow satis es:* $Pr\left(D^f \geq \frac{\sigma^f}{R^f} + E^f\right) \leq \mathcal{F}(\sigma^f)$.

4.4 An Expedited Forwarding Per-domain Behavior

To obtain per-domain PSRG for a flow f in presence of flow aggregation, we have assumed in above that $R_{s+1}^{f_s+1} \geq R_s^{g_s}$ for all $s = 1, \ldots, h-1$. Here comes a question: is this requirement reasonable? If not, the obtained results for per-domain PSRG could then be of no use. Fortunately, from the following discussion, we believe that in DiffServ networks, the requirement can be satisfied and hence PSFA can be used to aggregate EF flows to provide per-domain PSRG.

From the end-user's point of view, a service guarantee such as PSRG makes more sense end-to-end than per-hop. Per-hop guarantee does not necessarily result in per-domain guarantee and consequently e2e guarantee. Besides the reason of flow aggregation, another reason is that packets of a microflow could tranverse a domain through different paths that may provide different levels of service guarantees. In consequence, packets of a microflow could experience different delays and even be out-of-order at the egress point. To avoid these, the DiffServ WG is currently working on defining per-domain behaviors (PDBs). Each PDB specifies a forwarding path treatment of a traffic aggregate [19]. Note that various route pinning mechanisms can be used to ensure that the forwarding path along which a flow traverses keeps unchanged. One such example is MPLS [21]. Particularly, if L-LSPs with bandwidth reservation, defined in [11], are used as forwarding paths for EF traffic, the requirement mentioned above is implicitly satisfied. This is because there is no separation along an L-LSP and in the case of L-LSP merging, the reserved bandwidth for the downstream of the merged point is required to be sufficient to carry the sum of merged traffic [11].

Finally, as for EF PHB, we define an Expedited Forwarding Per-Domain Behavior (EF PDB) as:

Definition 9. *A Di Serv domain that supports EF PDB to the EF aggregate between an ingress-egress interface pair at some con gured rate R must satisfy*

$$d^i \leq F^i + E \qquad (33)$$

where with $F^0 = 0; d^0 = 0$, F^i *is iteratively de ne d by*

$$F^i = max[a^i, min(d^{i-1}, F^{f,i-1})] + \frac{l^i}{R}. \qquad (34)$$

Here, a^i is the arrival time of the ith packet of the EF aggregate to the ingress interface, d^i is the departure time of the packet from the egress interface, l^i is the length of the packet, F^i is the target departure time of the packet, and E is the error term for the treatment of the EF aggregate traversing the domain through the ingress-egress interface pair. Indeed, function (34) is the domain virtual finish time function (27) if all packets in the EF aggregate traverse the domain through the same path.

While looking similar, the defined EF PDB differs from EF PHB in several aspects. First, for EF PHB, the referred EF aggregate is the aggregate of all EF flows destined to an output interface. However, in Definition 9, the referred EF aggregate is the aggregate of EF flows that have the same ingress interface and the same egress interface. Second, for EF PHB, a packet departs from the same node as it arrives to. However, for the defined EF PDB, the node a packet departs from can be different from what it arrives to. Third, for the defined EF PDB, there can be multiple forwarding paths between the ingress-egress interface pair, which however do not exist for EF PHB.

On the other hand, the defined EF PDB has similar dual characterization as EF PHB. In Definition 9, if the ith packet refers to the ith departure of the EF aggregate from the egress interface, then (33) and (34) define the "aggregate behavior" per-domain PSRG. If the ith packet refers to the ith arrival of the EF aggregate to the ingress interface, (33) and (34) defines the "packet-identity-aware" per-domain PSRG. If all packets in the EF aggregate traverse the domain through the same path, there is no difference between these two sets of definitions. However, if packets in the EF aggregate traverse the domain through different paths, the "aggregate behavior" per-domain PSRG can be different from the "packet-identity-aware" per-domain PSRG. Nevertheless, the results presented earlier lay a theoretical foundation to determine per-domain PSRG along each path and consequently the defined EF PDB.

5   Conclusion

This paper has made several contributions in the context of Expedited Forwarding service with special focus on per-domain PSRG. First, we introduced a new concept called LR-WSG. We proved that if a server provides LR-WSG, it also provides PSRG. We showed that a wide family of schedulers belong to LR-WSG servers. Appealingly, these schedulers include not only one-level schedulers but also hierarchical schedulers. Second, we proved that per-domain PSRG is provided by networks of PSRG servers if per-flow scheduling is implemented. The proof is notable in that it relies only on the definitions of PSRG, which include the initial nodal PSRG definition and the generalized domain PSRG definition. With the definition of domain PSRG virtual finish time function, the proof is simple. Third, we developed a framework for realizing per-domain PSRG in presence of flow aggregation. Specifically, we proposed to use PSFA to aggregate flows. In addition, we introduced a method to implement PSFA based on the concept of MSC. Furthermore, we showed that with PSFA, per-domain PSRG can be provided in spite of flow aggregation. Finally, we discussed the viability of using PSFA in DiffServ networks and introduced a definition of EF PDB.

References

1. Agrawal, R., Cruz, R. L., Okino, C. M., and Rajan, R.: A framework for adaptive service guarantees. In *Proc. Allerton Conf. on Comm., Control, and Comp.*, 1998.
2. Bennett, J. C. R., et al: Delay jitter bounds and packet scale rate guarantee for Expedited Forwarding. *IEEE/ACM ToN*, 10(4):529–540, August 2002.
3. Bennett, J. C. R., and Zhang, H.: WF^{2}Q: Worst-case fair weighted fair queueing. In *Proc. IEEE INFOCOM'96*, 1996.
4. Bennett, J. C. R., and Zhang, H.: Hierarchical packet fair queueing algorithms. *IEEE/ACM ToN*, 5(5):675–689, Oct 1997.
5. Blake, S., et al.: An architecture for Differentiated Services. *IETF RFC 2475*, Dec. 1998.
6. Charny, A., et al.: Supplemental information for the new definition of the EF PHB. *IETF RFC 3247*, March 2002.
7. Charny, A. and Le Boudec, J.-Y.: Delay bounds in a network with aggregate scheduling. In *Proc. QoFIS'2000.*
8. Cobb, J. A. Preserving quality of service guarantees in spite of flow aggregation. *IEEE/ACM ToN*, 10(1):43–53, Feb. 2002.
9. Cruz, R. L.: SCED+: Efficient management of quality of service guarantees. In *Proc. INFOCOM'98*, 1998.
10. Davie, B., et al: An Expedited Forwarding PHB. *IETF RFC 3246*, March 2002.
11. Faucheur, F. L., et al: Multiprotocol label switching (MPLS) support of Differentiated Services. *IETF RFC 3270*, May 2002.
12. Goyal, P., Lam, S. S., and Vin, H. M.: Determining end-to-end delay bounds in heterogeneous networks. *Springer Multimedia Systems*, 5:157–163, 1997.
13. Goyal, P., Vin, H. M., and Cheng H.: Start-time Fair Queueing: A scheduling algorithm for Integrated Services packet switching networks. *IEEE/ACM ToN*, 5(5):690–704, 1997.
14. Jacobson, V., Nichols, K., and Poduri, K.: An Expedited Forwarding PHB. *IETF RFC 2598*, June 1999.
15. Jiang, Y.: Delay bounds for a network of Guaranteed Rate servers with FIFO aggregation. *Computer Networks*, 40(6):683–694, Dec. 2002.
16. Jiang, Y.: Per-domain packet scale rate guarantee for Expedited Forwarding. Technical report, Institute for Infocomm Research, 2003. (http://www.icr.a-star.edu.sg/ jiangym/publications/ef-pdb.pdf)
17. Le Boudec, J.-Y. and Charny, A.: Packet scale rate guarantee for non-FIFO nodes. In *Proc. IEEE INFOCOM'2002.*
18. Lee, K.: Performance bounds in communication networks with variable-rate links. In *Proc. ACM SIGCOMM'95.*
19. Nichols, K. and Carpenter, B.: Definition of differentiated services per domain behaviors and rules for their specification. *IETF RFC 3086*, April 2001.
20. Parekh, A. K. and Gallager, P. G.: A generalized processor sharing approach to flow control in intergrated services networks: The single-node case. *IEEE/ACM ToN*, 1(3):344–357, 1993.
21. Rosen, B., Viswanathan, A., and Callon, R.: Multiprotocol label switching architecture. *IETF RFC 3031*, January 2001.
22. Yin, Q., Jiang, Y., Jiang, S., and Kong, P. Y.: Analysis on generalized stochastically bounded bursty traffic for communication networks. In *Proc. IEEE LCN'02*, 2002.
23. Zhang, Z.-L., Duan, Z., and Hou, Y. T.: Fundamental trade-offs in aggregation packet scheduling. In *Proc. ICNP'01.*

On Achieving Weighted Service Differentiation: An End-to-End Perspective*

Hung-Yun Hsieh, Kyu-Han Kim, and Raghupathy Sivakumar

School of Electrical and Computer Engineering
Georgia Institute of Technology
Atlanta, Georgia, 30332, USA
{hyhsieh,siva}@ece.gatech.edu, khkim94@cc.gatech.edu

Abstract. In this paper, we consider the problem of weighted rate differentiation using purely end-to-end mechanisms. Existing approaches to solving the problem involve changes in the AIMD congestion control mechanism used by TCP. However, such approaches either do not scale well to large weights, or make impractical assumptions. We use a new multi-state transport layer solution called *pTCP* to achieve end-to-end weighted service differentiation. A pTCP flow of weight w consists of w TCP *virtual flows* that collectively achieve w times the throughput of a default TCP flow. pTCP scales significantly better than approaches that change the AIMD congestion control mechanism of TCP. On the other hand, pTCP achieves more effective service differentiation and incurs less host overhead than the simplest form of a multi-state solution using multiple TCP sockets through application striping. We substantiate our arguments through simulations, and testbed experiments based on a user-level implementation of pTCP.

1 Introduction

Approaches to achieve relative service differentiation are inherently much simpler to deploy and manage. Hence, the paradigm of relative service differentiation has gained considerable attention over the last few years [1,2]. In this work, we consider the specific problem of achieving weighted rate differentiation using purely end-to-end mechanisms. A solution to such a problem will have the added benefit of supporting scalable QoS without any infrastructure change.

An important instantiation of such an end-to-end weighted rate differentiation solution lies in the incorporation of weighted fairness within the TCP transport protocol design. Essentially, under a weighted fairness model, a TCP flow of weight w is to be provided with w times the throughput of a default TCP flow (with unit weight). In this context, several related works have been proposed to modify the AIMD (additive increase, multiplicative decrease) congestion control of TCP for achieving the desired throughput. For example, MulTCP [3] changes the AIMD parameters according to the weight of the flow. While such a weighted AIMD (WAIMD) scheme requires minimal changes to TCP, simulation and testbed results [3,4] have shown that WAIMD can provide weighted rate differentiation only for a small range of weights (less than 10). For

---

* This work was funded in part by NSF grants ANI-0117840 and ECS-0225497, Motorola, Yamacraw, and the Georgia Tech Broadband Institute.

K. Jeffay, I. Stoica, and K. Wehrle (Eds.): IWQoS 2003, LNCS 2707, pp. 440–457, 2003.
© Springer-Verlag Berlin Heidelberg 2003

larger weights, it suffers from frequent packet losses, and does not provide consistent service differentiation. TCP-LASD [5] is an approach proposed to improve the performance of WAIMD by adapting the AIMD parameters to the packet loss rate as well as the flow weight. Although TCP-LASD exhibits higher scalability in terms of weight (up to 100), it relies on accurate loss estimation that is difficult to achieve using purely end-to-end schemes without any network support [5].

The fact that WAIMD maintains only one TCB (TCP control block) [6] per connection makes it vulnerable to deviation from the ideal behavior under severe loss conditions. Specifically, given an identical distribution of packet losses, a connection maintaining only one TCB will be impacted by timeouts far more than one that maintains multiple TCBs. When timeouts occur in the former, the whole connection will stall until the loss is recovered, but in the latter, only the affected TCB(s) will stall. While an application-striping approach using multiple TCP sockets (and hence multiple TCBs) has been studied and experimented in a different context [7,8,9,10], it has thus far not been considered as a potential solution for achieving weighted service differentiation due to the following reasons: (i) The throughput gain is not consistently proportional to the degree of parallelism (number of sockets used) even for a small number of sockets (around 10). Hence it is difficult to decide (in a distributed fashion) the number of parallel sockets to use for achieving the desired weighted fairness under any given network condition. (ii) Striping is usually done by dividing the application data into same-sized partitions equal to the number of sockets before transmission commences. Each partition of data is therefore transferred asynchronously by the corresponding streams (sockets) and is reassembled after all transmissions are complete (offline reassembly). This approach thus cannot be used by applications that require strict TCP semantics including in-sequence data delivery. The added complexity imposed on applications to perform the sophisticated striping techniques (e.g. data partition and reassembly) also renders this approach less desirable.

In this paper, we first study the performance of an application-striping approach when used as a solution to achieve weighted service differentiation. We show that it fares better than WAIMD in terms of scalability to increasing weights, but still does not achieve the ideal expected weighted service differentiation beyond small weight values. We provide insights into the performance limitations of application striping. We then use a multi-state transport layer protocol called **pTCP** (parallel TCP) that maintains multiple TCBs per connection but avoids the pitfalls of application striping, for achieving the desired weighted differentiation. pTCP was originally proposed in [11] to aggregate bandwidths on a mobile host with multiple network interfaces. We tailor the design of pTCP for the specific goal of achieving weighted service differentiation. A pTCP connection of weight w consists of w mini-flows called *TCP-v* (TCP-virtual) flows. TCP-v is a simple variation of default TCP that employs the same congestion control mechanisms, but does not deal with the actual application data. A central entity called the pTCP engine manages the send and receive socket buffers, and handles reliability and flow control for the pTCP connection. Through both simulation results and real-life evaluation of a user-level implementation of pTCP, we show that pTCP is able to achieve effective weighted service differentiation, exhibiting a much higher scalability to the range of weights than both WAIMD and application striping.

The rest of this paper is organized as follows: In Section 2 we explain the goals and scope of this paper, and in Section 3 we discuss related work that uses end-to-end mechanisms to achieve weighted service differentiation. In Section 4 we present the pTCP design and protocol. Section 5 presents simulation and prototype implementation results showing the performance of pTCP. Section 6 discusses some critical issues in the pTCP design, and finally Section 7 concludes the paper.

2   Goals and Scope

- **Weighted Rate Differentiation:** The *DiffServ* framework supports absolute service differentiation with guarantees on absolute performance levels, as well as relative service differentiation with assurances for relative quality ordering between classes [1,12]. Many approaches and architectures have been proposed to achieve relative service differentiation for different service parameters and applications [2, 5,13,14,15]. It is shown in [1] that relative service differentiation requires a "tuning knob" to adjust the relative QoS spacing between classes, and hence the *proportional differentiation* model, where the performance experienced by a certain class is proportional to the service differentiation parameters, stands out for its ability to achieve *controllable* and *predictable* service differentiation. The goal of this paper is to provide such a "tuning knob" for achieving relative service differentiation. We consider data rate differentiation and hence a user (a TCP flow in particular) with weight or differentiation parameter w is to be provided w times the data rate of a user with unit weight.
- **End-to-End Approach:** We aim to provide the weighted rate differentiation using purely end-to-end mechanisms. While a complete model for providing relative service differentiation requires appropriate pricing and policing enforced at the edge routers, we do not rely on network support to achieve service differentiation. No assumptions are made in terms of network support except for a fair dropping mechanism such as RED. Note that the fair dropping requirement is also essential for TCP to achieve the default (non-weighted) proportional fairness [16,17,18].
- **TCP Friendliness:** We define TCP friendliness in the context of weighted service differentiation as follows: A weighted TCP flow of weight w will receive exactly the throughput that would have been enjoyed by w default TCP flows (which replace the weighted flow under the same network condition) in total. Note that given our TCP friendliness goal, the behavior of a TCP flow with weight w should be exactly that of an aggregation of w unit TCP flows. This in turn means that the weighted flow will still exhibit any undesirable property that TCP might have (such as RTT bias). While it is not the goal of this paper to change the behavior of a default TCP flow, any improved congestion control mechanism used by TCP should be easily incorporated by the weighted flow to achieve the desired service differentiation.
- **TCP Semantics:** We limit the scope of this paper to applications that require the end-to-end semantics of TCP in terms of reliability and in-sequence delivery. The conventional application-striping approach [7,8] that partitions application data and transfers different portions through different TCP connections thus falls outside the scope of this paper, since it requires the receiving application to perform *offline processing* to reassemble the collected data portions.

3   Motivation

There are two broad classes of approaches that can be used to achieve end-to-end weighted rate differentiation: (i) *Weighted AIMD:* A single-state approach that uses a single TCP flow with a modified AIMD congestion control mechanism, and (ii) *Application Striping:* A multi-state approach that stripes across multiple default TCP sockets. The first class of approaches has been studied in quite some detail by related work [3, 5]. However, the latter class of approaches, although proposed in other contexts [7,8], has not been investigated as a viable option for achieving weighted rate differentiation. In the rest of the section, we first outline the reasons for the *non-scalability* of vanilla WAIMD, and discuss the limitations of a variant called TCP-LASD. We then study the performance of application striping in the context of weighted rate differentiation, and provide insights into its benefits and limitations.

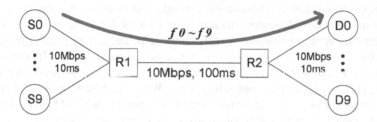

Fig. 1. Network Topology (Single Link)

We use simulation results based on the *ns-2* network simulator [19] to illustrate and substantiate our arguments during the discussion. The topology used consists of a single link topology with 2 backbone routers and 20 access nodes as shown in Fig. 1 The end-to-end path traversed by the 10 TCP flows (flow i originates from S_i and terminates at D_i) has bottleneck capacity of 10Mbps and base round-trip time of 240ms. The backbone routers use the RED queue with buffer size of 320KB (approximately the bandwidth-delay product of the end-to-end path), and the access nodes use the DropTail queue. $f0$ is a weighted flow with weight w, and $f1$ through $f9$ are regular TCP flows with unit weight. We use TCP-SACK for all TCP flows.

3.1   Limitations of Weighted AIMD

Ideally, the throughput of a weighted flow with weight w should be w times that of the average throughput enjoyed by the unit flows. However, it is clear from Fig. 2(a) that[1] WAIMD does not scale beyond a weight of even 10. The reasons for such poor performance stem from the following two properties of WAIMD:

– **Burstiness:** For a flow with weight w, WAIMD modifies the increase (α) and decrease (β) parameters in AIMD to be αw, and $\frac{\beta}{w}$ respectively. It is clear that the

---

[1] The performance of pTCP shown in Fig. 2 and Fig. 3 will be discussed in Section 5.1.

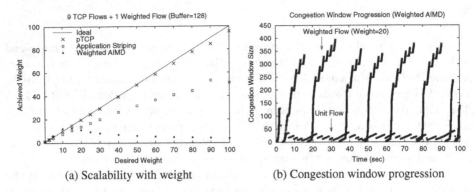

(a) Scalability with weight   (b) Congestion window progression

Fig. 2. Limitations of Weighted AIMD

congestion window progression for a weighted flow becomes more bursty with increasing weights. Burstiness induces packet losses due to queue overflows, which eventually result in timeouts if sufficiently large number of packets are lost from within one congestion window, or a retransmitted packet is lost. It is shown in [5] that the loss probability at a bottleneck link increases proportional to the *square of the sum of weights* of all contending flows. While the SACK option can ameliorate the impact of losses to some extent, due to the limited number of SACK blocks available in the TCP header, its benefits do not scale with the amount of losses. Hence, WAIMD becomes more bursty with increasing weights, and consequently experiences increasing chances of timeouts. Fig. 2(b) presents the congestion window evolution of the WAIMD flow. The burstiness is evident through the steep increases in the congestion window. Moreover, as the figure shows, 8 timeouts occur during the period of 100 seconds, substantiating our argument that the bursty nature of the traffic induces frequent timeouts in WAIMD.

– **Single State:** Timeouts in general degrade TCP's throughput performance. However, they drastically impact WAIMD's performance because of its single state strategy. Specifically, WAIMD maintains only one TCB per connection (just as TCP). Hence, when a timeout occurs, irrespective of the weight w of a flow, the flow is completely shutdown. In contrast, if the flow were really replaced with w default TCP flows, even if one of the flows experiences a timeout, the remaining flows would have been able to continue without interruption. However, WAIMD cannot emulate such a behavior because of its single state design.

While WAIMD cannot achieve the desired service differentiation due to the inability to handle packet losses induced by its burstiness, in [5] the authors propose a *loss-adaptive* variant of WAIMD, called TCP-LASD, that adapts its increase and decrease parameters as a function of the loss rate (p) observed–e.g., by setting $\alpha \propto \frac{1}{p}$, or $\beta \propto p$. They show that TCP-LASD can scale considerably better than WAIMD if accurate loss rate information is available at all sources. However, such an assumption, even the authors agree, is not pragmatic in a distributed environment. This is due to the fact that even when network routers attempt to provide a *fair dropping probability*, they merely strive to achieve a fair expected loss probability for all packets in the *long term* (several round-trip times), and do not try to reduce the variance in the loss probabilities accorded to different flows. However, the fact that TCP-LASD relies on accurate loss estimation to drive the congestion window progression on a per-packet basis, makes its performance sensitive to even *short-term* loss rate estimation. While the authors argue that the problem can be offset with accurate loss rate information feedback from the network, this solution deviates from the scope of this paper in terms of providing service differentiation through purely end-to-end mechanisms.

3.2   Limitations of Application Striping

In the application-striping approach, the application opens multiple sockets to the destination, and explicitly stripes data across the different sockets in an attempt to achieve better throughput performance. Specifically, we assume that a sending application will open w socket connections with the destination for achieving the desired weight of w. In keeping with the TCP semantics of in-sequence delivery, we assume that the receiving application will read only from the socket buffer that has the next expected application layer sequence number. The application can perform such an in-sequence read by setting the *peek* flag in the socket read options (which will prevent the last read packet from being dequeued from the socket buffer), and performing an actual read only when it knows that the socket buffer has the next expected packet.[2]

We observe from Fig. 2(a) that the performance of application striping is considerably better than that of WAIMD. This can be attributed to the *multiple-state* strategy adopted by the application-striping approach. In other words, in application striping, one TCB is maintained per unit TCP flow. Hence, even when one of the flows experiences a timeout, the other flows are still free to continue transmitting. The limiting factor, however, will be the *head-of-line blocking* at the receiver-side buffer. Since the application reads only in-sequence, although flows not experiencing a timeout can continue transmitting, the receiving application will not read from their socket buffers if the next in-sequence packet is carried by the timeout-stalled flow. When their buffers thus become full, the TCP receivers of those flows will advertise a window size of zero and force the TCP senders to enter the *persist* mode [20], eventually stalling the flows.

Note from Fig. 2(a) that the performance of application striping deviates from the ideal behavior for weights larger than 10. We now proceed to evaluate and explain its performance in terms of the buffer requirement, and when the per-unit-flow fair share of the bandwidth amounts to a small (and hence timeout-prone) congestion window. Fig. 3(a) studies the impact of the receive buffer size per TCB on the performance of the aggregate connection. Since the bandwidth-delay product for each TCB is approximately 24KB, it can be observed that application striping is able to achieve close to the ideal performance only for significantly large buffers (of 512KB or above for a weight of 20). In other words, close to *twenty times the bandwidth-delay product worth of buffering is required for each socket* for the performance of the application striping to even reach

---

[2] While we take such an approach to reduce the application complexity and overhead (in terms of the resequencing process required), note that any performance degradation due to the apparent lack of an application resequencing buffer can be compensated by using a large TCP socket buffer. We do study the impact of the buffer size at the receiving TCPs later in this section.

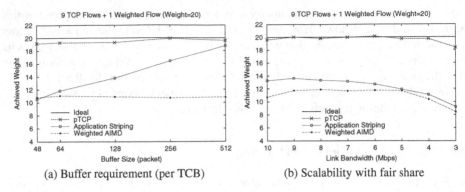

(a) Buffer requirement (per TCB)   (b) Scalability with fair share

Fig. 3. Limitations of Application Striping

close to the ideal performance (the total amount of buffering used by the application is the per-socket buffer size times the number of sockets open). Clearly, application striping fails to *scale* to large weights, from purely the standpoint of the amount of memory expended at the receiver. The dependence on such large buffers is due to the head-of-line blocking otherwise experienced, either (i) when striping is performed in a manner disproportionate with the instantaneous rate of the individual TCP flows by an unaware application, or more importantly (ii) when packet losses or timeouts occur.

Fig. 3(b) studies the impact of the fair share per TCB (unit flow) on the performance of the aggregate connection. Note that the congestion window size of a TCP flow is reflective of the fair share available. When the average congestion window size goes down below a value of *six*, it has been shown in [21] that TCP is more prone to timeouts due to the unavailability of sufficient data packets to trigger fast retransmit (3 duplicate ACKs) after a loss event. When timeouts do occur, although application striping does not suffer from the single-state problem in WAIMD, it is still vulnerable to the head-of-line blocking problem due to the filling up of the individual receive buffers (when one or more flows are recovering from a timeout). The results shown in Fig. 3(b) are obtained by varying the bandwidth of the bottleneck link from 10Mbps to 3Mbps, which in turn changes the average congestion window size per TCB (the queue size of RED routers and the buffer size per TCB scale accordingly). It is clear that while application striping achieves only about half the desired throughput when the bandwidth is 10Mbps (the average congestion window size is around 20), its performance degrades even more as the bandwidth reduces. Hence, application striping fails to *scale* to large weights when the available fair share per TCB is such that flows are prone to timeouts.

In summary, although application striping performs better than WAIMD by virtue of its multiple-state strategy, it still has the following limitations:

– **Disproportionate Striping:** When the application performs striping without transport layer support, only simple strategies such as *round-robin striping*, or *write until block* can be used. However, such simple strategies can result in the amount of data assigned to the individual TCP flows being disproportionate with the actual instantaneous data rates of the TCP flows. This will in turn result in out-of-order (in terms of application sequence numbers) packets being delivered at the receiver causing the receive buffers to fill up, and hence potentially resulting in some of the flows stalling due to buffer limitations.

- **Inefficient Buffer Sharing:** While disproportionate striping by itself causes the undesirable phenomenon of more out-of-order delivery at the receiver, the problem is exacerbated due to the inefficient use of the aggregate receive-side buffer. Similar to the problem identified in [22], if the instantaneous rates of the individual TCP flows are different (due to window fluctuations), the constant buffer allocation at the receive side (per TCP flow) is clearly inefficient as the faster flows require a larger portion of the aggregate buffer. However, when application striping is used, no buffer sharing is possible between the individual TCP flows unless an explicit, dynamic buffer re-allocation technique like the one proposed in [22] is used.

- **Timeouts:** Due to the multiple independent states (one per unit TCP) maintained, application striping does not suffer from the drastic consequences that WAIMD faces upon the occurrence of timeouts. However, as explained earlier, the aggregate connection is still vulnerable to stalls because the unaffected TCP flows are also blocked due to unavailability of receive buffer during the course of a timeout. While over-allocation of buffer can reduce the intensity of the problem, it is clearly not a scalable solution.

- **Application Complexity:** Finally, another key drawback of application striping is the additional complexity that the application has to bear in terms of performing intelligent striping, and more importantly performing an elaborate resequencing process at the receiver in order to emulate TCP's in-sequence delivery semantics. Such a resequencing process will involve the use of application layer sequence numbers, intelligent reading from the socket buffer, and efficient maintenance of the application buffer. Requiring every application that needs weighted service differentiation to perform the same set of tasks is clearly undesirable.

4   The pTCP Protocol

pTCP is a multi-state transport layer protocol that maintains multiple TCBs per connection [11]. While it was originally proposed for achieving bandwidth aggregation on multi-homed mobile hosts with heterogeneous network interfaces, we discuss in this section how the basic principles of pTCP, combined with an appropriate tailoring of its mechanisms to the problem of weighted service differentiation (WSD), can help in achieving the desired goal.

4.1   Design Elements

- **Multiple States:** Similar to application striping, pTCP maintains multiple states for a weighted connection to avoid the performance degradation exhibited in WAIMD. A pTCP connection with a weight of w consists of w TCP-v mini-flows (pipes). The state that each TCP-v maintains (TCB-v) is identical to the TCB maintained by TCP, except that no real application data is stored or manipulated in the TCB-v. Note that while pTCP mimics application striping in maintaining multiple TCBs, the other design elements are targeted toward avoiding the pitfalls in application striping that we identified in Section 3.2.

- **Decoupled Functionality:** pTCP is a wrapper around TCP-v, and it controls the socket send and receive buffers across all TCP-v pipes. Each TCP-v performs congestion control and loss recovery just as regular TCP, but it does not have access to the application data and has no control over which data to send. Any segment transmission by a TCP-v (called "virtual segment" that contains only the TCP header) is preceded by a function call to pTCP requesting for data binding. Therefore, TCP-v controls the *amount* of data that can be sent while pTCP controls *which* data to send. A retransmission in the TCP-v pipe does not necessarily mean a retransmission of the application data. pTCP thus decouples congestion control from reliability. By virtue of the design of decoupled functionality, pTCP is able to incur significant less overhead than application striping (we elaborate on this in Section 6.2).

- **Congestion Window Based Striping:** pTCP does not explicitly perform any bandwidth estimation along individual TCP-v pipes to decide the amount of data to distribute across pipes. Instead, pTCP reuses TCP's congestion window adaptation to perform intelligent striping. Specifically, in pTCP the application data is "bound" (assigned) to a TCP-v pipe for transmission only when there is space in its congestion window (recall that TCP-v controls the amount of data to be sent). As bandwidth along each pipe fluctuates, the congestion window of the concerned TCP-v adapts correspondingly, and the amount of data assigned to the pipe also varies, thus achieving packet allocation across multiple pipes. Note that when used for achieving bandwidth aggregation across different paths, the congestion window based striping needs to be complemented with packet scheduling algorithms to tackle the delay differential problem (where different paths exhibit RTT mismatches). However, such a sophisticated and high-overhead packet scheduling algorithm is not required for achieving WSD since all pipes share the same physical path.

- **Dynamic Reassignment:** An important design element in pTCP to avoid head-of-line blocking is the dynamic reassignment of data during congestion. We refer to the process that unbinds application data bound to a virtual segment, so as to rebind it to another virtual segment, as restriping. In [11], pTCP uses a restriping strategy that "blindly" unbinds data bound to virtual segments falling outside the congestion window of a TCP-v pipe that cuts down its congestion window due to congestion or probe losses. It then reassigns such unbound data to pipes that request to send more data. However, for the target environment, a more intelligent restriping strategy that incurs less overhead can be used. Note that since all segments dispatched by pTCP traverse the same physical path, pTCP can leverage the FIFO delivery nature of the single path to perform more intelligent loss detection. Essentially, pTCP can infer a loss as long as it receives 3 or more ACKs for any packets transmitted after the lost packet, irrespective of the specific TCP-v pipes they are bound to. This enables pTCP to "fast reassign" lost packets to another pipe, much before individual TCP-v pipes detect those losses. Therefore, when the fair share of each TCP-v pipe is low, even if individual TCP-v pipes might experience timeouts due to insufficient data to trigger fast retransmit, pTCP will not suffer.

- **Redundant Striping:** Another design element in pTCP to avoid head-of-line blocking is the redundant striping. We refer to the process of binding the same application data to more than one virtual segment as redundant striping. In [11], a TCP-v pipe that cuts down its congestion window to one (after a timeout) will be assigned data that can be bound to another TCP-v pipe. In this way, the concerned TCP-v can keep probing for the state of the path it traverses, without stalling the progress of the whole pTCP connection (since it is possible that the path suffering a timeout is currently experiencing a blackout). However, for achieving WSD, we use a different redundant striping strategy. Not that there is no need to redundantly stripe the first segment of the recently-stalled pipe, since all segments experience the same dropping probability irrespective of which pipe they belong to. Instead, pTCP redundantly stripes any segment that is retransmitted due to the fast retransmit mechanism. This is because, in TCP, the loss of a retransmitted segment will cause a timeout. By redundantly striping the retransmitted segment, pTCP ensures no head-of-line blocking will occur even the concerned pipe might eventually experience a timeout. Although redundant striping might appear to be an overhead, the overhead is small when compared to the benefits such striping brings to the aggregate connection in terms of preventing a stall.

- **Simplified Connection Setup:** When used on multi-homed mobile hosts with heterogeneous network interfaces, the peers of a pTCP connection need to exchange the number of interfaces to use and the corresponding IP addresses during connection establishment. As shown in [11], it takes at least two round-trip times to fully establish all TCP-v pipes (the first round-trip time is needed to convey the IP addresses used by subsequent TCP-v pipes). However, for the target environment, all TCP-v pipes of a pTCP connection terminate at the same pair of IP addresses, and hence only a field in the packet header that carries the desired weight (hence the number of TCP-v pipes to open) is needed. The connection setup time thus is the same as a normal TCP connection. Note that in [11] a new IP layer socket hashing function is necessary to map incoming segments with different IP addresses to the same pTCP socket. Such hashing function is not required for achieving WSD.

4.2 Protocol

Fig. 4 provides an architectural overview of the pTCP protocol. pTCP acts as the central engine that interacts with the application and IP. When used with a weight of w, pTCP spawns w TCP-v pipes. TCP-v is a slightly modified version of TCP that interacts with pTCP using the 7 interface functions shown in Fig. 4. The *open()* and *close()* calls are same as the default TCP ones to enter or exit its state machine [20]. The *established()* and *closed()* interfaces are used by TCP-v to inform pTCP when its state machine reaches the ESTABLISHED and CLOSED state respectively. The *receive()* call is used by pTCP to deliver virtual segments to TCP-v, and the *send()* call is used by TCP-v to send virtual segments to pTCP which will then bind the segments to real data for transmission. Finally, the *resume()* call is used by pTCP to throttle the amount of data each TCP-v can send.

pTCP controls and maintains the send and receive data buffers for the whole connection. Application data writes are served by pTCP, and the data is copied onto the send_buffer. A list of active TCP-v pipes (that have space in the congestion window to transmit) called active_pipes is maintained by pTCP. A TCP-v pipe is placed in active_pipes initially when it returns with the *established()* function call. Upon the availability of data that needs to be transmitted, pTCP sends a *resume()* command to

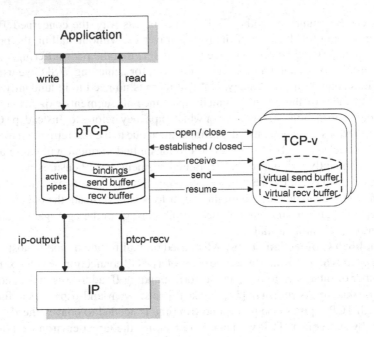

Fig. 4. pTCP Architecture

the active TCP-v pipes, and remove the corresponding pipes from `active_pipes`. A TCP-v pipe that receives the command builds a regular TCP header based on its state variables (e.g. sequence number) and gives the segment (sans the data) to pTCP through the *send()* interface. pTCP binds an unbound data segment in the `send_buffer` to the "virtual" segment TCP-v has built, maintains the binding in the data structure called `bindings`, appends its own header and sends it to the IP layer. A TCP-v pipe continues to issue *send()* calls until there is no more space left in its congestion window, or pTCP responds back with a FREEZE value (note that the TCP-v needs to perform a few rollback operations to account for the unsuccessful transmission). When pTCP receives a *send()* call, but has no unbound data left for transmission, it returns a FREEZE value to freeze the corresponding TCP-v, and then adds the corresponding pipe to `active_pipes`.

When pTCP receives an *ACK*, it strips the pTCP header, and hands over the packet to the appropriate TCP-v pipe (through the *receive()* interface). The TCP-v pipe processes the *ACK* in the regular fashion, and updates its state variables including the virtual send buffer. The virtual buffer can be thought of as a list of segments that have only appropriate header information. The virtual send and receive buffers are required to ensure regular TCP semantics for congestion control and connection management within each TCP-v pipe. When pTCP receives an incoming data segment, it strips both the pTCP header and the data, enqueues the data in the `recv_buffer`, and provides the appropriate TCP-v with only the skeleton segment that does not contain any data. TCP-v treats the segment as a regular segment, which is then queued in the virtual receive buffer.

5 Performance Evaluation

In this section, we compare the performance of pTCP against that of weighted AIMD and application striping using both simulation and testbed results.

5.1 Single Link Configuration

We first evaluate the performance of pTCP using the network topology and scenario described in Section 3 that we used for evaluating WAIMD and application striping. We observe in Fig. 2(a) that pTCP scales considerably better than WAIMD and application striping with increasing w, and follows the ideal curve closely even when w scales to 100. While it is clear that WAIMD suffers from its single-state design, pTCP outperforms application striping due to its design elements to prevent head-of-line blocking explained in Section 4.1.

Considering the scalability of pTCP in terms of buffer requirement and bandwidth fair share (i.e. congestion window size), we find in Fig. 3(a) and Fig. 3(b) that pTCP also achieves much better performance than WAIMD and application striping. Note that in Fig. 3(a), the bandwidth-delay product is around 24KB, and hence the ideal (minimum) buffer requirement is 48KB [22]. The reason for the marginal decrease of pTCP in the achieved weight can be explained by the coupling of the individual TCP-v pipes. Although pTCP attempts to mask such coupling to the maximum extent possible, it may still fail in some cases given a tight buffer allocation. However, even when the buffer allocation is significantly reduced, pTCP's performance reduces more gracefully than the other two schemes as shown in Fig. 3(a). Similarly, in Fig. 3(b) we observe that the performance of pTCP does not degrade until the link bandwidth is reduced to 4Mbps at which point the average congestion window size is approximately 8, while both WAIMD and application striping exhibit performance degradation from their already lower performance, at a much earlier point. When the bandwidth is eventually reduced to 3Mbps (the average congestion window size is around 6), individual unit TCP flows become prone to frequent timeouts [21]. However, the performance of the aggregate pTCP connection does not degrade by much even under such circumstances because of its restriping and redundant striping strategy.

5.2 Multiple Link Configuration

In this section, we extend the simulation scenario to a more sophisticated network topology with multiple backbone routers as shown in Fig. 5. The multi-link topology consists of 5 backbone routers and 28 access nodes (access nodes for flows $f10$ to $f13$ are not shown for clarity). Flows $f0$ to $f9$ are "long" flows with round-trip time of 240ms, while flows $f10$ to $f13$ are "short" flows with round-trip time of 90ms and are used as background traffic. As shown in Fig. 5 we also introduce 60 on-off UDP traffic ($c0$ to $c59$) in both directions to emulate the flash crowds in the Internet. Each UDP traffic is generated using the Pareto distribution, where the mean burst time is set to 1s, the mean idle time is set to 2s, the data rate during the burst time is set to 200Kbps, and the shape parameter is set to 1.5. Finally, we introduce another UDP traffic using CBR source on

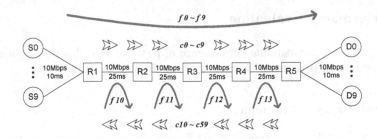

Fig. 5. Network Topology (Multiple Links)

the bottleneck link (from R1 to R2) to explicitly control bandwidth fluctuations experienced by TCP flows along the bottleneck link. The data rate of the background UDP traffic varies from 500Kbps to 3.5Mbps and fluctuates in a 1-second interval throughput the duration of the simulation (600 seconds).

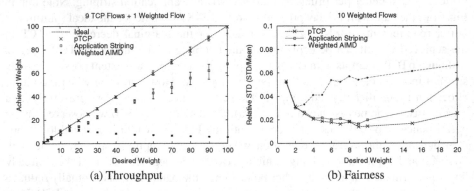

(a) Throughput   (b) Fairness

Fig. 6. Performance of pTCP using Multiple Link Topology

In Fig. 6(a) we show the throughput ratio between the weighted flow ($f0$) and the average of the other 9 unit flows ($f1$ to $f9$)–recall that the weighted rate differentiation is with respect to flows along the same path. It is clear that pTCP achieves a much higher scalability than WAIMD and application striping as in the single bottleneck topology, despite the sophisticated traffic distribution and bandwidth fluctuations. In Fig. 6(b), we increase the number of weighted flows to 10 ($f0$ to $f9$), and vary the weight of individual flows from 1 to 20 (all weighted flows have the same weight) to study the fairness property of the 3 schemes. We obtain the throughputs of individual flows, and use the relative standard deviation as a metric to measure the "unfairness" experienced by all flows. As Fig. 6(b) shows, WAIMD has the highest variance when the weight increases due to frequent timeout occurrences. While application striping achieves similar performance to pTCP when the weight is small, its performance degrades significantly with larger weights. This again is attributed to the head-of-line blocking at the receiver (note that the per-socket buffer requirement in application striping increases with weight).

Fig. 7. Testbed Topology

5.3   Testbed Results

We now present evaluation results for a prototype implementation of pTCP tested over a real-life campus network. We use the campus network shown in Fig. 7 as the testbed. In order to avoid sub-millisecond round-trip times, the client and the server communicate through a campus-wide wireless LAN. The server is a DELL Optiplex GX110 desktop with a Pentium III 733Mhz CPU and 256MB RAM, and the client is an IBM Thinkpad T-20 laptop with a Pentium III 700Mhz CPU and 128MB RAM. Both the client and the server are equipped with the Orinoco IEEE 802.11b network card operating at a data rate of 2Mbps, and run the RedHat 7.3 Linux operating system. The round-trip time between the client and the server is approximately 15ms. The background traffic in the network is not under our control.

We build pTCP upon a user-level implementation of TCP,[3] and follow closely the design and architecture presented in Section 4. The socket interface exported by pTCP resembles that of TCP, except that it allows the specification of the desired weight w. A simple client-server file transfer application is implemented, and the client and the server use pTCP to communicate. We also use a modified version of the file transfer application that explicitly opens w TCP sockets of unit weight and performs striping over the w sockets. We use this to evaluate the performance of application striping, and compare its performance against that of pTCP. We start two FTP applications between the server and the client: one with unit TCP flow and one with weighted flow using either pTCP or application striping.

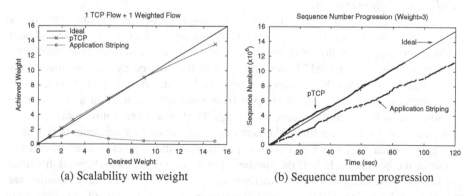

| (a) Scalability with weight | (b) Sequence number progression |

Fig. 8. Testbed Results

---

[3] We thank Jia-Ru "Jeffrey" Li for sharing his user-level implementation code of TCP with us.

In Fig. 8(a), we present the ratio of the throughput enjoyed by the weighted flow to the throughput enjoyed by the default TCP flow, for different values of w. We show both the results for pTCP and application striping. The ideal curve is also shown for comparison. It can be observed that pTCP scales significantly better than application striping for all weights, except for $w = 15$, where the ratio observed is 14:1. The reason for the deviation from the ideal behavior is due to the implementation of pTCP at the user-level. The maximum throughput of a user-level process is limited by the CPU scheduling policy in the kernel. Since the server serves the two flows using two independent user-level processes, each process obtains approximately equal share of the CPU cycles. While this does not serve as a limitation for smaller weights, for the weight of 15, the CPU cycles become a bottleneck resulting in the marginally lower performance. We note that such an overhead will not exist in a true kernel implementation.

On the other hand, we observe that the application striping results in Fig. 8(a) are significantly worse than the ideal performance. Upon close inspection, it is determined that severe head-of-line blocking is consistently observed due to both wireless channel losses and congestion losses, resulting in the individual flows stalling repeatedly. Fig. 8(b) substantiates this observation where the sequence number plot of application striping exhibits multiple timeouts, and has a much smaller slope than that of the ideal curve. Note that pTCP, although tested in the same wireless environment, does not exhibit performance degradation owing to the design elements described in Section 4.1.

6 Discussion

6.1 Scalability Limit

As we have shown in Section 5, pTCP exhibits a much higher scalability than weighted AIMD and application striping. An application that requires weighted rate differentiation of w can simply open a pTCP socket with w TCP-v pipes and enjoys the desired service (subject to the policing mechanism of the service model). An interesting question that arises is: *what is the upper bound on the maximum weight that pTCP can support for weighted rate differentiation?*

The answer is determined by the *network storage* defined as the sum of the queue length of the bottleneck router and the bandwidth-delay product of the end-to-end path. Since a weighted pTCP flow with weight w essentially consists of w TCP mini-flows, the maximum weight that pTCP can support is in fact limited by the maximum number of TCP connections the network can support. It is shown in [21] that since TCP's fast retransmit mechanism cannot recover from a packet loss without a timeout if its window size is less than 4 packets, on average TCP must have a minimum send rate of 6 packets per round-trip time. The network hence needs to store roughly 6 packets per active connection, which places an upper limit on the number of connections that can share the bottleneck link. If the number of connections increases beyond this limit, timeouts become the norm and TCP will experience a high degree of delay variation and unfairness. Although pTCP is designed to function even when some of the component mini-flows experience timeouts (pTCP will not stall as long as one of the mini-flow is not stalled), nonetheless it is undesirable to use pTCP in such a scenario.

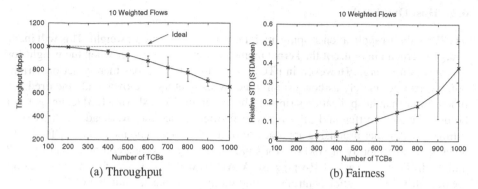

(a) Throughput (b) Fairness

Fig. 9. Setting Weight Beyond the Network Limit

To illustrate the phenomenon when the network is operated beyond its limit, we use the same network topology as shown in Fig. 1. We introduce 10 pTCP flows with the same weight to study their throughput performance when the total number of TCBs open is greater than the network limit. For the network considered, the bandwidth-delay product is 300 packets and the router's buffer size is 320 packets, so the network can store at most 620 packets at any instant. If we roughly apply the "6 packets per connection" rule, then the maximum number of TCBs the network can support is around 100. When the number of TCBs used is beyond this limit, Fig. 9(a) shows the average throughput enjoyed by each flow and Fig. 9(b) shows the throughput unfairness among them. We observe that the average throughput degrades and the unfairness increases due to the frequent timeout occurrences. In fact, when the number of connections is greater than network storage (in terms of packets), each connection on average cannot send more than 1 packet per round-trip time, which inevitably will induce timeouts.

A first look into the limitation of maximum weight might indicate that pTCP's design of maintaining one TCB per unit weight causes the problem, since a pTCP flow with weight w needs at least $6w$ packets of storage in the network. However, we contend that for any TCP-based protocol, the maximum weight achievable will indeed be a function of the network storage. Recall that a flow with weight w should achieve throughput w times the throughput of a flow with unit weight. Since TCP has a minimum send rate of 6 packets per round-trip time, the flow with weight w needs to send at the rate of at least $6w$ packets per round-trip time to achieve the desired service differentiation. Hence, as long as the unit flows are TCP-based, the maximum achievable weight for a single flow (or alternately, the maximum of the sum of the weights of contending flows) will be bounded by $\frac{\eta}{6}$, where η is the amount of network storage available.

Note that the design of pTCP by itself does not preclude the use of any other congestion control mechanism that is different from that of TCP. Conceivably, if a congestion control mechanism does not require transmission of at least one packet every round-trip time, the limitation imposed by the network storage on the maximum weight achievable can be eliminated. Such a scalable congestion control scheme can be used in tandem with pTCP through the well-defined interface described in Section 4.2.

6.2   Host Overhead

pTCP, similar to application striping, maintains one TCB per unit weight. This will incur a large overhead in terms of the kernel memory spent at the sender when the weight for a connection is large. However, in pTCP, since the TCP-v pipes merely act on virtual buffers, and act merely as congestion window estimators, the overheads incurred are much lower than in application striping. Moreover, the TCB sharing [23] technique can be used between different TCP-v pipes to further reduce the overheads such as RTT estimation. Another promising approach to reduce the overhead incurred by pTCP is to leverage the scalability of WAIMD for small weights by using a combination of pTCP and WAIMD, where each TCP-v pipe uses WAIMD with a small weight (instead of using the default TCP congestion control with unit weight). Hence, the number of TCP-v pipes used in pTCP to achieve weight w can be reduced to at least $\frac{w}{2}$ (since WAIMD will scale to weight of 2 easily under all conditions), thus reducing the overheads and complexity in pTCP. Mixing different congestion control schemes within pTCP is possible due to its design of decoupled functionality.

7   Future Work and Conclusions

While we present pTCP as a solution to achieve weighted service differentiation, the pTCP design can have a wider range of applications. Some examples are: (i) Each TCP-v flow can traverse a different path, and hence the performance of pTCP will not be limited to a single bottleneck path. (ii) For an environment where the network can provide absolute QoS assurances, achieving bandwidth aggregation of QoS guarantee service and best-effort service is a non-trivial problem [24]. pTCP can address such a problem by dedicating one TCP-v for the guaranteed service, and one TCP-v for the best-effort service, and effectively providing the application with the desired service. In this paper, we use a transport layer protocol called pTCP to achieve weighted rate differentiation. A pTCP flow of weight w consists of w TCP-v mini-flows that collectively achieve throughput w times the throughput of a TCP flow. pTCP achieves more effective service differentiation and incurs less host overhead than an approach using multiple sockets. On the other hand, pTCP avoids the pitfalls of the approach that changes the AIMD congestion control of TCP to resemble aggregate TCP flows, i.e. propensity to timeouts and poor scalability. We present evaluation results showing that pTCP is able to achieve end-to-end weighted service differentiation with better scalability and fairness than those presented in related work.

References

1. Dovrolis, C., Ramanathan, P.: A case for relative differentiated services and the proportional differentiation model. IEEE Network **13** (1999) 26–34
2. Banchs, A., Denda, R.: A scalable share differentiation architecture for elastic and real-time traffic. In: Proceedings of IWQoS, Pittsburgh, PA, USA (2000)
3. Crowcroft, J., Oechslin, P.: Differentiated end-to-end internet services using a weighted proportional fair sharing TCP. ACM Computer Communication Review **28** (1998) 53–69

4. Gevros, P., Risso, F., Kirstein, P.: Analysis of a method for differential TCP service. In: Proceedings of IEEE Globecom, Rio de Janeiro, Brazil (1999)
5. Nandagopal, T., Lee, K.W., Li, J.R., Bharghavan, V.: Scalable service differentiation using purely end-to-end mechanisms: Features and limitations. In: Proceedings of IWQoS, Pittsburgh, PA, USA (2000)
6. Postel, J.: Transmission control protocol. IETF RFC 793 (1981)
7. Allman, M., Kruse, H., Ostermann, S.: An application-level solution to TCP's satellite inefficiencies. In: Proceedings of Workshop on Satellite-Based Information Services (WOSBIS), Rye, NY, USA (1996)
8. Sivakumar, H., Bailey, S., Grossman, R.: PSockets: The case for application-level network striping for data intensive applications using high speed wide area networks. In: Proceedings of IEEE Supercomputing (SC), Dallas, TX, USA (2000)
9. Lee, J., Gunter, D., Tierney, B., Allcock, B., Bester, J., Bresnahan, J., Tuecke, S.: Applied techniques for high bandwidth data transfers across wide area networks. In: Proceedings of Computers in High Energy Physics (CHEP), Beijing, China (2001)
10. Hacker, T., Athey, B., Noble, B.: The end-to-end performance effects of parallel TCP sockets on a lossy wide-area network. In: Proceedings of IPDPS, Fort Lauderdale, FL, USA (2002)
11. Hsieh, H.Y., Sivakumar, R.: A transport layer approach for achieving aggregate bandwidths on multi-homed mobile hosts. In: Proceedings of ACM MobiCom, Atlanta, GA, USA (2002)
12. Blake, S., Black, D., Carlson, M., Davies, E., Wang, Z., Weiss, W.: An architecture for differentiated services. IETF RFC 2475 (1998)
13. Dovrolis, C., Stiliadis, D., Ramanathan, P.: Proportional differentiated services: Delay differentiation and packet scheduling. In: Proceedings of ACM SIGCOMM, Cambridge, MA, USA (1999)
14. Nandagopal, T., Venkitaraman, N., Sivakumar, R., Bharghavan, V.: Delay differentiation and adaptation in core stateless networks. In: Proceedings of IEEE INFOCOM, Tel-Aviv, Israel (2000)
15. Shin, J., Kim, J.G., Kim, J.W., Kuo, C.C.: Dynamic QoS mapping framework for relative service differentiation-aware video streaming. European Transactions on Telecommunications 12 (2001) 217-230
16. Kelly, F., Maulloo, A., Tan, D.: Rate control for communication networks: Shadow prices, proportional fairness and stability. Journal of the Operational Research Society 49 (1998) 237–252
17. Massoulie, L., Roberts, J.: Bandwidth sharing: Objectives and algorithms. In: Proceedings of IEEE INFOCOM, New York, NY, USA (1999)
18. Kunniyur, S., Srikant, R.: End-to-end congestion control schemes: Utility functions, random losses and ECN marks. In: Proceedings of IEEE INFOCOM, Tel-Aviv, Israel (2000)
19. The Network Simulator: ns-2. http://www.isi.edu/nsnam/ns (2000)
20. Wright, G.R., Stevens, W.R.: TCP/IP Illustrated, Volume 2. Addison-Wesley Publishing Company, Reading, MA, USA (1997)
21. Morris, R.: Scalable TCP congestion control. In: Proceedings of IEEE INFOCOM, Tel-Aviv, Israel (2000)
22. Semke, J., Mahdavi, J., Mathis, M.: Automatic TCP buffer tuning. In: Proceedings of ACM SIGCOMM, Vancouver, Canada (1998)
23. Touch, J.: TCP control block interdependence. IETF RFC 2140 (1997)
24. Feng, W., Kandlur, D., Saha, D., Shin, K.: Understanding and improving TCP performance over networks with minimum rate guarantees. IEEE/ACM Transactions on Networking 7 (1999) 173–187

IX Storage

Online Response Time Optimization of Apache Web Server

Xue Liu[1], Lui Sha[1], Yixin Diao[2], Steven Froehlich[2], Joseph L. Hellerstein[2], and Sujay Parekh[2]

[1] Department of Computer Science
Univ. of Illinois at Urbana-Champaign
Urbana, IL, 61801, USA
[2] IBM T. J. Watson Research Center
Hawthorne, NY 10532, USA

Abstract. Properly optimizing the setting of configuration parameters can greatly improve performance, especially in the presence of changing workloads. This paper explores approaches to online optimization of the Apache web server, focusing on the MaxClients parameter (which controls the maximum number of workers). Using both empirical and analytic techniques, we show that MaxClients has a concave upward effect on response time and hence hill climbing techniques can be used to find the optimal value of MaxClients. We investigate two optimizers that employ hill climbing—one based on Newton's Method and the second based on fuzzy control. A third technique is a heuristic that exploits relationships between bottleneck utilizations and response time minimization. In all cases, online optimization reduces response times by a factor of 10 or more compared to using a static, default value. The trade-offs between the online schemes are as follows. Newton's method is well known but does not produce consistent results for highly variable data such as response times. Fuzzy control is more robust, but converges slowly. The heuristic works well in our prototype system, but it may be difficult to generalize because it requires knowledge of bottleneck resources and an ability to measure their utilizations.

1 Introduction

The widespread use of eCommerce systems has focused attention on quality of service, especially response time. One challenge here is adapting systems to changing workloads by online optimization of configurations. This paper explores approaches to such online optimization in the Apache web server with an emphasis on techniques that are minimally invasive and are applicable to a wide range of parameters and systems.

How much can be achieved by optimizing the settings of configuration parameters? Consider the Apache MaxClients parameter, which governs the number of requests being processed in parallel by the web server. In Table 1, we show average response times measured at different MaxClients settings under different workloads [1]. The testbed used to collect this data is discussed later in this

K. Jeffay, I. Stoica, and K. Wehrle (Eds.): IWQoS 2003, LNCS 2707, pp. 461–478, 2003.

Table 1. Response time (sec.) for different workloads

| MaxClients | Workload | |
	Dynamic	*Dynamic+Static*
150	50	
650	1	15
900	30	2

paper. We see clearly that the best `MaxClients` value to use depends on the type of pages being accessed at the site. Since real-world workloads can change rapidly, there is the potential of obtaining order-of-magnitude improvements by doing online optimization of such key parameters.

This paper describes a generic approach to the online optimization of response times for the widely used Apache web server[2]. One area of related work is differentiated service in which the intent is to achieve response time objectives for different classes of work. In [3,4], the authors use proportional-integral controllers to achieve response time regulation and differentiation. In [5], multiple-input multiple-output controller design is used to regulate server CPU and memory utilization within specified QoS value. [6] describes an approach that combines queueing theory and control theory to regulate response times for response time regulation. Unfortunately, the regulation problems addressed by these approaches is quite different from optimization. In essence, regulation (e.g., ensuring target response times for gold and silver service) determines how to "cut the pie" whereas optimization (e.g., minimize response time across service classes) addresses how to "make the pie bigger" by adjusting resource allocations to the workload. Some work has been done in the area of online optimization of resources in computing systems. [7] describes an Apache implementation that manages web server resources based on maximizing revenue (e.g., responding within 8 seconds so that users are not discouraged). While the results are encouraging, the approach requires substantial modifications to the Apache resource management schemes. [8] considers maximizing SLA profits for web server farms, but this is done in a way that depends on having an accurate analytic model of the system being controlled. More recently, [1] proposes a fuzzy control approach to minimize response time using a combination of feedback control system and qualitative insights into the effect of tuning parameters on QoS. Unfortunately, the convergence times are long.

Figure 1 displays the architecture we propose. The target system (e.g., Apache) exposes one or more configuration parameters (e.g., `MaxClients`) that are dynamically modified by the optimizer to optimize measured variables (e.g., response times). In the specific case of Apache and `MaxClients`, we proceed as follows. First, we show that `MaxClients` has a concave upward effect on response time and hence hill climbing techniques can be used to find the optimal value of `MaxClients`. We investigate two optimizers that employ hill climbing—one based on Newton's Method and the second based on fuzzy control. A third tech-

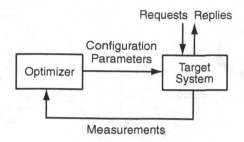

Fig. 1. General architecture for online optimization. The target system is controlled by configuration parameters that are dynamically changed by the optimizer in response to changing workloads.

nique is a heuristic that exploits the observed relationships between bottleneck utilizations and response time minimization. Newton's method does better than the default Apache scheme but yields inconsistent results because response times are variable. Fuzzy control is more robust, but converges slowly. The heuristic works well in our prototype system, but it may be difficult to generalize because it requires knowledge of bottleneck resources and an ability to measure their utilizations.

The remainder of the paper is organized as follows. Section 2 discusses the Apache architecture and response time measurements. Section 3 describes a queueing system that explains how `MaxClients` affects response times. Section 4 presents and evaluates several approaches to online optimization. Our conclusions are contained in Section 5.

2 Apache Architecture and Measurements

Apache [2] is typically structured as a pool of workers that handle HTTP requests. Our studies use release 1.3.19 in which workers are processes, although we believe that the central ideas are broadly applicable.

The flow of requests in Apache is displayed in Figure 2. Requests enter the TCP Accept Queue where they wait for a worker. A worker processes a single request to completion before accepting a new request. The number of worker processes is limited by the parameter `MaxClients`.

Many of the insights in this paper are based on experimental results. Throughout, these experiments use the Apache 1.3.19 server software running on a Pentium III 600 MHz server with 256 MB RAM running the Linux 2.4.7 kernel. We use synthetic workload generators running on a set of similar machines, connected via a 100Mbps LAN. The distribution of files sizes is the same as Webstone 2.5 [9]. We employ both a static and a dynamic workload. Requests for dynamic pages are processed by the Webstone 2.5 CGI script. A detailed description of the Apache testbed and workload generator can be found in [5].

Further details are needed to describe the manner in which requests are generated. Our workload model is based on WAGON [10], which has been shown

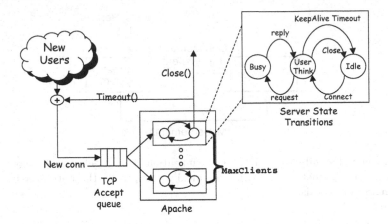

Fig. 2. Apache architecture and session flow.

to apply to a wide range of web requests. This model structures the workload into multiple sessions (which represent a series of user interactions). As illustrated in Figure 3, a session consists of multiple page requests. A page contains a number of embedded objects, which is parameterized by the burst length. Thus, the workload parameters are: session arrival rate, session length (number of clicks or web page requests in a session), burst length (number of objects in a burst), and think time (time between successive clicks). Table 2 summarizes the parameters used in this paper, which are based on data reported in [10] for a public web site. We use the httperf program [11] to generate HTTP/1.1 requests based on a synthetic web log that is generated according to the WAGON model.

Table 2. Workload Parameters

Parameter Name	Distribution	Parameters
$SessionRate$	Exponential	$mean = 0.1$
$SessionLength$	LogNormal	$mean = 8, \sigma = 3$
$BurstLength$	Gaussian	$mean = 7, \sigma = 3$
$ThinkTime$ (s)	LogNormal	$mean = 30, \sigma = 30$

The metric we choose to minimize is the server-side response time. Although client side response time measure is the most user-relevant metric, this information is generally not available at the web server in real-time. Moreover, even if the client side response time can be approximated using server side measurements and a TCP model [12], only the server side response time can be controlled by the server. Hence, we consider the server side response time, in particular, per page

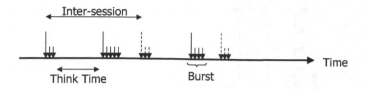

Fig. 3. Elements of the WAGON workload model. Two sessions are shown, as depicted by the solid and dashed lines. The longer arrows indicate the HTML text of a web page, and the short arrows indicate requests for objects in the web page.

response time (RT) in this paper. Since delivering a page may involve multiple requests, this quantity needs to be estimated. We use the following equation:

$$RT = AQT + BL \times ST \tag{1}$$

The accept queue time (AQT) is collected from the Linux kernel where we have added instrumentation for measuring the average delay for connections that enter the accept queue within a time window. The service time (ST) is measured by instrumenting the first and last steps in the Apache request processing loop (i.e., at the points where the request enters and the reply is sent). The average number of embedded requests per page is also known as the burst length and denoted as BL. It can be calculated as the number of requests serviced in all the worker processes divided by the number of connections serviced in the TCP accept queue. Due to persistent connections in HTTP/1.1, an established TCP connection remains open between consecutive HTTP requests of a burst so that only the first request needs to set up the TCP connection and enter the TCP accept queue. This gives us the above equation.

Figure 4 displays the results of experiments in which Apache is configured with different settings of MaxClients. The circles indicate mean response times, and the vertical lines specify the standard deviations. Note that the circles line is a pronounced concave upward shape to this curve. Further, the curve indicates that MaxClients has in excess of a ten-fold effect on response times for this workload.

This concave shape can be explained in terms of the Apache architecture. If MaxClients is too small, there is a long delay due to waits in the TCP Accept Queue. Indeed, it is possible that the queue overflows, which causes requests to be rejected. On the other hand, if MaxClients is too large, resources become over-utilized, which degrades performance as well. In extreme cases, there may be an internal server error if the limit on the number of processes is exceeded. The combined effect of these factors is that response time is a concave upward function of MaxClients. In essence, worker processes can be viewed as logical resources that are needed to process a request. However, to do so, physical resources are required, such as CPU, memory, and input/output bandwidth.

Our interest is in online optimization and thus we must change MaxClients dynamically. To this end, a mechanism similar to graceful restart was imple-

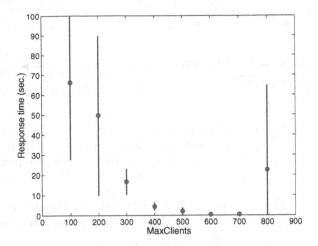

Fig. 4. Effect of MaxClients on response times.

mented to allow for a way to change MaxClients without shutting down Apache. Doing so required having an agent on the Apache system. This agent also provides instrumentation such as CPU utilizations, memory utilizations, and server side response times.

While this paper focuses on MaxClients, we believe that the approach taken has broader application. For example, we are currently investigating KeepAlive-TimeOut, another Apache parameter that determines the time that a session may remain idle if persistent connections are used. Other systems have configuration parameters similar to MaxClients, such as the number of servlet threads and EJB threads in an application server.

3   Analytic Model

This section develops an analytic model for how MaxClients affects response times in the Apache web server. We have two objectives. First, we want to demonstrate that the concave upward effect of MaxClients on response times can be explained in terms of a simple model. Second, we believe that this model provides a general framework in which other similar studies can be done.

We model interactions with Apache using an $M/M/m/K/N$ queueing system [13]. That is, interarrival times are exponentially distributed with a rate of λ, there are m servers (Apache workers), service times are exponentially distributed with a rate of μ_m (i.e., the service rate depends on the number of servers), the buffer size is K, and there are N customers. The model is evaluated using data from our Apache testbed.

Figure 5 depicts the $M/M/m/K/N$ queueing system as applied to Apache using the WAGON workload model. User sessions are modeled as the N customers

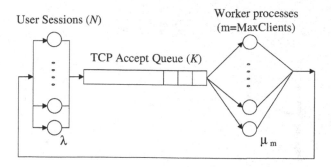

Fig. 5. Modeling Apache with an $M/M/m/K/N$ queueing network model.

in the queueing system. Users remain idle (in "think time") for an exponentially distributed period with mean $1/\lambda$. At the end of a think time, a page request is generated and enters the queue. (Note that a request represents a page, not a session.) This queue represents the TCP Accept Queue. The queue has a finite length of K. Requests wait until one of the m servers is available, where a server represents a worker and $m = $ MaxClients. The time a request spends in service is exponentially distributed with rate μ_m.

We calibrate the model parameters based on the Apache architecture and the workload model.

- Request generation rate λ: The reciprocal of λ is the user think time, which is the time between bursts (clicks) within a user session. Thus, for our testbed, we use the (reciprocal of) the mean of the think time distribution of the WAGON model.
- Number of servers m: This is the number of worker processes in Apache, i.e., MaxClients.
- Service rate μ_m: The service rate for a page is computed as the reciprocal of the inter-page request time. That is,

$$\mu_m = \frac{1}{BurstLength \times ST_m + KeepAliveTimeOut} \tag{2}$$

where ST_m is the service time for an HTTP request processed by Apache. The subscript indicates that service time depends on the value of MaxClients. Once all objects in a page have been processed, the worker waits for the minimum of a think time and the KeepAliveTimeOut time. We assume that the user think time distribution generates values that are mostly larger than the KeepAliveTimeOut value (default value is 15 seconds). We obtain burst length from the workload model, service time is computed as an average based on our instrumentation of the Apache request processing loop.

- Buffer size K: This is the buffer size of the TCP Accept queue. We can either get its value from the Linux kernel, or assume it to be ∞ if there is almost no request lost. We assume $K = \infty$ for the simplicity of calculation.

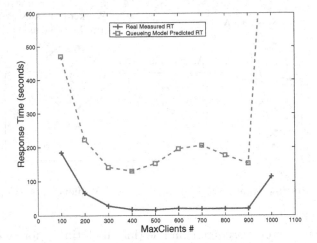

Fig. 6. Comparison of measured and predicted response times.

– Number of customers N: The number of customers in the system should approximate the number of concurrent user sessions. This can be estimated using Little's Result.

$$N = SessionRate \times SessionDuration$$
$$= SessionRate \times (\frac{1}{\mu_m} \times SessionLength$$
$$+ThinkTime \times (SessionLength - 1))$$

These parameters can all be obtained from the WAGON workload model.

Based on the $M/M/m/K/N$ queueing formula in [13] and the foregoing description of how to obtain the model parameters, response time can be computed. Figure 6 plots predicted response times using this model and the measured values obtained from experiments at different values of MaxClients. We see that the model consistently overestimates the true response times, sometimes by a large amount. Possible reasons for the model's inaccuracy include the distributional assumptions (e.g. exponential inter-arrivals and service times) and the variation of $ThinkTime$ we used in the experiment.

Even though the model is inaccurate in an absolute sense, it does *track* measured response times well. In particular, we see that predicted response times are concave upward in MaxClients. This gives us assurance that Figure 4 is not an artifact of the measurement environment. Further, it may be that the model can be applied more broadly, such as to the configuration of application servers (e.g., the maximum number of servlet or enterprise Java Bean (EJB) threads).

Another potential application of the queueing model is to aid in online optimization. This is possible since the model tracks the measurement results reasonably well. Unfortunately, we cannot use the model in this way, at least not without additional online measurement data. The problem is the manner in which model parameters are obtained. Many depends on characteristics of the workload that are not known a priori. Other model parameters require new instrumentation, such as state-dependent service time information to estimate service rates.

4   Online Optimization

This section describes ways to minimize response times by dynamically adjusting MaxClients based on the insight that response time is concave upward in MaxClients. Several schemes are explored: Newton's Method, fuzzy control, and a heuristic. These techniques are compared as to how well they minimize response time and the speed of convergence to the steady state value. The former is desirable in terms of improving quality of service. The latter is important in order to adapt to changing workloads.

All of the approaches considered involve feedback. Thus, MaxClients is adjusted based on the observed effect on response time or other metrics. An alternative would be to employ a feed-forward scheme in which the optimal value of MaxClients is computed based on an analytic model. Feed-forward is appealing in that it avoids problems with stability and speed of convergence. However, such a scheme requires an analytic model that (a) tracks the measured values of response time and (b) has inputs that can be readily estimated. While the model developed in Section 3 satisfies (a), it does not satisfy (b). For example, the service rate μ_m depends on the number of servers, i.e., $\mu_m = f(m)$, but we do not know this function. Possibly, a model could be developed that satisfies both (a) and (b). However, lacking such a model, we focus on feedback approaches.

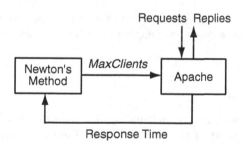

Fig. 7. Architecture of online optimization of Apache using Newton's Method to dynamically adjust MaxClients based on measurements of response times.

4.1   Newton's Method

Figure 7 displays an architecture in which Newton's Method [14] is employed for online optimization of Apache response times by dynamically adjusting

`MaxClients`. Newton's method, a widely used approach to optimization, uses the gradient of the function to be minimized (e.g., Figure 4) to estimate the value of `MaxClients` that minimizes response times. For example, if y is response time and x is `MaxClients`, we might use the approximation $y = f(x) \approx a(x-x^*)^2 + b$, where $a, b \geq 0$ are unknown constants estimated from the data and x^* is the value of `MaxClients` that minimizes response time. Newton's method is described by the following equation

$$x_{k+1} = x_k - (\nabla^2 f(x_k))^{-1} \nabla f(x_k) \tag{3}$$

where x_k is the value of x at discrete time k. Equation (3) starts from an initial value x_0 at $k = 0$. The gradient $\nabla f(x_k)$ is computed at x_k, and its negation indicates the direction of steepest descent. The value $\nabla^2 f(x_k)$ (the second partial derivative of $f(x)$) indicates the update step size. The introduction of the second partial derivative removes the local linear search, allowing a potentially faster convergence. But this also makes the algorithm more sensitive to measurement noise.

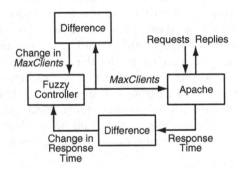

Fig. 8. Architecture of online optimization of Apache using Fuzzy Control to dynamically adjust `MaxClients` based on changes in `MaxClients` and response times.

4.2   Fuzzy Control

Fuzzy control is another approach for online optimization [1]. We explore this approach in the context of the present study. Figure 8 displays an architecture in which fuzzy control is employed for online optimization of Apache response times by dynamically adjusting `MaxClients`. The fuzzy controller uses changes in `MaxClients` and response times to dynamically optimize `MaxClients`.

The actions of the fuzzy controller are guided by a set of IF-THEN rules. For example, "IF *change-in-MaxClients* is *neglarge* and *change-in-response-time* is *neglarge*, THEN *next-change-in-MaxClients* is *neglarge*." The terms *change-in-MaxClients* and *change-in-response-time* are linguistic variables; *neglarge* is a linguistic value. Linguistic variables are a natural way to handle uncertainties created by the stochastics present in most computer systems. Linguistic variables exist in one-to-one correspondence with numeric variables. Fuzzy control systems provide a way to map between numeric variables and linguistic variables (referred to as fuzzification and de-fuzzification). More details on fuzzy control can be found in [15].

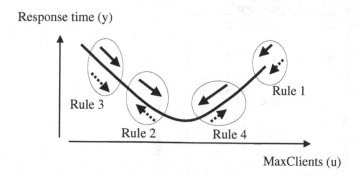

Response time (y)

Rule 3

Rule 1

Rule 2   Rule 4

MaxClients (u)

Fig. 9. Illustration of fuzzy rules.

Table 3. Fuzzy rules

Rule	IF			THEN
	change in	AND	change in	change in
	MaxClients	AND	Response Time	next MaxClients
1	neglarge	AND	neglarge	neglarge
2	neglarge	AND	poslarge	poslarge
3	poslarge	AND	neglarge	poslarge
4	poslarge	AND	poslarge	neglarge

The optimization problem we address can be easily represented in fuzzy rules. The rules, which are listed in Table 3, are structured as follows. (They are also illustrated in Figure 9 where the dashed arrow lines indicate the *IF* premise parts and the solid arrow lines indicate the *THEN* consequent parts.) The *IF* part determines the position on the response time curve relative to the optimal MaxClients. For example, *Rule 4* considers the case in which MaxClients is increased and the result is a larger response time. This suggests that we are to the right of the optimal MaxClients. The *THEN* part indicates how MaxClients should be changed—*neglarge* is a decrease, and *poslarge* is an increase. *Rule 1* and *Rule 3* describe situations in which MaxClients was last changed in the correct direction in that the result is a decrease in response time. Conversely, *Rule 2* and *Rule 4* handle "incorrect actions", where the previous action caused the response time to increase. The magnitude of the change in MaxClients determines the speed of convergence and the extent of any oscillation at steady state. Clearly,

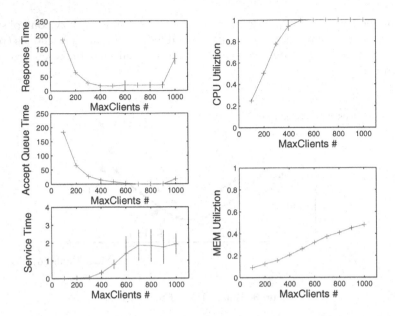

Fig. 10. Apache measurements for a dynamic workload.

if the curve is steep, small changes in `MaxClients` are best. For a more gradual slope, larger changes are better.

4.3 Saturation-Based Heuristic Optimization

This method is motivated by a desire to achieve fast convergence while being robust to noise and the specifics of the function being optimized.

Our heuristic is based on the following observation: response time is minimized when `MaxClients` is increased to the point where the CPU is 100% utilized. This is apparent in the measurements of static and dynamic workloads in Figure 10 and Figure 11. For different `MaxClients` values the average accept queue time and service time are measured, and the response time is computed using Equation (1). The CPU and memory utilizations are also measured for monitoring system resource usage. In Figure 10, response time decreases as `MaxClients` is increased from 200 to 480, at which point CPU utilization is approximately 100%. In Figure 11, this saturation occurs when `MaxClients` is approximately 800.

Our intuition as to why this works is as follows. `MaxClients` determines a set of logical resources—the Apache workers. These logical resources share the same physical resources, such as CPU, memory, and input/output bandwidth. By increasing `MaxClients` up to the point at which a physical resource saturates, we allow more of the logical resources to operate in parallel. However, once a physical resource saturates, further increases in the logical resource do not

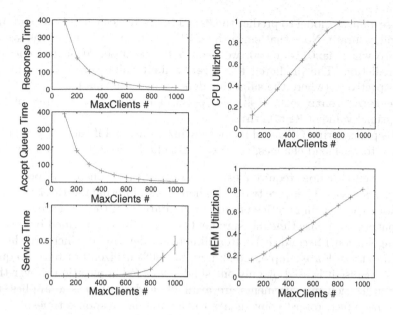

Fig. 11. Apache measurements for a static workload.

increase parallelism. Instead, such increases add overhead (e.g., due to process switches).

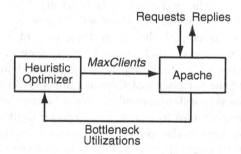

Fig. 12. Architecture of online optimization of Apache using a saturation-based heuristic to dynamically adjust MaxClients based on changes in bottleneck utilizations.

The foregoing observations motivate the architecture displayed in Figure 12 in which the heuristic controller dynamically determines the minimum value of MaxClients that maximizes the utilization of the bottleneck resource. The major steps are given as follows.

1. Given an initial MaxClients value MC_0, measure the CPU utilization CPU_0 and the memory utilization MEM_0.

2. Use a linear model to predict the MaxClients values when CPU and memory will saturate. Note that since the CPU and memory utilizations are always zero when MaxClients=0, we need only one observation to generate this prediction. The predicted MaxClients limit values are $\frac{MC_0}{CPU_0}$ and $\frac{MC_0}{MEM_0}$, respectively (where the subscript denotes discrete time).

3. Set MaxClients to $\min(\frac{MC_0}{CPU_0}, \frac{MC_0}{MEM_0})$. This goes to a vicinity of the real optimal value of MaxClients.

4. Keep measuring CPU and memory utilizations, and if they vary significantly due to workload changes, go to step 2 to find a new MaxClients value.

Our heuristic does require measurements of utilizations for all potential bottleneck resources. There are two issues here. First, internal metrics are sometimes difficult to acquire in practice because of limitations of the measurement system. (In contrast, response time measurements can readily be provided by an external probing station.) Second, it is often difficult to determine which are the bottleneck resources. For example, a disk may be 100% utilized but have no queueing delays because it is used by only one single-threaded application. Never-the-less, if the utilization measurements are available and the heuristic applies, then it can provide fast, robust convergence to the minimal response times.

4.4 Experimental Results

This section compares the techniques for online optimization in terms of the minimum value of response time that is achieved, the speed of convergence, and robustness.

Figure 13 compares the performance of Newton's Method with the default Apache scheme. The figure contains three sub-figures, each with two plots. In each sub-figure, the upper plot shows the trajectory of MaxClients, and the bottom plot displays the associated response times. Note that Newton's Method does improve response times compared to those in the default Apache scheme. However, because of the variability of response times, different runs of Newton's Method can produce very different results. This is because obtaining the Hessian matrix requires three samples to compute the second derivative, *at each step of the algorithm*. This increases the convergence time and also the algorithm is more sensitive to noise in response time measurements. Unfortunately, response times are typically quite noisy, unless they are averaged over many samples (something that reduces the speed with which the controller can respond to changes in workloads). Because of this noise sensitivity, we do not consider Newton's Method in the remaining comparisons.

Next, we compare the default Apache scheme with fuzzy control and the heuristic method presented earlier. Figure 14 displays the results for a dynamic workload. (The results are structured in the same manner as Figure 13.) We see that the heuristic converges its MaxClients value after 2 minutes. For fuzzy control, convergence takes approximately 14 minutes. On the other hand, fuzzy control does achieve a smaller response time. Figure 15 displays the results for a static workload. Once again, the heuristic converges faster than fuzzy control.

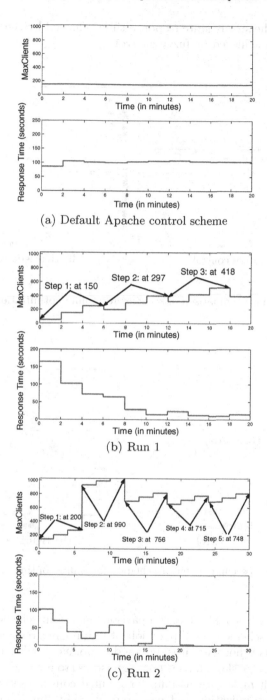

(a) Default Apache control scheme

(b) Run 1

(c) Run 2

Fig. 13. Comparison of the default Apache scheme with Newton's method under a dynamic workload. While Newton's method does achieve lower response times, its behavior is not consistent due to the variability of response times.

Here, however, the steady state response time achieved by the heuristic is about the same as that achieved by fuzzy control.

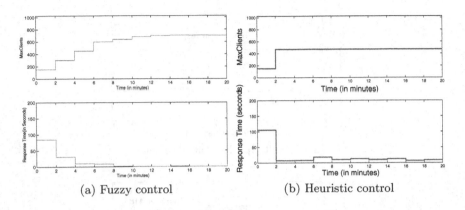

(a) Fuzzy control   (b) Heuristic control

Fig. 14. Performance comparison of schemes for online optimization under a dynamic workload.

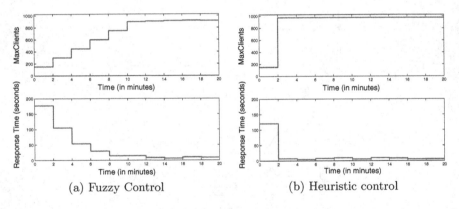

(a) Fuzzy Control   (b) Heuristic control

Fig. 15. Performance comparison of schemes for online optimization under a static workload.

Table 4 provides a qualitative comparison of the four schemes considered. The default Apache scheme does a poor job of minimizing response times, in large part because this is not what it is designed to do. Newton's method improves on this, but it converges slow and has poor robustness to noise. Fuzzy control is quite robust because it makes few assumptions, but it converges slowly. Our heuristic provides good optimization and converges quickly, but it makes assumptions about the bottleneck resources that may not always hold.

Table 4. Qualitative comparisons of techniques

	Optimization	Speed	Robustness
Default Apache	Poor	Fast	Good
Newton's Method	Fair	Slow	Poor
Fuzzy Control	Good	Slow	Good
Heuristic	Good	Fast	Fair

5 Conclusions

This paper explores approaches to online optimization of configuration parameters of the Apache web server with an emphasis on techniques that are minimally invasive and are applicable to a wide range of parameters and systems. We focus on the MaxClients parameter, which controls the maximum number of workers. First, we show that MaxClients has a concave upward effect on response time and hence hill climbing techniques can be used to find the optimal value of MaxClients. This is demonstrated both in measurements and with an analytic model. The underlying intuition is that MaxClients controls the trade-off between delays in the TCP Accept Queue and delays due to contention for operating system resources.

We investigate two optimizers that employ hill climbing—one based on Newton's Method and the second based on fuzzy control. A third technique is a heuristic that exploits relationships between bottleneck utilizations and response time minimization. In all cases, online optimization reduces response times by a factor of 10 or more compared to using a static, default value. The trade-offs between the online schemes are as follows. Newton's method is well known but does not produce consistent results for highly variable data such as response times. Fuzzy control is more robust, but converges slowly. The heuristic works well in our prototype system, but it may be difficult to generalize because it requires knowledge of bottleneck resources and an ability to measure their utilizations.

Our future work will address a number of issues. Foremost, we want to simultaneously optimize multiple parameters. This may involve other dynamically adjustable parameters in Apache such as KeepAliveTimeOut, which specifies how long the TCP connection to be kept for a client before the connection is torn down. Second, while we have studied the Apache web sever performance tuning, there are other more complex systems such as database servers and application servers where online optimization have a more dramatic effect on end-user response times. Last, we want to explore the effect of distributed architectures, especially the trade-off between doing local optimization with accurate knowledge of local state versus global optimization with somewhat dated information.

References

1. Y. Diao, J. L. Hellerstein, and S. Parekh, "Optimizing quality of service using fuzzy control," in *Proceedings of Distributed Systems Operations and Management*, 2002.
2. Apache Software Foundation. http://www.apache.org.
3. Y. Diao, J. L. Hellerstein, and S. Parekh, "A business-oriented approach to the design of feedback loops for performance management," in *Proceedings of Distributed Systems Operations and Management*, 2001.
4. C. Lu, T. Abdelzaher, J. Stankovic, and S. Son, "A feedback control approach for guaranteeing relative delays in web servers," in *Proceedings of the IEEE Real-Time Technology and Applications Symposium*, 2001.
5. Y. Diao, N. Gandhi, J. L. Hellerstein, S. Parekh, and D. M. Tilbury, "Using MIMO feedback control to enforce policies for interrelated metrics with application to the Apache web server," in *Proceedings of Network Operations and Management*, 2002.
6. L. Sha, X. Liu, Y. Lu, and T. Abdelzaher, "Queuing model based network server performance control," in *Proceedings of the IEEE Real-Time Systems Symposium*, 2002.
7. D. Menasce, V. Almeida, R. Fonsece, and M. Mendes, "Busines oriented resource management policies for e-commerce servers," *Performance Evaluation*, vol. 42, pp. 223–239, Oct. 2000.
8. Z. Liu, M. S. Squillante, and J. L. Wolf, "On maximizing service-level-agreement profits," in *Proceedings of the ACM Conference on Electronic Commerce (EC'01)*, 2001.
9. I. Mindcraft, "Webstone 2.5 web server benchmark," 1998. http://www.mindcraft.com/ webstone/.
10. Z. Liu, N. Niclausse, C. Jalpa-Villanueva, and S. Barbier, "Traffic model and performance evaluation of web servers," Tech. Rep. 3840, INRIA, Dec. 1999.
11. D. Mosberger and T. Jin, "httperf: A tool for measuring web server performance," in *First Workshop on Internet Server Performance (WISP 98)*, pp. 59—67, ACM, June 1998.
12. D. P. Olshefski, J. Nieh, and D. Agrawal, "Inferring client response time at the web server," in *Proceedings of the ACM SIGMETRICS Conference on Measurement and Modeling of Computer Systems*, 2002.
13. S. S. Lavenberg, ed., *Computer performance modeling handbook*. Orlando, FL: Academic Press, INC, 1983.
14. A. L. Perssini, *The Mathematics of Nonlinear Programming*. Springer-Verlag, 1988.
15. K. M. Passino and S. Yurkovich, *Fuzzy Control*. Menlo Park, CA: Addison Wesley Longman, 1998.

A Practical Learning-Based Approach for Dynamic Storage Bandwidth Allocation*

Vijay Sundaram and Prashant Shenoy

Department of Computer Science
University of Massachusetts Amherst
{vijay,shenoy}@cs.umass.edu

Abstract. In this paper, we address the problem of dynamic allocation of storage bandwidth to application classes so as to meet their response time requirements. We present an approach based on reinforcement learning to address this problem. We argue that a simple learning-based approach may not be practical since it incurs significant memory and search space overheads. To address this issue, we use application-specific knowledge to design an efficient, practical learning-based technique for dynamic storage bandwidth allocation. Our approach can react to dynamically changing workloads, provide isolation to application classes and is stable under overload. We implement our techniques into the Linux kernel and evaluate it using prototype experimentation and trace-driven simulations. Our results show that (i) the use of learning enables the storage system to reduce the number of QoS violations by a factor of 2.1 and (ii) the implementation overheads of employing such techniques in operating system kernels is small.

1 Introduction

Enterprise-scale storage systems may contain tens or hundreds of storage devices. Due the sheer size of these systems and the complexity of the application workloads that access them, storage systems are becoming increasingly difficult to design, configure, and manage. Traditionally, storage management tasks have been performed manually by administrators who use a combination of experience, rules of thumb, and in some cases, trial and error methods. Numerous studies have shown that management costs far outstrip equipment costs and have become the dominant fraction of the total cost of ownership of large computing systems [15]. These arguments motivate the need to automate simple storage management tasks so as to make the system self-managing and reduce the total cost of ownership.

In this paper, we address the problem of automating the task of storage bandwidth allocation to applications. We assume that the storage system is accessed by applications that can be categorized into different classes; each class is assumed to impose a certain QoS requirement. The workload seen by an application class varies over time, and we address the problem of how to allocate storage bandwidth to classes in presence of varying workloads so that their QoS needs are met. Since data accessed by applications may be stored on overlapping set of storage devices, the system must dynamically partition the device bandwidth among classes to meet their needs.

---

* This research was supported in part by NSF grants CCR-9984030, ANI-9977635 and EIA-0080119.

K. Jeffay, I. Stoica, and K. Wehrle (Eds.): IWQoS 2003, LNCS 2707, pp. 479–497, 2003.

Our work on dynamic storage bandwidth allocation has led to several contributions. First, we identify several requirements that should be met by a dynamic allocation technique. We argue that such a technique (i) should adapt to varying workloads, (ii) should not violate the performance requirement of one class to service another class better, and (iii) should exhibit stable behavior under transient or sustained overloads.

Second, we design a dynamic bandwidth allocation technique based on *reinforcement learning* to meet these requirements. The key idea in such an approach is to learn from the impact of past actions and use this information to make future decisions. This is achieved by associating a cost with each action and using past observations to take an action with the least cost. We show that a simple learning approach that systematically searches through all possible allocations to determine the "correct" allocation for a particular system state has prohibitive memory and search space overheads for practical systems. We design an enhanced learning-based approach that uses domain-specific knowledge to substantially reduce this overhead (for example, by eliminating searching through allocations that are clearly incorrect for a particular system state). A key advantage of using reinforcement learning is that no prior training of the system is required; our technique allows the system to learn online.

Third, we implement our techniques into the Linux kernel and evaluate it using prototype experimentation and simulation of synthetic and trace-driven workloads. Our results show that (i) the use of learning enables the storage system to reduce the number of QoS violations by a factor of 2.1 and (ii) the implementation overheads of employing such techniques in operating system kernels is small. Overall, our work demonstrates the feasibility of using reinforcement learning techniques to automate storage bandwidth allocation in practical systems. Moreover, our techniques are sufficiently general and can be used to manage other system resources as well.

The rest of the paper is structured as follows. In Section 2, we define the problem of dynamic storage bandwidth allocation. Section 3 presents a learning-based approach for dynamic bandwidth allocation. Section 4 presents details of our prototype implementation in Linux. Section 5 presents the results of our experimental evaluation. Section 6 discusses related work, and finally, Section 7 presents our conclusions.

2   Dynamic Storage Bandwidth Allocation: Problem Definition

2.1   Background and System Model

An enterprise storage system consists of a large number of disks that are organized into disk arrays. A disk array is a collection of physical disks that presents an abstraction of a single large logical storage device; we refer to this abstraction as a logical unit (LU). An application, such as a database or a file system, is allocated storage space by concatenating space from one or more LUs; the concatenated storage space is referred to as a logical volume (LV). Figure 1 illustrates the mapping from LVs to LUs.

We assume that the workload accessing each logical volume can be partitioned into *application classes*. This grouping can be determined based on either the files accessed or the QoS requirements of requests. Each application class is assumed to have a certain response time requirement. Application classes compete for storage bandwidth and the bandwidth allocated to a class governs the response time of its requests.

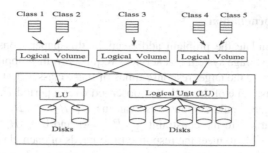

Fig. 1. Relationship between application classes, logical volumes and logical units.

To enable such allocations, each disk in the system is assumed to employ a QoS-aware disk scheduler (such as [7,18,23]). Such a scheduler allows disk bandwidth to be reserved for each class and enforces these allocations at a fine time scale. Thus, if a certain disk receives requests from n application classes, then we assume that the system dynamically determines the reservations $R_1, R_2, \cdots R_n$ for these classes such that the response time needs of each class are met and $\sum_{i=1}^{n} R_i = 1$ (the reservation R_i essentially denotes the fraction of the total bandwidth allocated to class i; $0 \leq R_i \leq 1$).

2.2 Key Requirements

Assuming the above system model, consider a bandwidth allocation technique that dynamically determines the reservations $R_1, R_2, ..., R_n$ based on the requirements of each class. Such a scheme should satisfy the following key requirements.

Meet class response time requirements: Assuming that each class specifies a target response-time d_i, the bandwidth allocation techniques should allocate sufficient bandwidth to each class to meet its target response-time requirements. Whether this goal can be met depends on the load imposed by each application class and the aggregate load. In scenarios where the response time needs of a class can not be met (possibly due to overload), the bandwidth allocation technique should attempt to minimize the difference between the observed and the target response times.

Performance isolation: Whereas the dynamic allocation technique should react to changing workloads, for example, by allocating additional bandwidth to classes that see an increased load, such increases in allocations should not affect the performance of less loaded classes. Thus, only spare bandwidth from underloaded classes should be reallocated to classes that are heavily loaded, thereby isolating underloaded classes from the effects of overload.

Stable overload behavior: Overload is observed when the aggregate workload exceeds disk capacity, causing the target response times of all classes to be exceeded. The bandwidth allocation technique should exhibit stable behavior under overload. This is especially important for a learning-based approach, since such techniques systematically search though various allocations to determine the correct allocation; doing so under overloads can result in oscillations and erratic behavior. A well-designed dynamic allocation scheme should prevent such unstable system behavior.

2.3 Problem Formulation

To precisely formulate the problem addressed in this paper, consider an individual disk from a large storage system that services requests from n application classes. Let $d_1, d_2, \ldots, d_n$ denote the target response times of these classes. Let $Rt_1, Rt_2, \ldots, Rt_n$ denote the response time of these classes observed over a period P. Then the dynamic allocation technique should compute reservations $R_1, R_2, \cdots, R_n$ such that $Rt_i \leq d_i$ for any class i subject to the constraint $\sum_i R_i = 1$ and $0 \leq R_i \leq 1$. Since it may not always be possible to meet the response time needs of each class, especially under overload, we modify the above condition as follows: instead of requiring $Rt_i \leq d_i, \forall i$, we require that the response time should be less than or as close to the target as possible. That is, $(Rt_i - d_i)^+$ should be equal to or as close to zero as possible (the notation x^+ equals x for positive values of x and equals 0 for negative values). Instead of attempting to meet this condition for each class, we define a new metric

$$sigma_{rt}^+ = \sum_{i=1}^{n} (Rt_i - d_i)^+ \tag{1}$$

and require that $sigma_{rt}^+$ be minimized. Observe that, $sigma_{rt}^+$ represents the aggregate amount by which the response time targets of classes are exceeded. Minimizing a single metric $sigma_{rt}^+$ enables the system to collectively minimize the QoS violations across application classes.

We now present a learning-based approach that tries to minimize the $sigma_{rt}^+$ observed at each disk while meeting the key requirements outlined in Section 2.2.

3 A Learning-Based Approach

In this section, we first present some background on reinforcement learning and then present a simple learning-based approach for dynamic storage bandwidth allocation. We discuss limitations of this approach and present an enhanced learning-based approach that overcomes these limitations.

3.1 Reinforcement Learning Background

Any learning-based approach essentially involves learning from past history. Reinforcement learning involves learning how to map situations to *actions* so as to maximize a numerical *reward* (equivalent of a *cost* or *utility* function) [21]. It is assumed that the system does not know which actions to take in order to maximize the reward; instead the system must discover ("learn") the correct action by systematically trying various actions. An *action* is defined to be one of the possible ways to react to the current system state. The system state is defined to be a subset of what can be perceived from the environment at any given time.

In the dynamic storage bandwidth allocation problem, an action is equivalent to setting the allocations (i.e., the reservations) of each class. The system state is the vector of the observed response times of the application classes. The objective of reinforcement learning is to maximize the reward despite *uncertainty* about the environment (in our

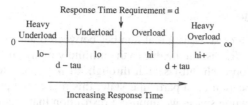

Fig. 2. Discretizing the State Space

case, the uncertainty arises due to the variations in the workload). An important aspect of reinforcement learning is that, unlike some learning approaches, no prior training of the system is necessary—all the learning occurs online, allowing the system to deal with unanticipated uncertainties (e.g., events, such as flash crowds, that can not have been anticipated in advance). It is this feature of reinforcement learning that makes it particularly attractive for our problem.

A reward function defines the goal in the reinforcement learning; by mapping an action to a reward, it determines the intrinsic desirability of that state. For the storage allocation problem, we define the reward function to be $-sigma_{rt}^{+}$—maximizing reward implies minimizing $sigma_{rt}^{+}$ and the QoS violations of classes. In reinforcement learning, we use reward values learned from past actions to estimate the expected reward of a (future) action.

With the above background, we present a reinforcement learning approach based on *action values* to dynamically allocate storage bandwidth to classes.

3.2 System State

A simple definition of system state is a vector of the response times of the n classes: $(Rt_1, Rt_2, \ldots, Rt_n)$, where Rt_i denotes the mean response time of class i observed over a period P. Since the response time of a class can take any arbitrary value, the system state space is theoretically infinite. Further, the system state by itself does not reveal if a particular class has met its target response time. Both limitations can be addressed by discretizing the state space as follows: partition the range of the response time (which is $[0, \infty)$) into four parts

$$\{[0, d_i - \tau_i], (d_i - \tau_i, d_i], (d_i, d_i + \tau_i], (d_i + \tau_i, \infty)\}$$

and map the observed response time Rt_i into one of these sub-ranges (τ_i is a constant). The first range indicates that the class response time is substantially below its target response time (by a threshold τ_i). The second (third) range indicates that the response time is slightly below (above) the target and by no more than the threshold τ_i. The fourth range indicates a scenario where the target response time is substantially exceeded. We label these four states as lo^-, lo, hi and hi^+, respectively, with the labels indicating different degrees of over- and under-provisioning of bandwidth (see Figure 2). The state of a class is defined as $S_i \in \{lo^-, lo, hi, hi^+\}$ and the modified state space is a vector of these states for each class: $S = (S_1, S_2, \ldots, S_n)$. Observe that, since state of a class can take only four values, the potentially infinite state space is reduced to a size of 4^n.

3.3   Allocation Space

The reservation of a class R_i is a real number between 0 and 1. Hence, the allocation space $(R_1, R_2, \ldots, R_n)$ is infinite due to the infinitely many allocations for each class. Since a learning approach must search through all possible allocations to determine an appropriate allocation for a particular state, this makes the problem intractable. To discretize the allocation space, we impose a restriction that requires the reservation of a class be modified in steps of T, where T is an integer. For instance, if the step size is chosen to be 1% or 5%, the reservation of a class can only be increased or decreased by a multiple of the step size. Imposing this simple restriction results in a finite allocation space, since the reservation of a class can only take one of m possible values, where $m = 100/T$. With n classes, the number of possible combinations of allocations is $\binom{m+n-1}{m}$, resulting in a finite allocation space. Choosing an appropriate step size allows allocations to be modified at a sufficiently fine grain, while keeping the allocation space finite. In the rest of this paper, we use the terms *action* and *allocation* interchangeably.

3.4   Cost and State Action Values

For the above definition of state space, we observe that the response time needs of a class are met so long it is in the lo^- or lo states. In the event an application class is in hi or hi^+ states, the system needs to increase the reservations of the class, assuming spare bandwidth is available, to induce a transition back to lo^- or lo. This is achieved by computing a new set of reservations $(R_1, R_2, \ldots, R_n)$ so as to maximize the reward $-sigma_{rt}^+$. Note that the maximum value of the reward is zero, which occurs when the response time needs of all classes are met (see Equation 1).

A simple method for determining the new allocation is to pick one based on the observed rewards of previous actions from this state. An action (allocation) that resulted in largest reward $(-sigma_{rt}^+)$ is likely to do so again and is chosen over other lower reward actions. Making this decision requires that the system first try out all possible actions, possibly multiple times, and then choose one that yields the largest reward. Over a period of time, each action may be chosen multiple times and we store an exponential average of the observed reward from this action (to guide future decisions):

$$Q_{(S_1, S_2, \ldots, S_n)}^{new}(a) = \gamma * Q_{(S_1, S_2, \ldots, S_n)}^{old}(a) + (1 - \gamma) * -sigma_{rt}^+(a) \qquad (2)$$

where Q denotes the exponentially averaged value of the reward for action a taken from state $(S_1, S_2, \ldots, S_n)$ and γ is the exponential smoothing parameter (also known as the *forgetting* factor). Learning methods of this form, where the actions selected are based on estimates of action-reward values (also referred to as action values), are referred to as *action-value methods*.

We choose an exponential average over a sample average because the latter is appropriate only for stationary environments. In our case, the environment is non-stationary due to the changing workloads and the same action from a state may yield different rewards depending on the current workload. For such scenarios, recency-weighted exponential averages are more appropriate. With 4^n states and $\binom{m+n-1}{m}$ possible actions in each state, the system will need to store $\binom{m+n-1}{m} * 4^n$ such averages, one for each action.

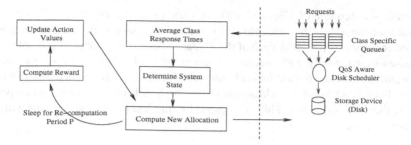

Fig. 3. Steps involved in learning.

3.5 A Simple Learning-Based Approach

A simple learning approach is one that systematically tries out all possible allocations from each system state, computes the reward for each action and stores these values to guide future allocations. Note that it is the discretization of the state space and the allocation space as described in Sections 3.4 and 3.2 which make this approach possible. Once the reward values are determined for the various actions, upon a subsequent transition to this state, the system can use these values to pick an allocation with the maximum reward. The set of learned reward values for a state is also referred to as the *history* of the state. As an example, consider two application classes that are allocated 50% each of the disk bandwidth and are in (lo^-, lo^-). Assume that a workload change causes a transition to (lo^-, hi^+). Then the system needs to choose one of several possible allocations: $(0, 100)$, $(5, 95)$, $(10, 90), \ldots, (100, 0)$. Choosing one of these allocations allows the system to learn the reward $-sigma^+_{rt}$ that accrues as a result of that action. After trying all possible allocations, the system can use these learned values to directly determine an allocation that maximizes reward (by minimizing the aggregate QoS violations). This quicker and suitable reassignment of class allocations is facilitated by learning. Figure 3 shows the steps involved in a learning based approach.

Although such a reinforcement learning scheme is simple to design and implement, it has numerous drawbacks.

Actions are oblivious of system state: A key drawback of this simple learning approach is that the actions are oblivious of the system state—the approach tries all possible actions, even ones that are clearly unsuitable for a particular state. In the above example, for instance, any allocation that decreases the share of the overloaded hi^+ class and increases that of the underloaded lo^- class is incorrect. Such an action can worsen the overall system performance. Nevertheless, such actions are explored to determine their reward. The drawback arises primarily because the semantics of the problem are not incorporated into the learning technique.

No performance isolation: Since the system state is not taken into account while making allocation decisions, the approach can not provide performance isolation to classes. In the above example, an arbitrary allocation of $(0, 100)$ can severely affect the lo^- class while favoring the overloaded class.

Large search space and memory requirements: Since there are $\binom{m+n-1}{m}$ possible allocations in each of the 4^n states, a systematic search of all possible allocations is impractical. This overhead is manageable when $n = 2$ classes and $m = 20$ (which corresponds to a step size of 5%; $m = 100/5$), since there are only $\binom{21}{20} = 21$ allocations for each of the $4^2 = 16$ states. However, for $n = 5$ classes, the number of possible actions increases to 10626 for each of the 4^5 states. Since the number of possible actions increases exponentially with increase in the number of classes, so does the memory requirement (since the reward for each allocation needs to be stored in memory to guide future allocations). For $n = 5$ classes and $m = 20$, 83MB of memory is needed per disk to store these reward values. This overhead is impractical for storage systems with large number of disks.

3.6 An Enhanced Learning-Based Approach

In this section, we design an enhanced learning approach that uses the semantics of the problem to overcome the drawback of the naive learning approach outlined in the previous section. The key insight used in the enhanced approach is to use the state of a class to determine whether to increase or decrease its allocation (instead of naively exploring all possible allocations). In the example listed in the previous section, for instance, only those allocations that increase the reservation of the overloaded class and decrease the allocation of the underloaded class are considered. The technique also includes provisions to provide performance isolation, achieve stable overload behavior, and reduce memory and search space overheads.

Initially, we assume that the allocations of all classes are set to a default value (a simple default allocation is to assign equal shares to the classes; any other default may be specified). We assume that the allocations of classes are recomputed every P time units. To do so, the technique first determines the system state and then computes the new allocation for this state as follows:

Case I: *All classes are underloaded (are in lo^- or lo).* Since all classes are in lo or lo^-, by definition, their response time needs are satisfied and no action is necessary. Hence, the allocation is left unchanged. An optimization is possible when some classes are in lo^- and some are in lo. Since the goal is to drive all classes to as low as state as possible, one can reallocate bandwidth from the classes in lo^- to the classes in lo. How bandwidth is reallocated and history maintained to achieve this is similar to the approach described in Case III below.

Case II: *All classes are overloaded (are in hi or hi^+).* Since all classes are in hi or hi^+, the target response times of all classes are exceeded, indicating an overload situation. While every class can use extra bandwidth, none exists in the system. Since no spare bandwidth is available, we leave the allocations unchanged.

An additional optimization is possible in this state. If some class is heavily overloaded (i.e., is in hi^+) and is currently allocated less than its initial default allocation, then the allocation of all classes is set to their default values (the allocation is left unchanged otherwise). The insight behind this action is that no class should be in hi^+ due to starvation resulting from an allocation less than its default. Resetting the allocations to their default values during such heavy overloads ensures that the system performance is no worse than a static approach that allocates the default allocation to each class.

Case III: *Some classes are overloaded, others are underloaded (some in hi^+ or hi and some in lo or lo^-).* This is the scenario where learning is employed. Since some classes are underloaded while others are overloaded, the system should reallocate spare bandwidth from underloaded classes to overloaded classes. Initially, there is no history in the system and the system must *learn* how much bandwidth to reassign from underloaded to overloaded classes. Once some history is available, the reward values from past actions can be used to guide the reallocation.

The learning occurs as follows. The application classes are partitioned into two sets: *lenders* and *borrowers*. A class is assigned to the lenders set if it is in lo or lo^-; classes in hi and hi^+ are deemed borrowers. The basic idea is to reduce the allocation of a lender by T and reassign this bandwidth to a borrower. Note that the bandwidth of only one lender and one borrower is modified at any given time and only by the step size T; doing so systematically reassigns spare bandwidth from lenders to borrowers, while learning the rewards from these actions.

Different strategies can be used to pick a lender and a borrower. One approach is to pick the most needy borrower and the most over-provisioned lender (these classes can be identified by how far the class is from its target response time; the greater this difference, the greater the need or the available spare bandwidth). Another approach is to cycle through the list of lenders and borrowers and reallocate bandwidth to classes in a round-robin fashion. The latter strategy ensures that the needs of all borrowers are met in a cyclic fashion, while the former strategy focuses on the most needy borrower before addressing the needs of the remaining borrowers.

Regardless of the strategy, the system state is recomputed P time units after each reallocation. If some classes continue to be overloaded, while others are underloaded, we repeat the above process. If the system transitions to a state defined by Case I or II, we handle them as discussed above.

The reward obtained after each allocation is stored as an exponentially-smoothed average (as shown in Equation 2). However, instead of storing the rewards of all possible actions, we only store the rewards of the actions that yield the k highest rewards. The insight here is that the remaining actions do not yield a good reward and, since the system will not consider them subsequently, we do not need to store the corresponding reward values. These actions and their corresponding reward estimates are stored as a link list, with the neighboring elements in the link list differing in the allocations of two classes by the step size T, that of one lender and one borrower. This facilitates a systematic search of the suitable allocation for a state, and also pruning of the link list to maintain a size of no more than k. By storing a fixed number of actions and rewards for any given state, the memory requirements can be reduced substantially. Further, while the allocation of a borrower and a lender is changed only by T in each step during the initial learning process, these can be changed by a larger amount subsequently once some history is available (this is done by directly picking the allocation that yields the maximum reward).

As a final optimization, we use a small non-zero probability ϵ to bias the system to occasionally choose a neighboring allocation instead of the allocation with the highest reward (a neighboring allocation is one that differs from the best allocation by the step size T for the borrowing and lending classes, e.g., $(30, 70)$ instead of $(35, 65)$ when $T = 5\%$). The reason we do this is that it is possible the value of an allocation is underestimated as a result of a sudden workload reversal, and the system may thus select the best allocation based on the current history. An occasional choice of a neighboring allocation ensures that the system explores the state space sufficiently well to discover a suitable allocation.

Observe that our enhanced learning approach reclaims bandwidth only from those classes that have bandwidth to spare (lo and lo^- classes) and reassigns this bandwidth to classes that need it. Since a borrower takes up bandwidth in increments of T from a lender, the lender could in the worst case end up in state hi^1. At this stage there would be a state change, and the action would be dictated by this new state. Thus, this strategy ensures that any new allocation chosen by the approach can only improve (and not worsen) the system performance; doing so also provides a degree of performance isolation to classes.

The technique also takes the current system state into account while making allocation decisions and thereby avoids allocations that are clearly inappropriate for a particular state; in other words, the optimized learning technique intelligently guides and restricts the allocation space explored. Further, since only the k highest reward actions are stored, the worst case search overhead is reduced to $O(k)$. This results in a substantial reduction from the search overheads of the simple learning approach. Finally, the memory needs of the technique reduce from $\binom{m+n-1}{m}$ to $4^n * k$, where k is the number of high reward actions for which history is maintained. This design decision also results in a substantial reduction in the memory requirements of the approach. In the case of 5 application classes, $T = 5\%$ (recall $m = 100/T$) and $k = 5$, for example, the technique yields more than 99% reduction in memory needs over the simple learning approach.

4   Implementation in Linux

We have implemented our techniques in the Linux kernel version 2.4.9. Our prototype consists of three components: (i) a QoS-aware disk scheduler that supports per-class reservations, (ii) a module that monitors the response time requirements of each class, and (iii) a learning-based bandwidth allocator that periodically recomputes the reservations of the classes on each disk. Our prototype was implemented on a Dell PowerEdge server (model 2650) with two 1 GHz Pentium III processors and 1 GB memory that runs RedHat Linux 7.2. The server was connected to a Dell PowerVault storage pack (model 210) with eight SCSI disks. Each disk is a 18GB 10,000 RPM Fujitsu MAJ3182MC disk[2]. We use the software RAID driver in Linux to configure the system as a single RAID-0 array.

We implement the Cello QoS-aware disk scheduler in the Linux kernel [18]. The disk scheduler supports a configurable number of application classes and allows a fraction of the disk bandwidth to be reserved for each class (these can be set using the scheduler system call interface). These reservations are then enforced on a fine time scale, while taking disk seek overheads into account. We extend the *open* system call to allow applications to associate file I/O with an application class; all subsequent read and write operations on the file are then associated with the specified class. The use of our enhanced open

---

[1] The choice of the step size T is of importance here. If the step-size is too big the overloaded class could end up in underload and vice versa and this could result in oscillations.

[2] The Fujitsu MAJ3182MC disk has an average seek overhead of 4.7 ms, an average latency of 2.99 ms and a data transfer rate of 39.16 MB/s.

system call interface requires application source code to be modified. To enable legacy application to benefit from our techniques, we also provide a command line utility that allows a process (or a thread) to be associated with an application class—all subsequent I/O from the process is then associated with that class. Any child processes that are forked by this process inherit these attributes and their I/O requests are treated accordingly.

We also add functionality into the Linux kernel to monitor the response times of requests in each class (at each disk); the response time is defined to the sum of the queuing delay and the disk service times. We compute the mean response time in each class over a moving window of duration P.

The bandwidth allocator runs as a privileged daemon in user space. It periodically queries the monitoring module for the response time of each class; this can done using a special-purpose system call or via the $/proc$ interface in Linux. The response time values are then used to compute the system state. The new allocation is then determined and conveyed to the disk scheduler using the scheduler interface.

5 Experimental Evaluation

In this section, we demonstrate the efficacy of our techniques using a combination of prototype experimentation and simulations. In what follows, we first present our simulation methodology and simulation results, followed by results from our prototype implementation.

5.1 Simulation Methodology and Workload

We use an event-based storage system simulator to evaluate our bandwidth allocation technique. The simulator simulates a disk array that is accessed by multiple application classes. Each disk in the array is modeled as a 18GB 10,000 RPM Fujitsu MAJ3182MC disk. The disk array is assumed to be configured as a RAID-0 array with multiple volumes; unless specified otherwise we assume an array of 8 disks . Each disk in the system is assumed to employ a QoS-aware disk scheduler that supports class-specific reservations; we use the Cello disk scheduler [18] for this purpose. Observe that the hardware configuration assumed in our simulations is identical to that in our prototype implementation. We assume that the system monitors the response times of each class over a period P and recomputes the allocations after each such period. We choose $P = 5s$ in our experiments. Unless specified otherwise, we choose a target response time of $d_i = 100ms$ for each class and the threshold τ_i for discretizing the class states into the lo^-, lo, hi and hi^+ categories is set to 20ms.

We use a two types of workloads in our simulations: trace-driven and synthetic. We use NFS traces to determine the effectiveness of our methods for real-world scenarios. However, since a trace workload only represents a small subset of the operating region, we use a synthetic workload to systematic explore the state space.

We use portions of an NFS trace gathered from the Auspex file server at Berkeley [12] to generate the trace-driven workload. To account for caching effects, we assume a large LRU buffer cache at the server and filter out requests resulting in cache hits from the original trace; the remaining requests are assumed to result in disk accesses. The resulting NFS trace is very bursty and has a peak to average bit rate of 12.5.

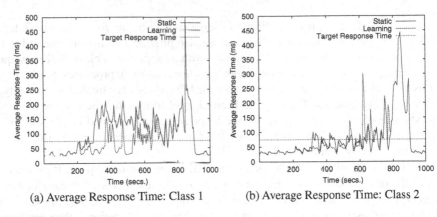

(a) Average Response Time: Class 1   (b) Average Response Time: Class 2

Fig. 4. Behavior of the learning-based dynamic bandwidth allocation technique.

Our synthetic workload consist of Poisson arriving clients that read a randomly selected file. File sizes are assumed to be heavy-tailed; we assume fixed-size requests that sequentially read the selected file. By carefully controlling the arrival rates of such clients, we can construct transient overload scenarios (where a burst of clients arrive in quick succession).

Next, we present our experimental results.

5.2   Effectiveness of Dynamic Bandwidth Allocation

We begin with a simple simulation experiment to demonstrate the behavior of our dynamic bandwidth allocation approach in the presence of varying workloads. We configure the system with two application classes. We choose an exponential smoothing parameter $\gamma = 0.5$, the learning step size $T = 5\%$ and the number of stored values per state $k = 5$. The target response time is set to 75ms for each class and the re-computation period was 5s. Each class is initially assigned 50% of the disk bandwidth.

We use a synthetic workload for this experiment. Initially both classes are assumed to have 5 concurrent clients each; each client reads a randomly selected file by issuing 4 KB requests. At time $t = 100s$, the workload in class 1 is gradually increased to 8 concurrent clients. At $t = 600s$, the workload in class 2 is gradually increased to 8 clients. The system experiences a heavy overload from $t = 700$ to $t = 900s$. At $t = 900s$, several clients depart and the load reverts to the initial load. We measure the response times of the two classes and then repeat the experiment with a static allocation of $(50\%, 50\%)$ for each class.

Figures 4 depicts the class response times. As shown the dynamic allocation technique adapts to the changing workload and yields response times that are close to the target. Further, due to the adaptive nature of the technique, the observed response times are, for the most part, better than that in the static allocation. Observe that, immediately after a workload change, the learning technique requires a short period of time to learn and adjust the allocations, and this temporarily yields a response time that is higher than that in the static case (e.g., at $t = 600s$ in Fig 4(b)). Also, observe that between $t = 700$ and $t = 900$ the system experiences a heavy overload and, as discussed in Case II of

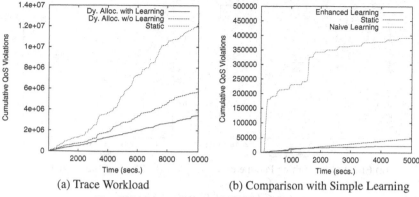

(a) Trace Workload   (b) Comparison with Simple Learning

Fig. 5. Comparison with Alternative Approaches

our approach, the dynamic technique resets the allocation of both hi^+ classes to their default values, yielding a performance that is identical to the static case.

5.3   Comparison with Alternative Approaches

In this section, we compare our learning-based approach with three alternate approaches: (i) *static*, where the allocation of classes is chosen statically, (ii) *dynamic allocation with no learning*, where the allocation technique is identical to our technique but no learning is employed (i.e., allocations are left unchanged when all classes are underloaded or overloaded as in Cases I and II in Section 3.6, and in Case III bandwidth is reassigned from the least underloaded class to the most overloaded class in steps of T, but no learning is employed), and (iii) the *simple learning* approach outlined in Section 3.5.

We use the NFS traces to compare our enhanced learning approach with the static and the dynamic allocation techniques with no learning. We configure the system with three classes with different scale factors[3] and set the target responses time of each class to 100ms. The re-computation period is chosen to be 5s. We use different portions of our NFS trace to generate the workload for the three classes. The stripe unit size for the RAID-0 array is chosen to be 8 KB. We use about 2.8 hours of the trace for this experiment.

We run the experiment for our learning-based allocation technique and repeat it for static allocation and dynamic allocation without learning. In figure 5(a) we plot the cumulative $\sum sigma_{rt}^+$ (i.e., the cumulative QoS violations observed over the duration of the experiment) for the three approaches; this metric helps us quantify the performance of an approach in the long run. Not surprisingly, the static allocation techniques yields the worst performance and incurs the largest number of QoS violations. The dynamic allocation technique without learning yields a substantial improvement over the static approach, while dynamic allocation with learning yields a further improvement. Observe that the gap between static and dynamic allocation without learning *depicts the benefits of dynamic allocation over static*, while the gap between the technique without learning

---

[3] The scale factor scales the inter-arrival times of requests and allows control over the burstiness of the workload.

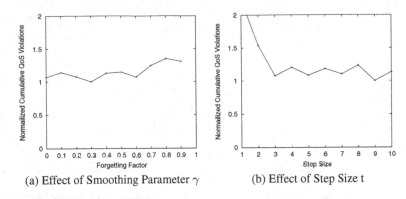

(a) Effect of Smoothing Parameter γ (b) Effect of Step Size t

Fig. 6. Impact of Tunable Parameters

and our technique *depicts the additional benefits of employing learning*. Overall, we see a factor of 3.8 reduction in QoS violations when compared to a pure static scheme and a factor of 2.1 when compared to a dynamic technique with no learning.

Our second experiment compares our enhanced learning approach with the simple learning approach described in Section 3.5. Most parameters are identical to the previous scenario, except that we only assume two application classes instead of three for this experiment. Figure 5(b) plots the cumulative QoS violations observed for the two approaches (we also plot the performance of static allocation for comparison). As can be seen, the naive learning approach incurs a larger search/learning overhead since it systematically searches through all possible actions. In doing so, incorrect actions that exacerbate the system performance are explored and actually worsen performance. Consequently, we see a substantially larger number of QoS violations in the initial period; the slope of the violation curve reduces sharply once some history is available to make more informed decisions. Consequently, during this initial learning process, a naive learning process under-performs even the static scheme; the enhanced learning technique does not suffer from these drawbacks, and like before, yields the best performance.

5.4   Effect of Tunable Parameters

We conduct several experiments to study how the choice of three tunable parameters affects the system behavior: the exponential smoothing parameter γ, the step size T and the history size k that defines the number of high reward actions stored by the system.

First, we study the impact of the smoothing parameter γ. Recall from Equation 1 that $\gamma = 0$ implies that only the most recent reward value is considered, while $\gamma = 1$ completely ignores reward values. We choose $T = 5\%$ and $k = 5$. We vary γ systematically from 0.0 to 0.9, in steps of 0.1 and study its impact on the observed QoS violations. We normalize the cumulative QoS violations observed for each value of γ with the minimum number of violations observed for the experiment. Figure 6(a) plots our results. As shown in the figure, the observed QoS violations are comparable for γ values in the range (0,0.6). The number of QoS violations increases for larger values of gamma—larger values of γ provide less importance to more recent reward values and consequently, result in larger QoS violations. This demonstrates that, in the presence of dynamically varying workloads, recent reward values should be given sufficient importance. We suggest choosing a γ between 0.3 and 0.6 to strike a balance between the recent reward values and those learned from past history.

Next, we study the impact of the step size T. We choose $\gamma = 0.5$, $k = 4$ and vary T from 1% to 10% and observe its impact on system performance. Note that a small value of T allows fine-grain reassignment of bandwidth but can increase the time to search for the correct allocation (since the allocation is varied only in steps of T). In contrast, a larger value of T permits a faster search but only permits coarse-grain reallocation. Figure 6(b) plots the normalized QoS violations for different values of T. As shown, very small values of T result in a substantially higher search overhead and increase the time to converge to the correct allocation, resulting in higher QoS violations. Moderate step sizes ranging from 3% to as large as 10% seem to provide comparable performance. To strike a balance between fine-grain allocation and low learning (search) overheads, we suggest step sizes ranging from 3-7%. Essentially, the step size should be sufficiently large to result in a noticeable improvement in the response times of borrowers but not large enough to adversely affect a lender class (by reclaiming too much bandwidth).

Finally, we study the impact of varying the history size k on the performance. We choose $\gamma = 0.5$, $T = 5\%$ and vary k from 1 to 10 (we omit the graph due to space constraints). Initially, increasing the history size results in a small decrease in the number of QoS violations, indicating that additional history allows the system to make better decisions. However, increasing the history size beyond 5 does not yield any additional improvement. This indicates that storing a small number of high reward actions is sufficient, and that it is not necessary to store the reward for every possible action, as in the naive learning technique, to make informed decisions. Using a small value of k also yields a substantial reduction in the memory requirements of the learning approach.

5.5   Implementation Experiments

We now demonstrate the effectiveness of our approach by conducting experiments on our Linux prototype. As discussed in Section 4, our prototype consists of a 8 disk system, configured as RAID-0 using the software RAID driver in Linux. We construct three volumes on this array, each corresponding to an application class. We use a a mix of three different applications in our study, each of which belongs to a different class: (1) *PostgreSQL database server:* We use the publicly available PostgreSQL database server version 7.2.3 and the *pgbench 1.2* benchmark. This benchmark emulates the TPC-B transactional benchmark and provides control over the number of concurrent clients as well as the number of transactions performed by each client. The benchmark generates a write-intensive workload with small writes. (2) *MPEG Streaming Media Server:* We use a home-grown MPEG-1 streaming media server to stream a 90 minute videos to multiple clients over UDP. Each video has a constant bit rate of 2.34 Mb/s and represent a sequential workload with large reads. (3) *Apache Web Server:* We use the Apache web server and the publicly available SURGE web workload generator to generate web workloads. We configure SURGE to generate a workload that emulates 300 time-sharing users accessing a 2.3 GB data-set with 100,000 files. We use the default settings in SURGE for the file size distribution, request size distributions, file popularity, temporal locality and idle periods of users. The resulting workload is largely read-only

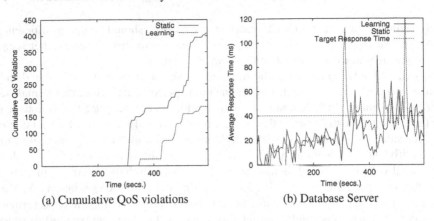

(a) Cumulative QoS violations   (b) Database Server

Fig. 7. Results from our prototype implementation.

and consists of small to medium size reads. Each of the above application is assumed to belong to separate application class. To ensure that our results are not skewed by a largely empty disk array, we populated the array with a variety of other large and small files so that 50% of the 144GB storage space was utilized. We choose $\gamma = 0.5, T = 5\%$, $k = 5$ and a recomputation period $P = 5s$. The target response times of the three classes are set to 40ms, 50ms and 30ms, respectively.

We conduct a 10 minute experiment where the workload in the streaming server is fixed to 2 concurrent clients (total I/O rate of 4.6 Mb/s). The database server is lightly loaded in the first half of the experiment and we gradually increase the load on the Apache web server (by starting a new instance of the SURGE client every minute; each new client represents 300 additional concurrent users). At $t = 5$ minutes, the load on the web server reverts to the initial load (a single SURGE client). For the second half of the experiment, we introduce a heavy database workload by configuring pgbench to emulate 20 concurrent users each performing 500 transactions (thereby introducing a write-intensive workload).

Figure 7(a) plots the cumulative QoS violations observed over the duration of the experiment for our learning technique and the static allocation technique. As shown, for the first half of the experiments, there are no QoS violations, since there is sufficient bandwidth capacity to meet the needs of all classes. The arrival of a heavy database workload triggers a reallocation in the learning approach and allows the system to adapt to this change. The static scheme is unable to adapt and incurs a significantly larger number of violations. Figure 7(b) plots the time-series of the response times for the database server. As shown, the adaptive nature of the learning approach enables it to provide better response times to the database server. While the learning technique provides comparable or better response time than static allocation for the web server, we see that both approaches are able to meet the target response time requirements (due to the light web workload in the second half, the observed response times are also very small). We observe a similar behavior for the web server and the streaming server. As mentioned before, learning could perform worse at some instants, either if it is exploring the allocation space or due to a sudden workload change, and it requires a short period to readjust the allocations. In figure 7(b) this happens around $t = 400$ s when learning performs worse than static, but the approach quickly takes corrective action and gives better performance.

Overall, the behavior of our prototype implementation is consistent with our simulation results.

5.6   Implementation Overheads

Our final experiment measures the implementation overheads of our learning-based bandwidth allocator. To do so, we vary the number of disks in the system from 50 to 500, in steps of 50, and measure the memory and CPU requirements of our bandwidth allocator. Observe that since we are constrained by a 8 disk system, we emulate a large storage system by simply replicating the response times observed at a single disk and reporting these values for all emulated disks. From the perspective of the bandwidth allocator, the setup is no different from one where these disks actually exist in the system. Further, since the allocations on each disk is computed independently, such a strategy accurately measures the memory and CPU overheads of our technique. We assume that new allocations are computed once every 5s.

We find that the CPU requirement for our approach to be less than 0.1% even for systems with 500 disks, indicating that the CPU overheads of the learning approach is negligible. The memory overheads of the allocation daemon are also small, with the percentage of memory used on a server with 1 GB RAM varies (almost linearly) from 1 MB (0.1 %) for a 50 disk system to 7 MB (0.7 %) for a 500 disk system.

Finally, note that the system call overheads of querying response times and conveying the new allocations to the disk scheduler can be substantial in a 500 disk system (this involves 1000 system calls every 5 seconds, two for each disk). However, observe that, the bandwidth allocator was implemented in user-space for ease of debugging; the functionality can be easily migrated into kernel-space, thereby eliminating this system call overhead. Overall, our results demonstrate the feasibility of using a reinforcement learning approach for dynamic storage bandwidth allocation in large storage systems.

6   Related Work

Recently, the design of self-managing systems has received significant research attention. For instance, the design of workload monitoring and adaptive resource management for data-intensive network services has been studied in [9]. The design of highly-dependable ("self-healing") Internet services has been studied [15].

From the perspective of storage systems, techniques for designing self-managing storage have been studied in [2,4]. The design of such systems involves several sub-tasks and issues such self-configuration [2,4] , capacity planning [8], automatic RAID-level selection [5], initial storage system configuration [3] , SAN fabric design [22] and on-line data migration [13]. These efforts are complementary to our work which focuses on automatic storage bandwidth allocation to applications with varying workloads.

Dynamic bandwidth allocation for multimedia servers has been studied in [20]. Whereas the approach relies on a heuristic, we employ a technique based on reinforcement learning. Several other approaches ranging from control theory to online measurements and optimizations can also be employed to address this problem. While no such study exists for storage systems, both control theory [1] and online measurements and optimizations [6,16] have been employed for dynamically allocating resources in web servers. Utility-based optimization models for dynamic resource allocation in server clusters have been employed in [11]. Feedback-based dynamic proportional share allocation to meet real-rate disk I/O requirements have been studied in [17]. While many feedback-based methods involve approximations such as the assumption of a linear relationship between resource share and response time, no such limitation exists for reinforcement learning—due to their search-based approach, such techniques can easily handle non-linearity in system behavior. Alternative techniques based on linear programming also make the linearity assumption, and need a linear objective function which is minimized; such a linear formulation may not be possible or might turn out to be inaccurate in practice. On the other hand, a hill-climbing based approach can handle non-linearity, but can get stuck in local maxima.

Finally, reinforcement learning has also been used to address other systems issues such as dynamic channel allocation in cellular telephone systems [19] and adaptive link allocation in ATM networks [14].

7   Concluding Remarks and Future Work

In this paper, we addressed the problem of dynamic allocation of storage bandwidth to application classes so as to meet their response time requirements. We presented an approach based on reinforcement learning to address this problem. We argued that a simple learning-based approach is not practical since it incurs significant memory and search space overheads. To address this issue, we used application-specific knowledge to design an efficient, practical learning-based technique for dynamic storage bandwidth allocation. Our approach can react to dynamically changing workloads, provide isolation to application classes and is stable under overload. Further, our technique learns online and does not require any *a priori* training. Unlike other feedback-based models, an additional advantage of our technique is that it can easily handle complex non-linearity in the system behavior. We implemented our techniques into the Linux kernel and evaluated it using prototype experimentation and trace-driven simulations. Our results showed that (i) the use of learning enables the storage system to reduce the number of QoS violations by a factor of 2.1 and (ii) the implementation overheads of employing such techniques in operating system kernels is small. Overall, our work demonstrated the feasibility of using reinforcement learning techniques for dynamic resource allocation in storage systems. As part of future work, we plan to explore the use of such techniques for other storage management tasks such as configuration, data placement, and load balancing.

References

1. T. Abdelzaher, K.G Shin and N. Bhatti. Performance Guarantees for Web server End-Systems: A Control Theoretic Approach. *IEEE Transactions on Parallel and Distributed Systems.* 13(1), January 2002.
2. G. A. Alvarez et al. Minerva: An Automated Resource Provisioning Tool for Large-scale Storage Systems. *ACM Transactions on Computer Systems* (to appear). *Technical report HPL-2001-139, Hewlett-Packard Labs*, June 2001.

3. E. Anderson et al. Hippodrome: Running Circles Around Storage Administration. *In FAST'02, Monterey, CA*, pp. 175–188, Jan. 2002.
4. E. Anderson et al. Ergastulum: An Approach to Solving the Workload and Device Configuration Problem. *HP Laboratories SSP technical memo HPL-SSP-2001-05*, May 2001.
5. E. Anderson, R. Swaminathan, A. Veitch, G. A. Alvarez and J. Wilkes. Selecting RAID levels for Disk Arrays. *In FAST'02, Monterey, CA*, pp. 189–201, January 2002.
6. M. Aron et al. Scalable Content-aware Request Distribution in Cluster-based Network Servers. *Proceedings of the USENIX 2000 Annual Technical Conference, San Diego, CA*, June 2000.
7. P. Barham. A Fresh Approach to File System Quality of Service. *In Proceedings of NOSSDAV' 97, St. Louis, Missouri*, pages 119–128, May 1997.
8. E. Borowsky et al. Capacity planning with phased workloads. *In Proceedings of the Workshop on Software and Performance (WOSP'98), Santa Fe, NM*, October 1998.
9. A. Brown, D. Oppenheimer, K. Keeton, R. Thomas, J. Kubiatowicz, and D.A. Patterson. ISTORE: Introspective Storage for Data-Intensive Network Services. *In Proceedings of the 7th Workshop on Hot Topics in Operating Systems (HotOS-VII), Rio Rico, Arizona*, March 1999.
10. J. Carlström and E. Nordström. Reinforcement learning for Control of Self-Similar Call Traffic in Broadband Networks. *Proceedings of the 16th International Teletraffic Congress, ITC'16*, P. Key., D. Smith (eds.), Elsevier Science, Edinburgh, Scotland, 1999.
11. J. Chase et al. Managing Energy and Server Resources in Hosting Centers. *Proceedings of the Eighteenth ACM Symposium on Operating Systems Principles (SOSP)*, Oct. 2001.
12. M. Dahlin et al. A Qualitative Analysis of Cache Policies for Scalable Network File Systems. *In Proceedings of the ACM SIGMETRICS '94*, May 1994.
13. C. Lu, G. A. Alvarez, and J. Wilkes. Aqueduct: Online Data Migration with Performance Guarantees. *In FAST'02, Monterey, CA*, pp. 219–230, January 2002.
14. E. Nordström and J. Carlström. A Reinforcement Learning Scheme for Adaptive Link Allocation in ATM Networks. *IWANNT '95*, J. Alspector, T.X. Brown, pp. 88–95, Lawrence Erlbaum, Stockholm, Sweden, 1995.
15. D.A. Patterson et al. Recovery-Oriented Computing (ROC): Motivation, Definition, Techniques, and Case Studies. *UC Berkeley Computer Science Technical Report UCB//CSD-02-1175*, March 15, 2002.
16. P. Pradhan, R. Tewari, S. Sahu, A. Chandra and P. Shenoy. An Observation-based Approach Towards Self-managing Web Servers. *In Proceedings of ACM/IEEE Intl Workshop on Quality of Service (IWQoS), Miami Beach, FL*, May 2002.
17. D. Revel, D. McNamee, C. Pu, D. Steere and J. Walpole. Feedback Based Dynamic Proportion Allocation for Disk I/O. Technical Report CSE-99-001, OGI CSE, January 1999.
18. P. Shenoy and H. Vin. Cello: A Disk Scheduling Framework for Next Generation Operating Systems. *In Proceedings of ACM SIGMETRICS '98, Madison, WI*, pp. 44–55, June, 1998.
19. S. Singh and D. Bertsekas. Reinforcement Learning for Dynamic Channel Allocation in Cellular Telephone Systems. With D. Bertsekas. *In NIPS 10*, 1997.
20. V. Sundaram and P. Shenoy. Bandwidth Allocation in a Self-Managing Multimedia File Server. *Proceedings of the Ninth ACM Conference on Multimedia, Ottawa, Canada*, Oct. 2001.
21. R. S. Sutton and A G. Barto. *Reinforcement Learning: An Introduction.* MIT Press, Cambridge, MA.
22. J. Ward, M. O'Sullivan, T. Shahoumian, and J. Wilkes. Appia: Automatic Storage Area Network Design. *In FAST'02, Monterey, CA*, pp. 203–217, January 2002.
23. R. Wijayaratne and A. L. N. Reddy. Providing QoS Guarantees for Disk I/O. Technical Report TAMU-ECE97-02, Department of Electrical Engineering, Texas A&M University, 1997.

CacheCOW: QoS for Storage System Caches

Pawan Goyal, Divyesh Jadav, Dharmendra S. Modha, and Renu Tewari

IBM Almaden Research Center, San Jose CA 95120, USA

Abstract. Managed hosting and enterprise wide resource consolidation trends are increasingly leading to sharing of storage resources across multiple classes, corresponding to different applications/customers, each with a different Quality of Service (QoS) requirement. To enable a storage system to meet diverse QoS requirements, we present two algorithms for dynamically allocating **cache** space among multiple classes of workloads. Our algorithms dynamically adapt the cache space allocated to each class depending upon the observed response time, the temporal locality of reference, and the arrival pattern for each class. Using trace driven simulations collected from large storage system installations, we *experimentally* demonstrate the following properties of CacheCOW. First, the CacheCOW algorithms enable a storage cache to meet the feasible QoS requirements that class-unaware cache management algorithms such as LRU do not. Second, if an offline, static partitioning of the cache can meet the QoS requirements, our algorithms also meet them and discover the allocations **online**. Third, the CacheCOW allocations achieve the same feasibility region as that of the offline static algorithms. Finally, the algorithms not only meet the QoS requirements, but also increase the throughput by achieving a higher hit rate whenever feasible.

1 Introduction

Enterprises are increasingly out-sourcing the management of their data and applications to managed hosting services that collocate multiple sites, applications, and multiple customer types on the same host machine or a cluster and provide different quality of service (QoS) to them based on various pricing options. One of the central challenges in shared environments is to manage resources such that applications and customers are isolated from each other and their performance can be guaranteed as in a dedicated environment. Numerous mechanisms for service differentiation and performance isolation have been proposed in the literature in the context of collocated web servers [1,14,16]. However, QoS-aware resource management for storage systems has not been adequately investigated and is the subject of this paper.

To provide QoS in storage systems, resources such as CPU and cache at the NAS and block servers, SAN network bandwidth, and disk bandwidth have to be managed. Techniques for allocating CPU, network, and disk bandwidth have been investigated in the literature for web servers and other applications and can potentially be applied to storage systems. Also, techniques for automated provisioning and load-balancing have been investigated in [2]. However, techniques

K. Jeffay, I. Stoica, and K. Wehrle (Eds.): IWQoS 2003, LNCS 2707, pp. 498–515, 2003.

for allocating cache space, which is an important factor in storage system performance, to provide QoS differentiation have not been adequately investigated and are the focus of this paper.

Caches differ fundamentally from other resources such as CPU and network bandwidth in two aspects. First, if CPU (or network bandwidth) is allocated to a class, it can be immediately used to improve the performance for a class. In contrast, the allocation of cache space does not yield immediate performance benefits for a class; performance benefits accrue in future only if there are cache hits. Furthermore, unlike CPU, current cache space allocation for a class can significantly impact the future cache performance of all other classes. With ephemeral resources such as CPU and network bandwidth, adaptation is faster with immediate reallocation, while with cache allocation any adaptation technique requires a window into the future. Second, the performance benefit of cache space allocation depends on the workload characteristics of the class. More cache space does not necessarily imply better performance (e.g., if the workload has no hits). Due to these fundamental differences, techniques for meeting the QoS requirements of multiple classes that have been developed for resources such as CPU and network bandwidth cannot be directly applied to caches.

One approach for cache allocation is to statically partition the cache among different classes. However, such an approach has two main drawbacks. First, due to the dynamic nature of the workload, it is difficult to determine the appropriate partition size *a priori*. Second, static partitioning tends to under-utilize the cache and cannot benefit from statistical multiplexing effects. Hence, in this paper, we develop dynamic cache allocation algorithms for meeting the QoS requirements of multiple classes. The primary and secondary goals of the dynamic cache allocation algorithms are, respectively:

- **QoS differentiation and performance isolation**: To allocate cache space to provide desired QoS such as response time or throughput to various classes.
- **Performance Maximization**: To allocate cache space to maiximize the system performance–when all the QoS goals have been met.

CacheCOW is used to collectively refer to two dynamic cache allocation algorithms, namely, PERIODIC ALLOCATION and CONTINUOUS ALLOCATION, that achieve the above goals. Both algorithms manage pages in each class using LRU, but either periodically or continuously control the size of the cache for each class. The cache allocation algorithms can use any other suitable cache replacement policy instead of LRU, for example, [11]. Using traces collected from large storage system installations, via simulations, we demonstrate that these algorithms are indeed able to achieve the above goals. We *experimentally* show that: (1) Our algorithms enable a storage cache to meet the QoS requirements that class-unaware cache management algorithms such as LRU do not; (2) If an o ine static partitioning of cache can meet the QoS requirements, our algorithms can also meet them and discover the allocations *online*; (3) Our algorithms can achieve the same feasibility region as that of offline static algorithms; and (4) The algorithms not only meet the QoS requirements, but also optimize the throughput by achieving a higher hit rate whenever feasible. For some traces the hit rate improvements are twice that of the LRU achieved values.

The rest of the paper is organized as follows. Section 2 formulates the cache allocation problem. The algorithms for dynamically allocating cache are presented in section 3. Section 4 presents the results of our trace driven simulations. We present related work in Section 5. Finally, Section 6 summarizes the results of the paper.

2   QoS Based Cache Allocation

In this section, we first present our assumptions about the cache architecture in a storage subsystem. We then define the problem of cache allocation to meet the QoS requirements.

2.1   Caches in Storage Systems

Caches are deployed in a storage system at the local server file system, a NAS (network-attached storage) server, a block server such as a SAN-based in-band virtualization engine, or an enterprise storage system such as IBM TotalStorage/EMC Symmetrix. The caches in these systems are managed in a similar way, using a cache replacement policy (primarily LRU) that has been modified to handle sequential accesses. The CacheCOW allocation algorithms that support QoS can be applied to caches at all the various components of the storage system. For simplicity, in the rest of the paper, we assume that the cache is deployed at the SAN virtualization engine.

The cache at the SAN virtualization engine is used for multiple purposes: for caching reads, prefetching data (read-ahead for sequential accesses), and implementing write-backs (i.e., acknowledging writes without actually writing to the disk but destaging to the disk at a later time). There are two general approaches for implementing the cache: (1) Partitioned: In this approach the read and write caches are physically separate with the write cache being NVRAM; (2) Unified: In this approach, the same cache is used for reads and writes. We assume that the write blocks are periodically being destaged; the study of a destage policy and its interaction with cache allocation is beyond the scope of this paper.

In our presentation, we assume that the cache is unified. Our algorithms, however, are applicable directly for the partitioned case as well.

2.2   I/O Request Class Identification

To provide differentiated QoS to the classes the storage system has to be able identify the class to which an I/O request belongs. The specific classification algorithm will depend on the storage protocol employed. In case of SCSI (either over Fiber Channel or IP protocol) which is the most widely deployed protocol in enterprises, we use the *initiator* address, *target* address, and *logical-unit* attributes of a request for classification. The classification system classifies each I/O request as belonging to one of class $1, 2, ..., N$. Associated with each class is a QoS specification which can consist of multiple performance or availability requirements, however, in this paper, for concreteness, we assume that the QoS requirement is that of average response time guarantees. Our algorithms can be adapted to other performance metrics such as throughput as well.

2.3   Cache Allocation Problem

Cache allocation controls the response time by effecting the cache hit-ratio. To observe the role played by the caching algorithm in controlling the average response time, let h_i denote the hit-ratio for class i. Further, let r_i^{hit} and r_i^{miss} be the average response time in case of a hit and miss, respectively. Thus, the average response time r_i can be expressed as:

$$r_i = h_i \times r_i^{hit} + (1 - h_i) \times r_i^{miss} \tag{1}$$

The caching algorithm, by appropriately allocating cache space among the classes, can effect the hit ratios for each class, and thus the average response time.

The objective of the cache allocation algorithm is to allocate cache such that the measured average response time (over a defined time interval) r_i for class i is at most R_i where R_i is the response time requirement for class i (i.e., $r_i \leq R_i$). Two natural questions that arise are: (i) If a QoS requirement is feasible, what is the appropriate criteria for choosing among the multiple feasible allocations? and (ii) If a QoS requirement is infeasible (i.e., can not be satisfied by any cache allocation), what is the criteria for selecting a cache allocation? We chose, for simplicity, maximizing hit ratios as the criteria for selecting the cache allocations when multiple or non-feasible cache allocations exist. This criteria is used by an offline cache allocation algorithm as follows.

2.4   Offline Cache Allocation

Offline procedures for static cache partitioning have been considered in the past, for example, in [10] and [13,15]. These papers, however, did not consider QoS and were interested primarily in maximizing the hit ratio. The fundamental idea in [13,15] is to look at the hit ratio versus cache size curves for all the classes where LRU is used as the replacement policy. They seek to find a cache size for each curve such that the hit ratio derivatives for each curve at its chosen cache size are equal. Essentially, the same idea is considered in [10] who solved the problem of finding the static offline optimal partitioning using dynamic programming. The ideas presented below are similar in spirit, but differ to accommodate the QoS constraints.

We consider the offline case where request streams associated with each of the classes are known a priori. Let us suppose that LRU replacement is employed for each class. The choice of replacement policy will affect the feasibility region defined below. Let the *hit-ratio function* $\hat{h}_i$, $1 \leq i \leq N$, of a class i, map a given cache size to a hit ratio. Since LRU is known to be a stack algorithm, we know that the functions $\hat{h}_1, \hat{h}_2, \ldots \hat{h}_N$ are non-decreasing.

Observe that response time depends on the the hit ratio. In general, this dependence is complicated, non-linear, and time-variant. We assume that the response time for a stream decreases as the hit ratio for that workload increases, as shown in [15]. Under this assumption, we can determine the smallest cache size, say, L_i, $1 \leq i \leq N$, that must be allocated to class i so as to guarantee the desired response time for that class (i.e., $r_i \leq R_i$). Now, we say that a feasible static partitioning of the cache exists if: $\sum_{i=1}^{N} L_i \leq c$ where c is the total cache size. Assuming that a feasible partition exists, we allocate cache space L_i to class i. In general, there may still be cache space left over. In this case, we assign the remaining space so as to maximize the overall hit ratio. We assign remaining space to various classes in a block-by-block manner. For every additional block, we assign it to the class that delivers the largest additional hits for that extra block. It is easy to see that this greedy procedure is optimal. When no feasible partition exists, we order L_i in the increasing order, and start allocating the classes requiring smaller space to be satisfied first. The properties of the offline algorithm are: (i) When multiple feasible allocations exist, the algorithm selects the minimal allocation that meets the QoS requirements and then resorts to an additional allocation that maximizes overall hit ratio. (ii) In case no feasible allocation exists, the algorithm selects the minimal allocation that maximizes the number of classes that can meet their QoS requirements and then resorts to an additional allocation that maximizes overall hit ratio.

Offline static or dynamic partitioning algorithms are not feasible in practice. Hence, we would like online algorithms for cache partitioning that perform as well as the static offline algorithm. An ideal online algorithm would: (1) find a feasible solution whenever a offline static partitioning exists, and (2) achieve the same (or possibly higher) hit ratio than the offline static algorithm by doing dynamic allocation. Next, we present two algorithms that closely reach this ideal.

3   Online Algorithms for Dynamic Cache Allocation

Cache allocation algorithms may adjust cache allocation: i) periodically, i.e., after some time interval, number of arrivals or number of cache misses, or ii) continuously, i.e., after every request arrival. Whereas the continuous cache allocation may be more responsive to workload changes, the periodic allocation may have lesser overhead. Hence, we explore both periodic and continuous allocation algorithms as part of CacheCOW.

To allocate cache such that the goals are met, the cache allocation algorithms need to know the effectiveness of allocating additional cache space to each class. To determine such information, we use a common concept of history.

3.1   History

The precise amount of history maintained for each class is determined in a fashion that is inspired by [11]. In particular, for each class i, we maintain two LRU lists: A_i and B_i. The list A_i contains buffers in the cache. The list B_i contains buffers that were recently evicted. Let a_i denote the size of A_i and b_i denote the size of B_i and c be the total cache size. We will maintain target sizes T_i and S_i, for the lists A_i and B_i , respectively. Because of the cache size constraint, we must have that $\sum_{i=1}^{N} a_i = c$. Also, for consistency, we will require that $\sum_{i=1}^{N} T_i = c$. The issue is what should be the total size of the history lists. Large history size leads to better estimates about the effectiveness of a cache but at the expense of higher overhead. We balance the competing objectives of overhead and accuracy, by choosing history size equal to cache size, $\sum_{i=1}^{N} b_i = c$. We allocate history to a class i that is proportional to the amount of cache space allocated to all other classes, i.e., $S_i = \frac{c-a_i}{(N-1)}$.

The two algorithms presented below differ in how the target sizes for the cache lists A_i are set. They also differ in how often these target sizes are updated and the amount of statistics that needs to be maintained.

3.2   Periodic Re-allocation Algorithm

The periodic re-allocation algorithm builds upon the static off-line algorithm presented in Section 2 to allocate cache dynamically and online. The cache re-allocation can be triggered after a fixed time interval, number of arrivals or number of cache misses. Ideally, the adaptation should be triggered whenever the workload pattern has changed. Intuitively, the rate of cache misses is a good indicator of workload change. Hence, we trigger a cache allocation adaptation after every M cache misses where M is a parameter of the algorithm. In all our experiments, we set M to 0.1% of the total cache size in number of blocks.

The cache allocation algorithm first satisfies the QoS requirements of all the classes and then optimizes the overall cache hit ratio. The two cases are considered below.

Meeting QoS Requirements: Consider the case where the QoS requirements of some classes are not being met. We call a class dissatisfied if the observed response time r_i is larger than the desired response time R_i (i.e., $r_i > R_i$) and satisfied otherwise, i.e., $r_i \leq R_i$. When the average response time is r_i, the corresponding hit ratio using (1) is:

$$h_i = \frac{r_i^{miss} - r_i}{r_i^{miss} - r_i^{hit}}$$

Let h_i^+ be the desired hit ratio for $r_i = R_i$. Observe that for satisfied classes, $h_i \geq h_i^+$ and for dissatisfied classes $h_i < h_i^+$. In general, the hit-ratio can be an arbitrary function of the cache size. We assume that in the region of our interest, the hit-ratio function is piece-wise linear and has a slope of m_i. To reallocate cache, we compute the amount of cache space, $spare_i$, the satisfied class i, can give up and the amount of cache space, $need_j$, the dissatisfied class j, needs. Thus:

$$spare_i = \frac{h_i - h_i^+}{m_i}$$

$$need_j = \frac{h_i^+ - h_i}{m_i}$$

In the above equations we need the slope m_i. We determine that using the history list as follows. We know the hit-ratios for the previous (and current) cache allocation for a class. Using the history list, we also know the hit-ratio for a cache size equal to sum of actual cache size and the history-list. Thus we always have at least two points, one in the past and one in the future, to compute the slope. In practice the slope is computed by averaging over different intervals of the cache size and over multiple instantaneous measurements. To prevent oscillations, at each adaptation cycle we bound the total readjusted space to be M buffers (for simplicity, we selected the same number of buffer allocations that were required in an adaptation cycle due to a miss). Therefore, the actual readjusted space $\hat{M}$ is limited to $\min(\Sigma spare_i, M, \Sigma need_j)$.

Given the total amount of space that can be reallocated, we do the reallocation of the cache using a greedy approach. The satisfied classes are ordered in descending order of $spare_i$, $spare_i \geq spare_{i+1}$. The dissatisfied classes, on the other hand, are ordered in ascending order of $need_j$, $need_j \leq need_{j+1}$. Then, the one at the top of the satisfied list (with most spare capacity) reduces its target and increases the target of the one on top of the dissatisfied list (with the least need), thereby, minimizing the number of dissatisfied classes. At each adaptation cycle, cache space is not physically moved around by reassigning buffers. Instead, only the target value T_i is adjusted. For the satisfied classes it is:

$$T_i - = \min(\hat{M}, spare_i), 1 \leq T_i \leq a_i + b_i$$

For the dissatisfied classes it becomes:

$$T_j + = \min(\hat{M}, need_j), 1 \leq T_i \leq a_i + b_i$$

The target value is bounded such that it never goes below 1 and never goes above the sum of the total cache size and history size. The lower bound ensures that a class should not get starved of all cache space. The upper bound is governed by the computation of the slope m_i. Since the slopes are determined based on the history list, any adjustment that sets the cache size to be larger than the sum of current cache size and the history size will not be accurate.

On a miss in class i, when a buffer is required and the cache size is below target, some other class j, whose cache size is most above target, releases a buffer. Specifically, $j = \max_k(a_k - T_k)$.

Maximizing Performance: In the case when the QoS requirements have been met, the objective is to maximize overall hit-ratio. To do that, we determine the excess cache allocation for each class using the method presented above and reallocate greedily to the cache with the largest hit-rate density which is defined as hit rate per unit cache size. Observe that we use hit-rates instead of hit-ratio to take into account the arrival rates in each of the classes. If a class has low arrival rate but very high hit-ratio, it may not benefit the overall system performance by adding to its cache size.

The algorithm as described above is directly applicable for read requests. To use it for write requests, we modify it slightly. The reads and writes share the same LRU ordering in the cache. In case of writes, however, a read buffer is always released, to prevent blocking as far as possible. A new write request blocks only if it has to wait for a destage of a dirty buffer. Once it has been destaged it is treated as a read buffer. The hits on a write buffer are treated the same as that of reads. A read hit on a write buffer is the same as a read hit on a read. However, a write hit on a read buffer changes the data in the read buffer and also marks it as dirty. Since buffering writes accrues immediate performance benefit the adaptation algorithm considers it as a hit in the history list.

3.3   Continuous Allocation Algorithm

The periodic reallocation algorithm presented above adapts only after every M misses. The choice of M affects how the algorithm responds to workload changes. Also it maintains statistics to predict the slope of the hit-ratio curve which could be inaccurate when the slope rapidly changes. To eliminate these drawbacks, we next present a dynamic algorithm that continuously reallocates cache space amongst various classes and immediately responds to workload changes. The idea of continuous allocation is to adjust the target cache size for each class incrementally, essentially on some misses (that are hits in the history), without requiring an explicit ordering of the classes or maintaining hit statistics. The target balancing game increases the target of a class with a corresponding decrease in target of the other classes such that the total target remains bounded. When a class becomes satisfied it gets out of the target increase game.

The complete cache management algorithm is presented in Figure 1. The algorithm uses two control variables, namely, "satisfied(i)" and "AllSatisfied" that are set to true if the class i is satisfied and if all classes are satisfied, respectively. These variables are used to determine the classes that are eligible for target increase. As with the periodic reallocation algorithm, a write request is treated differently and viewed as a hit in the history list for target adjustment.

4   Experimental Evaluation

4.1   Methodology

To evaluate the various cache allocation algorithms we use an event-driven disk-array simulator. The architecture of the simulator that we used for our experiments is shown in Figure 2(a). The requests from each customer class go through a storage system virtualization engine that contains the common cache. Our cache allocation algorithms control the behavior of this cache. The requests

---

Input: new request x for class i
begin
    if (Hit in cache: x is in A_i) then
        Move x to the MRU position in A_i.
    endif
    if (Hit in history: x is in B_i) then
        $\delta = \max\{1, a_i/b_i\}$
        if (!satisfied(i) || AllSatisfied) then
            Adjust Tragets: $T_i \mathrel{+}= \delta$ and $T_q \mathrel{-}= \delta/(N-1)$ for all $q \neq i$.
        endif
        RELEASEBUFFER(i).
        Remove x from B_i and move it to the top of A_i. $a_i = a_i + 1$. $b_i = b_i - 1$.
    endif
    if (Miss: x is not in A_i or B_i) then
        RELEASEBUFFER(i).
        Move x to the MRU position in A_i. $a_i = a_i + 1$.
    endif
    Adjust history targets: $S_j = \frac{c - a_j}{(N-1)}, 1 \leq j \leq N$.
    while ($b_i > S_i$) Remove LRU buffer from B_i and $b_i = b_i - 1$. endwhile
end

RELEASEBUFFER(i):
begin
    Let j denote the class with maximum $a_j - T_j$
    if ((($a_q - T_q) = 0$ for all classes $1 \leq q \leq N$) or (satisfied(i)) then
        $j = i$
    endif
    Delete the LRU buffer in A_j and move it to the top of B_j. $a_j = a_j - 1, b_j = b_j + 1$.
    if ($b_j > S_j$) then
        Delete the LRU buffer in B_j and $b_j = b_j - 1$.
    endif
end

Fig. 1. Algorithm for Continuous Adaptation

that miss in the cache are forwarded after translation from a virtual VLun to a target/Lun pair that is handled by the Logical Unit (LUN) layer. Each customer request resembles a SCSI command and consists of the tuple $<$ id, command, LBA, size $>$, where id is the identifier for the customer, command is either CMD_READ or CMD_WRITE, along with the logical block address and the size of the request in bytes. In the simulator, we use the customer id to classify the request into the corresponding QoS class. In reality we need to rely on the initiator, target ids, and the LUN of the SCSI command to do the classification. Each customer class in our experiments issues SCSI commands by reading a trace file consisting of block access data gathered from different sources. We use 4 types of traces in our experiments: i) SPC1 trace: which was generated by running the SPC-1 [7] benchmark and capturing the disk requests of each of the individual 8 streams separately to create different types of workload. Thus, while one stream is predominantly sequential access, one has a random access pattern with high locality of reference. ii) Financial: This trace was collected by monitoring requests to disks of an OLTP application at a large financial institution. This trace had reads and writes with random access patterns which strong locality and very little sequential access. iii) Ecommerce trace: This disk access trace was collected from a large company running ecommerce transactions. It shows very high locality of reference and hardly any sequential accesses. iv) Search Engine: Here the disk accesses are caused by web requests at a large search engine and are predominantly reads. The characteristics of the traces are shown in Table 1. The achievable read hit ratios for the traces for different cache sizes is shown in Figure 2(b). The default drive characteristics consisted of a 9GB disk, with 4 heads and 800 sectors per track. The rotational latency per revolution was 6 ms and a track-to-track seek of 50 μs with a 100 and 1000 track seek of 1.2ms and 5ms respectively.

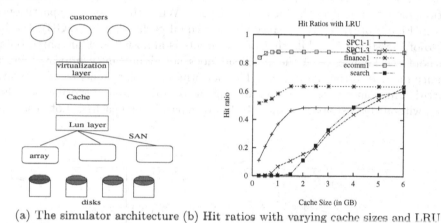

(a) The simulator architecture (b) Hit ratios with varying cache sizes and LRU

Fig. 2. Simulator architecture and trace characteristics

Table 1. Summary of the Traces

Name	Reads	Writes	Max. Read Hit Ratio	Avg. Bytes/IO	Pattern
SearchEngine1	1055236	212	60.1% @ 6GB	15509	random
SearchEngine2	4578819	990	82.0% @ 7.9GB	15432	random
SearchEngine3	4259646	1259	82.0% @ 7.9GB	15771	random
Financial	1235633	4099354	63.7% @ 1.85GB	3465	random
Ecommerce	3046112	653082	87.9% @ 1.63GB	2448	random
SPC1-1	933050	932178	48.4% @ 1.83GB	4096	random
SPC1-2	6316209	6304796	91.1% @ 7.0GB	4096	random
SPC1-3	3631793	0	81.6% @ 7.0GB	6881	seq. cycle

4.2   Shared and Partitioned Cache

The CacheCOW algorithms are designed to dynamically partition the cache to meet the QoS requirements and maximize the overall hit ratios. As an alternative, we can rely on LRU to share the cache across classes or use a static partitioning scheme. Figure 3(a,b,c) show the performance of LRU: i) when the cache is shared among all the customer classes, ii) when the entire cache is available to each class, and iii) when the cache is statically partitioned among each class. The three classes use three different workloads derived from the SPC1 trace streams, i.e., SPC1-1, SPC1-2, SPC1-3 respectively. For a cache size of 1GB, a shared cache with LRU (Figure 3(a)) has a Class0 hit ratio of 16%, while the other classes are almost at 0%. When the entire cache is available to a class (Figure 3(b)), for a 1GB cache size, Class0 has a hit ratio of 38%. The shared LRU cache, by allocating space among all classes without any performance isolation, more than halves the hit ratio of Class0. When the classes are partitioned (as in Figure 3(c)) with each receiving an equal cache share (1/3GB), the hit ratio of Class0 is 17% while that of the others is almost 0%. Thus partitioning without the knowledge of the workload does not significantly improve performance relative to the shared case. The performance isolation achieved by static partitioning comes at the cost of reducing the overall system performance. Thus even without QoS support, a shared LRU or a partitioned cache is not desirable.

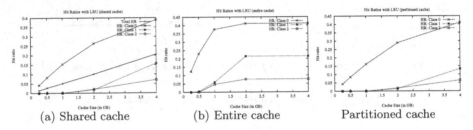

(a) Shared cache   (b) Entire cache   Partitioned cache

Fig. 3. SPC trace: Performance of LRU with different cache configurations

4.3   Providing QoS Support

To understand the behavior of both the CacheCOW algorithms with different QoS requirements per class, we configure the simulator to use the same trace for each customer class. By using the same trace, each class becomes equally competitive and the continuous and periodic adaptation algorithms cannot exploit the statistical multiplexing advantages and dynamic partitioning gains. We selected this worst-case scenario (for the CacheCOW allocation) to evaluate the performance because it ensures that the only differentiator among the classes is the QoS requirement and the miss response time. In this set of experiments we selected the same disk characteristics for all classes such that the average miss response time per class is the same (approximately 200 ms). The hit response time was also common across all classes and set to 50 μs. The disk requests consisted of only reads and there was no sharing of cache buffers across classes as each customer was directed to different target LUNs. The QoS requirements per class are set as an absolute response time (average) guarantees. One of the classes was set to have the tightest QoS requirement that is feasible for the given cache size and the others had a lax requirement. Figures 4(a,b) and 5(a,b) show the achieved average response time per class for varying total cache space for 2 different trace types (SPC-1, Financial). A selection of different traces per class one with sequential and another with random accesses will significantly bias the results in our favor compared to LRU.

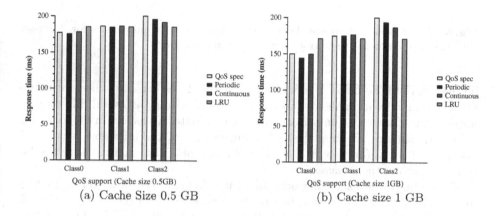

(a) Cache Size 0.5 GB   (b) Cache size 1 GB

Fig. 4. QoS Support: Response Time with different QoS requirements for 3 classes with identical disks and same trace per class. SPC-1 trace

While LRU settles for an identical cache partitioning among the classes, the periodic and continuous allocation algorithms select the largest partition for the class with the most stringent requirement and less for the others. The periodic allocation is greedy in nature and allocates more space than necessary to the most stringent class and reduces it for the others while maintaining the QoS requirements for all. The continuous allocation is more fair to the classes with not so stringent requirements. For these experiments both periodic and continuous allocation meet the QoS requirements for all classes, while LRU misses it for the most stringent class.

4.4   Maximizing Hit Rates

So far we have focused on the adaptiveness of the cache allocation algorithms to meet the QoS requirements for the classes. However, all QoS requirements may not be feasible as hit rates are workload specific and may not increase with increasing cache space. On the other hand, the QoS requirements could

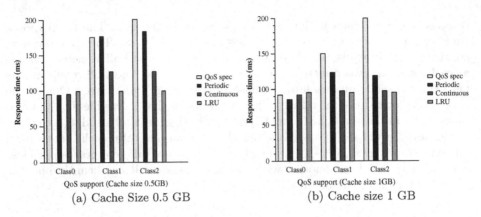

Fig. 5. QoS Support: Response Time with different QoS requirements for 3 classes with identical disks and same trace per class. Financial trace

be met and still be below the feasible hit rates. In either case, the continuous and periodic allocation algorithms revert to maximizing the overall hit rates to improve the storage system performance. To evaluate this aspect in the following set of experiments, we drop the QoS requirements to the infeasible region < 1 ms, 1 ms, 1 ms > (or view it as no QoS constraints exist) and measure the hit rates for each of the 3 classes.

To evaluate the effect of workloads with different access patterns, in Figures 6(a,b,c), each class is attached to different streams of the SPC1 workload. Here SPC1-1 has random accesses with medium locality, SPC1-2 has random accesses with poor temporal locality, and SPC1-3 has sequential accesses. Observe in this case, for a 1GB cache, the total hit ratios for LRU, continuous and periodic are 4.5%, 9.3% and 4.6% respectively. While the continuous allocation does much better (almost 2 times better hit ratio), the periodic allocation does slightly better.

Since the periodic allocation does not adapt continuously it misses some of the gains of statistical multiplexing and sequential access isolation. For a larger cache of 1.5GB, the total hit ratios for LRU, continuous and periodic are 6.6%, 10.8% and 13.0% respectively. Here periodic allocation with it's greedy swapping does much better as there is more available space to allocate to the best performing class (i.e., the class with the largest hit rate density). The continuous allocation consistently does much better than LRU. Thus, for skewed workloads, where some classes dominate in hits, LRU does not isolate the classes, thereby, reducing the overall hit ratio.

4.5   Reads and Writes

The earlier experiments used only the read accesses to evaluate the performance. However, a significant fraction of the storage requests are writes. The writes are buffered and destaged to disk at a later time based on the destage policy. In

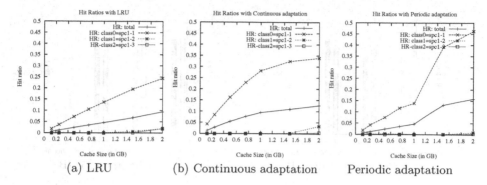

Fig. 6. Maximizing hit ratios: Performance without QoS controls and different traces per class. SPC1-1, SPC1-2, SPC1-3 trace.

our architecture the reads and writes share the same cache. The read and write blocks belonging to the same class follow the same LRU ordering. A write is always serviced as long as a buffer exists (evicting a read) and has the same response time cost as a read hit. When a write blocks in order to wait for a dirty buffer to be destaged it adds the response time cost of a read miss. In case a read miss triggers a write to be destaged, the response time cost is twice that of a read miss (one disk write and one disk read). The policy we assume destages a write block periodically (the time interval being twice that of the miss response time).

Figures 7(a,b) show the QoS performance when the reads and writes are combined using the Ecommerce trace. The miss times for the 3 classes < Class0, Class1, Class2 > were on an average < 50ms, 100ms, 200ms > respectively, while the QoS requirement was identical. The same Ecommerce trace, with 80% reads and 20% writes, was used for each class. The experiments in Figure 7(a,b) show the hit ratios per class with identical QoS requirements but varying disk miss times. The class with the largest miss time (Class 2 with 200ms) has the most stringent QoS requirement and is allocated the largest space, and consequently the largest hit ratio, by the periodic and continuous allocation. LRU, on the other hand, again has equal partitioning with equal hit ratios per class. In these experiments LRU does not achieve the requirement of Class2 which had the largest miss time. There were no blocking writes for the cache sizes that were used. The behavior with writes is closely tied to the destage policy which is beyond the scope of this paper.

4.6 Feasibility Region

Apart from providing QoS support one of the goals of the CacheCOW algorithms is to find a dynamic partitioning of the cache that can achieve the same (if not better) performance of an offline approach. The key difference is that the CacheCOW algorithms find the optimum partitioning in an online manner without any a priori knowledge of the workload. To evaluate this aspect, we measure

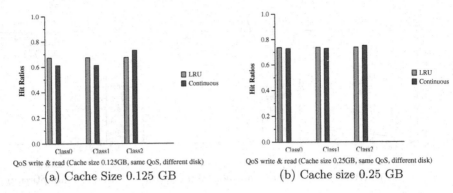

(a) Cache Size 0.125 GB   (b) Cache size 0.25 GB

Fig. 7. Reads and Writes: Total Hit Ratios (reads and writes) with identical QoS requirements for 3 classes with different disks and same trace per class. Ecommerce trace.

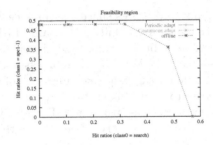

Fig. 8. Feasibility curve: Hit ratios with two classes. SPC1-1 and Searchengine trace.

offline the feasible hit ratios for a class attached to a particular workload for different cache sizes. For a given total cache size, there are different partitions possible among two classes. From the offline measurements we can determine the hit rates possible for the two classes for each of the different partitions of the cache. This is the offline feasibility region for the hit ratios for the two classes. Using these hit rates we can compute the feasible response time goals per class and use them to determine the feasibility region for the continuous and periodic allocation. Figure 8 compares the feasibility regions using two classes and two workloads (SPC1-1 and SearchEngine1) for the offline case with the periodic and continuous allocation. The experiment shows that the CacheCOW algorithms can dynamically find the feasible partitions and do as well as the offline algorithm. In some cases CacheCOW can do better for workloads where statistical multiplexing can be exploited.

4.7   Dynamic Adaptation

To demonstrate the adaptiveness of the continuous and periodic allocation, we change the workload attached to a class midway in the experiment. In the experiment (shown in Figure 9) there are two customer classes with one class using the SPC1-1 workload for the first half and the SPC1-3 workload for the second half while the other class does exactly the reverse. Figure 9(a) shows that for continuous allocation the cache size among the classes dynamically adjusts after the workload switch happens. The periodic adaptation (Figure 9(b)), although triggered later, rapidly reallocates the cache space due to its greedy nature while the continuous adaptation gradually changes the cache size allocation.

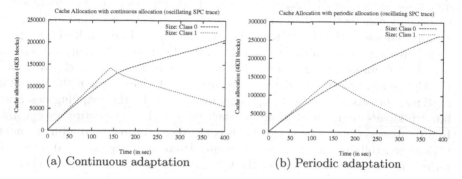

(a) Continuous adaptation   (b) Periodic adaptation

Fig. 9. SPC trace: Dynamic adaptation without QoS controls

5 Related Work

In the recent past, resource management for service differentiation in web servers has received significant attention [5,3,12]. These resource management techniques focus on CPU, network bandwidth, and software resources such as number of processes. As explained in Section 1, these resource management techniques cannot be directly employed for cache allocation. Cache partitioning techniques have been investigated in [6,9]. The objective of cache partitioning in [6] is to allocate the file system cache among multiple disks, some slower than others, such that the average cost of a miss in the cache is minimized. However, partitioning to provide service differentiation is not considered. In [9] an algorithm for partitioning a web cache between multiple classes is considered. The objective is to partition the cache such that the ratio of the hit rate between any two classes is as specified. The objective of our cache allocation algorithm, in contrast, is to meet the response time requirements of the various classes and optimize the system throughput. A related but orthogonal work on object replacement algorithm that maximizes the cache utility when different objects derive different utility from hits is presented in [8].

Our concept of history lists is variously known in the literature as a ghost cache or as a shadow cache. Such ideas have been widely used before especially in cache replacement algorithms. There is a close relationship between CacheCOW and ARC [11]. The latter is an adaptive policy for cache replacement. In particular, the precise amount of history allocated to each class is inspired by the formula used in ARC. Moreover, there is a even closer tie between our Continuous Adaptation Algorithm and ARC. For the case of two classes that are assumed to be satisfied, the former becomes virtually identical to the latter. However, our Continuous Adaptation Algorithm can be applied to arbitrary number of classes. Finally, unlike our work, ARC has no notion of QoS.

In the context of storage systems, [4] has developed an architecture for a quality-of-service-based "attribute-managed" storage system. The basic idea is to formally convey QoS goals to the storage system which uses automated provisioning and load-balancing to meet the QoS targets. In later work, [17] proposed an information model, namely, Rome, that can be used to formally capture and represent all important elements of a storage system, for example, the workloads, the QoS goals, the storage devices, the network devices, various device configurations, the storage network topology and protocols, the mapping describing how workloads are mapped to various devices, as well as the entire system state. In a running system, various QoS goals could be monitored, and adjustments to various controllable variables can be made. However, they do not describe the techniques or algorithms to meet the QoS goals in a storage system cache.

6 Conclusions

In this paper we proposed two online algorithms that periodically and continuously allocate cache space in a storage system to maintain the QoS requirements of different classes of workload while maximizing the hit ratios. We presented the online CacheCOW algorithms, namely periodic and continuous allocation, that: i) select the minimal allocation that meets the QoS requirements and then resorts to an additional allocation that maximizes overall hit ratio, ii) empirically achieve the same feasibility region as that of offline static algorithms; and iii) optimize the throughput by achieving a higher hit rate whenever feasible. Through trace driven simulations, collected from large storage system installations, we experimentally demonstrated that these algorithms are indeed able to achieve the above goals. In future, we wish to examine: (i) interaction between QoS requirements and the write destage policy; (ii) interaction between QoS requirements and read-ahead (prefetching); and (iii) employing different cache replacement policies for each class, for example, using LRU for one class and ARC [11] for another.

References

1. T. Abdelzaher, K. G. Shin, and N. Bhatti. Performance guarantees for web server end-systems: A control-theoretical approach. *IEEE Trans. Parallel and Distributed Systems*, 13(1), January 2001.

2. E. Anderson, M. Hobbs, K. Keeton, S. Spence, M. Uysal, and A. Veitch. Hippo-drome: Running circles around storage administration. In *Proc. Usenix Conf. File and Storage Technology (FAST'02), Monterey, CA*, pages 175–188, January 2002.

3. M. Aron, P. Druschel, and S. Iyer. A resource management framework for pre-dictable quality of service in web servers.
http://www.cs.rice.edu/~druschel/publications/mbqos.pdf, 2001.

4. E. Borowsky, R. Golding, A. Merchant, L. Schreier, E. Shriver, M. Spasojevic, and J. Wilkes. Using attribute-managed storage to achieve QoS. In *Proc. 5th Int. Workshop on Quality of Service (IWQoS), Columbia, NY*, pages 75–91, June 1997.

5. A. Chandra, M. Adler, P. Goyal, and P. Shenoy. Surplus fair scheduling: A proportional-share cpu scheduling algorithm for symmetric multiprocessors. In *Proc. Fourth Symp. Operating System Design and Implementation (OSDI 2000), San Diego, CA*, October 2000.

6. B. Forney, A. C. Arpaci-Dusseau, and R. H. Arpaci-Dusseau. Storage-aware caching: Revisiting caching for heterogeneous storage systems. In *Proc. USENIX Conf. File and Storage Technologies*, 2002.

7. S. A. Johnson, B. McNutt, and R. Reich. The making of a standard benchmark for open system storage. *J. Comp. Resource Management*, 101:26–32, 2001.

8. T. P. Kelly, Y. M. Chan, S. Jamin, and J. K. Mackie-Mason. Biased replacement policies for web caches: Differential quality-of-service and aggregate user value. In *Fourth International Web Caching Workshop, San Diego, California*, 1999.

9. Y. Lu, T. Abdelzaher, C. Lu, and G. Tao. An adaptive control framework for QoS guarantees and its application to differentiated caching services. In *Proc. Tenth Int. Workshop on Quality of Service*, 2002.

10. R. L. Mattson. Partitioned cache – a new type of cache. In *IBM Research Report*, 1987.

11. N. Megiddo and D. S. Modha. ARC: A self-tuning, low overhead replacement cache. In *Proc. USENIX Conf. File and Storage Technologies (FAST'03), San Francisco, CA*, 2003.

12. D. Steere, A. Goel, J. Gruenberg, D. McNamee, C. Pu, and J. Walpole. A feedback-driven proportion allocator for real-rate scheduling. In *Proc. Symp. Operating Systems Design and Implementation*, February 1999.

13. H. S. Stone, J. Turek, and J. L. Wolf. Optimal partitioning of cache memory. *IEEE Tran. Comp.*, 41(9), September 1992.

14. V. Sundaram, A. Chandra, P. Goyal, P. Shenoy, J. Sahni, and H. Vin. Application performance in the qlinux multimedia operating system. In *Proc. Eighth ACM Conference on Multimedia, Los Angeles, CA*, pages 127–136, November 2000.

15. D. Thiebaut, H. S. Stone, and J. L. Wolf. Improving disk cache hit-ratios through cache partitioning. *IEEE Tran. Comp.*, 41(6), June 1992.

16. T. Voigt, R. Tewari, D. Freimuth, and A. Mehra. Kernel mechanisms for ser-vice differentiation in overloaded web servers. In *Proc. Usenix Annual Technical Conference*, June 2001.

17. J. Wilkes. Traveling to Rome: QoS specifications for automated storage system management. In *Proc. Int. Workshop on Quality of Service (IWQoS), Karlsruhe, Germany*, pages 75–91, June 2001.

Author Index

Lecture Notes in Computer Science

For information about Vols. 1–2579

please contact your bookseller or Springer-Verlag

Vol. 2616: T. Asano, R. Klette, C. Ronse (Eds.), Geometry, Morphology, and Computational Imaging. Proceedings, 2002. X, 437 pages. 2003.

Vol. 2617: H.A. Reijers (Eds.), Design and Control of Workflow Processes. Proceedings, 2002. XV, 624 pages. 2003.

Vol. 2618: P. Degano (Ed.), Programming Languages and Systems. Proceedings, 2003. XV, 415 pages. 2003.

Vol. 2619: H. Garavel, J. Hatcliff (Eds.), Tools and Algorithms for the Construction and Analysis of Systems. Proceedings, 2003. XVI, 604 pages. 2003.

Vol. 2620: A.D. Gordon (Ed.), Foundations of Software Science and Computation Structures. Proceedings, 2003. XII, 441 pages. 2003.

Vol. 2621: M. Pezzè (Ed.), Fundamental Approaches to Software Engineering. Proceedings, 2003. XIV, 403 pages. 2003.

Vol. 2622: G. Hedin (Ed.), Compiler Construction. Proceedings, 2003. XII, 335 pages. 2003.

Vol. 2623: O. Maler, A. Pnueli (Eds.), Hybrid Systems: Computation and Control. Proceedings, 2003. XII, 558 pages. 2003.

Vol. 2625: U. Meyer, P. Sanders, J. Sibeyn (Eds.), Algorithms for Memory Hierarchies. Proceedings, 2003. XVIII, 428 pages. 2003.

Vol. 2626: J.L. Crowley, J.H. Piater, M. Vincze, L. Paletta (Eds.), Computer Vision Systems. Proceedings, 2003. XIII, 546 pages. 2003.

Vol. 2627: B. O'Sullivan (Ed.), Recent Advances in Constraints. Proceedings, 2002. X, 201 pages. 2003. (Subseries LNAI).

Vol. 2628: T. Fahringer, B. Scholz, Advanced Symbolic Analysis for Compilers. XII, 129 pages. 2003.

Vol. 2631: R. Falcone, S. Barber, L. Korba, M. Singh (Eds.), Trust, Reputation, and Security: Theories and Practice. Proceedings, 2002. X, 235 pages. 2003. (Subseries LNAI).

Vol. 2632: C.M. Fonseca, P.J. Fleming, E. Zitzler, K. Deb, L. Thiele (Eds.), Evolutionary Multi-Criterion Optimization. Proceedings, 2003. XV, 812 pages. 2003.

Vol. 2633: F. Sebastiani (Ed.), Advances in Information Retrieval. Proceedings, 2003. XIII, 546 pages. 2003.

Vol. 2634: F. Zhao, L. Guibas (Eds.), Information Processing in Sensor Networks. Proceedings, 2003. XII, 692 pages. 2003.

Vol. 2636: E. Alonso, D, Kudenko, D. Kazakov (Eds.), Adaptive Agents and Multi-Agent Systems. XIV, 323 pages. 2003. (Subseries LNAI).

Vol. 2637: K.-Y. Whang, J. Jeon, K. Shim, J. Srivastava (Eds.), Advances in Knowledge Discovery and Data Mining. Proceedings, 2003. XVIII, 610 pages. 2003. (Subseries LNAI).

Vol. 2638: J. Jeuring, S. Peyton Jones (Eds.), Advanced Functional Programming. Proceedings, 2002. VII, 213 pages. 2003.

Vol. 2639: G. Wang, Q. Liu, Y. Yao, A. Skowron (Eds.), Rough Sets, Fuzzy Sets, Data Mining, and Granular Computing. Proceedings, 2003. XVII, 741 pages. 2003. (Subseries LNAI).

Vol. 2641: P.J. Nürnberg (Ed.), Metainformatics. Proceedings, 2002. VIII, 187 pages. 2003.

Vol. 2642: X. Zhou, Y. Zhang, M.E. Orlowska (Eds.), Web Technologies and Applications. Proceedings, 2003. XIII, 608 pages. 2003.

Vol. 2643: M. Fossorier, T. Høholdt, A. Poli (Eds.), Applied Algebra, Algebraic Algorithms and Error-Correcting Codes. Proceedings, 2003. X, 256 pages. 2003.

Vol. 2644: D. Hogrefe, A. Wiles (Eds.), Testing of Communicating Systems. Proceedings, 2003. XII, 311 pages. 2003.

Vol. 2645: M.A. Wimmer (Ed.), Knowledge Management in Electronic Government. Proceedings, 2003. XI, 320 pages. 2003. (Subseries LNAI).

Vol. 2646: H. Geuvers, F, Wiedijk (Eds.), Types for Proofs and Programs. Proceedings, 2002. VIII, 331 pages. 2003.

Vol. 2647: K.Jansen, M. Margraf, M. Mastrolli, J.D.P. Rolim (Eds.), Experimental and Efficient Algorithms. Proceedings, 2003. VIII, 267 pages. 2003.

Vol. 2648: T. Ball, S.K. Rajamani (Eds.), Model Checking Software. Proceedings, 2003. VIII, 241 pages. 2003.

Vol. 2649: B. Westfechtel, A. van der Hoek (Eds.), Software Configuration Management. Proceedings, 2003. VIII, 241 pages. 2003.

Vol. 2651: D. Bert, J.P. Bowen, S. King, M, Waldén (Eds.), ZB 2003: Formal Specification and Development in Z and B. Proceedings, 2003. XIII, 547 pages. 2003.

Vol. 2653: R. Petreschi, Giuseppe Persiano, R. Silvestri (Eds.), Algorithms and Complexity. Proceedings, 2003. XI, 289 pages. 2003.

Vol. 2656: E. Biham (Ed.), Advances in Cryptology – EUROCRPYT 2003. Proceedings, 2003. XIV, 649 pages. 2003.

Vol. 2663: E. Menasalvas, J. Segovia, P.S. Szczepaniak (Eds.), Advances in Web Intelligence. Proceedings, 2003. XII, 350 pages. 2003. (Subseries LNAI).

Vol. 2665: H. Chen, R. Miranda, D.D. Zeng, C. Demchak, J. Schroeder, T. Madhusudan (Eds.), Intelligence and Security Informatics. Proceedings, 2003. XIV, 392 pages. 2003.

Vol. 2667: V. Kumar, M.L. Gavrilova, C.J.K. Tan, P. L'Ecuyer (Eds.), Computational Science and Its Applications – ICCSA 2003. Proceedings, Part I. 2003. XXXIV, 1060 pages. 2003.

Vol. 2668: V. Kumar, M.L. Gavrilova, C.J.K. Tan, P. L'Ecuyer (Eds.), Computational Science and Its Applications – ICCSA 2003. Proceedings, Part II. 2003. XXXIV, 942 pages. 2003.

Vol. 2669: V. Kumar, M.L. Gavrilova, C.J.K. Tan, P. L'Ecuyer (Eds.), Computational Science and Its Applications – ICCSA 2003. Proceedings, Part III. 2003. XXXIV, 948 pages. 2003.

Vol. 2670: R. Peña, T. Arts (Eds.), Implementation of Functional Languages. Proceedings, 2002. X, 249 pages. 2003.

Vol. 2675: M. Marchesi, G. Succi (Eds.), Extreme Programming and Agile Processes in Software Engineering. Proceedings, 2003. XV, 464 pages. 2003.

Vol. 2692: P. Nixon, S. Terzis (Eds.), Trust Management. Proceedings, 2003. X, 349 pages. 2003.

Vol. 2707: K. Jeffay, I. Stoica, K. Wehrle (Eds.), Quality of Service – IWQoS 2003. Proceedings, 2003. XI, 517 pages. 2003.